JESUS
and the GOD
of Classical Theism

JESUS
and the GOD
of Classical Theism

Biblical Christology in Light
of the Doctrine of God

STEVEN J. DUBY

Baker Academic
a division of Baker Publishing Group
Grand Rapids, Michigan

© 2022 by Steven J. Duby

Published by Baker Academic
a division of Baker Publishing Group
PO Box 6287, Grand Rapids, MI 49516-6287
www.bakeracademic.com

Paperback edition published 2023
ISBN 978-1-5409-6711-4

Printed in the United States of America

The Library of Congress has cataloged the hardcover edition as follows:
Names: Duby, Steven J., author.
Title: Jesus and the God of classical theism : biblical Christology in light of the doctrine of God / Steven J. Duby.
Description: Grand Rapids, Michigan : Baker Academic, a division of Baker Publishing Group, [2022] | Includes bibliographical references and index.
Identifiers: LCCN 2021043093 | ISBN 9781540961389 (cloth) | ISBN 9781493420575 (ebook) | ISBN 9781493420582 (pdf)
Subjects: LCSH: Jesus Christ—History of doctrines. | Jesus Christ—Person and offices.—Biblical teaching. | Theism.
Classification: LCC BT198 .D7685 2022 | DDC 232—dc23
LC record available at https://lccn.loc.gov/2021043093

Unless indicated otherwise, Scripture translations are those of the author.

Baker Publishing Group publications use paper produced from sustainable forestry practices and post-consumer waste whenever possible.

For Charlie, Evie, Wyatt, and George

Contents

Acknowledgments

The encouragement, wisdom, and feedback of various friends, colleagues, and colaborers in Christian theology have helped to bring this book to completion. To Dave Nelson in particular I am grateful. His support of the work from the beginning and his incisive contributions as a dialogue partner and editor have been excellent.

I am thankful to friends at Phoenix Seminary for their outstanding love, support, and hospitality—and their willingness to let me bother them with exegetical questions. Several individuals, especially Ivor Davidson and Tyler Wittman, have graciously interacted with me on the questions addressed in this study and have read portions of the manuscript to give feedback. I am grateful for their steady wisdom and good judgment in the work of theology.

My parents continue to be a great source of encouragement. I am thankful for their interest in what I do and admire their perseverance through the course of life's challenges. My wife, Jodi, continues to reflect the love of Christ to me and our four children. I want to dedicate this book to our children (Charlie, Evie, Wyatt, and George), each an expression of God's goodness to us, in the hope that they may grow up always following the eternal Son, who took on flesh for us and for our salvation.

Introduction

In 2008 Richard Bauckham published a collection of essays under the title *Jesus and the God of Israel*, offering a description of the person of Jesus Christ in relation to the identity of the God revealed in the Old Testament. Other biblical scholars also have taken up the challenge of exploring the interface of Christology and theology proper in the Bible and early Christianity.[1] In view of contemporary interest among systematic and historical theologians in recovering and implementing earlier Christian accounts of God,[2] it seems fitting to take another step and work on explicating the relationship between biblical Christology and a doctrine of God in which divine attributes like aseity, immutability, impassibility, eternity, and simplicity play a significant role and inform one's Christology.[3] It is crucial to emphasize, however, that in the project laid out here—"Jesus and the God of 'classical theism'"—it

1. E.g., Hurtado, *Lord Jesus Christ*; Gathercole, *The Pre-existent Son*; Rowe, *Early Narrative Christology*; W. Hill, *Paul and the Trinity*; Tilling, *Paul's Divine Christology*; Bates, *The Birth of the Trinity*; Fletcher-Louis, *Jesus Monotheism*; Kirk, *A Man Attested by God*; Bird, *Jesus the Eternal Son*; Pierce, *Divine Discourse in the Epistle to the Hebrews*.

2. E.g., Weinandy, *Does God Suffer?*; Gavrilyuk, *The Suffering of the Impassible God*; Levering, *Scripture and Metaphysics*; Emery, *The Trinitarian Theology of St Thomas Aquinas*; Ayres, *Augustine and the Trinity*; Dolezal, *God without Parts*; S. Holmes, *The Quest for the Trinity*; Webster, *God without Measure*; Duby, *Divine Simplicity*; Long, *The Perfectly Simple Triune God*; Wittman, *God and Creation in the Theology of Thomas Aquinas and Karl Barth*; Duby, *God in Himself*.

3. There are of course various authors already making noteworthy contributions on this front. See, e.g., Weinandy, *Jesus: Essays in Christology*; Luy, *Dominus Mortis*; White, *The Incarnate Lord*; Pawl, *In Defense of Conciliar Christology*; Pawl, *In Defense of Extended Conciliar Christology*; Riches, *Ecce Homo*; Legge, *The Trinitarian Christology of St Thomas Aquinas*; M. Gorman, *Aquinas on the Metaphysics of the Hypostatic Union*; Williams, *Christ the Heart of Creation*; Daley, *God Visible*.

is not that the God of Israel and the God described by the orthodox church fathers are taken to be two different Gods. In fact, I intend to argue that the revelation of God in Christ and Holy Scripture implies and is illumined by the theological claims of the catholic fathers.[4]

I should also mention that the phrase "classical theism" is an imprecise one. I use it here only because it has been used by many as an expedient designation for an account of the triune God holding that he is simple, immutable, impassible, and eternal (words to be defined later on). I have no particular interest in defending the phrase "classical theism" or employing it for constructive ends, which is why it ends up appearing infrequently in this study and typically in quotation marks. The aim of this volume is not to quibble about the fecundity of a single phrase but rather to deal with substantive issues in Christology and trinitarian doctrine. Given the nature of this book, it should be clear that I am not implying that "classical" theological commitments should be exempt from all analysis. Nor am I implying that there is complete uniformity to be found across the Christian tradition in authors like Athanasius, Augustine, Thomas Aquinas, and others. Nevertheless, I will maintain that, at a general level at least, such authors do present a broadly cohesive set of exegetical and theological resources that will prove fruitful in contemporary Christology.

I also want to recognize here that words and phrases like "traditional," "more traditional," and "catholic tradition" appear in various places throughout this volume. The use of such words and phrases is not intended to discourage or replace actual exegetical and theological reasoning. The goal is not to try to conserve what is older simply because it is older—as if that might be an end in itself—but rather to set forth the christological teaching of Holy Scripture and to explore the extent to which certain theological resources that do happen to be older can help us to interpret Scripture well. When speaking about accounts of Christ or the Trinity that are "traditional" or part of the "catholic tradition," I have in mind a body of Christian teaching on central topics about which there is a broad agreement, expressed in statements from the ecumenical councils of the patristic period, in biblical commentaries and topical treatments of theological questions in the medieval period, and in early modern Protestant confessions of faith. My sense is that even in the midst of their diverse ways of handling certain matters, one can find this kind

---

4. I agree with Katherine Sonderegger's programmatic statement that the Christian doctrine of God does not have to be derived exclusively from the incarnation: "Not all is Christology!" (*Systematic Theology*, 1:xvii). Cf. Webster, "The Place of Christology in Systematic Theology." Yet I do hope to show in this study that a robust doctrine of God that is not exclusively based upon the incarnation still has a multitude of positive connections with it.

of broad agreement in figures such as Gregory of Nyssa, Augustine, Cyril of Alexandria, John of Damascus, Peter Lombard, Bonaventure, Thomas Aquinas, and Protestant orthodox theologians.

Any study of this sort must face the reality that modern treatments of the person of Christ have cast doubt on whether a "more traditional" doctrine of God can fit with an exegetically driven Christology. As one author puts it, in the eyes of many, older Christian accounts of God and the person of Christ have a "biblical Jesus problem."[5] As we will see in chapter 1, the relevant concerns often relate to upholding the biblical depiction of Christ's relationship to the Father and Spirit, the unity of the person of Christ, and the genuineness of Christ's human life and suffering. In addition, some modern studies in Christology have questioned whether traditional concepts and categories themselves (e.g., "essence," "substance") still enable insight into the Bible's portrayal of Christ's life and work. Roughly two hundred years ago, Friedrich Schleiermacher, for example, criticized talk of Christ's "two natures." In his judgment, a person—an "I" that is "the same in all one's successive elements over time"—cannot remain intact under a "duality of natures."[6] One recent study of Pauline Christology is critical of using an "Aristotelian ontology" in biblical exegesis, for, according to the author, it diminishes the ontological significance of relations and yields a misguided focus on "substance" or "static being."[7]

This volume will take concerns like these into consideration and offer a constructive treatment of the person of Christ. It will draw upon earlier Christian descriptions of God and incorporate concepts and patterns of reasoning from catholic Christology in an effort to illumine and set forth the biblical portrayal of Christ's relationship to the Father and Spirit, the unity of his person, and the genuineness of his human life and suffering. In other words, this study will argue that such a doctrine of God and attendant christological insights provide valuable resources for securing the pertinent biblical desiderata in our understanding of the person of Christ today.

With this aim in mind, the volume possesses three distinct features. First, it devotes space to biblical exposition and works to display how different tenets of orthodox trinitarianism and Christology contribute to setting forth the identity and work of Jesus described in the Bible. Accordingly, the book draws together scriptural exegesis and ontological concerns, encouraging biblical scholars and systematic theologians to engage in conversation and take

---

5. J. Hill, "Introduction," 3.
6. Schleiermacher, The Christian Faith, §96 (585).
7. Tilling, Paul's Divine Christology, 37, 47, 267–68.

seriously the contributions that can be made from both sides. Second, this study will draw upon the catholic theological tradition as inherited and advanced by Reformed orthodox theologians. Patristic and medieval authors will play a significant part, and often their thinking will be taken up in connection with the later elaborative work of the Reformed orthodox. After frequently being caricatured or ignored in past decades, the Reformed orthodox continue to gain recognition as important dialogue partners for constructive theology and biblical interpretation.[8] Thus, the volume aims to be ecumenical in scope and tenor. Third, the volume will keep in view the three themes mentioned above—the relationship of Christ to the Father and Spirit, the unity of the person of Christ, and the genuineness of Christ's human life and suffering—and at key points examine how the account offered here provides insight into these essential features of biblical Christology.

Chapter 1 will outline ways in which some modern treatments of biblical Christology have called into question the claims of "classical theism" and have criticized the use of "Greek" philosophical concepts in scriptural exegesis. I will then respond with a brief rationale for affirming divine attributes like aseity, immutability, impassibility, and simplicity and for continued use of the broadly Aristotelian philosophical apparatus employed in older Christology. Chapter 2 will begin the material and constructive work of the book. It will focus on the Son's eternal relation to the Father and coordinate the real relations among the divine persons with the doctrine of divine simplicity. Chapter 3 will discuss the Son's election and mission, framing these in light of God's immutability and transcendence of time. Chapter 4 will then address the Son's relationship to his human nature in more detail and discuss matters like the doctrine of the *communicatio idiomatum* in connection with God's immutability and simplicity. Chapter 5 will treat the Son's dependence on the Holy Spirit in his earthly ministry, which will involve a discussion of the Spirit's distinct manner of acting in relation to the Son and his communication of spiritual gifts to the Son. Chapter 6 will discuss the Son's obedience to the Father, including his human striving under the pressures of temptation. Finally, chapter 7 will treat the Son's suffering and seek to integrate it with the doctrine of divine impassibility.

As we begin, it may be worth noting a comment made by the nineteenth-century German theologian Hermann Cremer regarding the interest (or lack

8. See, e.g., Muller, *Post-Reformation Reformed Dogmatics*; Bac, *Perfect Will Theology*; te Velde, *Paths beyond Tracing Out*; Pedersen, "Schleiermacher and Reformed Scholastics on the Divine Attributes." Some of my efforts in this area include "Atonement, Impassibility and the *Communicatio Operationum*"; *Divine Simplicity*; "Election, Actuality and Divine Freedom"; "Divine Immutability, Divine Action and the God-World Relation"; and *God in Himself*.

of interest) among Christian believers in a traditional doctrine of God. Cremer remarked that out of all the theological claims present in the church's dogmatic tradition, those concerning the attributes of God "sounded through" the least in the church's proclamation in his own day, especially among those who appeared to care most about the gospel. For Cremer, this was because many of those statements could be seen as independent of God's revelation in Christ and containing nothing distinctly Christian.[9] Perhaps some would say the same about the contemporary landscape of Christian theology and ministry. However, instead of attributing this to a deficiency in the theology of writers such as John Chrysostom, John of Damascus, Peter Lombard, or Francis Turretin, this book will attempt to address the problem by showing how such a theology might help us to set forth the Christology of the Bible in a fresh and energizing way for those who believe and proclaim the gospel of Jesus Christ.

9. Cremer, *Die christliche Lehre von den Eigenschaften Gottes*, 7–8.

Abbreviations

AB	Anchor Bible
ACO	*Acta Conciliorum Oecumenicorum*. Edited by Eduard Schwartz. Vols. 1.1.1, 5–7. Berlin: de Gruyter, 1927–29.
Ad monachos	Cyril of Alexandria, *Epistula ad monachos*
Ad Theodosium	Cyril of Alexandria, *Oratio ad Theodosium*
Altera ad Nestorium	Cyril of Alexandria, *Epistula altera ad Nestorium*
BBR	*Bulletin for Biblical Research*
BDAG	Frederick W. Danker, Walter Bauer, William F. Arndt, and F. Wilbur Gingrich. *A Greek-English Lexicon of the New Testament and Other Early Christian Literature*. 3rd ed. Chicago: University of Chicago Press, 2000.
BDB	Francis Brown, S. R. Driver, and Charles A. Briggs. *The Brown-Driver-Briggs Hebrew and English Lexicon*. Reprint, Peabody, MA: Hendrickson, 1979.
BECNT	Baker Exegetical Commentary on the New Testament
BS	*Bibliotheca Sacra*
CBQ	*Catholic Biblical Quarterly*
CBR	*Currents in Biblical Research*
CCSL	Corpus Christianorum Series Latina
CD	Karl Barth, *Church Dogmatics*
CIT	Current Issues in Theology
CO	John Calvin. *Ioannis Calvini opera quae supersunt omnia*. 59 vols. Edited by Guilielmus Baum et al. Brunswick: Schwetschke, 1863–1900.
Conf.	Augustine, *Confessionum libri XIII*
Contra Orientales	Cyril of Alexandria, *Apologia XII capitulorum contra Orientales*
Contra Theodoretum	Cyril of Alexandria, *Apologia XII capitulorum contra Theodoretum*
CPHST	Changing Paradigms in Historical and Systematic Theology
CSEL	Corpus Scriptorum Ecclesiasticorum Latinorum
De civ.	Augustine, *De civitate Dei*
De doct.	Augustine, *De doctrina christiana libri IV*

De hebdomadibus	Thomas Aquinas, *Expositio libri Boethii De hebdomadibus*
De incarn.	Girolamo Zanchi, *De incarnatione Filii Dei*
De pot.	Thomas Aquinas, *De potentia*
De scientia Christi	Bonaventure, *Quaestiones disputatae de scientia Christi*
De trin.	Augustine, *De trinitate libri XV*
De trin.	Boethius, *De trinitate*
De unione	Thomas Aquinas, *Quaestio disputata De unione Verbi incarnati*
Dial.	John of Damascus, *Dialectica*
Disp.	Robert Bellarmine, *Disputationum Roberti Bellarmini de controversiis Christianae fidei*
EDNT	*Exegetical Dictionary of the New Testament*. Edited by Horst Balz and Gerhard Schneider. 3 vols. Grand Rapids: Eerdmans, 1990–93.
EPR	Elements in the Philosophy of Religion
Explanatio XII cap.	Cyril of Alexandria, *Explanatio XII capitulorum*
Expos. fidei	John of Damascus, *Expositio fidei*
GNO	Gregory of Nyssa. *Gregorii Nysseni opera*. Vols. 1–3.1. Edited by Wernerus Jaeger. Leiden: Brill, 1958–60.
HBT	*Horizons in Biblical Theology*
Hebrews	John Owen, *An Exposition of the Epistle to the Hebrews*
HNTC	Harper's New Testament Commentaries
HTR	*Harvard Theological Review*
HUCA	*Hebrew Union College Annual*
ICC	International Critical Commentary
IJST	*International Journal of Systematic Theology*
In Acta	John Calvin, *Commentarius in Acta Apostolorum*
In De div. nom.	Thomas Aquinas, *In librum beati Dionysii De divinis nominibus expositio*
In harm.	John Calvin, *Commentarius in harmoniam evangelicam*
In Heb.	John Calvin, *Commentarius in epistolam ad Hebraeos*
In Heb.	John Chrysostom, *Homiliae XXXIV in epistolam ad Hebraeos*
In Iohann.	Augustine, *In Iohannis Evangelium tractatus CXXIV*
In Joann.	Cyril of Alexandria, *In d. Joannis Evangelium*
In Johann.	John Chrysostom, *Homiliae CXXXVIII in Johannem*
In Matt.	John Chrysostom, *Homiliae in Matthaeum*
In Metaphys.	Thomas Aquinas, *In duodecim libros Metaphysicorum Aristotelis expositio*
In Phil.	John Calvin, *Commentarius in epistolam ad Philippenses*
In Phil.	John Chrysostom, *Homiliae XV in epistolam ad Philippenses*
In Phil.	Girolamo Zanchi, *In d. Pauli apostoli epistolam ad Philippenses*
In Rom.	John Calvin, *Commentarius in epistolam Pauli ad Romanos*
In Rom.	John Chrysostom, *Homiliae XXXII in epistolam ad Romanos*
In Rom.	Peter Vermigli, *In epistolam S. Pauli Apostoli ad Romanos*
In Sent.	Bonaventure, *Commentaria in quatuor libros Sententiarum*, vols. 1 and 3

Inst.	Francis Turretin, *Institutio theologiae elencticae*
IPQ	*International Philosophical Quarterly*
ITQ	*Irish Theological Quarterly*
JAT	*Journal of Analytic Theology*
JBL	*Journal of Biblical Literature*
JECS	*Journal of Early Christian Studies*
JRT	*Journal of Reformed Theology*
JSNTSS	Journal for the Study of the New Testament Supplement Series
JTC	*Journal for Theology and the Church*
JTI	*Journal of Theological Interpretation*
KD	Karl Barth, *Die kirchliche Dogmatik*
La Trinité	Hilary of Poitiers, *La Trinité*
LCL	Loeb Classical Library
LXX	Septuagint
MAJT	*Mid-America Journal of Theology*
MT	Masoretic Text
MT	*Modern Theology*
NICNT	New International Commentary on the New Testament
NICOT	New International Commentary on the Old Testament
NIDNTT	*The New International Dictionary of New Testament Theology.* Edited by Colin Brown. 4 vols. Grand Rapids: Zondervan, 1986.
NIDNTTE	*New International Dictionary of New Testament Theology and Exegesis.* Edited by Moisés Silva. 5 vols. Rev. ed. Grand Rapids: Zondervan, 2014.
NIDOTTE	*New International Dictionary of Old Testament Theology and Exegesis.* Edited by Willem A.VanGemeren. 5 vols. Grand Rapids: Zondervan, 1997.
NIGTC	New International Greek Testament Commentary
NSBT	New Studies in Biblical Theology
NSD	New Studies in Dogmatics
NTL	New Testament Library
NTS	*New Testament Studies*
NZSTh	*Neue Zeitschrift für Systematische Theologie und Religionsphilosphie*
Oratio I	Athanasius, *Orationes I et II contra Arianos*
Oratio II	Athanasius, *Orationes I et II contra Arianos*
Oratio III	Athanasius, *Oratio III contra Arianos*
Oratio IV	Athanasius, *Oratio IV contra Arianos*
OSAT	Oxford Studies in Analytic Theology
OSHT	Oxford Studies in Historical Theology
OTL	Old Testament Library
PG	Patrologia Graeca [= *Patrologiae Cursus Completus.* Series Graeca]. Edited by J.-P. Migne. 162 vols. Paris, 1857–86.
PNTC	Pillar New Testament Commentary
RB	*Revue Biblique*
RHT	Reformed Historical Theology

RS	*Religious Studies*
SBT	Studies in Biblical Theology
SC	Sources Chrétiennes
SCDS	Studies in Christian Doctrine and Scripture
SCG	Thomas Aquinas, *Summa contra Gentiles*
Scholia	Cyril of Alexandria, *Scholia de incarnatione Unigeniti*
Select. disp., pars prima	Gisbertus Voetius, *Selectarum disputationum theologicarum, pars prima*
Select. disp., pars sec.	Gisbertus Voetius, *Selectarum disputationum theologicarum, pars secunda*
Sent.	Peter Lombard, *Sententiae in IV libris distinctae*
Sent. De anima	Thomas Aquinas, *Sentencia libri De anima*
Sent. Ethic.	Thomas Aquinas, *Sentencia libri Ethicorum*
Serap.	Athanasius, *Epistulae I–IV ad Serapionem*
SHBC	Smyth & Helwys Bible Commentary
SJT	*Scottish Journal of Theology*
SNTSMS	Society for New Testament Studies Manuscript Series
SP	Sacra Pagina
ST	Thomas Aquinas, *Summa theologiae*
Super De trin.	Thomas Aquinas, *Super Boetium De trinitate*
Super Eph.	Thomas Aquinas, *Super epistolam ad Ephesios lectura*
Super Heb.	Thomas Aquinas, *Super epistolam ad Hebraeos lectura*
Super Ioann.	Thomas Aquinas, *Super Evangelium S. Ioannis lectura*
Super Matt.	Thomas Aquinas, *Super Evangelium S. Matthaei lectura*
Super Phil.	Thomas Aquinas, *Super epistolam ad Philippenses lectura*
Super Rom.	Thomas Aquinas, *Super epistolam ad Romanos lectura*
Super Sent.	Thomas Aquinas, *Scriptum super libros Sententiarum*
Sur Matt. I	Hilary of Poitiers, *Sur Matthieu I–II*
Sur Matt. I	Jerome, *Commentaire sur Saint Matthieu I–II*
Sur Matt. II	Hilary of Poitiers, *Sur Matthieu I–II*
Sur Matt. II	Jerome, *Commentaire sur Saint Matthieu I–II*
TDNT	*Theological Dictionary of the New Testament.* Edited by Gerhard Kittel and Gerhard Friedrich. Translated by Geoffrey W. Bromiley. 10 vols. Grand Rapids: Eerdmans, 1964–76.
Tertia ad Nestorium	Cyril of Alexandria, *Epistula tertia ad Nestorium*
THNTC	Two Horizons New Testament Commentary
TPT	Petrus van Mastricht, *Theoretico-practica theologia*
TS	*Theological Studies*
TZ	*Theologische Zeitschrift*
USQR	*Union Seminary Quarterly Review*
VCSup	Supplements to Vigiliae Christianae
WBC	Word Biblical Commentary
WTJ	*Westminster Theological Journal*
WUNT	Wissenschaftliche Untersuchungen zum Neuen Testament
ZAW	*Zeitschrift für die alttestamentliche Wissenschaft*
ZECNT	Zondervan Exegetical Commentary on the New Testament

ONE

Biblical Christology and "Classical Theism"

I. Introduction

The goal in this first chapter is to exhibit how treatments of the Bible's Christology have called into question older Christian accounts of God and then to begin to sketch a response to such criticisms, though ultimately the response will be developed throughout the subsequent constructive chapters of the book. First, we will consider how various interpreters of Scripture have drawn from christological and trinitarian considerations to express doubts about divine attributes like simplicity, immutability, impassibility, and eternity. Then we will consider how some have argued that traditional concepts and categories themselves ("essence," "nature," "substance," and so on) create problems for understanding the Bible's portrayal of the person and work of Christ. Along the way, I will draw attention to three common themes already flagged in the introduction of the book: (1) the concern for adequate description of Christ's relationship to the Father and Spirit, (2) the concern to uphold the unity of the person of Christ, and (3) the concern to affirm the genuineness of Christ's human life and suffering. After examining these criticisms, we will consider why older theologians (whose primary aim was in fact to interpret Scripture) have thought it fitting to call God simple, immutable, impassible, and eternal in the first place. Then I will respond to worries about traditional metaphysical concepts and categories, rethinking how the conceptual resources of a broadly Aristotelian ontology might be deployed to explicate rather than subvert the Bible's christological teaching. This will require us to

1

move beyond misunderstandings and caricatures of such concepts while still carefully delimiting their role in exegesis.

II. Christological Challenges to "Classical Theism"

Theologians, historians, and biblical scholars of various traditions have objected to accounts of God that include divine attributes like simplicity, immutability, impassibility, and eternity (often taken to mean "timelessness"). Here key objections raised on christological and trinitarian grounds must be taken into consideration. While an inductive presentation of these objections, proceeding chronologically from one major author to the next, would provide a sense of the historical development of the material, I have thought it more expedient to orient the reader to the material by way of a topical presentation of it. What follows is thus a canvassing of relevant objections organized under the three aforementioned concerns about the relationship of Christ to the Father and Spirit, the unity of the person of Christ, and the genuineness of Christ's human life and suffering.

First, some writers have argued that Christ's relationship to the Father and Spirit conflicts with the doctrine of divine simplicity. The doctrine of divine simplicity is often unfamiliar to contemporary Christians and will be explained in more detail below, but for now it is sufficient to note at a general level that it involves a denial of God having any "parts" and an affirmation that there is just one divine intellect and will shared by the three divine persons (rather than three sets of faculties that might be included in what distinguishes one divine person from another). This rejection of multiple intellects and wills in God, taken together with an older habit of calling the divine persons "modes of subsisting" or "subsisting relations," has become a cause of concern. According to some, such a teaching cannot comport with the Bible's portrayal of Christ's distinction from and interaction with the Father and Spirit. Jürgen Moltmann, for example, contends that if the persons are called "modes of being," they are "degraded": the "subjectivity of acting and receiving is transferred from the divine Persons to the one divine subject," reviving the error of Sabellianism. Moltmann affirms that the divine persons exist only in relation to one another, but he emphasizes that they are three divine "subjects" in fellowship together.[1] Colin Gunton argues that divine simplicity or an "Augustinian" representation of God's unity undermines adequate distinction of the divine persons and their mutual

1. Moltmann, *The Trinity and the Kingdom*, 139, 171–76.

"relatedness" that "constitutes" God's being.[2] While Gunton denies that a divine person is an "individual centre of consciousness" with a discrete will, he still insists that the "persons are not relations, but concrete particulars in relation to one another."[3]

There are similar concerns among philosophical theologians. Thomas Morris, for example, explores the notion of communion within the Trinity and reasons that calling the persons mere "modes of subsisting" would preclude genuine interpersonal communion.[4] William Lane Craig stresses that "on no reasonable understanding of *person* can a person be equated with a relation." He asserts that "God is a soul which is endowed with three complete sets of rational faculties, each sufficient for personhood." On this view, "God, though one soul, would not be one person but three, for God would have three centers of self-consciousness, intentionality and volition."[5] William Hasker also comments that it is "exceedingly difficult to understand what a divine 'mode of being/subsistence' can be, given that it is not a *person* as we now understand that notion." He contends that this view leads to exegetical and logical problems. It implies that "the Gospels portray for us a single person praying to himself, talking to himself, answering himself, and crying out to himself in protest for having forsaken himself." By contrast, Hasker proposes that a divine person is a "distinct center of knowledge, will, love, and action."[6]

In addition, some authors suggest that the related teaching of the "inseparable operations" of the persons—the Father, Son, and Spirit always exercise the one divine will and power together in God's outward works—conflicts with the Bible's description of God's economic activity. Gunton, though affirming the axiom that the outward works of the Trinity are undivided (*opera Trinitatis ad extra indivisa sunt*), suggests that construing the persons as relations in an Augustinian manner will lead to neglect of the persons' distinct "forms of action" in the economy.[7] This concern, taken in conjunction with Gunton's emphasis on the Holy Spirit's distinct work of empowering the Son in his incarnate ministry,[8] raises the question of whether the doctrines of divine simplicity and inseparable operations will yield a Christology that obscures the Son's personal interaction with the Father and his dependence on the Spirit in the Gospels. Indeed, in view of such concerns, influential

---

2. Gunton, *The Promise of Trinitarian Theology*, 38–48, 74, 92–94, 152, 195–96, 200.

3. Gunton, *The Promise of Trinitarian Theology*, 39, 94–96, 195–96, 198, 200–201. Cf., e.g., A. Torrance, *Persons in Communion*, 115–16, 251–62.

4. Morris, *The Logic of God Incarnate*, 210–18.

5. Craig, "Toward a Tenable Social Trinitarianism," 91, 99.

6. Hasker, *Metaphysics and the Tri-personal God*, 193–95.

7. Gunton, *The Promise of Trinitarian Theology*, xxv, xxvi–xxviii, 3–4, 57, 94, 172, 198.

8. E.g., Gunton, *The Promise of Trinitarian Theology*, 51, 66–69, 131–33, 144, 189.

evangelical theologian Wayne Grudem has recently advocated abandoning the doctrine of inseparable operations altogether.[9]

Second, various authors maintain that the unity of the person of Christ in the Scriptures conflicts with certain logical implications of traditional descriptions of God. The nineteenth-century kenoticist Gottfried Thomasius argues that if the Son remains immutable in the incarnation, "if he persists in his trans-worldly position, in the unlimitedness of his world-ruling and world-embracing governance, then the mutual relation of [his divine mode of being and action and his finite human nature]. . . . remains afflicted by a certain duplication."[10] That is,

> the divine then, so to speak, surpasses the human as a broader circle does a smaller one; in its knowledge, life and action the divine extends infinitely far over and above the human, as the extra-historical over the temporal, as that which is perfect in itself over that which becomes. . . . The consciousness that the Son has of himself and of his universal governance does not come together as one with the consciousness of the historical Christ—it hovers, as it were, above him; the universal activity which the Son continuously exercises does not coincide with his divine-human action in the state of humiliation. . . . Thus the Logos still is or has something which is not merged into his historical appearance, which is not also the man Jesus—and all this seems to destroy the unity of the person, the identity of the ego; thus there occurs no living and complete penetration of both sides, no proper being-man of God.[11]

Albrecht Ritschl faults medieval theologians of the Western church in particular for keeping the immutable divine nature at a distance from the person of Christ in his historical work. If the divinity of Christ remains unaffected by the incarnation, then it appears "as if Godhead did not belong to him at all."[12] In their own ways, Thomasius and Ritschl are raising the question of whether within the logic of "classical theism" there must be a divinity above or behind Christ that is never truly united with his humanity. Eberhard Jüngel's emphasis on the death of God in Christ also brings up this question. Jüngel holds that a traditional doctrine of God would undermine God's "identification" with the man Jesus. He asks, "How can the divine essence be thought

9. Grudem, "Doctrinal Deviations in Evangelical-Feminist Arguments about the Trinity," 19–28. For recent defenses of inseparable operations, see, e.g., S. Holmes, "Trinitarian Action and Inseparable Operations"; Vidu, "The Incarnation and Trinitarian Inseparable Operations"; Vidu, *The Same God Who Works All Things*; Wittman, "On the Unity of the Trinity's External Works."

10. Thomasius, *Christ's Person and Work*, 46.

11. Thomasius, *Christ's Person and Work*, 46–47.

12. Ritschl, *The Christian Doctrine of Justification and Reconciliation*, 390–91.

of together with the event of death without destroying the concept of God?" Though conscious of the great "cloud of witnesses" from patristic, medieval, and early Protestant contexts who would disagree, Jüngel reasons that God's "unity with perishability" in Christ compels us to abandon an understanding of God in which he is complete in himself and unaffected by the world.[13] Recent discussions in philosophical theology have touched upon a similar point in relation to the concept of divine "timelessness." Thomas Senor, for example, has drawn attention to an apparent incompatibility between an entirely "timeless" deity and the temporal existence of Christ. Senor writes that if God the Son is "atemporal," then he is a person "with a human body whose actions (both the acts and their consequences) are temporally ordered but who is nevertheless timeless." According to Senor, "this account of the Incarnation is incoherent."[14]

Building on the work of Karl Barth, Bruce McCormack has taken a different approach in which he seeks to preserve God's immutability without compromising the unity of the person of Christ. However, in aiming to uphold God's immutability and the unity of the person of Christ, McCormack does argue that the doctrine of divine impassibility must be rejected. He posits that God constitutes his own essence by his eternal decision for the incarnation and thus includes in his own essence, in an anticipatory manner, the suffering of the Son. The impetus for this move, at least in my understanding of it, lies in McCormack's conviction that the Son's suffering cannot be restricted to his human nature. For restricting it in this manner would require that the human nature either be a mere "instrument" (a mere outward object) upon which the Son acts or else assigned to a second person. Thus, the suffering of the Son in his deity is invoked to confirm that he truly is the subject of suffering in the incarnation. It is the constitution of God's essence by his decision for the incarnation, then, that allows God to remain the same God that he eternally is while assuming a human nature in history and undergoing suffering. God's immutability remains intact, but, in order to avoid the error of Nestorianism, the doctrine of God's impassibility is abandoned.[15] McCormack argues that his constructive proposal not only upholds the unity of the person of Christ but also ensures the full deity of the *Logos ensarkos* since the *Logos asarkos* is, in his own divine essence, also *Logos incarnandus* (predestined to be incarnate).[16]

13. Jüngel, *God as the Mystery of the World*, 100, 199–225.

14. Senor, "Incarnation, Timelessness, and Leibniz's Law Problems," 224.

15. McCormack, "Karl Barth's Christology as a Resource for a Reformed Version of Kenoticism"; McCormack, "'With Loud Cries and Tears,'" 43–44, 47, 50–52; McCormack, "Divine Impassibility or Simply Divine Constancy?," 168–69, 177; McCormack, "The Only Mediator," 256–57, 262–64.

16. E.g., McCormack, "Grace and Being," 93–99; McCormack, "Seek God Where He May Be Found," 68; McCormack, "The Lord and Giver of Life," 231. McCormack has recently

Third, some have suggested that the genuineness and gravity of Christ's human life and suffering come into conflict with a traditional Christian view of God. In using words like "genuineness" and "gravity" I attempt to signal the importance of the fact that in the Gospels the Son himself lives a human life immediately—without merely wielding a human nature that remains external to him. There is real drama, exertion, and costly suffering in the Son's accomplishment of his mission. Isaak Dorner, for example, makes a case that God's simplicity, immutability, and eternity have been developed in the Christian tradition in a manner that renders divine action in the world "docetic." In the "old dogmatics," God's actuality and causal activity are "uniform," so his presence is not "differentiated." History then becomes only a "dogmatic repetition and rehearsal of something already eternally accomplished"; "temporal succession" becomes "merely an illusion." On such a view, Dorner suggests, the incarnation cannot involve a distinct assumption of and subsistence in a human nature on the part of the Son, for there could be at most only a special receptivity of this human nature to the general presence of God. Dorner, of course, insists that this is insufficient, so he maintains that the incarnation is "a new being of God himself in the world, which previously existed only according to potence or decree, and first achieves actuality in Christ."[17]

Various philosophical theologians today have similar concerns. Richard Holland, for example, makes the case that a traditional understanding of divine eternity, taken to mean divine "timelessness," would prevent us from taking seriously the events of Jesus's life that unfold in Scripture: "If the classical model of God's relation to time is true, then the biblical statements describing what took place in the Incarnation simply cannot be taken to mean what they might be interpreted to mean on a straightforward reading of the text." However, Holland suggests, if the incarnation is the starting point of our theologizing about God's being, this will lead us to posit "sequence in the divine life."[18] In addition, some authors have claimed that the Son's assumption of a human nature cannot cohere with the doctrine of divine simplicity. For that assumption, the implications of which are traditionally explicated in connection with the doctrine of the *communicatio idiomatum*, entails the introduction of human "properties" in the person of the Son. But it seems that the Son being a composite person with such human properties conflicts with God being simple.[19]

---

worked to refine and draw together the different elements in his approach in his new monograph *The Humility of the Eternal Son.*

17. Dorner, *Divine Immutability*, 101–2, 124–26, 129, 187–89.

18. Holland, *God, Time, and the Incarnation*, 125–26, 165.

19. See Senor, "The Compositional Account of the Incarnation," 58; Mullins, *The End of the Timeless God*, 184.

Related to the question of the authenticity of the Son's human experience are the practices of "partitive exegesis" and reduplicative speech in Christology: predicating certain attributes of Christ *as God* and predicating other attributes and experiences of Christ *as human*.[20] If it is legitimate to ascribe divine perfections to Christ *qua Deus* while also ascribing certain human attributes and experiences to the same Christ *qua homo*, this would help us to clarify that divine attributes like immutability, impassibility, eternity, and simplicity cohere with the Son's distinctly *human* weakness and suffering. However, a number of authors have challenged the practice of reduplication. Senor, for example, critiques a "compositional" view of the incarnation that has been used to ground reduplication, on which view, in Senor's description, God the Son is "a proper part of the individual who is Jesus Christ." For Senor, the problem is that the whole (the person of Christ) either will truly have the properties of its "parts" (the divine and human) and will be unable to have mutually exclusive properties (e.g., omniscience and ignorance) or will not "genuinely borrow a property from a part" and will ultimately not have that property *simpliciter*.[21] Jonathan Hill also notes objections to "compositional" Christology and comments that reduplicative description of the person of Christ needs a "metaphysical strategy."[22]

One might add that some recent treatments of the Son's *kenōsis* in Philippians 2:6–11 also seek to underscore the genuinely human experience of the Son and the drama and humiliation of the incarnation by implicitly revising or discarding the doctrines of divine immutability and simplicity. While a number of exegetes comment that the Son does not actually give up anything belonging to his divinity in the language of Philippians 2—the phrase "emptied himself," after all, is not accompanied by a "genitive of content"[23]—some still conclude that the Son's assumption of a servant's form must entail a cessation of the exercise of certain divine attributes on his part.[24] But in their more traditional formulations, divine immutability and simplicity do not admit of any idleness or inactivity on the part of God and, indeed, preclude a real distinction between act, on the one hand, and would-be passive capacities or faculties in God, on the other.

---

20. On partitive exegesis, see, e.g., Behr, *The Formation of Christian Theology*, 347–52; Jamieson, "1 Corinthians 15.28 and the Grammar of Paul's Christology."

21. Senor, "The Compositional Account of the Incarnation," 55, 69.

22. J. Hill, "Introduction," 5–6, 14. Cf., e.g., Le Poidevin, "Incarnation," 707–9. For positive work on reduplication, see, e.g., M. Gorman, "Christological Consistency and the Reduplicative Qua"; Moser, "Tools for Interpreting Christ's Saving Mysteries in Scripture."

23. Hawthorne and Martin, *Philippians*, 117.

24. E.g., MacLeod, "Imitating the Incarnation of Christ," 318–19, 329–30. See also Schreiner, *New Testament Theology*, 326.

These christologically driven criticisms of "classical theism" emerge from various disciplinary milieus and call for a careful response. However, before beginning the constructive work of this study and addressing the material concerns of such authors along the way, we should consider some reservations about the formal concepts and categories employed in the history of Christian description of the person of Christ.

III. Opposition to "Metaphysics"

Theologians and biblical scholars who have questioned the viability of using traditional concepts to shed light on the Bible's Christology have done so for a variety of reasons. I do not wish to force those reasons to fit under the three types of concerns that have been discussed in this chapter so far, but I will attempt to note certain connections to those concerns where it is appropriate. More broadly, I will try to accomplish two things in this section: first, to take into account a general aversion to classical metaphysics in modern study of theology and the Bible; and, second, to show more specifically how some theologians and biblical scholars question particular uses of metaphysical concepts that are present in traditional Christology.

A. General Aversion to Classical Metaphysics

For most of church history Christian interpreters of the Bible thought it fitting to make use of various concepts taken up and analyzed in the classical metaphysical tradition. They did this in order to exhibit what Scripture teaches about the triune God and to confess not just what God has done in history but also who God is in himself (insofar as that is knowable to us). However, certain factors at work over the past few centuries have altered the theological and exegetical landscape, yielding a reluctance to utilize the older concepts and categories and, in some cases, a tendency to locate the meaning of God's revelation strictly within the compass of history, or at least within the context of God's relationship to creation.

While many names bear mentioning here, it is difficult to engage modern theological discussion of metaphysics without including Immanuel Kant. In his quest to secure a kind of human knowledge marked by necessity and independence from the contingency associated with sense perception, Kant argued that the mind possesses various a priori concepts and judgments that shape the "raw material" of sense perception.[25] The proper objects of human

---

25. Kant, *Critique of Pure Reason*, A1–2.

knowledge are in fact mental representations, not outward things themselves (especially not those things that transcend sense perception altogether).[26] In this account of human knowing, traditional concepts and categories in metaphysics (substance, quality, relation, action, passion, and so on) are a priori features of the mind, not something introduced in the mind by an encounter with the structures of outward reality itself.[27] Since the mind will seek to find a "because" that answers its "why" questions, human persons end up positing God in order to account for and complete our knowledge of conditioned, limited beings. But this move, designated by the term "ontotheology," does not provide any knowledge of God as an actual extramental being.[28] For Kant, then, it is not theoretical but practical reason (deliberation about the actions that human beings should undertake) that provides a better pathway to obtaining certainty about the existence of God. Human awareness of moral obligation involves an awareness of the freedom of the human subject that cannot be accounted for merely by reference to the sensible realm. The awareness of moral obligation also engenders a belief and certainty about God and the prospect of a future life to come, if not a strict "knowledge" of God with objective grounds.[29]

In post-Kantian philosophy, various thinkers sought to explain the relationship between nature or the sensible world, on the one hand, and the thinking subject, on the other hand. In Frederick Beiser's words, German idealists sought to clarify the sense in which "reality depends upon the ideal or the rational." According to Beiser, some emphasized that from within the human subject the ideal or the rational gives form to the content of outward reality ("subjective idealism"), while others emphasized that the ideal in the human subject and in outward reality itself are "equal instances" of an "archetypical" rationality ("objective idealism").[30] Fichte provides one example of what Beiser calls "subjective idealism." According to some of his critics, Fichte seemed to eliminate altogether the outward reality of things in themselves. He seemed to reason that the human subject in solipsist fashion posits

26. Kant, *Critique of Pure Reason*, Bxxxix, A30/B45, A36–B53, A104, B146, A368–76, A490–91/B518–19.

27. Kant, *Critique of Pure Reason*, A77–83/B102–9, A92–95/B125–29, B406–13; Kant, *Prolegomena to Any Future Metaphysics*, 4:265–66.

28. Kant, *Critique of Pure Reason*, A290–92/B347–49, A296/B352–53, B593–95, A578–91/B606–19, A592–620/B620–48, A632/B660, A845–46/B873–74; Kant, *Prolegomena to Any Future Metaphysics*, 4:350–60.

29. Kant, *Critique of Pure Reason*, Bxxix–xxx; A3/B6–7; A820–31/B848–59. Kant's more expansive treatments of morality and its connection with the concepts of God, freedom, and immortality can be found in his *Groundwork of the Metaphysics of Morals*; *Critique of Practical Reason*; and *Religion within the Bounds of Mere Reason*.

30. Beiser, *German Idealism*, 11–14.

the external world, though whether this was Fichte's intention is disputed.[31] Schelling and Hegel provide examples of an "objective idealism." Schelling advances a philosophical system in which an absolute ideal realizes itself through a mutual determination of nature and mind.[32] In Hegel's system, absolute being or absolute Spirit proceeds through a historical dialectic in which it attains to self-consciousness. Hegel's framing of the progression of the divine toward self-realization envisions a contribution to be made by human subjectivity and includes a reinterpretation of the central events of the Christian faith.[33]

Offering an adequate account of German idealism is well beyond the bounds of this study, but the point here is just to observe that it did involve a tendency to locate God (or that which is absolute) within the horizon of the world and its history. Without attempting to identify all the points at which Kant and later idealists influenced modern theologians and exegetes, I want to convey here at least a sense of the backdrop against which many of those theologians and exegetes have gone about their work.[34] Reservations about classical metaphysics appear throughout modern theology and take various forms. Like Kant, some writers expressly argue that metaphysics must be circumvented in an effort to find a more secure path to knowledge of God. Like certain strands of German idealism, some writers focus on God's historical activity rather than God himself or God's immanent acts. To borrow a description from Hans Urs von Balthasar, amid these authors' diverse concerns lies the common construal of classical metaphysics as "the mischief-maker."[35]

In his speeches to religion's "cultured despisers," Friedrich Schleiermacher, for example, echoes the idea that metaphysical thinking is a matter of human persons proactively using mental constructs to classify things instead of responding to outward reality. Metaphysics "classifies the universe and divides it into this being and that, seeks out the reasons for what exists, and deduces the necessity of what is real while spinning the reality of the world and its

31. See, e.g., Fichte, *A Crystal Clear Report*, 39–115. On Fichte, see Beiser, *German Idealism*, 217–345; Pinkard, *German Philosophy, 1760–1860*, 105–30; Dorrien, *Kantian Reason and Hegelian Spirit*, 65–74.

32. See Schelling, *System of Transcendental Idealism*. On Schelling, see Beiser, *German Idealism*, 491–505, 551–64; Pinkard, *German Philosophy, 1760–1860*, 172–98; Dorrien, *Kantian Reason and Hegelian Spirit*, 160–73.

33. See Hegel, *The Phenomenology of Spirit*; Hegel, *Lectures on the Philosophy of Religion*. On Hegel, see Pinkard, *German Philosophy, 1760–1860*, 217–304; Pinkard, *Hegel: A Biography*. Note also these more constructive works: Hodgson, *Hegel and Christian Theology*; De Nys, *Hegel and Theology*.

34. Useful background material can be found in Zachhuber, *Theology as Science in Nineteenth-Century Germany*; Zachhuber, *Zwischen Idealismus und Historismus*.

35. Von Balthasar, *Theo-Drama*, 62.

laws out of itself." In metaphysics, the human subject takes the initiative as the "condition of all being and the cause of all becoming." By contrast, Schleiermacher says, religious "intuition" or "immediate perception" of the infinite in its mysterious and evocative character affords a surer connection with God. In religion, one is acted upon by the universe in a "childlike passivity." Human attempts to reflect upon the religious intuition and to represent it in the "abstract expressions" of dogma inevitably lose something of its responsive awareness of the mystery of God.[36]

Ritschl develops a sharp distinction between metaphysical thinking and Christian knowledge of God and contends that the former reduces God to a feature of "nature" or an impersonal "world-ground." For Ritschl, metaphysics as the study of "things in general" or the "universal grounds" of things focuses on "nature and her laws" and fails to account for a crucial distinction between nature, on the one hand, and "spirit" or "personality," on the other. When Greek philosophers or scholastic theologians try to develop a "rational" concept of God through cosmological or teleological arguments, they arrive at only the idea of a "world-unity" or "world-ground" to which the Christian idea of God might then be arbitrarily attached. Indeed, this way of thinking proves God's existence only "in thought," not his "objective existence." And it does not arrive at a personal God who transcends the impersonal structures of nature. In this connection, Ritschl is critical of a concept of the "Absolute" set over against the "personality" and the love of the biblical God. Stuck within the field of impersonal "nature," this "Absolute" is simply an idol.[37]

Consequently, Ritschl criticizes medieval and Protestant scholastic theologians for neglecting to begin their accounts of God with God's revelation in the person of Christ, who is the only source of genuine knowledge of God.[38] In Ritschl's view, human beings cannot truly know God with a "theoretical," "disinterested" sort of knowledge. We must know God with a faith that apprehends him as the true source of our blessedness, which is found only in God's kingdom. Indeed, we "know the nature of God and Christ only in their worth for us."[39] In his discussion of the knowledge of God, Ritschl also argues that it is a mistake to presume to know what a thing is in itself over against

36. Schleiermacher, *On Religion*, 19–24, 26–29, 31–33, 48–53.

37. Ritschl, *The Christian Doctrine of Justification and Reconciliation*, 16–17, 24–25, 208, 214–19, 221, 222, 225–28, 238. Kant's moral arguments for God's existence fare better here, since they at least proceed from the assumption of "man's self-distinction from nature" (219–20).

38. Ritschl, *The Christian Doctrine of Justification and Reconciliation*, 4–5, 7–8, 193–94, 202, 212–13, 237. Of the older theologians, Ritschl suggests, Luther alone understood the importance of this approach to the knowledge of God.

39. Ritschl, *The Christian Doctrine of Justification and Reconciliation*, 6–7, 203–7, 212–13, 218.

its operations and "phenomenal effects." How could one presume to know what a thing is "at rest" or "apart from its effects" when in fact one knows it only by its operations and effects? Here Ritschl remarks that "scholastic dogmatics" erred in its treatment of "the essence and attributes of God" in distinction from the "operations of God upon the world and for the salvation of mankind."[40] In Ritschl, then, one can find an aversion to a metaphysics that fails to secure knowledge of God in his transcendence of created being. One can also find the suggestion that once one has committed to knowing God in Christ, one primarily deals with God in his activity toward us, rather than what God is in himself.

Adolf Harnack's treatment of the formation of Christian dogma also registers concerns about the role of Greek metaphysics in theology. In Harnack's view, both early Gnostic sects and early catholic Christians undertook an "acute secularising of Christianity" in order to transform the gospel of Jesus into a metaphysical system that would secure the place of Christianity in the ancient world. Harnack calls this an "indulgent remodeling" of the Christian faith, or an accommodation to the "Greek spirit." Though he endeavors to provide a historical description of Christian dogma, Harnack clearly laments what he takes to be a corruption of the Christian message in its accommodation to Greek concepts and speculative tendencies.[41] In Harnack's estimation, retelling the history of dogma is instrumental to "emancipating" the church from Greek metaphysical thinking.[42]

Finally, some of Karl Barth's comments on metaphysics in theology should be included here. Barth takes issue with a theological method that involves attending to the limits of created being (or "non-being") and then extrapolating from those limits what "true being" (i.e., God) must be.[43] In Barth's judgment, human beings should not be confident that we can develop an accurate idea of a perfect being that will in fact correspond to God's being. The movement from "mere consciousness" to the "apprehension of the truth of being" cannot be wrought by our own efforts. In his assessment of authors like Aquinas and Melanchthon on the doctrine of God, Barth criticizes them for beginning with a "doctrine of being" or a "concept of being which comprehends God and what is not God." Such a "general idea of God" is developed "arbitrarily" according to the whims of (fallen) reason and inevitably

40. Ritschl, *The Christian Doctrine of Justification and Reconciliation*, 18–23. On Ritschl's understanding of metaphysics in relation to theology, see further his *Theology and Metaphysics*, 151–217.

41. Harnack, *History of Dogma*, 15–17, 21, 46–53, 223–28.

42. Harnack, *Outlines of the History of Dogma*, 7–8.

43. Barth, *CD*, II.1, 303–4.

stands against the particular content of God's revelation in Christ, which cuts through our subjective assumptions about what God must be like. This particular revelation is what secures a connection between us and God as an object of knowledge.[44]

From within a general resistance toward classical metaphysics, there is a tendency in some circles to label certain claims about God "metaphysical" in a negative sense, particularly those claims that speak of God in himself without reference to his economic works. It seems to me that the connection between these two phenomena lies in the fact that natural or metaphysical reasoning, over against the economy or the incarnation, is often taken to be what grounds claims about God in himself in his transcendence of the economy.[45] This of course presupposes that God's revelation in the economy or the incarnation does not reveal God to be complete in himself without reference to his economic activity—a point that will be challenged later on.

Schleiermacher, for example, takes the teaching of the eternal equality and distinctions among the divine persons in God himself to be a matter of mere "speculation" with no bearing on "our living communion with him."[46] Hermann Cremer criticizes earlier theologians for embracing "philosophical speculation" in the doctrine of God. The fathers, Cremer argues, adopted an Aristotelian notion of God as "first mover," "pure being," or "the absolute," to which the fathers inconsistently added the concrete attributes of the God revealed in Christ. For Cremer, the Aristotelian approach or the Dionysian "threefold way" to God's attributes does not yield knowledge of the true God. Consideration of the world around us does not produce real theological knowledge. Philosophy seeks a solution to the "mystery of conditioned being," while faith seeks a practical knowledge of God for salvation. Accordingly, "statements about God which do not stand in direct connection with our salvation are useless for faith and doctrine." Christians know God by his revelatory action in history. According to Cremer, though God does not need us, he has determined himself to be "God for and with others." God is the one "who wills to be all that he is for us and with us" and "wills to have us for himself." Indeed, that is "his innermost essence, which fulfills him" (*sein Wesen, das Innerste, das ihn erfüllt*). In this regard, his activity toward us "belongs to his essence." Accordingly, for Cremer, we must "join

---

44. Barth, *CD*, II.1, 259–64, 272–74, 288, 310–12, 329; III.1, 346–49.

45. Katherine Sonderegger (*Systematic Theology*, 2:xvi) also points out a tendency in modern theology to associate reflection on God's inner life with "speculation" and "rationalism" over against biblical teaching.

46. Schleiermacher, *The Christian Faith*, §171 (1023–24), §172 (1032, 1035). For a recent argument that Schleiermacher is still not dismissive of the doctrine of the Trinity on the whole, see Poe, *Essential Trinitarianism*.

all our statements about the essence of God more closely and immediately to his revelation in Christ." Once we understand that *this* God is the subject of all true statements about God, then it is possible to use the concept of God to identify divine attributes that will suit him.[47]

Barth called Cremer's work on the divine attributes "extraordinarily informative," but he also faulted Cremer for "yielding to a revulsion against the idea of being as such." Here Barth is eager to emphasize that "God is not swallowed up in the relation and attitude of himself to the world." That is, God is who he is even without his outward works: "They are bound to Him, but He is not bound to them."[48] At the same time, Barth clearly opposes any approach to the doctrine of God that begins with a "common" or "neutral" (i.e., "metaphysical") concept of being rather than the incarnate Christ. He writes, "God is who He is in His works"; "in Himself He is not another than He is in His works." In other words, God's being is a "being in act," in the act of his revelation in Christ. Therefore, when inquiring about God's being, we have to focus exclusively on his works. For we will "encounter [the essence of God] at the place where he deals with us as Lord and Saviour, or not at all."[49] Since God has eternally willed the incarnation, we are not authorized to "bracket" God's decision in an attempt to know a Godhead or a *Logos asarkos* behind Jesus.[50] Indeed, in a move that sounds reminiscent of Cremer, Barth insists not only that we cannot know God apart from the incarnation but also that there just is "no such thing as Godhead in itself. Godhead is always the Godhead of the Father, the Son and the Holy Spirit. But the Father is the Father of Jesus Christ and the Holy Spirit is the Spirit of the Father and the Spirit of Jesus Christ."[51]

A number of theologians after Barth make similar statements regarding "metaphysical" claims about God. T. F. Torrance, for example, rejects a "metaphysical conception of the inertial Nature or Being of God" in favor of a "powerful soteriological approach" to the doctrine of God that is "governed by the self-revelation of God as Father, Son and Holy Spirit in the history of salvation." In this soteriologically oriented approach, God enters "relations of love with others thereby opening himself to them and establishing reciprocal relations with them."[52] Jüngel also takes up a "critical position over against

---

47. Cremer, *Die christliche Lehre von den Eigenschaften Gottes*, 7–11, 13–20, 23, 25, 31–33, 106–8. With his emphasis on God's revelation in Christ in particular, Cremer seeks to address what he considers to be shortcomings in Ritschl and Wilhelm Herrmann.

48. Barth, *CD*, II.1, 260.

49. Barth, *CD*, II.1, 260–64, 272–75.

50. Barth, *CD*, IV.1, 52–53.

51. Barth, *CD*, II.2, 115.

52. T. F. Torrance, *The Christian Doctrine of God*, 248.

the traditional metaphysical conception" by emphasizing God's "unity with perishability" in Christ.[53] Similarly, Robert Jenson writes that "Greece identified deity by metaphysical predicates" (e.g., impassibility, timelessness, and simplicity). Jenson contrasts the "metaphysical principles of the Greeks and the storytelling of the gospel," the latter portraying a God who completes his identity through his eschatological action.[54]

Wolf Krötke's treatment of the divine perfections (*Klarheiten*, in his description) discusses the "metaphysical doctrine of the attributes of God" and then "ways out of the metaphysical doctrine of the attributes of God." The "metaphysical doctrine" is exemplified by Aquinas and proceeds from an understanding of God as first cause. In Krötke's assessment, the "metaphysical" notion of God as the self-sufficient first cause does not permit adequate description of the biblical God's activity in the world.[55] In Bruce McCormack's critique of a metaphysical doctrine of God (one that originates from outside the doctrine of the incarnation), he writes that "classical theism" operates with a "very robust Creator-creature distinction." God's being is "understood to be complete in itself with or without the world." It is "characterized by . . . a 'static' or unchanging perfection." This metaphysical approach to God strives to "deny to God any similarity to created reality through a process of negating the limits thought to belong to the creaturely."[56]

In addition to the cautions of systematic theologians, there are prominent voices in recent biblical scholarship who contend that Scripture has little or nothing to say about ontological matters or "Greek" philosophical speculation, particularly God in his aseity and transcendence of history.[57] It seems to me that a broader account of this phenomenon would require some discussion of the origin and predominance of historical-critical study of the Bible, together with the rise of biblical studies as a specialization influenced by German idealist or historicist philosophies and often isolated from the concerns of theology and worship.[58] However, a few examples will have to

53. Jüngel, *God as the Mystery of the World*, 184.
54. Jenson, *Systematic Theology*, 64–66, 94–95, 111–12, 234.
55. Krötke, *Gottes Klarheiten*, 49–59.
56. McCormack, "The Actuality of God," 186–88.
57. See, e.g., Brueggemann, *An Unsettling God*, 1–2, 4–5, 9; Fretheim, *What Kind of God?*, 19, 41, 104, 121, 159–61, 326; Feldmeier and Spieckermann, *God of the Living*, 109, 330, 361, 403–8.
58. Figures like Baruch Spinoza (see his *Tractatus theologico-politicus*, 7.97–117) and J. P. Gabler (see his *De iusto discrimine theologiae biblicae*, esp. 183–84 on the distinction between "biblical" and "dogmatic" theology) have significantly shaped how biblical interpretation is carried out. On the influence of certain strands of German philosophy, see, e.g., Noonan, "Hegel and Strauss"; Rogerson, *Old Testament Criticism in the Nineteenth Century*; Hayes and Prussner, *Old Testament Theology*, esp. chaps. 2–3; Rogerson, *W. M. L. de Wette*; Baird,

suffice here to illustrate concerns about the intrusion of "metaphysics" in scriptural exegesis.

In the case of the divine name ("I AM WHO I AM") in Exodus 3, for example, commentators have often restricted its significance to God's relationship to Israel or God's historical action. While premodern exegetes typically see in the divine name a testimony to God's eternal plenitude,[59] Gerhard von Rad, for instance, writes that the name does not concern God's absolute being or aseity: "Such a thing would be altogether out of keeping with the Old Testament."[60] Put differently, "One must take care not to introduce into [the verb "to be"] the metaphysical notion of Being in itself, of aseity as elaborated by Greek philosophy."[61] Again, the name does not teach us "something about God's substance or essence but something about a personal identity and history."[62] In other words, the name does not reveal God's "static being" but rather his "dynamic being" or "efficacious being."[63]

Other examples of the presupposition that the biblical text does not deal with God's own being can be found in analyses of the Johannine statements "God is spirit," "God is light," and "God is love" (John 4:24; 1 John 1:5; 4:8, 16). Though the restriction of the content of these statements to God's external works is not universal, Rudolf Bultmann, for example, expresses well a tendency toward such a restriction in his comments on John 4:24:

> This is not a definition in the Greek sense. It is not, that is, an attempt to define the mode of being proper to God as he is in himself, by referring to it as the mode of being of a phenomenon from the observable world, i.e., the πνεῦμα. It does however "define" the *idea* of God, by saying what God *means*, viz. that

History of New Testament Research, chap. 8; Howard, *Religion and the Rise of Historicism*; Harrisville and Sundberg, *The Bible in Modern Culture*, esp. chaps. 5–6; Zachhuber, *Theology as Science in Nineteenth-Century Germany*. For responses to the separation of biblical studies and constructive theology, see, e.g., Fowl, *Engaging Scripture*; Legaspi, *The Death of Scripture and the Rise of Biblical Studies*; Stanglin, *The Letter and Spirit of Biblical Interpretation*; Carter, *Interpreting Scripture with the Great Tradition*; Sarisky, *Reading the Bible Theologically*; Macaskill, "Identifications, Articulations, and Proportions in Practical Theological Interpretation."

59. E.g., Hilary of Poitiers, *La Trinité* 1.5 (1:211–12); Augustine, *De trin.* 5.3 (1:207–8); John of Damascus, *Expos. fidei* 1.9 (31). In this study, where older cited works include numerical designations for book, chapter, paragraph, and so forth, the page numbers from the edition used appear afterward in parentheses.

60. Von Rad, *Old Testament Theology*, 180.

61. De Vaux, "The Revelation of the Divine Name YHWH," 70.

62. Seitz, *Figured Out*, 140.

63. Abba, "The Divine Name of Yahweh," 327; Mowinckel, "The Name of the God of Moses," 127; von Rad, *Old Testament Theology*, 180. However, for recent alternatives to such approaches, see Allen, "Exodus 3 after the Hellenization Thesis"; Saner, *"Too Much to Grasp"*; Macaskill, "Name Christology, Divine Aseity, and the I Am Sayings in the Fourth Gospel"; Bauckham, *Who Is God?*, 42–45.

for man God is the miraculous being who deals wonderfully with him just as the definition of God as ἀγάπη (I Jn 4.8, 16) refers to him as the one who deals with men out of his love and in his love.[64]

Similarly, Raymond Brown states that this is "not an essential definition of God, but a description of God's dealings with men. . . . God is Spirit toward men because he gives the Spirit."[65] Likewise Adolf Schlatter: "πνεῦμα names God according to his works within the world. The statement remains in this respect parallel with ὁ θεὸς φῶς ἐστιν, I, 1, 5 and ὁ θεὸς ἀγάπη ἐστίν, I, 4, 8. All these statements describe God's behavior and works."[66]

B. Aversion to Particular Uses of Metaphysical Concepts in Christology

Now that we have considered some of the broader thinking about metaphysics in modern theology and exegesis, we can observe more specific objections to the use of metaphysical concepts in traditional Christology. Schleiermacher, for example, critiques creedal and scholastic description of the person of Christ on the grounds that the term "nature" denotes an "aggregate of modes of conduct or a body of laws according to which life circumstances not only change but are also contained within a distinct course of life." According to Schleiermacher, a person—an "I" that is "the same in all one's successive elements over time"—cannot remain intact under a "duality of natures" without either "the one yielding to the other when the one offers a larger and the other a narrower course of life" or "the two natures blending into each other, in that the two systems of law and conduct actually become one in the one life." To illustrate what he calls the "total fruitlessness of this mode of presentation," Schleiermacher draws attention to the claim that Christ has two wills. He reasons that if Christ has two wills pertaining to two natures, one must be "superfluous, no matter whether the divine will is supposed to accompany the human or vice versa." Indeed, the object of the human will could never be that of the divine will ("simply the entire world in the totality of its development").[67]

At the beginning of the twentieth century, authors like P. T. Forsyth and H. R. Mackintosh argued for a "moralizing" of Christology, by which they meant translating it out of Aristotelian concepts and categories and into categories that, in their judgment, would bring the personal, ethical action of

---

64. Bultmann, *John*, 191.
65. R. Brown, *John I–XII*, 172.
66. Schlatter, *Der Evangelist Johannes*, 162. Cf. Beasley-Murray, *John*, 62.
67. Schleiermacher, *The Christian Faith*, §96 (585–87).

Christ into focus. Forsyth contends that within a two-natures christological framework the divinity and humanity of Christ could exist only in "mutual externality." Accordingly, Forsyth advocates a view in which the ethical action of Christ, beginning with his *kenōsis* and culminating in his sacrificial death, unites the divine and human in his person.[68] Mackintosh insists that the two-natures doctrine "imports into the life of Christ an incredible and thoroughgoing dualism": the "simplicity and coherence of all that Christ was and did vanishes, for God is not after all living a human life. On the contrary, he is still holding Himself at a distance from its experience and conditions." For the Chalcedonian formulation assumes that "there exists a complex whole of attributes and qualities, which can be understood and spoken about as a 'nature' enjoying some kind of real being apart from the unifying or focal Ego." This leads either to a "duplex personality" or, if the personal unity remains, to the "impersonal manhood" found in the doctrine of the *anhypostasis* of Christ's human nature.[69] In Schleiermacher, Forsyth, and Mackintosh, hesitations about the traditional terminology are connected to an interest in upholding the unity of the person of Christ and the authenticity of his human life.

Developing theological trajectories that he finds in Barth's work, McCormack questions the use of the category of "substance" in theology proper and Christology. McCormack's concern about the term "substance" turns on what he takes to be its designation of an "abstract" divine essence or nature that is not informed by God's decision for the incarnation. In McCormack's "actualist" ontology, God constitutes himself as God or "assigns" himself his own being by his act of deciding to be God for us in the incarnation. There is thus no "metaphysical gap" between God *in se* and God *pro nobis*. In McCormack's program, this is important for retaining the immutability of God the Son in the incarnation. For God the Son must remain unchanged and undiminished in his divinity in his incarnation and passion, lest the efficacy of his saving work be jeopardized. But, McCormack argues, the Son suffers in his divinity and not merely in his human nature. Thus, if his divinity is to remain unchanged in the midst of his incarnation and suffering, it must include in an anticipatory manner the suffering that he will undergo. Insofar as an "abstract" divine substance would prevent God's own essence from including Christ's redemptive suffering, it should be abandoned.[70]

---

68. Forsyth, *The Person and Place of Jesus Christ*, 216–35, 318–20.
69. Mackintosh, *The Doctrine of the Person of Jesus Christ*, 293–96.
70. See McCormack, "Grace and Being," 93–101; McCormack, "Seek God Where He May Be Found," 68; McCormack, "The Actuality of God," 221–23; McCormack, "Election and the Trinity," 210, 214, 222; McCormack, "The Lord and Giver of Life," 231, 246–47.

There are comparable lines of thinking in the writings of New Testament scholars who aim to prioritize concepts and categories that they believe are more suited to the Jewish milieu of the incarnation. Not all New Testament scholars follow this line of thinking, but some who advocate an early "high Christology" in the New Testament do take this sort of approach. Richard Bauckham, for example, has proposed that the notion of "identity" can open up New Testament Christology in a way that illumines the high Christology of the early church without getting preoccupied with "Greek" conceptions of a "divine nature" or "metaphysical attributes." Bauckham takes the term "identity" here to refer to "the personal identity of self-continuity," which is applied to God "by analogy with human personal identity, understood not as a mere ontological subject without characteristics, but as including both character and personal story (the latter entailing relationships)." In Bauckham's judgment, the notion of the "identity" of the God of Israel "appropriately focuses on *who* God is rather than what divinity is"—"rather than divine essence or nature, which are not the primary categories for Jewish theology." For Bauckham, using the notion of identity enables us to circumvent the false choice between a "functional" and an "ontic" Christology, for it is precisely the functions or actions performed by the God of Israel (particularly his work of creating and ruling the world) that are "intrinsic" to his identity and thus mark him out as the true God. This means that when such actions are ascribed to Jesus in the New Testament, the biblical authors are including him in the identity of God and evincing a Christology of the very highest sort.[71]

To be sure, Bauckham is sympathetic to the way the church fathers sought to "transpose" the Christology of the New Testament in their Hellenistic context by teaching the consubstantiality of the divine persons in the Nicene Creed. Indeed, Bauckham's account confirms that the fathers were not developing a high Christology out of thin air but were attempting to expound the apostolic teaching about Jesus. However, Bauckham does believe that the fathers' reflection on the "divine nature" is problematic in that it kept the cross at a distance from God's identity. In Bauckham's view, it is not only that Jesus is included in God's identity but also that God's identity is enacted in the humility and suffering of Jesus: "Not only the pre-existent and the exalted Jesus, but also the earthly, suffering, humiliated and crucified Jesus belongs to the unique identity of God." Indeed, "The story of Jesus is not a mere illustration of the divine identity; Jesus himself and his story are intrinsic to the divine identity." After all, the Old Testament itself teaches that God would "reveal his glory and demonstrate his deity" through "the witness,

71. Bauckham, *Jesus and the God of Israel*, ix–x, 6–8, 30–31, 35, 52.

the humiliation, the death and the exaltation of the Servant of the Lord." According to Bauckham, "the shift to the categories of divine nature and the Platonic definition of divine nature which the Fathers took for granted proved serious impediments to anything more than a formal inclusion of human humiliation, suffering and death in the identity of God. . . . Adequate theological appropriation of the deepest insights of New Testament Christology . . . was not to occur until Martin Luther, Karl Barth and more recent theologies of the cross."[72]

Another New Testament scholar who has expressed concern about the distorting influence of traditional philosophical concepts is N. T. Wright. Though he affirms that Jesus understood himself as the embodiment of YHWH, Wright comments that Jesus himself would have found talk of a "hypostatic union" to be "puzzling," not least because it is a product of the "abstract, dehistoricized mode in which much systematic theology has been conducted." Instead of theorizing about substances or natures or "cleaning up with the categories of Aquinas, Calvin, or anyone else," Wright proposes that Jesus's relation to God should be understood in terms of the prophesied return of YHWH to his temple, a move that would, in Wright's estimation, "slice through the denser thickets of theological definitions and enable us to talk more crisply, more Jewishly, and for that matter more intelligibly, about Jesus and about God."[73] In a work written for a more popular audience, Wright states that "the canonical gospels and the creeds are not in fact presenting the same picture" of Jesus because the latter are largely silent about the Savior's life, passing quickly from his birth to his passion.[74] For Wright, the decidedly Jewish character of the life and teaching of Jesus must come to the fore. Though not altogether dismissive of the christological statements of the ecumenical councils, Wright suggests, "From at least the fourth century onwards, Christian theology has constantly been trying to make theological bricks without the biblical straw." Wright wonders whether by deploying "the language of substance and nature" theologians "forgot, perhaps deliberately (?), the Jewish narrative within which what they wanted to say made much better sense."[75] It might be said that Wright, like others, is calling attention to the importance of Christ's earthly life, but rather than making the point in general terms Wright is accentuating the Jewishness of that life.

72. Bauckham, *Jesus and the God of Israel*, x, 33, 35–37, 45–46, 50–53, 58–59. Among the more recent theologies that Bauckham lists are those of Moltmann and Jüngel.

73. Wright, "Jesus' Self-Understanding," 52–59.

74. Wright, *How God Became King*, 11–13.

75. Wright, "Historical Paul and 'Systematic Theology,'" 157–58.

A final example is Chris Tilling's work on Pauline Christology, which is critical of traditional theological use of Aristotelian concepts. Tilling endeavors to shed light on Paul's "divine Christology" by considering "the relation between the risen Lord and believers." Along the way he takes issue with "Aristotelian ontology" (as mediated by LeRon Shults's characterization and criticism of it). Tilling calls attention to "Paul's relational and commitment oriented monotheism," which prioritizes "language and categories drawn from the complex of interrelated themes and concepts that describe the relation of Jewish believers with YHWH." Tilling faults Gordon Fee, for example, for operating with an Aristotelian ontology, which involves an "emphasis on the substance or essence of Christ" and a "suppression of 'relation' as 'accidental' to a thing." In Tilling's judgment, a focus on "static being" makes it difficult to take seriously the subordination of the Son to the Father without concluding that one must compromise Paul's account of the divinity of Christ.[76]

Toward the end of his study, Tilling emphasizes that one finds in Paul a "relational" theology and epistemology more than "static and intellectualised propositional statements." This way of representing the person of Christ can, according to Tilling, accommodate Paul's subordination language without threat to Christ's divinity, for "it could embrace mystery, paradox and tension. Christ was subordinate to God yet was grasped in Paul's relational pattern of language in a manner which affirms a divine-Christology." Tilling suggests that "recent employment of relational concepts" in philosophical discourse provides an opportunity for exegetes to "reengage with the relational mode of Christology and monotheism . . . that one finds in Paul's letters." This approach "pushes the matter beyond a merely functional conception of the significance of Christ for Paul, but neither is it stated especially in terms of Christ's 'being' or 'essence,' as in the later church creeds—even if the creeds can be fairly posited as a faithful 'translation' of the significance of Paul's Christ-relation." A little later Tilling appears to express a somewhat lower estimation of Nicene Christology's connection to the Bible. He writes that "the Jesus who said 'Why do you call me good? No one is good but God alone' (Mark 10:18) is unlikely to have said in the next breath, that he is 'true God from true God.'" Indeed, "whether creedal statements are a faithful translation of biblical material from one context to another need not even be questioned because translations of concepts like this . . . by necessity involve development." One need not emphasize either continuity or discontinuity between the New Testament and "orthodox Christology," because the latter

76. Tilling, *Paul's Divine Christology*, 34, 36, 39, 47, 103–4.

is neither a "necessary interpretation of the historical Jesus" nor an "illegitimate development from the same." Tilling roots this assessment in the idea that being in relation to Christ is more fundamental than testimony about Christ, an ordering that, Tilling holds, allows the church's understanding of Christ to develop over time. Again, prioritizing relations is the key, and Paul's "relational intuitions," along with philosophy's "turn to relationality," confirm "the demise of recourse to static substance." Drawing upon Shults, Tilling muses that Darwinian biology also undermines the notion of fixed substances, which gives further incentive to explore the use of other categories in contemporary Christology.[77]

In the previous section we considered how a number of theologians, philosophers, and biblical scholars have argued that the Bible's Christology conflicts with various claims found in traditional Christian accounts of God (e.g., that he is immutable, impassible, eternal, simple). Though they are not the only issues one could highlight, we noted three recurring themes that come up: (1) a concern to set forth the Son's relationship to the Father and Spirit, (2) a concern to preserve the unity of the person of Christ, and (3) a concern to honor the authenticity of Christ's human life and suffering. We have now also examined some important challenges to the concepts and categories traditionally used in Christian description of God and the person of Christ. These challenges are related to our three aforementioned themes, but it should be added that the biblical scholars included here have a particular interest in working with the grain of Jewish representations of Jesus in the New Testament. In the next two sections, I will begin a response to these concerns and prepare for the constructive work to be done in the following chapters. The next section sketches a brief rationale for affirming divine attributes like aseity, immutability, impassibility, eternity, and simplicity. The following section will address the more formal questions about the concepts and categories used in Christology.

IV. Revisiting God's Perfections

In setting out a more traditional Christian view of God that can shape the doctrine of the person of Christ, it will be helpful to define terms like "aseity," "immutability," "impassibility," "eternity," and "simplicity." Theologians of the past have defined such terms in diverse ways, but I would hasten to add that there are broadly cohesive accounts of them in catholic theology proper.

---

77. Tilling, *Paul's Divine Christology*, 246–49, 260–65, 268–69.

Throughout this volume, I will attempt to provide an account that is informed by scriptural revelation and the insights of the catholic tradition. This section, however, is merely a précis. It is meant only to adumbrate key lines of reasoning to be developed through subsequent chapters and to give some sense of why it is worth exploring how this doctrine of God links up with Christology.

(1) Divine aseity lies at the heart of this doctrine of God. It is an attribute that signifies that God is not dependent on anything or anyone else to be the God that he is but instead has life in and of himself. This is a life eternally fulfilled in the fellowship of the Father, Son, and Holy Spirit. That God is not dependent on anything or anyone to be the God that he is can be seen in various places in the Old and New Testaments. Unlike other ancient Near Eastern origins accounts, the opening chapter of the Bible tellingly lacks a theogony, a divine becoming in which God might strive to obtain an identity of his own and an authority over the world. Instead, the God of the Bible just is who he is: "In the beginning God created the heavens and the earth" (Gen. 1:1). He creates the world not from a deficiency in himself or a need to have others accomplish things for him but from a generous will to communicate life, to provide for the human race, and to invite the human race into the cultivation of his world (1:26–30).[78] Already in its creation account Holy Scripture begins to convey that God does not need us but has freely chosen to bring us into being. Moreover, as the Creator of all things, God is not a constituent part of a greater encompassing reality. Athanasius aptly states that to think God might be one part within the system of the world is a "Greek thought."[79] The fact that God does not stand in a mutually constitutive relation to created being and is not caught up in a zero-sum game with the creature's presence and agency has significant implications for God's freedom to be directly present in our midst, a point that comes up later in this volume.

God's independence and plenitude are displayed throughout the history of Israel. In Exodus, when God reveals his name, I AM WHO I AM, he is making it clear that Moses and the people of Israel do not determine who he is or what he will do, though they can count on his covenant faithfulness (Exod. 3:13–15).[80] The name is characterized by God in terms of his freedom to be gracious to whom he will be gracious and to have mercy on whom he will have mercy (33:19).[81] This note of divine prevenience comes through in the

---

78. On the contrast with surrounding ancient Near Eastern mythologies, see, e.g., Walton, *Ancient Near Eastern Thought and the Old Testament*, 87–88, 104–5; cf. also Oswalt, *The Bible among the Myths*.

79. Athanasius, *Oratio II*, 22,1 (198).

80. Cf. Bauckham, *Who Is God?*, 42–45.

81. Cf. Childs, *Exodus*, 596; Cassuto, *Exodus*, 436.

establishment of the covenant with Israel: "I am YHWH, your God, who brought you up out of Egypt, out of the land of slavery" (20:2). YHWH chose Israel to be his treasured people and delivered them from Egypt not for any benefit they could bestow upon him but simply because he loved them and because he is faithful to his promises (Deut. 7:7–8). According to Psalm 50, God does not need the worship of his people. All things already belong to him because all things are from him: "If I were hungry, I would not tell you, for the world and all that is in it is mine. Do I eat the flesh of bulls or drink the blood of goats?" (50:12–13 NRSV). Isaiah's prophecy likewise attests the underived life and prevenience of God. This takes place in a number of texts that echo the giving of the divine name in Exodus 3 by use of the nominal clause אֲנִי הוּא ("I am he").[82] Speaking of his sovereignty over all things, God declares, "I am YHWH, the first and with the last, I am he" (Isa. 41:4). In reaffirming his plan for Israel, God assures them that he is trustworthy, unlike the false gods, again emphasizing "I am he" and adding, "Before me no God was formed, and after me none will be." He alone is the true God who can save: "Yes, from of old I am he, and there is none who can deliver from my hand. I act, and who will reverse it?" (43:10–13). "Even to your old age I am he, even in your gray hair I will sustain you" (46:4). YHWH distinguishes himself from the idols by pointing out that he foretold the fall of Babylon and will tell of things still to come. "I am he," he says, "I am the first and I am the last. And my hand founded the earth, and my right hand stretched out the heavens" (48:12–13). The book of Isaiah presents God as the one who cares deeply about the future of Israel and as the one who can bring about Israel's future hope precisely because he is the God who is *a se* and is not dependent on or limited by another.

In the New Testament, God's aseity is reiterated and also disclosed in its trinitarian aspect. According to John's Gospel, God has life in himself and grants creatures participation in that life (John 1:3–4). It is a life that is trinitarian: "In the beginning was the Word, and the Word was with God and the Word was God" (1:1). The Father has "life in himself" and "gives to the Son to have life in himself" (5:26). Since this is a communication of the life by which the Son can raise the dead by his mere speech (5:25), this life is a divine life that belongs to the Son as God and thus to his eternal relation to the Father, not merely to his human capacities or even primarily to his economic office.[83] In this way the Gospel of John conveys that God is not inactive prior to the

---

82. For the connection back to Exodus, see, e.g., Goldingay and Payne, *Isaiah 40–55*, 1:149–51.

83. Cf. Rainbow, *Johannine Theology*, 101–2.

existence of creation. The Father is already active in sharing life with the Son. The Father and Son have dwelt together in love and glory "before the foundation of the world" (17:5, 24). As we will discuss in chapter 2, the divine love is already fulfilled in the relations and processions of the divine persons, the Father having the Son as his perfect image and the adequate object of his love, which obviates any need of an external counterpart. Hilary of Poitiers expresses this well in stressing that God is not a "solitary" God.[84]

In Paul's speech at Athens, the apostle continues the scriptural portrayal of God as independent and self-sufficient. Unlike the idols, the true God is the one who does not live in temples built by human hands, and he is not served by human hands as though needing anything. Rather, this God gives life and breath and all things to the rest of us (Acts 17:24–25). As Paul puts it in Romans 11, "Who has known the mind of the Lord, or who has been his counselor? Or who has given to him, and he will repay him? For from him and through him and to him are all things. To him be glory into the ages" (11:34–36). John's Apocalypse also teaches about God's eternal fullness and independence of the created order. Invoking the divine name from the Old Testament, John calls God "the one who is and who was and who is coming," "the Alpha and Omega" who has established the beginning and the end of all creation and history (Rev. 1:4, 8; 11:17; 16:5).[85] God brings all things into being not out of necessity but by his sovereign will (4:11).[86] And at the consummation of all things God is again the one who initiates and gives: "I am making all things new" (21:5). "I am the Alpha and the Omega, the beginning and the end. To the one who is thirsty I will give to drink of the fount of the water of life" (21:6; 22:1).

Divine aseity signifies that God is independent and entirely self-sufficient, not constituted as God by another. In its full material content, it entails that God is always fully himself and needs no further actualization of his being. He is not contained within a system of things where he would have to be distinct from others by lacking something that they possess (as it is in the distinction of one creature from another). Positively, the triune God is complete in himself in trinitarian fellowship and enjoys a fullness of life from which he can freely communicate life and love to creatures. He is distinct from creatures not negatively by lacking something that they have but positively by being the only one who has in an eminent manner all the perfections that can be found in creatures.

84. Hilary of Poitiers, La Trinité 5.39 (2:168); 7.3 (2:282).
85. On the divine name in Revelation, see Bauckham, The Theology of the Book of Revelation, 28–30.
86. Cf., e.g., Smalley, The Revelation to John, 125–26.

Upholding God's aseity is not, as some have suspected, a way of implying that God is aloof or uninterested in the history of the world. Rather, it implies that God acts from a rich benevolence and liberality in the economy, without ever looking upon the creature as an instrument of his own self-realization. As John Webster has put it, the "non-reciprocity of the creator-creature relation . . . is the ground of the creatures' worth. The dignity of creatures does not consist in furnishing God with an object without which his love would be undirected; it consists simply in creatures being themselves, having proper creaturely integrity, order and movement in prospect of an end."[87] Moreover, by not being just one more part within the system of the world, God does not have to "make room" for us by changing or withdrawing himself or by undermining the integrity of our presence and agency. Instead, he can remain truly himself while sustaining the world from within and can therefore commune with us creatures in the original integrity and richness of his triune life.

(2) Following on divine aseity, divine immutability signifies that God cannot be changed, improved, or diminished. God's immutability concerns both God's own being and his relationship to the world. God is constant in his perfections and in the eternal relations of the Father, Son, and Spirit. He is also constant in his good plan for the world. Holy Scripture does not provide a single extended treatment of God's immutability, but the fact that God's immutability is often described briefly and in connection with God's relationship to us does not mean that it is a negligible doctrine. What is true of God is foundational to everything else that appears in the biblical teaching on God's outward works.

In Psalm 102, the days of the afflicted writer pass away "like smoke." His heart and life wither "like grass" (102:3–4, 11). YHWH, however, remains enthroned forever and always ready to act for the good of Zion (102:12–22). He is the one who laid the foundations of the earth and created the heavens. They perish, but he remains. They wear out like old garments, but, the psalmist observes, "you remain the same [וְאַתָּה־הוּא], and your years never end" (102:25–27). In his speech about impending divine judgment, the prophet Malachi also affirms that God does not change. After God has said that he will bear witness against evildoers and oppressors, God declares, "For I, YHWH, do not change, so you, children of Jacob, are not brought to an end" (Mal. 3:6). That God does not change is presented as the basis of Israel's hope. Because God does not change, Israel may still return to him after their rebellion, at which point God would also "turn" to them (3:7). If God's readiness

87. Webster, "Trinity and Creation," 14.

to receive Israel back (the inward readiness itself) is not conditioned upon Israel's actual turning, it follows that God's "turning" would not be a change in his goodness or love but a new action produced by God in which he blesses Israel once more.

Second Timothy 2:13 expresses the central point of the doctrine of divine immutability: God cannot deny himself, which is an encouragement to the weak in faith. James 1 also exhibits how God's changelessness has pastoral significance. According to James, God "cannot be tempted by evil, and he himself tempts no one" (James 1:13). The unchanging God is never to blame for evil. He is, rather, the source of all good things: "Every good and perfect gift from above is coming down from the Father of lights, with whom there is no change or shadow of turning" (1:17). The language used draws our attention to the heavens and instructs us that God's constancy surpasses even that of the heavenly lights.[88]

God's purpose for the world also is constant. In the book of Isaiah, idols are recognizable by their ignorance of what is to come, whereas the true God can tell what is to come and need not change his plans. In Isaiah 46, he declares the end from the beginning, from ancient times things not yet done. His counsel will stand. He will accomplish his purpose (46:9–10). In Isaiah 46, the "beginning" is creation itself, and the end that God already knows and declares is correspondingly broad—namely, the full scope and consummation of history.[89] In Hebrews, the writer speaks of God's unchangeable promise to Abraham in order to assure his readers of the benefits of persevering in faith. In keeping with human custom, God swore on oath to Abraham that he would bless and multiply Abraham's descendants, in order that "through two unchangeable things"—arguably, God's promise and the accompanying oath[90]—"in which it is impossible for God to lie, we might have strong encouragement" (Heb. 6:16–18).

There are of course questions that arise from biblical passages in which God is said to "repent" or "regret" doing something (e.g., Gen. 6:6; Exod. 32:14; 1 Sam. 15:11, 35; 2 Sam. 24:16; Jer. 18:5–11; Jon. 3:10). There are even questions to be asked about whether a robust doctrine of divine immutability can fit with the fact that God performs new actions at diverse times in history. For the moment, I will only gesture toward the approach that this volume will take in responding to these questions, leaving the formation of more substantial arguments to later chapters. Here I will note that if it belongs to God as God over against the idols that he should know what is to

88. E.g., Johnson, *James*, 197.
89. Cf. the reading of Goldingay and Payne, *Isaiah 40–55*, 2:82–83.
90. So, e.g., Ellingworth, *Hebrews*, 342.

come (esp. Isa. 41:21–24; 44:6–8; 45:21; 46:9–10), then the biblical text itself requires us not to take God's repentance or regret as a literal advancement in knowledge with an attendant change of volition.[91] But this does not mean that God's repentance is meaningless. On the contrary, catholic accounts of God's perfections have stressed that God's repentance signals that God is working a change in the course of history. The early Reformed theologian Amandus Polanus, for example, writes that divine repentance is not a divine "perturbation" or "change of counsel" but rather a "change of works." In fact, because God's counsel already encompasses the developments of history, it is not abrogated but rather executed precisely by God changing the conditions of his creatures.[92] Similarly, Francis Turretin comments that repentance should be understood in a manner that befits God: "not by reason of counsel but of event, not by reason of his will but of the thing willed, not by reason of affect and internal sorrow but of effect and external work, because he acts as a penitent man is accustomed to act." That is, God repents not "pathetically" but "energetically."[93]

While some theologians have suggested revisions to more traditional understandings of God's immutability in order to take into account the novelty and diversity of God's historical action,[94] I will argue later on that a more traditional doctrine of God is capacious enough to account for the diversity in God's action without suggesting that God's own actuality must fluctuate over time. In particular, some of the Reformed orthodox theologians point toward a distinction between God's essential, constant actuality and the "egression" or "termination" of that actuality with different effects at different times.[95] If God is already active and satisfied in the loving fellowship of the Trinity and yet also produces new and diverse effects in the world, it seems to me that this distinction is well grounded and may be useful later on in this study.

(3) Following on God's aseity and immutability, impassibility signifies that God is not susceptible to being harmed or deprived of any good that is constitutive of his well-being. He is never acted upon so as to become disposed in a manner contrary to his well-being and sufficiency. Thus, he is not subjected to emotional distress like creatures. Instead, God remains constant in his goodness and sufficiency. In spite of certain misguided representations of

91. For a fuller discussion, see chap. 7, sect. IV.

92. Polanus, *Syntagma*, 2.13 (152); 2.35 (194).

93. Turretin, *Inst.*, 3.11.11 (1:227).

94. See, e.g., Dorner, *Divine Immutability*; Barth, *CD*, II.1, 496–99. Note also Chalamet, "Immutability or Faithfulness?"

95. See, e.g., Owen, *A Dissertation on Divine Justice*, 1.1 (498–500); 2.8, 11 (562, 577). For further discussion, see Duby, "Divine Immutability, Divine Action and the God-World Relation"; Duby, "Divine Action and the Meaning of Eternity," 363–65, 373–75.

the doctrine, divine impassibility is actually good news for human beings. For impassibility entails that God cannot be deterred or discouraged in his pursuit of our good.

As mentioned in the comments on Genesis 1 above, the being of the God of Scripture is not established by an interchange with forces outside himself. And he is not served by others as though needing anything, so his goodness and fulfillment do not depend on something that we have either to offer or withhold. According to the apostle Paul's preaching in Acts, this distinguishes the true God from human beings. To dissuade the people of Lystra from worshiping him and Barnabas, Paul cries out, "Why are you doing these things? We also are human beings ὁμοιοπαθεῖς ["of like passions" or "affected in similar ways"[96]] with you, evangelizing you to turn from these empty things to the living God, who made heaven and earth and the sea and all things in them" (Acts 14:15). The worship of beings "of like passions" with humanity is an "empty" thing to be given up in favor of worshiping the Creator. Paul teaches in Romans 1:23 as well that the corruptibility of creatures makes them unfit to be worshiped, whereas the true God is "incorruptible." In Pauline theology, then, the God who transcends passion and corruptibility is called "blessed" and the "God of peace" (2 Cor. 13:11; Phil. 4:9; 1 Tim. 1:11; 6:15). Moreover, the Bible's Christology itself implies that God—even the God-man with respect to his deity—is impassible. According to Hebrews, Christ had to be "made like" his brothers and sisters in order to suffer with them and to deliver them (Heb. 2:17). Indeed, Christ *became* a merciful and sympathetic high priest (2:18; 4:15). Christ's firsthand experience of suffering was new; it was not included in his divine life. The drama and remarkable pastoral force of the incarnation and passion of God the Son imply the backdrop of divine impassibility.

Of course, certain biblical texts have raised questions about divine impassibility. Many of these fall into the category of the divine repentance texts already touched upon here, but one prominent example is Hosea 11. After speaking of Israel's sin and judgment, God asks, "How will I give you up, Ephraim? How will I hand you over, Israel? How will I give you up like Admah? How will I make you like Zeboyim? My heart is altogether changed within me, my compassion is excited" (11:8). If God's heart is changed and his compassion excited, is this not a description of God being affected from without and undergoing some kind of emotional flux? As one writer puts it,

96. Cf. Erich Beyreuther and Günter Finkenrath, "ὅμοιος κτλ.," in *NIDNTT* 2:501; Louw and Nida, *Greek-English Lexicon*, 25.32 (292); Johnson, *Acts*, 249. Mounce, *The Analytical Lexicon to the Greek New Testament*, 338, especially brings out this emphasis, defining ὁμοιοπαθής as "being affected in the same way," "subject to the same incidents, of like infirmities, subject to the same frailties and evils."

it appears that God is suffering an "internal conflict" and posing for himself an "existential question."[97] But the passage continues, "I will not execute my burning anger, I will not destroy Ephraim again, for I am God and not a man, the holy one in your midst, and I will not come in wrath" (11:9). God will bring judgment upon Israel's sin (11:1–7, 10–11), but he will not bring a judgment "on the order of Admah and Zeboiim."[98] And it is in fact not a change of heart but rather God's determination not to destroy Israel entirely in verse 9a that is rooted in what God is as God in verse 9b ("for I am God and not a man"). As the holy one, God remains faithful, unlike human beings, who so readily abandon their promises when they are wronged.[99] The holy one of Israel is not deflected from his love for Israel, so a text like Hosea 11:9 actually provides a reason for affirming that God is impassible, unlike temperamental and capricious pagan deities, who are, Athanasius remarks, "pseudonymous gods" (ψευδώνυμοι θεοί) and "faithful neither in being nor in promising."[100] This does not empty Hosea 11:8 of its significance, for the passage conveys that from his own goodness, love, and holiness God will produce a change in history, graciously preserving and restoring Israel after he has judged their sin. More will be said about the meaning of impassibility and about possible objections to it in chapter 7.

(4) Divine eternity signifies, in the classic formulation of Boethius, God's "whole, simultaneous, and perfect possession of interminable life."[101] That is, divine eternity expresses that God is without beginning or end and without the temporal succession that creatures undergo. He already has fullness of life in himself and does not acquire or lose that fullness over time. There are many scriptural texts that tell us God has no beginning or end. The psalmist declares, "From everlasting to everlasting you are God" (Ps. 90:2; cf. 102:27; Isa. 43:10; Rev. 1:8; 21:6; 22:13). He is the only immortal one (1 Tim. 6:16). Scripture also teaches us that God does not experience time in the way that creatures do: "A thousand years in your sight are like yesterday when it is past, or like a watch in the night" (Ps. 90:4 NRSV; cf. 2 Pet. 3:8).

A more challenging point about the doctrine of divine eternity is that God has a fullness of life and actuality that does not need to be enhanced and cannot be attenuated over time. Accordingly, divine eternity is simply an inflection of divine aseity viewed with respect to creatures' passing, temporal mode of existence. Divine eternity is not a strategy for removing God from

97. Janzen, "Metaphor and Reality in Hosea 11," 12, 18–19, 22–23, 25–26.
98. Janzen, "Metaphor and Reality," 11.
99. Cf. Stuart, *Hosea–Jonah*, 181–83; Carroll R., "Hosea," 286.
100. Athanasius, *Oratio II*, 10,1 (186).
101. Boethius, *Philosophiae consolationis* 5.6 (422–23).

history but a reiteration of God's plenitude in the midst of history.[102] Boethius, for example, says that God was in the past, is in the present, and will be in the future. But God abides in time in a "divine now" in that he remains fully himself and is not moved from without.[103] Anselm takes a similar approach and insists that it is "repugnant" to God's essence that he should not exist in space and time, for if God created all things, a withdrawal of his presence and sustaining power would entail the annihilation of all things. Unlike created beings, God is in time but without being "contained" by it. He is "in" and "with" time, but his life is whole, "without parts," and never "dissimilar to itself."[104] In this line of thought, God's eternity is shorthand for his being without beginning or end and having fullness of life without that fullness being acquired or lost through temporal succession. That such an understanding of divine eternity does not preclude or compromise the genuinely historical acts of God—chiefly, the Son's assumption of a human nature—will be discussed in chapter 3.

(5) Divine simplicity signifies that God is not composed of parts but is identical with his own essence, existence, and attributes, each of which is identical with God's whole being viewed under some particular aspect. And each divine person is not a "part" that composes God but is really identical with God or God's essence, though each person is distinct from the other two.[105] There are several approaches to the doctrine of divine simplicity in the Christian tradition, including those of Thomas Aquinas, John Duns Scotus, and Gregory Palamas.[106] My articulation and use of this doctrine in the present study reflects Aquinas's work in particular.[107] In my judgment, a Christian understanding of God's simplicity is ultimately based on God's aseity, so the exegetical considerations informing the teaching of God's aseity are the strongest foundation for affirming simplicity as well. God is not composed of parts because (a) he does not draw upon something other than himself in order to be the God that he is, (b) there is no one above or behind him that might compose him or put him together, and (c) there is no modal structure above or behind him that might determine the necessary unity of his being

102. On this point, see also Muller, *Post-Reformation Reformed Dogmatics*, 3:345–62; Pasnau, "On Existing All at Once"; Duby, "Divine Action and the Meaning of Eternity."

103. Boethius, *De trin.* 4 (20–23).

104. Anselm, *Monologion* 20 (35); 22 (40–41); 24 (42).

105. A "real" distinction is between one "thing" (Latin *res*) or being and another. The doctrine of divine simplicity excludes this sort of distinction from God, but it does not exclude all distinctions in God.

106. For one attempt to integrate all three of these approaches, see M. Spencer, "The Flexibility of Divine Simplicity."

107. For a brief overview, see Duby, *Divine Simplicity*, 80–89.

and perfections. God is identical with his essence because there is no principle of being other than God himself that might establish what he is and how he acts. He is identical with his existence because there is no source of being other than himself in which he would have to participate in order to be. He is identical with each of his attributes because his wisdom, goodness, and so on are not qualities added to his essence (as in the case of creatures). As Augustine points out, to be God just is to be perfectly wise, perfectly good, and so on.[108]

It is important to note that the Christian doctrine of divine simplicity does not yield an assimilation of God to abstract philosophical ideas. In fact, it does precisely the opposite: it clarifies that there is no abstract "being," "goodness," "substance," and the like existing beyond the God of Holy Scripture, in which both he and the creature alike would have to participate. Rather the only ultimate being just is the tripersonal God himself, who is the source and exemplar of all others. And instead of having one part of what it is to be God—instead of being a partial version of a more ultimate deity—each of the coequal divine persons has all the fullness of God in him (cf. Col. 1:19; 2:9). Indeed, rather than having the divine essence plus some additional "thing" that individuates him, each of the persons really *is* the divine essence. What distinguishes one person from another is not matter or a set of accidents but simply a certain relationship to another divine person. The Son, for example, has all that is the Father's; the distinction between the two lies in that he has it from the Father (so, e.g., John 1:14; 5:26; 16:15; Heb. 1:3). That the eternal relations in God constitute the distinctions among the divine persons will come to the fore in chapter 2 in particular.

This sketch of some of the key divine attributes by no means addresses every potential challenge, but it will hopefully suffice to show why they should be taken seriously by Christian theologians and exegetes and why they should be of interest in exploring their relationship to Christology. Our last task before launching into that constructive work is to offer a response to concerns about the use of certain metaphysical concepts and categories in Christology today.

V. Revisiting the Role of Metaphysical Concepts

A. Responses to Critiques

I will first address challenges brought up by some of the key philosophers and theologians from section III above and then move on to recent challenges

---

108. Augustine, *De trin.* 7.4 (1:260).

by biblical scholars like Bauckham, Wright, and Tilling. After this, I will venture a brief positive sketch of the function of concepts like "essence," "substance," and so forth in this study.[109]

(1) Despite his profound influence over modern conceptions of the task of Christian theology, Kant's epistemology ought not to be taken as an unassailable given or starting point for the present discussion. One can affirm that the human mind has an inchoate aptitude for embracing certain patterns of reasoning without positing that the mind's concepts and judgments are themselves innate or detached from outward reality. Christians in particular will want to affirm that we know things (and, indeed, persons) that exist outside our own minds. For we are made to know and love God and one another. In Paul's words, we know God by encountering "the things which have been made" and by discerning from them something of God's "eternal power and divinity" (Rom. 1:19–20). One can affirm this biblical teaching about a natural knowledge of God as the cause of creation without minimizing our need for the supernatural revelation of the gospel. And if we are not compelled to take up Kant's epistemological agenda, we are in a position to consider the possibility that classical metaphysical concepts and categories are reflective of extramental reality and may have some use in Christology. Furthermore, if we decline to make Kant's problems our problems, we may excuse ourselves from the sort of idealist speculations about the subject-object relation that led figures like Schelling and Hegel to replace the biblical God with an "absolute" whose potential has to be realized over time. We may also recognize that theological discourse can faithfully express God's revelation in Christ while still granting to a figure like Schleiermacher that scientific reasoning cannot capture the full depth of human experience of God.

(2) Authors like Ritschl and Cremer have set "metaphysics" in opposition to the realm of the personal and ethical and suggested that if metaphysical reasoning is applied to God and created persons, it will distort our understanding of them. However, these authors have made "metaphysics" a cipher for something that is different from the philosophical and theological work undertaken by earlier authors like Augustine, John of Damascus, Aquinas, or the Reformed orthodox. It is understandable that one would want to draw a strong distinction between the impersonal material realm, on the one hand, and the personal, spiritual, moral realm, on the other. However, the way in which such a distinction is used to vilify "metaphysics" yields a picture of metaphysics that does not correspond to its actual practice in history.

---

109. For a fuller discussion of the relationship between metaphysics and theology that is envisaged in this volume, see Duby, *God in Himself*, chap. 5.

For the metaphysical engagement of the term "being" that one finds in the catholic tradition does not stipulate that being applies to all things in the same way. "Being" is not a univocal or neutral concept, especially where God is concerned (see the next section below).[110] Moreover, while Aquinas, for example, writes that the mind "resolves" all its objects into "being," this does not entail a ruthless assimilation of the personal and transcendent to the impersonal and material. The point is innocuous: knowing subjects consider everything they know to be a "being" because, quite simply, "being" is a term that signifies "that which is," and everything that we encounter and know in some way *is*. This does not involve a negation (what Aquinas calls a *separatio in re*) of the distinct modes of existing of particular things, be they personal or impersonal. It is only a matter of considering things under a certain aspect that is (by analogy) common to other things.[111] It may sound pious or inspiring to assert that "being" and "metaphysics" (the study of being *qua* being) have nothing to do with religion or theology, but in order to sustain this claim one would, strictly speaking, have to claim that religion and theology do not recognize that God or created persons in some way *are*. Surely practitioners of Christian theology who wish to stress the personal and ethical character of its subject matter will still want to affirm that God and created persons exist. If so, Christian theologians should resist the temptation to place theology in conflict with the analogical concept of being that is treated in metaphysical science.

(3) In light of the Bible's testimony to God's aseity, the simplistic pairing of teaching about God in himself with idle philosophical speculation, alongside the pairing of teaching about God in the economy with true Christian knowledge, is something that needs to be challenged. Authors like Cremer, Barth, and a number of biblical scholars have given the impression that only the practice of metaphysics or natural theology can lead to making statements about God that do not have immediate reference to his economic activity. However, Scripture points us in another direction. For it sometimes tells us what is true of God without respect to the being of the world or the plan of salvation. The Word was with God and would have always been with God even if he had not given life and light to the world. The fact that this is so is precisely what brings out the decisive and surprising nature of the incarnation in John's prologue and elsewhere in the New Testament.

110. For more on univocity and analogy, see Duby, *God in Himself*, chap. 6. I am aware that Duns Scotus in particular advocated a univocal concept of being, but I still do not think that what he advocates would inevitably cause the problems Ritschl and Cremer have in mind.

111. See Aquinas, *Quaestiones disputatae de veritate* 1.1 (5); Aquinas, *Super De trin.* 5.3 corp. (147–48); Aquinas, *ST* Ia.5.2 corp. (58); 85.1 ad 1 (331).

(4) With respect to more concrete objections to the use of metaphysical concepts, Schleiermacher makes an important point in questioning the wisdom of speaking about a divine "nature" alongside a human nature in Christ, especially when he observes that the term "nature" often denotes a "restricted being, which is engaged in some contrast."[112] Unlike creatures in their distinction from God and from one another, God is not limited or constituted by lacking what others have. If God and the creature stood in a mutually delimiting relation to one another, it would appear that the union of a divine and human nature in a single subject could not be sustained. It would appear that the divine activities and human activities of that subject must stand in a competitive relation to one another, either moving in conflicting directions at the expense of the unity of the person of Christ or one ceasing its operation at certain times so that the other might begin to contribute to Christ's work. On such a view, it is understandable that a dyothelete Christology would seem superfluous. If the two wills operated within a shared genus of being and acting and were directed toward the same aspects of the same works, the efficacy of the divine operation would appear to obviate the human operation. However, it is worth mentioning that the New Testament itself speaks of a divine "nature" (φύσις; Gal. 4:8; cf. 2 Pet. 1:4) and of "divinity" (θειότης; Rom. 1:20) and "deity" (θεότης; Col. 2:9), which standard lexica often render as "divine nature."[113] James Dunn notes that the word θεότης in Colossians 2:9 signifies "the nature or essence of deity, that which constitutes deity," and that this became a "principal building block of subsequent Christology."[114] Significantly, Scripture itself authorizes us to speak of a divine "nature," and it would be a mistake to position ourselves above the vocabulary of the Holy Spirit and the human authors of the Bible. At the same time, it is appropriate to be clear about what we mean in using the term—namely, what God is as God or that which constitutes God as God, not a principle governing his being and actions and placing him within the system of the world alongside creatures.

(5) The comments from Forsyth and Mackintosh about breaking away from traditional categories are open to criticism from a few different angles. For example, if Forsyth's claim that the two natures of Christ must have a "mutual externality" means only that there is an ongoing distinction between Christ's divinity and humanity, then that claim can actually be granted. If, however, it means that the two cannot subsist in a single person, then it

---

112. Schleiermacher, The Christian Faith, §96 (584).
113. E.g., BDAG, 446, 452; Louw and Nida, Greek-English Lexicon, 12.13 (140). On the decidedly "ontological" use of φύσις in Gal. 4:8, cf. Hafemann, "'Divine Nature' in 2 Pet 1,4," 91.
114. Dunn, The Theology of Paul the Apostle, 205–6.

elicits the same sort of response given above to Schleiermacher's concerns. Furthermore, Forsyth's assertion that a traditional Christology leaves out the "personal action" of the Son in becoming poor for our sake and privileges only the miraculous nature of the virgin conception is not accurate.[115] The older theologians were devoted to the task of expounding the Bible and could hardly avoid texts like Philippians 2 that speak about the Son's humble assumption of his human nature.[116] In addition, if Forsyth takes the union of Christ's deity and humanity to be a product of the Savior's work, this seems to leave unexplained why that work should have had its unique character and salvific efficacy in the first place.

Mackintosh's concern about the Chalcedonian framework positing the existence of "natures" or sets of "qualities" existing apart from the person of Christ also is mistaken on at least two accounts. First, insofar as the doctrine of the person of Christ is set forth in concert with God's simplicity, there can be no question of a hypostatized divine nature above or behind the Son that might serve to govern what he is and does. The divine nature or essence is just what God is as God and what is common to the three divine persons in whom there is all the fullness of deity. Second, catholic Christology's assertion of the anhypostatic and enhypostatic mode of Christ's human nature decisively rules out an independent human nature from which Christ might keep his distance. (There seems to be considerable irony in Mackintosh criticizing the purported assertion of independent natures while also lamenting the teaching of the *anhypostasis* of Christ's human nature.) The Son's human nature is not an independent thing from which he insulates himself or into which he can deposit his human experiences without himself undergoing them. That nature subsists only and directly in him, a point that will be developed later in this volume.

(6) McCormack's reservations about the category of substance or the concept of a divine essence that is constituted without reference to God's decision for the incarnation can be addressed both with respect to the doctrine of divine aseity and with respect to the christological claims that are central to McCormack's revision of the doctrine of God. I will comment only on the former here and will leave it to later chapters to discuss God the Son suffering just in his human nature without this undermining the unity of his person or the genuineness and salvific efficacy of his suffering. The key point to be made here is that if one is convinced from Scripture that God is not constituted by a relation that he assumes toward the world (even toward the Son's own

---

115. Forsyth, *The Person and Place of Jesus Christ*, 223.
116. See, e.g., Aquinas, *Super Phil.* 2.57–58 (101).

human nature), then McCormack's critique of the term "substance" will not be compelling. If God just is the God that he is with or without reference to his economic work, then theologians and exegetes should have no problem speaking of a divine essence that is not constituted by God's action *ad extra*. Of course, from within the logic of a more traditional doctrine of God, there are a number of reasons to be cautious about talk of a divine "substance" (see the next section), but the worry about "substance" language precluding God's self-constitution by the act of election is not one of them.

(7) Before addressing the specific arguments of Bauckham, Wright, and Tilling, it may be worth commenting on the general reluctance of some biblical scholars to find statements in Scripture that pertain to God's being. In light of the remarks included above on the divine name in Exodus 3, it seems that some tend to assume that one cannot speak of God's being or essence without giving the impression that God is a lifeless object who could not perform the works he does in the history of redemption. It is understandable that exegesis of individual passages of the Bible will often not yield protracted discussion about God in himself. Unfolding the meaning of a passage in a short essay or even a whole commentary simply may not afford the best opportunity for undertaking such discussion. In addition, human beings encounter and come to know God by his outward works (creation, providence, redemption). Yet, while God's outward works provide the occasion and means of our knowledge of God, the content revealed about God in his outward works pertains not just to the outward works themselves but also to who and what God is. Scripture itself conveys that God would be God even if he had chosen not to create the world, for he does not become the God that he is by virtue of his relation to us (see again, e.g., Ps. 50:12–13; Acts 17:24–25). Take, for example, Psalm 119:68: "You are good and do good [טֽוֹב־אַתָּ֥ה וּמֵטִ֗יב]." The psalmist speaks of God himself being good and then speaks of God's outward display of that goodness. Simply put, God has a life of his own. To be sure, it is a life in which he graciously invites us to participate, but it is a life already established and active in triune love before the foundation of the world. That God is already active in himself can hardly be taken to imply that he is unable to act in the world. Precisely as the one who is completely active in himself, God is always ready to act outwardly. As Aquinas observes, since God is entirely in act, he is the one for whom "acting is especially suitable."[117]

(8) In my judgment, Bauckham's discussion of the "divine identity" is a significant contribution to the ongoing task of expounding the Bible's doctrine of God and Christology. He uses it to good effect in shedding light on

---

117. Aquinas, *De pot.* 1.1 corp. (9).

how the early church's conceptions of the person of Christ exhibit a "high Christology." It also seems to me that the inclusion of Jesus in the "divine identity" could be used today to explain the underpinnings of Chalcedonian Christology to believers who may need a more gradual pathway into the use of concepts like "essence," "substance," and so on. At the same time, the notion of identity is a regular feature in the classical metaphysical tradition just as much as the notion of essence or substance. "Identity" is often set in contrast to "diversity" or "distinction." An early Reformed philosopher and theologian like Johann Alsted, for example, construes *identitas* in terms of one's "agreement" with oneself, which is far from being inimical to Bauckham's identity of "self-continuity."[118]

Further, it is not clear that the discussion of an identity of "self-continuity" can succeed in bifurcating the question of who God is and the question of what God is.[119] Even in the case of composite created beings, those distinguishing features that mark off one individual from another (the "who") are not present or intelligible apart from that which constitutes that individual in a certain kind (the "what"). One's identity or agreement with oneself across time involves not just a sameness of distinguishing or individuating features (e.g., what makes someone *this* human being) but also a sameness of essence (humanity). This would apply all the more in God's case, especially if God—since he is the only God—is not composed of one thing that would distinguish him from other would-be deities and another thing that would place him in a common species of deity. The identity or agreement of God with himself across time therefore involves a sameness of who he is (*this God*, the Father, Son, and Spirit) and a sameness of what he is (his God-ness, which is represented to us by various attributes like goodness, righteousness, and omnipotence that are common to the divine persons).[120]

In addition, Bauckham's inclusion of "personal story" in God's identity, together with his statements about the "functions" of God being "intrinsic"

118. Alsted, *Metaphysica*, 1.29 (232).

119. Bauckham himself uses the word "deity" several times (*Jesus and the God of Israel*, 35, 51, 57).

120. In light of this, any movement back and forth between "who" and "what" in the doctrine of God is not a shift from one "thing" to another. As Aquinas notes, it is the same to be God and to be *this* God (*ST* Ia.11.3 corp. [111]). The abstract term "deity" or "divine essence" signifies what God is as God, what is common to the three divine persons, and what distinguishes the true God from false gods, in order to help facilitate knowledge of God in creatures like us who are accustomed to distinguishing what is common and what is proper in other objects of knowledge. But shifting to the use of the concrete term "God" does not mean that an unactualized, abstract essence has just now been individuated. The use of the concrete term is fitting because God in his God-ness never was an abstract idea but always the God who subsists, lives, and acts.

to God's identity, raises the question of whether Bauckham takes God's action *ad extra* to be not only revelatory but also constitutive of who and what God is. Bauckham's statements that the crucified Christ "belongs to the unique identity of God" and that "Jesus himself and his story are intrinsic to the divine identity" appear to point in that direction. However, while various actions of Jesus certainly show that he belongs within the identity of God, that does not entail that such actions are what constitute who or what God is. For Scripture reveals that God's identity and completeness are not established by his economic acts or his relation to us. Further, if the cross in some sense completed or secured God's identity, this would imply that the efficacy of the cross could not be rooted in the fact that one who already is fully God offers himself to die for our sins. This might then invite a quite speculative account about how the cross possesses its salvific efficacy in the first place, grounding that efficacy in certain aspects of God that were already complete prior to the cross as distinct from other aspects of God that were purportedly not yet complete. That line of thought would be contrary to Scripture's teaching on God's aseity. Presumably, it would also be contrary to Bauckham's own desire to avoid metaphysical speculation. However, if Bauckham's discussion of "personal story" means only that God himself in the person of the Son has directly faced the suffering of the cross, that would be entirely resonant with the sort of theology proper and Christology advocated in this volume.

(9) Wright criticizes systematic theology as a discipline often carried out in a "de-historicized mode." It is in fact happily true that much that needs to be said in the Christian doctrine of God does not pertain primarily or immediately to history. For the God of Holy Scripture would be complete in wisdom, goodness, and love in his triune life even if the world and its historical development had never existed. When systematic theologians work through the doctrine of God, one of their tasks is to remind us that history is not everything and, indeed, that the history of God's dealings with his people derives its gravity, its universal significance, and its hopeful outcome from the fact that the triune God never needed the history of the world and that, precisely by virtue of this, he acts within history as the God who is mighty to save. Of course, everything else that systematic theology treats (God's economic acts, God's creatures, God's government of the church and its mission) is tied to history, but history unfolds in the hands of the God who lives and acts *a se*. Christology is a topic in Christian teaching where description of the God who both transcends history and acts within it is joined to description of a divine person's human, historical life and activity. *Theologia* and *oikonomia* meet here in a unique way that invites systematic theologians and biblical

scholars to cooperate in bearing witness to God and all that he has done for our salvation.

Wright is also concerned that the Gospels and the ecumenical creeds do not present the same picture of Jesus, because the latter speak so little of the life Jesus lived in a first-century Jewish context between his birth and crucifixion. In some Christian circles today, there is a lack of understanding that Jesus came in fulfillment of Israel's Scriptures to complete the story begun through Adam and Abraham. In that regard, Wright's emphasis is salutary. At the same time, the creeds do reflect the teaching of Scripture, and they do not purport to give a full treatment of Jesus's activity. The confession of faith in the God who made heaven and earth reflects the teaching of the Old Testament (rather than non-Christian philosophy). The identification of that God as Father reflects Jesus's own teaching about our relation to God. And the creeds focus on only a few aspects of the picture of Jesus, without negating that he is the Jewish Messiah who fulfilled Israel's Scriptures. As is well known, the Nicene Creed emerged under the pressure felt by the bishops of the early church to articulate the divinity of Jesus in a manner that would be faithful to the apostolic writings and would expose the deficiencies of the teaching of Arius and others who denied the Son's full equality with the Father. Indeed, the church's use of the concept of "substance" or "essence" (οὐσία) to express the Son's equality with the Father is not a departure from apostolic patterns of speech, since the New Testament itself incorporates the concepts of "divinity," "deity," and "divine nature" to speak of what God is as God. Further, the statement of the Son's consubstantiality with the Father not only clarifies that he is equal to the Father but also frees us up to affirm and to study the genuinely human (and Jewish) life of Jesus without being nervous about undermining his deity. For the Son who shares the one, incorruptible divine essence is firmly established as the God that he is and can therefore fully partake of the human condition without compromising his deity.

Wright has also suggested that the biblical theme of the temple will enable us to understand how the New Testament presents Jesus as the embodiment of YHWH. The temple is a rich theme in biblical theology and ought to play a role in our understanding of the fulfillment of God's purposes in the person of Jesus.[121] But the temple is not the only theme to be taken up in our Christology. Nor is it, by itself, adequate to guard against serious error in our Christology. This can be seen in historical discussions of John 2:19–22,

---

121. For recent discussion, see Levering, *Christ's Fulfillment of Torah and Temple*, part 2; Beale, *The Temple and the Church's Mission*; Perrin, *Jesus the Temple*; Behr, *John the Theologian and His Paschal Gospel*, chap. 3.

where Jesus identifies his own body as God's temple. Does God dwell in the body of Jesus like he did in Solomon's temple? Is the man Jesus only a special locus of God's general presence in the world? Or is the man Jesus YHWH himself? A teaching commonly linked with Paul of Samosata posited that Jesus was a mere man on whom God's grace rested in a special way. However, patristic authors discerned that this was an erroneous Christology and that the meaning of the temple language had to be clarified with other language. For example, Athanasius affirms the contribution that the temple theme can make to our Christology and soteriology, but he also points out that when the Son invites the disciples to touch his resurrected body (Luke 24:39), he invites them to touch *himself*, not an additional man joined to himself. Athanasius therefore remarks that the ὑπόστασις of the Son cannot be separated from "the man from Mary." It is necessary, then, to affirm the true deity (θεότης) of that man, which keeps use of the temple language from veering off into the teaching that Jesus might be a mere man specially indwelt by God.[122] Such use of concepts like ὑπόστασις and θεότης does not require us to neglect the theme of the temple, but it does show that words like these are needed to specify what Jesus's body as the dwelling place of God does and does not entail.

In his comment that Jesus would have found the concept of the hypostatic union "puzzling," Wright seems to be suggesting that the explicit vocabulary of the Scriptures should be prioritized in the exposition of Christian teaching. But the Pauline corpus itself already includes terms like "deity" or "nature," and, as the Philippians learned (Phil. 3:2–6), Paul will suffer no one to doubt his Jewish credentials. The author of Hebrews even writes of the ὑπόστασις of the Father that is represented by the Son (1:3). In addition, Wright himself has made significant use of the term "worldview" in his various writings, a term drawn not from the Bible but from Enlightenment philosophy.[123] Ultimately, as Athanasius points out, though it is ideal to use a term that is explicitly scriptural (ἔγγραφον), there are occasions when scriptural teaching must be set forth by use of an extrabiblical or "unwritten" (ἄγραφον) turn of phrase that brings out the "judgment" (διάνοια) of Scripture.[124]

(10) Tilling's study of Paul's Christology makes a significant contribution in explaining how Christ's relation to believers reflects YHWH's relation to Israel and thus confirms that Christ is a divine person. Like Bauckham's discussion of Jesus's inclusion in the divine identity, Tilling's work can help exegetes make sense of how the earliest Christians understood Jesus to be

122. Athanasius, *Oratio IV*, 34–35 (520–21).
123. So Naugle, *Worldview*, chaps. 3–4.
124. Athanasius, *De decretis* 31–32 (27–28). Cf., e.g., Gregory of Nyssa, *Contra Eunomium, pars prior* 1.535–48 (1:181–85).

the God of Israel in their midst. However, Tilling's understanding of classical metaphysics and theology proper is mistaken on some important points. Tilling's lament that traditional theological use of metaphysical concepts has "suppressed" the category of relation as merely "accidental" to a thing warrants a brief look at the categories of Aristotelian ontology.

In Aristotelian metaphysics there are ten categories of being, ten ways in which things exist in reality. The first is that of substance, which is something that exists (or, more precisely, "subsists") in its own right (e.g., a human being, an angel) and does not have to inhere in another thing in order to be. A substance "stands under" and is foundational to the existence of other things ("accidents") that must accede to or inhere in another in order to be. Contemporary use of the term "accident" often suggests that what is accidental is unimportant and does not truly affect the thing of which it is an accident, but in earlier usage it signifies a thing that inheres in something else and may be quite important to it. There are nine categories of accidents, though philosophers (and Christian theologians) have historically debated the exact sense in which some of these can be identified as true accidents that require their own category: quantity, quality, relation, action, passion, place ("where"), time ("when"), position (the comportment of a thing's constituent parts), and habit. The aim here is not to debate the finer points of this list but to make a few key observations regarding this general approach to ontological matters.[125]

First, the category of substance is not a category of "static being" if that phrase signifies things that do not act or undergo change in relation to other things. In the primary use of the term, "substance" is just a designation for those things that exist without having to inhere in something else, those things that exist in fundamental self-continuity while still undergoing various sorts of changes. A substance's features (e.g., the quality of love or justice) will change over time. Those features can grow or weaken, come to be or pass away. "Substance" is used in a second sense as well, to signify the essential constitution of an individual thing (i.e., the constitution it has in common with others of the same species). This use of the word also should not be particularly controversial, for a human being, for example, remains human while changing in any number of ways.[126]

---

125. My understanding of typical metaphysical treatments of the following issues especially reflects Aristotle, *Aristotelis Metaphysica*, ed. Jaeger; John of Damascus, *Dialectica*, ed. Kotter; Aquinas, *In duodecim libros Metaphysicorum Aristotelis expositio*, ed. Cathala and Spiazzi; Keckermann, *Scientiae metaphysicae*, 2013–40; Alsted, *Metaphysica*; Maccovius, *Metaphysica*.

126. *Pace* the suggestion of Tilling and Shults, this line of thinking need not stand in conflict with the idea of theistic evolution, for, within that idea, individual beings constituted in a

Second, substances in general are not insulated from being affected by accidents or impoverished by the loss of accidents. Intriguingly, this makes the term "substance" more suited to those theological programs that seek to portray God as mutable and passible. This is why Augustine, for example, insists that God can be called a *substantia* only "improperly" (*abusive*).[127] Similarly, Boethius contends that God is *ultra substantiam*, for God does not possess his attributes as accidents. With regard to his justice, for example, "God himself is the same as what is just."[128] John of Damascus calls God ὑπερούσιος ("super-substantial" or "super-essential"), because his life and perfections are not derived from without. God is subsisting life itself, subsisting goodness itself, and so on.[129] Such an understanding of God takes issue with the term "substance" because of its tendency to signify created, mutable things, but the Christian tradition has often still incorporated and qualified the term to designate (a) God (or, indeed, each divine person) as one existing or subsisting without needing to be a part of another or (b) what God is as God and what is common to the three divine persons. More recent attempts to revise the Christian understanding of God sometimes take issue with the term "substance" because they wrongly conceive of substance as something that suggests detachment from other things. They then often discard the term in an effort to maintain that God is constituted by his outward relation to the creature. Such attempts miss both the signification of the classical metaphysical terminology and the Bible's teaching about God's aseity.

Third, the idea that the category of relation has been "suppressed" or overlooked in the Christian doctrine of God is inaccurate. The Aristotelian and Christian scholastic traditions have offered various analyses of the concept of relation. Aquinas and others discuss distinctions to be drawn among "real," "rational," and "mixed" relations. In a "real" relation the two things related to one another are both informed and determined by one another in some way (e.g., a father and son who would not be who they are without this relation). In a strictly "rational" or logical relation (*relatio rationis*) the two related things are not mutually determined by one another in extramental reality, but the mind conceives of them in relation to one another. In a "mixed" relation, one thing is really related to and determined by the other (e.g., a human subject informed by an object of sense perception), but the other is not really related to and determined by that first thing (e.g., the object of the

---

certain species presumably would not cease to be members of that species over the course of their lifetime, even if the distinction between one species and another might be unclear at times.

127. Augustine, *De trin.* 7.4 (1:260).

128. Boethius, *De trin.* 4 (18).

129. John of Damascus, *Expos. fidei* 1.8 (18).

sense perception).[130] The relations among the persons of the Trinity are real relations, for the persons are constituted in their personal distinctness by their relations to one another. They are not merely related to one another in the human mind. The Father is who he is by his relation to the Son; the Son is who he is by his relation to the Father; the Spirit is who he is by his relation to the Father and Son. There are some debates about the precise import of the relations among the persons in earlier trinitarian theology,[131] but the concept of relation lies at the heart of trinitarian doctrine and, by implication, at the heart of the sort of Christology being explored and advocated in this study.

Of course, for an author like Aquinas, God's relation to the creature is not constitutive of God's being and is thus considered a "rational" relation on God's side (in the aforementioned technical sense of the word "rational"). God certainly creates, sustains, and acts to produce various effects in the world, but he is not established in some aspect of his being by the existence or agency of creatures.[132] But the clarification that God is not "really" related to the world in this highly specified, technical sense is not at all contrary to the central point of Tilling's book, that Jesus stands in relation to believers as YHWH stands in relation to Israel. In response to Tilling, then, it needs to be emphasized that carefully qualified talk of God's "substance" has had and can continue to have a role to play in Christology, without this undermining the important concept of relation.

Fourth, Tilling has written that the Jesus who said "No one is good but God alone" is "unlikely to have said in the next breath, that he is 'true God from true God.'" This seems to be an attempt to make creedal formulae sound at least unexpected or awkward, perhaps even misguided. However, this appears to indicate not just an interest in moving the Christology of the creeds to a lower position in Christian thought but also a neglect of certain things that the Jesus of the New Testament actually said and did, especially if the Gospel of John is taken to give reliable information on Jesus's view of himself. Jesus calls the Father the "true God" (John 17:3) and says that he is "from" this true God and has received from him life and glory (5:25–26; 6:46; 7:29; 17:5, 24; cf. 1:14). And throughout his ministry Jesus shows himself in various ways to be the true God (see, e.g., Mark 2:1–12; John 8:58). Jesus thus gives us all the elements of the creedal formula "true God from true God" in the Gospels: (a) the Father as true God, (b) the coming forth of Jesus the Son from the true God, (c) Jesus himself as true God. There are

---

130. Aquinas, *ST* Ia.13.7 (152–54).

131. See, e.g., the difference between Bonaventure (*In Sent.* 1.27, art. un., q. 2 [468–70]) and Aquinas (*ST* Ia.40.2 corp. and ad 4 [413–14]) on the Father's relation to the Son.

132. Turretin, *Inst.*, 5.1.11 (1:476), expresses this balance well.

of course elements of the Nicene Creed and of later dogmatic Christology that are not explicitly found in the New Testament (e.g., the teaching of the *homoousia* of the Father and Son). But if these are implications contained in and legitimately drawn out from the New Testament teaching, this is not a problem, for the Bible must be interpreted and errors must be met with more than bare repetition of biblical statements to which anyone might appeal. In light of all this, it is important not to drive a wedge between what the creedal formulae teach and what the Gospels teach.

This response to critiques of some metaphysical concepts and categories found in theology proper and Christology is intended to help us take on board important points made by critics and also move beyond misunderstandings of these concepts and categories, clearing a way to explore again their exegetical usefulness. Next, I will try to clarify in a more positive manner how the broadly Aristotelian resources under discussion here can be put to use in Christology without us losing sight of the uniqueness of Christology's subject matter. This will take us once more into the sphere of technical ontology, but, to the extent that this encourages clarity in trinitarian theology and Christology, I take it to be worthwhile. I will break up the next section into three points.

B. Use and Adaptation of Aristotelian Resources

(1) Metaphysics is a discipline that treats "being" taken as a universal or as applicable to the many, rather than particular kinds of being or particular beings themselves that are treated under particular sciences. Anything that is, is a being (τὸ ὄν, *ens*)—not because things that exist must be assimilated to and governed by our mental or semantic constructs but because things exist and, in response to this, human beings have for some time used this word *ens* or "being" to designate "that which is." Metaphysics is the science that treats being and those things that pertain to it as being (its modes, its causes, and so on). That is, metaphysics' proper subject matter is *ens* as such, or "that which is" (*id quod est*), "that which has essence," "that which has existence [*esse*]."[133] But *ens* as that which "has" essence and "has" existence is created, finite being. A created being "has" or partakes of an essence; it is not the subsisting fullness of its essence (e.g., no one human being is the full

133. The conception of "being" and metaphysics laid out here reflects the accounts of Aristotle, *Metaphysica* 4.1003a–1005a (59–64); 5.1017a–1017b (98–100); Aquinas, *Super De trin.* 5.4 (153–55); Aquinas, *De hebdomadibus* 2 (270–71); Aquinas, *Quaestiones de quolibet* 2.2.1 [3] ad 2 (215); Keckermann, *Scientiae metaphysicae*, 1.1–2 (2013–16); Alsted, *Metaphysica*, praecognita (18–19, 23–24); Maccovius, *Metaphysica*, 1.1 (1–3); 2.1, 6 (180, 265).

embodiment of humanness). Furthermore, the essence that a created being has is limited and lacking certain features that are constitutive of other kinds of created things. A created being "has" or partakes of *esse*; it does not exist by virtue of what it is but receives its existence from another. Moreover, the *esse* that it has is shaped by the limitations of its essence. Such a being's essence and existence are in a sense "really" distinct. While they are not two distinct "things" (*res*) in the strictest sense, essence is what something is and existence is the actuality and restriction of that essence in an individual being. Accordingly, metaphysics does not include God in its subject matter, though its exploration of the causes of created being can yield some knowledge of God as cause of its subject matter. Already this (broadly Thomistic and Reformed orthodox) conception of the discipline of metaphysics alerts us to the fact that its conceptual resources will not pass over into the work of theological description without significant qualification.

(2) Accordingly, metaphysical concepts may be applied to God only analogically—not univocally, as though God and the creature were two equals located under a common genus. On the one hand, these concepts may indeed be utilized in our description of God. They can clarify or express the sense and implications of what is taught in Scripture. Some of them are even explicitly found in Scripture. Paul brings the term φύσις ("nature") into his account of God in Galatians 4:8. The writer of Hebrews insists on Christians confessing that God "is" (ἐστίν, a form of the verb εἶναι, "to be") (Heb. 11:6). Paul's letter to the Philippians speaks of Christ "subsisting" (ὑπάρχων) in the form of God (Phil. 2:6). Hebrews teaches that the Son represents the ὑπόστασις of the Father (Heb. 1:3). The use of the term ὑπόστασις in Hebrews 1:3 (though perhaps less so in 3:14 and 11:1) overlaps with metaphysical usage.[134] Some older analyses assert that ὑπόστασις there pertains directly to the Father as one individual "substance" or distinct person;[135] some of the recent lexica translate it "substantial nature" or "essence."[136]

The aim of these observations is not to suggest that the New Testament gives us a technical ontology consciously imitating Aristotelian usage in the closest possible manner. However, these observations do indicate an overlap and commensurability of biblical modes of speech with classical metaphysical modes of speech. Accordingly, they also signal that it is fitting to explore how metaphysical resources may be used to illumine and set forth the material content of biblical teaching. Some of the technical definitions and

---

134. Cf. Johnson, *Hebrews*, 69–70.
135. E.g., Polanus, *Syntagma*, 3.1 (198–99). For further discussion, see Owen, *Hebrews*, 3:85, 88–95.
136. E.g., BDAG, 1040; cf. Harm W. Hollander, "ὑπόστασις," in *EDNT* 3:407.

arrangements of these concepts will be formally extrabiblical, but certainly the need to interpret the Bible and clarify its sense, coupled with the connection of these resources to the ordinary language of Scripture, suggests that it is appropriate to deploy such resources in the service of scriptural exegesis. Indeed, they are no more alien to the Bible than Bauckham's phrase "divine identity," for example, and can readily cooperate with this sort of contribution from Bauckham in expounding the Bible's Christology.

On the other hand, if God is *a se* and radically distinct from created being, these metaphysical concepts must undergo modification in their use in theology proper and Christology. As Turretin puts it, these terms are "sanctified by ecclesiastical custom" and applied to the mystery of God in an "eminent" manner.[137] The reason for calling God a "being" is not that he "has" or participates in an essence that can be instantiated beyond himself or in an *esse* more ultimate than himself. Rather, God may be called a "being" in an analogical sense simply because he is and because he is *this one* distinct from others. It is necessary to speak of a divine "essence" or "nature" not because God is governed by a delimiting principle that facilitates his actions but because God is God with all the perfections that pertain to him as God, and what God is as God is common to the three divine persons and distinguishes him from false gods.[138] It is fitting to call a divine person a "substance" in what is historically that term's primary sense: one that subsists *per se* and without needing to inhere in another as a part of it, eventually designated by the Greek ὑπόστασις according to catholic custom. This is not because any of the persons takes up accidents added to the divine essence but simply because each person does subsist, without inhering in something else as a mere part of it, and because each person has his own distinct mode of being or personal "property." Throughout this study, I will attempt to remain alert to possible misuse of metaphysical concepts and to deploy them in a manner that befits the uniqueness of Christology's subject matter.

(3) When dogmatic theology collates and expounds the major topics of Christian teaching, often taking up metaphysical resources to do so in the topics of theology proper and Christology, it is not a departure from biblical exegesis. Rather, in an important sense dogmatic theology is just one form of biblical exegesis. On the one hand, dogmatic theology differs from exegesis if "exegesis" is taken to mean an explanation of an individual biblical text,

---

137. Turretin, *Inst.*, 3.23.9 (1:282).

138. It is fitting to speak of a divine "substance" in what is historically its secondary sense (the essential constitution of a thing, eventually designated by the Greek οὐσία according to catholic custom) not because God has some constitution that can receive or lose additional qualities but for the same reasons that it is fitting to speak of God's essence.

with relative brevity and relatively little engagement with the whole canon of Scripture and the church's hermeneutical and theological tradition across the centuries. On the other hand, dogmatic theology is but one form of exegesis if "exegesis" simply means an unfolding and setting forth of what is already there in the biblical text. Even dogmatic theology's use of certain metaphysical concepts is an exegetical move. For the fact that those concepts have been analyzed in the scientific discipline of metaphysics ought not to obscure the fact that they are first and foremost just ordinary features of human knowledge about reality. For example, a carefully expressed distinction between ὑπόστασις and essence is merely a reflection of the fact that human beings perceive that there are individual beings in the world that also belong to common kinds. Therefore, although deploying a distinction between ὑπόστασις and essence in biblical exegesis might at first sound overly clever, it can be simply a matter of taking ordinary features of human knowledge and utilizing them in an analogical way to clarify, for example, that while the Son of God and Jesus are one person, that one person is both divine and human at the same time. And offering that sort of clarification is hardly an obstacle to confessing that the God with whom he is identified is the God of Israel and that, in his humanity, he fulfills the vocation of the first Adam and the messianic hopes of the prophets.

Though its formal presentation of Christian doctrine is different from that of Scripture itself, dogmatics treats the same subject matter that is found in Scripture. This formal difference concerns the ordering of the material and also some of the concepts and distinctions utilized. John Owen helpfully addresses both of these aspects. Owen praises the benefits of how revealed truth is "distributed" in the books of Scripture, which are so often tied to particular occasions. For, according to Owen, the books of the Bible are designed by God to meet the concrete situations of the church's life. Yet Owen still acknowledges that the "methodical disposition" of Christian doctrine in "our catechisms and systems of divinity" does much to "help the understandings and memories of men."[139] The arrangement and mutual ordering of the articles of faith (the *dogmata*) in dogmatic topics or commonplaces is not an attempt to look away from the Bible or to discredit its own order of teaching. It is, instead, an attempt to provide a way of impressing this teaching on the minds of believers that has heuristic and integrative advantages. With regard to the peculiar concepts and distinctions used, Owen writes that "use is to be made of words and expressions as, it may be, are not literally and formally contained in Scripture, but only are, unto our conceptions and

139. Owen, *Pneumatologia*, 6.2.6 (4:188–91).

apprehensions, expository of what is so contained. And to deny the liberty, yea, the necessity hereof, is to deny all interpretation of the Scripture—all endeavors to express the sense of the words of it unto the understandings of one another, which is, in a word, to render the Scripture itself useless."[140] The "expository" role of extrabiblical language is expressed well in the notion that theology's use of philosophical concepts is strictly "ministerial" rather than "magisterial," serving and opening up the sense of Scripture to the Christian mind rather than dictating what scriptural revelation can and cannot teach. In other words, any philosophical apparatus brought into the work of Christian theology has an ancillary function and should help us remain faithful to the apostolic teaching and to refute erroneous representations of it.[141] It will be an aim throughout this study to clarify why certain metaphysical concepts appear at particular points in the doctrine of the person of Christ and how they can illumine pertinent biblical teaching.

VI. Conclusion

In this chapter we have considered a number of important criticisms of "classical theism" brought forward on the basis of biblical Christology. We have observed how these criticisms often focus on (1) a concern to provide adequate description of Christ's relationship to the Father and Spirit, (2) a concern to uphold the unity of the person of Christ, and (3) a concern to uphold the immediacy and authenticity of the Son's human experience and suffering. After this, we considered some criticisms of the use of Aristotelian metaphysical concepts in Christology, a number of which have certain connections to the three aforementioned concerns. In response to the first set of criticisms, the next section began to sketch a rationale for embracing a doctrine of God that affirms his aseity, immutability, impassibility, eternity, and simplicity in the hope of showing why Christian theologians and exegetes still ought to be interested in how such an understanding of God might fit with the Bible's Christology. The next section then addressed the criticisms of certain philosophical concepts and categories, first touching upon specific criticisms brought up by various authors and then providing a positive description of how use of such concepts and categories is both warranted and seriously chastened by the uniqueness of the subject matter of Christian theology. From here we begin the constructive work of the book and come first to the Son's eternal relation to the Father.

140. Owen, *Doctrine of the Trinity*, 379.
141. So, e.g., Turretin, *Inst.*, 1.13.1–14 (1:49–53).

TWO

"The Word Was with God": The Son's Eternal Relation to the Father

I. Introduction

In this chapter the aim is to examine the Son's eternal relation to the Father and to explain how that relation coheres with and is illumined by God's simplicity. This will involve considering scriptural texts that disclose the Son's eternal relation to the Father and expounding the scriptural teaching with the use of concepts like essence, substance, person, relation, and so on. First, we will work through pertinent biblical material on the Son's eternal relation to the Father in order to ground and orient our discussion throughout the chapter. Next, I will consider how this thread of scriptural teaching may be connected to the Bible's emphasis on the unity and simplicity of God, particularly with respect to God's intellect, will, and power. The next section will then attempt to integrate the two previous sections and elaborate on the way in which the personal distinctions and personal communion in God fit together with God's unity and simplicity. The final main section of the chapter will respond to two potential challenges related to the claim that in the Son's eternal relation of origin from the Father the Son receives from the Father the divine essence.

II. Biblical Description

It is not idle curiosity that gives rise to discussion of the Son's eternal relation to the Father in Christology and the doctrine of the Trinity. Rather, God's own self-revelation necessitates such discussion, since God's self-revelation includes that eternal relation within the body of scriptural teaching given to all believers for their growth in the faith. The goal here is to show that this relation is a relation of origin in which the Son eternally comes forth from the Father and, in so doing, receives from the Father the divine essence.

Recapitulating and expanding the opening of Genesis, John's prologue announces, "In the beginning was the Word, and the Word was with God and the Word was God" (John 1:1). Just as the Genesis creation account eschews a divine becoming and implicitly conveys that the God who created the universe already is the God that he is, so John tells us that even prior to the world's existence the Word was with God the Father. This is what explains the gravity of the incarnation: the one who was with God the Father and already was himself true God is the very one who took on flesh and dwelt among us.

The beginning of John's Gospel arguably echoes the description of wisdom in Proverbs 8:22–31, where wisdom is with God at the beginning of creation and active in God's creative work.[1] On the one hand, John's account of the Word differs from the personification of wisdom in Proverbs 8 and from various ancient wisdom traditions, perhaps underscoring that Jesus the Word is greater than any other wisdom.[2] Indeed, John's articulation of the Word's eternal relation to the Father before the work of creation may make it difficult to find a straightforward precedent in Proverbs 8. For in Proverbs 8:22 wisdom declares, "YHWH originated me [קָנָנִי] in the beginning of his way." The Hebrew verb קנה can be used to express an act of making (e.g., Gen. 14:19, 22) and thus locate its object within the created order.[3] In addition, the verb is translated with the Greek ἔκτισέν ("created") in the LXX, which is why the church fathers sought to clarify that Proverbs 8 does not envision the Son to be a mere creature.[4]

On the other hand, if John does draw broadly from the conception of wisdom in Proverbs 8, then it may be instructive to note certain elements of Proverbs 8 that indicate that wisdom has an origin that ultimately transcends the

1. A variety of Old and New Testament scholars affirm this connection: e.g., Whybray, *Wisdom in Proverbs*, 11–12; Waltke, *Proverbs*, 126–33; M. Thompson, *The God of the Gospel of John*, 136; Keener, *John*, 1:300–302, 367–70, 379–81; Hurtado, *God in New Testament Theology*, 65–67.

2. See esp. Jobes, "Sophia Christology," 238–43. Cf. Waltke, *Proverbs*, 129–32; Longman, *The Fear of the Lord Is Wisdom*, 246–50.

3. In a number of places the verb expresses not an act of producing per se but an act of possessing or acquiring, though producing might be considered a means of possessing or acquiring (see Fox, *Proverbs 1–9*, 279).

4. For the view that the act of creating in Prov. 8:22 concerns only the Word's human nature, see, e.g., Athanasius, *Oratio II*, 44–45 (220–22); Hilary of Poitiers, *La Trinité* 12.44–45 (3:446–50); Ambrose, *De Spiritu Sancto* 2.6,51 (106).

created order.[5] In 8:24–25, wisdom proclaims, "When there were no watery depths I was brought forth [חוֹלָלְתִּי]"; "Before the hills I was brought forth."[6] This begetting evidently occurs before the existence of the world. Hilary of Poitiers, for example, picks up on this and contends from Proverbs 8:24–25 that the Son is in fact begotten of the Father before the ages.[7] Though the link between John's prologue and the material on wisdom in Proverbs 8 does not mean that the teaching of the former is wholly determined by the latter, it does suggest that, insofar as John presents Jesus the Word as the wisdom of God, the Word being "with" God before creation in John 1:1 may entail that he is also begotten of God like wisdom was brought forth from God before the founding of the world in Proverbs 8:24–25. The point here is not that Proverbs 8 by itself establishes the doctrine of the eternal generation of the Son but only that John's prologue has in its Old Testament background the notion of personified wisdom coming forth from God before the world began.

At any rate, that the Word is "from" the Father appears explicitly in John 1:14: the Word who was with God became flesh, and "we have seen his glory, glory as of the only Son from the Father [μονογενοῦς παρὰ πατρός], full of grace and truth." It is not the glory per se but the glorious Son that is παρὰ πατρός here.[8] The preposition παρά is indicative of origin ("the only Son who originates from the Father").[9] In 1:6, where John the Baptist is said to be a man sent παρὰ θεοῦ, the preposition παρά concerns an origination in time only. Some interpreters reason that the Son's origination from the Father in 1:14 also refers to a temporal mission only, not least because human beings have seen the glory under consideration and because of the various places in John where Jesus has come from the Father into the world (3:17, 34; 4:34; 5:23–24, 30, 36–38; 6:29, 38–39, 44, 57; 7:16, 18, 33; 8:16, 18, 26, 29, 42; 9:4; 10:36; 11:42; 12:44–45, 49; 13:20; 15:21; 16:5; 17:3, 18, 23, 25; 20:21).[10]

Certainly the language of coming or being "from" in John does not automatically stipulate an eternal origination or procession, but that does not

5. The semantic range of קנה in 8:22 itself does not require this conclusion but does leave open the possibility (cf. Waltke, *Proverbs*, 408–9; Turretin, *Inst.*, 3.29.12 [1:326]).
6. On the Hebrew verb, see Fox, *Proverbs 1–9*, 282.
7. Hilary of Poitiers, *La Trinité* 12.37–38 (3:434, 436). For Hilary, those who hold that the Son is a mere creature have failed to allow the subject matter of the text to inform the interpretation of the words: *non sermoni res sed rei est sermo subiectus* (4.14 [1:40]; 12.35 [3:432]).
8. Cf. Barrett, *John*, 139.
9. For the use of the preposition, see, e.g., Robertson, *A Grammar of the Greek New Testament*, 614–15; Wallace, *Greek Grammar beyond the Basics*, 378; Harris, *Prepositions and Theology*, 175.
10. Cf. R. Brown, *John I–XII*, 14; Michaels, *John*, 80–81; Harris, *Prepositions and Theology*, 175.

mean that it cannot do so.[11] In John 1:14, whether the word μονογενής is translated "only begotten," "only Son," or something similar, the μονογενής is "from the Father" in such a way that this origin explains his sharing the glory, grace, and truth ascribed to YHWH in Exodus 33:17–34:7.[12] But temporal origin like that of John the Baptist in John 1:6 does not entail that the one sent is equal in glory to YHWH or full of divine grace and truth. For YHWH's own glory and his infinite grace and truth are just not something that can be acquired at a point in time. It seems to me, then, that the relation of origin that the μονογενής has toward the Father in 1:14 is something that transcends the economy of salvation and is thus eternal.

Perhaps one could respond that the Son's being from the Father in John 1:14 implies that the Son eternally existed with the Father before his outward mission but does not necessarily specify that in eternally existing *with* the Father he also eternally existed *from* the Father. But the designation μονογενής and the name "Son," used throughout John's Gospel, are not arbitrarily assigned. The term "Son" is not applied to one divine person without a real reason, as though the one called "Son" might just as fittingly have been called "Father." The terms "Son" and "Father" express who the persons truly are. The Son decisively reveals the Father because he eternally *is* the beloved μονογενής in the "bosom" of the Father (1:18; cf. 17:24).[13] As Gregory of Nyssa observes, it is vital not to separate the word "Son" from its signification, and what it signifies is a relation of essential kinship to one who begets.[14] Thus, in addition to the use of the preposition παρά in John 1:14, the names of the persons themselves inform us that the relation of the Word or Son to the Father is a relation of origin. To be sure, there are certain elements in John's teaching that rule out a univocal use of the term "generation" in the case of God. In particular, the generation was not corporeal, since God is incorporeal (cf.

11. Herman Ridderbos comments that this language in John is "unsystematized" (*John*, 526).

12. Regarding the connection of John 1 to Exod. 33–34, see, e.g., Craig A. Evans, *Word and Glory*, 78–83; Hengel, "The Prologue of the Gospel of John," 286–87; Bauckham, *Gospel of Glory*, 46–52.

13. Even if μονογενής should be translated "only" or "unique," its use in the LXX and NT shows that it still often signifies an only or beloved *child* (see John 3:16, 18; 1 John 4:9; cf. Luke 7:12; 8:42; 9:38; Heb. 11:17; so Keener, *John*, 412–16; cf. Hengel, "The Prologue of the Gospel of John," 287; Michaels, *John*, 80). While there are several ways in which sonship language is applied to created beings in Scripture (e.g., angels, human rulers), various texts in the Gospels, such as John 1:18 and 17:24, attest that Jesus's sonship is unique, being that of the coeternal, consubstantial Son of the Father.

14. Gregory of Nyssa, *Contra Eunomium, pars altera* 3.1, 126 (2:46); 3.1, 135–37 (2:48–49). Gregory's point here focuses on the essential equality of the persons, but it includes the notion that sonship necessarily involves being begotten of the Father. Cf. Cyril of Alexandria, *Scholia* 28 (552); Cyril, *Ad Theodosium* 7,13 (50–51).

John 4:24). Also, the Son never began to exist, since he eternally was with the Father. Not everything that applies in ordinary father-son relations applies in God's case.[15] But John's Gospel does teach that the name "Son" means something: the Son receives from the Father divine life and glory and is the eternal object of the Father's delight (e.g., 1:18; 5:26; 16:15; 17:5, 24). So Gregory of Nyssa: "Calling him 'Son,' we say that he truly is what he is called, being shone forth by generation from the unbegotten light."[16] In short, the Son is eternally begotten of the Father and eternally proceeds from the Father.

To expand on John's witness to the Son's procession from the Father, it is important to consider several other texts as well. In John 5, Jesus has angered his interlocutors by implicitly "making himself equal with God" (5:18). Jesus clarifies that he is not in competition with the Father by emphasizing that he always acts according to what he sees the Father doing (5:19–23; cf. 5:30). Jesus explains that whoever hears his word and believes the Father will have eternal life (5:24). Indeed, the dead who hear the Son's voice will live (5:25). Jesus then grounds this statement in another: "For just as the Father has life in himself [ζωὴν ἐν ἑαυτῷ], so also he has given to the Son to have life in himself [ζωὴν ... ἐν ἑαυτῷ]" (5:26). The life that the Father communicates to the Son is a life by which the Son can raise the dead by his mere speech. It is thus a divine life, not a life or power that pertains merely to Jesus's human nature or economic office and not a life reducible to the eternal life that all believers receive (cf. 1:4; 11:25–26). Indeed, in his conversation with Nicodemus, Jesus has already ruled out the idea that humanity in its weakness ("flesh") might have the life by which one could grant spiritual life to others (3:5–6). The Son receives from the Father the fullness of the divine life, a life that pertains to what God is as God. The Son's reception of this life assumes, then, an eternal going forth or procession on the Son's part, a procession that is, as a procession of the Son rather than the Holy Spirit, fittingly called "generation" or "filiation."

In light of John 5, certain passages where the Son comes from the Father are suggestive of the Son's eternal generation. Some of the statements in John about the Son coming from the Father seem to pertain primarily to his mission, his being sent from the Father into the world, rather than his eternal procession (e.g., 8:42; 13:3; 16:27–28). In other cases, the situation appears to be different. In John 6:45–46, Jesus says that those who learn from the Father

15. See again Gregory of Nyssa, who lists various material or creaturely aspects of generation that do not apply in the Son's case and who also finds that what remains in the Son's case is being from another (τὸ ἐξ αἰτίας εἶναί) and an attendant natural kinship (*Refutatio confessionis Eunomii* 88 [348]; 94 [350–51]).

16. Gregory of Nyssa, *Contra Eunomium, pars altera* 3.7, 47 (2:231).

come to him, adding, "not that anyone has seen the Father except he who is from God [ὁ ὢν παρὰ τοῦ θεοῦ], he has seen the Father." An ordinary human hearer of Jesus's message might be "one who is of God" (ὁ ὢν ἐκ τοῦ θεοῦ) in that he or she is disposed by the Spirit to receive Jesus's message (so 8:47), but in 6:45–46 Jesus is "of" or "from" God in such a way that he has uniquely "seen" the Father and is the only one who can reveal him to others. In this case, the Son's coming forth from the Father has reference not merely to his mission but to his eternal procession, in which the Father communicates the fullness of divine knowledge to him. In this connection, John Chrysostom comments that the phrase "from God" in 6:46 is said "not by reason of cause [i.e., by creation]" but "according to the way of essence [κατὰ τὸν τρόπον τῆς οὐσίας]."[17] Likewise Aquinas: "Because [the Son] perfectly receives the whole nature of the Father by eternal generation, the Son totally sees and comprehends him."[18]

Jesus makes a similar statement in John 7, where he addresses some who question his messiahship in the temple: "I have not come from myself, but the one who sent me is true, whom you do not know. I myself know him, for I am from him [παρ' αὐτοῦ], and he sent me" (7:28b–29). This text certainly has reference to the Son's mission in the world and his coming from the Father in that respect in the last clause of verse 29 ("he sent me"). But, as in John 6:46, the Son is "from" the Father in the second clause of verse 29 ("I am from him") in such a way that it explains why the Son (indeed, the Son alone) truly knows the Father. Augustine catches up both elements of the text by pointing out that Jesus's statement "I am from him" pertains to the Son being "God of God, light of light," while the statement "he sent me" pertains to the coming of the Son into the world whereby his hearers see him in the flesh.[19]

In Colossians, Paul calls Christ the "image of the invisible God" and the "firstborn of all creation" (1:15). The concept of Christ as "image" has bearing on our understanding of the Son's eternal relation to the Father, though the term "firstborn" in this context is not tied to the doctrine of the Son's eternal generation. Various authors of the Christian exegetical tradition have been quick to point out that the phrase "firstborn of all creation" here does not pertain to the relation that the Son has to the Father. For that would imply that the Son is a mere creature, which is against Paul's teaching in 1:16, where the Son in fact operates with God the Father to create all things (1:16).[20] Jesus

17. John Chrysostom, *In Johann.* 46.1 (258).
18. Aquinas, *Super Ioann.* 6.5.5.947 (178).
19. Augustine, *In Iohann.* 31.4 (295).
20. Cf. Athanasius, *Oratio II*, 63–64 (239–41); Hilary of Poitiers, *La Trinité* 8.48 (2:454–56); Cyril of Alexandria, *Ad Theodosium* 7,16 (52), 30 (61), 39 (69).

is the "firstborn" of all creation in the sense that he is its author, heir, and leader, the one who, having assumed humanity and become the "firstborn from the dead" (1:18), brings creation to its fulfillment by the resurrection.[21] However, because Colossians 1 teaches that Christ created all things and is therefore not a mere creature, the sense in which Christ is the "image of the invisible God" transcends his human life and activity. Indeed, if the Son is the image of the *invisible* God, then the likeness in view cannot be something that pertains to him merely in his outward visibility. Further, in Colossians 1:19 and 2:9, Christ is the one in whom the divine fullness dwells, which implies that he reflects the Father in his deity. At the same time, if the use of the word "image" in this passage concerns how the invisible God makes himself known to creatures, then it likely does include the aspect of visible representation.[22] It is appropriate, then, to draw the conclusion that Christ images the Father in both his deity and his humanity. In his deity, he has and does what the Father has and does. In his humanity, he visibly represents and reveals God for the benefit of human beings.[23] The former is what fits him for the latter.[24] In connection with the line of argument being developed in this section, the Son who is eternally from the Father and given divine glory by the Father in John is the perfect image of the Father in Colossians. The teaching of John that the Son is beloved of the Father before the world began (John 1:18; 17:24) is illumined and reinforced by the teaching of Colossians that in the Son the Father beholds his own image that far surpasses Adam's likeness to God.

The writer of Hebrews teaches something similar in slightly different terms. He tells us that God has spoken "in these last days in his Son," whom he appointed to be heir of all things and through whom he made the ages (1:2). Describing the Son further, the author writes, "who, being the radiance of glory and the imprint of [God the Father's] substance [ὢν ἀπαύγασμα τῆς δόξης καὶ χαρακτὴρ ὑποστάσεως αὐτοῦ], bearing all things by the word of his power, after making purification of sins, sat down at the right hand of the majesty in the heavens, becoming superior to the angels inasmuch as the name he has inherited is superior to theirs" (1:3–4). Francis Turretin points out that Christ is the effulgence of the Father's glory and the representation of the Father as the God-man in his mediatorial office, so that whoever has

21. Cf. G. K. Beale's reading of "firstborn" that stresses the concept of sovereignty (*Colossians and Philemon*, 90–91).

22. So Hilary of Poitiers, *La Trinité* 8.48–51 (2:454–60). Cf. Owen, *Christologia* 5 (70–73); Dunn, *Colossians and Philemon*, 87–90; M. Thompson, *Colossians and Philemon*, 28–30.

23. On the inward and outward aspects of the imaging, cf. M. Thompson, *Colossians and Philemon*, 29–30; Moo, *Colossians and Philemon*, 115–17; Seitz, *Colossians*, 94–95.

24. Cf. Wright, *The Climax of the Covenant*, 115–17; Beale, *Colossians and Philemon*, 80–86, 89–91.

seen Christ has seen the Father (cf. John 14:9). Nevertheless, Turretin adds, it is "not excluded but assumed" that the Son is the "essential image" of the Father, "because that substantial image shines forth in Christ incarnate . . . whence he is called 'God manifest in the flesh'" (cf. 1 Tim. 3:16).[25] Similarly, John Owen observes in his Hebrews commentary that while the author aims "to show how the Father expressed and declared himself unto us in the Son, yet this could not be done without manifesting what the Son is in himself and in reference to the Father." In other words, the text treats the supremacy of Christ not only "consequentially to his discharge of the office of mediator, but also antecedently, in his worth, fitness, ability, and suitableness to undertake and discharge it," which is from his divine nature.[26] This line of interpretation corresponds well to the fact that in Hebrews 1 the author highlights the preeminence of Christ both with respect to his fulfillment of his economic office and with respect to his being YHWH himself, the unchanging Creator revealed in the Old Testament (1:10–12, quoting Ps. 102:25–27).[27]

If the Son is the image or representation of the Father's ὑπόστασις in his eternal, personally constitutive relation to the Father in Hebrews 1:3, and if he is one and the same God with the Father, then the meaning of ὑπόστασις must be treated carefully. For an image is distinct from that of which it is the image. If the Son were the image of the divine essence, then he would be distinct from the divine essence and, by implication, in possession of another essence numerically distinct from the Father's. Therefore, it is appropriate to take the term ὑπόστασις in 1:3 to denote the individual person of the Father.[28] This aligns with the technical sense that the term ὑπόστασις acquired over time in contrast to the term οὐσία in early Christian articulation of the doctrine of the Trinity. If ὑπόστασις were taken to signify God's essence or nature, then, to avoid the implication that the Son and the Father might have two distinct essences and be two distinct Gods, one would have to explain that the point is that the Son has the same essence as the Father and in that sense images the essence as it is in the Father.[29] At any rate, Owen rightly

25. Turretin, *Inst.*, 3.29.17, 19 (1:328–29).

26. Owen, *Hebrews*, 3:90–91.

27. On Heb. 1:3, see also Swain, "The Radiance of the Father's Glory," 40–42.

28. So Polanus, *Syntagma*, 3.1 (198–99). Thus, Turretin notes that the Son is the image of God with the term "God" taken "hypostatically" for the Father (not "essentially"). The alterity of the image (the Son) and that of which he is the image (the Father) holds because the Son images another mode of subsisting of the essence (i.e., the Father) (*Inst.*, 3.29.17 [1:328]). Cf. Owen, *Hebrews*, 3:95: "The hypostasis of the Father is the Father himself. Hereof, or of him, is the Son said to be the 'express image.'"

29. See, e.g., Athanasius's remark that in sharing the Father's essence the Son is the "image and radiance of the whole" (ὅλου εἰκὼν καὶ ἀπαύγασμα; *Serap.* 1.16,17–20 [492]).

sums up that "this agreement, likeness, and conveniency between the Father and Son is essential. . . . What the Father is, doth, hath, that the Son is, doth, hath; or else the Father, as the Father, could not be fully satisfied in him, nor represented by him."[30]

Authors like Turretin and Owen assert that the teaching of the Son as the image of the Father is rooted in the Father's eternal generation of the Son and eternal communication of the divine essence to the Son.[31] First, it should be observed that the word ἀπαύγασμα ("radiance" or "reflection") in Hebrews 1:3 already indicates that the Son has from the Father his divine perfection. Recent scholars typically exercise caution about whether to render ἀπαύγασμα actively as "radiance" or passively as "reflection," some suggesting it is passive since it is closely linked with χαρακτήρ, which is a received impression.[32] The same word is used in Wisdom of Solomon 7:26, where wisdom is called "the ἀπαύγασμα of eternal light and the spotless mirror of the working of God and the image of his goodness." In both Hebrews 1:3 and Wisdom 7:26, one could argue that ἀπαύγασμα is complementary to the concept of an "imprint" and is therefore a grammatically active radiating or shining forth. Alternatively, in both cases one could argue that ἀπαύγασμα is parallel to the concept of an "imprint" and is therefore a grammatically passive thing that receives an impression or light. It seems to me that, either way, the doctrinal implications are materially the same.[33] Either the Son is the radiance of light that comes forth from the Father and therefore reflects the Father, or the Son reflects the Father and must therefore receive the light of the Father and thus go forth from him. What is grammatically passive (reflection, receiving light) still signifies something that is on the Son's part really active (radiating and going forth). With a look back to the glory of God that shone among the people of God in the Old Testament, Owen captures well the key point, that the writer directs his readers to "the eternal glory of God, with the essential beaming and brightness of it in the Son, in and by whom the glory of the Father shineth forth unto us."[34]

Second, Hebrews 1:5 speaks of the Father "begetting" the Son: "For to which of the angels did [God] formerly say, 'You are my Son, today I have begotten [γεγέννηκά] you?' And again, 'I will be a Father to him and he will be a Son to me.'" The first quotation is from Psalm 2, a messianic psalm in

30. Owen, Hebrews, 3:95.

31. Turretin, Inst., 3.29.19 (1:329); Owen, Hebrews, 3:89, 96.

32. See, e.g., Ralph P. Martin, "ἀπαύγασμα," in NIDNTT 2:289–90; Otfried Hofius, "ἀπαύγασμα," in EDNT 1:117–18; Ellingworth, Hebrews, 98–99.

33. Cf. Johnson, Hebrews, 69.

34. Owen, Hebrews, 3:93.

which God proclaims the Davidic king's sovereignty over the nations. The second quotation is from 2 Samuel 7:14, where YHWH promises David that his line will continue and that his son will build the temple. Psalm 2:7 and Hebrews 1:5 appear often in traditional discussions of eternal generation, but in light of their messianic themes some interpreters do not think these verses refer to the Son's eternal generation.[35]

Owen's exposition, however, attends to the literary context and still ultimately confirms the Son's eternal generation. He notes that the use of Psalm 2:7 in Hebrews 1:5 assumes a typological connection between David and Christ, which would be compromised if the begetting of Christ in Hebrews 1:5 referred directly to his (unique) eternal generation.[36] At the same time, Owen observes that verse 5 is meant to explain that Jesus is superior to the angels, so the peculiar application of the name "Son" to Jesus must be intended to set forth his divine glory, which surpasses that of any creature.[37] On the one hand, Owen maintains the typological connection between David and Jesus by reasoning that just as "God raised [David] up, and established him in his rule and kingdom," so God outwardly "reveals" or "declares" Jesus to be the Son of God on pivotal "occasions" in his economic work, chiefly his resurrection (cf. Acts 13:33; Rom. 1:4). As God raised up and exalted David, so he has raised up and exalted Jesus. On the other hand, Owen maintains that naming Jesus "Son" and declaring his begetting displays his superiority over created beings. For the outward declaration of Jesus's sonship is ultimately an economic reiteration of the "natural and eternal sonship" of Jesus that renders him capable of fulfilling this work in the first place: "There is, indeed, included in this reasoning . . . an intimation of a peculiar filiation and sonship of Christ. Had he not been so the Son of God as never any angel or other creature was, he never had been called so in such a way as they are never so called."[38] In other words, the Father's pronouncement of the sonship of Jesus in Hebrews 1:5a is an economic declaration and exaltation (hence the parallel with David), but in the case of Jesus the *content* of that declaration ultimately includes the Son's eternal generation by the Father, by which the Son is uniquely fit to accomplish his work.

Owen continues in this vein in his exposition of the quote from 2 Samuel 7:14 ("I will be a Father to him, and he will be a Son to me"). For Owen, the appearance of this paternal statement in Hebrews 1:5b is not intended

---

35. For reflection on the history of interpretation of this text, see Bates, *The Birth of the Trinity*, 62–76.

36. Owen, *Hebrews*, 3:133–37.

37. Owen, *Hebrews*, 3:135.

38. Owen, *Hebrews*, 3:135–37.

directly to "prove the natural sonship" of Christ or to describe his human nature and activity as such. Instead, it is first and foremost a statement about the Son's fulfillment of his unique economic office as "the revealer of the will of God in the gospel." After all, it would be problematic to imply that the eternal relation of the Son to the Father had to be established by an economic promise. Nevertheless, Owen writes, "If it be asked on what account God would thus be a father unto Jesus Christ in this peculiar manner, it must be answered that the radical, fundamental cause of it lay in the relation that was between them from his eternal generation; but he *manifested* himself to be his father, and engaged to deal with him in the love and care of a father, as he had accomplished his work of mediation on the earth and was exalted unto his throne and rule in heaven."[39] Owen's reading makes sense of both the economic and the eternal dimensions of the biblical author's argument in Hebrews 1 and sheds light on the relation between those dimensions. The Father's eternal begetting of the Son accounts for the Son's unique fitness for his incarnate work, and that eternal begetting is what the Father ultimately expresses and underscores in his economic declaration of the Son's supremacy over all creatures.[40]

Drawing together the material explored in this section, we can say that the Son's eternal, personally constitutive relation to the Father that distinguishes him from the Father (and the Spirit) is an active one in which he is begotten of the Father and eternally comes forth from the Father. In light of this, it is rightly called a "relation of origin."[41] This has given rise to the traditional naming of the Son's personal "property" (that which is proper to him as the distinct person that he is) as γέννησις ("generation," "birth") or filiation.[42] This eternal generation involves the Father sharing or communicating the divine essence and life to the Son so that the Son has and is all that the Father essentially has and is. Eternal generation entails that the Son is personally distinct from the Father (since he receives from the Father the divine essence, while the Father receives it from no one) and essentially one with the Father (since the Son does indeed receive the fullness of the essence). By this generation the Son is the perfect image of the Father and the perfect object of the Father's eternal love.[43] The next section will examine the divine unity and

39. Owen, *Hebrews*, 3:138–39, 145. Though Heb. 1:6 goes on to call Christ the "firstborn," Owen judges that it does not refer to the Son's eternal generation per se, because it is a relative term inclusive of others who will become adopted children of God (*Hebrews*, 3:157–59).

40. See also the reading of Pierce, "Hebrews 1 and the Son Begotten 'Today.'"

41. See Aquinas, *ST* Ia.29.4 corp. (333).

42. So, e.g., John of Damascus, *Expos. fidei* 1.8 (26–27); Aquinas, *ST* Ia.32.2 (351–52).

43. As Owen puts it, "The divine nature in the Son is the only full, resting, complete object of the love of God the Father" (*Posthumous Sermons, Part IV* 22 [613]).

simplicity in coordination with which the personal relations in God should ultimately be treated.

III. The Unity and Simplicity of God

Here I will attempt to present Scripture's teaching on God's unity by looking at certain passages that call God "one," certain passages that call each of the persons the one God, and certain considerations that indicate the unity of God's intellect, will, and power that is common to the divine persons. I will do this under the following main points.

(1) Prior to its disclosure of the distinctions among the Father, Son, and Spirit, the Bible emphasizes that there is only one true God (e.g., Deut. 4:35, 39; 6:4–5). Whatever the people of Israel may have believed at any given point in their often inconsistent religious life, the Old Testament canon teaches that YHWH alone is the true God. It is not just that he has a distinct claim to Israel's worship but rather that in his own being and action he is unlike the false gods, which are in fact "no gods." For YHWH is sovereign over the nations and alone can kill and make alive (Exod. 15:11; Deut. 32:17, 21, 31, 36–39). He alone is the one who is eternal and made the heavens and the earth, while the idols are products of their craftsmen and ultimately have no power to do good or evil (Isa. 37:19; 40:18–19; 41:21–29; 43:10; Jer. 10:1–16). There are qualified senses in which beings other than YHWH may be called "gods." For example, "angels and magistrates are called 'gods' in Scripture on account of some participation of dominion and dignity" (e.g., Pss. 8:5; 82; 97:7). But YHWH alone is God "properly and originally." Others are mere "so-called gods" (λεγομένως), but YHWH alone is God in reality (cf. 1 Cor. 8:5).[44] Put differently, some created beings are called gods in an analogical and secondary sense (ἀναλόγως, δευτέρως); idols are called gods only "apparently" and "imitatively" (φαινομένως, μιμητικῶς); YHWH is called God "essentially" (οὐσιωδῶς).[45]

When Holy Scripture reveals that there are three distinct divine persons, it does not withdraw its claim that there is only one God (e.g., John 17:3; Rom. 3:30; 1 Tim. 1:17; James 2:19). This claim shows up in an especially pointed way in 1 Corinthians 8, where Paul offers a "Christianized" version of the

44. Turretin, *Inst.*, 3.3.4 (1:199).
45. Mastricht, *TPT*, 2.2.9 (88). One recent study of Paul's teaching on idols in 1 Cor. 8–10 notes that Paul calling them "so-called gods" gestures toward both their "non-deity (people only call them gods) and their existence in the world (which he will claim is related to demonic activity)" (T. Rogers, *God and the Idols*, 175–76).

Shema: "There is one God, the Father, from whom are all things and we are for him, and there is one Lord, Jesus Christ, through whom are all things and we are through him" (8:6).[46] Paul's expansion of the Shema does not set up two deities, one called "God" and one called "Lord." Instead, the words θεός and κύριος (the common Septuagint stand-in for יְהֹוָה) both reflect the designation of the one God as יְהֹוָה אֱלֹהֵנוּ ("YHWH, our God") in Deuteronomy 6:4.[47] Accordingly, Jesus as κύριος, together with God the Father, is the one God, though Paul's use of the prepositions "from" and "through" still indicates the order in the divine persons' being and acting.[48] If this is the case, then each person does not merely have a quality that renders him divine or an instantiation of a species of divinity alongside other members of the species. Rather, each person, while being distinct from the other, is somehow identical to *this* God, the God of Israel.

This point is corroborated by other New Testament passages. In Philippians 2:9–11, for example, the Son is distinct from the Father, by whom he is exalted, but is also identified as YHWH. Here Paul calls Jesus κύριος again, declaring that every knee will bow before him and every tongue confess that he is κύριος, alluding to Isaiah 45:23, where YHWH, the only God, is the object of the same sort of worship.[49] Something similar takes place in Hebrews 1:10–12, where the author names the Son the κύριος of Psalm 102:25–27, the one who made the world and remains unchanging in contrast to the world.

In the Johannine literature, the Son is named "God" where the Father also is named "God." In John 1:1, the Word was with God (the Father) and also was God (ὁ λόγος ἦν πρὸς τὸν θεόν, καὶ θεὸς ἦν ὁ λόγος). Since the Word is "with" the Father, he is clearly distinct from the Father. Indeed, the anarthrous θεός at the end of John 1:1 helps us not to infer that the Word might be the same as God the Father in every respect. Yet, while the Word is not wholly identical to the Father, he is still the same God. Again in John 1:18 the Word is with God the Father ("in the bosom of the Father") and reveals God the

46. See Wright, *Climax of the Covenant*, 129–32.

47. Cf. Ciampa and Rosner, *First Epistle to the Corinthians*, 382–83.

48. If Jesus is identified as YHWH himself in 1 Cor. 8:6, it makes little sense to conclude that this order implies that the Son has a lesser deity (*pace*, e.g., Schrage, *Unterwegs zur Einzigheit und Einheit Gottes*, 148, 155). Further, if Jesus shares YHWH's unique authority, one ought to avoid positing a "functional subordination" of the Son in his deity (*pace*, e.g., Fee, *First Epistle to the Corinthians*, 413–14). The prepositional distinction here does not require a divine obedience of the Son to the Father. For the prepositional distinction is adequately accounted for by the Son eternally receiving from the Father the divine power and thus exercising from the Father divine power in all of God's works.

49. See, e.g., Hays, "The Story of God's Son," 194–95, where Hays comments that Isa. 45:22–23 is a "relentlessly monotheistic text."

Father, but he is also μονογενὴς θεὸς,[50] evoking an English paraphrase like "the unique and beloved one, [himself] God."[51] Toward the end of the Gospel, Jesus is named by the noun θεός with both the article and a subsequent genitive of possession marking θεός as a definite noun, which "lays stress on individual identity" (not mere "membership in a class").[52] Thomas exclaims, "My Lord and my God ['Ο κύριός μου καὶ ὁ θεός μου]" (John 20:28).[53] In 1 John 5:20b, Jesus is arguably named by the noun "God" as a definite noun once more: "he is the true God and eternal life [οὗτός ἐστιν ὁ ἀληθινὸς θεὸς καὶ ζωὴ αἰώνιος]." In 1 John 5:20a, Jesus is the Son of God and then in 5:20b, assuming he is the referent of the pronoun οὗτος, he is named "the true God."[54]

According to the New Testament, then, there is only one God, and each divine person is this one God. To use technical metaphysical terminology, this is a "real" identity (from the Latin res, "thing"), in which one and another (here, a divine person and the one God) are one and the same being, though there are still important distinctions to be found within that one being (particularly between one divine person and another). If it is the case that each person is really identical to this one God, then it follows that God's essence (what God is as God) is not unified merely by common genus or species or by an aggregate of separate individuals. Instead, God's essence is numerically one. There is only one instance of it. To say that God or God's essence is "one in number" is not to imply that there is a series of deities (a first and then perhaps a second, a third, etc.) but to express that God is the only or unique God, beyond whom there is no other.[55]

50. On the strength of the reading μονογενὴς θεὸς over against μονογενὴς υἱός or just ὁ μονογενής, see Metzger, A Textual Commentary on the Greek New Testament, 169–70.

51. Carson, John, 134.

52. Wallace, Greek Grammar beyond the Basics, 245. I take it that this pattern of biblical description rules out the idea that in the claim "the Son is God" the "is" does not pertain to identity but only expresses that the Son is "divine" (pace, e.g., Craig, "Toward a Tenable Social Trinitarianism," 96; Yandell, "How Many Times Does Three Go into One?," 152, 166).

53. Of course, in John 17:3 the Father has already been called the "only true God" (τὸν μόνον ἀληθινὸν θεὸν), but the "only" modifies not "Father" but "God." It is not that only the Father is God but that the Father is the only God in contrast to false gods (so, e.g., Gregory Nazianzen, Discours 27–31, 30.13 [252–56]). See also the Dutch Reformed author Wilhelmus à Brakel, for example, who adds that the Father is distinguished from Christ here not with respect to his deity but with respect to his "mediatorial office" (The Christian's Reasonable Service, 174, 498–99).

54. See, e.g., R. Brown, The Epistles of John, 625–26; Wallace, Greek Grammar beyond the Basics, 326–27. A similar line of reasoning could be undertaken with regard to the Spirit in texts like Acts 5:3–4 and Heb. 3:7–11.

55. Polanus, Syntagma, 2.5 (135–36). Polanus observes that "one" in this case is used "absolutely" to signal by remotion that God is undivided, rather than "relatively" in anticipation of a sequence of divine beings. In classical metaphysics, one in this "absolute" use is a transcendental that is convertible with being (not adding something to a being but just signifying that the being is constituted a distinct unity and is undivided).

(2) In sharing the one essence of God, the Father, Son, and Spirit share one divine intellect, will, and power. This is a claim to be substantiated first by looking briefly again at the Son's procession from the Father and then by noting some attendant reasons for taking this position. Regarding the Son's procession, it is significant that in John 16, where Jesus says that the Spirit receives and speaks from him, Jesus teaches that the Spirit's reception from him is grounded in the reality that "all things, as many as the Father has, are mine" (16:15). On the one hand, some things that Jesus has with and from the Father are matters included in the outward economy of salvation, particularly the authority to bring life and judgment (5:22, 27; 13:3; 17:2, 7–8) and the people of God themselves (6:37, 39; 10:29). On the other hand, these things do not exhaust what Jesus has that is the Father's according to John's Gospel. For what Jesus has that is the Father's includes divine life in himself (5:26), divine knowledge (5:19; 6:46), divine volition (5:21), divine power to act (5:19), and divine glory before the foundation of the world (17:5, 24; cf. 1:14). In other words, it will not work to drive a wedge between God's outward works and God's inward life and argue that what Jesus has is also the Father's in the case of the former but not in the case of the latter. Jesus's divine act of knowing is the Father's divine act of knowing; his divine act of willing is the Father's divine act of willing; his divine operation *ad extra* is the Father's divine operation *ad extra*. This is why when Jesus and the Father are working they produce the same works, not merely complementary works done side by side (5:17, 19–20).

If the divine persons share all that it is to be God and to act as God, how are they still distinct persons? They are distinct in the ways in which they have all that it is to be God and to act as God. According to the logic of John 16:15, the Son has this from the Father, the Spirit has this from both the Father and the Son, and the Father has this from no one, being the only divine person without an origin or hypostatic principle from whom he might receive what it is to be God. The persons are economically distinct in a number of ways, but the persons are eternally distinct or constituted as distinct persons in God by the relations of origin alone, from which follow their respective ways of willing and acting and their suitedness to undertake their distinct economic offices. Each of the persons does not have or express a distinct act of knowing, willing, or effecting things. But each of the persons has and expresses the one act distinctly.

In Pauline terms, Jesus the Son who is the Father's perfect image has "all the fullness of deity" (Col. 2:9). He lacks nothing of what it is to be God.[56]

---

56. Commentators who do not wish hastily to find a fully developed patristic Christology in Col. 2:9 still affirm that θεότης ("deity") signifies God's nature or what God is (e.g., Dunn, *Colossians and Philemon*, 151).

He is not distinct from the Father by virtue of having his own instance or version of what it is to be God. In the context of Colossians 2, the point is that believers have to "walk" in Christ and avoid getting caught up in vain philosophical thinking (2:6–8). The fact that in Christ all the fullness of deity dwells bodily is the rationale for the exhortation not to pursue such vain thinking. Whatever the specifics of the vain philosophies the Colossians may have encountered, it appears that what Paul has to warn against is not an outright denial of the importance of Christ but rather an account of Christ according to which he is a secondary divine figure, "only an indirect reflection of the divine principle."[57] According to Paul, "It is not as if Christ has a portion of deity, as if deity were a substance or characteristic that could be divided up among any number of entities, so that the Colossians could look elsewhere for divine reality."[58] Again, "it is not just part of the 'Divine fullness' that dwells in Christ, but 'all' of it dwells in him."[59]

In this respect, Christology and the doctrine of the Trinity elicit the doctrine of divine simplicity. To confirm that Christ is fully God and to set forth the spiritual claim this makes on the people of God requires the observation that Christ (or any divine person) does not have part of—does not participate in—a deity that, as a composite whole, would be greater than Christ's deity and leave open the question of whether there is need of further access to the divine. One could still ask whether each divine person having the fullness of deity might still allow for that fullness itself to be composed of inseparable parts or a plurality of inseparable intellects, wills, and powers. Could it be that within the fullness of God there are distinct divine intellects, wills, and powers? If a distinction between two intellects, wills, or powers would presuppose that one lacks something that the other has, then at least one of the intellects, wills, or powers would be finite. Therefore, if Christ's divine intellect were distinct from that of the Father, he would have not all but *some* of the "storehouses of wisdom and knowledge" in himself (see Col. 2:3). Presumably, Paul did not have in mind fine-tuned debates about divine simplicity while writing Colossians, but, at the same time, his insistence that in Christ there is the fullness of deity, including all divine wisdom and knowledge, precludes the idea that Christ might have one (finite) actualization of divine faculties beside or behind which there might be another.[60]

---

57. Pokorný, *Colossians*, 119.
58. M. Thompson, *Colossians and Philemon*, 55.
59. Beale, *Colossians and Philemon*, 177.
60. On distinction involving negation or not having what another has, see Aquinas, *Super De trin*. 4.1 corp. (120–21); Aquinas, *ST* Ia.11.3 corp. (111); Turretin, *Inst*., 3.8.15 (1:216). Matthew Levering has argued recently that if the divine persons had distinct knowledge, volition, energy,

(3) There are several additional reasons for holding the position that in sharing the one divine essence the divine persons share one and the same intellect, will, and power. First, the divine intellect and will are characterized by other divine perfections or virtues like truth, goodness, love, mercy, patience, and justice. An attempt to situate the divine intellect and will in that which distinguishes the persons from one another seems to imply that a swath of such attributes also will have to be resituated in that which distinguishes the persons from one another. But this is problematic, because it is the glory of the one true God—to put it clumsily, it is the YHWH-ness of YHWH—to be full of divine truth, goodness, love, mercy, patience, and justice (Exod. 33:19; 34:6–7; John 1:14). There is, then, only one instance of the divine truth, goodness, love, mercy, patience, and justice. And if that is so, then Christ shares this one instance with God the Father. It is what unifies Christ and the Father and confirms that Christ, in having this, is the true God. Therefore, Christ shares what such attributes characterize (i.e., the divine intellect and will) with the Father, though each person has and exhibits the divine knowing, willing, and acting in his own manner.

Second, there are also biblical texts in which the divine intellect, will, and power are overtly included in what God is and what sets him apart from false gods. In Isaiah, for example, YHWH's knowledge of the future verifies that he alone is the true God (Isa. 41:21–24; 44:6–8). In Jeremiah and Daniel, too, YHWH's wisdom and understanding distinguish him from the idols (Jer. 10:12; Dan. 2:21–23, 47; cf. Ps. 104:24; Prov. 3:19–20). YHWH's volition also sets him apart from the idols and from human beings, for his is the one purpose that inexorably prevails: "Our God is in the heavens, he does all that he pleases" (Ps. 115:3). "Many are the purposes in the heart of a human being, but the counsel of YHWH stands" (Prov. 19:21). "The LORD of hosts has sworn: As I have designed, so shall it be; and as I have planned, so shall it come to pass" (Isa. 14:24 NRSV). "I am God, and there is no one like me. . . . 'My purpose shall stand, and I will fulfill my intention'" (Isa. 46:9–10 NRSV). This inexorability of will is bound up with God's omnipotence, which characterizes him as the true God and distinguishes him from

---

and so on, they would be "three finite entities" (*Engaging the Doctrine of the Holy Spirit*, 33). To elaborate, if the Son, for example, does not have the Father's relation to the Son, this means just that the Son is not the Father (which is indeed true). However, if the Son did not have the Father's power or act of knowing, then one or both of these persons must have a finite power or act of knowing. One divine person not having the peculiar relation of another divine person is innocuous, since it does not concern what is common to the persons (e.g., intellect or knowledge) or render the persons finite. But one person not having another's power or act of knowing is problematic, since it does concern something common to the persons (intellect or knowledge) and would render them finite.

false gods. God alone can do his mighty works (Deut. 3:24). God performs his awesome deeds before Israel's eyes, "so that you would acknowledge that the LORD is God; there is no other besides him" (Deut. 4:34–35 NRSV; cf. Josh. 4:23–24; Ps. 66:1–7). If the divine intellect, will, and power pertain to what God is as God, and if there is only one instance of what God is as God, then the Son shares this one instance of the divine intellect, will, and power with the Father. It is what unifies the Son and the Father and confirms that the Son, in having this, is the true God.

(4) Relevant New Testament passages, where the Son in his knowing, willing, or acting is distinguished from the Father in his knowing, willing, or acting, are illumined by the New Testament's teaching on the incarnation and on the Son's procession from the Father. These passages do not require the postulate of distinct intellects or wills in God. On the one hand, when Jesus states that he does not know the time of his return and when he asks in Gethsemane that the Father's will be done, Christian exegetes have appealed to the Son's human intellect and will to account for his ignorance or his deference to the Father's will.[61] On the other hand, it seems to me that the incarnation alone cannot account for the teaching of certain Johannine texts that deal with the Son's divine knowing, willing, or acting. However, the Son's procession from the Father accounts for this teaching without pressing us to posit distinct divine intellects or wills.

In John 5:17–18, Jesus "makes himself equal with God" in the eyes of certain Jewish leaders. Then, in 5:19–30, he explains why his work does not place him in competition with the Father. Jesus tells his listeners that "the Son is able to do nothing from himself except what he sees the Father doing. For the things that he [the Father] does, these things also the Son likewise does. For the Father loves the Son and shows him all things, the things that he himself does, and greater works than these will he show him, so that you may wonder" (5:19–20). These works include giving new life to the dead and judging the human race, so that all should honor the Son just as they honor the Father (5:21–23). The dead who hear the Son's voice will live, for the Father has given to the Son to have life in himself (5:24–27). Jesus then reiterates, "I am able to do nothing from myself. Just as I hear, I judge, and my judgment is just, for I do not seek my own will but the will of him who sent me" (5:30).

Although the outward works of giving eschatological life and rendering judgment pertain to the Son's fulfillment of his economic office, they do in-

---

61. E.g., Athanasius, *Oratio III*, 46,8–10 (357); Gregory Nazianzen, *Discours 27–31*, 30.15 (256, 258); Cyril of Alexandria, *Contra Theodoretum* 169,38–39 (124); Cyril, *Le Christ est un* 755d–756d (438–42).

volve not only human but also divine action on the Son's part. Yet the Son's procession from the Father accounts for the distinction here between the Son in his divine knowing, willing, and acting and the Father in his divine knowing, willing, and acting. The Son does not know, will, or act "from himself" because he does not subsist from himself. He knows, wills, and acts from the Father since he subsists from the Father and receives from the Father the divine life, understanding, volition, and power (John 5:21, 26; 6:46; 7:29). Thus, Athanasius, for example, roots the Son doing what he sees the Father doing in the fact that the Son is the "offspring" (γέννημα) who is "from the essence" of the Father.[62] In his commentary on John, Augustine similarly reasons, "Whatever the Son has that he does, he has from the Father that he does. Why does he have from the Father that he does? Because he has from the Father that he is the Son." In being the Son from the Father, the Son receives from the Father the divine knowledge or "seeing" and the divine power, which, in light of God's simplicity, are nothing other than the divine essence itself.[63] There is an order of acting that reflects the order of subsisting: the Son proceeds from the Father and acts from the Father, while the Father generates the Son and acts through the Son.

The Son receiving from the Father the divine essence and consequently always acting from the Father likewise accounts for the statements that Jesus judges as he "hears" from the Father and that he seeks the Father's will in John 5:30. John Chrysostom notes that the Son does not "hear" as though needing "instruction" from someone who knows more than he does or has already made a prior decision. Rather, Jesus makes this statement to convey the "concord and identity of the decision." Chrysostom paraphrases Jesus's words: "Thus I judge as if the Father himself was the one judging."[64] Chrysostom fittingly applies the same line of reasoning to Jesus's statement that his judgment is just since he seeks not his own will but that of the Father. Jesus

---

62. Athanasius, *De synodis* 48,4–49,2 (272–73). I take it that various church fathers are correct in arguing that the "seeing" of the Son and the "showing" of the Father in John 5 are not a matter of corporeal perception but of divine knowledge communicated in a way that befits the spiritual nature of the divine persons. Cf. Ambrose, *De fide* 4.4.41, 44 (2:488, 490); 5.62 (2:506), where Ambrose points out that those who would insist on a corporeal seeing by the Son would mistakenly imply a "use of corporeal operation in the Father."

63. Augustine, *In Iohann.* 20.4, 8 (205, 208). According to this exegetical approach, the Father "showing" the Son what he does is a matter of the Father communicating divine knowledge to the Son, and the futurity of the showing in John 5:20b ("And greater works will he show him, so that you may wonder") has to do not with an increase in the essential divine knowledge of the Son but with the future execution and outward manifestation of certain divine works through the Son (e.g., the resurrection from the dead and final judgment in 5:21–22) (so Aquinas, *Super Ioann.* 5.4.754, 760 [142, 143]).

64. John Chrysostom, *In Johann.* 39.4 (225–26).

intends to communicate not that he and the Father must have two distinct wills but that he wills in unity with the Father. According to Chrysostom, Jesus effectively says, "My will is not other than the Father's and proper [ἴδιον] to me, but if he wills anything, I also will this, and if I will anything, he also wills this. Therefore, just as no one ever would object to the Father judging, so neither to me."[65]

The key point here is that the Son's relation to and procession from the Father entails a particular order of being and acting among the persons, which accounts for the distinction between the Son in his knowing, willing, and acting and the Father in his knowing, willing, and acting. The Son always acts from the Father even as he and the Father are effecting the same thing (e.g., the resurrection of the dead). Polanus, for example, elaborates on this matter by distinguishing between a *voluntas essentialis* and *voluntas personalis* in God. The two are "really" one will, but the former is that will considered as common to the divine persons, while the latter is that will considered "singularly" or as modified and enacted in each person's proper mode of being and operating.[66]

(5) In light of the scriptural teaching about the distinctions and the unity of the divine persons, several expressions from catholic Christology and trinitarian doctrine help to clarify and summarize this teaching and help us to bear in mind certain principles or rules that ought to inform our theologizing. A few examples will have to suffice here. Gregory of Nyssa, for instance, highlights well that each divine person's "mode of being"—"how he is" (πῶς ἐστιν)—alone is what distinguishes him from the other two. "How" each one is distinguishes; "what" each one is (τί ἐστιν) unifies. From the unity of nature follows the unity of operation (ἐνέργεια). The operation itself is never "proper" (ἰδιάζουσά) to any one divine person, but the operation issues "from" the Father, proceeds "through" the Son, and is completed "in" the Holy Spirit.[67]

John of Damascus notes that in God there is one deity, one will, one power, and one energy. This is a matter of identity (ταυτότης), not mere similarity (ὁμοιότης).[68] Accordingly, the Father, Son, and Spirit are not distinguished by essence, will, power, or energy. The three have all in common except their relative "hypostatic idioms" or personal properties: unbegottenness (ἀγεννησία),

---

65. John Chrysostom, *In Johann.* 39.4 (226). If space permitted, it would work to offer a similar reading of John 6:37–40 and 10:17–18.

66. Polanus, *Syntagma*, 2.29 (160); 3.6 (219). The adjective "modified" here means not that the persons "change" the divine will but just that each person has the divine will according to his proper mode of being (e.g., the Son has it as the one who subsists from the Father).

67. Gregory of Nyssa, *Ad Ablabium*, 47–48, 55–56.

68. John of Damascus, *Expos. fidei* 1.8 (19, 28).

generation (γέννησις), and (in the Spirit's case) procession (ἐκπορεύσις).[69] From the Latin side of patristic theology, Augustine takes up a similar line of reasoning. Just as there is one divine "substance" (taking *substantia* to be equivalent to "essence"), there is one divine wisdom, goodness, omnipotence, and so forth. These attributes, then, are predicated of God as God. Thus, since God as God is one, they are predicated of God in his unity and they are common to the three divine persons. In Augustine's language, these attributes are predicated of God and of any of the divine persons "with respect to himself" and "substantially" (*ad se* and *substantialiter*). The Father and Son, then, are not distinguished by such attributes; they do not have distinct sets of such attributes. The Father and Son are distinguished only by their relations to one another (*secundum relativum, ad invicem* or *ad aliquid*).[70]

In slightly different terms, what pertains to God as God or to each of the divine persons absolutely is common to the divine persons and one in God; what pertains to a divine person relatively distinguishes the persons and is three in God. While rules of this sort can seem austere, it is worth remembering that they are just glosses and summaries of Scripture's teaching on the divine persons. And rather than keeping us from further exegetical work, they function only to discipline our thinking, accommodating our thinking from the outset to prior biblical learning in order to provide a better starting point for future readings. Just as it is good to remember, for example, who Abraham is whenever one goes back to reading Scripture, so it is good to remember who the Father, Son, and Spirit are and how they are distinct from each other whenever one goes back to reading Scripture.

The first two main sections of this chapter have contended that what fundamentally distinguishes the Son from the Father is the Son's relation of origin, in which the Son eternally proceeds from the Father and receives from the Father the divine essence. The Son has all that the Father has, though the fact that he has from the Father what the Father has distinguishes him from the Father. Among other things, this entails that the Father and Son share one divine intellect and will. At this point it is worth dealing with the question of whether this approach to the distinctions in the Trinity ends up undermining the persons' communion and interaction with one another. The next section will offer a response to that question and will involve, among other things, discussion of what the term "person" means in trinitarian theology and why the persons are sometimes called "modes of subsisting" or "subsisting relations."

---

69. John of Damascus, *Expos. fidei* 1.8 (26–27). The procession of the Spirit will be discussed in chap. 5.

70. Augustine, *De trin.* 5.5–6, 8, 10 (1:210–12, 215–16, 218); 7.2 (1:249–50).

What follows is an excursus working through some of the technical terms to be employed in a moment (e.g., "substance," "subsistence," "person," "essence") and then an employment of those terms in the next section that aims to integrate the numerical unity of essence, intellect, and will in God, on the one hand, and the personal distinctions and personal communion in God, on the other hand.

‖‖‖ **EXCURSUS** ‖‖‖

To elucidate the approach taken here, it will be useful to pause and revisit the meaning of certain terms like "substance," "subsistence," "person," and "essence." The definitions taken up in this section are gathered broadly from various authors in the Christian theological tradition, with the recognition that there are subtle differences in their explanations.[71]

"Substance" classically signifies something that exists or is sustained by itself, in the sense that it does not have to inhere in something else in order to exist (as an accident does). More particularly, "substance" can signify either a distinct, singular, individual thing of a given nature (e.g., a human being) or an individual thing's natural or essential constitution that is common to others of its kind (e.g., human nature). Within that first signification, "substance" can signify in a less restricted way just an individual that exists by itself and singularly or, in a more restricted way, an individual that exists by itself *and* is the subject of a certain individuating property or set of accidents that will be incommunicable to others (i.e., unable to be shared with or made constitutive of another individual). In the strictest use of the language, the former is sometimes called οὐσίωσις or *subsistentia*, whereas the latter is called ὑπόστασις or *prima substantia*.[72] However, *subsistentia* and ὑπόστασις are sometimes used synonymously. If the ὑπόστασις is of a nature with rational intellect and will, it is customarily called a "person."

"Substance" in its secondary sense is equivalent to "essence," which is what something is or the internal constituting principle by which it is what it is and

---

71. See, e.g., Boethius, *Contra Eutychen* 3 (84–93); John of Damascus, *Dial.*, fus. λ´-λα´ (93–95); μ´-μδ´ (106–9); Bonaventure, *In Sent.* 1.23.1.3–2.1 (408–12); Aquinas, *De pot.* 9.1 corp. and ad 4 (266); Aquinas, *ST* Ia.29.2 (330–31); Polanus, *Syntagma*, 3.1–2 (199); Turretin, *Inst.*, 3.23.1–7 (1:280–82); Mastricht, *TPT*, 2.24.6 (237).

72. The latter is also sometimes designated by the Latin *suppositum*, which names an individual thing according to it being the subject of a mental "supposing" or intention (cf. Aquinas, *ST* Ia.29.2 corp. [330]).

which facilitates its actions.[73] Essence is sometimes called "abstract" in that it is mentally prescinded or isolated from nonessential features of the thing or person whose essence it is.[74] But the mental prescinding of it from those nonessential features and from the whole individual has a foundation in the individual itself. Although the essence is not a separate being (ens) in its own right, it is a real principle in a created thing that constitutes or establishes what something is, and it does not automatically contain in itself something's nonessential, individuating features.[75]

Ὑπόστασις is something in which essence is actuated and individuated and thus something by which essence is not just an abstract universal, insofar as, pace Plato, abstract universals do not exist by themselves. As something in which essence is actuated and individuated, subsistentia or ὑπόστασις is something constituted as what it is by that essence.[76] The word subsistentia can also be used to signify the act of subsisting of something that exists by itself, but the verb subsistere especially fulfills that role regarding individual subsistentiae in the strict sense, while the verb substare fulfills that role regarding ὑποστάσεις in the strict sense. Subsistere is used to signify an individual thing's act of subsisting (sometimes called ὕπαρξις), and if subsistere is used in a way that includes the substance "standing under" a property that distinguishes it from others (i.e., in a way that includes substare), then subsistere signifies an individual thing's peculiar mode of subsisting (τρόπος ὑπάρξεως) that distinguishes it from other individuals and constitutes its incommunicability.[77]

73. Though Aristotle's Metaphysics employs the Greek οὐσία in the first and second uses of the term (Metaphysica 4.1017b [99–100]), οὐσία eventually became associated with the second use in particular, which is what one finds in the trinitarian formula "one οὐσία, three ὑποστάσεις" (see, e.g., First Council of Constantinople, "A Letter of the Bishops Gathered in Constantinople," in N. Tanner, Decrees of the Ecumenical Councils, 28).

74. For this meaning of abstraction, see Aquinas, De hebdomadibus 2 (272); Aquinas, ST Ia.85.1 ad 1 (331); Turretin, Inst., 3.5.4 (1:206).

75. In corporeal beings especially the constitutive essential principle (sometimes just called "form" even though the essence includes both form and matter) is distinct from the whole individual. See, e.g., Aquinas, De pot. 9.1 corp. and ad 6 (226–27); Aquinas, ST Ia.29.2 ad 5 (331). Note also Keckermann, Systema logicae, tribus libris adornatum, I, sect. prior, 17 (624), where forma particularly is the potissima pars of a corporeal creature's essence, since it is the active factor (ἐντελέχεια) in essence that shapes and perfects matter. But even in incorporeal beings there is a sense in which the essential constitutive principle is distinct from the whole individual in that the essence itself does not contain in itself its own existence and must receive existence or actuality from an efficient cause (cf. Aquinas, De pot. 7.4 corp. [195]; Aquinas, Quaestiones de quolibet 2.2.2 [4] [215–18]).

76. For Aquinas, the subsisting of a ὑπόστασις is dependent upon its essence: forma est principium subsistendi (ST Ia.29.2 ad 5). This point poses a problem for certain strands of Thomistic "existentialism" that might suggest an independence of esse from essentia.

77. Cf. John of Damascus's distinction between ὕπαρξις (which might be used to signify just a nature in act or a distinct individual in the fullest sense) and ἰδιοσύστατος ὕπαρξις (which

With respect to the doctrine of the Trinity, if God exists without having to inhere in something else in order to exist, then he may be analogically called a "substance" in this sense. More particularly, if God is not an abstract essence or species to be individuated, then God may be analogically called a "substance" in the primary sense noted above (i.e., a distinct substance subsisting in his own right; *this* God). Clarifying how all of this should be stated in the doctrine of the Trinity has led to some diversity (and confusion) in the use of the language. Augustine, for example, hesitates to call the Father, Son, and Spirit three distinct *substantiae*. For, if a "substance" is an individual of a given nature (e.g., a human being), then it would sound as though three divine *substantiae* might be three Gods.[78] Like Augustine, Boethius emphasizes that there is one divine essence and adds that there is thus one divine οὐσίωσις or *subsistentia*, but he also notes that many have still spoken of three divine *substantiae* by connecting the Latin term to the Greek custom of speaking about three ὑποστάσεις.[79] In accord with the connection of *substantia* to ὑπόστασις, Boethius offers his definition of a *persona* as "an individual substance of a rational nature" (*naturae rationabilis individua substantia*).[80]

---

would signify only a distinct individual in the fullest sense) (*Dial.*, fus. μγ' [108]). Subsistence or *subsistere* in the strict sense would be incomplete on its own. But if subsistence or *subsistere* is used as a synonym of *substare*, then it is what perfects or actualizes a nature (cf. the discussion in Polanus, *Syntagma*, 6.16 [375]; Turretin, *Inst.*, 3.23.5 [1:280–81]; cf. also Mastricht, *TPT*, 5.4.6 [538]). Aquinas notes that *subsistere* and *substare* are distinct only in reason or with respect to their conceptual content, for the subsisting of anything in reality will always include a proper mode of subsisting (*De pot.* 9.1 ad 4 [226]). Yet it seems to me that in the doctrine of the Trinity at least the ὕπαρξις–τρόπος ὑπάρξεως or *subsistere-substare* distinction does have a role to play. On the one hand, the divine essence is never without the mode of subsisting or personal property of any given divine person. On the other hand, the essence as such is not a species to be participated in by multiple would-be deities, so the essence taken absolutely does subsist per se (an act normally expressed with *subsistere*). But this occurs without the essence taken absolutely being a fourth ὑπόστασις in its own right or being characterized by its own incommunicable mode of subsisting (i.e., an act normally expressed with *substare*). In this case, then, the distinction between the ὕπαρξις or *subsistere* of the essence taken absolutely and the τρόπος ὑπάρξεως or *substare* of a given divine person is not purely in the human mind. The distinction here may be fittingly called a "modal" distinction (see below in section IV).

78. Augustine, *De trin.* 7.6.9–11 (1:259–65). Augustine observes that even if one explains that *substantia* does not signify *essentia* but rather "something singular and individual," like *this* man (*hic homo velut Abraham, velut Isaac, velut Iacob*), it still sounds like the three divine *substantiae* will have three essences (7.6.11 [1:263]).

79. Boethius, *Contra Eutychen* 3 (90).

80. Boethius, *Contra Eutychen* 3 (84). Based on a rejection of the language of three divine *substantiae*, Richard of St. Victor in the twelfth century rejected the use of Boethius's definition of *persona* in the doctrine of the Trinity. For Richard, there are not three divine substances, so the divine persons should not be called "individual substances" (*De trinitate* 4.21 [278–80]). According to Richard, then, it is preferable to give a definition of *persona* that is particularly applicable to God: *divinae naturae incommunicabilis exsistentia* (4.22 [280–82]).

According to Bonaventure's reading, Augustine associated *substantia* with the Greek οὐσίωσις (that which subsists in its own right, but without respect to any distinguishing property), which explains Augustine's concern that three divine *substantiae* would imply three Gods. According to Bonaventure, Boethius associated *substantia* with the Greek ὑπόστασις (which has reference to a distinguishing property), which explains Boethius's willingness to speak of three divine *substantiae*. Either way, Bonaventure seems to think that οὐσίωσις has to be linked with that which is common to the three divine persons and that ὑπόστασις should be linked with that which distinguishes the persons. For Bonaventure, one can associate *substantia* with οὐσίωσις and *subsistentia* with ὑπόστασις, leaving *substantia* to be one in God and *subsistentia* to be three in God (so Augustine). Alternatively, one can associate *subsistentia* with οὐσίωσις and *substantia* with ὑπόστασις, leaving *subsistentia* to be one in God and *substantia* to be three in God (so Boethius).[81] Aquinas's approach is somewhat different. He recognizes that *substantia* can be used equivocally to signify either essence or ὑπόστασις, and he of course maintains that there is one divine essence common to the divine persons. Aquinas recognizes the Latin custom of using *substantia* to signify essence (with the attendant use of *subsistentia* to signify a distinct individual), but he also affirms that *substantia* is aptly used to render the Greek ὑπόστασις. Aquinas also tends to connect both οὐσίωσις and *subsistentia* with ὑπόστασις. For Aquinas, it seems that οὐσίωσις pertains to essence only in that distinct, individual substances always do their subsisting in their various constitutive essences.[82]

The approaches of Augustine and, to some extent, Boethius and Bonaventure arguably allow for an analogical application of the primary signification of "substance" (a distinct individual of a given nature) to God taken absolutely or with regard to what is common to the three divine persons. However, Boethius's and Bonaventure's approaches also seem to allow an application of this signification to God taken relatively or with regard to what distinguishes the three divine persons. The approach of Aquinas seems to discourage application of the primary signification of "substance" to God taken absolutely. It encourages the application of this signification just to the three distinct persons. A number of the Reformed orthodox may prove helpful

---

81. Bonaventure, *In Sent.* 1.23.2.1 (412).

82. Aquinas, *ST* Ia.29.2 corp. and ad 4 (330). In the response to the fourth objection here, Aquinas both criticizes the Platonic doctrine of subsisting universals and also offers an explanation of why Boethius connects οὐσίωσις to essence. Aquinas also reasons that one can liken οὐσίωσις to form not because οὐσίωσις signifies essence but because form is that by which something exists by itself and is an οὐσίωσις, whereas matter (at least in composite substances) is that by which something has individuating accidents and is an individual ὑπόστασις (*ST* Ia.29.4 ad 5 [331]).

here in pointing out that since God as God is distinct (*this* God) and not a species, then God taken absolutely or with respect to what is common to the three persons can be said to subsist in a broad sense. However, this does not mean that God taken absolutely is a primary substance in the fullest sense. For ὑπόστασις or *prima substantia* signifies not just a distinct being that does not have to inhere in another but a distinct individual that does not have to inhere in another *and* is the subject of a property or mode of subsisting that distinguishes it from others and constitutes its incommunicability.[83] God as God subsists *per se*, but not incommunicably; God as Father, as Son, as Spirit subsists both *per se* and incommunicably. Therefore, *subsistentia* in a broader sense applies to God as one with respect to his subsisting *per se*; ὑπόστασις or *prima substantia* in a stricter sense applies to God as three with respect to his subsisting both *per se* and incommunicably.[84]

||||||||||||||||||||||||||||||||||||||||||||||||||||||||||||||||||||||||||||||||||||||||||||||||||||||||||||||||||||||||||||||||||||||||||||||||||||||||||||||

IV. Essence, Persons, and Relations

After examining scriptural teaching on the Son's relation to the Father and on God's unity of essence, intellect, and will, I will now aim to make use of some technical language to set out the coherence of these two elements of Christian doctrine. In order to do this, I will focus on describing (1) the relationship between essence and person in God; (2) the significance of the terms "person," "mode," "relation," and "property" in trinitarian doctrine; (3) the way in which the divine persons' distinct modes of subsisting are determined by their relations to one another; (4) the way in which the divine persons are identical to the same essence and still distinct from one another; and (5) the meaning of the personal communion of the divine persons.

(1) If each of the divine persons is really identical to the one God, then the divine essence with the essential divine intellect, will, and power common to the persons does not subsist behind or outside of the Father, Son, and Spirit. Polanus, for example, rightly observes that "the essence is not anterior or

83. I am attempting to use the word "individual" with some caution here. If the term is taken to imply that the divine essence has to be divided up among the persons or that a person has his own actualization of deity or can be separated from the other two persons, then it is a problematic designation. However, if the term is taken to signify only that each person is distinct and incommunicable, then it can be a useful designation.

84. See Polanus, *Syntagma*, 2.5 (136); Maccovius, *Metaphysica*, 2.1 (179, 181–83); Maccovius, *Loci communes* 29 (238–39). Turretin remarks that the divine essence itself exists singularly, but, because it does not have incommunicability, it cannot be termed a "person" (*Inst.*, 3.25.24 [1:299]). Cf. also Mastricht, *TPT*, 2.24.19 (241).

exterior to the three persons but is the same and individual and whole in the singular persons."[85] If the essence were ontologically prior or external to the three, that would entail a divine "quaternity," with a would-be fourth subsistence that alone would directly possess intellect and will. That would create a scenario in which concerns about a depersonalization of the persons would carry real weight. However, in the coordination of essence and person undertaken here in concert with the doctrine of divine simplicity, that is not the case. Rather, the divine essence with the essential intellect, will, and power of God subsists only in and as the Father, Son, and Spirit. As Turretin puts it, the essence does in a certain sense subsist "more widely" (latius) than any one of the persons, for it subsists not just in one but in all three. Yet, Turretin adds, the divine essence considered with respect to all three persons does not extend beyond them but rather is identified with them. While each person does not have the essence "wholly" or "adequately"—as though his was the only way in which the essence could subsist—each one still has the "whole" essence.[86] This is expressed in a number of Reformed orthodox definitions of a divine person. A divine person is, for example, "the essence modified, that is, the essence contracted to a certain and peculiar mode of subsisting";[87] "the Godhead restrained with his [one person's] personal property";[88] "nothing but the divine essence . . . subsisting in an especial manner."[89]

The concept of "person" will be discussed more in a moment, but here it is the real identity of essence and person that must be underscored. Given this real identity, to say that intellect and will are essential and common in God rather than idiomatic or proper to each person is not at all to diminish the personhood of the persons. Each person truly has the divine understanding and will. He does not have a really distinct understanding and will, but he has the one understanding and will in his own distinct manner.[90] In fact, given the real identity of essence and person in God, each person, strictly speaking, does not "possess" (much less have to acquire) God's essential knowing, willing, and loving but rather is that knowing, willing, and loving in his proper manner of being. Traditional habits of calling the persons "modes" or "relations"

---

85. Polanus, Syntagma, 3.2 (199).

86. Turretin, Inst., 3.15.24 (1:299). Cf. Mastricht, TPT, 2.24.8 (238); 5.4.5, 9 (537, 539).

87. Alsted, Methodus s.s. theologiae, 3.2 (203).

88. Leigh, A Treatise of Divinity, 2.16 (128).

89. Owen, Doctrine of the Trinity, 407. Cf. also Mastricht, TPT, 2.24.8 (238); 5.4.9 (539), where he writes that the essence is "restricted" by a person's mode of subsisting.

90. Owen, for example, comments that each divine person has the understanding and will "not as that person" (i.e., as though the understanding or will as such were peculiar to him) but "as the person is God" (i.e., as one who has the divine essence) (Brief Declaration and Vindication, 407).

will be discussed below, but already the real identity of essence and person in God should clear away some misunderstandings of this language of "modes" and "relations." For the Father, Son, and Spirit are not mere abstract modes but rather modes *of something*—namely, God's rich and active essence with his essential wisdom, will, and power. Or, as Aquinas articulates it, a divine person is not a mere relation but instead a *subsisting* relation with the fullness of God's essence.[91] In other words, a divine person is not merely that which distinguishes him from the other two persons (i.e., a certain mode of being or relation); rather, each person is all that the biblical God is, subsisting in a certain manner.

(2) The term "person" in trinitarian doctrine can be taken in a concrete sense as well as an abstract sense.[92] Exploring this concrete-abstract distinction here will help to show, on the one hand, that the persons are not *mere* modes or relations and, on the other hand, that they are still suitably called "modes" or "relations" in a very particular sense. The concrete use of the term "person" is one that signifies both the essence and the person's peculiar mode of subsisting, while the abstract use isolates and signifies chiefly the person's peculiar mode of subsisting. The former way is exemplified by Boethius's definition of "person," which incorporates the term *substantia* as an equivalent of ὑπόστασις: "an individual substance of a rational nature" (*naturae rationabilis individua substantia*).[93] The concrete designation of each divine person as a ὑπόστασις of the divine essence is fitting since each one subsists distinctly and has the fullness of the essence. While each person is not a discrete actualization of the divine essence (as though there might be three Gods), each one nevertheless has the one essence in himself and thus knows, wills, and acts.

The abstract use of "person" (i.e., the one that chiefly signifies what distinguishes one person from another) does not posit an extramental separation of person from essence but involves only a mental prescinding of that which distinguishes—namely, the persons' modes of subsisting. A brief look at the historical usage of this modal language can help us to understand its purpose in trinitarian doctrine and allay certain reservations about it. The Reformed orthodox frequently credit Justin Martyr and John of Damascus with the designation of the persons as τρόποι ὑπάρξεως.[94] However, the

---

91. Aquinas, *ST* Ia.29.4 corp. (333).

92. For the distinction, see, e.g., Maccovius, *Loci communes* 29 (236); Turretin, *Inst.*, 3.23.8 (1:282).

93. Boethius, *Contra Eutychen* 3 (84).

94. E.g., Keckermann, *Systema s.s. theologiae*, 1.2 (71–72) (incorrect pagination in original); 1.4 (84–86); Alsted, *Metaphysica*, 1.29 (240); Turretin, *Inst.*, 3.23.8 (1:282).

Expositio rectae fidei, formerly attributed to Justin, is now taken to be a later work of Theodoret of Cyrus.[95] According to this *Expositio*, the Father is unbegotten (ἀγέννητος), the Son is begotten (γεγέννηται), and the Spirit proceeds (προῆλθεν). This leads to a discussion of how "that which begets differs from that which is begotten and that which proceeds from that from which it proceeds." "Unbegotten," "begotten," and "proceeding" are not "names of essence [οὐσίας]" but names that "characterize" distinct "modes of subsisting" (τρόποι ὑπάρξεως). Thus, in the case of the Father, Son, and Spirit, there is "something the same according to the reason of essence [τὸ ταὐτὸν . . . κατὰ τὸν τῆς οὐσίας λόγον]" and a "difference . . . according to the mode of subsisting [κατὰ τὸν τῆς ὑπάρξεως τρόπον]." The modal nature of the personal distinctions is expressed adverbially, though it sounds awkward in contemporary English: the Father has being (τὸ εἶναι) "unbegottenly" (ἀγεννήτως); the Son has being "begottenly" (γεννητῶς); the Spirit has being "processionally" (ἐκπορευτῶς).[96]

In his philosophical work, John of Damascus considers that which distinguishes one ὑπόστασις from another, where the term ὑπόστασις signifies not essence (οὐσία) but the proper act of subsisting of an individual (τὴν καθ' αὐτὸ καὶ ἰδιοσύστατον ὕπαρξιν).[97] An individual ὑπόστασις has both essence and accidents and must subsist "according to itself" and "in act." The ὑπόστασις is individuated by its accidental, "characteristic properties" (τὰ χαρακτηριστικὰ ἰδιώματα) and its distinct act of subsisting (ὕπαρξις).[98] John reiterates later that when the term ὑπόστασις applies to that which subsists by itself, it signifies an act of subsisting. He adds that in the holy Trinity a ὑπόστασις is the "mode of eternal subsisting of each."[99] In his exposition of Christian doctrine, John emphasizes that the Father, Son, and Spirit have all in common, except that the Father is without principle and unbegotten, the Son is begotten, and the Spirit proceeds. But the begetting, being begotten, and proceeding are not expressions of essence but of "relation toward one another and of the mode of subsisting [τῆς πρὸς ἄλληλα σχέσεως καὶ τοῦ τῆς ὑπάρξεως τρόπου]."[100] Speaking more generally of what unifies and

---

95. See Clayton, *Theodoret of Cyrus*, 89–103. Theodoret's Christology was, of course, heavily criticized and ultimately condemned at the Second Council of Constantinople (see the council's "Sentence against the 'Three Chapters,'" in N. Tanner, *Decrees of the Ecumenical Councils*, 107–13).

96. *Expositio rectae fidei* 3 (6, 8).

97. John of Damascus, *Dial.*, fus. μγ' (108).

98. John of Damascus, *Dial.*, fus. λα' (95); cf. μδ' (109); μθ' (114).

99. John of Damascus, *Dial.*, fus. ξζ' (140). The Greek reads: ὑπόστασίς ἐστιν ὁ ἄναρχος τρόπος τῆς ἐκάστου ἀϊδίου ὑπάρξεως.

100. John of Damascus, *Expos. fidei* 1.10 (32).

individuates persons, Aquinas states that the phrase "some man" (*aliquis homo*) "signifies nature, or the individual on the part of the nature, with a mode of existing which belongs to singulars."[101]

These patterns of speaking stand behind Reformed orthodox use of modal language in the doctrine of the Trinity. Girolamo Zanchi, for example, writes that "the essence is the same in each, but there are diverse modes with which it subsists in each. By these diverse modes of subsisting the diverse persons are constituted." Zanchi comments further, "When you say 'essence,' you signify substance without a certain mode of subsisting; but when you say 'subsistence,' you contract essence to a certain mode of subsisting."[102] In keeping with this line of thought, Turretin states that the subsisting of a ὑπόστασις "superadds some mode of existence of a singular substance, which is called an entitative mode, ultimately terminating and completing the substantial nature and also giving incommunicability to it."[103]

When such comments are taken into account, an abstract definition of "person" that employs modal language in the doctrine of the Trinity may be less puzzling. In the Christian philosophical and theological tradition, what individuates a distinct ὑπόστασις has customarily been identified as an individual's "mode of subsisting." Accordingly, the phrase "mode of subsisting" is just shorthand for that which distinguishes one ὑπόστασις from another in a given essence. Taking up an abstract definition of "person" in trinitarian theology and calling the Father, Son, and Spirit "modes of subsisting" serves the purpose of expressing that each one is distinct from the others by the peculiar manner in which he has the divine essence. This expression focuses precisely on what distinguishes the persons and underscores that the persons are indeed distinct within the divine essence, not merely in outward appearance. That is the most robust sense in which the persons could be distinct without compromising the truth that there is only one God. Thus, the use of the abstract definition of "person" with the accompanying modal language is not a pathway but in fact an antidote to the error of Sabellianism, according to which the persons were supposed to be three *ad extra*, serial iterations of one immanent mode of being.

(3) Once it is stated that what distinguishes the persons is their diverse modes of subsisting, it is important to specify that in the case of the divine persons those diverse modes are determined by (or just *are*) the persons' relations to one another. This explains why an abstract use of the term "person" in

101. Aquinas, *ST* Ia.30.4 corp. (341).
102. Zanchi, *De tribus Elohim*, 4.6.9 (699, 701).
103. Turretin, *Inst.*, 3.23.5 (1:280–81). See also 3.23.8 (1:282).

trinitarian doctrine involves calling the persons not only "modes of subsisting" but also "subsisting relations," a point articulated well by Aquinas. Taking the principles of individuation in the Trinity to be the relations of origin, Aquinas calls the persons "relations" in an article of the *Summa theologiae* that is sometimes misunderstood. Aquinas observes, "Person in any nature signifies that which is distinct in that nature, as in human nature it signifies *this flesh* and *these bones* and *this soul*, which are principles individuating a human being." Since the divine persons' individuating principles are the relations of origin, the persons can be called "relations of origin." This has nothing to do with claiming that the persons are *mere* relations without the divine knowing, willing, loving, and acting. In this very question Aquinas makes clear that the Father, Son, and Spirit are concrete *hypostaseis* of the divine nature. Aquinas is not reducing a divine person to a pure relation but simply taking the term "person" to bring to the fore that which individuates— namely, a relation of origin.[104]

This explanation of the signification of the phrases "mode of subsisting" and "relation of origin" also helps to reinforce that the distinctions among the divine persons cohere with God's simplicity. For the diverse modes of subsisting in God's case are unlike those found in creatures. In creatures, one ὑπόστασις is distinct from another by its matter, by its actualization of essence, and by its various accidents, all of which, it might be said, are factors in an individual creature's proper mode of subsisting. An individual, composite creature, then, is not identical with its essence or with what individuates it (i.e., its mode of subsisting). In God's case, however, if one ὑπόστασις is distinct from the others by a relation of origin alone, then what distinguishes the person does not introduce a plurality of "things" or parts in God. For a relation is not a "thing" in its own right. It is a way in which one tends toward another or comports oneself toward another.[105] Each person's mode

104. Aquinas, *ST* Ia.29.4 (333–34). Cf. also Aquinas, *De pot.* 9.3 corp. (230), where Aquinas straightforwardly calls a person—even a person in God—"a certain [intellectual] nature with a mode of subsisting." See also Emery, *The Trinitarian Theology of St Thomas Aquinas*, 117–18, 121. Aquinas reasons that *persona* may be said to signify the relation directly and the divine essence indirectly. Alternatively, *persona* can be said to signify not the relation as such but as a *hypostasis*. In that case, since *hypostasis* is identical to essence in God, *persona* may signify the essence directly, though even in that case it will still include the notion of relation (Aquinas, *ST* Ia.29.4 corp. and ad 1 and 3 [333–34]). At any rate, describing the designation of "subsisting relations" in trinitarian theology as an "unintelligible formula" (Hasker, "The One Divine Nature," 74–75) reveals less about Aquinas's thinking and more about the contemporary reader's unfamiliarity or impatience with earlier texts in Christian theology.

105. On relations not introducing multiple "absolute" entities—not composing but only modifying—see Aquinas, *ST* Ia.40.2 ad 1 and 2 (413–14); Keckermann, *Systema s.s. theologiae*, 1.4 (84–86); Turretin, *Inst.*, 3.27.18 (1:309).

of having the divine essence is determined by a relation of origin, and the relation of origin is the way in which one person is ordered toward another.[106] Thus, unlike created ὑποστάσεις, the Father, Son, and Spirit are really identical with their proper modes of subsisting and not composed of essence plus an extra "thing."[107]

If that is so, then talk of the persons' distinct "properties" also coheres with God's simplicity. In order to express more readily that by which the persons are distinguished from one another, each person's mode of subsisting may be represented abstractly as a "property." The Father's proper mode of subsisting (i.e., eternally begetting the Son and communicating the divine essence to him) may be represented as "paternity"; the Son's proper mode of subsisting (i.e., eternally proceeding from the Father and receiving from the Father the divine essence) may be represented as "filiation"; the Spirit's proper mode of subsisting (i.e., eternally proceeding from both the Father and Son and receiving from both the Father and Son the divine essence) may be represented as "spiration."[108] Given that what each property signifies is not an accidental thing added to the divine essence but just a relation of origin within the essence, the persons' properties do not introduce composition in God.[109] Given that in some contemporary philosophical or theological circles the term "property" is used quite differently, this note about traditional usage

106. In light of this, the term "mode" might be applied in two senses in trinitarian doctrine. Each person has or is his own *mode* of subsisting in the divine essence. But the mode of subsisting is determined by a relation of origin, and a relation is not a thing itself but a *mode* or way in which one comports oneself toward another.

107. Cf. Polanus: "The divine essence is not composed from the persons but merely distinguished in the persons. Nor is any divine person composed from essence and a proper mode of subsisting, because the mode of subsisting does not compose but merely distinguishes. Similarly, relation in divine things . . . distinguishes one correlate from another but does not compose" (*Syntagma*, 2.9 [144]).

108. Cf. Aquinas, *ST* Ia.32.2 corp. (351–52). Aquinas writes that in trinitarian doctrine "essence" addresses the question of *quid* ("what"), "person" the question of *quis* ("who"), and "property" the question of *quo* ("by which"). There is a certain sense in which the Father's paternity, for example, can be called his individual "form" (*ST* Ia.40.1 corp. and ad 3 [411–12]), but "form" in that case means not "essence" but an abstract representation of the Father's distinct personal character.

109. Since the relations are active relations of origin, the persons' properties are sometimes called "notional acts," "notion" here signifying an abstract representation of the distinct character of a given person (on which, see, e.g., Aquinas, *ST* Ia.32.2–4 [351–52, 355, 357]; 40.4, [418]; Turretin, *Inst.*, 3.23.14–15 [1:284]). The five notions identified in the doctrine of the Trinity are the innascibility and the paternity of the Father, the filiation of the Son, the active spiration (the origination of the Spirit) of the Father and Son, and the passive spiration or procession of the Spirit. Four of these are also properties that belong to just one person (innascibility, paternity, filiation, procession). Four are relations (paternity, filiation, active spiration, procession). Three are personally constitutive properties (paternity, filiation, procession). The "notional acts," then, are the originating actions signified here (generation, being generated,

is important to bear in mind in order to avoid confusion in the doctrine of the Trinity today.[110]

(4) While the divine persons are really identical with the same essence, they are still truly distinct from one another in reality, not merely in our apprehension. The real identity of person and essence in God is compatible with the presence of other kinds of distinctions in God. If each person's mode of having the divine essence is what distinguishes him from the other two persons and, therefore, from the essence itself taken absolutely, each is rightly said to be "modally" distinct from the other two and from the essence as such.[111] And because the persons are distinct in God's own essence, some of the Reformed orthodox point out that this modal distinction is a *real* modal distinction, not in the sense that it might be between one "thing" and another but in the sense that it is a distinction in reality and not just in our minds.[112] There is a real identity of person and essence with respect to what exists or what is absolute (i.e., the divine essence as such).[113] But each person is constituted not only by the essence but also by his relative opposition or comportment toward another person.[114] That relative opposition or comportment, though not an absolute "thing" in its own right, is still distinct in reality from the divine essence as such. Thus, the modal distinction determined by the relative opposition is still a distinction in reality, which means that the distinctions

spiration, procession). A relation, personal property, and notional act signify the same reality but in different ways (so Aquinas, *De pot.* 2.5 ad 8 [36]; Aquinas, *ST* Ia.41.1 ad 2 [421–22]).

110. It seems to me that in some cases the term "property" is diluted and used to signify any predicate applied to a subject. Strangely, the term is then also sometimes reified so that whatever it denotes is taken to be a thing that introduces complexity in its subject. For this phenomenon, see, e.g., Moreland and Craig, *Philosophical Foundations for a Christian Worldview*, 524–25; Yandell, "How Many Times Does Three Go into One?," 162–63, 166–68 and passim.

111. E.g., Keckermann, *Systema s.s. theologiae*, 1.4 (84); Ames, *Medulla theologica*, 1.5.5 (16); Maccovius, *Loci communes* 29 (238); Turretin, *Inst.*, 3.27.3, 10–11 (1:306–8). This point circumvents the idea that if one person is identical to the essence, then he must be identical with the other persons (see, e.g., Hasker, "One Divine Nature," 63–64).

112. See Keckermann, *Systema s.s. theologiae*, 1.4 (85–86); Alsted, *Metaphysica*, 1.29 (240). Cf. Turretin, *Inst.*, 3.27.10–11 (1:307–8), who calls the modal distinction a *distinctio realis minor*, not "between things and things" but "between a thing and a mode of the thing, or among the modes themselves." See also Mastricht, *TPT*, 2.24.9 (238), who maintains the "real modal" distinction among the persons but also says that the "essence and the persons" (perhaps the plural "persons" is significant) are distinct in "reasoned reason" (*in ratione ratiocinata*, in reason with a basis in reality) (2.24.19 [241]).

113. On there being just one absolute being here, cf. Aquinas, *ST* Ia.28.3 corp. (324); Turretin, *Inst.*, 3.27.18 (1:309). In this respect, there is one absolute *fundamentum* of the relations among the persons (so Zanchi, *De natura Dei*, 2.2 [89]; Keckermann, *Systema s.s. theologiae*, 1.3 [72] [incorrect pagination in original]).

114. The term "opposition" here signifies not a "conflict" but rather a person's standing opposite to another person to whom he is connected by origination. Cf. Polanus's distinction between relative opposition and "repugnance" in *Logicae libri duo* 1 (32–34).

among the divine persons are distinctions in reality.[115] There are therefore three distinct persons living in relation to one another in God's being.[116]

Perhaps a question will emerge at this point about an apparent logical tension: Can it be the case that there are three modes of subsisting in God whose distinction and plurality is constituted by their real relations of origin when in fact real relations seem to presuppose distinction and plurality?[117] This question might be connected to an older question about whether the Father is the distinct person that he is prior to his relation to the Son. Bonaventure intriguingly argues that the Father prior to his relation to the Son is already a distinct person by his unbegottenness and by a certain "fontal plenitude" that he has. There is the Father as a distinct person, then the Father's act of generating the Son, and then the relation of the Father to the Son.[118] Bonaventure's approach could be used to make an argument that, at

115. As a certain comportment or ordering toward another, a relation always exists in something. It has *esse* (or *inesse*). But in God's case, what has *esse* is just God's essence, so, Aquinas reasons, a relation or personal property with respect to its *esse* is just the divine essence. But a relation between two terms in the same order of being also involves a real opposition or comportment toward another, and that opposition is distinct from the essence. In this way, Aquinas is able to articulate that even if there is not a real distinction in God with regard to what is absolute (essence, *esse*) there are still (*pace* Sabellianism) real distinctions among the persons in God with respect to what is relative (see *ST* Ia.28.1–3 [318–19, 321–22, 324]; 39.1 [396–97]; 40.2 ad 2 [414]). At certain points, Aquinas describes the distinction between one person's relative opposition to another and the divine essence as a distinction *in ratione*, though he does uphold that the distinction between one person and another is a "real" distinction according to what is relative (*ST* Ia.28.2 corp. [321]; 28.3 ad 1 [324]; 39.1 corp. [396]; 40.1 ad 1 [411]). Due to the potential ambiguity in labeling something a distinction *in ratione*, I appreciate where the Reformed orthodox go beyond stating that relation and essence are distinct *in ratione*. They do this by expressing that the distinguishing factor in one person is really modally distinct from the distinguishing factor in each of the other persons.

116. The account of the divine persons' relations and distinctions that is offered here is not to be conflated with recent proposals about the idea of "relative identity" (see van Inwagen, "And Yet They Are Not Three Gods but One God"; see also the critique in Rea, "Relative Identity and the Trinity"). Proponents of "relative identity" suggest, roughly, that things that are regarded as identical may be identical with respect to one sort of thing and distinct with respect to another sort of thing. There have been debates about whether the idea of relative identity actually holds up in the illustrations often given to explain it and about whether the idea is sufficiently grounded in reality to secure the truthfulness of distinctions made in human predication. Whatever the future of the idea of relative identity in philosophy, the subject matter of Christian theology proper is unique. Faithful exposition of it does not rest on the feasibility of the idea of relative identity in creaturely scenarios. And the real modal distinctions among the divine persons provide an ontological basis upon which the theologian can avoid logical contradiction in speaking about what is common and proper to the persons.

117. Cf. Craig, "Is God the Son Begotten?," 31.

118. Bonaventure, *In Sent.* 1.27, art. un., q. 2 (468–70). The question in Bonaventure's commentary on the *Sentences* is *Utrum generatio sit ratio paternitatis, an e converso* ("Whether generation is the rationale of paternity, or the reverse"), and Bonaventure answers that the act of generation is indeed the *ratio* or way toward the relation of paternity. Aquinas takes a

least in the Father's case, a prior distinction can be assumed in the relation of one person to another. However, insofar as this account means that the Father would be the distinct person that he is even without reference to the Son, there is a problem here. For if that were so, then the Father would be the distinct person that he is by virtue of something absolute in God rather than relative. And if he were the distinct person that he is by something absolute, then his personal property would characterize the divine essence as such. If the Father then communicated the divine essence to the Son and Spirit, the essence communicated to the Son and Spirit would be either characterized by his personal property in them (confusing the persons) or a secondary iteration of the essence (undermining the persons' equality).[119] It is more prudent, then, to stress that the Father (indeed, any divine person) is distinct not prior to but only *in* a relation to another. In addition, the line of reasoning set out here does not conclude that real relations are present without distinction and plurality. That claim would involve logical contradiction. Instead, the claim is only that, while real relations may ordinarily involve antecedent distinction and plurality, in this case they involve an eternally concomitant distinction and plurality in God's eternal being.

(5) In light of the previous points, the persons of the Trinity can be said genuinely to live in communion with one another, even if that divine communion is in some ways unlike that of creatures. The persons do not possess their own distinct sets of personal faculties, but they neither lack understanding and will nor possess these derivatively by a participation in something more ultimate than themselves. The Father, Son, and Spirit really are the divine

different approach. He does not posit an ontological priority or posteriority between a relation of origin and an act of origin in God. Relation and act of origin signify the same reality in God. But Aquinas does recognize a conceptual order, pointing out that relation might have conceptual priority in one way and action might have conceptual priority in another way. If relation were taken to signify an accident added to a person already distinct by an act of origin, then action would have conceptual priority and relation would follow and "manifest" the person distinguished by an act of origin. However, if, as Aquinas argues, relation in God is taken to signify what intrinsically distinguishes one person from another, then, since an act of origin signifies not what is intrinsic to a person who acts but a way to or from a person, relation has conceptual priority and action follows (see *ST* Ia.40.1–2 [411–14]). For Aquinas, one can still acknowledge the legitimacy of taking the relations to "manifest" the persons when one focuses on the concept of relation under the aspect of opposition or comportment toward another rather than something subsisting (*ST* 40.2 ad 4 [414]; 40.4 corp. [418]). As Turretin puts it, if relation is viewed "in its own external and respective *esse*," it is "declarative" (rather than constitutive) of a distinct person in an a posteriori manner (*Inst.*, 3.27.19 [1:309–10]).

119. To be sure, the Father is the first person of the Trinity and has priority in the sense that he communicates deity to both the Son and the Spirit. He is called "first" not because he is who he is apart from the Son but because he is the only divine person who gives without ever receiving from another person the divine essence.

essence with God's essential knowing, willing, and loving. Indeed, the three persons, not an abstract essence behind them, perform all of God's actions. According to the older authors drawn upon here, concrete ὑποστάσεις (not essences) perform actions. This is why ὑπόστασις or person is often called the *principium quod* of action (the "principle which" acts), while essence is called the *principium quo* of action (the "principle by which" the ὑπόστασις acts). That understanding of personal agency is expressed in the axiom *actus sunt suppositorum*.[120]

Furthermore, the persons modify the divine understanding and volition in distinct ways. Though the persons do not have three discrete actualizations of the divine understanding and volition, by the persons' diverse modifications of the common act of understanding and volition there is the plurality in God that is ingredient in mutual knowledge and love.[121] There is a relative plurality in which the Father eternally beholds his perfect goodness in its distinct modification and expression in the beloved Son. While the Bible does not supply a lengthy treatment of the eternal, mutual love of the divine persons, the Father's delight in the Son who is his perfect image gives us a glimpse of that love. Christ's prayer in John 17 is especially significant here: "Father, that which you have given me, I will that where I am those also may be with me, in order that they may see my glory, which you have given me because you loved me before the foundation of the world" (17:24). Such eternal fellowship and love is the backdrop to the economy of salvation, in which we are united to the Trinity as adopted sons and daughters in the consubstantial Son.[122]

This section has attempted to coordinate the real relations among the Father, Son, and Spirit with the unity and simplicity of God. I have argued that, according to Scripture itself, what distinguishes the Son from the Father is his

---

120. E.g., Aquinas, *ST* Ia.39.5 ad 1 (405); Maccovius, *Loci communes* 30 (242); Turretin, *Inst.*, 14.2.2–3 (2:411–12). Of course, the application of this axiom to the doctrine of the Trinity is not without its challenges. The point of the axiom is that actions are performed by substances that exist *per se*, not by abstract, common essences. God taken absolutely exists *per se* and may be called the *principium quod* of divine action. And yet within that *principium quod* there are three distinct *supposita*, each of whom is always active in producing God's works. In God's case, then, the axiom *actus sunt suppositorum* applies in a unique manner: efficient causality belongs to God absolutely, but proper modes of acting within the efficient causality belong to God relatively (or to the distinct persons of Father, Son, and Spirit).

121. The account offered here is different from that of Karl Rahner, for example (see *The Trinity*, 106), who hesitates to affirm that the persons love one another *ad intra*.

122. For a comparable line of thought that seeks to avoid both the idea of multiple wills in God and the temptation to overreact to "personalist" or "social" accounts of the Trinity, see Anatolios, *Retrieving Nicaea*, 219–20; Anatolios, "Personhood, Communion, and the Trinity in Some Patristic Texts." Note also McCall's argument that theologians who have various disagreements about the doctrine of the Trinity all should be able to affirm the intratrinitarian love of the persons (*Analytic Christology*, chap. 5).

relation of origin. I have also argued that there is still a distinction among the persons in their knowing, willing, and loving, a diversity that corroborates the presence of eternal fellowship and love in the Trinity. In the final main section of this chapter, I will try to address two challenges that might still be brought up against this account of the Son's relation to the Father.

V. Two Challenges

If the Son is distinct from the Father only by his eternal generation, there may be at least two challenges that need addressing. First, if the three divine persons share one power and energy, does the Father alone still perform the act of eternally generating the Son? Put differently, if the Son shares the power and energy by which the Father generates him, must he in some sense be involved in constituting himself a distinct person in God? These questions link up with medieval discussion about the "power of generating" in God.[123] Given the preceding account of the essential intellect, will, and power of God, it may seem that one must either (1) multiply the divine power and compromise the claim that the persons are distinct by relations alone or (2) concede that the Son would somehow constitutively act upon himself and render himself a distinct divine person.[124] A second potential challenge concerns the Son receiving from the Father the divine essence. If the Son receives the essence, does that not imply that the essence is somehow multiplied in the persons and, therefore, that even a more traditional trinitarianism will undermine divine simplicity? This objection would suggest that one must either give up on divine simplicity or compromise the personal distinctions described above. In this section, I will address each of these potential challenges in turn.

A. Essential Unity and the Potentia Generandi

In the *Sentences*, Peter Lombard includes a relevant discussion of the "power of generating" (*potentia gignendi* or *potentia generandi*) whereby the Father

---

123. One might suggest bypassing the older discussion of a "power of generating" and simply affirm the act of the Father generating the Son. However, while there is no power in God really distinct from his essence or immanent acts, there is still a common actuality and energy shared by the three persons, which leaves the question of whether the act of generating belongs to the Father alone. Furthermore, insofar as acts are wrought by power, discussion of the notional acts in the Trinity still has a natural connection to the medieval discussion of the "power of generating" (cf. Aquinas, *De pot.* 2.1 corp. [26]).

124. Even if the Son constituting himself a distinct person were not a logical conundrum, there would still be the problem of the Son (if he constituted himself as Son) taking up a relation that the Father alone has toward the Son.

generates the Son. Lombard's treatment is brief, stressing that the Father does not have a power that the Son lacks and that, nevertheless, the same power in the Son is not a power to generate but rather a power to be generated by the Father.[125] In later commentaries on the *Sentences* and other medieval works, the treatments of the topic become more elaborate.[126] It is not possible to examine all the pertinent works, so I will focus on Aquinas's account of the *potentia generandi* in his *De potentia* and then look at how Polanus's treatment of the *opera Dei* can be helpful on this issue.

In *De potentia*, Aquinas insists that the Son is distinguished from the Father not by essence but by relation only—that is, by being generated and having from the Father the divine essence. Such a relation is the only individuating principle in this case.[127] Yet, Aquinas writes, the *potentia generandi* is not purely "notional" or pertaining to a distinct characteristic of one person (the Father). Nor is it strictly essential, since it agrees with the Father alone as the one who generates. Aquinas therefore holds that the *potentia generandi* is both essential and notional.[128] This power is included in the divine essence but only as modified by the personal property of the Father: "Although generation in the Father is in some way a work of the divine nature, nevertheless it is [a work of the divine nature] with some concomitance of the personal property of the Father." Thus, the Father communicates all that is absolutely in the divine nature to the Son, including the divine power taken absolutely, but without the "concomitance" or "adjunction" of the Father's personal property.[129] The *potentia generandi*, then, is not God's omnipotence *simpliciter* or as common to the three divine persons; rather, it is God's omnipotence taken in the Father's mode of existing or under his relation to the Son.[130]

To broaden our theological resources on this issue, it will be useful to examine briefly Polanus's methodical treatment of the works of God in which he locates the procession of the Son from the Father. Polanus offers a synthesis of the insights of patristic and medieval authors and identifies several kinds of divine works, distinguishing them according to their principles and terms (both *termini a quo* and *termini ad quem*). The "personal" (as opposed to "essential") works are of special interest here, and the adjective "personal" applies chiefly to certain inward acts of God and then in a qualified way to certain outward acts that are terminated upon created objects. The *opera*

125. Lombard, *Sent.* 1.7.2.4 (94).
126. See, e.g., Bonaventure, *In Sent.* 1.7, art. un., qq. 1–2 (134–40); Aquinas, *Super Sent.* 1.7.2.1–2 (1:181–84).
127. Aquinas, *De pot.* 2.1 ad 3, 10, 12 (26, 27).
128. Aquinas, *De pot.* 2.2 corp. (28).
129. Aquinas, *De pot.* 2.4 ad 1–2 (33).
130. Aquinas, *De pot.* 2.5 (35–36).

personalia, Polanus writes, have both a "singular" principle and "singular" terms—"singular" here meaning proper to one of the divine persons—while the *opera essentialia* have a common principle (i.e., the divine essence absolutely) and common terms (i.e., effects wrought by all three persons).[131]

In the personal works, one person acts according to his proper personal character or *personalitas* as a formal principle. Put differently, the *principium* of a personal work is the essence in the person "operating according to his own proper relation." By contrast, the *principium* of an essential work is the essence taken absolutely or as common to the three. Personal works *simpliciter* are works whose *terminus a quo* and *terminus ad quem* alike are proper to one divine person. In these works, one person operates toward another according to the relation between them, which has led to the alternative name *opera relationis*. These works are the notional acts of the Father's generation of the Son, the Son's being born of the Father, and the Spirit's proceeding from the Father and Son. By contrast, some of God's works have a common principle (i.e., the divine essence) and common effect (a created object) but somehow reflect or express one person's property or role in the economy. These Polanus calls personal works in a qualified sense (*opera personalia certo modo*). Examples include the Father's speech at the Son's baptism, the Son's mission, incarnation, mediation, and satisfaction for sin, the Spirit's appearance in the form of a dove at the Son's baptism and in the form of fire at Pentecost.[132]

How do Aquinas's and Polanus's reflections on the *potentia generandi* and the various works of God help to advance the argument of this chapter? They underscore that divine power as such is not a proper distinguishing mark of any of the divine persons. Instead, it is included in the one essence of God that is shared by the persons. Yet the reflections of authors like Aquinas and Polanus also indicate that this does not entail that the Father's generation of the Son should be performed by the Son too as a reflexive, self-constitutive act. Though the Father and Son share one power, the Father alone performs the act of eternally generating. For while there is one essence and one essential power in God, that power is distinctly modified by and active in the Father under his relation to the Son so that the essence as modified by the Father is the *principium quo* of the eternal begetting and the Father alone is the *terminus a quo* of the begetting. There is no multiplication of an absolute divine perfection like power, but there is still a genuine distinction between the Father's mode of subsisting as the one who gives and the Son's mode of

131. Polanus, *Syntagma*, 4.2 (236). The "essential" works are called essential not because they are necessary but because they have the divine essence as common to the Father, Son, and Spirit as their *principium*.

132. Polanus, *Syntagma*, 4.2 (236–37). See also 5.1 (256–57).

subsisting as the one who receives the divine essence. In this important sense, the inward personal works of God are "divided," having the essence not as common to the three but as determined or modified relatively in one of the persons as their *principium quo*. And such works do not have the divine essence as common to the persons but rather just one of the three persons as their peculiar *terminus a quo*. Further, these works do not have the creature but rather just one of the three persons as their peculiar *terminus ad quem*. This is different from the Trinity's outward works, which have the essence absolutely as their *principium quo*, even if these outward works in some cases might still have just one person as their distinct *terminus ad quem*. These elaborative resources help us to confirm that the Father, Son, and Spirit share the one divine essence and power even as the Father's generative mode of subsisting and the Son's generated mode of subsisting are distinct from one another. The Father alone generates the Son rather than there being a self-generation of the Son.

B. The Father's Communication of the Essence to the Son

We now come to the second potential challenge: Does the Father's communication of the divine essence to the Son imply that the essence is multiplied, present in one version in the Father and in another version in the Son? There are various descriptions of the begetting of the Son in the Christian tradition, some of which might appear to suggest that the essence would be duplicated. For example, Basil of Caesarea speaks of the Son as "begotten light" in that the Son is life itself and goodness itself "proceeding from the life-giving font and paternal goodness" (ἐκ τῆς ζωοποιοῦ πηγῆς καὶ τῆς πατρικῆς ἀγαθότητος προελθόντα).[133] Though it is sometimes thought that strong statements about the Father as the font of deity are peculiar to the Greek fathers, they appear in the works of the Latin fathers too, even in contexts that stress the simplicity of

133. Basil of Caesarea, *Contre Eunome* 2.25 (2:104). The Eastern Orthodox theologian John Zizioulas has advocated this "Greek" position, arguing that the "ontological 'principle' or 'cause' of the being and life of God does not consist in the one substance of God but in the *hypostasis*, that is, *the person of the Father*." Indeed, "The one God is not the one substance but the Father, who is the 'cause' both of the generation of the Son and of the procession of the Spirit" (*Being as Communion*, 39–44). From a Protestant angle, T. F. Torrance maintains that Gregory Nazianzen rightly distanced himself from Basil and Gregory of Nyssa on this point in order to avoid the implication that there are degrees of deity in the persons (*Trinitarian Perspectives*, 29–32). By contrast, Bruce McCormack has developed—whether in faithfulness to Barth or not must be judged by Barth scholars—what he sees as a fecund "Basilian" thread in Barth's trinitarianism, according to which "God is triune because the Father has freely willed to be so" by his "command" in God's self-constituting act of election ("The Doctrine of the Trinity after Barth").

the essence and the consubstantiality of the Father and Son. Hilary of Poitiers, for example, explicitly denies that the divine essence is a "thing anterior" (*res anterior*) to the Father and Son in which both would have to participate. Instead, the Father gives the essence to the Son so that it is "born" in the Son and the Son is "God from the nature of God."[134] Similarly, Augustine can say that the Son "individually" (*singillatim*) is "essence from essence."[135]

These descriptions are interpreted charitably by medieval and early Protestant theologians. In the *Sentences*, Lombard, for example, asks "whether the Father has generated the divine essence or the essence [has generated] the Son, whether essence has generated essence or neither has generated nor is generated." He recalls comments from Hilary and Augustine of the aforementioned sort and does not take them to mean that the essence generates or is generated. Rather, Lombard writes, based on the full range of relevant statements from such authors, it should be concluded that "the Son, co-eternal with the Father, is from the Father, so that he is the same with him in nature, or of the same nature." For Lombard, this interpretation is not just a matter of historical interest but of theological accuracy as well. In Lombard's judgment, to hold that the Father generates the essence is to render the essence something relative to the Father, which precludes it truly being the essence that is absolute and common to the three. Lombard gives several other reasons for taking this view. Because the essence is one and the same in the Father and Son and because each of the persons is the same "thing" as the essence, it is illogical to say, for example, that the Father generates something that he himself really is.[136]

Aquinas also interprets the fathers along this line in his work *Contra errores Graecorum*. With Lombard, Aquinas reasons that the essence that is common to the three divine persons ought not to be regarded as something that distinguishes the persons, and what distinguishes the persons is that "one generates and another is generated and another proceeds." The distinct persons therefore are the proper subjects of generation and procession. Still, in light of statements from Athanasius, Basil of Caesarea, and Cyril of Alexandria, Aquinas readily acknowledges that the word "God" can signify the essence as it is in one of the persons, which means it is acceptable to say that "God generates God" or "God is born."[137] Although it is an "improper" way of speaking, Aquinas even explores the viability of using abstract "essence"

134. Hilary of Poitiers, *La Trinité* 4.4 (2:16–18); 5.11 (2:116); 5.35 (2:160).
135. Augustine, *De trin.* 7.2.3 (250). See further Ayres, *Nicaea and Its Legacy*, 377–80.
136. Lombard, *Sent.* 1.5.1 (80–87).
137. In *ST*, Aquinas observes that *Deus* can designate all three persons (i.e., God without respect to any personal distinctions) or the essence as it is in one person (Ia.39.5 corp. [405]).

language here. Because *Deus* and *deitas* are really identical, one might say that in the Son there is "essence from essence," but this must be parsed to mean that "the Son who is the essence is from the Father who is the same divine essence." In other words, the Son is not generated by the essence but rather "receives the essence by generation."[138] From the period of Protestant orthodoxy, Polanus concurs with this approach to the fathers, emphasizing that the Father generates "not as the essence but as the Father." Actions are performed by persons, and the fathers, according to Polanus, held that the essence generates or is generated not οὐσιωδῶς ("essentially," as the essence as such) but ὑποστατικῶς ("hypostatically," as a person in whom the essence subsists). The basic intent in the patristic use of the "essence" language at this point is to ward off the Arian notion that the Son was generated "outside the essence."[139]

In the early Reformed tradition, there was debate about whether it is appropriate to say that the Father communicates the essence to the Son. In the sixteenth century, John Calvin argued adamantly that the Son is *autotheos* (God of himself), bringing this emphasis into trinitarian polemics at the time and provoking discussion over the viability of his own position.[140] Calvin writes that the fathers characterize God the Father as the *principium* of the Son but also sometimes assert that the Son "has both the divinity and the essence from himself." For Calvin, Augustine sheds light on this by articulating that Christ with respect to himself (*ad se*) is God while Christ with respect to the Father (*ad Patrem*) is the Son. *Ad se*, then, the Son is *a se*. The essence in the Son is therefore "unbegotten," though the Son with respect to his person is from the Father. The Son as God exists *a se*, while the Son as Son exists from the Father. In Calvin's estimation, to say otherwise is to undermine the true deity of the Son.[141] Brannon Ellis observes that Calvin fundamentally objected to understanding generation in terms of a "communication" of the essence, because this would violate the distinction between the absolute and relative aspects of God's being and compromise the Son's divine self-existence.[142]

Calvin's doctrine and the question of Reformed "autotheanism" were discussed by various Roman Catholic and Protestant authors in the sixteenth and seventeenth centuries. On the other end of the spectrum from Calvin was Jacob Arminius, who contends that the *autotheotēs* of the Son is contrary to

138. Aquinas, *Contra errores Graecorum* 1.4–5 (74–75).
139. Polanus, *Syntagma*, 3.4 (203–4).
140. On Calvin, see Ellis, *Calvin, Classical Trinitarianism, and the Aseity of the Son*.
141. Calvin, *Institutio Christianae religionis*, 1.13.19, 25 (105–6, 112–13).
142. Ellis, *Calvin, Classical Trinitarianism, and the Aseity of the Son*, 12–13, 34, 62–63, 68–69.

"the word of God and the whole ancient Greek and Latin church," which held, against the threats of tritheism and Sabellianism, that "the Son has his own deity from the Father by eternal generation."[143] Leaning in the other direction (seemingly farther than Calvin himself), the English Reformed theologian Thomas Ridgley registers concerns about a communication of either the essence or a distinct "personality" to the Son. Ridgley wonders which way of speaking is "the least exceptionable" and is particularly opposed to saying that the Father "gives" the essence to the Son, for in Ridgley's view such an "unguarded expression" provides a foothold to the Arians. Ridgley includes eternal generation in his body of divinity in keeping with historical precedent, but he confesses that he has considered whether "it would be the safest and most eligible way to pass over it as a doctrine less necessary to be understood."[144]

How might we take into account the different positions of these authors regarding the coherence of generation, communication, and divine simplicity? In view of relevant biblical material, I would suggest that taking the path laid out by the likes of Lombard, Aquinas, and a majority of the Reformed orthodox is best. There are several biblical texts that indicate that the Son comes forth from the Father in such a way that he has received what the Father has (John 1:14; 5:26; 6:45–46; 7:28–29; 17:24; Col. 1:15; Heb. 1:3). This teaching implies a communication of the divine essence, a paternal sharing of the divine essence and life with the Son, by which the Son can perfectly represent the Father to us. By the Son's receptive mode of subsisting, the Son "is in his person distinct from the Father, another not the Father, but yet the same in nature, and this in all glorious properties and excellencies."[145]

At the same time, while retaining the communication language, it is vital to uphold the absolute-relative distinction invoked by Lombard, Aquinas, Calvin, and others. Among the Reformed orthodox, Bartholomäus Keckermann captures the importance of preserving that distinction, even if, in my judgment, he could have made the point without opposing the communication of the divine essence. Keckermann argues that to say the Father "communicates" the essence is to imply that what is absolute is multiplied, yielding more than one God. Indeed, the divine essence is underived (*autousia*), so if the Son had a generated or communicated version of the essence, the Son would not be true God.[146] For similar reasons, Turretin agrees that the essence is not begotten in

---

143. Arminius, *Declaratio sententiae*, 125. The *autotheotēs* of the Son could be taken to entail tritheism if it meant that there were three underived divine essences. It could be taken to entail Sabellianism if it were to make what is characteristic of the Father (subsisting *a se*) proper to the Son and Spirit as well.

144. Ridgley, *A Body of Divinity*, 258–59.

145. Owen, *Hebrews*, 3:91.

146. Keckermann, *Systema s.s. theologiae*, 1.4 (86–87).

the Son: "What generates and what is generated is necessarily multiplied."[147] But, unlike Keckermann, Turretin and other Reformed authors illumine how the communication of the essence in fact fits with the absolute-relative distinction. Certainly, the Father does not take the essence as a direct object and pass on some part or second instance of it to the Son as an indirect object of the generative action. Rather, as Turretin suggests, just as the *terminus a quo* of generation is the Father, so the *terminus ad quem* of generation is the Son— not the essence but the person.[148] Yet, if the Father generates another mode of subsisting that is his perfect image, it must be the case that this second mode of subsisting is a mode of subsisting *of the divine essence*.[149] Accordingly, the Father's communication of the essence is not precluded but required by God's simplicity. For person and essence are really identical in accordance with God's simplicity. Therefore, if the Father generates a divine person, that person is inevitably a mode of subsisting of the divine essence and inevitably receives the essence in this manner. Aquinas similarly states that the Father does not generate or spirate the deity but rather "in generating and spirating communicates it."[150] There is an important distinction between procession and communication: what is communicated does not proceed; rather, it is communicated to the one who proceeds.[151] While the Son does not have an essence that is "from the Father" (with the adjectival prepositional phrase), he still has "from the Father" (with the adverbial prepositional phrase) the one divine essence that is not multiplied or diminished.[152] In his study of Calvin, Ellis has argued that it is still a violation of the absolute-relative distinction to say that the Father and Son have the same essence but with distinct "modes of possessing" the essence.[153] I am sympathetic to the concerns of Ellis's work, but if the Son is from the Father a personal mode of the essence, then it follows that the Son has from the Father that essence. In addition, I do not regard this as a compromise of the absolute-relative distinction, because it is the essence as such that is absolute, not the way in which a given person has or modifies the essence.

147. Turretin, *Inst.*, 3.29.6 (1:322).

148. Turretin, *Inst.*, 3.29.6 (1:322).

149. Cf. the logic in Athanasius, *Serap.* 1.25,7–8 (513). Hilary repeatedly makes a similar point in *La Trinité* 3.4 (1:340–42); 5.11 (2:116); 5.37 (2:162–64); 6.11–13 (2:188–94); 6.31 (2:232–34); 7.11 (2:296–98); 7.13–15 (2:302–8); 7.25 (2:332–34); 8.43 (2:448). Cf. Polanus: *quod est in Deo, subsistit ut Deus* (*Syntagma*, 3.4 [203]).

150. Aquinas, *ST* Ia.39.5 ad 6 (405).

151. Polanus, *Syntagma*, 3.6 (219). Generation and communication are one act but taken under different aspects (as that act concerns the persons and as that act concerns the essence).

152. Cf. Turretin, *Inst.*, 3.28.40 (1:320–21).

153. Ellis, *Calvin, Classical Trinitarianism, and the Aseity of the Son*, 69, 100, 167–68.

That the essence is not multiplied or attenuated in the Father's communication of it is corroborated by the fact that, according to the doctrine of divine simplicity, essence and existence are identical in God. Unlike created essence, which is individuated by various actualizations of it, God's essence just is his existence, which means the Father communicates the one essence with the one *esse* to the Son.[154] Further, God's essence is indivisible and infinite, without any limit or extension. Therefore, as the Father generates another mode of subsisting of the essence, the Son must be a mode of subsisting of the very same essence, not (*per impossibile*) a second actually infinite essence.[155] Petrus van Mastricht nicely articulates the approach advocated here, agreeing with Calvin that the Son is not "essenced" or in possession of a derivative essence (*Deus essentiatus*) and yet holding that the Son has from the Father the divine essence. The Son therefore has an *aseitas essentialis*, though not an *aseitas personalis*; he is *autotheos*, though not *autoprosōpon*.[156] This approach enables us to confirm both that the Father has communicated the divine essence to the Son without undermining the simplicity of the essence and also that the Father has in his Son a perfect image whose goodness and glory he eternally knows and loves.

VI. Conclusion

This chapter has examined scriptural teaching on the Son's eternal, personally constitutive relation to the Father, that relation within and from which the Son does all that he does in the economy. In addition, this chapter has examined scriptural reasons to maintain that in being one and the same God, the Father, Son, and Spirit share one divine intellect, will, and power, though they modify that intellect, will, and power in diverse ways. The next section sought to clarify the coherence of the personal distinctions in God and the unity and simplicity of God's essence, which led to an affirmation of mutual knowledge and love in the Trinity, even if the fellowship of the divine persons is also dissimilar to that of created beings. Finally, I sought to address two

154. Cf. Aquinas, *Super Sent.* 1.2.1.4 ad 1 (1:74); Aquinas, *De pot.* 2.1 corp. (25); *ST* Ia.40.2 ad 2 (414). Turretin helpfully notes that the Father does not originate a distinct "absolute existence" in the Son but only a distinct "mode of subsisting" (*Inst.*, 3.29.31 [1:330]).

155. So Polanus, *Syntagma*, 3.4 (203). On a related note, God's simplicity is properly upheld by the orthodox affirmation of the identity of the essence in the Father, Son, and Spirit, not by the heretical teaching of a lesser, quasi-divine nature in the Son and Spirit (cf., e.g., Athanasius, *Serap.* 1.2,9–20 [452–53]; 1.17,1–3 [493]; 1.29,8–10 [522]; Hilary of Poitiers, *La Trinité* 5.25 [2:142]; 7.26 [2:336]).

156. Mastricht, *TPT*, 2.26.29 (259).

potential challenges to the argument of this chapter, which pertained to the Father's generation of the Son and his communication of the divine essence to the Son.

Before beginning the next chapter, it is appropriate to note how treating the Son's relation to the Father in concert with the doctrine of divine simplicity can help secure the biblical desiderata identified in the introduction of this volume (the genuineness of the Son's relationship to the Father and Spirit, the unity of Christ's person, and the authenticity of his human life and suffering). It bears repeating that a description of the persons as "modes of subsisting" or "subsisting relations" does not reduce the persons to mere modes or relations. Rather, the persons have, are, and modify the essential perfection of God, including his knowing, willing, and loving. The persons are really modally distinct from one another and love one another even without reference to the economy. Moreover, the Son is eternally constituted as the Son by his relation to the Father, not by anything else. This constrains us to view all that the Son is and does in the economy in the light of his fellowship with the Father. Though the material in this chapter does not bring us directly to the unity of the person of the Son in the incarnation or the authenticity of his human suffering, it does alert us to the fact that the Son, who is the divine essence (subsisting in a certain mode), will remain true God and cannot be separated from the essence in his incarnation and passion. The one who takes on human flesh and suffers will not be less than true God in so doing. The next chapter will consider the election and mission of the Son, which ground all that he does in his earthly sojourn.

THREE

"Foreknown before the Foundation of the World": The Son's Election and Mission

I. Introduction

The previous chapter focused on the Son's eternal relation to the Father, and this chapter begins to contemplate the work of the Trinity *ad extra*. In order to understand the Son's role in this work, the chapter starts by examining relevant biblical material on God's eternal decree and the Son's election and on the Son's mission and historical act of assuming a human nature. The following sections of the chapter will then expound this material and seek to exhibit how it is illumined by a consideration of divine perfections like immutability, eternity, and simplicity. This will involve discussing God's complete actuality in relation to his decree, God's immutability and simplicity in relation to the act of election and the doctrine of the *pactum salutis*, and God's transcendence of time in relation to the Son's historical mission and assumption of a human nature. The end of the chapter will then point out how this account of the divine decree and the mission of the Son corroborates the biblical emphasis on the Son's constitutive relation to the Father and the unity of his person.

II. Biblical Description

The Bible leads us to speak of the triune God's eternal decision to create the world and redeem sinners. Of course, if God just is the God that he is with

97

or without the world, he knows and wills and loves in the immanent fellowship of Father, Son, and Spirit even without reference to the plan of salvation.
The fulfillment of God's knowing, willing, and loving does not require the
existence of an outward object (this world or another, this elect people or
another). Nevertheless, according to the Bible, God has indeed directed his
wisdom and volition toward the world. He has chosen to create, sustain, and
act within the world, a choice often called God's "decree" in Christian dogmatics. There are scriptural uses of decretive language that pertain to what
God commands human beings to do rather than what God himself intends to
actualize (e.g., Deut. 4:45; 6:2; Ps. 119). However, Scripture does often speak
of God's "counsel," "purpose," "plan," or "decree" with regard to what God
wills to bring about, by himself alone or by the involvement of secondary
causes (e.g., 1 Kings 22:23; Job 38:2; 42:2; Pss. 33:11; 149:9; Prov. 16:4; 19:21;
Isa. 4:28; 10:22–23; 11:2; 28:22, 29; 50:45; 51:29; 55:11; Lam. 2:17; Hab. 1:12;
Zech. 8:14–15; Rom. 9:17; Heb. 6:17; Rev. 17:17). Various texts convey that
God's decree precedes created existence. It is an eternal decree, established
"before the foundation of the world" (e.g., Ps. 139:4–5, 15–16; Isa. 46:9–10;
Acts 2:23; 4:28; 1 Cor. 2:7; Eph. 3:11; 2 Tim. 1:9). God's decree includes the
full scope of created existence and its historical development, but in Scripture
it focuses especially on the destiny of human beings, particularly those chosen
to inherit salvation in Christ. God elects and determines to save a people for
the glory of his name (Mark 13:20, 22, 27; Rom. 8:28–30, 33; 9:11; 11:2, 7;
Eph. 1:3–14; 2 Tim. 2:10; Titus 1:1; 1 Pet. 1:1–2; 2 Pet. 1:10).

According to Holy Scripture, the divine decision to create the world and to
save this chosen people has for its end the glory of the Son, the manifestation
of the excellence of Jesus Christ, the one in whom all things are "summed
up" (Eph. 1:10). Christ is the "image of the invisible God and the firstborn
of all creation." It is "by" or "in" him that "all things were created in the
heavens and on the earth, things seen and things unseen, whether thrones
or dominions or rulers or authorities; all things were created through him
and for him" (Col. 1:15–16). The "invisible God," the Father, is revealed and
glorified in his image, the Son. This Son is the "firstborn of all creation" in
that he is its head, the one in connection with whom it has its purpose and
meaning. The Son is the one whom God appointed to be "heir of all things"
(Heb. 1:2). The people of God will ultimately be with him and behold his
glory (John 17:24; cf. Rev. 22:4–5). The saints' salvation will forever exhibit
the "surpassing richness of [God's] grace in kindness to us *in Christ Jesus*"
(Eph. 2:7; cf. 3:10–11). Thus, Christ is "the Alpha and Omega, the first and
the last, the beginning and the end" (Rev. 22:13).

The divine decree and act of election are not only *for* the Son but also wrought *by* and *in* the Son. Several texts speak directly of the Son acting to elect human persons, particularly the first disciples (John 13:18; 15:16, 19; Acts 9:15), but all scriptural teaching on election assumes the active involvement of the Son with the Father and Spirit insofar as all three persons act in all the works of God directed toward creatures. Perhaps more striking for the purposes of this chapter is the fact that election occurs "in Christ." The apostle Paul proclaims that God has "blessed us with every spiritual blessing in the heavenly places in Christ, just as he chose us in him in order that we should be holy and blameless before him" (Eph. 1:3–4). God has "predestined us to adoption through Jesus Christ, to himself, according to his good pleasure, to the praise of the glory of his grace, with which he has gifted us in the beloved" (1:5–6). God blesses us "in Christ" because he has chosen us, in the first place, "in Christ." Even if God's act of election is not constitutive of the identity of the Son, it does involve God eternally and immutably establishing that the Son will assume a human nature and bear the name Jesus Christ. In this regard, the Son is "the Lamb slain before the foundation of the world" (Rev. 13:8).

In fact, God's act of election "in Christ" is also an election "of Christ," an act having Christ as its object. After Peter greets "the elect . . . according to the foreknowledge of God the Father, in the sanctification of the Spirit, for obedience and sprinkling of the blood of Jesus Christ," Peter tells us that Christ himself was "foreknown before the foundation of the world" and then "made known in the last times on account of us" (1 Pet. 1:1–2, 20). The point is not that God merely perceived in advance that Christ would take on flesh in history but rather that God has eternally planned and delighted in the Son's incarnation.[1] In other passages as well Christ is chosen by God to undertake his mission. He is the chosen servant in whom God delights (e.g., Isa. 42:1). He is the chosen Son to whom the disciples must listen (Luke 9:35).

Commenting on 1 Peter 1 (and Eph. 1), William Ames writes that "all [God's] special blessings that pertain to our salvation depend on election." Indeed, "the foundation and source of all our happiness and consolation is established in this, that we are chosen by God." The opening of 1 Peter conveys that the Father, Son, and Spirit all work together to bring about our salvation: "The beginning is from the Father, the dispensation is through the Son, the application is through the Holy Spirit." Just as the persons operate together, the works appropriated to each of them are linked together. And if election is directed toward cleansing by the blood of Christ (1 Pet. 1:2), we should not "separate Christ from election, or election from Christ." For "God

---

1. Cf., e.g., P. Jacobs and H. Krienke, "προγινώσκω," in *NIDNTT* 1:693; Jobes, *1 Peter*, 68.

has constituted him [Christ] mediator of our redemption by virtue of his own election." Christ is "from all eternity predestined to the office of mediator." As "second Adam," he is "head of all the elect."[2]

In both Ephesians 1 and 1 Peter 1, there are signs that although God's election of Christ is eternal, it is not constitutive of his deity or personal relation to the Father. Predestination and election occur "according to the good pleasure of [God's] will [κατὰ εὐδοκίαν τοῦ θελήματος αὐτοῦ], to the praise of the glory of his grace" (Eph. 1:5–6). Here in the talk of God's "good pleasure" the emphasis falls on the "sovereign and gracious will of God."[3] As Ames puts it, "There is no cause or reason of our election to salvation beyond the *beneplacitum ipsius Dei* [the good pleasure of God himself]."[4] It is, after all, designed to incite praise to God for the richness of his grace. If the act of election were a matter of God establishing his own deity or if it were a necessary outworking of his deity, that would undermine the gracious character of it. It would no longer elicit praise for God's astounding generosity. Likewise, 1 Peter 1:20 tells us that the revelation of Christ in time—and, implicitly, the eternal predestination of Christ for this incarnate revelation—took place "on account of us" or "for our sake" (δι' ὑμᾶς). God is not fulfilling himself here but working outwardly for our good.

A number of other texts open up the trinitarian and christological dimensions of the decree. While teaching the disciples about the role of service in the kingdom of God, Christ reveals to them that he is conferring upon them the kingdom just as the Father has conferred upon (διέθετό) him the kingdom (Luke 22:29–30). The disciples only participate derivatively in a reign that the Father has first entrusted to Jesus. The verb διατίθεμαι and its cognates are used in the making of covenants.[5] Thus, Jesus is saying that he "covenanted with the Twelve 'as *my* Father covenanted with *me.*'"[6] In conjunction with the Father giving eschatological kingship to Jesus, the Father gives him a people for whom he serves as mediator. When Jesus describes himself as the "bread of life," he tells his listeners, "All that the Father gives me will come to me, and the one who comes to me I will never cast out" (John 6:37). Again, "This is the will of him who sent me, that all that he has given me I should not lose from him but should raise it up at the last day" (6:39). Later Jesus insists that his sheep will never perish, for the Father, who has given the sheep to him, is greater than all (10:29). In John 17, Jesus prays, "Glorify your Son, in order

2. Ames, *Utriusque epistolae divi Petri Apostoli explicatio analytica*, 5–8, 22–23.
3. H. Bietenhard, "εὐδοκέω," in *NIDNTT* 2:819.
4. Ames, *Utriusque epistolae divi Petri Apostoli*, 5.
5. See J. Guhrt, "διαθήκη," in *NIDNTT* 1:365, 369.
6. James R. Edwards, *Luke*, 636.

that your Son might glorify you, just as you have given him authority over all flesh, in order that all that you have given him, he might give eternal life to them" (17:1–2). Jesus has revealed the Father's name to those whom the Father gave him out of the world (17:6). He prays for the ones given to him by the Father, that they would be with him and see his glory (17:9–10, 24). The seventeenth-century English commentator Matthew Poole observes that some interpreters take the Father's giving of a people to the Son in John 6:37 to be an "eternal designation of Persons to eternal Life," while others take it to be "the infusing the Habits of special saving Grace, by which Persons are enabled actually to believe."[7] However, as Poole points out, at least in the other pertinent texts the giving is clearly something already established prior to God's saving action in time. It precedes the Son's historical mission and thus signifies "an Act of [God's] Eternal Counsel."[8]

The eternal appointment of the Son has its redemptive-historical unfolding in the Abrahamic covenant. According to Paul, Christ is in fact one of the parties of the Abrahamic covenant: "To Abraham the promises were spoken, and to his seed. It does not say 'and to his seeds' as to many but as to one: 'and to your seed,' who is Christ" (Gal. 3:16; cf. Gen. 13:15; 15:18; 17:7–8; 22:17–18). The law of Moses then came into effect until the coming of the seed (i.e., Christ) to whom the promises were made (Gal. 3:19). The noun σπέρμα ("seed") is a collective noun, capable of signifying that which includes multiple individuals, and Paul uses it in this way in Galatians 3:29: "If you [plural] are Christ's, then you are Abraham's seed." In 3:16 and 3:19, Paul takes the seed who received the Abrahamic promise to be the singular person of Christ, but the collective aspect is still present in that Christ is the head and representative to whom all of Abraham's true descendants are united by faith.[9] Significantly, then, Christ is not merely the one who fulfills the promises given to Abraham; he is the one to whom the promises were made in the first place. From the outset, Christ's mediation and covenantal headship envelop God's dealings with Abraham's family. Accordingly, "the promises made to Abraham, were but the Exhibition of the Eternal Covenant of Grace, made between the Father and his Son Christ Jesus, who was in it both the Mediator and Surety."[10]

The Abrahamic covenant is advanced through the future deliverance promised by Israel's prophets. Here too God has Christ as covenant partner and mediator in his new covenant. Christ is the servant with whom God the

---

7. Poole, *Annotations upon the Holy Bible*, on John 6:37, 39.
8. Poole, *Annotations upon the Holy Bible*, on John 17:6.
9. Cf. Schreiner, *Galatians*, 230; Moo, *Galatians*, 229.
10. Poole, *Annotations upon the Holy Bible*, on Gal. 3:16.

Father establishes his covenant and who faithfully does the will of the Father (e.g., Isa. 42:1; 49:5–6; 52:13). Indeed, YHWH gives Christ, the true Israel, to be a covenant for the people and a light for the nations (וְאֶתֶּנְךָ לִבְרִית עָם לְאוֹר גּוֹיִם) (Isa. 42:6; cf. 49:8). Here the addressee of YHWH's statement (Christ) "not only mediates but embodies the thing." He "embodies and expresses Yhwh's commitment."[11] He is the one "through whom the covenant is mediated," and "all the blessings of the covenant are embodied in, have their root and origin in, and are dispensed by him."[12] In the New Testament, Paul emphasizes, "There is one God, and one mediator between God and human beings, the man Christ Jesus" (1 Tim. 2:5). Hebrews in particular highlights Jesus's mediatorial role in the new covenant. YHWH swore on oath to the Davidic Messiah that he would be a priest after the order of Melchizedek (cf. Ps. 110:4). By this oath God appointed Jesus to be μεσίτης ("mediator") and ἔγγυος ("guarantor," one who ensures fulfillment) of the new and "better" covenant (Heb. 7:20–22, 28; 9:15; 12:24).

The eternal election of the Son to be mediator and head of the covenant people results in the Father sending the Son into the world to assume a human nature in history and to live and act as the God-man. In the Old Testament, YHWH anoints the Isaianic servant to preach good news to the poor and sends him to bring healing and deliverance (Isa. 61:1). The theme of sending can be found in the Synoptic Gospels too (Mark 9:37; 12:6; Luke 4:18, 43; see also Acts 3:26), but it is richly developed in John's Gospel especially. Although John the Baptist is sent by God in the Fourth Gospel (1:6, 33; 3:28), the unique filial relationship to God the Father is "conspicuous by its absence" in the Baptist's case and applies to Jesus alone.[13] In various contexts in John, Jesus identifies the Father as the one who sent him and identifies himself as the one sent by the Father (e.g., 3:34; 5:23, 24; 6:29, 44, 57; 7:33; 8:18; 10:36; 11:42; 13:20; 15:21; 16:5; 17:3, 18, 21, 23, 25; 20:21). As the one sent by the Father,

11. Goldingay and Payne, *Isaiah 40–55*, 1:227. Even if the phrase לִבְרִית עָם were rendered "a covenant people" (so Paul, *Isaiah 40–66*, 189), it would still be the case that God addresses Christ as the true Israel and establishes his covenant with Christ.

12. Young, *Isaiah*, 120. Another text that might bear mentioning here is Zech. 6:9–15, but its syntax is debated. In this passage a kingly figure called the "branch" (cf. Isa. 4:2; 11:1; Jer. 23:5; 33:15; Zech. 3:8) will rebuild the temple. A priest will sit on his throne, and there will be a "counsel of peace [וַעֲצַת שָׁלוֹם]" between them." But there is debate about whether (1) the "branch" himself is the priest and the "between them" refers to him and YHWH or (2) the "branch" and the priest are two distinct human figures between whom there is a counsel of peace. For recent discussion, see Jauhiainen, "Turban and Crown Lost and Regained"; Kashow, "Two Philological Notes on Zechariah 6,12–13." Taking the former approach, a number of early Reformed theologians include the text in treatments of the *pactum salutis*. See, e.g., Coccejus, *Prophetae duodecim minores*, 504–5; Coccejus, *Summa doctrinae*, 5.88 (86); Witsius, *De oeconomia foederum Dei*, 2.2.7 (104–5).

13. M. Thompson, *The God of the Gospel of John*, 92.

he does the will and work of the Father (e.g., 4:34; 5:30, 36–38; 6:38–39; 7:16, 18; 8:16, 26, 29, 42; 9:4). He is sent into the world to bring salvation: "For God did not send his Son into the world in order to judge the world but in order to save the world through him" (3:17). Since salvation and eternal life center on communion with God, the Son is sent into the world to reveal the Father (12:44–45, 49; cf. 14:24; 17:8). In a similar way, John's Gospel also speaks often of the Son "coming" into the world (1:9, 11, 15; 3:19; 9:33, 39; 10:10).

The sending and coming of the Son are connected to his divine transcendence and eternal relation to the Father. The sending of the Son from the Father and the working of the Son from the Father correspond to his receiving from the Father the divine life (John 5:16–30). The Son sent of the Father is the one who (eternally) *is* from the Father (6:44–46; 7:28–29). He who comes into the world is the one who made the world (1:9–10). Thus, the way of his coming points back to the fact that the coming does not constitute his personal existence. Positively, the Son's mission corresponds to an identity he has in his eternal relation to the Father. "The one who comes from above is above all. The one who is from the earth is from the earth and speaks from the earth. The one who comes from heaven is above all" (3:31; cf. 6:51; 8:23). This is what accounts for the decisiveness of the Son's testimony: he attests what he has seen and heard from the Father (3:32–36; cf. 5:19–20; 8:26). The "condition of origin" is what determines the "dignity of doctrine." "Although the body of Christ has come materially from the earth, he nevertheless comes actively from heaven inasmuch as his body has been formed by divine power. He also comes from heaven because the eternal and uncreated person of the Son comes from heaven by the assumption of the flesh." Having proceeded from the Father and received from the Father divine life and knowledge, the Son comes into the world and gives testimony that is more certain than that of any mere human being.[14] Significantly, these elements of John's Gospel anchor the Son's temporal mission back in his eternal procession and his receiving from the Father the divine essence.

The Pauline epistles also contribute to our understanding of the Son's mission. The apostle ties the Son's mission to his incarnation: God did what the law was incapable of doing by "sending his own Son in the likeness of sinful flesh" (Rom. 8:3). Galatians 4 especially presses us to consider the temporal nature of the Son's mission and the fact that this one who is eternal God is now existing in a human nature bound by time. Paul writes, "But when the fullness of time came, God sent forth his Son, born of a woman, born under the law, in order that he might redeem the ones under the law, in order that

14. Aquinas, *Super Ioann.* 3.5.8–9 (100–101).

we might receive adoption. And because you are sons, God has sent forth the Spirit of his Son into our hearts, crying 'Abba, Father'" (4:4–6). Reflecting on the arrival of the "fullness of time," N. T. Wright comments, "This is the time when the ancient prophecies are being fulfilled. This is the moment at which Paul can say that he and his communities are those 'upon whom the ends of the ages have now come'" (cf. 1 Cor. 10:11; Eph. 1:10).[15] There is a "chronological sequence in which the coming of the Messiah and the spirit [sic] occur at a late stage in a long process."[16] Even if one wishes to underscore the disjunctive nature of the incarnation (as in the "apocalyptic turn" in Pauline studies), it remains true that God's action in the Son's assumption of human flesh is temporal and historical. Likewise, the Son's birth and ensuing life "under the law" locate him in time. The sending of the Spirit "into our hearts" also has a temporal character inasmuch as he is given to human beings existing in time. Thus, Paul's teaching in Galatians 4 compels us to take into account God's action in time in any Christian affirmation of divine eternity.

In this section, we have examined scriptural teaching on God's eternal decree (particularly its trinitarian and christological shape) and on the Son's mission and assumption of a human nature in time. God has eternally elected us "in Christ." Indeed, God's eternal act of election has Christ as its object (and us in Christ). The Father has eternally appointed the Son, covenanted with the Son, to be the mediator of the people of God. We cannot get back to a time before God decreed that the Son would take on human flesh. At the same time, we have to recognize that the act of election is rooted in God's "good pleasure." Election does not fulfill God. The outward execution of the decree involves the Father sending the Son into the world. The Son's mission corresponds to his prevenient generation by the Father and eternal receiving from the Father. The mission and coming of the Son into the world indicate that he is not constituted as the person that he is by his being sent. He already is the eternal Son whose identity is determined by his immanent relation to the Father. At the same time, the Son's mission is decidedly temporal and historical and will not allow us to envision a God stuck outside of time.

In light of all this, the scriptural material elicits a consideration of how the election and sending of the Son comport with a doctrine of God that emphasizes his aseity and includes attributes like immutability and eternity. On the one hand, we cannot neglect the covenantal plan of God and its temporal execution. On the other hand, we cannot allow our description of that plan and temporal execution to suggest that the God driving it forward is

15. Wright, *Paul and the Faithfulness of God*, 1:552.
16. Wright, *Paul and the Faithfulness of God*, 2:876.

constituted by his works *ad extra*, for at precisely that point we would not only have an inaccurate view of God but also undermine the truly free and decisive character of God's acts of electing us and sending his Son into the world. With this in mind, we will discuss in the next three sections the completeness and actuality of God in relation to his eternal decree, the immutability and simplicity of God in relation to election and the *pactum salutis*, and God's transcendence of time in relation to the Son's temporal mission and assumption of a human nature.

III. Eternal Actuality and the Divine Decree

Given Scripture's teaching on the eternal decision of God to send the Son into the world to take on human flesh, does biblical Christology problematize the notion that God is completely and fully in act in himself without reference to the economy? Does biblical Christology stipulate that the identity of the Son must either be constituted by his election or else undergo some sort of change under the act of election? Put differently, might the Bible's teaching be granted its full force without us having to give up either the Son's independence of the economy or his immutability? This section will address the question of whether God's decree and act of election undermine the notion that the Son is eternally complete and in act without reference to the economy. The next section, on the election of the Son, will deal more directly with the question of the personal constitution of the Son in connection with God's immutability and simplicity. In this section, I will break up the material under the following three points and clear the way toward some more overtly christological reflections in the next section.

(1) To understand the importance of affirming God's complete actuality without reference to the existence of the world or the incarnation, it is necessary to consider what his aseity and completeness entail. It is straightforward enough to recall that the Latin phrase *a se* means "of himself" and that the predicate "aseity" signifies that God exists "of himself." He is independent and not caused by something else. Likewise, it is straightforward to say that God's perfection or completeness signifies that God has whatever is included in what it is to be God. But such statements about God's aseity and perfection do not penetrate beyond the purely formal level of inquiry. Etymological considerations have some value in the doctrine of the divine attributes, but ultimately Christian theology has to deal with the positive material content and entailments of the divine attributes. In other words, Christian theology must not merely affirm that God is *a se* or perfect and

then stop there. Rather, in light of the biblical revelation, which teaches us about the goodness and life and wisdom and triunity of God, Christian theology has to ask what it is about this God that grounds our affirmation of his aseity and perfection.

Given that the God of the Bible is not an impersonal object but the spiritual, good, living, and wise God of love, a proper treatment of the material content of God's aseity and completeness will touch upon his knowing and willing and loving. It will not insulate the notion of aseity from a consideration of these matters but will allow aseity to be informed by them and will apply the notion of aseity to them. In such an approach, God's existence, mentally prescinded from his various attributes, is not the sole focal point of aseity. God's goodness, knowledge, will, and love also are included in the meaning of aseity. Accordingly, it is not just the existence of God but the goodness, knowledge, will, and love of God that are *a se*. Thus, the goodness of God, which is the source of all enjoyment and satisfaction, is not derived from without but is complete in God himself (cf., e.g., Pss. 16:2, 5–6, 11; 34:8, 10; 36:8–9; 145:16, 19; Jer. 2:13). God's love, then, God's rejoicing in what is good, is antecedently fulfilled in God himself (cf. Matt. 3:17; 17:5; John 17:24). In light of this, God's aseity entails an antecedent actuality and contentment of God in himself whereby he does not need to create the world in order to fulfill himself. He is not only free of external constraint in his decree to create the world. He is also free of any natural or internal and automatic propensity (a "necessity of nature" in scholastic terms) in his decree to create the world. God acts with a freedom of "spontaneity" (freedom from external compulsion) and also a freedom of "indifference" (not a carelessness but a freedom either to do something or not to do something without detriment to one's own well-being) in his decision to create the world and send the Son to take on flesh for our salvation.

Some accounts of God's decision to create the world and elect us in Christ have suggested that while God acts with a freedom of spontaneity in doing so, he still acts with something like a necessity of nature.[17] While it is true that one could affirm a necessity of nature relative to God's decree and point out that the act of volition would still originate in God and not somewhere else, there is still the problem of the act of cognition, volition, and enjoyment being elicited by something else and having to terminate on some other existent in order for God to be fulfilled. Such a necessary termination would imply that God's own goodness is not sufficient for God and not sufficiently

---

17. See, e.g., Jonathan Edwards, *Concerning the End for Which God Created the World*. On Edwards's position, see Crisp, *Jonathan Edwards on God and Creation*, chap. 7.

shared already in the divine processions. Thus, Aquinas rightly observes that "because the goodness of God is perfect and can be without others, because nothing of perfection accrues to him from others, it follows that his willing things other than himself is not absolutely necessary."[18] Or, as Barth puts it, in God there is no "urgent necessity to stand in a relationship of reciprocity to something other outside Himself." The creature's existence is "superfluous," an overflow of God's fullness.[19] A sufficiently capacious understanding of God's aseity will therefore acknowledge that God's knowing and willing and loving are complete with reference to God himself and do not have to assume a reference toward creatures in order to be fulfilled. By implication, God's direction of his knowledge, will, and love toward the world in his decree is not something that fulfills or constitutes God's being or life.

(2) The immanent activity and fulfillment of God is opened up further by God's revelation of the processions of the Son and Spirit. The scriptural testimony to the Son's procession, which was discussed in chapter 2 (the Spirit's procession appears in chap. 5) underscores that God's knowledge and will are active in God himself without reference to the world and that God's goodness is eternally shared in the love and fellowship of the divine persons. There is a significant tradition in orthodox trinitarianism that explicates the procession of the Son as a distinctly intellective sort of procession and the procession of the Spirit as a distinctly volitional sort of procession. In Aquinas's reasoning, if the processions are immanent actions, and if the immanent actions of an "intellectual nature" are an "action of intellect" and an "action of will," then the procession of the Son or the Word is a procession "according to intelligible action" and the procession of the Spirit is a procession "according to the operation of the will" or a "procession of love."[20] The Reformed author Bartholomäus Keckermann follows a Thomistic pattern of thought here and asserts that in God's knowledge of himself there is a "conception" of the Word and in God's willing and loving himself, particularly in the Father and Son loving one another, there is a procession of the Spirit as "most perfect love."[21]

In my judgment, while this approach to the processions may have an illustrative use in the doctrine of the Trinity, it should not bear the weight

18. Aquinas, *ST* Ia.19.3 corp. (235). To clarify, if God willed to create the world with a "necessity of nature," his willing in that case would have an "absolute" necessity (the same sort of necessity the divine nature itself has). The kind of necessity that does apply here is a "hypothetical" or "suppositional" necessity: a necessity that is not absolute but turns on a free decision that subsequently cannot be revoked.

19. Barth, *CD*, IV.1, 201.

20. Aquinas, *ST* Ia.27.2 (311). For more on the development of these lines of thinking, see Friedman, *Intellectual Traditions at the Medieval University*.

21. Keckermann, *Systema s.s. theologiae*, 1.3 (72–76).

of argument for the doctrine of the processions.[22] Yet, even if it may be un-necessary to assert that the Son proceeds in a distinctly intellective manner while the Spirit proceeds in a distinctly volitional manner, it remains that the knowledge and will of God are active in the communication and love involved in the processions. The Father communicates the divine knowledge to the Son (John 6:46; 7:29), and the Father and Son have a unique knowledge of one another (Matt. 11:25–27). The Son is the shining forth of the Father's glory and the Father's perfect image and thus the object of the Father's love "before the foundation of the world" (John 17:5, 24; Heb. 1:3). It is viable at this point to speak of the love of God in both the absolute and the relative aspects of trinitarian doctrine. Owen aptly points out that "God's loving of himself absolutely as God is nothing but his eternal blessed acquiescence in the holy, self-sufficing properties of his nature." Yet there is also an "ineffable mutual love of the blessed persons in the holy Trinity, which Jesus Christ wonderfully sets out in John xvii."[23]

On the one hand, in the activity of the divine will in the Father's genera-tion of the Son, there is no use of the will that precedes the generation, no antecedent freedom of the divine will as though the Father might not have generated the Son. Such a claim would imply that the Father was indifferent to the Son's existence and then made the Son along with created beings. In-stead, Athanasius clarifies, "begetting his own Word from himself by nature [ἐξ αὐτοῦ φύσει], he does not deliberate beforehand [οὐ προβουλεύεται]." Indeed, the Father always acts *with* his Word in his counsel. But this does not mean that the Father generated the Son by a necessity that runs contrary to his will (ἀνάγκῃ καὶ μὴ θέλων). The Son is the Son "of the essence of the Father" (τῆς οὐσίας τοῦ πατρός) and "according to nature" (κατὰ φύσιν), but this does not entail that the Son's generation is against the Father's will (παρὰ γνώμην, ἀθέλητός) any more than God being essentially good or merciful is against God's will. Though the Father does not possess a "preceding will" (προηγουμένην βούλησιν), the Father, who is "generative by nature" (τῇ φύσει γεννητικὸς), does indeed willingly generate and love the Son.[24]

Thus, on the other hand, the negation of a "preceding will" does not stipulate a prior idleness in God. Peter Lombard strikes a helpful balance in reasoning that while the Father does not generate with a "preceding will"

22. Regarding the due caution about specifying the exact manner of generation and spiration in God, cf. John of Damascus, *Expos. fidei* 1.8 (25–26). For cautious discussion of analogies in the Reformed orthodox authors, see, e.g., Ames, *Medulla theologica*, 1.5.15–16 (16–17); Turretin, *Inst.*, 3.29.31 (1:332); 3.31.3 (1:339); Owen, *Hebrews*, 3:91–92.

23. Owen, *Posthumous Sermons, Part IV* 22 (613–14).

24. Athanasius, *Oratio III*, 60–67 (372–81). See also Gregory Nazianzen, *Discours 27–31*, 29.2, 6–8 (178–80, 186–92).

(*voluntate praecedenti*), he does still generate with a certain activity of the will. Just as the Father generates as powerful, as good, as wise (*potens genuit, et bonus genuit, et sapiens genuit, et huiusmodi*), so he generates as willing (*volens genuit*).[25] If one who is God (i.e., the Son) cannot be brought into being by a contingent act of will, then the Father generates the Son with a "necessity of nature."[26] Yet the necessary action does not exclude but rather includes the divine volition eternally operating under the Father's relation to the Son and in the Father's enjoyment of the Son. In this sense, the Son is generated not "by the will of the Father" but "by the Father who is willing."[27]

In some significant authors of the Christian tradition the mutual love of the Father and Son proceeds hypostatically as the Holy Spirit, who is regarded as the "bond of love" between the Father and Son and the one by whom the Father and Son love each other.[28] Some of the early Reformed writers reject this approach, while others express an openness to it.[29] The argument here does not turn on this approach to the Holy Spirit as the bond of love, nor does it preclude that approach. The point here is simply that the trinitarian life of God confirms that the divine knowledge, will, and love are not idle without God's decision to create the world and take on flesh for our redemption.[30] Furthermore, if there are no parts in God, then the activity of God's intellect and will with reference to God himself would preclude inactive potency or idleness in God altogether. For really distinct parts would be required in order for God to have mutually exclusive modes of being like actuality, on the one hand, and inactive potency or idleness, on the other.[31] But God does not have

25. Lombard, *Sent.* 1.6 (89–91).

26. Cf. Zanchi, *De natura Dei*, 3.4 (356).

27. Polanus, *Syntagma*, 3.5 (215). Though the Father does not will the Son with a *libertas antecedens*, he does will the Son with a *libertas concomitans*: not an indifference toward the Son's subsisting but a freedom from outward compulsion that the Father has as he rests in the Son (cf. Aquinas, *ST* Ia.41.2 [422–23]; Mastricht, *TPT*, 2.15.14 [160]).

28. See Augustine, *De trin.* 15.17.27–31 (501–7); Aquinas, *ST* Ia.37.1–2 (387–90). Cf. Levering, *Engaging the Doctrine of the Holy Spirit*, 51–70.

29. Polanus (*Syntagma*, 2.22 [173]) flatly says that "Holy Scripture nowhere teaches this" and goes on to list certain logical problems with it. By contrast, despite his reluctance to provide details on the processions of the Son and Spirit, Owen speaks of the "ineffable, eternal love that the Father had unto the Son, and the Son unto the Father, by the Spirit" (*Posthumous Sermons, Part IV* 22 [613]).

30. To the extent that the theological commitments of patristic, scholastic, and Protestant orthodox theologians are reflected in such a statement, it runs contrary to Barth's claim that these theologians could not properly identify God as "the living God" since, according to Barth, they sought to conceive of God without respect to his decision for the economy of salvation (see *CD*, II.1, 79).

31. On the mutual exclusivity or "privative opposition" of actuality and inactive potency, see Aquinas, *Super Sent.* 1.8.3.1 ad 2 (1:212); Aquinas, *SCG* 1.16 (44); Alsted, *Metaphysica*, 1.13 (122, 132).

parts, since God is neither composed by something else nor held together by a more ultimate modal system. Thus, God is completely active in himself and without unactualized potential.

(3) Given God's perfect goodness and self-sufficiency and given the perfect, mutual love of the Father, Son, and Holy Spirit, God himself is the only absolutely necessary object of the divine will. Consequently, any divine willing of the creature's existence will be directed not toward enriching God's goodness but toward communicating and manifesting God's goodness.[32] The termination of the divine will on any creaturely object is accordingly a free termination. However, it might be asked whether the pure actuality of God and the consequent denial of passive potency in God would circle back to undermine the freedom of God and the contingency of creation and the incarnation. For if God is pure act, he has no unactualized potential that might be taken to ground the freedom of his determination for creation and salvation, which means that his essential, necessary actuality is the actuality with which he decrees the world and brings it into being.[33]

To respond to this question, I would offer the following three points.[34] First, given that God is the God of eternal wisdom and triune love, it is clear that he cannot be without his act of knowing and willing.[35] But this does not entail that God must terminate his act of knowing and willing upon this or that creaturely object or, indeed, upon any creaturely object at all. Since he is a God who knows and wills, he necessarily wills something, but he could will only himself (i.e., delight and repose in himself) and choose not to create anything. In this regard, a number of early Reformed authors observe that God's decree to create the world is necessary with respect to the decree's "foundation and exercise" (i.e., relative to God's act of willing itself), but free with respect to the decree's "specification and termination" (i.e., its direction toward this or that created object, or any created object at all).[36]

Second, a complementary way of expressing the point is to clarify that while the act or actuality itself of the decree is identical with God's own act

32. Cf., e.g., Turretin, *Inst.*, 3.14.8 (1:242).

33. A number of recent authors have sought to address this question (or something like it) in terms of whether God's simplicity and pure actuality entail a "modal collapse" in which the necessity of God's own being and actuality overrides the contingency of creation. See the discussion in Duby, *Divine Simplicity*, 193–95. Note also Mullins, "Simply Impossible," 194–99; Tomaszewski, "Collapsing the Modal Collapse Argument"; Nemes, "Divine Simplicity Does Not Entail Modal Collapse"; Lenow, "Shoring Up Divine Simplicity."

34. I have sought to develop a response to this difficult question elsewhere, including *God in Himself*, 52–54, 221–23.

35. See Mastricht, *TPT*, 3.1.21 (276).

36. See, e.g., Alsted, *Theologia naturalis*, 1.16 (140); Voetius, *Select. disp., pars prima*, 1.13 (249–51); Turretin, *Inst.*, 3.14.11 (1:243); 4.1.13, 16 (1:343–44).

of being and is thus necessary, the tendency of the act to this or that object is not intrinsic to God's own act of being and is thus free. That is, no particular outgoing tendency or termination is built into or included in God's own act of being. Any such outgoing tendency or relation is ontologically subsequent to God's own necessary act of being, knowing, and willing and is thus taken up freely by God.[37] The tendency *ad extra* is ontologically subsequent to God's own act of being, knowing, and willing because of God's perfect goodness and self-sufficiency. Because God does not gain something from creatures, he does not have to complete himself by terminating his actuality or activity on creatures. His being therefore does not entail the being of creation and is in this particular sense "naturally indifferent" to creation.[38] Indeed, it is not inactive potential in the willing subject but rather the subject having perfect goodness and fulfillment in himself that grounds the freedom to do one thing or another (in this case, to create and act in the world or not to create and act in the world).[39]

Third, if it is the case that God's decretive assumption of a relation to us is entirely free and yet also wrought by an actuality that is identical with God's own act of being, then we are in a position to reiterate something that was said above about the scriptural teaching on election: we cannot get back to a time when God had not yet chosen us in Christ. We can affirm the freedom of the act of election and do so without having to moor this freedom in a scenario where God would have to transition from idleness to act or would have to proceed through a succession of moments before coming to the decision to be our God in Christ. The decree is not necessary, but it is eternal.[40] And because the act of decreeing is nothing but God's own act of knowing and willing turned toward the contingent order, the God who has determined to live in fellowship with us is the same God who is preveniently complete in himself.

In this section, I have sought to confirm that God's act of being, knowing, and willing is perfect in the triune love of God without reference to the economy or created being. I have also sought to confirm that this does not conflict with the scriptural teaching on God's eternal decree. In the decree, God directs his self-sufficient actuality toward created being and assumes a relation to created being, so the decree is free but also eternal. Indeed, though

---

37. If space permitted, one might explore whether God taking up such a tendency would still imply some transition from prior potency to actuality. For arguments that this is not the case, see Duby, *God in Himself*, 222n106; Duby, "Goodness, Gratitude, and Divine Freedom."

38. See Turretin, *Inst.*, 4.2.13 (1:346); Mastricht, *TPT*, 3.1.21 (276).

39. Cf. Aquinas, *De pot.* 3.15 ad 7 (84); Aquinas, *SCG* 1.82 (228). Maccovius comments that inactive potential is the *radix contingentiae* ("root of contingency"), but this is an inactive potential in the patient or object of an action (*Metaphysica*, 1.9 [78]).

40. See again Turretin, *Inst.*, 4.2.13 (1:346).

God does not constitute himself as God by the decree or election, he is emphatically the same God with the direction or tendency of his act of willing toward the world and the incarnation. This point can be corroborated by considering the more specifically christological dimension of the decree—namely, the election of the Son and the *pactum salutis*.

IV. Election, Immutability, and the *Pactum Salutis*

The aim of this section is to address whether the scriptural teaching on the election of the Son coheres with and may even be illumined by God's independence of the economy and attendant divine attributes like immutability and simplicity. Does the eternal appointment of Christ to take on flesh in time place the unity and constancy of the person of Christ in conflict with the notion that there is a divine Son whose identity is already constituted without reference to the economy? Moreover, if the Bible's teaching on the trinitarian shape of the decree is expressed in the language of the *pactum salutis* (the covenant of redemption between the Father and Son), does this undermine the unity and simplicity of God and therefore also the unity of God's plan for salvation? Our main interlocutor here will be Karl Barth, whose critique and revision of earlier Protestant teaching on the decree and election lays out the key questions with characteristic verve. I will summarize the pertinent material in Barth and then offer a response to it in order to develop the claim that the scriptural teaching on the decree and the election of the Son fits well with a robust understanding of God's aseity, immutability, eternity, and simplicity.

A. Barth on Election, Christology, and Divine Immutability

There are several places throughout his *Church Dogmatics* where Barth discusses the significance of Christology for the doctrine of God. In some cases, Barth is highlighting an epistemological point he wants to make—namely, that we should not look beyond the incarnate Son to obtain knowledge of God. For Barth, human beings err when they attempt to describe God on their own and apart from God's self-revelation in Christ. "What God is as God, the divine individuality and characteristics, the *essentia* or 'essence' of God, is something which we shall encounter at the place where God deals with us as Lord and Saviour, or not at all." Though God is not "swallowed up" in his relation to the world, "God is who He is in His works." Thus, "in the development and explanation of the statement that God is we have always to keep exclusively to His works."[41] The meaning of "deity" is something that cannot be learned from contemplating "absolute being." It can be learned only in Christ.[42] Hence Barth is cautious about the teaching of the *extra Calvinisticum*, for in his view it may lead to "fatal speculation about the being and work of the λόγος ἄσαρκος, or a God whom we think we can know elsewhere, and whose divine being we can define elsewhere than in and from the contemplation of His presence and activity as the Word made flesh."[43]

Barth's emphasis on the decisiveness of the incarnation comes into focus in his discussion of the decree and election. In his discussion of election in II.2 and his discussion of the mission and obedience of the Son in IV.1, it is clear that Barth's concern is not merely epistemological but ontological as well. His line of thought yields certain statements that at least seem to suggest that the eternal identity of the Son within God's own being might be informed somehow by God's decision for the incarnation.[44] Barth deals with the question of whether there is a God or a divine Logos behind the decree, a Logos different from the incarnate Christ. In Barth's assessment, it is pastorally problematic to say that "the electing God himself is not Jesus Christ" and that Jesus only subsequently carries out the decree. For such a *decretum absolutum* opens up an "abyss of uncertainty" before a God "above and beyond Jesus Christ." There appears to be a capricious *beneplacitum Dei* ("good pleasure of God") behind the decree's "christological reference," which is left "standing in the air." The seemingly arbitrary christological focus of election means that the early Protestants' emphasis on Christ as the *speculum electionis* (the "mirror of election," the one in whom assurance of God's love and election can be found) turns out to be empty. Barth's response is to maintain that "Jesus Christ is the electing God." "In no depth of Godhead shall we encounter any other but Him." Indeed, "There is no such thing as Godhead in itself. Godhead is always the Godhead of the Father, the Son and the Holy Spirit.

41. Barth, *CD*, II.1, 260–62.
42. Barth, *CD*, IV.1, 177.
43. Barth, *CD*, IV.1, 181. The so-called *extra Calvinisticum* is the notion that the Son in his divine subsistence transcends the limitations of his own human flesh. It will be discussed further in chap. 4.
44. In speaking this way, I do not wish to choose a side in the recent debates about Barth's doctrine of election relative to divine aseity (on which see, e.g., McCormack, *Orthodox and Modern*, esp. part 3; Dempsey, *Trinity and Election in Contemporary Theology*; Molnar, *Faith, Freedom and the Spirit*, chaps. 5–6; Hunsinger, *Reading Barth with Charity*). In my view, Barth makes certain statements that sound as if he remains committed to God's independence of the economy and then other statements that sound as if he believes the Son's very identity is constituted by his eventual assumption of a human nature. For a level-headed treatment of Barth's thinking, see Wittman, *God and Creation in the Theology of Thomas Aquinas and Karl Barth*, chap. 6.

But the Father is the Father of Jesus Christ and the Holy Spirit is the Spirit of the Father and the Spirit of Jesus Christ." [45] Accordingly,

> there is no *decretum absolutum*. There is no such thing as a will of God apart from the will of Jesus Christ. Thus Jesus Christ is not only the *manifestatio* and *speculum nostrae praedestinationis*. And He is this not simply in the sense that our election can be known to us and contemplated by us only through His election, as an election which, like His and with His, is made (or not made) by a secret and hidden will of God. On the contrary Jesus Christ reveals to us our election as an election which is made by Him, by His will which is also the will of God. He tells us that He Himself is the One who elects us. [46]

In the beginning of IV.1, then, Barth stresses the inappropriateness of speaking about "the eternal Son or the eternal Word of God *in abstracto*." Barth still grants that such a person is "the content of a necessary and important concept in trinitarian doctrine" that points to the "free basis in the inner being and essence of God" for the act of election. Yet Barth also asserts that the eternal Son cannot have "another form than that which God Himself has given in willing to reveal Himself and to act outwards." According to the will of God, "the eternal Son of God is Jesus Christ as He lived and died and rose again in time, and none other" ("*Der ewige Sohn Gottes ist . . . Jesus Christus, wie er in der Zeit lebte, starb und auferstand, und nur er*"). The Son *is* the eternal decision of God to be God for us ("*Er ist . . . die von Ewigkeit her gefallene Entscheidung Gottes*"). The decision was made freely by God but also "bindingly," so we cannot "go back on it" or "bracket that which God has actually done." In short, "Jesus Christ is the content and form of the first and eternal Word of God." [47]

Barth's insistence on the correspondence between the economic activity of the Son and the being and identity of the Son in God's own life is developed further in his treatment of the Son's mission and obedience in IV.1. [48] To ensure the true deity and immutability of the Son in his economic activity (and thus the efficacy of the Son's mission), Barth argues that the Son's proper mode of being that constitutes his identity is marked by an obedience to the Father that anticipates his obedience in the economy. The true God alone can save.

45. Barth, *CD*, II.2, 63–67, 115.
46. Barth, *CD*, II.2, 115.
47. Barth, *CD*, IV.1, 52–53; Barth, *KD*, IV.1, 55. Cf. von Balthasar, *Theo-Drama*, 47–48, 256.
48. An earlier (and different) attempt to work out the correspondence between the historical Christ and the eternal being and activity of God can be found in Schleiermacher, *The Christian Faith*, §97 (594–95, 602–3), §105 (679–82). I am not positing a genetic relationship between Schleiermacher's and Barth's accounts here, but comparing and contrasting them might be a fruitful exercise.

Therefore, if Christ were an attenuated version of God, he could not save. Thus, there can be no "cleft or rift or gulf in God himself, between His being and essence in Himself and His activity and work as Reconciler of the world." Positively, only if God is "truly and altogether in Christ" can Christ accomplish our reconciliation with God. To secure the consistency and immutability of the Son in his eternal relation to the Father and in his economic activity, Barth contends that the "self-humbling of Jesus Christ as an act of obedience cannot be alien to God." Barth acknowledges that "to speak of obedience which takes place in God Himself" is "difficult" and "elusive," but he thinks it necessary to do so. According to Barth, there is in God an eternal obedience and subordination of the Son and thus an "above" that pertains to the Father and a "below" that pertains to the Son. Without this eternal subordination, the filial obedience that takes place in the economy would concern only a secondary or "improper being of Godhead" and would therefore not "bring us into touch with God Himself." With this eternal subordination affirmed, there is in Christ the "most proper and direct and immediate presence and action of the one true God." The Son's work in the incarnation, then, takes place not without correspondence to God's being but "in the strangely logical final continuation [in wunderbar konsequenter letzter Forsetzung] of the history in which He is God."[49]

Barth is aware that objections concerning "subordinationism" will arise at this point. Does the idea of eternal subordination not imply that there are two Gods, one who commands and a lesser one who obeys? Barth's initial response to the potential charge of subordinationism is to underscore that his approach will secure the original, undiminished being of God in Christ and avoid what he takes to be an implicit modalism that, in an effort to keep Christ's deity free from humiliation, renders the Christ who obeys the Father in the economy a mere "appearance" of deity. To flesh out Barth's logic, it seems that he takes the underlying assumption in this tacit "modalism" to be that only the Father's (unsubordinated) mode of being can be identified with true Godhead. Thus, the Son's mode of being is assimilated to the Father's and the Son's obedience in the economy is reduced to a mere outward appearance of deity. Barth next contends that an eternal subordination of the Son subverts "human ideas about the divine nature" but not necessarily the Son's divine nature itself. It is our responsibility to "find the key" to the concept of a "divine nature" in the person and work of Christ.[50]

---

49. Barth, *CD*, IV.1, 183–88, 192–210; Barth, *KD*, IV.1, 223. See also, *CD*, IV.2, 84–86.

50. Barth, *CD*, IV.1, 195–97, 199. For a recent summary and defense of Barth's subordination without subordinationism, see Sumner, "Obedience and Subordination in Karl Barth's Trinitarian Theology."

According to Barth, both the subordinationist move to reduce the humble Son to a secondary deity (or a creature) and the modalist move to insulate the Son's proper being from his humiliation and obedience are attempts to "evade the cross of Jesus Christ." But the mystery of the Son's eternal subordination that anticipates the cross should not be "juggled away." This leads to a reframing of God's unity, which "consists in the fact that in Himself He is both One who is obeyed and Another who obeys." God's is a unique unity, including more than one mode of being, a "living unity" with an "above" and a "below." Barth argues, then, that we will have to jettison the "all too human" tendency to associate subordination with "deprivation" or "inferiority." Rather than allow our human tendencies to dictate what must be true of God, we will have to allow the presence of subordination within the *homoousia* of the Father and Son to correct our tendencies. While our word "Son" can communicate the "natural determination of a son to subjection to a father, the self-evident presupposition that a son owes obedience to a father," this word comes short of adequately expressing that in God the Father and Son there are "different modes of one and the same personal God" whose fellowship is characterized by an "ontological necessity." Indeed, Barth clarifies that the meaning of the word "person" must be carefully considered in the doctrine of the Trinity. The divine "persons" with whom there is an "above" and "below" are not two "self-existent individuals" with "their own specific self-consciousness, cognition, volition, activity." Rather, the divine persons are "modes of being" of the one divine "subject."[51]

Barth's concerns about the being and identity of the Son in relation to the decree can be seen in his critique of the doctrine of the *pactum salutis* as well. It may be useful first to say a word about the *pactum salutis* prior to summarizing Barth's critique of it. The exegetical material treated in section II above has already invoked covenantal language to describe the Father's eternally giving to the Son a kingdom and a people over whom he is king (cf. esp. Luke 22:29–30). In Reformed orthodox thought, this covenantal aspect is often given expression in the doctrine of the *pactum salutis* or covenant of redemption between the Father and Son. Johannes Coccejus offers a typical definition of the doctrine. After first clarifying that it is a *pactum* involving not fallen humanity directly but rather a mediator for fallen human beings, Coccejus says the *pactum* is "the will of the Father giving a head and redeemer of a people foreknown, and the will of the Son setting himself up for this salvation to be procured," which has the *ratio* or formal character of an

51. Barth, *CD*, IV.1, 199–205, 209.

agreement or covenant (*conventio*).[52] Herman Witsius offers a similar definition. He writes that there are three "moments" of the *pactum* of the Father and Son that is the "foundation of our whole salvation." The first "moment" is found in the "eternal counsel of the Trinity," where "the Son of God from the Father, with the Holy Spirit approving, is constituted Savior of the human race, with this condition, that in the fullness of time he should be born of a woman and under the law, which the Son pledges himself to do."[53]

Barth challenges the doctrine of the *pactum salutis*, famously calling it "mythology." He defines the *pactum salutis* as "the free disposing of God the Father, by virtue of which He has once and for all ascribed to a chosen portion of sinful humanity righteousness and eternal life in the Son" with a "corresponding disposing of the Son of God in virtue of which He for His part has undertaken once and for all the cause of those sinful men who are elected to sonship." It is an "aspect of the decree of predestination," a "binding engagement" of "two divine partners, i.e., God with God." The discussion of the *pactum* in *Church Dogmatics* IV.1 takes place within Barth's broader critique of a seventeenth-century "federal theology" represented by figures like Coccejus. For Barth, Coccejus and other federal theologians erred in maintaining that God's "covenant of grace" comes into effect as an abrogation of a prior "covenant of nature" or "covenant of works" made with Adam. Barth finds this quite puzzling given that these theologians held that the covenant of grace was rooted in a *pactum* in God's own triune life, a *pactum* whose eternal institution "in the bosom of the Godhead itself" should logically have precluded any subordination of the covenant of grace to a covenant of works. "How was it possible to know of the eternal basis of the covenant of grace and then not to think exclusively in the light of it, to understand and present it as the one covenant of God, as though there were some other eternity in God or elsewhere, an eternity of human nature and its connexion with God and its law and the works of this law?" According to Barth, the subordination of the covenant of grace to a covenant of nature in fact downplays the heinousness of sin, for in the primacy of the covenant of grace it is evident that sin is nothing short of a "transgression of the law given to man as the predestined brother of the Son and child of the Father, as falling away from the special grace which the Creator had shown him from all eternity."[54]

However, Barth finds the early Reformed description of the doctrine of the *pactum salutis* to be problematic in its own right for three reasons. First, it

52. Coccejus, *Summa doctrinae*, 5.88 (85).
53. Witsius, *De oeconomia foederum Dei*, 2.3.2 (111).
54. Barth, *CD*, IV.1, 63–64.

assumes "the existence of a God who is righteous *in abstracto* and not free to be gracious from the very first, who has to bind to the fulfilment of His promise the fulfilment of certain conditions by man." It is then "only with the conclusion of this contract with Himself [i.e., the *pactum salutis*] that He ceases to be a righteous God *in abstracto* and becomes the God who in His righteousness is also merciful and therefore able to exercise grace." Within this framework, there is an essence of God that stands behind the covenant of grace, where, "in spite of this contract, His righteousness and mercy are secretly and at bottom two separate things." But, Barth emphasizes, there should not have to be a divine decree in order to secure the unity of God's righteousness and mercy toward us. A "strict looking to Jesus Christ" finds that in God there is a "righteous mercy and merciful righteousness from the very first," which precludes an "original covenant of works."[55]

Second, the notion of an "intertrinitarian pact as a contract between the persons of the Father and Son" presupposes that there are "two divine subjects" or, indeed, "two legal subjects who can have dealings," which is simply "mythology." "God is one God," "one subject," "one partner" whose other partner is the human race. Furthermore, the notion of a legal pact in God introduces a "dualism" that undermines the unconditional nature of the covenant of grace. For the presence of different "subjects" in God raises the specter of "a will of God the Father which originally and basically is different from the will of God the Son." God's will for salvation and the incarnation might turn out not to be the "first and final Word of God."

Third, the *pactum salutis* focuses on a relationship "of God with Himself" rather than God's relationship with humanity. In God's free and eternal act of election he is "no longer by Himself." He assumes "into unity with His own existence as God . . . the existence of the man whom He intends and loves from the very first," which is the existence of the man "in whom He wills to bind Himself with all other men." In other words, in the act of election "there pre-exists the Jesus Christ who . . . will become and be the Mediator of the covenant between God and men." Thus, in election "the Son of the Father is no longer just the eternal Logos, but as such, as very God from all eternity He is also the very God and very man He will become in time." According to Barth, because they missed this point and left open the possibility that "Jesus Christ was perhaps only a secondary and subsequent divine arrangement," Coccejus and the federal theologians could not truly say that Jesus was "the beginning of all the ways of God."[56]

---

55. Barth, *CD*, IV.1, 64–65.
56. Barth, *CD*, IV.1, 65–66.

While Barth frequently refers to God's freedom in the decree and election, a number of his statements about election, Christology, and divine immutability raise the following question: Given the importance of the correspondence between God's being and God's economic action, does notion of a divine completeness without reference to the economy put God's immutability at risk? While Barth certainly does not deny that God is *a se*, some of the material in the *Church Dogmatics* at least appears to suggest that Godhead as such includes God's act of turning toward the creature in election and the incarnation, which prompts discussion of whether the doctrine of God's aseity must stand in tension with God's immutability. For, it would seem, a God constituted without reference to the creature would have to undergo some sort of change in turning toward the creature and taking on human flesh. The next subsection offers a response to Barth on election and immutability and will argue that the decisiveness of God choosing to be God for us in Christ does not undermine God's self-referential completeness and may in fact be illumined by it. I will attempt to do this under the following six points.

B. Response

(1) It will be wise to recognize the importance of some of the key points Barth wants to uphold. He is eager to uphold the goodness and trustworthiness of God rather than leave Christian believers to wonder whether there is a God behind the God of the covenant who might not truly be for us. Consequently, Barth is rightly concerned to emphasize the decisiveness of God's electing grace as something God will never rescind and something that we cannot "go back on." In this connection, it important to uphold that Christ is the *speculum electionis*. In addition, Barth is rightly concerned to maintain the full deity and immutability of Christ as requisite to the fulfillment of the Savior's revealing and saving work. These are crucial points to make in our theology today, but I think the way in which Barth attempts to establish and expound them is problematic for a few reasons that I will set out here.[57]

(2) Barth suggests that if Christ himself—not just the Son but seemingly the Son somehow antecedently determined to take on flesh—is not the electing God, then this will open up a capricious *beneplacitum Dei* behind Christ and undermine Christ as the mirror of election. However, this seems to assume that, without an act of election that informs God's life, God would be unsettled in his goodness, love, and holiness. But a strong doctrine of divine aseity entails the opposite: God is perfect in goodness and love and holiness

---

57. For another exercise in bringing early Reformed thought on election and Christology into dialogue with Barth, see Gibson, "A Mirror for God and for Us."

with or without the act of election and thus entirely good and trustworthy in whatever he may will. For whatever God may will, he wills it in impeccable goodness and purity (Ps. 119:68; James 1:13, 17; 1 John 1:5). Whatever God does, he "cannot do anything unbecoming of his holiness and goodness." "He doth whatsoever he will . . . but he cannot do what he cannot will" (e.g., "will any unrighteous thing" or "punish an innocent").[58]

God's goodness just *is* God's essence, which means that God's essence is "entirely alien from unjust severity, cruelty, tyranny, pride."[59] Though God did not choose to create the world with a necessity of nature, his own communicative goodness is the rationale for creation.[60] He creates to share what is good (Gen. 1:31). He does not prefer anger but delights in steadfast love (Mic. 7:18). He does not take pleasure in death, so in an important sense the affliction of human beings is not from his heart (Lam. 3:32–33; Ezek. 18:23, 32). In this respect, wrath and judgment are not basic to the origin of created being (cf. John 3:17). God rejoices in doing good to his creatures, so it is principally the conferring of blessing that comes from his heart (Jer. 32:40–41).[61] Thus, it is a recurring axiom in early Reformed theology that God is "more inclined to mercy than to wrath" (*pronior est ad misericordiam quam iram*).[62] As God's "relative goodness," mercy is his "darling attribute which he most delights in."[63] When God exhibits his wrath, it is considered to be a "strange work" (using the language of Isa. 28:21), an application of God's righteousness and holiness that assumes certain external conditions wrought by another—namely, human persistence in the hatred of God and those who bear God's image (cf., e.g., Gen. 15:16; 18:22–33; Jer. 44:22).[64] It is not an affront to God's goodness to condemn any sinner who refuses to repent, but this does not render God cruel or capricious, and, indeed, it is why

58. Charnock, *The Existence and Attributes of God*, 2:27–28. Cf. Mastricht, *TPT*, 2.15.31 (166).

59. Zanchi, *De natura Dei*, 2.1 (68).

60. On which, see, e.g., Aquinas, *ST* Ia.19.3 (234–35); Owen, *Christologia* 4 (59); Mastricht, *TPT*, 2.15.8 (159); 2.17.4, 12 (179–80).

61. See further Thigpen, "The Storm of YHWH," 425–28.

62. Ursinus, *Doctrinae Christianae compendium*, 125; cf. Zanchi, *De natura Dei*, 2.1 (68–69); Watson, *A Body of Practical Divinity*, 53; Turretin, *Inst.*, 20.6.16 (3:673). In addition to other biblical texts included above, this discussion often incorporates texts like Exod. 34:6–7; Pss. 103:8–14; 145:8–9; Isa. 55:6–9; Hosea 11:8–9; Mic. 6:8; Eph. 2:4.

63. Watson, *A Body of Practical Divinity*, 53.

64. Some recent readings of Isa. 28:21 do not support the view that it is God's judgment per se that is called "strange" in this context, but others do suggest that the judgment may in fact be what is called "strange" in the sense that God would ordinarily display his kindness toward his chosen people but is here bringing judgment upon them (cf. Oswalt, *The Book of Isaiah: Chapters 1–39*, 520; Smith, *Isaiah 1–39*, 489–90).

grace is truly gracious. And since God cannot deny himself or contradict his own purpose (2 Tim. 2:13; Heb. 6:17–18), he cannot abrogate his decision to save a multitude of sinners in Christ, which is the foundation of Christian assurance and the reason to set forth Christ as the mirror of election.[65]

(3) The way in which Barth seeks to anchor the assurance of God's love in election raises questions about God's freedom in creation and salvation. At least in certain places in the *Church Dogmatics*, it is not so much the *Logos asarkos* but the *Logos incarnandus* (already predestined to be incarnate) who acts in election. On the one hand, Barth wishes to uphold the notion of the Son as such and without reference to the incarnation as a necessary placeholder that reminds us of God's freedom in election. On the other hand, he insists that Jesus Christ is the "content and form" of the eternal Son. If by using the phrase "Jesus Christ" in a statement like this Barth intends to signify the person of the Son with respect to his assuming the office of mediator and being both divine and human, then it would seem as though Barth may have included the incarnation (and, by implication, God's decision to create the world and to permit the sin according to which there is need of a mediator) in that which eternally constitutes the Son as the person that he is. Without the incarnation, it would seem, the Son would not be the Son. This appears to be corroborated where Barth says that "there is no such thing as Godhead in itself." Whether that in fact is Barth's line of reasoning or not, the point is that if it were, it would not fit well with Barth's ongoing insistence that election is a free act. If the decision for the salvation of sinners were a necessary entailment or even constituent of the Son's hypostatic identity and of God's essence, then it would follow that the act of election

---

65. On the one hand, God is not indebted to us or obligated to save us (Rom. 11:35), which means his will to save is free and gracious. On the other hand, Ursinus rightly points out, if God has created the world to communicate his goodness and love to the praise of his glory, and if God would not create the human race "in vain," then, given God's decision to permit sin, "it is necessary that some should be delivered." Since God could have chosen not to create the world or permit sin, this necessity of salvation is a *necessitas ex hypothesi* (*Doctrinae Christianae compendium*, 124). Intriguingly, Ursinus is prepared to take the discussion a step further and suggest that human reason "even without the word of God" can discover that it is at least "probable" that there will be some deliverance of human beings: (a) because it does not appear to be true that a "most excellent creature" should be made for "the greatest and indeed perpetual misery" and (b) because it does not appear to be true that God should institute his law without it ever being fulfilled (125). Building on Ursinus's discussion, one could say that God simply is not the sort of God who would create the world only in order to damn all human beings. To be sure, there is nothing in sinful creatures themselves that merits salvation. At the same time, given the sort of God that God is, if he decides to create, he will do so principally in order to communicate his goodness and love and not principally or merely in order to destroy wicked persons.

(and, indeed, the foreordination of sin) would be marked by a necessity of nature on God's part.[66]

(4) Barth's affirmation of an eternal obedience of the Son is open to serious criticism.[67] On the one hand, Barth is correct in saying that it is because God is God that God the Son can take on flesh.[68] In my view, however, the logic of this freedom to take on flesh does not require Barth's postulate of the Son's eternal obedience. God is not one more being within the order of created being, where natures and individuals are distinct from one another by lacking something that another has. God is distinct from all else not by lacking something but by having everything, which is to say by virtue of being the God of infinite, ineradicable plenitude and goodness. Not subject to corruption and not situated within the order of created being, God does not stand in a competitive relation to the creature and can and does, in the person of the Son, assume into union with himself a created nature without losing or changing what he always was as God.

On the other hand, Barth goes beyond this and argues that God the Son can become human because his eternal mode of subsisting is already characterized by the sort of obedience that the Son undertakes in the economy, clearing away any potential dissonance between the Son in himself and the Son in his incarnate life and thus any obstacle to the full presence of God in the humble Christ. But the idea that the Son's eternal mode of being is characterized by humility and obedience conflicts with the apostle Paul's account of the incarnation. In 2 Corinthians 8:9, the apostle writes, "For you know the gift of our Lord Jesus Christ, that on account of you he became poor although he was rich, in order that you by his poverty might become rich." The "poverty" of the Son's human life is contrasted with his divine life. Though the Son was not "prideful" in the sense of having an unduly high estimation of himself, neither was he lowly prior to assuming a human nature. In Paul's teaching, the incarnation is what inaugurates the Son's humble manner of life, and it is the union of what is humble with what is eternally rich and exalted (the Son's divine subsistence) that renders the incarnation such a striking event and a strong motive for humble service on the part of Christian believers.

66. Offering this critique does not necessarily imply an ontological "rift" between a *Logos asarkos* and *Logos incarnandus*. There need not be multiple actualities in God's life—which would generate a temporal succession in God—in order to affirm that God's assumption of a relation to creation is ontologically subsequent to his own act of being and therefore contingent (see section III above).

67. For an example of a critique by a sympathetic interpreter of Barth, see Molnar, *Faith, Freedom, and the Spirit*, chap. 7. See also White, *The Incarnate Lord*, chap. 6; Mansini, "Can Humility and Obedience Be Trinitarian Realities?"

68. E.g., *CD*, IV.1, 12, 203–4.

The same applies in Philippians 2:6–8: believers must think like Christ, "who, being in the form of God, considered it not ἁρπαγμός [perhaps something to be grasped or something invoked to avoid service] to be equal with God, but he emptied himself, taking the form of a servant, being made in the likeness of human beings. Being found in appearance as a man, he humbled himself, becoming obedient until death, even death on a cross." The adversative at the beginning of 2:7 ("*but* he emptied himself") indicates that the subsistence in the *forma Dei* contrasts with the *forma servi* in which the Son obeys the Father. The Son "empties himself" *by* taking the *forma servi*. The emptying *is* the assumption, the addition of the human nature in the unity of his person. And the humiliation occurs by the obedience until death. If God as God cannot die and if this is an obedience until death, then it is a human obedience. Thus, Barth's view of the Son's eternal lowliness and obedience appears to weaken the drama and novelty of the Son's incarnation and humiliation. If the Son's obedience until death were a "logical continuation" of the Son's eternal mode of subsisting, that seems to undermine the shock and scandal of the cross. And it is not enough that, on Barth's proposal, the cross would still disrupt our expectations of what an exalted God would or would not do. In the apostle's teaching, the cross is *in reality* unlike the Son's eternal subsistence. To say this is not to "evade the cross" but, on the contrary, to underscore its truly astonishing character as a revelation of God's love for us.

Certainly, the fact of the incarnation requires us to affirm that God as God has the freedom and power to take on human flesh without ceasing to be God. What it does not require us to affirm—and what is contrary to the teaching of Paul—is the idea that God could take on flesh because there was already in God an eternal lowliness and submission. It seems to me that Barth is led to his construal of the fittingness of the Son's earthly humiliation by an unspoken presupposition that the focal point of unity in the incarnation is not merely the person but, in some direct way, the person's divinity and humanity as such. It seems that, for Barth, what pertains to the Son as God and what pertains to the Son as man must somehow be assimilated to one another in order to secure the full deity of Christ. But Scripture requires us to say only that the one person of Christ is both divine and human. It does not require us to say that Christ's divine life or Godhead is like his humanity.[69] Indeed, if the brief exegesis of 2 Corinthians 8:9 and Philippians 2:6–8 above is on the right track, Scripture actually requires us to say that they are not alike. The unity in the incarnation is located in the person himself, not directly in

---

69. It is true that the Son's procession from the Father establishes the fittingness of his being sent by the Father, but Barth is going beyond this more modest claim here.

the essences.[70] The noncompetitive relation between God and created being taken together with the hypostatic or personal mode of union enables us to confirm the full deity of the incarnate Son without taking up Barth's proposal of eternal submission.

(5) Barth's defense of his position against the charge of subordinationism also is open to criticism. He actually begins his defense against the charge in IV.1 by going on the offensive, arguing that a more traditional view that denies eternal subordination implies modalism. However, it seems to me that Barth's accusation that this view leads to modalism presupposes the logic of Barth's own proposal and superimposes that logic on the view that he disputes. Barth's logic, according to which the Son must eternally obey the Father in order for the Son to be fully God or fully himself in his incarnate obedience, need not be taken up in order to maintain the full deity of Christ and in fact was not taken up in the view that he critiques. If an eternal obedience of the Son is not needed to constitute or distinguish the Son as the person that he is, then (*pace* modalism) without that eternal obedience the Son still has his own mode of subsisting in God that is distinct from the Father's. Subordination and superordination are just not distinguishing factors in God's eternal being, so the rejection of their presence in God's eternal being does not entail modalism. Likewise, if eternal obedience is not needed for the Son himself to take on flesh and become obedient as man, then (*pace* modalism) without that eternal obedience the Son himself still can and does take on flesh, so that his eternal mode of subsisting is truly communicated to the flesh and the incarnation is not a mere appearance of a divine person.

Barth also argues that we should submit our initial ideas about divinity to God's revelation and allow them to be challenged by the presence of subordination within the *homoousia* of the Father and Son. While we certainly should submit our thinking about God to God's own revelation, Scripture does not teach an eternal obedience of the Son. It teaches us that the Son was with the Father, begotten of the Father, and loved by the Father, but there are no texts that either state or imply that, in his hypostatically constitutive relation to the Father and without reference to his economic office, the Son is obedient to the Father. In effect, Barth has asked his readers to submit their thinking not so much to Scripture but to his own inference that there must be a subordination in Christ's divine subsistence in order to secure his full deity in the incarnation. But, as noted above, Barth's deduction does

70. For discussion of the "mode of union" in the incarnation, see, e.g., Aquinas, *ST* IIIa.2.1 (22–23); Keckermann, *Systema s.s. theologiae*, 3.2 (175); Turretin, *Inst.*, 13.6.3, 8 (2:337, 339); Mastricht, *TPT*, 5.4.7 (538). Note also Levering, "Christ, the Trinity, and Predestination," 269–70.

not necessarily follow from the full deity of the incarnate Son and, indeed, conflicts with Pauline teaching.

There is also a problem in Barth's discussion of the Son's obedience occurring within the being of the one God who has only one will. While Barth takes it to be the case that the difficulty of subordination in the Godhead is alleviated by the unity of essence, understanding, and volition in the Trinity, the idea of an eternal obedience is actually precluded by this unity. The idea of an eternal submission and obedience of the Son implies that in some way the Father, in possession of an authority (a right of commanding) that the Son himself does not have, lays down a rule of life to which the Son must subsequently conform in his proper mode of subsisting. The structure of command and obedience involves some interval of determination and assent, but such an interval is precluded by the one volition of the Father and Son. The one volition means that the Father does not make any prior determinations to which the Son must subsequently assent and conform. Of course, the one volition is modified by each of the persons according to his personal property, but that modification does not permit the discrete acts of willing involved in command and obedience.

If Barth were to respond that this line of thought does not take seriously his contention that the eternal submission of the Son would be predicated of the Son in a manner that befits the divine unity, then I think it would be important, first, to comment briefly on how the analogical nature of theological language works. Recognizing that there is a profound distinction between God and created being and that our language can therefore apply to him in only an analogical way does not authorize us to think that just any predicate can be ascribed to God in the hope that it might be sufficiently adjusted to suit him. The nature of God's life does in fact rule out some predicates altogether (e.g., divine corporeality, complexity, ignorance). In this case, the numerical unity of volition in the Trinity rules out a command-obedience structure in the eternal relation of the Father and Son. One might still suggest, since the knowledge of the Trinity depends on scriptural revelation, that the Bible could encourage us to rethink this presupposition about command and obedience, but the Bible does not do that. For, second, the revelation of the Trinity in Scripture does not ascribe to the Father a right of commanding that he alone might have in his eternal, personally constitutive relation to the Son and that the Son might lack in his eternal, personally constitutive relation to the Father.[71] And the eternal relations of the persons of which Scripture speaks so circumspectly should not be loaded with all the factors

71. This point will be discussed further in chap. 6.

of human fatherhood and sonship. While Barth asserts that the language of sonship by itself entails obedience,[72] to fill in paternity and filiation in God with such human phenomena will open the doctrine of the Trinity up to false inferences—for example, that the Father must be older or wiser than the Son in accordance with the ordinary way of human paternity and sonship. This is why Aquinas, for example, clarifies that if an *auctoritas* (which could be translated "authority") is predicated of one divine person relative to another, the term expresses not a relation of command but only the relation of origin: "There is no *auctoritas* in the divine persons of one toward another except insofar as one is eternally from another."[73]

In view of the unity of the divine essence, understanding, and volition, John of Damascus, for example, observes that in God there is "one authority, one dominion" (μία ἐξουσία, μία κυριότης).[74] In sharing the one essence and will, the Father and Son share the one divine authority or right of ruling and commanding. If sharing the one divine essence and will entails sharing the one divine authority, then the idea that there is a divine authority that the Father alone possesses in opposition to the Son denies that something included in God's essence applies to the Son. If that is so, then the idea of an eternal obedience of the Son in fact cannot be uncoupled from inferiority. There is no safe "functional" subordination at this point. Not to share the authority of the Father is to be a creature. "There are two things, creation and deity, creation, on the one hand, having been ordered to service and obedience, and deity, on the other hand, ruling and sovereign."[75]

(6) Finally, Barth's critique of the *pactum salutis* should be addressed. There are several things that might be said along the way about his critique of "federal theology" in general, but our focus here is primarily on the *pactum salutis* itself.[76] First, it needs to be emphasized that the doctrine of the *pactum salutis* does not envision a God who is righteous and merciful only *in abstracto* prior to forming a "contract with himself." The use of the phrase *in abstracto* has to be handled carefully here. If by *in abstracto* Barth means

72. It might have been expected that Barth would judge such an assertion to be an iteration of "natural theology" (in his pejorative use of that phrase).

73. Aquinas, *Contra errores Graecorum* 2.23 (97). Cf. *De pot.* 10.1 ad 17 (256).

74. John of Damascus, *Expos. fidei* 1.8 (19).

75. Basil, *Contre Eunome* 2.31 (2:128); cf. 3.2 (2:152).

76. For another influential critique of "federal theology" after Barth's time, see J. Torrance, "Covenant or Contract?" For efforts to clarify the development of covenant theology (including the *pactum salutis*) in early Reformed thought, see, e.g., Venema, "Recent Criticisms of the 'Covenant of Works'"; van Asselt, *The Federal Theology of Johannes Cocceius*; Beach, *Christ and the Covenant*; Muller, "Toward the *Pactum Salutis*"; Trueman, "From Calvin to Gillespie"; Fesko, *The Covenant of Redemption*; Woo, *The Promise of the Trinity*. A helpful constructive essay on the *pactum salutis* is Swain, "Covenant of Redemption."

only that when we consider God's essential perfections in ontological priority to the decree, we are considering them in abstraction from or without mental reference to the economy, then there is no problem with the phrase *in abstracto* in this limited epistemological sense. However, Barth's use of the phrase *in abstracto* may be suggesting more than this. It may be suggesting that the catholic account of God taken up by the Reformed orthodox implies that God's essential righteousness and goodness or mercy are ontologically separate from, and only in potency before, a more concrete form of the divine life that would follow on God's decision to create humanity and save sinners. If that is the drift of Barth's use of the phrase *in abstracto*, then it is an inaccurate description of early Reformed accounts of God. In the doctrine of God advocated by the early Reformed who developed the notion of the *pactum salutis*, each of God's perfections is fully actual and concrete in God even without respect to the economy. God's righteousness and goodness (inflected as mercy in relation to the creature) await no realization or concretion by way of the decree. Indeed, God's righteousness and goodness are really identical, so his righteousness is invariably good and his goodness invariably righteous. Thus, the *pactum salutis* does not imply that God's righteousness was not already characterized by goodness and mercy before the making of a "contract," or that God's righteousness was an obstacle to his mercy. Only as the one who is both righteous and merciful could he establish the *pactum* in the first place. Of course, it is still the case that God in his righteousness and goodness (or mercy) is not compelled or obligated to act in redemptive grace toward those who have broken his covenant and chosen a godless life, but, insofar as Barth would want to affirm the graciousness of grace, it seems that he would agree in some way.

Second, though Barth is right to deny that there are three wills in God, he neglects the exegetical material that pressed authors like Coccejus and Witsius to develop the doctrine of the *pactum salutis* even in connection with a strong affirmation of the numerical unity of God's will. On the one hand, Barth posits eternal obedience in God without specific scriptural evidence and then insists that its rough edges may be smoothed out by the unity of the divine will. On the other hand, Barth rejects the *pactum salutis* without engaging the pertinent texts of Scripture and then asserts that the Father and Son could not have eternally agreed to take up their distinct economic offices in something like a covenant given the unity of the divine will. As examples of early Reformed "federal theology," it seems to me that Coccejus and Witsius set out merely to expound various scriptural texts that speak of God's eternal decree for the Son to be the mediator for God's people.[77] A number of these texts have already appeared in section II of this chapter. The Father has "covenanted" (διέθετο) with the Son to give him a kingdom (Luke 22:29).[78] The Father has eternally given to the Son a people whose salvation the Son secures (John 6:37, 39; 10:29; 17:2, 6, 9, 24). In his incarnate work as servant of YHWH, the Son *is* a covenant for the people of God (Isa. 42:6; 49:8). In short, Holy Scripture itself leads us to affirm that the Father and Son have established a covenant with one another, according to which the Father gives a people to the Son and the Son will save that people through his reconciling work. In this respect, deciding whether covenantal language seems too difficult to integrate with the numerical unity of the divine will is not our prerogative.

At the same time, authors like Coccejus and Witsius rightly clarify that an eternal agreement between the Father and Son can be only analogous to a covenantal agreement between two human parties with two distinct human natures and volitions. The Father and Son are not two legal parties with distinct rational faculties. They are two persons within the one divine essence who share and distinctly modify the one divine volition. That distinct modification is what establishes a certain plurality in the volition that makes possible our talk of a "covenant." It is a plurality not of instantiation and act but of manners of subsisting and willing within the one act.[79] The Father subsisting and acting without coming forth from another and the Son subsisting and acting from the Father determine to establish a *pactum* according to which they will assume their distinct economic offices for our salvation. Unlike the case of command and obedience, the *pactum salutis* does not implicitly require discrete acts of willing. Rather, in the *pactum*, the persons in their distinct modes of subsisting and willing determine together in one act of will the shape that the economy will take. It is worth bearing in mind that the *pactum* does not stipulate that the divine persons are fundamentally, hypostatically constituted as legal parties who must form a contingent agreement in order to have some unity. The only diversity required in ontological priority to the *pactum* is just that of the persons' distinct modes of subsisting and willing. It is then in and under the *pactum* freely established by the persons that there is an *economic* diversity of legal parties with legal obligations to one another. In addition, authors like Coccejus and Witsius are clear that the

77. See the exegetical work in Coccejus, *Summa doctrinae*, 5.88–92 (85–91); Witsius, *De oeconomia foederum Dei*, 2.3 (111–23).

78. Cf. the use of cognate forms in, e.g., Gen. 9:17 LXX; 15:18 LXX; Ezek. 37:26 LXX; Acts 3:25; Heb. 8:10; 9:16; 10:16.

79. Cf. Owen, *Hebrews*, 2:77, 87–88; Coccejus, *Summa doctrinae*, 5.92 (91); Witsius, *Exercitationes*, 7.7 (80–81).

eternal institution of the *pactum salutis* does not involve an obedience of the Son. Both the Father and Son freely and authoritatively establish the *pactum*. It is then under the economic fulfillment of the *pactum* that the Son, being born of a woman and "under the law" (Gal. 4:4), submits to the Father in his mediatorial office.[80] Thus, given the unity of the will and authority of the Father and Son in the establishment of the covenant of redemption, there is no need to worry, as Barth did, about an eternal "dualism" in which there might have been a more ultimate will of the Father which, over against the Son, did not incline to the salvation of sinners.

Third, and more briefly, the doctrine of the *pactum salutis* does not leave human beings out of the picture. For this expression of the relevant scriptural texts affirms that the Son is eternally appointed to be the sponsor and head of a redeemed people. It is true that the *pactum salutis* does not *directly* have fallen humanity as one of its covenant partners, but the entire point of the doctrine is to express the fact that the divine persons have decreed that the Son will be mediator of God's people and the second Adam to whom all the elect are united federally and, in due course, by the act of faith. The covenant of redemption presupposes that God decides to create humanity and permit the fall, and it posits that the Son will be mediator of an elect people and will take on human flesh himself to complete his mediatorial task.

This response to Barth provides an opportunity to clarify a few key points. In particular, affirming God's aseity and independence of the economy does not involve a capricious *beneplacitum Dei* that cannot be trusted. Rather, God in himself is perfect in goodness with or without the decree to create the world. Furthermore, instead of having to transition from an "abstract" to a "concrete" form of life at the expense of his immutability, God is already fully in act in his transcendence of the economy and remains the same God with his assumption of a tendency toward the creature. Instead of having to take up a different kind of divine subsistence, the Son can and does retain the same divine mode of subsisting while also determining to be the mediator and to take upon himself a lowly human nature. Indeed, only if the Son's divine subsistence is radically dissimilar to his human subordination and obedience can Pauline teaching on the wonder of the incarnation be adequately set forth. In my view, then, Barth's proposal too hastily dismisses the prospects of a more traditional approach to the decree and the election of the Son and ends up generating new problems regarding divine freedom and eternal obedience. The final section of this chapter will now

---

80. See Coccejus, *Summa doctrinae*, 5.89–95 (89–95); Witsius, *De oeconomia foederum Dei*, 2.3.6–9, 16–22 (113–16).

turn to the outworking of the Son's election in his mission and assumption of a human nature.

V. Procession, Mission, and Historical Assumption

Section II of this chapter noted that the Son's mission expresses and reveals his eternal procession from the Father in the Gospel of John (cf. 3:31; 5:16–30; 6:44–46; 7:28–29; 8:23). In Aquinas's description, the mission of a divine person involves two things: "the habitude of the one sent toward him from whom he is sent" and "the habitude of the one sent toward the *terminus* toward which he is sent." The former presupposes a procession of one person from another (in this case, the Son from the Father). The latter entails that the person should begin to be present in the *terminus ad quem* in some new way (in this case, the Son in the human nature that he assumes). Though the Son was present in the world prior to the assumption of his human nature, he now "has begun to be in the world visibly by the flesh assumed."[81] Given the Son's new mode of existing in his human nature, at least this aspect of his mission has to be characterized as "temporal." The mission "includes the eternal procession and adds something, namely, a temporal effect."[82] In this section, the central task is to articulate the relationship between the temporal character of the Son's mission and assumption of a human nature and the divine attribute of eternity, leaving a more detailed examination of the Son's relationship to his human nature to the following chapter. Here the question is whether the temporal mission and assumption cast doubt on a "classical" doctrine of divine eternity: How is it that the Son acts in time and, indeed, begins to have a new mode of existing in time while still being eternal?

A number of theologians and philosophers maintain that the mission and incarnation of the Son should lead us to deny that God is eternal or "timeless." For it seems that a God who performs actions at particular points in time and even begins a new way of being in the world cannot be "timeless." Isaak Dorner, for example, argues that a traditional understanding of divine actuality and divine eternity would prevent God from doing something new in the world and would lead to a "docetic" view of the incarnation wherein there is no newly instituted existence of the Son in a human nature.[83] More recently, a number of philosophical theologians have argued that a "timeless"

81. Aquinas, *ST* Ia.43.1 (445).
82. Aquinas, *ST* Ia.43.2 (446).
83. Dorner, *Divine Immutability*, 101–2, 124–26, 129, 187–89.

cause cannot produce a temporal effect.[84] Nicholas Wolterstorff states that a "timeless" God has no "temporal aspects," whereas the God of Scripture is a "being among whose states there is temporal succession," someone who "has a history of acting and responding." If God "does one thing at one time and a different thing at a later time, there's change in [God's] life" and "a felt temporality in God's experience."[85] Similarly, Alan Padgett reasons, "The occurrence of an effect (which is itself a change) implies a change in the cause of the effect." Further, "whenever a change occurs the subject of the change goes through some interval of time." The implication is that "God is not absolutely timeless, and the traditional doctrine of eternity must be abandoned." Given God's production of temporally diverse effects, God's "power-to-act" cannot be timeless even if God might timelessly *will* that various effects occur at different times.[86]

Applying a similar line of thought to the incarnation, Richard Holland contends that divine "timelessness" would preclude the sort of life that God the Son lives in the Gospels. Holland writes that if "the classical model of God's relation to time is true," then the "biblical statements describing what took place in the Incarnation" cannot be interpreted by "a straightforward reading of the text." From Holland's perspective, a "classical" view of God should not be permitted to problematize the incarnation; instead, the incarnation should prompt us to affirm "sequence in the divine life."[87] R. T. Mullins likewise argues that the incarnation requires that real change take place in God the Son when he assumes a human nature. In addition, the Son's presence and activity in time require that he be able to have "*de se* beliefs" like "I am now doing such and such after I wasn't before," which involves mental sequence and temporality and precludes a traditional understanding of the Son's eternity.[88]

In what follows I will offer a response to these concerns about the coherence of the Son's mission and God's eternal life. This will involve (1) clarifying what a more traditional understanding of eternity involves, (2) offering some comments on the theological implications of this understanding, (3) applying these reflections to the nature of divine action in the Son's mission and assumption of a human nature, and (4) briefly commenting on the relationship between the Son's two natures.

84. E.g., Pike, *God and Timelessness*, 105; Davis, *Logic and the Nature of God*, 9–13; Mullins, *The End of the Timeless God*, 102–3.

85. Wolterstorff, *Inquiring about God*, 133–34, 138–39, 145, 149–50, 153–55, 157–58, 160–62, 173, 178.

86. Padgett, *God, Eternity and the Nature of Time*, 60–66, 122, 130–31, 146.

87. Holland, *God, Time, and the Incarnation*, 125–26, 165.

88. Mullins, *The End of the Timeless God*, 185–86, 192–93.

(1) Many of the criticisms of a "traditional" view of eternity equate it with divine "timelessness" or "atemporality." However, the contemporary use of this language seems to obscure what older theologians like Augustine or Boethius actually meant in their discussions of eternity. It should be noted, first of all, that in their accounts of divine eternity and creaturely time, major representatives of a "traditional" position state that only present things exist.[89] They do not appeal to something like what is now called "eternalism" in order to make it easier to discuss God's involvement in history.[90] In the *Confessions*, Augustine, for example, writes that God is "above all times" (*super omnia tempora*) and does not act "temporally."[91] Yet Augustine also writes that God's action in the baptism of Jesus, for instance, occurs in time. When the Father speaks to Jesus at his baptism ("You are my beloved Son . . ." [Mark 1:9–11]), his words take place in time (or are "done in time," *ad tempus facta*) and have a beginning and end in time. God wills and acts without succession, but his effects are temporal.[92] Indeed, Augustine speaks of God regenerating his mother, Monica, through baptism at a particular time and working in his own temporal life through teachers in his youth.[93] For Augustine, God is both immutable and actively bringing about temporal changes.[94]

Boethius's definition of eternity has been quoted through the ages: "whole, simultaneous, and perfect possession of interminable life" (*interminabilis vitae tota, simul et perfecta possessio*). Boethius envisions God in his possession of such life viewing history from above.[95] Yet Boethius also emphasizes that God intimately cares for all his creatures and "arranges" the changes in the world. God accomplishes his works through time (*per temporales ordines*), and God himself is "in" time. The key qualification is just that God remains himself without being moved, unlike creatures, whose lives unfold through change and succession. In Boethius's characterization, talk of God's eternity or God's *semper* (always existing) does not signify some "thing" in God or something predicated of God "according to himself" (*secundum se*). Rather, predicates like eternity or *semper* are employed with respect to God's

89. Augustine, *Conf.* 11.15.18 (203); 11.20.26 (206–7); Boethius, *Philosophiae consolationis* 5.6 (426–31); Anselm, *Monologion* 22 (40).

90. According to "eternalism," the past, present, and future all exist in some sense. They are differentiated not with respect to existence but only serially. For accessible descriptions of contemporary positions held regarding the nature of time, see, e.g., Craig, *Time and Eternity*; Mullins, *The End of the Timeless God*, chap. 2; Deng, *God and Time*.

91. Augustine, *Conf.* 11.1.1 (194); 12.11.13 (222); 12.15.18 (224–25); 13.29.44 (268); 13.37.52 (272).

92. Augustine, *Conf.* 11.6.8–8.10 (198–99).

93. Augustine, *Conf.* 1.12.19 (10–11); 9.13.34 (152).

94. Augustine, *Conf.* 1.4.4 (2).

95. Boethius, *Philosophiae consolationis* 4.6 (364–65); 5.6 (422–23, 432–33).

relationship to the world. Just as *ubique* is predicated of God because he is present throughout all of creation's space, so *semper* is predicated of God because he is present throughout all of creation's temporal existence.[96]

Anselm follows a similar line of thought and says it would be "repugnant" if God did not exist in time (if he existed "nowhere and never"). God's ongoing, sustaining presence is necessary for anything at any time to continue in existence.[97] God as the "highest essence" is *in tempore*. To clarify the meaning of the phrase *in tempore*, Anselm adds that when something is *in tempore*, this ordinarily means that it is present in its particular time and also contained by that time. In God's case, however, only the former applies: he is present in time, but not contained in it. God is in time "in his own way." For Anselm, then, it may be most fitting to say God is *cum tempore* ("with time") more than strictly *in tempore*.[98] Divine eternity, then, does not remove God from the world. It is simply an attribute that signifies God's perfect, unchanging life with respect to the temporal mode of created being.[99]

Aquinas draws together the emphasis on God's eternity signifying his complete and unchanging life and the emphasis on the genuinely temporal character of God's outward effects. Echoing Boethius, Aquinas writes that God is eternal in that God is "lacking beginning and end, having at once his own whole being." This wholeness of being turns on God not undergoing motion and succession, which is what time measures.[100] Positively, God's actuality remains constant. God's operation is really identical with God himself and never "departs" from him, so his life remains "whole" and has no succession.[101] In other words, in his pure actuality, God never transitions from inactive potential to activity and back again. In this sense God never undergoes motion, which is what gives rise to succession and temporality.[102] Yet God is certainly present and active in time. To be sure, Aquinas can describe God

96. Boethius, *Philosophiae consolationis* 1.6 (166–67); 3.12 (298–301); 4.6 (358–61); 5.6 (422–25); Boethius, *De trin.* 4 (20–23).

97. Anselm, *Monologion* 20 (35).

98. Anselm, *Monologion* 22 (40–41).

99. Anselm, *Monologion* 24 (42).

100. Aquinas, *Commentaria in octo libros Physicorum Aristotelis* 3.3.5.15 (114); Aquinas, *SCG* 1.15 (41–42).

101. Aquinas, *SCG* 1.99 (264); cf. Aquinas, *ST* Ia.10.2–3 (96–98). On the real identity of operation and essence in God in Aquinas's thinking, see *Super Sent.* 1.2.1.2 ad 2 (1:63); Aquinas, *De pot.* 1.1 ad 1 (9); 3.3 (43); Aquinas, *SCG* 2.8–9 (283–84); 2.35 (348); Aquinas, *ST* Ia.25.1 ad 2 (290); 45.3 ad 1 (467).

102. For pertinent discussion of motion taken broadly as transition from passive potency to act, see Aquinas, *Super Sent.* 1.8.3.1 ad 1 and 2 (1:211–12); 2.1.1.5 ad 11 (2:37); Aquinas, *Sent. De anima* 3.6 (229); Aquinas, *In De div. nom.* 4.7.369 (121); Aquinas, *SCG* 1.13 (30–34); 1.68 (198–99); 2.33 (348); Aquinas, *ST* Ia.18.3 (228); IaIIae.9.1 (74–75); 9.3 (77–78).

as being "outside" the continuum of time (*extra continuum*), but in using this language Aquinas is in fact stressing that God truly "coexists" with each passing moment along the continuum.[103] God acts "immediately" in all things to preserve their being through time, so that his eternity "includes all times."[104] In this connection, motion can be ascribed to God in that he knows, wills, and produces diverse effects in the world.[105] Indeed, given the temporal diversity of God's effects, Aquinas asserts that God's power, which is really identical with God's essence, is not always "conjoined" to its temporal effects (i.e., the effects themselves are not eternal but wrought at various times).[106]

Accordingly, for authors like Augustine, Boethius, Anselm, and Aquinas, God is eternal in the sense that he is complete in his life and actuality. He does not undergo change from inactive potential to actuality, or the sort of motion that yields succession and can be measured by temporal intervals. But God remains with creatures in the temporal world and brings into being different outward effects at different times.

(2) This brief historical survey of some significant contributors to a "traditional" doctrine of divine eternity can now be developed a little and unpacked with a view to its implications for the present line of argument. Here it needs to be emphasized that eternity signifies the fullness of God's life and actuality relative to the temporal mode of created being. It does not signify any discrete thing in God himself that becomes an obstacle to his presence in time. It does not eliminate the possibility of a positive relationship to temporal creatures. In fact, it is predicated of God only because he does have a positive relationship to the creature and because that relationship requires that we clarify the sort of duration that God has in contrast to that of the creature. Eternity is simply a relative inflection of God's plenitude and infinity.[107] Furthermore,

---

103. Aquinas, *SCG* 2.66 (185).

104. Aquinas, *ST* Ia.8.1 (82); 8.3 ad 1 (87); 10.2 ad 4 (96).

105. Aquinas, *Super Sent.* 1.8.3.1 ad 1 and 2 (1:211–12); Aquinas, *In De div. nom.* 9.4.840–42 (316); *ST* Ia.9.1 ad 1 and 2 (90); 18.3 ad 1 (228). In the commentary on *De divinis nominibus*, Aquinas expounds the sense in which rest (*statio, sessio*) and motion (*motus*) are applicable to God. *Statio* and *sessio* apply to God in that (a) he exists in himself without sustenance from another, (b) his operation remains constant since it is in knowing and loving himself that he does all that he does and does not become weaker or stronger in his operation, and (c) he is not caused or changed from without and in this sense is *immobilis* (9.4.835–37 [315–16]). *Motus* applies to God not as though he might be changed in quality, quantity, place, or knowledge, but in the sense that he produces and conserves diverse things at diverse places and times and providentially confers his operations and "processions of gifts" on creatures. In this regard, we should "praise the motion of the unmoved God." God both rests and "proceeds," so his rest is "generative" and his operation is "invariable" and "stable" (9.4.840–42 [316]).

106. Aquinas, *De pot.* 1.1 ad 8 (9).

107. See Turretin, *Inst.*, 3.8.1 (1:213); Mastricht, *TPT*, 2.9.1 (117). Cf. also Muller, *Post-Reformation Reformed Dogmatics*, 3:345–62; Pasnau, "On Existing All at Once." Note also

the approach taken here does not envision time as an independent thing or a framework into which created beings are deposited. Instead, there are created beings, and then, by undergoing change and motion, those created beings live a life of succession that is measurable by temporal intervals. In this approach, the eternal God does not have to discern how he might gain access to the temporal world. Instead, as the one who inwardly sustains the life of creatures that undergo motion and succession, he is inevitably present with them in their temporal mode of being. Given his presence with creatures in time, he can and does bring about diverse effects in the world at diverse times. In this regard, a "traditional" view of God's eternity simply does not burden Christology with some of the commitments and problems that have incited worry on the part of recent critics of divine "timelessness."[108]

More will be said below under the third point regarding the question of how the eternal God produces temporally diverse effects (insofar as something can be said about the indelibly mysterious fact that he does), but it will be helpful to note first that this understanding of divine eternity upholds well the drama of the Son's mission and assumption of a human nature, which is attested in a passage like Galatians 4:4–6 ("When the fullness of time came . . ."). For it is not as though the divine decree and election of the Son took place "long ago" on a time line that existed before the world and eventually led up to the creation of it. For there was no time without the world and thus no time in which the Son's election "before the foundation of the world" might have taken place in a quasi-temporal manner at the expense of the consequent mission's eschatological novelty.[109] God's eternal life and decree are ontologically but not temporally prior to the world. Thus, on the one hand, God precedes all times and is in this respect the "Ancient of Days," but, on the other hand, God is ever "new and young."[110] The only temporal

---

Christoph Schwöbel's discontentment with the options laid out in recent philosophical discussions of divine timelessness and temporality in "The Eternity of the Triune God," 345–48.

108. It is worth adding that appropriating the view of eternity and time found in an author like Aquinas does not require us to take up a complete system of Aristotelian physics or cosmology. There are notable contemporary defenses of an essentially Aristotelian view of motion and time (see Feser, "The Medieval Principle of Motion and the Modern Principle of Inertia"; Feser, "Motion in Aristotle, Newton, and Einstein"; Feser, *Aristotle's Revenge*, chap. 4), but my intention here is simply to show that recovering this sort of understanding of God's eternal life commits us fundamentally to the claim that God never has to transition from idleness to activity and that this understanding does not necessarily create the problems that critics of divine "timelessness" often associate with it.

109. Cf. Augustine on the novelty of creation itself where he points out that just as there was no space "where" God created the world, so there was no time "when" God created the world (*De civ*. 11.5–6 [2:325–26]).

110. Aquinas, *In De div. nom*. 10.2.860, 864 (324).

aspect of God's decree, then, is its historical execution, which takes place not before but only concurrently with the life of creatures. Hence the real historical drama of 1 Peter 1:20: Christ was, "on the one hand, foreknown before the foundation of the world, but, on the other hand, revealed in the last of times for your sake."

(3) Drawing from the material above regarding divine action in section III, I would suggest that eternity as God's complete actuality can be integrated with the temporal diversity of God's effects (including the Son's mission and incarnation) by way of considering the egression or termination of God's actuality toward his effects.[111] I will not restate the argument given above for the consistency of the pure actuality of God and the contingency of God's outward actions but will attempt to apply it here to the Son's mission and assumption of a human nature in time. On the one hand, the actuality of God is preveniently complete, so divine action taken with respect to God's actuality by which God produces his effects never requires any change. On the other hand, the egression or breaking forth and termination of God's actuality is variegated, so divine action taken with respect to this termination upon outward effects does involve change and novelty. In this account, the mission of the Son taken with respect to the eternal actuality of the Son's procession from the Father is nothing new. Yet the mission of the Son taken with respect to the outward breaking forth of this actuality—taken with respect to the Son's coming to be visibly present in the world in his human nature—is genuinely new.[112]

(4) Given the ongoing distinction between the Son's deity and humanity, divine eternity does not prevent the Son from beginning an authentically temporal life. The divine Son can and does continue to exist as God and therefore eternally (without succession) even as he exists as man and therefore temporally (with succession). Here the noncompetitive relationship between Creator and creature and the hypostatic mode of union in the incarnation come into play. Since God transcends the order of created being, and since the

111. The language of "egression" and "termination" can be found in various Reformed authors (e.g., Alsted, *Metaphysica*, 1.17 [150–51]; Voetius, *Select. disp., pars prima*, 1.13 [233]; Turretin, *Inst.*, 3.10.15 [1:225]; 5.3.16 [1:484–85]; Owen, *A Dissertation on Divine Justice*, 1.1 [498–500]).

112. It seems to me that reflection on the distinction between essential actuality and egression in connection with the Son's mission may also help to shed light on recent discussion of whether the Son's mission is an "accident" (on which see von Balthasar, *Theo-Drama*, 154–63, 168, 263, 509; see also McCormack, "Processions and Missions"). The actuality of the mission whereby the mission is accomplished is not something added to the actuality of the procession, so it certainly does not involve the accrual of an "accident" on the part of the Son. At the same time, the egression of the divine actuality upon a temporal *terminus ad quem* (i.e., the Son's human nature) is contingent and novel, not a constitutive or necessary feature of the Son's eternal relation to the Father.

incarnation involves the union of two distinct natures in one person rather than an immediate fusion of natures, what pertains to Christ *qua Deus* and what pertains to Christ *qua homo* need not be collapsed into one another. Some of what must be said here can only anticipate fuller discussion of the practice of "reduplication" in chapter 7, but the point for now is that the eternal life of the Son need not be conformed to the temporal succession of his human life in order to enable or "make room" for this succession. The suggestion that the incarnation requires sequence in God's life seems to rest on the mistaken idea that in the incarnation the Son's divinity must be assimilated to his humanity, with its various properties and modes of being. Taking up that mistaken idea might in principle lead to a qualification of any of the divine perfections: If God the Son had to undergo succession *qua Deus* in order to be human as well, would it be the case that he should have to be caused, circumscribed, mortal, or ignorant *qua Deus* in order to be human as well?

Moreover, the particular concern about the Son being able to have knowledge or "beliefs" with temporal or tensed content (i.e., "I am doing this after previously having not done this") appears to reflect two questionable assumptions. First, it appears to reflect the idea that the Son cannot have assumed a human nature with a human intellect and temporally acquired knowledge distinct from the divine intellect and divine act of knowing. But if the Son does indeed possess such a human intellect and distinctly human knowledge, then the Son can proceed through a series of (human) mental acts without this compromising his divine eternity. Second, the concern appears to reflect the idea that God's eternal act of knowing must either be continually "updated" in accord with the passing of time or else ignorant of what is taking place at particular times. However, this idea has at least two problems. First, it assumes that God's intellect is like ours in having to undergo successive acts of apprehension at different times. Thus, it does not pose a problem for the view that God truly undergoes no succession; it only reveals that (*per impossibile*) if God were to undergo succession, he would have to undertake a series of intellective acts in order to keep up with time and avoid slipping into ignorance. Second, it assumes that God's intellect can be true only if its manner of understanding (not merely the content understood) corresponds to outward reality. But someone like Aquinas, for example, might respond that the truth of the intellect concerns not whether the *manner* of the understanding is like the thing understood but the fact that the *content* of the understanding is like the thing understood.[113] Applied to the current

---

113. See Aquinas, *Quaestiones disputatae de veritate* 2.7, 13 (67–69, 87–90); Aquinas, *SCG* 1.58–59 (165–68); Aquinas, *ST* Ia.14.14–15 (194–95), where he describes God's knowledge of

line of argument, this means that God the Son with his divine intellect need not proceed through a series of mental acts in order to have divine knowledge of his successive human experiences and activities. He knows both *qua Deus* and *qua homo* in distinct ways what takes place at each moment in his human sojourn, without compromising his divine eternity.

VI. Conclusion

This chapter has focused on the election and mission of God the Son. It began by examining scriptural teaching on God's decree, on the Son's appointment to be the mediator for God's people, and on the Son's consequent coming forth into the world to take on human flesh. In order to expand our understanding of the Bible's teaching and engage with some important contemporary discussions about the Son's election and mission, the next sections considered ways in which the Son's election and mission may be connected to a doctrine of God that upholds attributes like eternity, immutability, and simplicity. First we considered the importance of God's prevenient completeness and actuality and its coherence with God's eternal decree. Then we considered some of Barth's claims about the Son's election and how they may imply a tension between the Son's independence of the economy and the Son's immutability and hypostatic unity. I offered a response to Barth attempting to confirm the unchanging goodness and mercy of God in his decretive freedom, challenging Barth's account of the Son's hypostatic unity and eternal obedience, and clarifying the meaning and scriptural logic of the *pactum salutis*. Finally, we considered God's eternity or transcendence of succession in relation to the Son's mission and assumption of a human nature. There I argued in response to Dorner and some recent philosophical theologians that God's eternal life facilitates his presence and action in time and does not obstruct the Son's mission and assumption of a human nature at a particular time.

　　To conclude this chapter, it is fitting to note how the preceding material helps us to secure the three desiderata observed in modern Christology's frequent critiques of "classical theism." First, the treatment of the decree and the *pactum salutis* reinforces that the Son always lives and acts within his eternal

---

singular things that exist temporally, which is unfolded in terms of God knowing "enunciables" (things that can be declared true or false with reference to their existence or nonexistence) without God's intellect undertaking "composition" or "division." If one stipulates that the manner of understanding must reflect the thing understood, then one would have to address a number of problems, such as God's (incorporeal) knowledge of corporeal things that are ordinarily known by sense perception.

relation to the Father. All that he will do in the economy will take place only within the context of his procession from the Father and on the basis of the divine decision wherein the Father and Son (with the Spirit) acted together to establish their economic offices. Second, our treatment of the Son's eternal subsistence reinforces that, in his divine transcendence of the created order and in the hypostatic mode of union in the incarnation, the Son remains the same divine Son that he always was when he takes on flesh. Third, our treatment of the Son's transcendence of time relative to his mission and incarnation reinforces the genuineness of his human experience. His eternal divine life not only allows for his direct subsistence in a human nature but enables the authenticity of his human nature and life, since his humanity is not mixed with his divine nature. Already the content of this chapter has pressed us to consider the Son's relationship to the human nature that he assumes, and the aim of the next chapter will be to offer a fuller account of this relationship.

FOUR

"And the Word Became Flesh": The Son's Relationship to His Human Nature

I. Introduction

The previous chapter began to discuss the Son's assumption of a human nature. The goal of this chapter will be to describe in more detail the Son's relationship to the nature that he has assumed. The first main section will exegete certain scriptural passages that illumine that relationship and provide an entryway into broader dogmatic considerations in catholic Christology (e.g., the way in which Christ "subsists" in his humanity or the way in which Christ is a "composite" person). The next main section will work through that broader dogmatic elaboration, highlighting how it sets forth the genuineness of the Son's human life and how it fits together with divine attributes like immutability and simplicity. After this, the chapter will address certain debates among Lutheran and Reformed authors about the notion of the *communicatio idiomatum* and the so-called *extra Calvinisticum*.

II. Biblical Description

In an important sense, John 1 and Philippians 2 contain all the central features of orthodox teaching on the person of Christ and his act of assuming a human nature. In this section I will lean on John 1, Philippians 2, and a few other scriptural texts and attempt to present these key features in terms of (1) the divine person who acts to assume the human nature, (2) the act of assumption and resultant union with the human nature, (3) the integrity of the nature assumed, (4) the unity and sameness of the person of the Son after the assumption of the human nature, and (5) the ongoing distinctness of the Son's divine and human natures.

(1) After telling us that the eternal Word was with God the Father in the beginning and that he was the one through whom the Father made all things (John 1:1–5), John also calls the Word the "true light" who illumines all things and comes into the world (1:9–11). "And the Word became flesh and dwelt among us [Καὶ ὁ λόγος σὰρξ ἐγένετο καὶ ἐσκήνωσεν ἐν ἡμῖν], and we have seen his glory, glory as of the only Son from the Father [μονογενοῦς παρὰ πατρός], full of grace and truth" (1:14). "No one has ever seen God; the only Son who is God [μονογενὴς θεὸς], who is in the bosom of the Father, he has revealed him" (1:18). Thus, the person who became flesh is the eternal Word, who was with God the Father before the creation of the world and was himself the true God and Creator described in Genesis 1.[1] Whether something like "only Son" or "only begotten Son" is the correct translation of μονογενής, it remains that the μονογενής is "from the Father" (παρὰ πατρός) in such a way that this relation of origin explains his sharing the glory, grace, and truth ascribed to YHWH in Exodus 33:17–34:7. In other words, the person who became flesh is the eternal Word or eternal Son who has (eternally) received from God the Father the divine essence.[2] In fact, in order to fulfill the purpose of his coming, he must be the true God. Unlike John the Baptist, a man sent from God, the incarnate Word must himself be the true light that illumines the world (John 1:5–9, 15). He must be the Son who is in the "bosom of the Father" and who can therefore decisively reveal the Father and grant the right of sonship to others (1:12, 18).

Like John's prologue, the hymn of Philippians 2 also teaches that it is the Son who is equal with God the Father that assumes a human nature. Christ is the one "who, being in the form of God [ἐν μορφῇ θεοῦ ὑπάρχων], considered it not ἁρπαγμός [KJV "robbery"; NRSV "something to be exploited"] to be equal with God [τὸ εἶναι ἴσα θεῷ], but he emptied himself [ἑαυτὸν ἐκένωσεν], taking the form of a servant, being made in the likeness of human beings" (2:6–7). While some biblical scholars have suggested that Christ being in

---

1. Regarding the links between John 1 and Gen. 1, see, e.g., Bauckham, *The Testimony of the Beloved Disciple*, 240–42.
2. On John 1:14 and the Son's eternal procession, see chap. 2, sect. II.

the *forma Dei* in 2:6 is akin to Adam bearing the image of God,[3] an "Adam Christology" by itself does not account for certain details of the text. First, the being in the *forma Dei* is a matter of being "equal with God."[4] Christ's subsistence in the *forma Dei* therefore signifies something beyond human likeness to God. Second, Christ becoming human is not mentioned until the next verse.[5] Third, the parallel between the *forma Dei* and *forma servi* implies that being in the *forma Dei* is not merely a matter of being *like* God insofar as having the *forma servi* is not merely a matter of being *like* a servant.[6] Fourth, if the initial being in the *forma Dei* concerned only a human likeness to God, that would undermine the flow and force of the whole passage: "What is the point of saying that a human being chose to become a human being and was found in appearance as a human being?"[7]

Scholars who have recognized that Christ being in the *forma Dei* transcends Adamic likeness to God have proposed different interpretations of what this "form" signifies: the divine nature,[8] a certain sphere of existence,[9] a high status or position,[10] an outward appearance or visible manifestation of divine glory.[11] In my view, it is justifiable to maintain that the "form of God" in this passage does signify the divine nature, not least because the signification of the parallel "form of a servant" includes human nature itself and not just the outward appearance of human nature or servanthood. However, it seems to me that even interpretations that hesitate to take the *forma Dei* directly to signify the divine nature will end up at least implying that Christ shares the divine nature with the Father. If biblical thought allows for no middle ground between Creator and creation, then the only "sphere" or "status" in which this person might exist prior to taking up a creaturely form is that of the one

---

3. E.g., Cullmann, *The Christology of the New Testament*, 176–77; Talbert, "The Problem of Pre-existence in Philippians 2:6–11"; Murphy-O'Connor, "Christological Anthropology in Phil., II, 6–11," 39–42, 49–50; Dunn, "Christ, Adam, and Preexistence," 74–79.

4. Cf. Käsemann, "A Critical Analysis of Philippians 2:5–11," 62; Fee, *Philippians*, 207; Silva, *Philippians*, 100–101; Hansen, *Philippians*, 138. The article in the phrase τὸ εἶναι ἴσα θεῷ appears to have an anaphoric function, indicating that Christ's "being equal with God" has the same referent as his "being in the form of God" (Wright, *The Climax of the Covenant*, 83; Hawthorne and Martin, *Philippians*, 114).

5. So, e.g., Wanamaker, "Philippians 2.6–11," 183.

6. Cf. Fee, *Philippians*, 203; Hawthorne and Martin, *Philippians*, 110–11.

7. Hansen, *Philippians*, 141.

8. John Chrysostom, *In Phil.* 2.6.2 (220); Aquinas, *Super Phil.* 2.2.54 (101); Zanchi, *In Phil.*, 131; Lightfoot, *Philippians*, 127–33; Fee, *Philippians*, 204; Thompson and Longenecker, *Philippians and Philemon*, 71.

9. Käsemann, "A Critical Analysis of Philippians 2:5–11," 61; Reumann, *Philippians*, 341.

10. Fowl, *The Story of Christ in the Ethics of Paul*, 54; Hawthorne, "In the Form of and Equal with God," 98, 104.

11. Bockmuehl, *Philippians*, 126–29; Fowl, *Philippians*, 91–94.

divine essence. And if Christ was in the outward appearance of divine glory in such a way that he was also equal with the Father, then, again, he shares the divine essence of the Father.[12] In short, the "form of God" might signify the divine essence directly and its outward manifestation indirectly, or vice versa.[13]

The importance of the divinity of Christ in his assumption of a human nature can be reinforced by examining what it means that he "considered it not ἁρπαγμός to be equal with God." Analyses of the meaning of ἁρπαγμός abound. Older interpreters often take the term to signify a prize seized (or to be seized) or an act of seizing something ("robbery").[14] More recent interpreters often assert that the meaning of "robbery" is impossible in Philippians 2.[15] They also break up the interpretive options in several categories with the use of Latin terms. The word ἁρπαγμός could be taken to signify (a) a thing seized (*res rapta*), (b) a thing to be seized (*res rapienda*), (c) an act of seizing (*actus rapiendi*), or (d) a thing to be clung to, perhaps for selfish ends (*res retinenda*).[16] Roy Hoover's influential study of the word ἁρπαγμός has led a number of exegetes to conclude that Christ did not consider equality with God something to be exploited for selfish ends as though it might excuse him from coming to serve others.[17] In my view, several possibilities could work: Christ considered being equal with God the Father (a) not something seized or gained since he always was in the form of God in the first place, (b) not something to be seized or gained (i.e., not something he had to seize or gain) since he always was in the form of God in the first place; (c) not something to be exploited to avoid an act of self-giving love toward others. Whichever option is best, the text affirms that Jesus always has been equal to the Father, for one can be said not to misuse or exploit only what one already has.[18]

On a related note, some interpreters have also debated whether the participle ὑπάρχων has a concessive function ("*although* he was in the form of God") or a causal function ("*because* he was in the form of God").[19] The

---

12. So Calvin, *In Phil.*, 2.6 (25–26). Cf. Zanchi, *In Phil.*, 132–33.

13. Cf. Coccejus, *S. Pauli apostoli epistola ad Philippenses*, 43, who writes that the *forma Dei* signifies "the true thing itself and this thing made manifest."

14. E.g., Ambrose, *De fide* 2.8.70 (2:296, 298); John Chrysostom, *In Phil.* 2.6.2–3 (220–22); Calvin, *In Phil.*, 2.6 (25–26). Cf. Aquinas, *Super Phil.*, 2.2.55 (101).

15. E.g., BDAG, 133; O'Neill, "Hoover on *Harpagmos* Reviewed," 448; Fee, *Philippians*, 205.

16. See Moule, "Further Reflexions on Philippians 2:5–11," 266–68, 271–76; R. Martin, *A Hymn of Christ*, 134–53; Wright, *The Climax of the Covenant*, 62–82; Fee, *Philippians*, 205–7; Bockmuehl, *Philippians*, 129–31; Hawthorne and Martin, *Philippians*, 115–16.

17. Hoover, "The HARPAGMOS Enigma"; Wright, *Climax of the Covenant*, 82–90; Bockmuehl, *Philippians*, 129; Fowl, *Philippians*, 94–95; M. Martin, "ἁρπαγμός Revisited."

18. So, e.g., Hoover, "The HARPAGMOS Enigma," 118; M. J. Gorman, "'Although/Because He Was in the Form of God,'" 155–56.

19. See M. J. Gorman, "'Although/Because He Was in the Form of God.'"

concessive approach seeks to honor the contrast between the *forma Dei* in Philippians 2:6 and the *forma servi* in 2:7. However, the causal approach affords more flexibility on the meaning of ἁρπαγμός and can still maintain the contrast between 2:6 and 2:7. On the one hand, the text could convey that because Christ subsisted in the fullness of divine majesty, he considered equality with God not something he had to gain, but he stooped low and took a servant's form. On the other hand, the text could convey that because Christ was in the form of the self-giving God, he considered equality with God not something to be exploited in order to avoid a display of self-giving love but rather emptied himself by taking a servant's form.[20] The first version of the causal approach may not fit well with what is now the prevalent understanding of ἁρπαγμός, but the second version may not fit well with the striking novelty of the Son's servanthood and obedience in 2:7–8.[21] Either way, the text highlights that the one who assumes the servant's form must be the true God who manifests God's love and whose astonishing example of condescending by taking a servant's form calls Christian believers out of arrogance and selfish ambition.

(2) As to the act of assuming the human nature, when God the Word comes into the world, he does not merely reside in the flesh by grace. His dwelling in the flesh is not merely another iteration of God's gracious presence with the saints or prophets. As Cyril of Alexandria repeatedly emphasizes, since God the Word *became* flesh, the flesh is not just an "instrument" (ὄργανον) with which the Word might have only an "external relation." Likewise, the person of Jesus Christ is not an additional person involved in the incarnation, an "assumed man" or "God-bearing man" (θεοφόρος ἄνθρωπος) used to accomplish certain tasks.[22] In the case of God the Word, the name "Emmanuel" means something much greater. The Word himself is "God-made-man" (θεός ἐνηνθρωπηκώς).[23] The Word "makes human traits his own."[24] The Word's flesh is proper to him— even permanently proper to him (John 2:18–22; 20:27). So Cyril: "It was not the body of another from among us but rather the proper body of him who is the Word from the Father that was begotten from [the virgin Mary]."[25]

20. Cf. Wright, *The Climax of the Covenant*, 90, 97; M. J. Gorman, "'Although/Because He Was in the Form of God.'"

21. Cf. Fee, *Philippians*, 208n65. The first version allows the whole of 2:6 to stand in contrast to 2:7, whereas the second version allows only a more restricted contrast between the last clause of 2:6 ("he considered it not something to be exploited") and 2:7 ("but he emptied himself").

22. E.g., Cyril of Alexandria, *Ad monachos* 1,19 (19); Cyril, *Tertia ad Nestorium* 6,4 (36); 6,12 (41); Cyril, *Contra Theodoretum* 169,54 (130); 169,83 (142).

23. E.g., Cyril of Alexandria, *Contra Theodoretum* 169,71 (137–38).

24. Cyril of Alexandria, *Contra Theodoretum* 169,39 (124).

25. Cyril of Alexandria, *Ad monachos* 1,20 (20).

In Philippians 2, when the Son is said to have the "form" of a servant, to be made in the "likeness" of human beings, and to be found in "appearance" as a man (2:7), the language does not imply that the Son is not really human. Instead, since the *forma servi* is parallel to the *forma Dei*, and since being in the *forma Dei* is a matter of being equal with God, this suggests that assuming the *forma servi* results in being equal with a servant or really being a servant.[26] That the Son really is a servant is borne out in 2:8, according to which Christ obeyed the Father to the point of death. While the use of the word "likeness" (ὁμοίωμα) in "being made in the likeness of human beings" arguably leaves room for some distinction between Christ and sinful humanity (cf. Rom. 8:3), the word can easily be taken to signify a shared condition or set of experiences,[27] which would presuppose having the same kind of nature according to which one could have such common experiences. And the word "appearance" (σχῆμα) in "being found in appearance as a man" is aimed not at denying Christ's authentic humanity but at declaring that his humanity was observable to others. It was a verifiable humanity (cf. 1 John 1:1–3).[28]

The writer of Hebrews also teaches that in order to help human beings the eternal Son came to associate himself with us in the closest way. As the children of Abraham have "shared in flesh and blood," so "*he himself* likewise partook of *the same things*" (αὐτὸς παραπλησίως μετέσχεν τῶν αὐτῶν) (Heb. 2:14).[29] To help Abraham's children, he had "to be made like his brothers and sisters according to all things" (2:17). Scripture further illumines the meaning of the Son's assumption of a human nature by simply calling him "a man." He is "Jesus of Nazareth, a man attested by God" (Acts 2:22; cf. 17:31). He is "the one man, Jesus Christ," through whom God's grace abounds to sinners (Rom. 5:15, 17). He is "the second man" through whom God will raise the saints from the dead (1 Cor. 15:21, 47). And he is the only mediator between God and human beings, "the man Christ Jesus" (1 Tim. 2:5). That he can be called "a man" entails a real union between the person of the Son and a human nature that is proper to him and individuated by him. And because of that real union of the person of the Son and the Son's flesh, the Son can say that he gives this flesh for the life of the world (John 6:51–59). Paul can say that Christ has reconciled us to God "by the body of his flesh through death" (Col. 1:22). Insofar as it is something by which the Son acts for our salvation, the flesh of the Son is an instrument (ὄργανον) of the Son—not a

---

26. Cf. Bockmuehl, *Philippians*, 135.

27. Cf. BDAG, 707.

28. E.g., Zanchi, *In Phil.*, 145; Fee, *Philippians*, 215; Hansen, *Philippians*, 153–54.

29. On the significance of the terms μετέχω and παραπλησίως, see BDAG, 642, 770; Ellingworth, *Hebrews*, 172.

mere external instrument but still an instrument of a sort, to be discussed in the next section. And as an instrument of the eternal Son, who is eternal life (John 5:26; 14:6; 1 John 5:20), this flesh is "life-giving."[30]

(3) What the Word became or assumed is called "flesh" (σάρξ) in John 1:14. In Scripture, the term "flesh" sometimes signifies the material component of created things (e.g., Gen. 2:21; 9:4; 17:11; 40:19; Exod. 4:7; 22:31; Lev. 4:11; Matt. 26:41; Luke 24:39; Rom. 1:3). The term can also function synecdochally, taking the material part for the whole of the human person or the human race, sometimes with an emphasis on humanity's weakness and mortality (cf. Gen. 6:3, 12; Pss. 56:4; 65:2; Isa. 40:5; 66:23; Ezek. 21:4–5; Matt. 16:17; Acts 2:17; 1 Cor. 15:50). Insofar as embodied persons often act wickedly in connection with their bodily desires, the apostle Paul in particular uses σάρξ to signify the sinful condition of human persons (e.g., Rom. 7:5, 14, 18, 25; 8:3–13; 1 Cor. 3:3; 2 Cor. 10:2–3; Gal. 5:13, 16–17, 19, 24; cf. 1 John 2:16).[31] Certainly when John teaches that the Word "became flesh," this does not have to mean only a material body. In fact, John himself uses "flesh" to speak in more general ways about human life and activity (John 1:13; 17:2). Yet John does present σάρξ as something that is weak, mortal, and in need of the renewing work of God's Spirit (3:6; 6:63), though John's use of σάρξ by itself does not convey all the Pauline connections with sin and evil desire.[32] In the case of the Word in John, "flesh" signifies humanity in its weakness and frailty, its mortality and dependence upon the Spirit's work.[33] Cyril of Alexandria fittingly comments that σάρξ in John 1:14 does not signify "soulless flesh" but rather humanity as a "composite" (both soul and flesh). But there is a certain strategy in using a term that often directly designates the most corruptible part of humanity in order to signify the whole. For this expression accentuates humanity's need to come to participate in the Word's immortal life. One recognizes the "wound" and the "medicine" at the same time.[34]

John's Gospel is clear that what the eternal Word has become or assumed includes a human soul or spirit. When Lazarus dies, the incarnate Word, Jesus, is "moved in spirit and troubled" (11:33, 38). In his last week, Jesus says, "Now my soul has been troubled" (12:27). At the Last Supper, Jesus is "troubled in spirit" and announces that one of the disciples will betray him (13:21). Other places in Scripture confirm this and shed light on why it is so important that

30. See Cyril of Alexandria, *In Joann.* 4.2 (1:530); Cyril, *Le Christ est un* 722e–724a (330–31).
31. See, e.g., Alexander Sand, "σάρξ," in *EDNT* 3:230–33.
32. Lee, *Flesh and Glory*, chap. 2, finds an especially strong emphasis on the goodness of flesh in Johannine thought.
33. Cf., e.g., Bauckham, *Gospel of Glory*, 125.
34. Cyril of Alexandria, *Commentaire sur Jean* 1,9 (530, 532, 534).

the eternal Son should have a human intellect and will. For example, Isaiah promises that the Spirit will communicate to the messianic figure virtues of the intellect and will like wisdom, righteousness, and the fear of YHWH (11:1–5). In some sense (to be explored in chap. 6), Jesus advances in wisdom as he grows older (Luke 2:40, 52). Furthermore, in his eschatological discourse, Jesus tells the disciples that he does not know the hour of his return (Mark 13:32). Though Jesus wills to remain unseen while in Tyre and Sidon, he is not able to do this (7:24), which implies that he has a created will that in some way can be frustrated. In Gethsemane he experiences profound sorrow and anxiety and submits his will to the Father's (Matt. 26:37–39, 42). At Golgotha he wills not to drink wine that is offered to him (Matt. 27:34; Mark 15:23), which implies that he has a human will that has some respect to bodily matters, a will by which he had chosen not to dull the corporeal pain of his crucifixion.[35]

Christ's role as the representative of God's people brings into focus the importance of the integrity of his human nature and of his human volition in particular. He is the true Israel and second Adam whose remit is to act in human righteousness and obedience to God the Father in order to bring justification to the people united with himself (Isa. 53:11–12; Matt. 3:15; Rom. 5:12–21). He takes on the *forma servi* in order to become obedient to the Father to the point of vicarious death (Gal. 3:13; Phil. 2:6–8; 1 Pet. 2:24). His being made like us and having a human volition that abhors the grievous elements of his earthly sojourn is what enables him to become a sympathetic high priest for us (Heb. 2:17–18; 4:14–15). Moreover, his human determination to do the Father's will in the face of suffering is an example and encouragement to the saints (e.g., Phil. 2:5; Heb. 12:2; 1 Pet. 2:21–23; 4:1–2). At a more general level, the scriptural account of human nature provides a rationale for the necessity of Christ having a human soul with intellect and will. For human nature involves a rational intellect and will by which one can apprehend spiritual and moral truth and make choices about spiritual and moral matters (Gen. 6:5; Ps. 32:8–9; Rom. 7:15–25; 12:2; Eph. 4:17–18, 22–23; Col. 3:10). In order for Christ truly to participate in the human condition, to be like the children of Abraham whom he comes to help, Christ's humanity must include the soul's rational intellect and will. In light of this, Maximus the Confessor points out that Christ possesses a "natural" human will (θέλημα φυσικὸν), by which he wills "according to essence" (κατ' οὐσίαν).[36]

---

35. Cf., e.g., Keener, *Matthew*, 677–78; Nolland, *Matthew*, 1190–91.
36. Maximus the Confessor, *Opusculum* 7, 77. Cf. John of Damascus, *Expos. fidei* 3.14 (137–38, 140–41).

(4) The Son who assumes the human nature in its integrity remains one and the same person after the assumption. According to John 1:14, the glory of the Word that is made visible to others in the incarnation is still the glory "as of the only Son from the Father," the particle "as" (ὡς) indicating not a comparison of a lesser thing to a greater thing but rather a specification that the glory of the Word made flesh is precisely that of the eternal μονογενής from the Father.[37] The visibility of the glory does not mean that the disciples fully comprehend the divine essence; nevertheless, the glory seen by finite creatures in a finite way is still that of the Word's eternal deity. As Cyril notes, the Word became human "not according to change or alteration but by the power of ineffable union."[38] Later in John's narrative, then, while Jesus is "not yet fifty years old," he announces that he remains the eternal, unchanging God who calls himself "I am" (8:57–58).[39]

The sameness of the Son across the time preceding the assumption of his humanity and the time after the assumption is necessary for the efficacy of his revealing and reconciling work. Only if he remains what he was as the divine Son who is "in the bosom of the Father" can he decisively reveal God to those who have never seen him (John 1:18). Only if he remains the one in whom all the fullness of God dwells can it be said that in beholding him believers have full assurance of spiritual knowledge (Col. 2:2–3, 9). Likewise, only if all fullness dwells in him can Christ atone for the world's sin and reconcile the world to himself (Col. 1:19–20, 22; 2:14–15; Heb. 1:3–4; 9:11–14; cf. 1 Pet. 1:18–20).

Though the Son's κένωσις in Philippians 2:7 has sometimes been taken to mean that the Son undergoes some change in the incarnation, the description of it in Philippians 2:7 actually corroborates the Son's sameness in his incarnate ministry. To be sure, a number of interpreters hold that the statement "he emptied himself" in this text signifies that Christ gave up the *forma Dei* or exchanged the *forma Dei* for the *forma servi*.[40] However, if Christ being in

37. "The point of ὡς ('as') is not that the glory of the Word is simply analogous to the glory of 'a father's One and Only,' but that it actually is that glory" (Michaels, *John*, 80n19). On the use of the particle ὡς to specify or restrict the consideration of something, cf. BDAG, 1104; John Chrysostom, *In Johann.* 12.1 (82).

38. Cyril of Alexandria, *Contra Theodoretum* 169,71 (138). Cf. more recently, e.g., Barrett, *John*, 138. *Pace*, e.g., Schnelle, *Antidocetic Christology in the Gospel of John*, 221–22, who, in a commendable effort to set forth the genuineness of Christ's humanity in Johannine thought, unfortunately ends up suggesting that the very "nature" of the Logos was changed in the incarnation.

39. On the "I am" sayings in John, see Bauckham, *The Testimony of the Beloved Disciple*, 246–50; Macaskill, "Name Christology, Divine Aseity, and the I Am Sayings in the Fourth Gospel."

40. Cf. Käsemann, "A Critical Analysis of Philippians 2:5–11," 64; Wanamaker, "Philippians 2.6–11," 183, 185; Fowl, *The Story of Christ in the Ethics of Paul*, 58, 64; Hurst, "Christ, Adam, and Preexistence Revisited," 86.

the *forma Dei* is a matter of Christ being equal with God the Father, and if God the Father cannot cease to be the true God, then Paul would not envision Christ divesting himself of the *forma Dei*. Positively, Paul actually explains the κένωσις not by subtraction but by addition, by the assumption of the *forma servi*.[41] Various exegetes still attempt to find something *of which* Christ emptied himself: for example, the exercise of certain divine attributes;[42] lordship over the world;[43] certain rights, privileges, or prerogatives that he once had;[44] a position of equality with God that he once had.[45] However, the passage simply states that Christ emptied himself and then follows this with two participial phrases: "He emptied himself, taking the form of a servant, being made in the likeness of human beings." The participles have an adverbial and instrumental or modal function, explaining how or in what way Christ emptied himself: *by* taking the form of a servant, *by* being made in the likeness of human beings.[46]

Philippians 2 therefore gives no basis for positing a change in the Son's exercise of certain divine perfections or in his divine lordship. After all, divine omniscience, divine omnipotence, divine providence, and so forth do not have an on-off switch.[47] At the same time, one can add that Christ's divine glory was generally hidden under the veil of the flesh in his humble human sojourn.[48] Indeed, this seems to be implied by the fact that, after the Son's obedience to death, the Father outwardly exhibits the divine glory of the Son (Phil. 2:9–11). Yet the transition from temporary economic veiling to economic display does not involve a change in the Son's divinity. In fact, it would be fitting for the Father to grant an outward manifestation of the Son's divine glory only if the Son always was and remained the true God. For this glory is that of YHWH himself, the only God and the unchanging God, before whom every knee must bow (Isa. 45:22–23).

41. So, e.g., Fee, *Philippians*, 210–11; Hawthorne and Martin, *Philippians*, 117–18; Schreiner, *New Testament Theology*, 325.

42. MacLeod, "Imitating the Incarnation of Christ," 329–30; Schreiner, *New Testament Theology*, 326.

43. Byrne, "Christ's Pre-existence in Pauline Soteriology," 317.

44. Bockmuehl, *Philippians*, 133–35; Hawthorne and Martin, *Philippians*, 118; cf. I. Marshall, *New Testament Theology*, 348; Reumann, *Philippians*, 368.

45. Fowl, *The Story of Christ in the Ethics of Paul*, 58.

46. Cf., e.g., Fee, *Philippians*, 210; Bockmuehl, *Philippians*, 133; Hawthorne and Martin, *Philippians*, 118. Barth is right that when it comes to the Son's κένωσις, "the decisive commentary is given by the text itself." Thus, the Son "never became a stranger to himself" (*CD*, IV.1, 180).

47. Intriguingly, a "kenotic" theologian like Gottfried Thomasius agrees on this point: with respect to attributes like omniscience or omnipotence, "renunciation of the use is thus here *eo ipso* divesting of the possession" (*Christ's Person and Work*, 71).

48. Cf., e.g., Aquinas, *Super Phil.* 1.3.71 (103–4); Turretin, *Inst.*, 13.6.13 (2:340–41); Witsius, *De oeconomia foederum Dei*, 2.3.17 (116).

At the same time, insofar as the eternal Son previously did not have a human nature united to himself, his assumption of a human nature does involve something new. He is no longer just the divine Son but the divine Son who is now both divine and human. As Cyril puts it, "From the complete *hypostasis* of God the Word and truly also from a humanity completely having its own inner logic, there is one Christ."[49] Formerly, the divine Son was an "incomposite" (ἀσύνθετος) person and now he is a "composite" (σύνθετος) person.[50] The person of Jesus Christ, then, is not the "bare" Word but rather the Word with flesh "woven" (without confusion) to himself.[51] How this fits together with divine immutability and divine simplicity will come up in the next section.

(5) Finally, the Word's divine and human natures remain distinct after his assumption of the human nature. The sense in which the Word "became" flesh in John 1:14 entails this ongoing distinction. Since the Word already was with God in John 1:1, his becoming flesh was not a creation of his ὑπόστασις. And since the Word who became flesh was still the Son full of the divine glory, grace, and truth, his becoming flesh evidently did not involve a confusion of his divinity with the flesh in all its weakness.[52] Indeed, the Word retains his divine fullness, from which we receive "grace upon grace" (John 1:16). Furthermore, since the divine fullness of the Word "tabernacles" or "dwells" in the flesh (John 1:14; cf. Col. 1:19; 2:9; 1 Tim. 3:16), his becoming flesh evidently was not a changing of his divinity into flesh. If that which indwells and that which is indwelt must remain distinct from one another in some way, then that which originally constituted the person of the Word (his eternal deity and personal relation to the Father) must remain the same. The fact that the person of the Word does not *merely* "indwell" the flesh but rather unites it to himself so that its properties now belong to him does not overturn this truth.[53]

In addition, Paul's logic in 2 Corinthians 8:9 indicates that the richness of Christ's divinity remains distinct from the poverty of his humanity. According to Paul, Christ became poor, although being rich [ἐπτώχευσεν πλούσιος ὤν],

49. Cyril of Alexandria, *Scholia* 8 (514).

50. So, e.g., John of Damascus, *Expos. fidei* 3.3 (114–16).

51. Cyril of Alexandria, *Ad Theodosium* 7,36 (66).

52. Note also Ambrose's caution against taking "to become flesh" or "to be made flesh" to mean "to be converted into flesh." Ambrose notes that when Christ is made sin for us (2 Cor. 5:21), he assumes our sin and guilt rather than being converted into sin (*De incarnationis dominicae sacramento* 6,60–61 [255–56]).

53. Cf. again Cyril of Alexandria, *Scholia* 27 (548); Cyril, *Contra Orientales* 24,11 (36); Cyril, *Le Christ est un* 735c–d (370). Cyril points out that the language of "becoming" in Gal. 3:13, where Christ "became" a curse for us, corroborates that the Son's "becoming" should not automatically be regarded as a changing into something.

so that by his poverty we too might become rich. The grammatical structure itself, with an aorist main verb followed by a present adverbial participle,[54] may (but does not necessarily) suggest that the "being rich" continues in its integrity even after the impoverishment. Either way, the material content of the verse does entail this continuation. For Christ even after his impoverishment is still the one who makes us rich. If he can give only what he has, and if he gives riches to us, then he does not compromise his divine richness by dissolving it into his human poverty.

All of this is confirmed by the fact that divinity as such is incorruptible (Rom. 1:23; 1 Tim. 1:17; cf. James 1:17), incapable of undergoing confusion or change in the first place.[55] It is also confirmed by the fact that Christ is the true representative of the people of God. While he is filled with the Spirit's gifts in an unprecedented way (so Isa. 11:1–5), Christ must remain genuinely human, not (per impossibile) a third sort of thing situated between God and created nature. He must remain genuinely human to be the second Adam and to be a sympathetic high priest with experiential knowledge of our weakness. A quasi-divine human being would not be "made like his brothers and sisters according to all things" (Heb. 2:17). In sum, in the case of the divine Son, becoming flesh is not a matter of converting into flesh; it is a matter of assuming and individuating a human nature that is proper to him but still remains distinct from his divine nature.

The main points covered in this section raise certain questions that invite further clarification and elaboration. First, if it is important that the divine Son should be joined to his humanity in a manner that exceeds the way in which God was already present in all things or present with someone like Moses in the Old Testament, how should this new mode of presence or this new mode of dwelling in the flesh be understood? Building from statements above about the Son individuating his human nature and making it proper to himself, the next section will expand on this by discussing the Son's communication of his subsistence to his humanity. Second, if it is vital to maintain the integrity of the human nature that the Son has assumed, how can this be done without suggesting that the Son assumed an actual human being (i.e.,

---

54. On the aspect and relative time of the present participle, see Robertson, *A Grammar of the Greek New Testament*, 891–92, 1115–16; Wallace, *Greek Grammar beyond the Basics*, 623–26. Commentators often assert that Christ being rich was antecedent to his impoverishment (e.g., R. Martin, *2 Corinthians*, 263–64; Best, *Second Corinthians*, 80; Matera, *II Corinthians*, 191), but this is typically due to questionable theological assumptions, in which Christ must somehow abandon his deity in order to become truly human. Insofar as Christ as true God cannot cease to be true God, his divine life, while prior to his human life, continues unabated even in the midst of his human life.

55. Cf. Cyril of Alexandria, *Ad Theodosium* 7,10 (48–49).

a second human person involved in the incarnation)? The next section will address this question by discussing the way in which the Son actualizes his human nature. Third, if the humanity of the Son is something by which the Son acts in the world, what does it mean (or what should it mean) to call the Son's humanity an "instrument" of a divine person? If is it an instrument, is the Son himself still truly human? Fourth, if the Son remains one and the same person in the incarnation, how does this fit with the fact that he has united to himself a human nature whose properties are newly communicated to him? If the Son is now a "composite" person, does this undermine the doctrines of divine immutability and divine simplicity? These four sets of questions will now be taken up under the following points in the next section.

III. Dogmatic Elaboration

(1) The exegetical point, that the Son *became* flesh and is joined to his humanity in a way that exceeds God's presence in creation in general or even in the lives of the prophets, is something that can be illumined by underscoring that in the Son's assumption of a human nature the Son communicates or shares his own subsistence or ὑπόστασις with his humanity. He brings it about that his ὑπόστασις is now a ὑπόστασις of not only eternal deity but also the human nature that he assumes.[56] In order to explain the intention behind this way of speaking about the incarnation and to show its exegetical benefit, it will be useful to recall from the excursus of chapter 2 the meaning of the language of "substance," "subsistence," and ὑπόστασις. In deploying these concepts again, I would emphasize that the point is not to know the concepts or the words themselves—as though words might be ends in their own right. Rather, the point is to bear in mind the distinct ways in which things exist (or "subsist"), how these are expressed carefully by certain terms, and how we might deploy such terms to explain and summarize the sense of Scripture's teaching on the incarnation.

If the divine Son became flesh, so that he himself is now man and there is no other man that the Son assumed in the incarnation, then the Son has established that he himself is the subsistence or ὑπόστασις of the human nature he assumed. That is, he is the one subsisting by himself in whom the

---

56. Cf., e.g., John of Damascus, *Expos. fidei* 3.11 (131); Polanus, *Syntagma*, 6.16 (376). Regarding the communication of the Word's ὑπόστασις, Turretin points out that the communication could be taken "effectively" (as though effecting a new ὑπόστασις in the flesh), "transfusively" (as though changing the ὑπόστασις into flesh and making the flesh a ὑπόστασις), or "assumptively" (as taking up the flesh into the unity of the one ὑπόστασις to be sustained in and only in the one ὑπόστασις, which is the correct sense) (*Inst.*, 13.6.22 [2:344]).

human nature is actuated and individuated and thus the one who becomes a man by this human nature. Even if God or God the Son already existed in all things or existed and specially acted in Solomon's temple and the souls of the prophets, those things or persons themselves were still the subjects in which their natures were actuated and individuated and were the subjects that were essentially constituted by their respective created natures.[57] In the case of the incarnation alone, the Son directly individuates and makes proper to himself a created nature. Only here can the Son be named from this created nature: the Son is man, the man Jesus. In communicating his subsistence to his humanity, the Son establishes that his proper act of subsisting (ὕπαρξις) distinguishes his humanity from any other instances of humanity. The Son is the one who gives his humanity its incommunicability, so that it subsists in and only in him and is not communicable or proper to anyone else, which is why there is no "assumed man" or second human being involved in the incarnation.

The Son's assumption of a human nature, in which he gives his eternal ὑπόστασις to be the ὑπόστασις of his humanity from its very conception, establishes the one person of Christ as the unifying factor of the divine and human in the incarnation. In other words, the union is *personal but not of persons.*[58] Negatively, because the Son does not merely dwell in the flesh (or in a second human being) and does not merely wear his humanity like a vestment, the unifying factor is not an accident like place or habit.[59] The mode of union, then, is not accidental.[60] And while the divine essence is united to the Son's humanity, it is not the divine essence as such but the divine essence in the person of the Son or under the Son's proper mode of subsisting that is immediately united to the Son's humanity.[61] Therefore, the unifying factor in the incarnation is not essence as such (or two essences confused with one another). The union is *of essences but not essential.*[62]

57. While it can be said that all things are (and are actuated and held together) in God (so Acts 17:28; Col. 1:17), this means that God has created all things and inwardly sustains all things, not that God would be the immediate subject of all created essences or would be essentially constituted by all created essences. Inward presence does not necessarily imply immediate subjectivity or essential constitution.

58. Polanus, *Syntagma*, 6.16 (376); Mastricht, *TPT*, 5.4.7 (538).

59. On the inadequacy of temple or "vestment" language to express the meaning of the incarnation, cf. Athanasius, *Oratio IV*, 34–35 (520–21).

60. Cf. Aquinas, *De unione* q. un., art. 1 corp. (423); Aquinas, *ST* IIIa.2.6 (36–37). In this connection, the phrase "grace of union" (see, e.g., *ST* IIIa.2.10 [48–49]; 6.6 [104]; Owen, *Christologia* 18 [227–28]) signifies the gift given to the Son's human nature that it should subsist in the divine Son, not that the union occurs by a mere man being graciously indwelt by the Son.

61. Cf. Lombard, *Sent.* 3.5.2 (46); Polanus, *Syntagma*, 6.13 (364); Turretin, *Inst.*, 13.4.7–9 (2:331–32); 14.2.20 (2:416); Mastricht, *TPT*, 2.24.8 (238); 5.4.5, 9 (537, 539).

62. Polanus, *Syntagma*, 6.16 (376); Mastricht, *TPT*, 5.4.7 (538). Where earlier authors like Cyril of Alexandria (*Contra Theodoretum* 169,30 [119–20]) and John of Damascus (*Expos.*

(2) While the eternal Son communicates his ὑπόστασις and his act of subsisting to his human nature, this does not precipitate a choice of either negating the human nature's integrity (its wholeness, which consists of body and soul with rational intellect and will) or securing that integrity by positing an additional human being in the incarnation. On the one hand, in this unique case, the Son is already (eternally) constituted a ὑπόστασις with intellect and will by his deity and eternal relation to the Father, even without reference to his human nature.[63] While the Son does not have an absolute existence (*esse*) that is numerically distinct from that of the Father and Spirit, he does have the divine *esse* in his own manner (from the Father), in which sense the Son already has his own personal act of subsisting. In the incarnation, then, the Son is not fundamentally constituted a ὑπόστασις or a person by his humanity. He does not receive from the humanity a fundamentally constitutive act of subsisting. Put differently, he subsists *by* his deity and just *in* his humanity.[64]

On the other hand, in giving his subsistence to be the subsistence of his humanity, the Son truly does individuate and characterize this humanity, so that he is newly constituted as man. He is one ὑπόστασις with one *act* of subsisting,

---

fidei 3.3 [114]) declare the union to be "natural" (φυσική) or "essential" (οὐσιώδης), their point is just that the union is not illusory, which ultimately does not conflict with later clarifications about the union being "personal."

63. In Aquinas's description, the Son is "simply constituted a substance [*simpliciter substantificatur*] by the divine nature." The Son is then constituted a substance just *secundum quid* ("according to something," in a qualified sense) by his humanity: "The eternal *suppositum* is constituted a substance [*substantificatur*] by the human nature inasmuch as he is this man" (*De unione* q. un., art. 4 corp. [432]).

64. Polanus, *Syntagma*, 6.16 (376). Cf. Owen, *Christologia* 18 (229). As discussed in chap. 2 and under point (1) above, a person's act and mode of subsisting individuates or distinguishes him from others. Therefore, since Christ is one person (not two), he has one *esse* or act of subsisting (not two) (cf. Aquinas, *ST* IIIa.17.2 [222–23]; Polanus, *Syntagma*, 6.16 [377]). While a divine person's mode of subsisting is incommunicable in that it cannot be transferred or made constitutive of another *person*, it is communicable and, in the Son's case, in fact is communicated to another *nature* (i.e., the humanity he assumes) (cf. Aquinas, *ST* IIIa.3.1 ad 2 [53]). At certain points, Cyril of Alexandria speaks about the Word having two ὑποστάσεις (e.g., *Contra Theodoretum* 169,13–14 [112]; *Contra Orientales* 24,19 [37]), but his intention is just that the Word's deity and humanity are not mere abstract forms but are in fact actual or concrete in the Word (cf. *Contra Theodoretum* 169,32 [120]; *Contra Orientales* 24,27–31 [39–40]; 24,40 [42]; 24,54 [46]; 24,72 [50]), which ultimately does not conflict with subsequent clarifications that the one person of Christ has one *esse* that applies to and individuates his humanity. See further John of Damascus, *Dial.*, κϛ′ (108); McGuckin, *Saint Cyril of Alexandria*, 212–16. In one place, Aquinas distinguishes between an *esse principale* and *esse secundarium* in Christ (*De unione* q. un., art. 4 corp. [432]), which, it seems to me, might be explained in terms of the one personal *esse* being communicated to a second (i.e., human) nature and actualizing and modifying that nature, but Aquinas's meaning is not entirely clear (see further M. Gorman, "Christ as Composite according to Aquinas"; Salas, "Thomas Aquinas on Christ's *Esse*"; Salas, "There Can Only Be One"; Froula, "*Esse Secundarium*"; Riches, *Ecce Homo*, chap. 7).

but he now has a twofold *way* of subsisting.[65] In other words, in assuming the humanity, the Son does not leave it to be an abstract essence but makes it the case that someone (i.e., the Son himself) has become an individual substance of human nature.[66] Accordingly, the point of the notion of the *anhypostasia* and *enhypostasia* of Christ's humanity is not that the humanity is never individuated or concrete but rather that the Son from the very creation of the humanity is the only one who ever has individuated it and made it concrete.[67]

65. Cf. Aquinas, *De unione* q. un., art. 3 ad 11 (431); Ames, *Medulla theologica*, 1.18 (73). To avoid confusion about whether the Son has one mode of subsisting or two modes of subsisting, it might be good to note that both Aquinas and Ames use the word *ratio* in the texts cited to speak of a diverse or double "way" of subsisting. The Son does not have two τρόποι ὑπάρξεως that equally constitute him a distinct person, for then the Son would be two persons. Rather, the point of using an expression like *duplex ratio* is that the Son's one act and mode of subsisting that modifies and characterizes the divine essence is now applied to his human nature as well, so that the one mode now modifies and characterizes two natures. There is one mode of subsisting, but, it might be said, that mode modifies in two ways, distinguishing the Son not only in his divine nature but also in his human nature. It could be added that there are two ways of viewing the Son's modification and individuation of his humanity. On the one hand, the Son's eternal relation to the Father is fundamental to the modification and distinct characterization of the Son's humanity and, indeed, of all that he wills and does as man. On the other hand, the peculiar matter and accidents of the Son's humanity are also, in a broad sense, factors in the individuation of the Son's humanity (cf. John of Damascus, *Expos. fidei* 3.7 [122–24]). Thus, the Son's one mode of subsisting in its application to the Son's humanity takes up the individuating factors of matter and accidents.

66. Cf. John of Damascus: "God the Word incarnate assumed neither the nature thought in bare theory (for this is not incarnation but a fraud and figment of incarnation) nor the nature thought in species (for he does not assume all *hypostaseis*), but the nature in an individual [ἐν ἀτόμῳ]"—"not according to this nature subsisting and formerly being an individual . . . but [according to this nature] subsisting in the *hypostasis* of himself" (*Expos. fidei* 3.11 [131]). In this connection, while the Son's humanity never subsists on its own apart from the Son, it has its own subsistence that is the Son's since the Son himself has individuated and terminated it in himself (cf. Polanus, *Syntagma*, 6.16 [375]; Maccovius, *Loci communes* 57 [492]). The Son's humanity does not have a new subsistence with a proper mode of subsisting that did not already belong to a person subsisting in another nature (i.e., the divine nature). In that respect, the Son's humanity does not have its own complete subsistence (Turretin, *Inst.*, 3.23.5 [1:281]) or its own *personalitas* that completes nature (so Mastricht, *TPT*, 5.4.6 [538]). But insofar as the Son's humanity is individuated by the Son himself and subsists in the Son himself—he subsists in it and is constituted a man by it—it can be said to have complete subsistence and a proper mode of subsisting in him. The adjective "proper" here indicates not that the subsistence or mode of subsisting modifies no other nature at all (for it does eternally modify the divine nature) but only that the subsistence or mode of subsisting truly modifies and individuates this human nature, and no other human nature. On the one hand, then, Christ's humanity is not a ὑπόστασις or *prima substantia* in its own right; its actualization does not yield a new *prima substantia*. On the other hand, though, by the actualization of that nature a preexisting *prima substantia* (the Son) is now a *prima substantia* of the human nature. The Son is not a *prima substantia* by the human nature, but he is a *prima substantia* of the human nature.

67. John of Damascus, *Expos. fidei* 3.12 (134–35); Owen, *Christologia* 18 (233). Cf. Ian McFarland's statement that "the claim 'Jesus does not have a human hypostasis' does not

And even as the Son's prevenient act of subsisting is that which actualizes and individuates his humanity, this does not truncate the content of the human nature or displace its intellect and will. For the divine person with divine intellect and will in whom the human nature is actualized is the *terminus* of the human nature with all that the human nature includes.[68] The person, then, is not that which introduces rational intellect and will to an otherwise nonrational nature, for intellect and will as such are not what distinguishes human persons but are rather ingredient in the common meaning of humanity. If what distinguishes a person were that which introduces intellect and will to nature, then presumably the Son's divine intellect and will would displace the human intellect and will. Instead, however, person is the individuating endpoint of everything encompassed in the common nature, including rational intellect and will, so the person of the Son truly has a human intellect and will. That the concreteness and integrity of Christ's human nature does not require a second person involved in the incarnation can be corroborated by the next point about the sense in which the human nature may be called an "instrument" of the Son.

(3) If the incarnate Son acts by his human nature to reveal the Father and accomplish our salvation, there is an important sense in which the human nature is an "instrument" (ὄργανον, *organum*) of the Son. To clarify the sense in which the Son's humanity is an instrument and to show that this coheres with the fact that the Son is a concrete man who acts as man, it is worthwhile to think carefully about Cyril of Alexandria's comments on the Son's humanity being an instrument. For Cyril's work on this is typically regarded as seminal, and whether Cyril's view minimizes the Son's humanity or human action is a matter of concern in some circles.[69]

In Cyril's writings, the Son's humanity is not an instrument of the Son in the way that a musical instrument is externally possessed and wielded by the one playing it. In fact, the Son's humanity can be an instrument—a life-giving instrument—in a Cyrilline sense only because it is his very own humanity.[70] The Son's body is "his own" (ἴδιον) just as our bodies belong to us. Thus, the Word offered up his own body and, indeed, his own soul for our redemption,

---

entail any diminishment or qualification of the claim that he has a fully human *nature*" (*The Word Made Flesh*, 8).

68. On person as the *terminus* of nature, cf. Aquinas, *ST* IIIa.19.1 ad 4 (241); Turretin, *Inst.*, 13.6.18 (2:343).

69. See, e.g., Beeke and Jones, *Puritan Theology*, 336–40; McCormack, "The Only Mediator"; McCormack, "Atonement and Human Suffering," 198.

70. Cyril of Alexandria, *In Joann*. 4.2 (1:530); *Le Christ est un* 722e–724a (330–31); 777a–e (509–10). Cyril remarks that "common flesh is not able to give life" (so John 6:63) (*Explanatio XII cap*. 148,29 [25]).

a body and soul in which the Word himself experienced infirmities and trials, like hunger, grief, and fear.[71] The point of calling the flesh an "instrument" is to help express that the Word, who is impassible in his deity, made the flesh his own so that by it he could suffer and die for us and bring us life.[72] Furthermore, in Cyril's account, the person who acts for our salvation is not just the "bare" Word but rather the God-man, Christ, acting not only *by* but, one might say, also *in* and *according to* his humanity. Cyril writes that "from the complete *hypostasis* of God the Word and truly also from a humanity completely having its own inner logic, there is one Christ."[73] Thus, the deity and the humanity both are "in the same one," Immanuel, who is "neither bare man nor truly the Word apart from the humanity and the flesh."[74] The "same one" (ὁ αὐτός) is both the only begotten and the human firstborn among many brothers and sisters.[75] Thus, the one speaking about worship with the Samaritan woman at the well is "the one and only Lord Jesus Christ, from the humanity which worships and the deity which is worshiped, truly having both to be God and to be called God and also to be man and to be called man." As God, Christ is the Lord of glory who is worshiped; as man, Christ seeks glory from the Father.[76] Indeed, according to Cyril, the Son as God is above the law, so only as man can the Son be subject to the law and obey it for our sake.[77] He does this as one Christ, "from both deity and humanity, according to an economic unity."[78]

One need not draw anachronistic conclusions about Cyril being a Reformed theologian in order to discern that his Christology can be reasonably explicated in terms of there being one incarnate Son who acts by both his deity and his humanity, and not just *by* but even *in* and *according to* the humanity and thus as man. Other major figures who speak about Christ's humanity being an "instrument" follow this trajectory.

John of Damascus, for example, speaks of Christ's humanity or his flesh as an "instrument of deity" (ὄργανον τῆς θεότητος).[79] But John's account clearly requires that the humanity that is an instrument of the Son must also

71. Cyril of Alexandria, *Ad monachos* 1,19–21 (19–20); Cyril, *Scholia* 27 (551); Cyril, *Ad Theodosium* 7,21 (55); Cyril, *Contra Theodoretum* 169,54 (131); 169,83 (142); 169,86 (143).

72. Cyril of Alexandria, *Explanatio XII cap.* 148,31 (25).

73. Cyril of Alexandria, *Scholia* 8 (514); 13 (526); Cyril, *Ad Theodosium* 7,36 (66).

74. Cyril of Alexandria, *Scholia* 35 (563).

75. Cyril of Alexandria, *Ad Theodosium* 7,30 (61–62).

76. Cyril of Alexandria, *Ad Theodosium* 7,32 (63).

77. See, e.g., Cyril of Alexandria, *Ad monachos* 1,18 (18); 1,23 (21); Cyril, *Tertia ad Nestorium* 6,5 (36–37); Cyril, *Explanatio XII cap.* 148,27 (24); Cyril, *Scholia* 5 (508).

78. Cyril of Alexandria, *Contra Theodoretum* 169,50–51 (129).

79. John of Damascus, *Expos. fidei* 3.15 (150); 3.19 (161).

essentially constitute the Son himself as man so that the Son can act as man. For Christ's humanity is an instrument in that through Christ's human volition and actions Christ's divine volition and actions are brought to bear in the economy. Subsisting in the Son, the human nature has its own distinctly human energy with which (together with the divine energy) the Son produces his effects.[80] The human energy and its effect (ἀποτέλεσμα) and the divine energy and its effect remain distinct even as they are inseparable in one "theandric energy."[81] The humanity and human energy of Christ is said to have been "deified" (τεθεῶσθαι), but without any change or confusion of the humanity or its "properties" (ἰδιώματα). Rather, according to John, there is a union and "mutual indwelling" (περιχώρησις) of the two natures so that the human efficacy is never isolated from the divine.[82] The point of the instrumentality of Christ's humanity or the concept of "theandric energy," then, is just that the divine volition and activity of Christ is what governs his human volition and activity, ensuring that his human operation always corresponds to the will of God. The human is not independent of the divine but rather ordered to and reflective of it. And because of the human energy's union with the divine, it contributes to works that exceed the capacity of any other human nature. In this sense, the humanity or human energy is an instrument by which the divine Son accomplishes his works. For example, Christ operates by his human nature to touch someone who is ill or to break loaves of bread, on the one hand, and he operates by his divine nature to produce a miraculous healing or to multiply loaves, on the other hand.[83] One and the same Christ wills and operates "divinely" and wills and operates "humanly."[84]

Aquinas also calls the humanity of Christ an *organum* and strongly emphasizes the difference between an "external" and "common" instrument like an axe and the "conjoined" and "proper" instrument of Christ's humanity. An

80. John of Damascus, *Expos. fidei* 3.15 (145–49).
81. John of Damascus, *Expos. fidei* 3.15 (148). The Greek here is ἄλλο . . . τοῦτο, κἀκεῖνο ἕτερον, εἰ καὶ ἀλλήλων ἀχώριστοι ὑπάρχουσιν ἐν τῇ θεανδρικῇ ἐνεργείᾳ. Cf. also 3.17 (156); 3.19 (162). While John suggests here that Christ acting by his two natures produces two ἀποτελέσματα, the Reformed theologians often stress that Christ acting by his two natures produces one ἀποτέλεσμα (esp. the work of mediation or redemption), though they recognize that the terms ἐνέργεια and ἀποτέλεσμα have sometimes been used synonymously (see Polanus, *Syntagma*, 6.16 [378]; Turretin, *Inst.*, 14.2.3 [2:412]). Aquinas may help us to see that the difference is largely semantic where he states that there is a *proprium operatum* of the divine nature (e.g., the healing of a leper) and a *proprium operatum* of the human nature (e.g., the corporeal touching of the leper), but "both operations concur toward one *operatum* as one nature acts with communion with the other" (*ST* IIIa.19.1 ad 5 [241]).
82. John of Damascus, *Expos. fidei* 3.17 (155–56).
83. John of Damascus, *Expos. fidei* 3.15 (145–46, 149–51), 17 (156), 18 (158–60).
84. John of Damascus, *Expos. fidei* 3.15 (146).

axe is an external, separable instrument that is common to and used by many. The operation of the axe is not proper to the one wielding it. For Aquinas, a better illustration of the instrumentality of Christ's humanity involves a human hand and human soul: "The axe is not a proper instrument like this hand. For by the axe many are able to operate, but *this* hand is assigned to the proper operation of *this* soul." Moreover, while other human beings can be considered instruments of God in the sense that God works through them to accomplish certain things, only the humanity of Christ is something by which God "instrumentally works these things which are operations proper to God alone, like to wash away sins, to illumine minds by grace, and to lead to the perfection of eternal life."[85] Calling Christ's humanity an *organum* expresses that the human nature in Christ is "moved and ruled by the divine." This means that Christ's divine operation "uses" the human operation to accomplish certain things. But, Aquinas insists, that which is moved by another has a "double action": one action according to its own proper form or virtue and another according to it being moved by another. Thus, Christ performs both divine and human operations, the divine using the human as an instrument and the human participating in the operation of the divine by which it is moved.[86]

If the divine Son has acted by his human nature to reveal the Father and reconcile us to God, it is important to understand the sense in which the human nature is an instrument of the divine Son. This sense is illumined in the works of authors like Cyril of Alexandria, John of Damascus, and Thomas Aquinas. Drawing insights from these authors, one can say that the Son's humanity is an instrument in two senses. First, the Son already was God and did not need his humanity in order to be constituted a person. The Son subsequently united the humanity to himself for the purpose of saving sinners and displaying the mercy of God. The humanity, then, is something by which the Son who already is the Son does a particular thing. Second, the Son's human volition and human action are ordered to and governed by the Son's divine volition and divine action. The humanity, then, is not by itself the principal agent in the incarnation. It is something by which the Son accomplishes his mediatorial works.

However, the contingency involved in the assumption of the human nature and the submission of the human volition and action to the divine volition and action does not cancel out the concreteness of the Son's humanity. Nor does

---

85. Aquinas, *SCG* 4.41 (141–42). Cf. Aquinas, *ST* IIIa.13.2 corp. and ad 2 (173).

86. Aquinas, *ST* IIIa.19.1 corp. and ad 1–2 (240–41). Like John of Damascus, when Aquinas mentions the *operatio theandrica*, he states that there is no "confusion of operations."

it cancel out the fact that the acting subject in the incarnation is essentially constituted as man and acts as man. This is expressed well in the statement that Christ's human nature is a *principium quo*—not merely an instrument but an internal formal principle by which he is in his own person capable of human action and suffering.[87] In fact, the sense in which Christ's humanity is an instrument requires that it be individuated by him and proper to him. For Christ's humanity is an instrument by which he unfailingly reveals the Father. Christ's humanity can be such an instrument only if the human volition and action is enclosed within and always characterized by the Son's relation to the Father.[88] Likewise, Christ's humanity is an instrument by which he pays the penalty of the world's sin. Christ's humanity can be such an instrument only if the human volition and action is that of a divine person laying down his life and offering his own precious blood on the cross (Acts 20:28; 1 Pet. 1:18–19).

(4) Finally, the Son remains the same person before and after the assumption of his human nature. His assumption of human flesh does not overturn his divine immutability or his divine simplicity. Of course, there should be no dispute that, having assumed human flesh, the Son according to his humanity undergoes change like other human beings do. The point here is that the Son according to his divinity underwent no change in the assumption of his humanity. And the point is an urgent one because the Son must remain the one from the Father full of the divine glory, grace, and truth in order to reveal the Father and atone for sin. He must remain rich in order to make us rich by his human poverty and suffering.

In light of the discussion of divine actuality in chapter 3, I would emphasize here that neither the divine essence nor the person of the Son had to undergo change in Son's assumption of a human nature.[89] The Son did exercise and outwardly terminate his divine actuality in a new way when he assumed the human nature. In that regard, he became present with us in a new manner.[90] Yet he did not have to reduce a previously unactualized divine power to actuality in order to create and simultaneously assume the human nature. Having

87. See, e.g., Aquinas, *De unione* q. un., art. 5 corp. and ad 4 (434); Turretin, *Inst.*, 14.2.2–3 (2:411–12); Mastricht, *TPT*, 5.4.13 (540).

88. See the excellent treatment in White, *Incarnate Lord*, chap. 5. If space permitted, it might be fruitful to reflect more on the concept of Christ's humanity as an instrument of a divine person and instrument of divine revelation in connection with Ian McFarland's recent monograph on the incarnation, where he argues that while the divine person of the Son is revealed in the incarnation, only the Son's humanity is perceived by us (*The Word Made Flesh*, 8–9 and passim).

89. If the person of the Son had undergone change by the act itself of assuming a human nature, then at that point, because he was subsisting in the divine nature alone before the incarnation, he would have (*per impossibile*) undergone change by some capacity of the divine essence.

90. Cf., e.g., Cyril of Alexandria, *Scholia* 2 (502–3); Cyril, *Contra Theodoretum* 169,41 (125); Aquinas, *ST* Ia.43.1–2 (445–46).

assumed the human nature whose capacities and faculties became proper to him, it was then that he, as human, began to experience the ordinary changes of human life. Insofar as Christ's human nature never became confused with his deity, Christ's human nature as a principle of change in him never introduced change into his deity.

Does the notion that the Son is now one person "from" two natures or the notion that the Son is now the subject of human properties stand in conflict with the doctrine of divine simplicity? In response to this question, I think there are two things that need mentioning, one pertaining to theology proper and the other more directly to Christology itself. First, it is important to avoid a superficial and overly austere reading of divine simplicity.[91] Divine simplicity does not stipulate that there are absolutely no distinctions in God's being or that a divine person could not be the subject of two distinct natures, one of which (i.e., the human) is composed of parts. As discussed in chapter 2, any Christian doctrine of divine simplicity will have to take into account that there are three distinct persons in God, each with his own proper mode of subsisting. Moreover, any Christian account will have to recognize that it is the divine essence (what God is as God or what each divine person is as God) that is simple. One divine person's assumption of a human nature that is not mixed up with his divine essence does not render the divine essence itself complex. Nor does any of this enervate the doctrine of divine simplicity or make it irrelevant. The doctrine still sets forth that God is not constituted as God by anything other than God, that God himself is the fullness of each of his divine attributes, and that the fullness of God subsists in each of the divine persons.

Second, the Son's assumption of a human nature in fact does not involve any confusion of that nature with the Son's simple deity. While the Father, Son, and Spirit act together by their common divine power to bring about the incarnation (Matt. 1:18; Luke 1:35; 2 Cor. 8:9; Phil. 2:7; Heb. 10:5), only the Son becomes flesh (i.e., assumes, individuates, and makes proper to himself the human nature). To anticipate some of the language to be used in the next chapter, only the Son is the *terminus ad quem* of the creation of the human nature in Mary's womb. Only the Son is the "endpoint" in whom that human nature comes to subsist. Accordingly, only the Son—not the divine essence as such—is the subject who individuates the human nature and is constituted as man by the human nature. It is the person of the Son, then, and not the divine essence that is constituted by two natures, one of which has parts (i.e., the human nature with body and soul, essence and qualities, and so forth).

91. An example of which can be found in Senor, "The Compositional Account of the Incarnation," 58–59.

The aim in calling Christ a "composite" (σύνθετος) person is just to specify that he is one person now subsisting in two natures, not that his divinity itself might have become complex. Cyril of Alexandria speaks of Christ being "from" deity and humanity or "from two things" (ἐκ δυοῖν . . . πραγμάτων).[92] At the same time, he emphasizes that when the Word became man, he did not change into something he was not, "for he is always the same [ὁ αὐτός] and does not endure to suffer a shadow of change" (so James 1:17). He does not mix or confuse his divine essence with the flesh. He has "remained God even in the assumption of the flesh and is one Son of God the Father, our Lord Jesus Christ, the same [ὁ αὐτός] also before every age and time insofar as he is understood as the Word . . . and in the last times economically a man on account of us." Before the incarnation the Word was the Word "without flesh" (ἄσαρκος), and after the incarnation the Word is "the same one embodied" (ὁ αὐτὸς ἐνσώματος).[93]

The notion of a σύνθεσις in the incarnation is formally taken up in the anathemas of the Second Council of Constantinople (553), where σύνθεσις is contrasted with σύγχυσις ("confusion"). The union of the Word with the flesh occurs "according to a synthesis"—that is, "according to the *hypostasis*." This "union according to synthesis" precludes both confusion and separation of the deity and humanity.[94] In accord with this usage, when John of Damascus calls Christ a ὑπόστασις σύνθετος, he provides important clarifications. According to John, there is a unity of Christ's two complete natures "not according to confusion" as Eutyches thought, "nor according to good pleasure" as Nestorius thought, but "according to synthesis, truly, according to *hypostasis* [κατὰ σύνθεσιν ἤτοι καθ' ὑπόστασιν], without change and without confusion." There is no "composite nature" (σύνθετος φύσις); instead the

92. E.g., Cyril of Alexandria, *Ad monachos* 1,18 (18). Cf. Cyril, *Altera ad Nestorium* 4,3 (26–27); Cyril, *Tertia ad Nestorium* 6,8 (38); Cyril, *Scholia* 8 (514); 27 (548); Cyril, *Ad Theodosium* 7,24–25 (57–58), 44 (72); Cyril, *Contra Theodoretum* 169,51 (129); 169,83 (142); Cyril, *Contra Orientales* 24,31 (40); 24,71–73 (50).

93. Cyril of Alexandria, *Explanatio XII cap.* 14,5 (17); 14,8 (17–18). Cf. Cyril, *Altera ad Nestorium* 4,3 (26–27); Cyril, *Tertia ad Nestorium* 6,3 (35); Cyril, *Scholia* 8 (510, 512); 27 (547–48); 37 (574–75); Cyril, *Ad Theodosium* 7,10 (48–49); 7,26 (58–59); Cyril, *Contra Theodoretum* 169,13 (112); Cyril, *Contra Orientales* 24,21–22 (38); 24,31 (40); Cyril, *Le Christ est un* 735d (370). Though some places in Cyril's works affirm the "one nature" (μία φύσις) of the Word (e.g., *Contra Orientales* 24,72 [50]; *Le Christ est un* 735a–737d [370–80]), he still maintains a clear distinction between the Word's divinity and humanity and, in those places, uses the term φύσις in the way that both he and others would use the term ὑπόστασις. Cf. Cyril's letter to John of Antioch included in the documents of the Council of Ephesus in N. Tanner, *Decrees of the Ecumenical Councils*, 72. See further McGuckin, *Saint Cyril of Alexandria*, 207–12; van Loon, *The Dyophysite Christology of Cyril of Alexandria*.

94. Second Council of Constantinople, "Anathema 4," in N. Tanner, *Decrees of the Ecumenical Councils*, 115.

two natures are "united to one another truly in one composite *hypostasis* [ὑπόστασιν σύνθετον]." "We declare their essential difference [τὴν οὐσιώδη διαφορὰν] to be preserved."[95] Otherwise, the Word would be neither true God nor true man, and the incarnation would be an illusion.[96]

When Aquinas treats the question of whether Christ is a "composite person" in the *Summa theologiae*, he responds that Christ is a composite person inasmuch as he is one subsisting (*unum subsistens*) in two natures with two distinct ways of subsisting (*alia et alia ratio subsistendi*). The "composition of the person from the natures is not said by reason of parts, but rather by reason of number, as everything in which two convene can be called 'composed' from these."[97] Thus, the human nature of Christ is not properly speaking a "part" in a whole. It remains, then, that Christ is "simple according to the divine nature but composed according to the human nature." [98] Among the Reformed orthodox, Polanus, for example, writes that consideration of the person of Christ is twofold: "one by reason of the essence of the Logos, another by reason of the gracious and salvific economy." In the former respect, Christ is an "ἀσύνθετος *hypostasis* generated by the Father in the divine essence"; in the latter respect, Christ is a "*hypostasis* σύνθετος, that is, the second person of the deity incarnate, and accordingly composed of two natures." But Polanus also specifies what is meant by the adjective "composite" in this case. On the one hand, nothing can "accede to" or come to inhere in the complete, eternally established subsisting (*esse completum*) of the Son, so he is not "composite" in this regard. In this connection, the human nature of the Son is not a part but an "instrument" of the Son. Yet, on the other hand, something can come into communion with the subsistence of the Son for the accomplishment of an end (i.e., our salvation). Hence the "composition of the person from the natures is not by reason of parts but rather by reason of number, because the human nature subsists in the person of Christ."[99] Likewise, Turretin observes that the Son is the God-man not by composition "properly so called," as though the divine and human natures were "incomplete parts" ordered to the constitution of a greater whole. Nothing accedes to the divine nature or renders it composite. Instead, the human nature is assumed, perfected, and sustained by

95. John of Damascus, *Expos. fidei* 3.3 (114–16). Cf. 3.7 (123–24).
96. John of Damascus, *Expos. fidei* 3.2–3 (110–12).
97. Aquinas, *ST* IIIa.2.4 (31).
98. Aquinas, *De unione* q. un., art. 2 corp. and ad 18 (427, 429). On a related note, Aquinas observes the limitation of the body-soul analogy used to illustrate the union of Christ's two natures in the Christian tradition (see *De unione* q. un., art. 1 corp. and ad 1 [424]; art. 5 ad 11 [435]). The use of the illustration focuses not on the body and soul being parts that compose a nature but on these two that are distinct from one another being united in a single person.
99. Polanus, *Syntagma*, 6.12 (362); 6.16 (374–75).

the person of the Son, whose divine subsistence is already eternally complete. Because this involves not a composition of essential parts (body and soul) or subject and accident but the unique assumption of an "essential adjunct" by an already complete subsistence, Turretin calls this a "hyperphysical" composition (i.e., one that transcends the ordinary workings of nature).[100]

In this section I have sought to shed some more light on the scriptural teaching set out in the previous section. The elaboration on the Son's subsistence in his humanity illumines the sense in which he is present in and united to his humanity in a manner that surpasses God's presence in all things or God's activity in the lives of the prophets. The elaboration on the Son's actualization and individuation of his humanity helps to confirm the concreteness and integrity of his humanity. The elaboration on the sense in which the humanity of the Son is an "instrument" helps to clarify the relationship between the human and the divine in Christ and, instead of undermining the Son's human volition and activity, actually confirms that the Son himself must be human and must will and act as human. Finally, elaborating on the sameness and simplicity of the Son across his act of assuming a human nature confirms that the radical novelty of the incarnation involves no change in the divine subsistence of the Son and thus that the Son remains fit for his climactic prophetic and priestly work.

So far I have taken what I consider to be a broadly catholic approach to the way in which what is proper to the Son's humanity truly belongs to him but does not affect his divinity. However, there will likely be questions asked about whether the communion or communication of the human and the divine in Christ can fit so neatly with God's immutability, impassibility, and simplicity. More specifically, some readers may wonder whether the debates among Lutheran and Reformed theologians regarding the *communicatio idiomatum* and the so-called *extra Calvinisticum* problematize the notion that Christ according to his divinity transcends the mutability and passibility of his own flesh. These issues will be addressed in the next two sections.

IV. Concerns about the *Communicatio Idiomatum* and the *Extra Calvinisticum*

In order to substantiate this chapter's account of the Son's relationship to his human nature—particularly the claim that the Son's subsistence in the

---

100. Turretin, *Inst.*, 3.7.7 (1:211); 13.6.8 (2:339). See also Turretin's comments on the use of the body-soul analogy in Christology in 13.7.16 (2:348–49).

flesh coheres with his divine immutability, impassibility, and simplicity—it will be important to address the concerns of some Lutheran and Reformed theologians surrounding the doctrine of the *communicatio idiomatum* (the communication or sharing of the properties of the two natures in the one person of Christ) and the related notion of the *extra Calvinisticum* (the teaching that Christ according to his divinity is not enclosed within his humanity but rather subsists *extra carnem*, beyond his finite flesh). These concerns give rise to different strategies for securing the unity of the person of Christ. Early Lutheran theologians maintained that the incarnation did not affect the deity of the Son, so their arguments ultimately do not undermine the claims of this volume. However, insofar as the early Lutheran criticisms of the *extra Calvinisticum* have sometimes been taken to open the way to divine passibility, it will be valuable to respond to their lines of reasoning.[101] Beyond the field of early modern Protestant theology, nineteenth-century "kenotic" Christologies emphasized that Christ's divinity actually was affected by the incarnation, undergoing certain limitations in order to facilitate the unity of the person of Christ during his earthly sojourn. The nineteenth-century Lutheran theologian Isaak Dorner opposed the kenotic teaching but also developed some of the Lutheran criticisms of Reformed Christology. His concern to avoid a docetic portrayal of the incarnation and to identify the point of union of Christ's two natures will be worth taking into account here. Finally, from the Reformed side, Karl Barth cautiously affirmed the *extra* but also registered concerns about it potentially undermining the unity of the person of Christ and the decisiveness of God's revelation in Christ. Each set of concerns noted here might warrant its own book-length analysis. My intention at present is not to provide an exhaustive response to these concerns but rather to describe them briefly in this section and then to show (or at least begin to show) in the next section that a catholic, Reformed account of the Son's relationship to his human nature has the resources needed to provide convincing responses.

(1) In the early development of Lutheran Christology, key authors took diverse paths in explicating the communication or sharing of the divine and human in Christ. Historical accounts of the sixteenth- and seventeenth-century discussions often set out distinctions among figures like Martin Luther, Philipp Melanchthon, Johannes Brenz, and Martin Chemnitz.[102] Melanchthon

---

101. Eberhard Jüngel, for instance, remarks that "Luther's Christology and Hegel's philosophy" are responsible for widespread revision of the doctrine of God (*God as the Mystery of the World*, 373). See also Ngien, "Chalcedonian Christology and Beyond."

102. See, e.g., Barth, *CD*, IV.1, 181–83; Wiedenroth, *Krypsis und Kenosis*; Haga, *Was There a Lutheran Metaphysics?*; McGinnis, *The Son of God beyond the Flesh*, chap. 4; Klinge,

is often regarded as being closer to Reformed Christology, whereas Brenz is often regarded as pressing in a more distinctively Lutheran or perhaps simply a more novel direction. My intention here is not so much to analyze the intra-Lutheran debates but to observe the common concerns of mainstream Lutheran orthodox theologians like Chemnitz, Johann Gerhard, and Johann Quenstedt about the doctrine of the *communicatio idiomatum*. There are caricatures of the early Lutherans that exaggerate their disagreement with Reformed Christology and need to be cleared away for the benefit of ecumenical, constructive Christology today.[103] At the same time, there are some serious Lutheran orthodox criticisms of Reformed Christology that will elicit clarification of the position developed in this chapter.

The Lutheran orthodox often speak of three genera or kinds of christological communication that follow on the hypostatic union of the two natures.[104] First, there is a *genus idiomaticum*, wherein the essential properties of each nature are really communicated to or belong to the one person of Christ, the divine properties being communicated to Christ on account of his deity and the human properties being communicated to Christ on account of his humanity. Second, there is a *genus majestaticum*, wherein the majesty or glory and excellence of the divine nature is communicated to the human nature on account of the hypostatic union, so that Christ's humanity has an excellence and power that surpasses that of ordinary humanity. To be clear, this is not just a communication that produces finite habitual graces; it is a communication of gifts that are "truly divine and infinite." According to the Lutherans, in the context of the second genus, the deity of Christ is eternally complete and therefore remains free of change or passion. It is not affected by the union with Christ's humanity even as it affects the humanity. Third, there is a *genus apotelesmaticum*, wherein the economic offices and works (*apotelesmata*) of Christ belong to the person of Christ on account of both his deity and his humanity because Christ always acts by both natures together to accomplish his works.[105]

Verheißene Gegenwart; Cross, *Communicatio Idiomatum*. For broader considerations about the development of the *extra*, see also Drake, *The Flesh of the Word*.

103. For helpful examples of clearing away such caricatures, see Luy, *Dominus Mortis*; S. Holmes, "Asymmetrical Assumption."

104. Sometimes the phrase *communicatio idiomatum* is used broadly to include more than one kind of communication; other times it is used more narrowly to signify just the first kind. So, e.g., the note in Gerhard, *Loci theologici*, 4.10.176 (528).

105. See Chemnitz, *De duabis naturis in Christo*, 12.153–69; Gerhard, *Loci theologici*, 4.10 (527–32); Quenstedt, *Theologia didactico-polemica*, 3.3.1.1 (93–108). For the quote about gifts that are "truly divine and infinite," see Gerhard, *Loci theologici*, 4.12.209 (551); Quenstedt, *Theologia didactico-polemica*, 3.3.1.1 (100).

   While the early Lutherans do not advocate a transfer of human properties and experiences to the divine nature of Christ, they do distinguish their view of the *genus idiomaticum* and especially the *genus majestaticum* from that of the Reformed theologians and accuse the Reformed of having Nestorian tendencies in their Christology. They argue that the Reformed allow only a "verbal" (rather than "real") communication of essential properties in the person of Christ, as though the divine attributes were only spoken of the man Jesus and did not belong to him in reality. According to the Lutherans, this enervates the hypostatic union and removes the ontological basis of statements ("personal propositions") like "God is man" and "man is God" or statements like "God bought the church with his own blood" (see Acts 20:28).[106]

   At the heart of this disagreement with the Reformed is the Lutheran contention that within the *genus majestaticum* divine attributes like omnipresence are shared by Christ's humanity. To be sure, omnipresence is not transferred to Christ's humanity in the abstract or on its own. It does not become a property of Christ's humanity on its own, but it is shared by Christ's humanity like fire may heat iron. The heat does not become proper to the iron in abstraction from the fire, but the iron becomes hot by virtue of its union with the fire. The sharing of divine omnipresence with the human nature means that the person of the Word never subsists outside of or beyond the flesh (*extra carnem*). Wherever the person of the Word is, there is the human nature and human flesh.[107]

   That Christ never subsists beyond the flesh is a key point for Lutheran sacramental theology—and a point that is strongly criticized in Reformed Christology. For their part, Reformed orthodox theologians do affirm that the divine properties or attributes (omnipresence, omniscience, and so on) belong to the man Jesus in reality. But they also reason that when the Lutherans go beyond this to affirm that the divine attributes are shared by *the human nature* of the man Jesus, then this implies, despite Lutheran arguments to the contrary, that the sharing would pertain to the human nature as such or in the abstract, thus suggesting a Eutychian confusion of Christ's two natures.[108] In turn, the Lutherans provide further clarifications of their own position to address the charge of Eutychianism and emphasize that the Reformed teaching of Christ subsisting beyond the flesh (pejoratively called the *extra Calvinisticum*

106. E.g., Gerhard, *Loci theologici*, 4.8.152 (517–18); 4.9.158–67 (521–24); 4.10.178 (529).

   107. Chemnitz, *De duabis naturis in Christo*, 12.158; 30.467–525; Gerhard, *Loci theologici*, 4.10.175 (528); 4.12.218–29 (555–64); Quenstedt, *Theologia didactico-polemica*, 3.3.1.2.5 (138–42).

   108. For Reformed accounts, see, e.g., Zanchi, *De incarn.*, 2.3 (338–41); Turretin, *Inst.*, 13.8 (2:349–61).

as though it were an innovation of the Reformed) severs the hypostatic union and compromises Christ's saving power and presence with us.[109]

By affirming the immutability and impassibility of Christ's divinity in the midst of the incarnation, the older Lutheran theologians align with the trajectory of the present chapter. However, the Lutheran contention that the Reformed maintain only a "verbal" communication of properties in the person of Christ and that the notion of the *extra Calvinisticum* undermines the hypostatic union is something that needs to be addressed in the next section in order to show that one can maintain a real communication of properties in Christology even in connection with a robust affirmation of Christ's divine essence transcending the features of his human flesh.

(2) Nineteenth-century kenotic Christology moved beyond the orthodox theological instincts of early Lutheranism and, in Barth's words, sought "to find a place for the historical form of Jesus in its human limitation" by embracing "the idea of a self-limitation of God in the incarnation (or . . . the possibility of a *genus tapeinoticum*)."[110] In the nineteenth century and more recently, various writers have offered different proposals under the heading of "kenotic" Christology, with diversity in the manner or extent to which they are willing to deny that Christ possessed or exercised certain divine attributes in his time on earth.[111] Here I will focus on one significant representative of nineteenth-century kenoticism, Gottfried Thomasius. Thomasius argues that the Son's assumption of a human nature "does not reach all the way in explaining the *historical* person of the God-man. We must go yet one step further, to the supposition of a self-limitation of the divine." For if the divine Son "remains in his divine mode of being and action in the finite human nature assumed by him, if he persists in his trans-worldly position, in the unlimitedness

109. For a pejorative reference to the *Calviniani* who maintain "that Nestorian *extra*" (*Extra illud Nestorianum*), see Quenstedt, *Theologia didactico-polemica*, 3.3.1.2.5 (139). On the "practical use" of the Lutheran position, see Gerhard, *Loci theologici*, 4.9.154 (518). For recent studies on the *extra Calvinisticum*, see E. Willis, *Calvin's Catholic Christology*; Aus der Au, "Das Extra Calvinisticum"; Habets, "Putting the 'Extra' Back into Calvinism"; van der Kooi, "The Identity of Israel's God"; Sumner, "The Twofold Life of the Word"; McGinnis, *Son of God beyond the Flesh*; Gordon, *The Holy One in Our Midst*.

110. Barth, CD, IV.1, 182. The phrase *genus tapeinoticum* signifies a kind of communication in Christology wherein the humble features of Christ's humanity would be shared by his divinity. This was not a genus accepted by the early Lutherans but is explored later in modern Christologies.

111. For more recent works, see, e.g., C. Stephen Evans, *Exploring Kenotic Christology*; D. Brown, *Divine Humanity*; Senor, "Drawing on Many Traditions"; Davis, "The Metaphysics of Kenosis"; Le Poidevin, "Kenosis, Necessity and Incarnation"; Loke, *A Kryptic Model of the Incarnation*; Archer, "Kenosis, Omniscience, and the Anselmian Concept of Divinity"; Youngs, *The Way of the Kenotic Christ*; Yang, "Kenoticism and Essential Divine Properties." For a critical assessment, see, e.g., Crisp, *Divinity and Humanity*, 118–53.

of his world-ruling and world-embracing governance, then the mutual relation of the two also remains always afflicted by a certain duplication." The
divinity is like a "broader circle" that "encompasses" the humanity. It is the
"extra-historical over the temporal," "that which is perfect in itself over that
which becomes." The divine "consciousness" of the Son is not unified with
that of the "historical Christ." The "universal activity" of the Son "does not
coincide with his divine-human action in the state of humiliation." "Thus here
is a twofold mode of being, a double life, a double consciousness; the Logos
still is or has something which is not merged into his historical appearance,
which is not also the man Jesus—and all this seems to destroy the unity of
the person, the identity of the ego." Accordingly, "there occurs no living and
complete penetration of both sides, no proper being-man of God," which is
fatal to the view that there is one subject in the incarnation. From Thomasius's
point of view, in order to confirm that in the incarnation the man Jesus is
God and not merely indwelt by God in a special way, it will be necessary to
posit that "what applies to the historical Christ must apply to both sides of
his being, i.e., to the one person on both its sides."[112]

To explain his view of the personal unity and self-limitation of Christ,
Thomasius sets out certain biblical grounds for it. He reasons that Christ's
state of humiliation, which includes things like sleep, ignorance, and mental
growth, involves an "alteration . . . in the relation of the Son to the Father."
In Thomasius's reading of Philippians 2, the Son "emptied himself of the
'form of God.'" The exchange of a "God-like relation to a humanly limited
and conditioned one" just "is the incarnation."[113] Given the historical realities of Christ's sleep, ignorance, and so forth, and given Thomasius's desire
to avoid positing a double consciousness and activity in Christ, he posits a
divine self-limitation of Christ in the incarnation. Because God's being is
not "rigid" but "self-positing" (*sich selber setzendes*) and "utterly master of
itself," God has the ability to give himself a new determination (*Bestimmung*)
to exist in a human mode of being. God is bound only to his will and his love
(the love among the divine persons and toward creatures), so he is free to limit
himself by beginning to exist under human conditions. Precisely because it
is included in his divine being that he can do this, and because he does this
in accordance with his love, his self-limitation is not an abrogation of or
alienation from himself but in fact a manifestation of himself. He "remains
identical with himself in the divesting of himself" and "bears in himself the
heaven from which he came." Thus, "God's determining of himself to actual

112. Thomasius, *Christ's Person and Work*, 46–47, 72.
113. Thomasius, *Christ's Person and Work*, 50–56.

participation in the human mode of being, i.e., in the human form of life and consciousness," is the origin of "the divine-human person."[114]

Thomasius argues that his approach to the union of the divine and human in Christ does not compromise Christ's deity or humanity. He contends that in the Son's self-limitation, the Son does not divest himself of anything that pertains to the divine essence. The Son does not give up divine presence, knowledge, or power *in itself*. In Thomasius's words, the Son does not give up any "immanent attributes." But, according to Thomasius, the Son does give up a certain divine mode of these attributes or the relation that these attributes have had toward the world, a relation in which God is everywhere, knows all things, and governs all things. Thomasius calls these attributes taken in relation to the world "relative attributes."[115] Christ is still in possession of the "immanent attributes" of "absolute power, truth, holiness and love." But in the incarnation the "absolute life that is the essence of deity exists in the narrow bounds of an earthly human life; absolute holiness and truth, these essential determinations of the divine, develop in the form of human thinking and willing; absolute love has attained human shape, it lives as human feeling." Put differently, "what belongs to the Logos is carried forward in the human thought, will and ability." Of course, this entails a denial of the *extra*: "The Son of God has not reserved a distinct being-for-himself outside the human nature assumed by him, a distinct consciousness, a distinct sphere of activity or possession of power; in no way and at no point does he exist outside the flesh." There is no longer "a dualism of divine and human modes of existence, of divine and human consciousness," but "one unitary movement, experience and development of life." In the incarnation, Christ's "divine thoughts come only gradually to consciousness for him through the mediation of the Holy Spirit." Such thoughts are already "contained in the depths of his being" and are "actually present" but undergo a "development" that takes place "in the form of human knowing." And Thomasius maintains that this does not compromise Christ's humanity, for Christ still has a human consciousness and activity. Furthermore, true humanity always has to be fulfilled by God's presence and activity: "The creature and man in particular exists only in

114. Thomasius, *Christ's Person and Work*, 47, 59–61, 73. For the German text quoted here, see Thomasius's *Christi Person und Werk*, 203–4. Another way in which Thomasius seeks to preserve the divine constancy of Christ in the incarnation is by suggesting that "the essential conditionedness of the creature by time and space" is already anticipated by a "trans-mundane analogue in the immanent trinitarian relationships" (61).

115. For Thomasius, without this distinction between an "immanent attribute" like power and a relation or "relative attribute" like "omnipotence," it would seem that God is necessarily related to or dependent on the world in order to be God. In other words, Thomasius uses the distinction to try to uphold God's aseity.

that God upholds and lives through him; he is and becomes what he ought
to be, physically and morally, only through the constant immanence of God
in him."[116]

(3) In his *History of the Development of the Doctrine of the Person of
Christ*, Dorner analyzes both Lutheran and Reformed positions and is not
entirely uncritical of his own Lutheran tradition (or at least some of its possible implications). Among other things, Dorner cautions against the view of
"Chemnitz and his adherents" that a Lutheran approach to the *communicatio
idiomatum* follows automatically from the hypostatic union itself. For, according to Dorner, even in the view of these early Lutherans the humanity of
Christ began to participate in divine ubiquity not from the very beginning of
the union but only from the moment of Christ's exaltation. And a distinction
between the "possession" and the "use" of an attribute like ubiquity does not
help, for in the case of such an attribute there can be no possession without
"at the same time an actuality."[117]

Yet even if the Reformed better represented "the traditional point of view,
especially that of the Council of Chalcedon and that of Dyotheletism," and
even if they "demonstrated the incompleteness and assailableness of the Lutheran view," Dorner does not hold back from critiquing Reformed Christology. He identifies "one spot of the Reformed Christology, where its apparent
simplicity and clearness changes into obscurity and indefiniteness; where
it is compelled to confess the superiority of the Lutheran view." Reformed
Christology is right in its "unwearied protest against the position, that veritable divinity is appropriated also to the humanity," but it is lacking where it
envisions "merely a fellowship of the divine with the human, instead of the
existence of a real point, which conjoined both divinity and humanity." It is
here that Reformed Christology cannot be reconciled with its own "persistent
assertion of the unity of the person."[118]

Dorner wonders how it could be that "the man Christ" is, say, ubiquitous
or omnipotent "through the person" while, at the same time, "nothing divine
could pertain to the human nature." For if the man Christ is ubiquitous or
omnipotent "through" the person of the Logos, and if the Logos is a person of
the divine essence, that would seem to challenge the view that nothing divine
pertains to the human nature. Dorner reasons that in order to uphold the
consistency of Reformed Christology, one would have to deny "the simplicity
of the divine essence" and "acknowledge a distinction between the person and

116. Thomasius, *Christ's Person and Work*, 48, 56–59, 62–63, 67–74.
117. Dorner, *History of the Development of the Doctrine of the Person of Christ*, 237–41.
118. Dorner, *History of the Development of the Doctrine of the Person of Christ*, 241, 243.

the essence of the Logos." Dorner comments, "At this point the Lutherans persist in maintaining, that the personality of the Logos cannot be conceived without the fulness of its attributes; consequently, if the person pertain to the human nature, so also must the attributes." One could try to evade this conclusion by suggesting that the person of the Logos "did not really become the property of human nature," but this move implies that "there is no real point of unity whatever, and the incarnation itself is reduced to a mere seeming." Deprived of a "veritable possession" of the person of the Logos, Christ's humanity is rendered "a selfless organ of the deity." One could attempt to justify the claim that the Logos did not become the "property" of Christ's human nature by suggesting that it is because the person is "nothing at all by itself" but merely the "distinctness" or "limit" of the (divine) nature, but this means that the phrase *unio personalis* "really signifies nothing," leaving us to conceive of a union of two natures without the person as the focal point of the union.[119]

From a more constructive perspective, Dorner argues that if only the person of the Logos and not what pertains to the divine essence becomes the "property" of Christ's humanity, then the possibility of a union of the divine and human in Christ vanishes, a point that, for Dorner, is expressed in the axiom *finitum non est capax infiniti*. It seems that, in Dorner's assessment, the options are (a) a docetic view of the incarnation, (b) a "commixture and confusion" of the divine and human, or (c) a better way forward that involves developing the notion of creaturely dependence upon God so that, in Christ, there is a "living susceptibility of His essence to a real union of Him with God, and of God with Him." In this account, against "the Reformed theologians and Chemnitz," the incarnation is not a "contra-natural miracle" but the "fulfilment of the needs of Christ's human nature itself." The divine essence is "no longer a heterogeneous element, but that in which human nature realized its own truth." For Dorner, this approach rises above the "clumsy" features of the older Lutheran formulae and shows that "human nature first truly possesses itself, when by grace it possesses the divine—when it has God, not merely as the Lord on whom it depends, but as the one who dwells in it." This approach removes the focal point of the union of the divine and human from the constraints of space and time and secures the Lutheran desideratum of an "illocal union of the Logos and humanity." The spatial, temporal aspects of Christ's flesh are "relatively accidental" to the incarnation; the "essential, fundamental element" of the incarnation is "the relation which the illocal and eternal Logos purposed to establish . . . between Himself and

---

119. Dorner, *History of the Development of the Doctrine of the Person of Christ*, 243–45.

humanity." Indeed, the Logos's "will of love constituted so completely, as it were, the very heart of His loving nature, that He in His entirety, or in His entire essence, was determined by it; and with all His infinitude or omnipresence, was in no instance without this most inward and real relation to this central act of love."[120]

(4) Finally, in accordance with his emphasis that we know God only by God's self-revelation in the incarnate Son, Barth is both opposed to kenotic Christologies and cautious about the doctrine of the *extra Calvinisticum*. For Barth, while the kenoticists had good intentions (namely, to "make possible a 'historical' consideration of the life of Jesus"), they paid too high a price in pursuit of their goal. Their program meant abandoning the immutable deity of Christ. In doing this, the kenoticists brought into question the biblical teaching that "God was in Christ." And if God were not truly in Christ, how would Christ reconcile the world to God? For Barth, then, the kenoticists left the revealing and reconciling work of Christ "hanging in the air."[121]

At the same time, in keeping with his commitment to the knowability of God in Christ alone, Barth expresses some concerns about the *extra*. Along the way, he is appreciative and critical of both Lutheran and Reformed Christology. In Barth's reading, Luther and the early Lutherans simply aimed to set forth the genuineness of God's gracious presence in Christ by affirming a "perichoresis between the Word of God and the human being of Christ." This is, according to Barth, a "reversal of the statement about the *enhypostasis* of Christ's human nature, to the effect that as the humanity only has reality through and in the Word, so too the Word only has reality through and in the humanity." There is a risk here of undermining the freedom and glory of the Word by "submerging" him in the flesh. Barth suggests that if "the Word was never anywhere henceforth without the flesh," then this sounds as though either the truth of the Word's deity or the truth of his humanity is in question.[122]

On the other side, the Reformed were carrying forward "all earlier Christology" in their contention that the Word does not exist "solely" in the flesh but "also exists outwith (*extra*) the flesh." They were not denying that the whole Word is in the flesh (*totus intra carnem*) but only asserting that the Word is also outside it (*etiam extra*). In Barth's judgment, the Reformed "did not want the reality of the λόγος ἄσαρκος abolished or suppressed in the reality of the λόγος ἔνσαρκος." But if the Lutherans were in danger of losing the Word's true deity and humanity, "the Reformed failed to show convincingly

120. Dorner, *History of the Development of the Doctrine of the Person of Christ*, 245–48.
121. Barth, *CD*, IV.1, 182–83.
122. Barth, *CD*, I.2, 166–68.

how far the *extra* does not involve the assumption of a twofold Christ, of a λόγος ἔνσαρκος alongside a λόγος ἄσαρκος, and therefore a dissolution of the unity of the natures and hypostatic union, and therefore a destruction of the unequivocal Emmanuel."[123] Later in the *Church Dogmatics*, Barth reiterates that the divine immutability of Christ in the incarnation requires the clarification that there was no "absolute *inclusio*" or "limitation" of the Word in a created essence, which is why the *extra Calvinisticum* still matters. Barth's concern about the *extra* is that it encourages speculation about a Word of God knowable apart from the work of the Word incarnate.[124]

Ultimately, Barth declares that he does favor Reformed Christology.[125] But he does not do this without developing a theological framework to retain the divine immutability of Christ in the incarnation while also blocking speculation about the *Logos asarkos*. That framework involves positing that the Word's eternal relation to the Father is already characterized by the humility and obedience manifested in his incarnate, earthly life. Thus, even if the concept of a *Logos asarkos* is a useful placeholder to remind us that the Word did not have to become incarnate, the identity of the Word remains the same in his incarnate work.[126] Barth's reasoning appears to be founded upon (a) the necessity of Christ's divine immutability for the efficacy of his work and (b) the belief that if the immutable Word himself is the one who takes on flesh and suffers for our salvation, then the Word cannot leave his deity behind in coming to us.[127] It seems to me that Bruce McCormack accurately reflects Barth's line of thinking at this point when he writes that the Word is "nothing in the absence of his divine nature but a contentless cipher,"[128] which is why not just the Word but even the divine essence of the Word is thought to be informed by or at least aligned with his human attributes and experiences. As God the Word is man and undertakes his human obedience and suffering.[129] In

123. Barth, *CD*, I.2, 168–70.
124. Barth, *CD*, IV.1, 180–81.
125. See *CD*, IV.2, 66–69. Here Barth discusses the key difference between the Reformed and the Lutherans and states that the Reformed tended to concentrate on the hypostatic union itself, whereas the Lutherans tended to have a greater interest in exploring the communion of the two natures in its own right. Though he sides with the Reformed, Barth is still sympathetic to that interest in discerning what takes place in the *communio naturarum*. See also his discussion of Reformed and Lutheran Christology in IV.2, 76–78, 80.
126. Barth, *CD*, II.2, 95–99; IV.1, 51–53, 183–88, 192–210; IV.2, 84–86.
127. Barth, *CD*, IV.1, 185–87.
128. McCormack, "'With Loud Cries and Tears,'" 44n11, 47.
129. Barth, *CD*, IV.2, 177. In this section Barth writes that "God *as God* [*Gott als Gott*] is capable, willing, and ready for such a lowering and such a humiliation" (*KD*, IV.1, 193). Again, Christ is "true God" and "as such also true man and so is a partaker of human nature" (*KD*, IV.1, 193).

fact, Barth can even say that only a "philosophical" and "deeply unchristian" concept of God would lead one to believe that the union with humanity left Christ's deity "untouched" (*unberührt*). Only such a concept of God would prevent one from affirming that the union could affect (*affizieren*) his deity.[130] But, in Barth's logic, divine immutability is upheld because it always was within God's divine power to take on human flesh and suffer.[131] Indeed, in some way, God's own essence itself is perhaps informed by or at least given its "determination" by the eternal act in which he elects to be God for us.[132] In God's eternal counsel, he does not first elect us but rather himself. "God elects and determines [*bestimmt*] himself to be the God of man."[133] Within this view of God and the incarnation, Barth can speak of a "mutual participation" (*beiderseitigen Teilnahme*) of the deity and humanity in the incarnation in which each essence "acquires" (*bekommt*) a certain "determination" (*Bestimmung*) toward the other. That determination is not symmetrical, for in it the deity is determined *to* the humanity and the humanity is determined *from* the deity. The deity gives and the humanity receives. Yet Barth is still willing to suggest that the early Lutherans may have been too scrupulous about avoiding a *genus tapeinoticum* in their Christology. For in his electing grace God is pleased to unite his deity with a human essence and "to give that telos and that form [*jenes Telos und jene Gestalt*] to his divine essence for the sake of man."[134]

V. Response to Concerns

Addressing the concerns laid out in the previous section will help to make the case that the unity of the incarnate Son and the genuineness and immediacy of his human life cohere with the teaching that the incarnate Son according to his divine essence remains immutable, impassible, and simple. Though a number of the concerns in the previous section have to do with early Reformed Christology, the point here is not to defend Reformed Christology simply

130. Barth, *CD*, IV.2, 84–85; *KD*, IV.2, 92–93.

131. Barth, *CD*, IV.1, 159, 164, 177, 185–87; IV.2, 86.

132. Recall the treatment of election in *CD*, II.2, 63–67, 95–99, 115–16, which came under discussion in chap. 3 of the present volume.

133. Barth, *CD*, IV.2, 84; *KD*, IV.2, 92.

134. Barth, *CD*, IV.2, 70–74, 78, 84–88; *KD*, IV.2, 75, 95–96. Barth maintains that this act of giving an end and form to the divine essence entails no alteration of it and no curtailment of God's freedom in the incarnation (e.g., *CD*, IV.1, 201; IV.2, 85–87). For broader reflections on the significance of Christ's humanity in Barth's view of God, see, e.g., Jones, *The Humanity of Christ*; Sumner, *Karl Barth and the Incarnation*.

because it bears the descriptor "Reformed." Instead, the point is to discern what is true about the person of Christ in conversation with pre- and post-Reformation theologians. The following considerations will include insights from Reformed authors because, in my view, they help to provide clarity on the meaning of the *communicatio idiomatum* and its relationship to the divine immutability of Christ.

(1) The Lutheran writers of the sixteenth and seventeenth centuries did not claim that the divinity of Christ was affected by his human properties or experiences, which means that there is ultimately no quarrel between their works and the argument of the present chapter. However, because their statements about the *communicatio idiomatum* have been used to suggest that attributes of one of Christ's natures must belong in some way to the other nature, I will attempt to address some of their reasoning here.

It is important to be fair to theologians like Chemnitz, Gerhard, and Quenstedt by bearing in mind that they deny a communication of divine properties to Christ's human nature in the abstract or on its own. But the Lutheran orthodox discussion of the sense in which the human nature might be a "concrete thing" (*concretum*) or an "abstract thing" (*abstractum*) can generate confusion. Gerhard, for example, holds not only that the person of the human nature is a *concretum* but also that the human nature itself is a *concretum* "to the extent that it is considered not in itself separately but in the person itself of the Son of God and in respect of the personal union." The human nature, then, is an *abstractum* only when considered "in itself, by itself . . . according to its own natural properties and according to its own proper definition" and apart from the union with the Word (*citra mutuum unionis complexum*).[135] When an author like Gerhard denies that divine properties belong to Christ's human nature *in abstracto*, he is denying only that divine properties would belong to the human nature in separation from the divine Word. This approach still affirms that in the context of the personal union not only the person but even the human nature itself (if not *by itself*) is a "partaker of divine properties." The human nature itself (if not *by itself*) is omnipresent, omnipotent, and so forth. Hence Gerhard writes that in the *genus majestaticum* the divine majesty and divine power are predicated of Christ not only "by and on account of the hypostatic union" but also "according to the human nature." For, according to Gerhard, not only the *concretum* of the person but also the *concretum* of the human nature is the subject to which divine attributes are ascribed in the New Testament. For example, in Mark 2:28, Jesus says, "The Son of Man is Lord of the Sabbath." The human

135. Gerhard, *Loci theologici*, 4.12.273 (581–82).

nature's partaking of divine attributes and being the subject of them is what enables it to be "life-giving" and a "saving and suitable instrument of divine works" (see, e.g., John 6:51).[136]

In my view, the early modern Reformed authors were right to pick up on an equivocation in the Lutheran discussion of the distinction between something concrete and something abstract.[137] Because of the traditional usage of the language, the restriction of the exchange of properties to the human nature *in concreto* initially suggests that the *person* of the human nature (who is also divine) is ubiquitous, omnipotent, and so forth.[138] But in fact the Lutheran claim is that the *human nature itself* (as long as it is not taken to be *by itself*) is ubiquitous and omnipotent. If that is an accurate expression of the claim being made, it is still important to be fair to the Lutherans by bearing in mind that they repudiate a Eutychian confusion of the two natures. And yet it has to be said that at the very least their approach raises serious questions about whether Christ's finite human nature can be both ubiquitous and circumscribed, omnipotent and finite in power. Even if the human nature is taken to be ubiquitous and omnipotent by participation in the divine but circumscribed and finite in power by its own natural principles (i.e., even if it acquires these properties in distinct ways), one and the same nature would still have to be infinite and finite. Indeed, there are serious questions about whether that which is not identical to the divine essence and which therefore has to participate in God's perfection can be ubiquitous and omnipotent. The very notion of participation itself implies not having the fullness of the divine perfection.[139]

Positively, one can reject the idea that the properties of one of Christ's natures are communicated to the other nature itself and still maintain a real (i.e., present in reality and not merely verbal or predicative) communication of properties in the one incarnate person.[140] All the properties pertaining to each nature really are common to one and the same person. Furthermore, contrary to the impression given by Thomasius and Dorner, although the human nature itself of the man Jesus is not ubiquitous or omnipotent, it can be said without hesitation that the man Jesus is ubiquitous and omnipotent.

136. Gerhard, *Loci theologici*, 4.10.182 (530); 4.12.201 (544).

137. See, e.g., Turretin, *Inst.*, 13.8.5 (2:350).

138. For some examples of standard usage, see Aquinas, *Super Sent.* 3.11.4; Aquinas, *De hebdomadibus* 2 (272); Aquinas, *ST* IIIa.16.1–2, 4–5 (197–98, 201, 203–5); Ames, *Medulla theologica*, 1.18.24 (79); Turretin, *Inst.*, 13.8.5 (2:350).

139. As Aquinas puts it, to participate in something is "to receive partially that which belongs to another wholly" (*De hebdomadibus* 2 [271]).

140. For Reformed emphasis on the *communicatio realis*, see, e.g., Zanchi, *De incarn.*, 2.2 (86–88); Polanus, *Syntagma*, 6.16 (379); Mastricht, *TPT*, 5.4.12 (539–40).

While the one person who is man is not ubiquitous or omnipotent according to his human nature, this one person who is man is ubiquitous and
omnipotent according to his divine nature.[141] And if it is this one person
and no other who has actualized and individuated the human nature so
that it subsists only in him, then the suspicion of Nestorianism ought to be
removed.

The real communication of properties in the person of Christ that is affirmed in this approach has implications for interpreting places in Scripture where the person of Christ signified by a name pertaining to one of his
natures is the subject of a statement whose predicate pertains to the other
nature. Such places include Acts 20:28, where Christ is called "God" and is
said to have bought the church with his own blood. Given that God the Son
has communicated his ὑπόστασις to his human nature so that both natures
and their attributes really and intrinsically belong to the Son, it is important
to exercise some caution about calling a statement like the one in Acts 20:28
"figurative" or "improper."[142] For in this case blood or death does not apply
to the Son only by a relation to an external instrument or by a metaphor.[143]
What the predicate signifies applies to the subject God the Son by virtue of a
nature intrinsic to him. Thus, given the real communication of properties to
the incarnate Son, a statement like the one in Acts 20:28 is not figurative in
an ordinary way. It is "indirect," using a predicate whose referent is indeed
intrinsic and proper to the subject according to one nature but naming the
subject by the other nature.[144]

141. Cf., e.g., Polanus, *Syntagma*, 6.16 (379): "The man Christ is God, eternal, everywhere
present, omnipotent, omniscient, and, indeed really, even most really and not merely by name."

142. Such statements are often identified as a figure or, more specifically, a synecdoche. See,
e.g., Calvin, *In Acta*, 469; cf. Polanus, *Logicae libri duo* 2 (128).

143. Cf. Melanchthon, *Erotemata dialectica* 1 (525), who treats the personal propositions in
Christology as a type of "improper" speech but still remarks that there are no other examples
of such propositions "in the whole universe." For a detailed analysis of figurative speech involving an extrinsic relation between predicate and subject or a conflict between the ordinary
signification of the predicate and the nature of the subject, see Keckermann, *Systema logicae,
tribus libris adornatum*, II, sect. post., 2 (732–34).

144. On the mode on speaking about Christ being either direct or indirect, see Turretin,
Inst., 13.8.3 (2:350); Mastricht, *TPT*, 5.4.12 (539–40). On the one hand, the early Reformed
authors (e.g., Polanus, *Logicae* 1 [128]; Mastricht, *TPT*, 5.4.12 [540]) recognize that statements
like the one in Acts 20:28 involve a synecdoche, which is a figure of speech in which the name
of a whole (in this case, the whole person of God the Son) is used to signify a part (in this
case, though it can be only analogically called a "part," the humanity of the Son) or vice versa.
On the other hand, in the place cited, Mastricht says that this sort of christological statement
pertains to a predication that is "*as it were*, tropical and *close* to a synecdoche" (*quasi tropicam
et synecdochae proximam*). The uniqueness of the incarnate Son makes it difficult to align
such a christological statement with a common instance of figurative or improper speech in a
straightforward manner.

It should also be noted that these cautions about applying divine attributes to Christ's human nature itself are compatible with a robust affirmation of certain unique graces or gifts being communicated to the human nature. These include the grace of union itself, a "grace of eminence" or dignity above all other instances of human nature, a "capital grace" that pertains to Christ as the head of his body, and the infused habitual graces that will come under discussion in chapter 5.[145] Under the next point I hope to corroborate that a rejection of the *genus majestaticum* is compatible with the biblical and patristic notion of Christ's flesh as a life-giving instrument.

(2) While it is the teaching of Holy Scripture that functions as the source and supreme rule of our christological claims, it is worth observing some relevant statements from patristic figures in relation to the debates about Lutheran and Reformed Christologies. In particular, I would like to suggest that the exegetical insights of figures like Cyril of Alexandria and John of Damascus, who were exemplary on the profound communion of Christ's deity and humanity, actually cohere with the firm distinction between Christ's deity and humanity that is represented by the Reformed tradition.

It should first be acknowledged that some of the patristic authors do use certain language that could be seen to anticipate some of the early Lutheran emphases. Cyril of Alexandria, for example, discusses the union of Christ's deity and humanity with the analogy of fire and wood or fire and metal. The Word transforms what he assumes "into his own glory and energy" like "fire comes into contact with wood and having penetrated into it, burns it." Though the Word preserves the authenticity of the humanity, he still puts in it "the energy of his own nature."[146] Thus, in the logic of Cyril's Christology, the Word's flesh, by belonging to him, is life-giving.[147] At the same time,

145. See, e.g., Aquinas, *ST* IIIa.2.10 (48–49); 7.13 (124–25); 8.5 (132–33); Turretin, *Inst.*, 13.8.1 (2:349); Owen, *Christologia* 18 (227–28). There are various ways in which the teaching on the hypostatic union and its consequents might be organized. And there are various ways in which material claims in that teaching might be reflected in the organization. For example, Aquinas's structure in the *Summa theologiae* locates the grace of union within the discussion about the mode of union itself, the habitual and capital graces within the discussion about what is "coassumed" with the human nature, and the communication of properties and unity of operations within the discussion about things that follow the union. While the Lutherans often take the *communicatio idiomatum* itself to include the *genus idiomaticum*, *genus majestaticum*, and *genus apotelesmaticum*, the Reformed can map out the consequents of the union in several ways while still denying that infinite gifts are communicated to Christ's humanity, sometimes distinguishing between those consequents pertaining to the person of the union and those pertaining more directly to the human nature of the person (see, e.g., Zanchi, *De incarn.*, 2.3 [332, 341–42, 344]; Keckermann, *Systema s.s. theologiae*, 3.2 [176–77]; Turretin, *Inst.*, 13.8.1–2 [2:349]).

146. Cyril of Alexandria, *Scholia* 9 (516).

147. Cyril of Alexandria, *Tertia ad Nestorium* 6,12 (41–42); Cyril, *Contra Theodoretum* 169,86 (143).

when Cyril discusses christological "sayings" (statements about Christ as God and about Christ as man), his approach seems not to fit well with the idea of Christ's divine perfections being communicated to Christ's humanity itself. Cyril does emphasize that those things that befit God and those that befit humanity both belong to "one Christ." But the Word truly takes up the finite "measure" of human knowledge, for example, so that in the form of a servant he is ignorant of certain things.[148]

John of Damascus speaks of the "hypostatic union" (ἡ καθ' ὑπόστασιν ἕνωσις) and the "mutual indwelling" or "interpenetration" (περιχώρησις) of the deity and humanity in Christ through which the Word "imparts his own [τῶν ἰδίων] to the flesh according to the way of an exchange [or "communication," ἀντιδόσεως]."[149] John also speaks about the deification (θέωσις) of the human nature and human will and affirms that through the identity of the ὑπόστασις in the incarnation and the "inseparable union" of natures, the human soul of Christ "is enriched with the knowledge of future things and the remaining miraculous powers [θεοσημίας]." By virtue of the union and deification, the flesh of Christ is "life-giving."[150]

At the same time, this περιχώρησις of natures and ἀντίδοσις of properties is significantly qualified. For "we do not predicate of the flesh the properties of the deity (for we do not say that the flesh or the humanity is uncreated)." Instead, we apply to the ὑπόστασις (signified by a name pertaining to just one nature or to both natures) the properties of both natures. John explains, "Whenever [Christ] is called man . . . he receives the properties and glories of the divine essence." For example, the man Christ is an "eternal child" and "man without beginning." But he is eternal and without beginning *as God* (καθὸ θεὸς) and not *as man* (καθὸ ἄνθρωπος). "This is the way of the communication of each of the natures, communicating to the other its properties on account of the identity of the *hypostasis* and the *perichōrēsis* of them in one another."[151] John insists that when the divine person deifies the flesh, the flesh undergoes no change of its "natural properties." Like fire united with metal, which acquires a "burning energy" not "naturally" but by union with the fire, the divine power of the Word works through the flesh, displaying its energy through the flesh.[152] Furthermore, John is one of the patristic figures

148. Cyril of Alexandria, *Contra Theodoretum* 169,37–38 (123–24).
149. John of Damascus, *Expos. fidei* 3.3 (115). Cf. also 3.7 (126); 3.15 (146, 150); 3.19 (160). Throughout these sections John underscores that while the deity imparts something to the flesh, the flesh imparts nothing to the deity.
150. John of Damascus, *Expos. fidei* 3.17 (155–56), 21 (163).
151. John of Damascus, *Expos. fidei* 3.5 (117).
152. John of Damascus, *Expos. fidei* 3.17 (156). Cf. also 3.19 (162), where the illustration of fire and metal once again underscores the distinction between the two natures.

who anticipates the *extra Calvinisticum* and shows that in substance it is not distinctively "Calvinistic" at all, for God the Word as God is "uncircumscribed, his flesh not being coextensive with his uncircumscribed deity."[153]

With these considerations in view, it is difficult to look at a theologian like Cyril of Alexandria or John of Damascus and conclude that their works anticipate the *genus majestaticum* in any straightforward way. John quite clearly focuses the ἀντίδοσις of properties on the person who is human rather than the human nature itself: the man Christ is indeed eternal or uncircumscribed, for example, but *as God* and not *as man*. And the deification of the humanity and the communication of "miraculous powers" does not indicate a bestowal of divine or infinite gifts to the human nature. It indicates the communication of extraordinary but still finite gifts and the instrumentality of Christ's human nature, according to which its operation contributes to works that exceed the capacity of ordinary humanity. For John, the Word's deification of his human will and energy does not alter their human finitude. Rather, the Word's human flesh and human energy are life-giving and saving in that Christ's divine operation works with and through his human operation so that the human operation is always joined with the divine. Christ's human power and activity is not "without participation" (ἄμοιρος) in his divine power and activity in that the two are always joined. The participation of the humanity in the divinity does not consist in the humanity itself becoming omnipotent but in the humanity's communion with the divine and in the humanity being an instrument of the divine.[154] With a figure like John of Damascus, one can fully affirm this doctrine of the theandric energy together with the teaching that Christ's flesh is a life-giving instrument and also affirm that the properties of each one of Christ's natures belong to the one person of Christ and not to the other nature itself.

(3) To the extent that the kenotic Christology of Thomasius was designed to set forth the unity of the person of Christ and the genuineness and immediacy of the divine Son's human, historical life, one can agree with Barth that there was at least something commendable in the basic intention behind it. Nevertheless, Thomasius's interpretation of the crucial statement in Philippians 2 (κένωσις as subtraction and not just addition) is simply incorrect. As noted in section II above, Paul does not teach that Christ emptied himself of the *forma Dei*. There is no identification in the text of something

153. John of Damascus, *Expos. fidei* 3.17 (126).
154. John of Damascus, *Expos. fidei* 3.15 (146); 3.19 (161–62). Cf. Turretin, *Inst.*, 13.8.35–36 (2:359), where he states that the humanity of Christ being a life-giving instrument does not mean that the humanity efficiently produces eternal life by its own virtue but rather that the humanity (or, better, Christ as human) acquires eternal life for us by his own death.

of which Christ emptied himself. The nature of the κένωσις is explained by the subsequent participles ("taking the form of a servant, being made in the likeness of humanity"). In fact, only if Christ unabatedly remained the true God would it make sense for Paul to say that in the end Christ will receive the glory and honor due to YHWH alone (Phil. 2:9–11; cf. Isa. 45:23). YHWH is not someone who ever stops being what he is or has to acquire what he is. Furthermore, Barth is right in pointing out that if Christ leaves behind something of his deity in coming to us in the flesh, then his revealing and atoning work is left "hanging in the air." A Christ who was not all that he once was as God would not provide the decisive revelation of the true God and would not decisively bring us back to the true God.

At the same time, it is still worth addressing elements of Thomasius's reasoning more specifically. Among other things, he is adamant about avoiding a "duality" or "duplication" in Christ's life and consciousness. There is of course a sense in which orthodox Christology can simply retort that if Christ is truly divine and truly human, then affirming duality here is unavoidable and, indeed, a positive good. But it seems to me that Thomasius also strives to avoid a duality that involves redundancy, on the one hand, and mutual exclusion, on the other. Orthodox Christology itself needs to clarify that two distinct intellects, volitions, and operations are united in the incarnate Son without redundancy or mutual exclusion. I think the key point here is that the two natures and operations do not occupy a common genus or order of being, so each contributes something that the other does not and neither excludes the other. Various examples could be given to show that Christ's divine and human activity are not redundant and that each contributes something that the other does not. For instance, it is only by his deity that Christ can will and operate sovereignly and inexorably to give up his human life exactly according to the divine plan; it is only by his humanity that Christ can will and operate submissively and obediently on our behalf to undergo death. And the recognition that deity and humanity do not occupy a common order of being clarifies that the one does not exclude the other from being in the same subject any more than, say, being tall and being musically talented would exclude one another from being in the same subject. Things that are not in the same category do not compete with one another, and deity is not in any creaturely category at all.[155]

---

155. Cf., e.g., the mundane example given by Aquinas in *SCG* 4.24 (91), where he notes that things that are not opposed, like "white" and "triangular," can be in the same thing. One could respond that divine and human volition, for example, are still analogous to one another, which might appear to mean that they could stand in competition with one another. But the analogical relationship itself confirms that they are not in the same category of being and do not stand

Furthermore, while Thomasius is right in seeking to uphold the integrity and development of Christ's human mental activity, his insistence on a single consciousness in Christ appears to presuppose a notion of personhood wherein that which individuates the person is what supplies mental capacities like intellect and will. If it were that which individuates a person that introduced intellect and will in human life rather than the common nature that a person individuates, then the personal unity of Christ would require that there be one intellect or consciousness and one will in Christ. However, if, as is the case, intellect and will are included in what a human being has in common with other human beings, then it is not what individuates a person but the common nature that supplies intellect and will. The person, then, individuates and terminates all that pertains to the nature, including its intellect and will.[156] This means that even if the one person of God the Son already has a (divine) intellect and will, then in his assumption of a human nature he still actualizes in himself a natural human intellect and will. His divine intellect and will do not render superfluous or supplant the human intellect and will. There is, therefore, one person who exercises the distinct power or capacity of each nature, but there are indeed two powers or capacities exercised, so that there is no abridgement of the divine Son's human mental operations.[157]

Because of the uniqueness of the Son of God, it is strange to think of one person with two intellects, with a divine act of understanding and a distinct human consciousness. However, I would suggest that Thomasius's attempt to combine the divine and human in a single consciousness and activity illustrates why such a move should be avoided. First, Thomasius's neat distinction between what is "immanent" and what is "relative" in the divine attributes is a dubious one. Although it is true that God did not have to assume a relation to the world, that does not mean that a divine attribute like knowledge, for example, has something like an inner core that can be isolated from its infinity and reduced to a finite mode. One can distinguish between immanent attributes of God that presuppose no relation to the

---

in competition with one another. For that analogical relationship one of the terms (human volition) is what it is by virtue of participation in or derivation from the other term (divine volition). The two are therefore not instances of something in the same category of being and therefore do not stand in competition.

156. In slightly different terms, person is not a constituent feature of a rational nature but rather the *terminus* of a rational nature (cf. Aquinas, *ST* IIIa.19.1 ad 4 [241]; Turretin, *Inst.*, 13.6.18 [2:343]).

157. This is an application of the dyothelete logic set out in Maximus the Confessor, *Opusculum* 7, 77; John of Damascus, *Expos. fidei* 3.14 (137–38, 140–41); Zanchi, *De incarn.*, 2.3.9 (238, 243). If God is simple and pure act, it is of course imprecise to speak of divine "capacities" as though these were distinct from the divine act of knowing and willing.

creature and relative attributes that do presuppose such a relation, but the infinite actuality of the former is not something added by virtue of the relation to the creature. Such attributes, therefore, have not gained something novel that might then be jettisoned in order to facilitate a divine "self-limitation." Second, while Thomasius duly points out that human fulfillment does not happen apart from God but only in union with God, there is still a problem in asserting that the development in the human soul of Christ is a development of divine knowledge or "divine thoughts." If the *content* of what is developed in Christ's human knowing and willing were something divine (albeit under a certain "self-limitation"), then even if the *mode* of the development were supposedly human there would still be a truncation of Christ's human knowledge, volition, and operation. He would not be like us in all things. He would not have an authentically human volition with which to obey the divine law where Adam failed to do so.[158]

(4) Dorner incisively raises the question of whether it is possible to identify a "real point" at which the divinity and humanity of Christ are joined together without the divine attributes of the Word being shared by his human nature. To elaborate, if the personal subsistence of the Word is that "real point," and if the person of the Word is really identical with his own divine essence and attributes (or, in McCormack's words, "nothing in the absence of his divine nature but a contentless cipher"), then how would the divine attributes of the Word not belong to the human nature? In my view, this is where a careful understanding of the doctrine of divine simplicity should come into play. The personal subsistence of the Word is indeed the "real point" of unity or that which is common to both the deity and the humanity. But the real identity of the person or personal subsistence of the Word and the divine essence does not preclude every kind of distinction in the Trinity.[159] To draw upon the argument presented in chapter 2, section IV, there is a modal distinction to be observed—even a "real" modal distinction where "real" means "present in reality and not merely in human reason"—between the person or personal subsistence of the Word, on the one hand, and the divine essence as such, on the other.

Certainly, as McCormack notes, the Word would be nothing without the divine essence. But being modally distinct from the essence as common to the three divine persons is not the same as being *without* the essence. A modal distinction does not involve a separation from the essence. Indeed, if

---

158. Cf. John of Damascus, *Expos. fidei* 3.14 (142–43), on the importance of avoiding the idea of a "composite will" in Christ.

159. It excludes only those sorts of distinctions that presuppose the presence of parts.

there were no such distinction between person and essence in God, then each person would not only have the whole essence but would have it wholly or without two other distinct persons also having the essence, yielding either a conflation of the persons or, if the persons remained distinct, a displacement of the other two persons from the essence and thus a subordination of them. Furthermore, if the real identity of person and essence in the Trinity left no room for a distinction between person and essence, then the Father and Holy Spirit, who also are persons of the one essence, would be incarnate. The modal distinction allows us to affirm that while the three persons are really identical to the one essence, they are also distinct from one another. It also allows us to affirm that it is not the divine essence as such or all three divine persons but rather the person of the Word that assumes the human nature.[160] While all three divine persons act to bring about the incarnation, only one of the persons (the Word) is the *terminus ad quem* of the divine act of assuming the human nature, so he is the only divine person who is incarnate.[161] Accordingly, it is not the divine essence as such but the divine essence in the person of the Son and under his proper mode of subsisting that is incarnate. Thus, John of Damascus comments that neither "the *hypostasis* alone" nor "the common nature of the *hypostaseis*" but "the common nature in the *hypostasis* of the Word" is incarnate.[162] Aquinas also makes the point well: "The divine nature is called 'incarnate,' as also 'assuming,' by reason of the person toward which the union is terminated. . . . The whole divine nature is called 'incarnate' not because it is incarnate in all the persons but because nothing about the perfection of the divine nature is lacking to the incarnate person."[163] In sum, the Word's subsistence or proper mode of subsisting is the factor common to both of his natures. The mode of union is not directly essential but hypostatic, which precludes Nestorianism and also confirms that while the properties of one of Christ's natures belong directly to him according to that nature, those properties belong to him according to that nature alone and not according to the other nature as well.

(5) Barth's desire to eliminate speculation about the Λόγος ἄσαρκος and his contention that the Word's eternal mode of being is marked by humility and obedience have been addressed in chapter 3, so I will focus more on some of his other statements about the *communicatio idiomatum* and the

---

160. Cf., e.g., Zanchi, *De incarn.*, 2.3 (104).

161. So, e.g., Zanchi, *De incarn.*, 2.3 (93–94, 104–5); Polanus, *Syntagma*, 6.13 (364).

162. John of Damascus, *Expos. fidei* 3.11 (132–33). Here John is explaining and defending Cyril of Alexandria's teaching that the φύσις of the Word became incarnate.

163. Aquinas, *ST* IIIa.3.4 ad 2 (62). Cf. Polanus, *Syntagma*, 6.13 (364); Turretin, *Inst.*, 13.4.7–9 (2:331–32); Mastricht, *TPT*, 2.24.8 (238); 5.4.5, 9 (537, 539).

extra Calvinisticum here. Barth's analyses of the debates among the Lutheran and Reformed orthodox on the person of Christ are often insightful. With respect to the Lutheran orthodox, his comments about them pressing beyond the hypostatic union to a consideration of the communion of natures in its own right are suggestive. I would add that the decision to undertake such a consideration may not be a neutral matter in which one could simply have more or less interest. It seems to me that if the Word's subsistence or proper mode of subsisting is the one factor that is common to both natures, then it is crucial to take the hypostatic union as the focal point itself of the communion of the natures rather than a starting point from which one might try to find additional factors ingredient in the communion. With respect to the Reformed orthodox, while Barth criticizes their teaching on election and the person of Christ at various points in the *Church Dogmatics*, it is important to note his affirmation of the basic validity of the *extra Calvinisticum*. Even in his efforts to shut down speculation about the Λόγος ἄσαρκος, Barth still sought to affirm the freedom of God in choosing the incarnation and the asymmetrical relation between Christ's deity and his humanity. For Barth, the former was never reduced to or "submerged" in the latter.

However, Barth did maintain that a truly Christian conception of God involves an acknowledgment that the deity of the Son (by his own choosing) was "touched" or "affected" by his humanity. It seems that Barth's reasoning may be exhibited in his way of speaking about God *as God* (*Gott als Gott*) being capable of and ready for humiliation and about Christ *as the one true God* being true man and undergoing his life in the flesh.[164] These claims warrant careful reflection. In analyzing what Barth has written on this in IV.1 and IV.2, I do not assume that he would subscribe to problematic implications that might be discerned here. Nevertheless, I still think it worthwhile to explore what his line of thought appears to imply.

On the one hand, there is a sense in which it is true that God the Son as God is capable of assuming human flesh. He was eternally capable of doing this by his divine omnipotence and, indeed, prior to the assumption of his flesh, had only this divine power by which he could accomplish any of his works, including the incarnation. In addition, deity and humanity are not in the same order of being, which underscores that it is *as God* or by virtue of his transcendent deity that the Son can take on flesh without ceasing to be what he was.[165]

---

164. See again *KD*, IV.1, 193: "Er [der eine wahre Gott] als solcher auch wahrer Mensch und also menschlicher Natur teilhaftig ist."

165. On this point and on the fact that it does not lead to the idea of divine passibility, cf. B. Marshall, "The Dereliction of Christ and the Impassibility of God," 297–98.

On the other hand, once the Son has actually taken on flesh, the use of the phrase "as such" becomes more complicated. With Barth, one could say, for example, "as God Christ is man." However, while it is true that Christ as God operated to assume his human nature and that Christ remains true God in union with his human nature, it is, strictly speaking, not the deity but the human nature of Christ by virtue of which he is man. Christ's human nature is the principle by which he undertakes human action and human suffering. Otherwise, if his deity were in a direct way that by virtue of which he was man and had human experiences, then his human nature would be an empty concept. Going beyond the statement quoted from Barth, one could say that "as God Christ as man obeys the Father and suffers." But, again, if the human nature is that by virtue of which Christ is true man, then the human nature is the principle by which he undertakes human action and human suffering. Accordingly, one cannot derive the conclusion that the deity of Christ is affected by his human suffering from the reality of his human suffering as such. In other words, divine passibility cannot be established by appeal to his human suffering.[166] Divine passibility would have to be established by arguing on other grounds that Christ's deity in its own right can and must suffer in the fulfillment of his economic work.[167] The key point here is that the immediacy of the divine Son's human suffering does not entail that the deity of the divine Son is affected by his suffering. Thus, the immediacy of the suffering requires no

166. One example of this sort of appeal can be found in Hunsinger, *Reading Barth with Charity*, 154–55. Hunsinger writes that, according to Gregory Nazianzen, "the unity of Christ meant that God suffered not only in his human nature but also in his deity." Thus, Hunsinger says that for both Gregory and Barth "the sufferings that God endured in his humanity did not remain restricted to that plane. Through his human nature they were mediated to his divine nature by which they were eternally destroyed." But the oration of Gregory that is cited here does not teach this idea. Gregory is clear in this oration that Christ's suffering, like his crying out in prayer, pertains to his servant-form, not to Christ "as the Word" (ὡς Λόγος). Again, Christ's suffering and agony pertain to his humanity, not to "the nature that is unchangeable and above suffering [οὐ τὴν ἄτρεπτον φύσιν καὶ τοῦ πάσχειν ὑψηλοτέραν]" (*Discours 27–31*, 30.6, 16 [236, 260]). The fact that it can be said that God suffers (cf., e.g., Acts 20:28) and the fact that it is indeed God the Son himself who undergoes the human suffering simply does not entail that God the Son *according to his deity* undergoes suffering.

167. There are places in which Barth affirms the possibility of a distinctly divine suffering. Though Barth does not envision a divine suffering imposed upon God from without, he does posit that God's perfection entails that rather than being unable to suffer he can freely choose to suffer (*CD*, IV.1, 187). Barth also affirms a divine suffering even of the Father (see, e.g., *CD*, IV.2, 357; IV.3.2, 414–15). To anticipate some of the arguments made in chap. 7 later on, I think the idea that divine plenitude or perfection entails the freedom to suffer misrepresents what suffering is. One does not remain fulfilled or perfect in suffering. To suffer just is to undergo the loss of fulfillment or well-being and thus to begin to have a disposition contrary to one's essence and telos. That remains the case even when God uses suffering to perfect the saints in their spiritual maturity. The suffering (e.g., of the body) is still real and has to be eradicated in the eschaton.

revision of the personal mode of the union in Christology, no direct assimilation of the two natures to one another. And that means that there is no need to choose either to give up the Son's divine immutability or to build into the Son's divine subsistence the lowliness that characterizes his human sojourn.

Before moving on from Barth, it may be good to comment on his talk of a "determination" (*Bestimmung*) of God's essence in election or in the union of Christ's two natures. Barth himself says even in the midst of his revision of the doctrine of election in II.2 that God has no need of creation and could remain satisfied in himself.[168] The Son's divine essence needs no actualization.[169] In view of this, it seems prudent to be cautious, in our interpretation of Barth as well as in our constructive theological work, about his assertion that God gives his essence a *Bestimmung* and a certain "telos" and "form" in his electing grace and in the union with Christ's humanity. If God is self-sufficient and is his own end, then his own essence is not constituted by the union with Christ's humanity. Perhaps, then, the *Bestimmung* Barth has in mind could be defined as a contingent direction or termination of God's eternal actuality toward a particular economic work. In any event, while one might wish Barth would have made it easier for us to integrate his thinking, the point is that in light of God's aseity and in light of the decidedly personal mode of union in the incarnation, Barth's claims about the *Bestimmung* of the divine essence in the incarnation need not lead us to question the coherence of the *communicatio idiomatum* and the divine immutability of Christ.

(6) Finally, a few direct and brief comments on the meaning of the *extra Calvinisticum* are in order. First of all, as noted in various studies by now, the material presence of the *extra* in patristic and medieval theology belies the idea that it is a distinctively "Calvinistic" notion.[170] The *extra* is not a parochial doctrine but an expression of the reality that the deity of the Word remains true (uncircumscribed) deity and the humanity of the Word remains true (circumscribed) humanity. It is an expression of the Word's divine transcendence of the limitations of his own human flesh. And it is not matter of envisioning the Word to be without his flesh in the sense of "apart from" his flesh.[171] There is no second Word existing apart from or alongside the Word incarnate. Rather, the one Word who is both divine and human subsists in his

---

168. Barth, *CD*, II.2, 121.

169. Barth, *CD*, IV.2, 113.

170. For relevant material in earlier Christian thought, see, e.g., Athanasius, *De incarnatione* 17 (174); Augustine, *In Iohann.* 12.8 (125); Cyril of Alexandria, *Scholia* 27 (550–51); John of Damascus, *Expos. fidei* 3.7 (123, 125–26).

171. Cf. Turretin on the phrase *extra humanitatem* indicating a "non-inclusion" of the deity in the humanity rather than a "separation" of the two (*Inst.*, 13.8.27 [2:357]).

uncircumscribed deity while always subsisting in his circumscribed humanity
as well. It could even be said that, after the incarnation, the Word is not only
never but also *nowhere* without the flesh in the sense that the Word who is
present everywhere is there in union with his flesh that remains circumscribed
in heaven.[172] The "whole Christ," who is God and man, is present everywhere even if the "whole of Christ" is not so (i.e., even if one of his natures
itself is not ubiquitous but circumscribed in heaven).[173] Though this is not
a book on sacramental theology, it may be fitting to end on the note that in
Reformed teaching on the Eucharist this understanding of the presence of
Christ's deity and humanity is not considered to be an obstacle to the people
of God receiving comfort from the gracious presence of the whole Christ and,
indeed, really partaking of the whole Christ in worship. By the Holy Spirit's
operation, believers partake not corporeally but still really and spiritually of
the body and blood of Christ by receiving the signs of the bread and the cup
(cf. 1 Cor. 10:16) for the nourishment of their souls to eternal life.[174]

VI. Conclusion

In this chapter, I have attempted to shed light on the divine Son's relationship
to the human nature that he has assumed. The first section set out scriptural
teaching on the divinity of the Son who assumes the human nature, the act
of assumption, the integrity of the nature assumed, the sameness of the person of the Son after his assumption of the human nature, and the ongoing
distinctness of the Son's divine and human natures. The next section then
sought to elaborate on this scriptural teaching by discussing matters like the
way in which the Son communicates his subsistence to his human nature,
the way in which the Son actualizes and individuates his human nature in
himself, the meaning of the instrumentality of the human nature, and the
sense in which Christ is a "composite" person. After this, I offered a summary of some Lutheran (and Reformed) reflections on the *communicatio
idiomatum* and *extra Calvinisticum* that might be taken to problematize the
claim that the divine Son really subsists in the flesh while remaining immutable, impassible, and simple according to his deity. In offering a response
to those reflections, I sought to confirm that a robust understanding of the

172. Cf. Zanchi, *De incarn.*, 2.3 (343).
173. For the *totus Christus* and *totum Christi* distinction, see, e.g., John of Damascus,
Expos. fidei 3.7 (126); Lombard, *Sent.* 3.22.3 (138–39); Keckermann, *Systema s.s. theologiae*,
3.2 (176); Turretin, *Inst.*, 14.8.23 (2:356).
174. See Heidelberg Catechism, QQ. 79–80 (787–88).

communicatio idiomatum does not require a communication of properties from one nature to the other and, indeed, positively coheres with the divine immutability of Christ.

This chapter has obvious implications for addressing modern concerns about the unity of the person of Christ and the genuineness and immediacy of his human life, most of which have already been drawn out in the preceding sections. For example, the communication of the Son's one subsistence to his human nature so that he himself is constituted a man by it rules out a Nestorian Christology. The way in which Christ's humanity is an instrument also precludes a Nestorian Christology, for the humanity is an instrument in the sense that he himself acts not only through it but in and according to it to bring about our salvation. In addition, the discussion of the *communicatio idiomatum* and *extra Calvinisticum* has bearing on the genuineness of the Son's humanity. For the humanity itself does not have divine properties. Christ as man remains finite and dependent upon divine operation for the fulfillment of his office. His dependence upon the Holy Spirit will be the subject of the next chapter.

FIVE

"The Spirit of the LORD Is upon Me": The Son's Dependence on the Holy Spirit

I. Introduction

A number of matters already touched upon in the preceding chapters converge here in our exploration of the Son's dependence upon the Holy Spirit: the eternal processions in God, the divine persons' distinct modes of acting, the unity of essence and power in God, and the abiding distinction between the Son's divinity and divine action, on the one hand, and his humanity and human action, on the other. All of this now needs to be developed further and applied to a discussion of the Son's relationship to the Holy Spirit. The goal will be to exhibit how Christ's relationship to the Spirit as it is described in the Bible may be illumined by a view of God that stresses God's simplicity and aseity. I will begin by examining pertinent scriptural teaching on the Son and Spirit, which includes material on the Spirit's procession, the unity and structure of God's triune action, and the Spirit's activity throughout the Son's incarnate life and ministry. The next sections will seek to develop the exegetical material further by addressing relevant concerns about the doctrine of God's inseparable operations and by elaborating on the Spirit's bestowal of certain spiritual gifts upon the Son. At the end of the chapter, I will then suggest ways in which the argument connects with the major emphases previously flagged up in recent Christology (i.e., the interaction of the divine persons, the unity of the person of Christ, and the authenticity of Christ's human experience).

193

II. Biblical Description

Chapter 2 of this volume dealt with the Son's procession or eternal generation by the Father. The exegetical material in this chapter will now have to
deal with the Holy Spirit's eternal procession in order to frame the Spirit's
activity in the Son's incarnate ministry. This procession will receive significant
attention here because it is foundational to the discussion of the unity and
order of the Trinity's outward action. In the revelation of the Spirit across the
whole canon of Scripture, he is identified as the true God and a person who
is distinct within the being of the true God even before he acts in creation
or comes to indwell the saints. Like the Father and Son, the Spirit is the true
God himself, not merely "divine" in an unspecified sense but identical with
the particular God revealed in Scripture (Acts 5:3; 1 Cor. 3:16–17; cf. 2 Cor.
3:17–18).[1] It follows that the Holy Spirit, together with the Father and Son,
has all that pertains to God as God (i.e., what is absolute in God). Therefore,
he is not distinct from the Father and Son by something that is absolute in
God. As the Spirit of the Father who raised the Son from the dead and as the
Spirit of the Son (Rom. 8:9, 11; Gal. 4:6; cf. 2 Cor. 3:17), he is distinct by his
relation to the Father and Son.

There are at least three interconnected reasons to uphold that the Spirit's
relation to the Father and Son is a relation of origin or an eternal procession:
the naming of the Spirit, the mission of the Spirit, and certain biblical statements about the Spirit coming forth and receiving from the Father and Son.
First, with respect to the naming of the Spirit, it has to be acknowledged that
the name "Holy Spirit" brings together two words that serve to describe the
divine essence that is absolute and common to all three persons.[2] In addition,
in the case of the other divine person who proceeds, the name "Son" overtly
involves a relation to a principle, whereas the name "Spirit" or "Holy Spirit"
does not immediately call to mind such a relation. However, the Spirit is not
just called "the Spirit" or "the Holy Spirit" but is also called "the Spirit of the
Lord," "the Spirit of him who raised Jesus from the dead," and (with some
variations in wording) "the Spirit of the Son" or "the Spirit of Christ" (Acts
16:7; Rom. 8:9, 11; 1 Cor. 6:11; 2 Cor. 3:17; Gal. 4:6; Phil. 1:19; 1 Pet. 1:11).
Even if the name "Son" has the more obvious reference to a principle, a name
like "Spirit of the Son" or "Spirit of Christ" certainly can have reference to

---

1. Regarding the identification of the Spirit as YHWH in 2 Cor. 3:17–18, cf. Ambrose, *De
Spiritu Sancto* 3.16,101–3 (192–93); Hays, *Echoes of Scripture in the Letters of Paul*, 143–44;
Belleville, *Reflections of Glory*, 293–96; W. Hill, *Paul and the Trinity*, 143–53.

2. On this point, see, e.g., Basil of Caesarea, *Contre Eunome* 3.3 (2:154–56); Gregory Nazianzen, *Discours 27–31*, 31.2 (278); Ambrose, *De Spiritu Sancto* 1.9,105–6 (61).

one who spirates or breathes forth.[3] That this relation is included in the person and name of the Spirit can be substantiated by a look at Old and New Testament descriptions of God's Spirit.[4]

On the one hand, the Old Testament's use of the term רוּחַ ("spirit") involves a range of meanings, some of which are not directly linked to the concept of breath or an act of breathing forth.[5] Furthermore, the Old Testament by itself does not provide a full-orbed pneumatology with a complete description of the Spirit as a distinct person together with the Father and Son. On the other hand, the Old Testament description of God's Spirit does include the notion that the Spirit is the breath of YHWH coming forth with divine power to give life.[6] In the prophecy of Ezekiel in particular, YHWH causes רוּחַ to enter Israel's dry bones and make them live (37:5). The רוּחַ "breathes" on the slain to give them life (37:9). And the prophecy confirms that it is YHWH's own רוּחַ that gives life (37:14; cf. 36:27).[7]

In the New Testament's more developed revelation of the Spirit as a distinct person in God, Jesus picks up on this Old Testament theme and makes the connection between the name "Spirit" and the act of breathing forth. When Jesus announces that he is sending out his disciples in John 20, John records that Jesus "breathed on [ἐνεφύσησεν] them and said, 'Receive the Holy Spirit'" (20:22). Jesus's statement recalls YHWH giving life to Adam and YHWH's breath giving life to the valley of dry bones in Ezekiel 37.[8] There have been extensive debates about how this event might be related to the Spirit's coming at Pentecost and about whether it is strictly symbolic,[9] but there is no need to drive a wedge between a real giving of some sort and an instruction about that giving. Given the great work set before the disciples, Jesus "fortifies them with an earnest of that more plentiful effusion of the Spirit . . . in the days

---

3. Cf. Ambrose, *De Spiritu Sancto* 1.3,44 (32–33); Aquinas, *ST* Ia.36.1 ad 2 (376).

4. For an insightful study of the naming of the Spirit in Scripture and the Christian tradition, see Sanders, "The Spirit Who Is from God." Sanders also provides an instructive reflection on the relationship between the verbal revelation of the divine persons in Scripture and the revelation of the persons in the divine missions; see *The Triune God*, chap. 3.

5. See BDB, 924–26.

6. See further Averbeck, "Breath, Wind, Spirit and the Holy Spirit in the Old Testament"; Block, "The View from the Top."

7. Cf. Block, "The View from the Top," 195: "The *rûaḥ* that will revitalize Israel is not the ordinary, natural life breath common to all living things; it is the Spirit of God himself."

8. So, e.g., Barrett, *John*, 474; Keener, *John*, 2:1204–6. The Greek verb ἐνεφύσησεν ("breathed on") or a cognate form appears in Gen. 2:7 and Ezek. 37:9 in the LXX. Given that the context of John 20:22 speaks about the disciples' evangelistic mission, Jesus's statement may present him as the giver of prophetic inspiration as well (cf. Keener, *John*, 2:1205).

9. The purely symbolic interpretation was anathematized at the Second Council of Constantinople (553) (see "Anathema 12," in N. Tanner, *Decrees of the Ecumenical Councils*, 119–20). On more recent interpretations, see Keener, *John*, 2:1196–200.

of Pentecost" and also helps them to understand his conferral of the Spirit by the "exterior sign" of breathing.[10] In the New Testament as well, then, the name "Spirit" has reference to one who spirates or breathes forth that which has divine power to give life. One could take the name "Spirit" with the reference to one who spirates as something purely economic, something arbitrarily assigned to a divine person whose true identity and relation to the Father and Son would remain undisclosed in the economy. However, even if, like the terms "Son" and "generation," the terms "Spirit" and "spiration" have to be divested of certain corporeal connotations when applied to God, what the name "Spirit" signifies in God's case ultimately transcends the contingency of the economy of salvation.[11] Jesus repeatedly clarifies the identity of the Paraclete who undertakes various economic tasks by naming him the Spirit (John 14:16–17, 26; 15:26; cf. 16:7, 13). Indeed, according to Hebrews, the Spirit is "the eternal Spirit" (Heb. 9:14).[12] This person is not someone who arbitrarily acts like a spirit breathed forth; rather, he *is* the Spirit originated by the Father and Son, coming forth with divine power.

Second, the mission of the Holy Spirit also entails that his relation to the Father and Son is a relation of origin or an eternal procession. Scripture speaks about the Spirit "coming" into the world (e.g., John 16:13; Acts 1:8), but it also speaks about him being "sent" by the Father and by the Son (e.g., John 14:16, 26; 15:26; 16:7; Gal. 4:6; cf. John 20:22; Acts 2:18, 33; Rom. 5:5). And being sent implies not only a relation to a *terminus ad quem* but also a relation in which one goes forth from a principle. Indeed, it often implies that the emissary receives counsel or jurisdiction from the sender.[13]

Why does Scripture speak of the Spirit not only "coming" but also being "sent"? With respect to the *terminus ad quem*, the Spirit takes up a new mode of presence in created effects (the form of a dove, the tongues of fire, the hearts of Christian believers). With respect to the act of going forth from a principle, one could posit a new act of going forth in which the Spirit receives new counsel or dominion from the Father and Son. But this would imply an

10. Poole, *Annotations upon the Holy Bible*, on John 20:22.

11. For clarifications about the meaning of the terms "Spirit" and "procession" in theology proper, see, e.g., Aquinas, *Super Sent.* 1.11.1.1 ad 4 and 6 (1:279); 1.13.1.1 (1:302), where Aquinas focuses on the basic truth of one person's act of going forth from a principle (*exitus a principio*).

12. For the view that the phrase "eternal Spirit" signifies the person of the Holy Spirit in Heb. 9:14, see Aquinas, *Super Heb.* 9.3.444 (434); Calvin, *In Heb.*, 111–12; Lane, *Hebrews 9–13*, 240; Koester, *Hebrews*, 410–11; Cockerill, *Hebrews*, 397–99. Cockerill (399) notes that just as the eternal sonship of Christ in Hebrews grounds the unique efficacy of his priesthood, so the Spirit being the "eternal Spirit" means that he is able to help Christ in his human operation to secure an "eternal redemption" (9:12).

13. Cf., e.g., Lombard, *Sent.* 1.15.9–10 (137); Bonaventure, *In Sent.* 1.15.1.1 (259–60); Aquinas, *Super Sent.* 1.15.2–3 (1:336–46); Aquinas, *ST* Ia.43.1 (445).

inferiority of the Spirit and stand in conflict with the Spirit's eternal deity and his sharing divine omniscience and dominion. By implication, if there is an act of going forth upon which the language of mission is based, it is an eternal act of going forth, in which, like the Son from the Father, the Spirit eternally receives from the Father and Son divine omniscience and dominion. That eternal act of going forth is the reason that when the Spirit comes, he is also said to be "sent." In other words, just as the Spirit has from the Father and Son the divine being, knowledge, power, and operation, so he has from the Father and Son his act of coming and taking up a new mode presence in the world, which is why, when he comes, he is said to be "sent."[14] Accordingly, what the word "mission" signifies here is the Spirit's act of eternally going forth from the Father and Son taken together with the new addition of a created *terminus*. The Spirit's mission, then, implies that his eternal relation to the Father and Son is a relation of origin or an eternal procession.

Third, certain biblical statements about the Spirit coming forth and receiving from the Father and Son more directly point us toward the Spirit's eternal procession. A few texts in John's Gospel and 1 Corinthians deserve a closer look here. In John's Gospel, Jesus tells the disciples, "Whenever the Paraclete comes, whom I will send to you from the Father [παρὰ τοῦ πατρός], the Spirit of truth that goes out from the Father [παρὰ τοῦ πατρὸς ἐκπορεύεται], he will testify concerning me" (John 15:26). The Spirit actively "comes" in this verse, which illustrates his "divine majesty" as one who "works as he wills" (cf. 1 Cor. 12:11). Yet the Spirit is also "sent." He does not change location, for "he himself fills the earth," but he "begins in a new mode by grace to dwell in those whom he makes the temple of God."[15] Jesus ascribes to himself the work of sending the Spirit (together with the Father), and it is possible to debate whether the first occurrence of the prepositional phrase παρὰ τοῦ πατρός has an adverbial function (Jesus sends *from the Father* the Spirit) or an adjectival function (Jesus sends the Spirit *who is from the Father*). Both approaches to the syntax fit the pattern of orthodox trinitarianism. More important here is the distinction between the being-sent to the disciples and the going-forth that is not tied to a historical event. It is logically possible that both of these descriptions pertain to the Spirit's outward mission or temporal procession, but it does seem that Jesus is elaborating on who the Spirit is when he clarifies that the Spirit is "the Spirit of truth that proceeds from the Father." Jesus has already said he will send the Spirit from the Father,

---

14. This logic is laid out by Aquinas in *SCG* 4.23 (86).
15. Aquinas, *Super Ioann.* 15.5.7.2061 (389).

so, if he is shedding light on the identity of the Spirit, it is reasonable to infer that his description of the Spirit as the one who proceeds from the Father goes beyond his description of the sending of the Spirit. In addition, in the context of John's Gospel, being sent by a divine person presupposes already being from that person and, by this relation of origin, being fit for outward mission and for revelation of the person from whom one proceeds (see John 1:14, 18; 5:16–30; 6:46; 7:29).

Jesus says something similar in John 16:

> Many things I still have to say to you, but you are not able to bear them now. But whenever he comes, the Spirit of truth, he will lead you in all truth, for he will not speak from himself, but as many things as he will hear he will speak, and the things coming he will declare to you. All things, as many as the Father has, are mine. On account of this, I said that from me he receives and will declare to you. (16:12–15)

The Spirit's coming into the world and illuminating the Son's work is rooted in his hearing, speaking, and receiving from the Son. This is not the only place in the New Testament where a divine person's knowledge and efficacy in revelation are rooted in a prevenient receiving. In Matthew 11:27 the Son knows the Father in a comprehensive manner and can thus reveal the Father since he is the one to whom the Father has "handed over" all things. In John 5:25–30 the Son hears and acts from the Father as one who has received from the Father the divine life. In John 6:46 and 7:29 the Son has divine knowledge since he is "the one who is from God." The operation from another is a sign of an antecedent procession from another. So Augustine: "Because [the Spirit] is not of himself but from that one from whom he proceeds, from whom he has the essence, from that one he has knowledge; from that one, then, is the hearing, which is nothing other than knowledge."[16]

Of course, in John 16:13–14 the Spirit *will* hear and speak and receive (future tense). Though this might at first seem to problematize the notion that the passage attests the Spirit's eternal procession, something similar occurs in John 5:20b regarding the Son: "Greater works than these *will* [the Father] show [the Son], so that you may wonder." Insofar as other scriptural texts throughout the canon teach that the Son and Spirit are divine persons equal to the Father, it seems that the futurity of the Son's seeing or the Spirit's hearing would not pertain to growth in a divine knowledge that the Father alone might have once possessed in full. Rather, it would pertain to the futurity of

16. Augustine, *In Iohann.* 99.4 (584–85).

the outward works that the Son and Spirit will effect.[17] If that is so, then the futurity of the Spirit's hearing and receiving in John 16:13–14 does not detract from the passage's reference to the Spirit's *eternal* relation to the Father and Son. In any event, the Spirit's receiving is not expressed in the future tense alone here. For in 16:15 the Son goes on to give the reason that the Spirit speaks from the Son—namely, that the Son himself has what the Father has. "All things, as many as the Father has, are mine. On account of this I said that from me he receives [λαμβάνει] and will declare to you."[18] Put in paraphrase, "All the Divine Essence, Wisdom, Power, which is in the Father, are mine; I am in all things that concern the Deity, one, and equal with the Father; and that was the reason that I said, that he should take of mine, and shew [*sic*] it to you."[19] In the farewell discourse, then, the Spirit goes forth from the Father (15:26) and in so doing receives from the Son (and Father) the divine life, knowledge, and power that the Son has from the Father.[20]

Another scriptural text that appears in early treatments of the Spirit's procession is 1 Corinthians 2:10–16.[21] In this passage Paul is explaining why those who prize worldly wisdom do not understand spiritual truths, whereas believers do understand. Believers understand because "God has revealed [the things of God] through the Spirit" (2:10a). God reveals himself this way because "the Spirit searches all things, even the deep things of God" (2:10b). Paul then explains further: "For who knows the things of a man except the spirit of that man in him? So also no one knows the things of God except the Spirit of God [τὸ πνεῦμα τοῦ θεοῦ]" (2:11). The apostle clarifies that this

17. Cf. Ambrose, *De Spiritu Sancto* 3.16,115 (199), where he takes the future verbs to be less about the "power of divine right" and "more about the office of the dispensation." Note also Augustine (*In Iohann.* 99.5 [585]) and Aquinas (*Super Ioann.* 16.3.5.2104 [397]), both of whom are unfazed by the use of the future tense insofar as God's eternity includes all times, making it acceptable to say that the Spirit was, is, and will be and that he knew, knows, and will know. Aquinas adds that the futurity of the verb may also be based upon the futurity of the things known by the Spirit (*aliquando dicitur audire in futuro propter hoc quia illa quorum notitiam habet sunt futura*).

18. Assessments of the significance in the change from the future to the present tense vary (see, e.g., Westcott, *John*, 231; R. Brown, *John XIII–XXI*, 707). While New Testament Greek does not necessarily have tense built into its individual verbs, a future verb in the indicative mood normally does point toward something taking place in the future (so, e.g., Campbell, *Advances in the Study of Greek*, 106–17). The change from the future to present tense in John 16:15 may have some significance, then, clarifying that the Spirit's act of receiving is not merely future.

19. Poole, *Annotations upon the Holy Bible*, on John 16:15.

20. Cf. Ambrose: "All the Father's things the Son has. . . . And these things which he accepts by a unity of nature, from him by the same unity of nature the Spirit also accepts. . . . What, therefore, the Spirit speaks, is the Son's, what the Son gives, is the Father's" (*De Spiritu Sancto* 2.12,134 [138–39]).

21. E.g., Athanasius, *Serap.* 1.22 (506–7); Ambrose, *De Spiritu Sancto* 2.11,124–29 (134–37).

is the very Spirit that has instructed believers: "And we received not the spirit of the world but the Spirit from God [τὸ πνεῦμα τὸ ἐκ τοῦ θεοῦ] so that we know the things given to us by God" (2:12). While the "natural" person does not receive "the things of the Spirit of God" (τὰ τοῦ πνεύματος τοῦ θεοῦ), the "spiritual" person receives and understands them (2:14–16).

God (the Father) operates through the Spirit to reveal himself and his will. The Spirit is called simply "the Spirit" in 1 Corinthians 2:10, "the Spirit of God" in 2:11 and 14, and the "Spirit from God" in 2:12. The "of God" in 2:11 and 14 may be a simple genitive of possession rather than a genitive of source (i.e., the Spirit is "God's Spirit"). But the addition of the preposition ἐκ in 2:12 encourages a translation of the phrase τὸ πνεῦμα τὸ ἐκ τοῦ θεοῦ with something like "the Spirit who issues from God."[22] This is another case of an operation from another (the Spirit's revelatory operation from the Father) (2:10a) being rooted in a coming-forth from another (2:10b–12). Is this a temporal coming-forth in mission or an eternal coming-forth in the divine life that transcends any historical mission? A temporal coming-forth in mission accords with Paul's emphasis on the Spirit coming to us and being given to us to reveal spiritual things and to illumine our minds. But Paul's comparison of the spirit of a human being and the Spirit of God in this passage concerns the Spirit in God's immanent life.[23] If this is a description of temporal procession that is based upon an actual coming-forth and receiving from the Father divine knowledge and divine operation to effect something in creatures, then, insofar as the Spirit did not recently learn the things of God but is coequal with the Father in eternal knowledge and counsel, then the act itself of proceeding and receiving is eternal, even as the outward *terminus* (i.e., the illumined mind of the believer) is new.[24] Alternatively, if the adjectival phrase τὸ ἐκ τοῦ θεοῦ more directly signifies that the Spirit antecedently issues from the Father with perfect knowledge and is thus antecedently fit for an outward mission of illumination, then, in that case too, the passage bears

22. Thiselton, *First Epistle to the Corinthians*, 261, 264. Thiselton is clear that he does not believe that 1 Cor. 2:12 by itself will "support a fully articulate doctrine of 'the procession of the Holy Spirit,'" but he then quotes (apparently with approval) another author who argues that the text "implies" the procession.

23. As a number of commentators point out (e.g., Fee, *First Epistle to the Corinthians*, 119), the analogy is not meant to suggest that there is an exact parallel between the human soul and the being of God. The point is that just as a human spirit is internal to the human person and knows the person's thoughts, so too does God's Spirit possess all the knowledge of God.

24. The Spirit's "searching" in this text is not a matter of learning what he formerly did not know. Instead, like the Father and Son, who also are said to "search" things (cf. Jer. 17:10; Rom. 8:27; Heb. 4:12; Rev. 2:23), the Spirit "searches" the deep things of God in that there is nothing that eludes him, nothing of which he is ignorant (so, e.g., Ambrose, *De Spiritu Sancto* 2.11,128 [136]).

witness to the Spirit's eternal procession. Either way, indirectly or directly, it seems to me that 1 Corinthians 2 attests the Spirit's eternal procession.

Like the Son, who eternally proceeds from the Father and in proceeding has all that the Father has, the Spirit eternally proceeds from the Father and Son and in proceeding has all that the Father and Son have. The Spirit's procession distinguishes him as the person that he is: only the Spirit proceeds from both the Father and the Son. At the same time, the Spirit proceeds from the Father and Son without any local motion or separation; he comes forth eternally without ever going away.[25] In proceeding, the Spirit receives from and shares with the Father and Son the one divine essence, power, and operation.[26] The Spirit's procession establishes both the distinctness in his mode of subsisting and acting and also the oneness of the divine essence, power, and operation that guide this chapter's treatment of the Spirit's activity in Christ's ministry.

One of the entailments of the Father, Son, and Spirit sharing one and the same divine essence is their mutual indwelling. In response to Philip's request to see the Father, Jesus says, "The one who has seen me has seen the Father. How do you say, 'Show us the Father'? Do you not believe that I am in the Father and the Father is in me? The words that I myself say to you I do not speak from myself, but the Father who remains in me does his works. Believe me that I am in the Father and the Father is in me" (John 14:9–11). The mutual indwelling of the divine persons includes the Holy Spirit too. Anticipating his imminent death, resurrection, and ascension, Jesus states in John 14 that he will ask the Father to give "another Paraclete," "the Spirit of truth," to the disciples, in order that the Spirit may be with them forever (14:16–17). Though Jesus will return to the disciples in his resurrected body for a short time (compare 14:18–19; 16:16), he will still be going away and will send the Spirit to dwell in them and continue his work (14:25–26; 15:26; 16:4–7). Of special importance here is that, according to Jesus, when the Spirit indwells a believer and the believer keeps and obeys the word of Jesus, then Jesus and the Father also reside within the believer (14:23; cf. 1 John 4:13). The Spirit in some peculiar way indwells believers, but the Spirit's indwelling still entails that the Father and Son also indwell them.

The situation is similar in Romans 8. The Spirit of God and of Christ lives in the saints, which entails that Christ himself lives in the saints (8:9–11).[27]

---

25. Ambrose, *De Spiritu Sancto* 1.11,116–20 (65–67).

26. In other words, this is not a creaturely reception of participation but a reception of consubstantiality (cf. Ambrose, *De Spiritu Sancto* 2.11,118 [132]; 2.12,134 [138–39]; Cyril of Alexandria, *Tertia ad Nestorium* 6,10 [39–40]; Aquinas, *Super Ioann.* 16.4.2.2108 [398]).

27. Against various recent authors who have claimed that Paul conflates Christ and the Spirit, see Gordon Fee's discussion of Pauline pneumatology wherein the Spirit is the one "who carries

Likewise, in 1 Corinthians 3:16, Paul asks the church, "Do you not know that you are the temple of God and the Spirit of God dwells in you?" Again, in 1 Corinthians 6:19 he asks, "Or do you not know that your body is a temple of the Holy Spirit in you, whom you have from God?" To be indwelt by the Holy Spirit is to be the temple of God in Paul's theology. The Spirit's presence and gracious operation is the presence and gracious operation of the Father and Son as well, which indicates and presupposes the mutual indwelling and common deity of the divine persons.[28] Thus, "where any divine operation of either the Father or the Son or the Spirit is designated, it is referred not only to the Holy Spirit but also to the Father, not only to the Father but also to the Son and Spirit."[29] According to figures like Athanasius and Ambrose, the mutual indwelling of the persons is not to be set against the unity of the divine essence as an independent explanation of the unity of the divine persons.[30] Rather, the mutual indwelling is an implication of the essential unity. The statement that the Father is in the Son and the Son in the Father is made intelligible by the fact that the Son is the "offspring of the Father's essence."[31] "We observe, then, that the Father and the Son and the Holy Spirit remain in one and the same [place or human person] by a unity of nature." In this "inseparable unity," "where either the Father or Christ or the Spirit is signified . . . there is all the fullness of the Trinity."[32]

The eternal processions, the eternal sharing of the one divine essence, and the mutual indwelling of the divine persons entail a unity of the Trinity's action *ad extra*. The Father's communication of the one Godhead to the Son and Spirit prompts us to expect a unity in the persons' action. For the one Godhead with the essential power common to the persons is the principle by which they accomplish their works. This is borne out in the Bible's concrete descriptions of the Trinity's activity in creation, providence, and salvation. The Father, Son, and Spirit always act together. Jesus makes this point with regard to the works of God in general: "Truly, truly, I say to you, the Son is able to do nothing from himself except what he sees the Father doing. For the

---

on the work of Christ following his resurrection and subsequent assumption of the place of authority at God's right hand" ("Christology and Pneumatology in Romans 8:9–11," 313–14). Max Turner argues that the naming of the Spirit as the Spirit of Christ, rather than identifying the Spirit as Christ, signals that the Spirit is the one through whom both the Father and Christ exercise their lordship in the world ("The Spirit of Christ and 'Divine Christology,'" 413–36).

28. See Athanasius, *Serap.* 1.19,31–50 (500–501); 2.12,16–25 (555–56); Ambrose, *De Spiritu Sancto* 1.11,122–25 (67–68).

29. Ambrose, *De Spiritu Sancto* 1.3,40 (31).

30. *Pace*, e.g., Moltmann, *The Trinity and the Kingdom*, 171–76.

31. Athanasius, *Oratio III*, 5,2 (310–11). Cf. Basil of Caesarea, *Sur le Saint-Esprit* 18,45 (406).

32. Ambrose, *De Spiritu Sancto* 3.9,55 (172–73); 3.13,91 (188).

things which he does, these things also the Son likewise does" (John 5:19; cf. 10:37–38). "The words that I myself say to you I do not speak from myself, but the Father who remains in me does his works" (14:10). The Son does not do certain works after the Father has done other works; rather, the persons effect the same work by their one operation.[33]

In creation, the Father acted with his Son, who is his wisdom and Word (Prov. 8:22–31; John 1:3, 10; 1 Cor. 8:6; Col. 1:16–17). The Father and Son acted with the Holy Spirit too, who gives life to God's creatures (Gen. 1:2; Job 33:4; Ps. 104:30). In the work of prophecy and inspiration, the three divine persons speak. Holy Scripture is the word of YHWH, the one God, but Scripture also attests the activity of each of the divine persons in its authorship. The Father speaks of and to his Son, the new Israel and servant of YHWH (e.g., Pss. 2; 110; Isa. 42:1–9; 52:13–53:12). The Son, chosen to be the incarnate one and the new Israel, speaks of his mission and addresses the Father (e.g., Pss. 22; 40:6–8; Isa. 49:1–7). The Spirit of Christ too speaks by the prophets in the Scriptures (e.g., Zech. 7:12; Acts 1:16; 4:25; 28:25; Heb. 3:7; 1 Pet. 1:10–12). In the incarnation of the Son, the three divine persons act together. The Father sends and gives his Son and prepares a body for him (Isa. 42:6–7; John 3:16; Gal. 4:4; Heb. 10:5); the Son comes and takes on flesh and dwells among us (John 1:9–14; 2 Cor. 8:9; Phil. 2:7; Heb. 2:14; 10:5); the Spirit enables the virgin Mary to conceive the Son according to his human nature (Matt. 1:18, 20; Luke 1:35). In the crucifixion all three persons are active. The Father gives up his Son and does not spare him (Isa. 53:10; Rom. 8:32; 2 Cor. 5:21); the Son lays down his own life (Isa. 53:12; Mark 10:45; John 10:17–18; Gal. 2:20; 3:13); the Spirit is the one by whose help the Son offers his life (Heb. 9:14). On the third day, the Father raises up and exalts the Son (Acts 2:24, 32, 36; 3:15; 4:10; 5:30; 10:40; 13:30, 34; Rom. 4:24; 8:11; 10:9; 1 Cor. 15:15; 2 Cor. 4:14; Gal. 1:1; Eph. 1:20; Col. 2:12; 1 Thess. 1:10; 1 Pet. 1:21). Yet the Son himself raises his own body as a sign of his divine authority (John 2:19; 10:18; cf. Matt. 27:63; Mark 8:31; Acts 17:3). And the "Spirit of holiness" is the one according to whom Jesus is "appointed Son of God in power by the resurrection from the dead" (Rom. 1:4).

In the early apostolic ministry, both the Son and Spirit are said to direct and empower and even speak in the apostles' proclamation and to advance the gospel throughout the world (Mark 13:11; John 20:21–22; Acts 4:31; 13:2, 52; Rom. 15:18–19; 1 Cor. 7:40; 2 Cor. 13:3; Phil. 1:19). In the mission of the Spirit, the Father and Son send and give while the Spirit actively comes

---

33. So Ambrose, *De Spiritu Sancto* 2.12,136 (140): "*Non ergo aliqui prior vel secundus est actus, sed idem unius operationis effectus est.*" Cf. Kathryn Tanner: "The Son does not replace the Father as his emissary. The Father works where the Son works" (*Christ the Key*, 153).

to dwell in human beings (John 14:16, 26; 15:26; 16:12–15; Acts 1:8; Rom. 5:5; Gal. 4:6). In baptism into the one name and authority of the triune God, the Father, Son, and Spirit act together to signify and seal the benefits of Christ and to initiate the baptized into the body of Christ (Matt. 28:19; Rom. 6:3–4). The Father and Son give the new birth and indwell the saints while the Spirit also quickens the dead and lives in us (Ezek. 36:26–27; Joel 2:28–29; Matt. 3:11; John 3:5; 5:21; 14:23; 17:21–23; Rom. 8:2, 11; 1 Cor. 12:13; 2 Cor. 3:6; Gal. 2:20; Eph. 2:10; 3:16–17; 1 John 3:24). In revelation and illumination, the Father, Son, and Spirit all act to enlighten us and enable us to receive spiritual truth in a saving manner (Matt. 11:25–27; John 1:9; 16:12–15; 1 Cor. 2:10–16; 12:3; Eph. 1:17–18). "As the Father is the light and the Son his radiance . . . it is right to see also in the Son the Spirit by whom we are enlightened. . . . When we are enlightened by the Spirit, Christ is the one enlightening in him" (cf. John 1:9; Heb. 1:3; 1 John 1:5).[34] In the work of sanctification, the Father elects us for holiness and consecrates us by the truth of the gospel, while Jesus purifies us by his blood and the Spirit of holiness also makes us holy (John 17:17; 1 Cor. 1:2; 6:11; 2 Cor. 11:3; Eph. 1:4; 5:26; 1 Thess. 3:11–13; 4:3, 7–8; 5:23; 2 Thess. 2:13; Heb. 13:12; 1 Pet. 1:2). Having defeated the ungodly powers by his death and resurrection, Christ distributes the spoils by giving spiritual gifts and officers to the church (Eph. 4:7–16), and yet the Spirit, too, apportions the gifts "just as he wills" (1 Cor. 12:4–11). Finally, in the culmination of God's plan, the Father judges the world with and through the Son (John 8:50; Acts 1:7; 17:31; Rom. 2:16; Heb. 12:23–24; 1 Pet. 1:17); the Son comes to execute the Father's will in the resurrection of the dead and the last judgment (Matt. 24:30–31, 36–39, 44; 25:31–46; John 5:22–24; 6:39–40, 44, 54; Acts 10:42; Rom. 2:16; 2 Tim. 4:1; James 5:8–9; Rev. 19:11–16; 22:12–13); the Spirit also is the living God to whom vengeance belongs and the one who goes forth from the throne of God in the new creation to sustain the saints' everlasting life (Heb. 10:29–31; Rev. 22:1–2, 17; cf. John 7:37–39).

In the midst of this unity of action there remains a diversity in the ways in which the persons act. Jesus's teaching in John 5:19–30 again is significant: he wills and acts outwardly from the Father in accordance with his receiving from the Father the divine life. The manner and order of acting reflects the manner and order of subsisting. Thus, for example, the Father creates the world "through" the Son (John 1:3, 10; 1 Cor. 8:6; Col. 1:16; Heb. 1:2). The Father saves and reconciles us through the Son (John 3:17; Rom. 5:9–11) and judges the world through the Son (John 5:22–23; Acts 10:42; 17:31; Rom. 2:16). The

---

34. Athanasius, *Serap.* 1.19,10–16 (498–99).

Father and Son both act "through" the Spirit. For example, the Father and Son work through the Spirit in revelation (John 14:26; 15:26–27; 16:12–15; Acts 1:2; 4:25; 1 Cor. 2:10). God has given us new life and has poured out his love into our hearts through the Holy Spirit given to us (Rom. 5:5; 8:11; cf. Eph. 3:16). The Spirit, then, acts from the Father and Son (John 14:26; 16:12–15). To be sure, in the Bible's account of God's actions, various prepositions ("of," "from," "through," "in") can be applied to each of the divine persons.[35] For example, the Father is not only the one "from whom" things are done but can also be described as the one "through whom" things are done (e.g., Rom. 6:4; 1 Cor. 1:9; Gal. 1:1). However, such texts do not teach that these are cases where it is the Son or Spirit acting through the Father, so these texts do not break up the biblical pattern of the Father acting through the Son and Spirit, the Son acting from the Father and through the Spirit, and the Spirit acting from the Father and Son. In light of this, theologians in the catholic tradition have often summarized scriptural teaching on the Trinity's outward action by noting that it always takes place *from* the Father, *through* the Son, *in* the Spirit. So Athanasius: "One is the ἐνέργεια of [the triad]. For the Father does all things through the Word in the Holy Spirit, and thus the unity of the holy triad is preserved, and thus one God is proclaimed in the church." Accordingly, "there is nothing that does not happen and is not wrought through the Word in the Spirit."[36] Gregory of Nyssa also exemplifies the ἐκ-διά-ἐν (from-through-in) prepositional pattern. He writes that every divine action occurs "from the Father" and "through the Son" and is completed "in the Holy Spirit." The action or "movement" is not proper (ἰδιάζουσά) to one person, but it is performed by each of the three in his own way according to his mode of being (πῶς ἐστι).[37]

There are places in Scripture where certain works are attributed or "appropriated" to individual persons because of a peculiar resonance between the work and the distinct character and economic office of the person. Often (though not exclusively) the biblical authors find it especially fitting to call the Father the one who predestines, creates, governs, and judges the world (John 8:50; Acts 2:23; 4:24–30; Rom. 2:16; 1 Cor. 15:24–28; Eph. 1:3–6, 9–11; 1 Pet. 1:20). They find it especially fitting to identify the Son as the one who undertakes the work of mediation, atonement, and redemption (Job 19:25; Isa. 53:10; Rom. 5:12–21; 2 Cor. 5:21; 1 Tim. 2:5; Heb. 7:22; 9:15; 12:24; 1 John 2:2) and to identify the Spirit as the one who applies and completes

35. See Basil of Caesarea, *Sur le Saint-Esprit* 5,7–12 (272–85).
36. Athanasius, *Serap.* 1.28,9–11 (520); 1.31,7–8 (526). Cf. 1.12,22–23 (483); 1.14,27–29 (488); 2.14,2–3 (558).
37. Gregory of Nyssa, *Ad Ablabium*, 47–48, 55.

the work of Christ in revelation and renewal, sealing and sanctification (John 16:12–15; Acts 1:8; Rom. 8:11, 13–14; 1 Cor. 2:10–16; Eph. 1:13–14; 2 Thess. 2:13; Titus 3:5–6; 1 Pet. 1:2). Given the unity of divine action discussed above, such peculiar appropriation of a certain work to one person should not be taken to exclude the activity of the other two persons: "The distribution of the economic task requires a twofold caution: I. that it should be understood to be made without any essential dependence and inequality"; "II. that any person has this economic office without excluding the other persons."[38] Yet it will be our task in the next section to discuss more adequately how the unity of the Trinity's outward action coheres with the indications of there being some diversity in God's action in the biblical narrative. This is particularly crucial with regard to the Spirit's work of empowering the Son in the fulfillment of his public ministry.

The Old and New Testaments bear witness to the Spirit empowering and leading the Son in his incarnate life. According to Isaiah 11:1–5, the messianic "branch" from the family of Jesse will be endowed with the Spirit of YHWH, the Spirit of wisdom and understanding and of counsel and strength, the Spirit of knowledge and the fear of YHWH, who will enable the branch to judge righteously and overthrow the wicked. Equipping the Messiah with such "mental endowments," the Spirit gives him "true knowledge showing itself in a life of reverence."[39] Later in Isaiah, YHWH's Spirit comes to rest upon YHWH's servant so that he brings forth justice, hope, light, and freedom for the nations (42:1–9). The servant proclaims, "The Spirit of the Lord YHWH is upon me, because YHWH has anointed me to bring good news to the poor. He has sent me to bind up the brokenhearted, to announce freedom for captives and liberation for the prisoners, to announce the year of YHWH's favor and the day of our God's retribution, to comfort all who mourn" (61:1–2). The Spirit's anointing of the Isaianic servant marks him out as both a prophet granted extraordinary knowledge of the will and ways of God and a king granted authority from God to carry out God's judgments (cf. Num. 11:17; Judg. 6:34; 1 Kings 19:16; 2 Kings 2:15–16; Ps. 45:6–7).[40]

Preparing the way of the Lord, John the Baptist declares that Jesus is the one endowed with God's Spirit and the one who will baptize with the Spirit and with fire (Matt. 3:11). When John baptizes Jesus in the Jordan, the Spirit descends upon him in the form of a dove (Matt. 3:13–17; Mark 1:9–11). Like the people of God in the Old Testament, who passed through the water in the

38. Mastricht, *TPT*, 2.24.12 (239).
39. Motyer, *The Prophecy of Isaiah*, 122.
40. Cf., e.g., Dempster, *Dominion and Dynasty*, 176.

presence of the Holy Spirit (so Isa. 63:11) and traveled into the wilderness, Jesus passes through the water as the new Israel in the power of the Spirit and will enter the wilderness for a time of testing.[41] Unlike the Israel of old, Jesus is, according to John the Baptist, permanently endowed with the Spirit: "I have seen the Spirit descending like a dove from heaven and remaining on him. And I did not know him, but the one who sent me to baptize in water said to me, 'On whomever you see the Spirit descending and remaining on him, this is the one who baptizes with the Holy Spirit. And I have seen and testified that this one is the Son of God" (John 1:32–34). "There was nothing very novel about God's Spirit coming upon someone." The Spirit could "come and go." But on Jesus the Spirit "stays." The "talk of the Spirit's 'staying' implies that in Jesus' entire story God's Spirit was indeed operating through him or that he was operating through God's Spirit."[42]

After Jesus's baptism, Matthew reports, "Then Jesus was led into the desert by the Spirit to be tempted by the devil" (Matt. 4:1). With his characteristic pace and brevity, Mark reports that after Jesus's baptism the journey to the desert happened "immediately." Mark also presents the Spirit as the subject of an active verb in his account: "And immediately the Spirit cast him out into the desert" (Mark 1:12). In Luke's account, Jesus is "filled with the Holy Spirit" and "led by the Spirit in the desert" (Luke 4:1). After Jesus's temptation by Satan, he returns to Galilee "in the power of the Spirit" (4:14). Teaching in the synagogue in Nazareth, he unrolls the scroll of Isaiah and applies Isaiah 61:1–2 (with the LXX wording) to himself: "The Spirit of the Lord is upon me because he has anointed me to preach good news to the poor, he has sent me to proclaim release for the captives and recovery of sight for the blind, to release the oppressed, to proclaim the year of the Lord's favor" (Luke 4:17–19). "When Jesus follows this reading by declaring, 'Today this scripture has been fulfilled in your hearing' (Luke 4:21), the reader of Luke's Gospel has been alerted that Jesus himself is the Spirit-anointed Servant figure whose mission is the liberation of Israel."[43] Jesus demonstrates that he is the one anointed with the Spirit throughout his ministry: "If by the Spirit of God I cast out demons, then the kingdom of God has come upon you" (Matt. 12:28; cf. Acts 10:38). In John's Gospel, the reason why Jesus speaks the words of God is that God has given him the Spirit "without measure" (3:34), a point that is anchored in the fact that "the Father loves the Son and has given all things into his hand" (3:35). Accordingly, Jesus says later, "The words that I have

41. See Beale, *A New Testament Biblical Theology*, 412–17.
42. Goldingay, *Biblical Theology*, 279–80.
43. Hays, *Echoes of Scripture in the Gospels*, 225.

spoken to you are spirit and are life" (6:64). "The Son speaks the words of God because he has been entrusted with all things, including the very words of God, as well as the Spirit, who quickens those words to the understanding of listeners and hence brings them life."[44]

In addition to the prophetic and kingly aspects of Jesus's work, the priestly aspect of it also is empowered by the Spirit: the blood of Jesus decisively cleanses from sin because "through the eternal Spirit he offered himself blameless to God" (Heb. 9:14). Some exegetes have held that the phrase "eternal Spirit" here signifies the Holy Spirit as a distinct divine person, while others have held that it signifies the eternal, spiritual divine essence subsisting in the Son. John Owen notes a "double interpretation" in the exegetical tradition. "Some say that the Lord Christ offered himself unto God in and by the acting of the Holy Ghost in his human nature. . . . Others say that his own eternal Deity, which supported him in his sufferings and rendered the sacrifice of himself effectual, is intended." Owen reasons that both (the divine nature in the Son and the person of the Spirit) necessarily "concurred" in Christ's sacrifice. The former was necessary with regard to the "efficacy and effect" of the offering, in that without the former the act of offering would have had only the dignity of a "mere creature." The latter was necessary with regard to the "manner" of the offering, in that the Son in his human nature was enabled by the Spirit to obey the Father and render an acceptable sacrifice.[45] Among other things, the peculiarity of the phrase "eternal spirit" as a designation for the divine essence in this passage arguably suggests that the phrase signifies the Holy Spirit as a distinct person.[46] Yet, as one recent commentator observes, if the phrase "eternal Spirit" signifies the Holy Spirit, it does so without any "diminution of all that [the author] has said about the Son's eternal being" (cf., e.g., 1:10–12).[47] Indeed, as we will discuss below, it is important not to place the Son's human empowerment by the Holy Spirit in competition with his divinity. As John 3:34–35 attests, the Son has the Spirit "without measure" since he has received from the Father all things. The Son as man is filled with the Spirit and acts by the Spirit since the Son as God receives all things from the Father, including the act of spirating the Spirit (cf. John 16:15).

In this section we have covered a number of important elements of scriptural teaching that frame the Son's relationship to the Holy Spirit: the eternal

44. M. Thompson, *The God of the Gospel of John*, 173.

45. Owen, *Hebrews*, 6:303–4. Owen ultimately favors the view that the phrase "eternal Spirit" in Heb. 9:14 signifies the divine essence.

46. For details on the rationale, see Lane, *Hebrews 9–13*, 240; Koester, *Hebrews*, 410–11; Cockerill, *Hebrews*, 397–99.

47. Cockerill, *Hebrews*, 398.

procession of the Spirit, the unity of the divine essence, the mutual indwelling of the persons, the unity of the persons' activity *ad extra*, the order of acting *ad extra*, the appropriation of certain works *ad extra* to certain persons, the Spirit's work of empowering and directing the Son in his incarnate life. This material raises some questions that deserve further attention in our study. For example, does the Bible's account of the diversity in God's action conflict with the unity and simplicity of God's essence and the consequent axiom *opera Trinitatis ad extra indivisa sunt* ("the outward works of the Trinity are undivided")? Does the Son's dependence on the Spirit conflict with the notion that the Son himself is always acting by the one divine essence in God's outward works? Does the Son's unique relationship to the Spirit and his reception of intellectual and moral endowments from the Spirit conflict with his authentic human experience? The next three sections of this chapter will elaborate on the exegetical material by setting forth relevant concerns about the unity of God's operations, by responding to those concerns, and then, finally, by addressing the question of the Son's reception of spiritual gifts from the Holy Spirit.

III. Concerns regarding the Unity of God's Operations

This section will explore in more detail whether Scripture's account of Jesus's dependence on the Spirit coheres with the unity of the Trinity's outward action. In other words, the aim is to consider whether Jesus truly depends on the Spirit if Jesus himself (with the Father and Spirit) is always acting by the simple divine essence throughout his incarnate life. This question might be broken up into three parts: (1) whether claiming that all three persons always act together still allows us to claim that one of the persons is especially manifested in a particular work; (2) whether the incarnate Son would have been in a position to have to depend on the Spirit in a meaningful way; and (3) whether the Spirit could have then been especially manifested in the divine empowerment of the incarnate Son's ministry. The second and third parts of the question connect with recent discussions about "Spirit Christology." Some of those discussions set the Spirit's work against a "Logos Christology" or a Chalcedonian Christology in which the personal identity and divine sonship of Christ are already established prior to the incarnation. Others suggest that taking the Spirit's work seriously might require only some modest revision or integration of Chalcedon.[48] I will argue here that the Spirit's empowerment

---

48. See the diverse proposals in Newman, *A Spirit Christology*; Haight, "The Case for Spirit Christology"; Moltmann, *The Way of Jesus Christ*, 73–94; del Colle, *Christ and the Spirit*; Dunn, *The Christ and the Spirit*, chaps. 7–9; Coffey, "The Theandric Nature of Christ"; Habets, *The*

of Christ coheres with and is illumined by Christ's deity and divine sonship. I will briefly observe how a number of authors have called attention to these three elements of the question that lies before us and then attempt to show that our understanding of the Son's dependence on the Spirit is actually enriched by the divine persons' unity in essence and operation.

(1) Some have argued that biblical teaching on the special prominence of one divine person in a particular economic work is problematized by the notion of the indivisibility of the Trinity's outward acts. In connection with this, some have argued that a commitment to the commonality or indivisibility of the Trinity's actions distances the doctrine of the Trinity from the concrete features of the economy of salvation. Catherine LaCugna, for example, raises these concerns by contrasting the theology of the Greek fathers with that of Augustine. According to LaCugna, the Greek fathers stressed that divine action "originates with the Father, passes through the Son, and is perfected in the Spirit. Thus, the Father creates, redeems, and divinizes through the Son in the power of the Holy Spirit." Augustine, however, prioritizes the one divine nature by which the Trinity works. Hence "the Trinity creates, the Trinity redeems, the Trinity sanctifies." But, LaCugna asks, "if it is a three-personed Godhead that acts in history, how is it possible to detect what is distinctive to each person?" LaCugna recognizes that there might be ways to harmonize what she views as the teaching of Augustine and the teaching of the Greek fathers, but she states that Augustine's view became "exaggerated" in medieval scholasticism when theologians flattened out God's action further in stating that any one of the persons could have become incarnate. In LaCugna's description of Augustine's theology, "essence precedes person." The indivisible operation of the one essence must then be shared by the persons. Thus, in LaCugna's judgment, there is a "modalist direction" in Augustine's theology, and this tacit modalism is not avoided by the appropriation or "assigning" of a particular work to a particular person. For the appropriations often appear "arbitrary." With the unity of the Trinity's operation in place, there is no longer "any need for a plurality of divine persons in the Godhead." It is "no longer possible to single out any one person in relation to a particular activity." Positively, LaCugna seeks

---

Anointed Son; Welker, *God the Revealed*, 217–22; Work, "Jesus' New Relationship with the Holy Spirit"; McFarland, "Spirit and Incarnation"; Crisp, *Revisioning Christology*, chap. 5; C. Holmes, *The Holy Spirit*, 123–30; Liston, "A 'Chalcedonian' Spirit Christology"; van der Kooi, *This Incredibly Benevolent Force*, chaps. 2–3; Kieser, "Is the *Filioque* an Obstacle to a Pneumatologically Robust Christology?"; M. J. Gorman, "The Spirit, the Prophets, and the End of the 'Johannine Jesus'"; Peppiatt, "Life in the Spirit." See also K. Tanner, *Christ the Key*, chap. 4; Abecina, "The Unity of Christ."

to uphold the "unique identity of the persons in the economy of salvation" and the "uniqueness of the missions of Son and Spirit." It is not a "generic Godhead" that sends the Son but rather "the Father alone." It is proper to the Son to be incarnate. It is proper to the Spirit (an "identifying characteristic" of the Spirit) to "make the creature holy." These "identifying characteristics" are not merely "appropriated" to the persons. LaCugna is concerned that the notion of the indivisibility of the Trinity's action prevents the doctrine of the Trinity from having a correspondence to the realities of the economy. It creates a "breach between *oikonomia* and *theologia*." The doctrine of appropriations is a "compensating strategy" here, but it does not truly express the *taxis* of the economy.[49]

Robert Jenson also criticizes Augustine for obscuring the distinctions among the persons in their action. According to Jenson, given Augustine's view that God is "metaphysically simple," he held that there could be no "self-differentiation" or "eventful" ("narrative") differentiation in God. The Cappadocians held that divine action "begins with the Father and is actual through the Son and is perfect in the Holy Spirit," but they still envisioned a "perfect mutuality of the agencies of the Father, Son, and Spirit each in his triune role." In his lack of subtlety, however, Augustine had to deny that "what God does *ad extra* is the *mutual* work of Father, Son, and Spirit, each exercising the mode of agency given by his inner-triune role as God." For Augustine, there is "no difference at all between the agencies of Father, Son, and Spirit." The bishop of Hippo writes with a strict dichotomy: either "Father, Son, and Spirit must simply do the *same* thing, or simply *different* things." Accordingly, "the Son's appearances in Israel could as well be called appearances of the Father or the Spirit." Moreover, according to the development of Augustine in Western scholasticism, any of the divine persons could have become incarnate. Likewise, the speaker who addresses Jesus at his baptism is "indifferently specifiable as the Father or the Son or the Spirit or the whole Trinity." Put bluntly, "The Augustinian supposition that there is no necessary connection between what differentiates the triune identities in God and the structure of God's work in time bankrupts the doctrine of the Trinity cognitively, for it detaches language about the triune identities from the only thing that made such language meaningful in the first place: the biblical narrative." Indeed, the root problem in Augustine's thought is that he refused to allow "the storytelling of the gospel" to determine his understanding of the identities of the divine persons. To provide an antidote to "the Western

---

49. LaCugna, *God for Us*, 97–100. On the relocation of the doctrine of the Trinity to an abstract realm of "metaphysics," cf., e.g., Kasper, *Jesus the Christ*, 245.

tradition" on this point, Jenson contends that the divine persons' works are undivided not because their "agencies" are "indistinguishable" but because they are "perfectly mutual."[50]

Because they are so intertwined, it will be best to treat parts (2) and (3) of the present question together (whether the Son was in a position to have to depend on the Spirit and whether the Spirit could have been the divine person especially manifested in the divine empowerment of the Son). Like LaCugna and Jenson, Colin Gunton faults Augustine for obscuring the divine persons' "characteristic ways of working" or "distinctive forms of action." In Gunton's assessment, the way in which Augustine absolutizes the undividedness of the Trinity's operations means that "the differences among the persons become effectively redundant." The "distinctiveness and particularity of the actions of Son and Spirit in the economy are overridden," so that "the doctrine of the Trinity is divorced from its basis in history and made an irrelevance."[51] Gunton applies this concern to Christ's dependence on the Spirit in his ministry. For Gunton, Jesus remained sinless throughout his earthly life "not through some inbuilt divine programming, though that is the way it has often been made to appear, but by virtue of his free acceptance of the Spirit's guidance." If the "motive force" of Jesus's life is taken to be "the eternal Word," the result is a problematization of the humanity of Jesus: the humanity is "either loosely joined to the Word as in classic Nestorianism or overridden by it." At this point, Gunton stresses the role of "the action of the Holy Spirit toward Jesus" and finds in John Owen's Christology a precedent for this move. Owen "limits the direct operation of the Word on the human reality of Jesus." "In answer to those who would in effect make the Holy Spirit redundant in christology Owen holds that 'The only singular immediate act of the person of the Son on the human nature was the assumption of it into subsistence with himself.'" "The humanity remains authentically human and is not subverted by the immanently operating Word." Gunton writes, "Such a conception does much to create space for a conception of the humanity of Jesus which gives due emphasis to his freedom, particularity, and contingency: they are *enabled* by the (transcendent) Spirit rather than *determined* by the (immanent) Word."[52] In addition to the theology of Augustine, Gunton faults the teaching of the *Filioque* as an obstacle to due recognition of the Spirit's work in Jesus's life. Gunton asserts that the "chief function" of the *Filioque* is to "prevent" a robust teaching of "the personal distinctness of the Holy Spirit." Moreover,

---

50. Jenson, *Systematic Theology*, 110–14.
51. Gunton, *The Promise of Trinitarian Theology*, xxv–xxvii, 3–4, 57, 94, 172, 198.
52. Gunton, *The Promise of Trinitarian Theology*, 66–69.

given that the *Filioque* underscores that the Son (together with the Father) originates the Spirit, it obscures the Son's dependence on the Spirit. However, "We have to speak of the Spirit's Jesus as much as of Jesus' Spirit."[53] Gunton gestures toward some specific ways in which the Spirit empowers the human Jesus in his ministry, including the performance of miraculous deeds and the giving of authority to proclaim the word of God.[54]

Alan Spence also has endeavored to set forth Christ's true human dependence on the Spirit. In his book *Incarnation and Inspiration*, Spence laments that the church's emphasis on the full divinity of Christ and on the subsistence of the humanity of Christ in union with the Logos has led to a neglect of Christ's human experience and empowerment by the Spirit (which Spence distills in the concept of "inspiration"). Positively, Spence aims to integrate the full divinity of Christ, on the one hand, and the human growth of Christ and empowerment of Christ by the Spirit, on the other. Christ is both "worthy of our worship" and "able in his faithfulness towards God to serve as a pattern for redeemed human life."[55]

Like Gunton, Spence finds Owen's work to be helpful in this regard. Owen affirmed the traditional teaching of the indivisibility of the Trinity's outward actions, but, according to Spence, "the difficulty facing this doctrine is the clear and repeated ascription by the Scriptures and the Church in its worship of various divine acts to particular persons of the Trinity." Spence notes that Owen attempts to address this problem by affirming the "appropriation" of certain works to certain persons: "Every activity of God, then, although generally assigned to each person, is particularly ascribed to the one whose characteristic property is manifested in it, or who in a particular way condescends to it." Spence argues that in certain places Owen qualifies the traditional commitment to the inseparable operations in order to uphold the incarnate Son's genuine dependence on the Holy Spirit.[56] Owen insists that the event of the incarnation, for example, is wrought by the Father, Son, and Spirit and yet the assumption of the human nature is "peculiar" to the Son. For Spence, the coherence of these two truths can be illumined by Owen's claim that certain works are appropriated to certain persons not only due to the order of their subsistence but also due to the "peculiar condescension" of one person to a particular work "wherein the others have no concurrence but by approbation and consent."[57]

53. Gunton, *The Promise of Trinitarian Theology*, 131, 133.
54. Gunton, *Father, Son and Holy Spirit*, 146, 153–54.
55. Spence, *Incarnation and Inspiration*, 5, 15.
56. Spence, *Incarnation and Inspiration*, 128–29.
57. Spence, *Incarnation and Inspiration*, 130–31.

This move, Spence reasons, undermines or qualifies the indivisibility of the Trinity's outward works inasmuch as "it admits a real distinction in the divine activity, maintaining only the common approval of the persons." Spence argues that Owen, building on material found in John of Damascus, allows for exceptions to the rule of inseparable operations in the Son's and the Spirit's fulfillment of their economic offices. The Son and Spirit, then, are "distinct agents of their own activity." According to Spence, Owen's qualification of the doctrine of inseparable operations is "somewhat disguised" as "an aspect of the principle of 'appropriation'" in order to avoid the appearance of theological novelty. In short, "the indivisibility of the external divine operations applies to the trinitarian persons only as they are considered divine persons absolutely and not as they condescend to their particular offices in the work of our salvation." Thus, Owen's "trinitarian interpretation of divine agency" enables him "to distinguish between the Son's action in assuming a human nature . . . and the Spirit's work in forming, sanctifying, and energizing that nature" and "to offer a coherent exposition of Jesus Christ both as the incarnate Son of God and also as a man of like nature with ourselves, inspired by the Holy Spirit."[58]

IV. Unity and Diversity in God's Operations

How might one respond to these concerns about the coherence of the Spirit's empowerment of Christ's ministry and the undividedness of the Trinity's outward works? Here I will attempt to shed light on this coherence under the following points.

(1) It may be helpful to make a few historical observations en route to making constructive comments. In particular, Augustine's work should be neither vilified nor made to bear the weight of everything one might want to say about the Trinity's outward action. Augustine acknowledges difficulties in understanding the unity and the diversity in God's works and in a number of places seeks to uphold both. On the one hand, the persons of the Trinity work "inseparably" and perform the same works. The speech of the Father at the baptism of Jesus was wrought by the Trinity (*trinitas fecerit*); the flesh

---

58. Spence, *Incarnation and Inspiration*, 131–37. Here Spence notes the patristic use of the indivisibility of the Trinity's operations to demonstrate the deity of the Holy Spirit. I take it that Spence might argue that a (qualified) notion of inseparable operations should form only part of the basis for affirming the Spirit's deity. For additional examples of recent concerns about the doctrine of inseparable operations, see, e.g., Baars, "'*Opera Trinitatis ad Extra Sunt Indivisa*'"; A. Torrance, "Reclaiming the Continuing Priesthood of Christ," 194–95.

of the Son was created by the Trinity (*trinitas creaverit*); the form of a dove in which the Spirit appears was wrought by the Trinity (*trinitas operata sit*). On the other hand, the Father's speech was the Father's alone (*non nisi patris fuit*); the Son's flesh was the Son's alone (*in qua non nisi filius de virgine natus est*); the Spirit's appearance in the form of a dove is the Spirit's alone (*in qua non nisi spiritus sanctus apparuit*).[59]

Later in *De trinitate* Augustine considers whether he is constrained to say that the Son sent himself into the world. He responds by noting that Scripture constrains us to say, for example, that the Father sanctifies the Son while the Son also sanctifies himself (John 10:36; 17:19), and that the Father delivers up the Son while the Son also delivers himself up on the cross (Rom. 8:32; Gal. 2:20). The divine persons evidently share "one will" and an "inseparable operation." Regarding the mission of the Son, then, the Father and Son (with the Spirit) both bring about the Son's appearing in the flesh (*hoc a patre et filio factum esset ut in carne filius appareret*), but the one who does not appear is said to "send," and the one who appears is said to "be sent" and assume the form of a servant.[60] Later in book 2 of *De trinitate*, where Augustine denies that Old Testament theophanies must have been appearances of the Son in particular, he still holds that while the Trinity wrought the human form in the virgin's womb, that form was the Son's alone.[61] Augustine says less than later scholastic theologians about how all of this fits together, but he affirms that while the whole Trinity effects the Father's speech or the Son's flesh or the Spirit's dove, "the inseparable operation of the Trinity" includes "singular things" that "pertain properly to the manifestation of either the Father or the Son or the Holy Spirit."[62]

It is entirely possible to take up Augustine's central point about the efficacy of all three persons in all of God's economic works and still affirm the *taxis* intrinsic to the Trinity's operations. Indeed, examining the prepositional phrases in texts like John 1:3, Romans 11:36, and 1 Corinthians 8:6, Augustine himself affirms the *taxis* intrinsic to the act of creation. He remarks that within the act of creation "singular things" are attributed to the Father, Son, and Holy Spirit: "*ex ipso*, from the Father; *per ipsum*, through the Son; *in ipso*, in the Holy Spirit."[63]

---

59. Augustine, *De trin.* 1.4.7–5.8 (1:35–36).

60. Augustine, *De trin.* 2.5.9 (1:90–93).

61. Augustine, *De trin.* 2.10.17–12.22 (1:101–9).

62. Augustine, *De trin.* 4.21.30 (1:202–3). Here the Latin reads, "*Cogniscitur inseparabilem in se ipsa trinitatem per visibilis creaturae speciem separabiliter demonstrari, et inseparabilem trinitatis operationem etiam in singulis esse rebus quae vel ad patrem vel ad filium vel ad spiritum sanctum demonstrandum proprie pertinere dicuntur.*"

63. Augustine, *De trin.* 1.6.12 (1:41).

Furthermore, a Greek father like Basil of Caesarea, for example, can offer a strong affirmation of the unity of divine operations: "No energy of the Son is severed from the Father, nor is there anything that is in the things belonging to the Son which is foreign to the Father. 'For all things,' he says, 'which are mine are yours, and yours are mine.'"[64] Likewise, the Spirit distributes gifts to the people of God just as the Father and Son do, so "the energy of the Holy Spirit is ordered with the energy of the Father and Son."[65] Put more strongly, "the Father is not beheld by a difference of works, by showing a proper and separate energy—for as many things as the Son sees the Father doing, these things the Son also likewise does."[66] Basil instructs his readers to learn the Spirit's "union" and "indivisibility" with the Father and Son in "every operation."[67] In this regard, it is important to avoid the simplistic idea that the Latin and Greek fathers produced two different versions of the doctrine of the Trinity or that we must choose between Augustine and the Cappadocians.[68]

One additional historical point bears mentioning. Owen's contribution on the indivisibility of the Trinity's outward action needs to be examined more carefully.[69] His view does accord with a traditional understanding of the undividedness of the Trinity's works. As noted, Owen says, drawing from John of Damascus, that the appropriation of a certain work to a certain person sometimes follows on "a peculiar condescension of any person unto a work, wherein the others have no concurrence but by approbation and consent."[70] However, an important text in Owen's *Christologia* sheds some light on this issue. Writing about the Son's assumption of a human nature, Owen explains, "As unto original efficiency, it was the act of the divine nature, and so, consequently, of the Father, Son, and Spirit. For so are all the outward acts of God—the divine nature being the immediate principle of all such operations." The "acting" of these works "belongs equally unto each person." Regarding the assumption, the "authoritative designation" and sending in this action are peculiar to the Father; the "formation of the human nature" is peculiar to the Spirit; the "term of the assumption, or the taking of our nature unto himself," is peculiar to the Son. It is then this point that Owen distills in the

---

64. Basil of Caesarea, *Contre Eunome* 2.34 (2:140).

65. Basil of Caesarea, *Contre Eunome* 3.4 (2:160).

66. Basil of Caesarea, *Sur le Saint-Esprit* 8,19 (314).

67. Basil of Caesarea, *Sur le Saint-Esprit* 16,37 (374).

68. Cf., e.g., Barnes, "De Régnon Reconsidered"; Barnes, "Augustine in Contemporary Trinitarian Theology"; Ayres, "'Remember That You Are Catholic'"; Butner, "For and against de Régnon." See also Turcescu, *Gregory of Nyssa and the Concept of Divine Persons.*

69. For a helpful analysis, see Wittman, "The End of the Incarnation."

70. Owen, *Pneumatologia*, 1.4 (3:94). Cf. 2.3 (3:160, 162).

important quotation from John of Damascus: the Son alone is the "term of assumption." It is with regard to the term of the assumption that "the other persons had no concurrence, but only . . . 'by counsel and approbation.'"[71] Accordingly, Owen does not hold that there are "real distinctions" among the actions of the Father, Son, and Spirit. The external acts are wrought by the Father, Son, and Spirit together, but certain facets of these acts are peculiar to certain persons. In short, Owen does not abandon or drastically qualify the teaching of the unity of God's outward works. His more thought-provoking contribution at this point arguably lies in his insights into the Son's dependence on the Holy Spirit, which will be noted below.

(2) Affirming the simplicity of God's essence and the attendant unity of God's operations does not obstruct the recognition that a certain divine work can pertain to a certain divine person in a special way. Here it will be helpful to clarify the senses in which various matters are common or proper to the persons.

First, since the eternal relations of origin in God are constitutive of the divine persons' distinct identities, these inward acts of God are "divided" among the persons. This means not that the divine persons can be divided or separated from one another but that there is just one person who generates the Son (the Father), one person who comes forth filially from the Father (the Son), and one person who comes forth from both the Father and the Son (the Spirit). The Son should not be said reflexively to generate himself, lest he be conflated with the Father, who alone has the property of paternity. The Spirit should not be said reflexively to spirate himself, lest he be conflated with the Father and Son, who share the notion of active spiration. The dividedness or unqualified peculiarity of these personally constitutive, inward acts may be set forth and clarified by speaking about the principle and terms of each of them.

71. Owen, *Christologia* 18 (225). The material in John of Damascus actually occurs right after John affirms the "simple deity and one simple energy" of God. He then comments on the distinct case of the things that belong to the σαρκώσις of the Word: "In these things neither the Father nor the Spirit in any way has participated [κατ' οὐδένα λόγον κεκοινώνηκεν], except according to good pleasure and according to the ineffable working of miracles" (*Expos. fidei* 1.10 [33]). Later on John clarifies that while the fullness of the divine essence was united with the human nature in the Son, only the Son was united with the human nature: "For in no way have the Father and the Holy Spirit participated in the incarnation [σαρκώσει] of God the Word, except according to good pleasure and counsel" (3.6 [120–21]). At the same time, John can still say in book 4 of the *Expositio fidei* that since the Son is "from" the Father, "likewise the things which he does, he does from and with him. For one and the same, not similar, but the same [οὐχ ὁμοία, ἀλλ' ἡ αὐτὴ] is the will, energy, and power of the Father and the Son and the Holy Spirit" (4.18 [212–13]). I suspect, then, that a more patient interpretation of John would involve something like the distinction between the common causation of the assumption and the peculiar union of the human nature with the Son, who alone is incarnate.

The *principium quo* (the principle or power "by which") they are wrought is the divine essence taken under one person's relation to another.[72] As noted in chapter 2, Aquinas, for example, points out that the power of generating is not only essential in God but "notional" as well. It is the essential power with the "concomitance" of the Father's personal property.[73] By implication, the *principium quo* of being begotten and coming forth filially from the Father is not the essence taken absolutely but the essence under the Son's relation to the Father. The *principium quo* of passive spiration or coming forth from both the Father and the Son is not the essence taken absolutely but the essence under the Spirit's relation to the Father and Son. Furthermore, as Polanus points out, the distinctness or peculiarity of what he calls the *opera Dei simpliciter personalia* (the "simply" or "absolutely" personal works of God) can be expressed by reference to their "terms" as well. These acts of God have both a proper (belonging to one person) *terminus a quo* and a proper *terminus ad quem*, the former in this case signifying the hypostatic "endpoint" from which an act goes forth and the latter in this case signifying the hypostatic "endpoint" toward which the act goes. The act of generation, for example, has only the Father as its *terminus a quo* and only the Son as its *terminus ad quem*. To offer clarification by way of contrast, these *simpliciter* personal acts are different from the essential divine act of knowing all things, for example, which has for its *principium* the essence as common to the three and has no distinct hypostatic *terminus*.

Second, given the unity and simplicity of God's essence and power, and given that the Father, Son, and Spirit are not constitutively distinguished by the acts of God *ad extra*, the acts of God *ad extra* have for their *principium quo* the essence common to the Father, Son, and Spirit.[74] Yet it is not just

72. In traditional discussions of agency, individual ὑποστάσεις or persons (rather than essences as such) perform actions; hence the axiom *actus sunt suppositorum* (actions belong to individual *supposita*). Thus, the individual ὑπόστασις is the *principium quod* in action (the "principle which" acts). Yet individuals perform actions by their essential power (or, in creatures, by some empowering qualities added to essence), so essence is considered the *principium quo* in action (the "principle by which" one acts).

73. Aquinas, *De pot.* 2.4 ad 1–2 (33); 2.5 (35–36). Cf. Polanus's distinction between the *principium* of the "essential works" of God and the *principium* of the "personal works" of God. The *principium* of the essential works is the divine essence "absolutely" or as common to the three. The *principium* of the inward personal works is one person in the divine essence operating according to his relation to another. The *principium* of the outward personal works is like the *principium* of the essential works in that it is the divine essence as common to the three, but this is qualified by the fact that a certain work may have a special correspondence to one person's personal property (*Syntagma*, 4.2–3 [236–37]).

74. It may be worth pausing to make a methodological observation here. The unity and simplicity of God's essential power that is shared by the persons would predispose one to assume that the acts of God will have the essence common to the persons as their *principium quo* and

that an essential unity of the persons implies the common *principium quo* and the unified activity of all three persons in the outward works. Scripture itself (see above in section II) explicitly attests the common activity of the three in these outward works. As Owen comments, the acts of God *ad extra* are "undivided, and are all the works of one, of the self-same God. And these things do not only necessarily follow, but are directly included, in the revelation made concerning God and his subsistence in the Scriptures."[75]

At the same time, while the *principium* or "beginning" of the outward operations of God is common to the three persons, it is possible to observe some distinctions within these operations. Most importantly, there are three distinct, irreducible modes of acting among the persons—modes of acting that correspond to and reflect the persons' distinct modes of subsisting. According to the logic of a passage like John 16:12–15, the Father acts through the Son and the Spirit; the Son acts from the Father and through the Spirit; the Spirit acts from the Father and the Son. Put slightly differently, all of God's operations proceed "from" the Father, who is the only unoriginated divine person, "through" the Son, who receives from the Father, "in" the Holy Spirit, who receives from both Father and Son and completes God's works.[76] Of course, the use of these prepositions is not intended to suggest that the Son or the Spirit is a mere "instrument" through which God the Father accomplishes his works.[77] Herman Witsius helpfully comments that "one divine person does not act by another as by a middle cause. Because the power of each is one and the same, they each achieve an effect by the same immediate tendency." Indeed, where there is no "diversity of essences and operations," there is no place for a "distinction of remote and proximate, mediate and immediate

---

will therefore involve the activity of all three persons. Since the persons are constituted and distinguished by the relations of origin in God, the assumption of an entirely common *principium quo* has to be qualified in the case of these relations of origin or notional acts. Significantly, it is not our responsibility to prove *why* the assumption of a common *principium quo* must be qualified in the case of the notional acts, for that would be tantamount to proving why God is triune. Our responsibility is simply to receive God's revelation of his triune existence and then seek to clarify its meaning, which in this matter prompts a qualification of the presupposition of an entirely common *principium quo* relative to the *opera ad intra*. However, since the persons are not fundamentally constituted by the *opera ad extra*, the presupposition of a common *principium quo* (and thus the active involvement of all the persons who share this *principium quo*) does not prompt the same sort of qualification in the case of the outward works.

75. Owen, *Doctrine of the Trinity*, 407.

76. For the from-through-in pattern, see again Athanasius, *Serap.* 1.28,9–14 (520); Gregory of Nyssa, *Ad Ablabium*, 47–48, 55.

77. For a misguided reading of the relevant prepositional phrases in Scripture, see, e.g., Schrage, *Unterwegs zur Einzigheit und Einheit Gottes*, 148, 155, where the author infers from the Pauline use of the preposition "through" in 1 Cor. 8:6 and elsewhere an unlimited subordination (*unübersehrbare Unterordnung*) of the Son to the Father.

cause." The application of these prepositions to the matter of divine action simply expresses the "hypostatic order of subsisting and operating."[78]

The persons' distinct modes of subsisting and acting ground the appropriation or special attribution of certain works to certain persons. The efficacy involved in the work remains common to the three persons, and the effect itself is produced by the three persons. At the same time, to borrow the language of Owen, there are cases where a work bears the "especial impression" of the personal property of one person. The work of creation, for example, bears the "impression" of the Father's personal property, so that it is assigned "peculiarly" and "eminently" to him. For creation is the first of God's outward works, and the Father is the first in the order of divine subsistence and action.[79] Such appropriation is particularly fitting when a given work reflects not only a given person's mode of subsisting and acting but also a peculiar economic office that that person takes up.[80] For example, the glorification of the incarnate Son can be appropriated to God the Father, since the Father has taken up the economic office of covenant head and Lord to whom the Son, according to his human will, renders obedience (e.g., John 17:1, 5; Phil. 2:9–11).[81] Redemption can be appropriated to God the Son since he has taken up the economic office of incarnate mediator who lays down his life for us (e.g., Mark 10:45; Eph. 1:7; 1 Tim. 2:5). Sanctification and the indwelling of the saints can be appropriated to God the Holy Spirit since he has taken up the economic office of applying and sealing what Christ procures for our salvation (e.g., 2 Cor. 1:22; Eph. 1:13–14; 2 Thess. 2:13).[82]

Furthermore, while the divine power and the production of the effects in God's economy are always common to the three divine persons, there are cases in which an effect may have a peculiar relation to one divine person. Of course, the primary instance of this is the created human nature of the Son, which belongs to him alone, so that he alone—not the Father or the Spirit—became flesh and was rightly called "man" (John 1:14; Rom. 5:15, 17; 1 Tim. 2:5). Though neither the voice from heaven nor the form of a dove at

---

78. Witsius, *Exercitationes*, 6.3 (66). Cf., e.g., Ames, *Medulla theologica*, 1.6.23 (24); Turretin, *Inst.*, 5.2.8 (1:479); Owen, *Pneumatologia*, 1.4 (3:93).

79. So Owen, *Pneumatologia*, 1.4 (3:93–94). According to Owen, each work is assigned "absolutely" to the whole Trinity but may be assigned "eminently" to one person.

80. Cf. Owen, *Pneumatologia*, 1.4 (3:94); Witsius, *Exercitationes*, 6.3 (65).

81. On the Father's office, cf. Mastricht, *TPT*, 2.24.12 (238–39); 2.25.7 (247–48).

82. One might add that each person's economic office itself has some correspondence to the person's mode of subsisting or his place in the order of subsisting. For example, the application and sealing of the Son's saving benefits especially aligns with the person (the Spirit) who has always received all things, including divine power and efficacy, from the Son (John 16:14–15) (so Witsius, *Exercitationes*, 6.3 [66]).

the baptism of Christ was assumed by a divine person like the Son's humanity was assumed by the Son,[83] the voice from heaven has a peculiar relation
to the Father, and the dove has a peculiar relation to the Spirit. Aquinas, for
example, points out that in this scenario the essence and operation of the
persons remain common, but the effects are "referred to diverse persons."[84]
The whole Trinity produces the voice and the dove, but each is an effect by
which one person appears and is manifested to us. "For as the Father and the
Son and the Holy Spirit are signified by diverse names, so also they are able to
be signified by diverse things."[85] Thus, the voice from heaven is a created effect
by which the Father's identity and relation to the Son are signified: "Only the
Father is declared in the voice."[86] Likewise, "the Holy Spirit has been shown
in some created things [e.g., the dove, the tongues of fire at Pentecost] as in
signs specially made for this." The dove is a created effect and a sign signifying the Spirit and the grace that the Spirit gives.[87]

   In the case of the Son's human nature, the relation of the created effect to
the one person of the Son is frequently expressed by noting that the assumptive
action "terminates" in the person of the Son.[88] In this connection, a number
of theologians have stated that the incarnation belongs "inchoatively" to all
three persons, but "terminatively" to the Son alone.[89] In other words, the
creation of the Son's humanity and the assumptive action itself belong to the
three persons, but the *terminus* or "endpoint" toward whom the assumptive

83. On the important distinction here, see Aquinas, *Super Ioann.* 1.14.4.270 (54); Aquinas,
ST Ia.43.7 ad 1 and 4 (452–53); IIIa.39.6 ad 2 (393).

84. Aquinas, *Super Matt.* 3.2.305 (47). Vidu, *The Same God Who Works All Things*, 159–63,
seeks to make a similar point by distinguishing between a divine "act," on the one hand, and
the resultant "state," on the other.

85. Aquinas, *ST* Ia.43.7 ad 3 (453).

86. Aquinas, *ST* IIIa.39.8 ad 2 (396).

87. Aquinas, *ST* Ia.43.7 ad 2 (453); IIIa.39.6 ad 2 and 4 (393–94). On Aquinas's approach,
see also B. Marshall, "What Does the Spirit Have to Do?"

88. See, e.g., Aquinas's distinction between the divine nature as the common *principium*
of the action and the person of the Son as the proper *terminus* of the action (*ST* IIIa.3.2 corp.
[56]; 3.4 ad 3 [62]). Aquinas writes, "Inasmuch as the divine nature assumes the human nature
to the person of the Word, it is said to assume [the human nature] to itself. But although the
Father assumes the human nature to the person of the Word, nevertheless, he does not on account of this assume it to himself. For the *suppositum* of the Father and Son is not the same.
And therefore it cannot be said properly that the Father assumes the human nature." The assumption of the human nature agrees with the divine nature "by reason of the person of the
Word" (IIIa.3.2 ad 1–2 [56]). In other words, the divine nature is "incarnate" only "by reason
of the person toward which the union is terminated" (IIIa.3.4 ad 2 [62]). Accordingly, the Son
alone is the one who subsists in the flesh and is constituted a man.

89. E.g., Zanchi, *De incarn.*, 2.2 (76); 2.3 (105); Polanus, *Syntagma*, 6.13 (364). Cf. Witsius's
distinction between the assumptive action taken "effectively" and the same action taken "terminatively" (*Exercitationes*, 6.2 [65]).

action is aimed and thus the one in whom the human nature will subsist is only the distinct person of the Son.

Girolamo Zanchi also applies the language of "termination" to the voice from heaven that manifests the Father at Christ's baptism and the dove that manifests the Spirit. The Trinity's outward actions "can be considered as an action and a certain work is terminated or has a term not outside the persons but in a certain one of those persons. In this case and in this respect, [the work] will not be common to all the persons but proper to that person in which it has a term and resides." Zanchi points out that the voice saying "This is my Son" cannot be that of the Son or Spirit (lest the statement be false). It is proper to the Father and resides in the Father. Similarly, the form of a dove in which the Spirit appears, "although it has been formed by the three persons, nevertheless it has not been a common symbol of the three persons. . . . For it has had a term in only the person of the Holy Spirit and under [the form of a dove] only the Holy Spirit has appeared."[90]

One example of a wider deployment of the word *terminus* can be found in Polanus's description of the works of God, where he mentions the acts of creation, redemption, and sanctification along with the speech of the Father at Jesus's baptism; the mission, incarnation, and mediation of the Son; and the appearance of the Spirit in the form of a dove all under the category of works that are "personal in a certain way" (*opera certo modo personalia*). In Polanus's treatment of these works, the divine power and action and the created effects are common to the three persons, but they occur "principally from one person of the deity according to a proper economy belonging to him alone." Aspects of Polanus's description sound very much like Zanchi's, but Polanus seems to go beyond Zanchi, adding that these works "have a foundation . . . in a certain one of the divine persons, namely, in a proximate act terminating itself in one person." These works are "proper to that person by whom principally, as it were, they emanate outwardly or in whom they have a term and reside." The operation is common, but the "proximate act" may be attributed to the Father, the Son, or the Holy Spirit. Polanus suggests that such works can have one person as their *terminus a quo*, *summus terminus*, or *proximus terminus*. According to Polanus, the Father is the *summus terminus* or *proximus terminus* of creation just as the Son is the *terminus* of redemption and the Spirit is the *terminus* of sanctification.[91]

---

90. Zanchi, *De incarn.*, 2.3 (104). The language of "residing" or "resting" is also used in Polanus, *Syntagma*, 4.2 (236–37); Alsted, *Methodus s.s. theologiae*, 1.4 (69).

91. Polanus, *Syntagma*, 4.2 (236–37). Cf. Ames, *Medulla theologica*, 1.6.31 (24–25).

It seems to me that the key factor in Polanus's more liberal use of the notion of termination is his willingness to identify one person as a *terminus a quo* in the economy—not only a hypostatic "endpoint" *toward which* a created effect might have a peculiar relation but even a hypostatic "endpoint" *from which* a divine operation impinges on a created effect. This takes the special resonance of a given work (e.g., creation) with a given person's property (e.g., the Father) and expresses that resonance by representing the person as the most prominent "endpoint" from which the operation goes forth. Polanus himself clearly continues to affirm the common operation of the persons, but there is at least some possibility of obscuring that affirmation in Polanus's statements about a work principally coming forth from one person. Witsius, for example, is more cautious on this matter. He cautions against identifying the Spirit, for example, as the "proximate and immediate principle of acting" in the work of sanctification. For all the persons have "one and the same power" and "achieve an effect by the same immediate tendency." For Witsius, sanctification may be attributed to the Spirit simply because sanctification follows on the grace and merits of Christ, and the Spirit follows the Son in the order of subsisting and acting. Thus, it is most fitting to attribute the work of the application of the Son's merits to the person who receives all things from the Son (John 16:14–15).[92]

In sum, certain features of the Trinity's outward works are common while others are proper to one person. The divine power, operation, and effects produced are common to all three divine persons. At the same time, each mode of acting is proper to one person. In addition, there may be a correspondence between the character of a given work and a mode of subsisting and acting that is proper to one person. Furthermore, the termination of an action and the consequent relation of an effect to God may be proper to one person.

(3) In bringing all of this to bear on our description of the mission, incarnation, and mediation of the Son, it is possible to consider various aspects of God's works and note the ways in which they may pertain to one of the divine persons. According to Scripture, the Father sends the Son into the world (e.g., John 3:17; Gal. 4:4), so, if one is treating the mission of the Son just with respect to the person from whom the Son proceeds and is sent, then one can say that the sending belongs to the Father. At the same time, according to Scripture, the Son actively comes into the world to save sinners (e.g., Luke

92. Witsius, *Exercitationes*, 6.3 (66). See also the recent discussion in Vidu, *The Same God Who Works All Things*, 166–71. Vidu notes a possible use of the word *terminus* in something like the way Polanus uses it (e.g., a given action may be "most proximate" to one person). At the same time, Vidu cautions against envisioning an "'agential chain' as a descending ladder of intermediaries" (168).

19:10; John 10:10). He actively takes upon himself the form of a servant (Phil. 2:7). With regard to the creation of the Son's human nature and the virgin conception, in the Synoptic Gospels the Spirit enables Mary to conceive the Son according to his human nature (Matt. 1:18, 20; Luke 1:35). Yet in Hebrews 10:5 Christ addresses the Father, who prepares a body for him. These various aspects of the mission and incarnation of the Son can pertain to a distinct divine person and can do so in diverse ways. On the one hand, the hypostatic origination of the Son that is ingredient in the Son's mission is proper to the Father in the strictest sense (i.e., he and he alone is the one from whom the Son eternally proceeds). On the other hand, the production of the Son's human nature in which he has a new mode of presence in the world, which is also ingredient in the Son's mission, is common to the three divine persons.[93] Nevertheless, the termination of the assumptive action is proper to the Son alone as the only person in whom the humanity begins to subsist and the only person who becomes incarnate. With regard to the virgin conception in the Synoptic Gospels, although the whole Trinity produces the Son's flesh in the womb of Mary, the conception may be appropriated to the Holy Spirit in a particular respect or for a particular reason. Aquinas, for example, discusses several possibilities here, including the fact that throughout Scripture the Holy Spirit is said to confer grace, sanctification, and sonship (see Luke 1:35; Rom. 1:4; 8:15–16; 1 Cor. 12:4; Gal. 4:6).[94] As to the preparation of Christ's body in Hebrews 10:5, this may be appropriated to the Father according to the fact that the Father is the hypostatic origin of the Son and, in the context of the economy of salvation, the one whom the Son obeys in the flesh.[95]

Since the Son is the hypostatic *terminus* of the assumption of a human nature, he alone is called mediator. The work of mediation, then, is appropriated to the Son. On the one hand, the whole Trinity is involved in accomplishing the work of mediation. "God was in Christ reconciling the world to himself" (2 Cor. 5:19). In Christ "all fullness was pleased to dwell and through him to reconcile all things to him, making peace through the blood of his cross" (Col. 1:19–20). Furthermore, it is the essential goodness and justice of the Trinity against which human beings have sinned, so it is the justice of the whole Trinity (or the just Trinity) that has to be satisfied through a mediatorial work. On the other hand, "there is one mediator between God and human beings, the man Christ Jesus" (1 Tim. 2:5). As the only incarnate one, the Son alone

---

93. See Aquinas's distinction between the *principium personae* in the mission and the *principium effectus* (*ST* Ia.43.8 [454]).

94. Aquinas, *Super Matt.* 1.4.112 (17); Aquinas, *ST* IIIa.32.1 corp. (333–34).

95. Cf. Aquinas, *ST* IIIa.32.1 ad 1 (334); Owen, *Christologia* 18 (225); Owen, *Pneumatologia*, 2.3 (3:162–63).

is the mediator and the guarantor of the new covenant who continually intercedes for us (Rom. 8:34; Heb. 7:20–22, 25, 28; 9:15; 12:24).[96] Accordingly, there may be different ways in which one person's economic office pertains to him. Though the office of covenant head and Lord whom the incarnate Son honors and obeys pertains to the person of the Father, the divine will, justice, and law that is the incarnate Son's rule of life belong no less to the Son or the Spirit. Thus, while the Father's economic office may be appropriated to the Father by reason of its correspondence to his mode of subsisting and acting in the Trinity, that appropriation cannot exclude the other two persons from the activity involved. Similarly, though the application of Christ's benefits pertains to the Spirit, the act itself of renewing and sanctifying God's people belongs no less to the Father or the Son. Thus, the appropriation of the Spirit's economic office by reason of his mode of subsisting and acting also cannot exclude the other two persons from the activity involved. The office of mediator, though, is somewhat different. It requires operation in the human nature that subsists in the Son alone. While the divine operation involved in mediation (e.g., offering up the Son's flesh on the cross) pertains to all three divine persons (John 10:17–18; Rom. 8:32; Heb. 9:14), the only person operating as both God and man is the Son. In this particular respect, the *theandric* work of mediation properly belongs to the Son. His economic office, then, is in a somewhat stricter sense his own.[97]

(4) These clarifications about the meaning of the unity and diversity in God's outward works may now be applied to the case of Christ's reliance on the Holy Spirit in his ministry. This concerns both the sense in which the Son was initially in a position to need the Spirit's help and the sense in which the Spirit then equipped the Son for his ministry. With respect to the Son's need of the Spirit's help, it is important to recall the hypostatic or personal mode of union in the incarnation.[98] In the incarnation, the divine nature as such does not assume the human nature; the human nature does not come to subsist in the divine nature as such. Instead, the Son communicates his personal

---

96. Cf. Turretin, *Inst.*, 14.2.14–15 (2:415); Coccejus, *Summa doctrinae*, 5.92 (91).

97. Cf. Witsius, *Exercitationes*, 6.2 (65). In response to Vidu's recent treatment of the sense in which all three divine persons might act through the Son's humanity as an instrument (*The Same God Who Works All Things*, 202–13), I would emphasize that, while all three persons act toward or upon the Son's humanity, only the Son performs the human actions. The divine movement of the Son's humanity is in an important sense distinguishable from the *actus secundus* of the Son's humanity (*actus secundus* being equivalent to operation or action in earlier metaphysics and theological discourse). Regarding the relationship and distinction between divine *praemotio* and *praecursus*, on the one hand, and human action, on the other, see, e.g., Turretin, *Inst.*, 6.5.13–15 (1:561–62).

98. On the mode of union, see chap. 4, sect. III.

subsistence to his human nature. Thus, the divine essence *in the person of the Son* is incarnate, leaving the genuine limitations of the humanity intact.[99] Owen brings this point out emphatically: "The only singular immediate act of the person of the Son on the human nature was the assumption of it into subsistence with himself." It follows that "the only necessary consequent of this assumption of the human nature . . . is the personal union of Christ, or the inseparable subsistence of the assumed nature in the person of the Son." Accordingly, "all other actings of God in the person of the Son towards the human nature were voluntary, and did not necessarily ensue on the union mentioned; for there was no transfusion of the properties of one nature into the other." For example, the Son's human nature did not become omniscient.[100] The distinction between Christ's two natures remains, so Christ as man could and did need the Spirit's help.

The Spirit, then, could and did equip Christ according to his humanity for the fulfillment of his ministry. Several factors in the Spirit's empowerment of Christ should be noted here. First, given that the Son (with the Father) eternally brings forth the Spirit and that the Son (with the Father) sends the Spirit in the New Testament (e.g., John 15:26; 20:21; Acts 2:33), it follows that the Son (with the Father) sends the Spirit upon himself according to his humanity. Paraphrasing in first-person language some of Jesus's words in John, Athanasius comments, "I myself being the Logos himself of the Father give the Spirit to myself having become man." Again, "remaining unchangeable, he is both the one who gives and the one who receives, giving, on the one hand, as the Logos of God and receiving, on the other hand, as man."[101] With Athanasius in mind, Aquinas writes that "Christ himself sent the Spirit from above as God the Son and he received the Spirit below as man."[102]

Second, the Spirit who comes upon Christ as man sanctifies and equips Christ from his conception onward and attests that sanctification and equipping by descending upon Christ in the form of a dove at Christ's baptism. The provision of grace to Christ according to his humanity is fittingly appropriated to the Spirit since the Spirit is the one who receives all power and gracious operation from the other two divine persons. Owen in particular connects the divine operation upon Christ in his humanity to the person of

---

99. On the essence being incarnate only as it is modified by the Son or determined under the Son's mode of subsisting or personal property, see, e.g., Polanus, *Syntagma*, 6.13 (364); Mastricht, *TPT*, 2.24.8 (238).

100. Owen, *Pneumatologia*, 2.3 (3:160–61).

101. Athanasius, *Oratio I*, 46,27–28 (156); 48,17–19 (158).

102. Aquinas, *Contra errores Graecorum* 2.1 (89). For helpful discussion of the outpouring of the Spirit on and by Christ, see Legge, *The Trinitarian Christology of St Thomas Aquinas*, 131–71.

the Spirit by reason of the Spirit's procession and place in the order of divine subsistence and action. For Owen, while the divine operation upon Christ in his humanity does not belong "absolutely" or "exclusively" to the Spirit, it can be said to belong "eminently" to the Spirit since the Spirit is the third person of the Trinity, who proceeds and acts from the other two.[103]

Third, the fact that the Spirit acts upon and empowers the Son according to his humanity coheres with the Son's divinity and divine operation in his incarnate life and ministry. The Spirit's activity and the Son's divinity and divine activity are not mutually exclusive. Indeed, the Spirit's activity in the Son's incarnate ministry is positively rooted in the Son's deity and eternal relation to the Spirit. Since the Spirit is the Spirit of the Son, who, from the Father, eternally spirates the Spirit, the Son according to his humanity of course has the Spirit "without measure" equipping and directing him (see John 3:34). And the biblical description of the Spirit's acting upon the Son's humanity does not negate the Son's divine acting upon and by his own humanity. For whenever the Spirit is acting, he is acting from the Son. And whenever the Son according to his divinity is acting, he is acting with and through the Spirit. This, it seems to me, is borne out in the New Testament's witness to the miracles of Christ. On the one hand, there are places where the miracles are attributed to the Spirit's presence and power (Matt. 12:28; cf. Acts 10:38).[104] On the other hand, there are places where the miracles show Christ's divine action to corroborate that he is God himself in the flesh (see, e.g., Mark 2:1–12). Cyril of Alexandria helpfully integrates the operation of the Spirit in the miracles of Christ and the operation of the Son according to his divinity. For Cyril, whenever Christ performs miracles by the Spirit, he is still exhibiting his own deity or divine power, because

---

103. Owen, *Pneumatologia*, 1.4 (3:92); 2.3 (3:161–63). Here Owen even attributes a certain "immediate efficacy" to the Spirit and calls the Spirit the "immediate operator" of God's acts, including the acts upon Christ's humanity. However, the idea that Owen might be rejecting the common efficacy of the three persons is ruled out by various other statements that Owen makes. The common divine nature is still the "immediate principle" by which God accomplishes his outward works, so that the acts belong "equally" to all three persons without any "succession" in their acting (see *Christologia* 18 [225]; *Pneumatologia*, 1.4 [3:94]; 2.3 [3:162]). Expressing the point that the Spirit is third or last in the order of acting in the Trinity by talk of the Spirit having an "immediacy" relative to an object of divine action may cause some confusion, but Owen's other statements clarify his commitment to the identity and indivisibility of the divine efficacy and operation. Despite the initial appearance of some of his terminology, Owen's description can fit with Witsius's statement above about all three persons having the same operation and even the same outward "tendency" toward a created effect.

104. For a discussion of the potential pedagogical reasons why Christ says that he, as man, casts out demons by the Spirit of God (Matt. 12:28), see Athanasius, *Oratio I*, 50,1–8 (160–61). Note also Owen, *Pneumatologia*, 2.4 (3:174).

in those cases he is still acting by the Spirit, who is *his own Spirit*, to accomplish the works of God.[105] From another angle, Owen also can help us to integrate Christ performing miracles by the Spirit and Christ acting as God. For Owen observes that whenever the Son operates in and by his human nature, he does so "by the Holy Ghost, who is his Spirit."[106] The Son as man performs miracles by the Spirit, and the Son as God performs miracles. These are really the same thing. An ellipsis in the former statement leaves it unstated that the Spirit is operating with and from the Son according to his divinity; an ellipsis in the latter statement leaves it unstated that the Son as God is operating with and through his Spirit and through the instrument of his humanity.[107]

(5) Finally, it may be good to finish up by pointing out some errors in the claims of the authors who dispute the undividedness of God's outward works. In particular, a theology of the Trinity's works that is influenced by Eastern and Western fathers (and medieval and early Protestant figures too) has ample room to note distinctions in God's outward works. For example, such a theology can say without hesitation that the Father alone is the person from whom the Son is sent, that the Son alone is the person who subsists in a human nature, and that the Spirit alone is the person who appears in the form of a dove at Christ's baptism. Rather than creating a conflict between *theologia* and *oikonomia*, a strong understanding of the indivisibility of the Trinity's operations can in various ways exhibit the rich correspondence between the two, without mistakenly implying that God's triune being is constituted by his outward operations. An exhaustive treatment of this is beyond the scope of this chapter, but, fundamentally, the eternal processions and modes of subsisting in God are revealed throughout the economy, with the Father sending the Son, the Son appearing in the flesh to mediate between us and God and to make us sons and daughters of God, and the Spirit, who receives from both Father and Son, coming to empower the Son according to his humanity and to apply the Son's benefits to believers.

105. Cyril of Alexandria, *Tertia ad Nestorium* 6,10 (39–40); Cyril, *Explanatio XII cap.* 148,25 (23); Cyril, *Contra Theodoretum* 169,63–64 (134–35); Cyril, *Contra Orientales* 24,77–79 (52–53).

106. Owen, *Pneumatologia*, 2.3 (3:162–63).

107. In light of all this, one could say that the Son as God acts by the Spirit in one sense, while the Son as man acts by the Spirit in another sense. As God, the Son acts by the Spirit in that he, with the Father, communicates the divine power to the Spirit; as man, the Son acts by the Spirit in that he exercises the capacities and follows the guidance that the Spirit grants. Further, the Spirit can be said to operate through the Son as man in that the Spirit enables the Son to fulfill his economic office. Likewise, the Spirit can be said to "send" the Son as man in that the Spirit directs various elements of this economic fulfillment (so, e.g., Mark 1:12) (cf. Aquinas, *Contra errores Graecorum* 1.14 [80–81]).

By taking into account a number of crucial elements in trinitarian doctrine—the Spirit's procession from the Father and Son, the mode of union in the incarnation, the ongoing distinction between the Son's two natures, the operation of the Spirit in the Son's incarnate life—we have now set the stage for more direct description of the Son's genuinely human activity and exertion. We will do well, however, to look more closely at the way in which the Spirit endows the Son with certain gifts for the fulfillment of his office before coming to the Son's human obedience and exertion in the next chapter.

V. The Gifts of the Spirit and the Human Experience of the Son

Having examined the ways in which a commitment to the undividedness of God's outward works is capacious enough to affirm and illumine the Son's dependence on the Spirit, we now have the task of considering the Spirit's communication of gifts to the Son and of describing how this communication coheres with the Son's genuinely human experience and ongoing reliance on the Spirit. This treatment of the notion of "habitual graces" in Christ will help till the ground for the next chapter's discussion of Christ's human obedience.

In section II above, we observed several biblical descriptions of the Son receiving intellectual, spiritual, and moral endowments from the Spirit. The pertinent Isaianic texts are striking here. In Isaiah 11:1–5, the "branch" from the family of Jesse who is anointed with the Spirit receives wisdom and understanding. He delights in the fear of YHWH. He acts with righteousness and faithfulness when he exercises judgment. Likewise, in Isaiah 42:1–9, the coming of the Spirit upon the servant of YHWH leads to the servant bringing justice to the nations. The Spirit-anointed servant is humble, gentle, patient, faithful in his work. Such teaching about the person and work of Christ has often been expressed in terms of Christ receiving "habitual graces" from the Spirit to equip him for his office. However, in the work of Karl Barth significant questions are raised about whether the notion of habitual grace should be used in expounding Christ's fitness for his office and his relationship to the Spirit. After examining Barth's concerns, I will offer a response regarding the way in which Christ's reception of habitual graces from the Spirit can fit together with a strong understanding of Christ's authentically human life in dependence on the Spirit.

In an important section of the *Church Dogmatics*, Barth considers how Christ's humanity is uniquely "determined" ("adapted" and "empowered") for the fulfillment of his mediatorial office, without this compromising the fact that Christ genuinely shares our humanity and is our brother. Here Barth critiques traditional Lutheran and Reformed approaches to the special "determination" of Christ's humanity. According to Barth, the early Lutheran and Reformed theologians alike located God's gracious empowerment of Christ in something that is given to Christ's humanity as such, in "a status mediated to him," as though the humanity in itself and in its own right might be a subject in permanent possession of certain gifts. For Barth, the Lutherans "divinised" the human nature in their unfolding of the *communicatio idiomatum* with the *genus majestaticum*. This is to treat the humanity of Christ in "one long abstraction," in isolation from the event or the actual history of the Son's incarnate life. Furthermore, the communication of divine properties to Christ's humanity would compromise his identification with our humanity.[108]

At this point, Barth says that the traditional Reformed objections to Lutheran Christology are "implicit" in his own critique, but he expands the critique in a distinct way. In Barth's judgment, if Christ's humanity as such is taken to be divinized and therefore capable of divinization, then humanity more broadly might be capable of divinization. This opens the door to a "secular philosophy" that wishes to break away from the "christological centre" of the faith and to define the relationship between God and the human race by way of a "general anthropology." In this respect, according to Barth, the diverse identifications of the divine and human that one finds in figures like Hegel and Feuerbach are just extensions of the logic intrinsic to classical Lutheranism.[109]

Barth is critical of the older Reformed authors as well. While the Reformed did not embrace the Lutheran *genus majestaticum*, they did speak of certain "habitual graces" communicated to or infused in Christ's human nature. Barth is wary of this since the word *habitus* connects back to the word *habere* ("to have"), meaning these habitual graces are held in "possession" by Christ's humanity, whereas true grace is a matter of "divine giving and human receiving." This rules out the notion of a *habitus* that properly belongs to Christ's humanity. Indeed, possession of a *habitus* on the part of Christ would place within Christ's humanity itself a grace that in fact pertains to his outward-facing dependence on the comfort of the Father and the power of the Spirit. Reformed accounts of "the full grace of God addressed to the human essence in Jesus Christ" risk offering a "docetic" portrayal of Christ's humanity that struggles to comport with the human limitations, weaknesses, desires, and temptations of Jesus in the Bible.[110]

108. Barth, *CD*, IV.2, 77–83.
109. Barth, *CD*, IV.2, 80–83.
110. Barth, *CD*, IV.2, 89–90, 94–96.

Positively, Barth reasons that God gives the divine essence a particular "determination" in the union with Christ's humanity and that, within a framework of "mutual participation," Christ's humanity is distinctly "determined" and "adapted" to his office by the electing grace of God. Barth conceives of this as a "filling out" of the doctrine of the *communicatio idiomatum* and a reconfiguration of the notion of a *communicatio gratiarum* (communication of certain graces or gifts to Christ as man). In Barth's view, the determination of Christ's humanity by the electing grace of God presses us to focus on the particular "event" or "history" of Christ's life and avoid "side-glances" away from this history toward an "abstract" empowerment of Christ's humanity. Furthermore, this approach, Barth argues, upholds the fact that Christ genuinely shares our human nature, for being human in the truest sense means living by God's electing grace. What is the concrete form of this determination of Christ's humanity by God's electing grace? Barth anchors the determination or "particularity" of Christ in what he calls a "grace of origin"—that is, in the fact that the "existence of the man Jesus Christ is an event by and in the existence of the Son of God." Barth then describes this particularity as an "exaltation" to an alignment with the divine will and a gratitude that corresponds to God's election of humanity. It is an exaltation to true human freedom in obedience to God's will. And in Christ's obedience he is sustained by the Father's blessing and by the comfort and guidance of the Holy Spirit.[111]

Barth contends that this conception of the unique "determination" of Christ's humanity allows us to take seriously his human limitations—his weakness, growth, temptations, and so forth. The "empowering" of Christ's humanity gives him a "capacity" and "authority" for his office, but the empowering is still not the giving of something like an infused habit. For the empowering comes not to the human nature of Christ as such but to the person of Christ and to his humanity only as an "organ" or "medium" by which he accomplishes his work. And Christ's humanity does not possess a preeminent human authority in its own right but just "bears" or "mediates and attests" divine power and authority. Thus, Christ's "grace of office" is not an "appropriated state" but a "history" in which Christ's humanity acquires divine authority.[112] My aim in the following points is to take into account Barth's concern for Christ's genuinely human life and Christ's ongoing need of the Spirit, while pointing out that Christ's reception of habitual graces from the Spirit actually fits together with his genuine humanity and his dependence on the Spirit.

111. Barth, *CD*, IV.2, 84–92, 94, 114.
112. Barth, *CD*, IV.2, 95–100.

(1) It seems wise to step back first and observe that Barth's treatment of the peculiar "determination" of Christ for his office may be moored within Barth's broader concern to move his description of God and the relationship between God and creation in what some have called an "actualist" direction.[113] Only a rough summary can be offered here, but in refusing to grant a knowability of God apart from God's self-revelation in the incarnate Son, Barth also refuses to grant that there is a being of God behind the act of election in Jesus Christ—an act that itself somehow already includes not just the volition of God the Son but the volition of the God-man Jesus Christ. For Barth, this shuts down the possibility of a more ultimate (and perhaps capricious) version of God behind the electing God who is for us in Christ.[114]

As Barth works out the implications of these commitments across the *Church Dogmatics*, the fact that God has chosen to be God only in willing to save sinners through the incarnation leads to a line of argument in which God's saving and reconciling grace is absolutely basic to any positive relationship that the human race can have with God. In the logic of Barth's thinking, this entails that the human person does not possess by nature anything in himself or herself according to which he or she might be like God or capable of fellowship with God, lest there be a "master concept" of being beyond the electing God, of which the creature and God alike would be instantiations and which would independently establish the terms on which creatures could be like God and could know God. There is thus no natural, given, static correspondence between the creature and God. The human person, then, can be like God or in fellowship with God only by God's electing, saving grace and by subsequent Christian faith and obedience. In addition, the human person's reception of electing, saving grace never involves an inward, permanent possession of grace. For that would entail a loss of God's freedom and transcendence, an immanentization of God's grace that obviates human need to look outward to the incarnate Son in order to correspond to God in our being and knowing. In Barth's memorable words, grace can never be something that we carry around "in our pocket."[115]

In accordance with these concerns, Barth resists ways of speaking about the peculiar grace afforded to Christ that might suggest that Christ's humanity possesses something in itself that sufficiently equips him for his saving work and obedience, something that immanentizes the correspondence between the man Jesus and the divine being and will. If some permanent factor in the

---

113. See the different readings of "actualism" in Nimmo, *Being in Action*; McCormack, "The Actuality of God"; Hunsinger, *Reading Barth with Charity*, 133–35, 178–79.

114. See chap. 3 above, sect. IV.A.

115. Barth, *CD*, IV.2, 123–24.

humanity of Jesus establishes his correspondence to the divine being and will, and if his humanity is truly like ours, then it is possible that there is such a permanent factor in all humanity, which leaves the door open to "wander right away from Christology" in pursuit of knowledge of God.[116] Instead, Christ's experience of the Spirit's empowerment is a matter of Christ being impelled by the Spirit at particular times to perform particular acts of filial obedience according to God's eternal act of willing our salvation. In short, within the logic of Barth's overarching program, the help that Christ receives from the Spirit is not an inward, permanent possession of something that Christ can call upon to accomplish his work. It is an impulsion from without. It is not under the control of the man Jesus but rather comes to him only as the Spirit sovereignly chooses to supply it and to display the power of God through the man Jesus.

Barth's treatment of Christ's "determination" for office and Christ's reliance on the Spirit connect back to some of Barth's underlying theological judgments, a point that ought to make us pause and reflect on whether his wariness of habitual graces in Christology is necessary for us. While all Christians will agree that the incarnation is the climax of God's self-revelation, many of us will still want to affirm the reality of God's self-revelation in nature, even if that revelation is distorted by sinful human minds. Indeed, many will still affirm the reality of a supernatural, scriptural revelation of God that contains true statements about God that do not have immediate reference to the incarnation and, furthermore, must be apprehended first in order for us to understand what takes place in the incarnation. Moreover, as argued in chapter 3, the God who is not constituted as the God that he is by the act of election or the incarnation is already the God of immutable goodness and never at odds with his revelation in the incarnation. If all this is so, there is no need to make God's electing, saving grace the exclusive basis of the creature's positive relationship with God. For human beings reflect God by virtue of creation, not just by virtue of saving grace.[117] In addition, if the Spirit's application of saving grace in regeneration involves the giving of a "new heart" with God's law written on it (Jer. 31:33; Ezek. 36:26–27), it is quite difficult to avoid the conclusion that the coming of this saving grace yields inward, permanent effects in the person, not just adventitious,

---

116. Barth, CD, IV.2, 81.

117. This is why the fall is contingent. By contrast, to suggest that *saving* grace is absolutely necessary for the human person's fellowship with God is to suggest that the fall (which is presupposed in the notion of salvation) is also absolutely necessary. This is also why the apostle Paul can speak of human persons in Christ being renewed or restored in the likeness of God (Eph. 4:23–24; Col. 3:10)—not just enjoying such a likeness for the first time by virtue of saving grace.

occasional promptings to obedience. These two factors—the human person's finite correspondence to God by virtue of creation and the inward, resident effects of regeneration—suggest that Barth's "actualism" need not govern the discussion of habitual graces in Christology.

(2) With these preliminary comments in mind about the broader context of Barth's revision of the *communicatio gratiarum*, we may turn more specifically to what Barth says in *Church Dogmatics*, IV.2, on this matter. I would agree with Barth that Lutheran orthodox Christology is susceptible to serious objections surrounding the coherence of the *genus majestaticum* and the true humanity of Christ (see chap. 4, sect. V of the present volume), though I do not think that Barth's inference about Hegel and Feuerbach necessarily follows. Moreover, Barth is right to reject a framing of the *communicatio gratiarum* under which Christ's humanity might be taken to function as a discrete thing or subject in its own right, and under which habitual graces would somehow eliminate Christ's ongoing dependence on the Spirit and his real historical activity and exertion. In my view, the problem in Barth's critique lies in that Barth's description of the infusion of habitual graces does not actually match the claims of the Reformed orthodox and ends up presenting a false dilemma, where habitual grace supposedly stands in competition with particular acts of filial obedience that are impelled by the Spirit's sovereign activity. In addition, there are questions that could be asked about the implications of Barth's statement that the humanity of Christ is only an "organ" or "medium" that "bears" and "mediates" a distinctly divine power and authority. In particular, after rejecting the notion of habitual graces in Christ in order to amplify the genuinely human existence of Christ, has Barth ended up downplaying the fact that the incarnate Son exercises not only divine power and authority but also human power and authority? In other words, has Barth's way of accentuating the Son's humanity at this point in the *Church Dogmatics* circled back to negate something integral to that humanity and its place in the fulfillment of the Son's mediatorial office?

(3) Regarding the suitability of the notion of infused *habitus* in Christology, it is necessary to consider both what Scripture teaches about the character of the Spirit-anointed Messiah and what the term *habitus* actually means in earlier psychological discourse. In texts like Isaiah 42:1–9 and 61:1–2, the emphasis falls on what the Spirit-anointed figure will do—namely, bring forth justice, liberate captives, and so forth. But in a text like Isaiah 11:1–5 there is a strong emphasis on what sort of person the Spirit-anointed figure will be:

> There shall come forth a shoot from the stump of Jesse,
>   and a branch from his roots shall bear fruit.

> And the Spirit of the LORD shall rest upon him,
>   the Spirit of wisdom and understanding,
>   the Spirit of counsel and might,
>   the Spirit of knowledge and the fear of the LORD.
> And his delight shall be in the fear of the LORD.
> He shall not judge by what his eyes see,
>   or decide disputes by what his ears hear,
> but with righteousness he shall judge the poor,
>   and decide with equity for the meek of the earth;
> and he shall strike the earth with the rod of his mouth,
>   and with the breath of his lips he shall kill the wicked.
> Righteousness shall be the belt of his waist,
>   and faithfulness the belt of his loins. (Isa. 11:1–5 ESV)

Certainly, the help that Jesus will receive from the Spirit leads him to act and to bring about various works. But the passage teaches more: the Spirit will rest upon him to impart wisdom, understanding, delight in reverence for YHWH, righteousness, and faithfulness.[118] Faithfulness or "steadfastness" (אֱמוּנָה) by definition implies an established formation of the person so that this person will be continually trustworthy. In other words, Jesus will not only intermittently receive promptings from the Spirit to do works marked by wisdom or righteousness or faithfulness; he will in fact *be* wise and righteous and faithful.[119]

This resonates with the Bible's broader account of the economy of salvation. For within the economy, sinful human beings do not just have a soul with various capacities or faculties that may be prodded to act in certain ways. Rather, sinful human beings have minds and wills that are now intrinsically depraved, determined or inclined toward evil and selfish gain. YHWH sees in Genesis 6:5 that "every inclination of the thought of [humanity's] heart is altogether evil" (וְכָל־יֵצֶר מַחְשְׁבֹת לִבּוֹ רַק רַע) (cf. 8:21). The word יֵצֶר (translated as "inclination" in NRSV, NIV) appears again in Deuteronomy 31:21, where YHWH says he knows that after entering the land Israel will break the covenant, because he knows what they are "inclined to do" (יָדַעְתִּי אֶת־יִצְרוֹ אֲשֶׁר הוּא עֹשֶׂה הַיּוֹם; literally, "I know his inclination which he [is] doing today") (cf. 1 Chron. 28:9; 29:18). The word is used elsewhere in the Old Testament to signify something "formed" or "shaped" by a potter

---

118. Turretin observes that the Spirit's "resting" is one element of the text that implies a "perpetuity of gifts, which Christ indeed possesses, not as an act, and as some transient or fleeting motion, but as permanent and fixed, which he has freely used" (*Inst.*, 13.12.4 [2:378]).

119. Not surprisingly, to explain Isa. 11:1–5, commentators often reach for the language of "qualities," "capacities," "skills," "endowments," "characteristics," or "attributes" (see, e.g., Oswalt, *The Book of Isaiah: Chapters 1–39*, 279–83; Watts, *Isaiah 1–33*, 209–11).

or craftsman (Isa. 29:16; Hab. 2:18; cf. Ps. 103:14; Isa. 45:16).[120] In texts like Genesis 6:5, 8:21, and Deuteronomy 31:21, YHWH is concerned not just about the evil actions of human beings but also about the way in which the human heart is "shaped" or "inclined" and "determined" toward evil actions.[121]

The apostle Paul expresses the problem in terms of the sinful mind's hostility toward God and, indeed, the sinful mind's inability to submit to God's law: "The mind of the flesh is hostile to God, for it does not submit to the law of God, for it is not able" (Rom. 8:7; cf., e.g., Rom. 1:21–23, 25, 28; 3:11; Eph. 4:17–19; James 1:14–15). Thus, in the execution of God's plan for salvation, sinful human beings are regenerated and reformed from the inside out. Our hearts are made new (Jer. 31:33; Ezek. 36:26–27). The judgment of the mind is enlightened and renewed so that the human person perceives Christ no longer as foolishness but as the very wisdom and power and image of God (1 Cor. 1:24; 2:6–16; 2 Cor. 4:6; cf. Col. 3:10). In the context of union with Christ and in the sealing of God's grace in baptism, the human person undergoes a death to sin, a mortification of sin's passions and desires by the circumcision of the heart, so that it is possible to bear good fruit (Rom. 6:1–4; 7:4–6; Gal. 5:22–24; Col. 2:11–13; cf. 1 John 3:9). The believer is transformed into a "new human being created in righteousness and true holiness" (Eph. 4:24). Paul's instruction to "put on" the "new human being" is not a matter of the believer working up toward an eventual attainment of righteousness and true holiness, but a matter of acting according to the Spirit's (already decisively wrought) transformation of the soul.[122] To be sure, the believer continues to struggle with indwelling sin and must actively pursue obedience (so, e.g., Rom. 7:13–25; 1 Cor. 9:24–27; Eph. 6:10–19; Heb. 12:14). Though we become "partakers of the divine nature" by God's gracious promises, we nevertheless have to "make every effort" to grow in faith and godliness (2 Pet. 1:3–11). Yet, as we grow, we do not just repeatedly engage in certain acts, but acquire certain aptitudes. As the author of Hebrews puts it, we "have, through practice, senses [or "faculties," τὰ αἰσθητήρια] having been trained for discernment of both good and evil" (5:14).

120. See BDB, 427–28.
121. The use of the translation "determination" (see A. H. Konkel, "יצר," in NIDOTTE 2:505) nicely brings together the idea of being formed in a certain way and the purpose of the human heart.
122. Cf., e.g., Lincoln, Ephesians, 287–88; Arnold, Ephesians, 289–90. On the insufficiency of exclusively "act-centered approaches" in theological ethics, note also Macaskill, Living in Union with Christ, 24: exclusive focus on acts of obedience to divine commandments, "without giving deeper consideration to the moral identity of the person who seeks to perform them, is simply superficial. It ignores the fact that much of our life is taken up by activities that are not regulated by divine commandments and that can be performed virtuously or viciously."

In recalling the inward depravity of human persons and the inward, resident effects of God's saving work, the point is not to develop a full theology of the Christian life here. The point is just that God is evidently concerned not only with the actions of human beings but also with the underlying, abiding inclinations of the soul according to which human beings perform actions. My contention is simply that Scripture's witness to the wisdom, righteousness, and holiness of the Messiah links up with God's concern about the determination or abiding disposition of the human mind and heart. If the Messiah is truly wise, righteous, holy, faithful, and so on, if he is truly pleasing to God and fulfills the will of God unlike the first Adam and unlike Israel, then he is holy not just in his outward acts but in the inclinations of his mind and heart. The Messiah's human intellect and will are not just media through which the Spirit may accomplish God's works but are themselves positively oriented toward God in wisdom and holiness. His heart is not merely a tabula rasa frequently prompted in the right direction by the Spirit; his heart in fact *is* right before God.

(4) All of this leads us to the consideration of whether the concept of *habitus* is helpful in Christology. In earlier metaphysical and psychological discussion, the term *habitus* can have two main senses, both being connected to the verb *habere* ("to have").[123] On the one hand, it can be used to signify the "medium" between a thing that "has" something and whatever it is that is "had," particularly where this "medium" is a focal point of something like action on the part of the "thing having" and something like passion or being affected on the part of the "thing had."[124] *Habitus* in this sense is typically identified as one "category" of being, alongside others like substance, quantity, quality, and so forth. On the other hand, *habitus* can be used to signify a particular kind of quality, and it is this sense that plays an important role in classical psychology. This use of *habitus* has a highly specified connection with the verb *habere*. A *habitus* in this sense is a certain way in which someone "has oneself" (comports oneself) either with respect to oneself (one's own nature and capacities) or with respect to something other than oneself. Put a bit differently, a *habitus* is a disposition or ordering of oneself or one's powers or capacities in a certain manner.[125] *Habitus* in this sense is a kind

123. What follows is an attempt to distill material from Aristotle, *Metaphysica* 5.1022b (113); Aquinas, *In Metaphys.* 5.20.1058–84 (277–80); Aquinas, *ST* IaIIae.49.1 (309–10); Keckermann, *Systema logica minus*, 1.5 (189–90 [correct pagination, 177–78]); 1.9 (182); Alsted, *Metaphysica*, 2.4 (257–58); 2.8 (266); Maccovius, *Metaphysica*, 2.3 (218–19).

124. A common example of a "thing having" (*habens*) and "thing had" (*id quod habetur* or *habitum*) would be a body and an item of clothing or vestment.

125. Aquinas clarifies that *dispositio* applies not only to bodily parts, place, and inchoate potencies but also to something already completely formed or ordered in a certain manner (*ST* IaIIae.49.1 ad 3 [310]).

of quality, something by which one is a person of a certain sort (*qualis*). As a determination and disposition of a person's intellectual or volitional capacity, a *habitus* is an inclination and aptitude for understanding or desiring something.[126] It is not a bare intellective or volitional power or capacity itself, nor just an inchoate disposition or readiness to do certain acts or eventually assume definite inclinations. It is one such established, definite inclination toward acting in a certain manner.[127]

Since a *habitus* is neither an entirely passive, unformed power of the soul nor an operation of the soul, the concept of *habitus* can be used to express the sense in which someone may be a wise or merciful person, for example, even if, for the moment, he or she is not performing an act of thinking or pursuing the good of someone who is in misery. It can be used to express the sense in which someone continues to have faith in Christ even when he or she is asleep and not performing a distinct mental and volitional act of agreeing with and reposing in the promises of the gospel. Some *habitus* are considered to be "natural" (i.e., following immediately on the constitution of one's nature, albeit under the formative influence of some external prompting).[128] Some *habitus* are considered to be "infused" in the human person by God, like knowledge given supernaturally to a human author of Scripture or like the mental tendency of judging rightly about spiritual things, which is necessary for sinners to exercise saving faith in Christ.[129] Others

126. In Keckermann's description, he calls a *habitus* a *facultas* or *aptitudo* for performing certain functions of which a human being is not capable by nature alone (*Systema logica minus*, 1.5 [189/177]). It may be helpful to note that the term "faculty" can be used to signify (1) a bare power or capacity of the soul (i.e., intellect or will) without a particular determination, (2) an inchoate inclination or readiness of such a power or capacity to perform certain actions or assume certain *habitus*, or (3) an already formed, abiding inclination or readiness—a *habitus*—for certain cognitive or volitional acts. Cf. the attempts to clarify the use of terms like *facultas*, *aptitudo*, and *habitus* in Keckermann, *Systema logicae, tribus libris adornatum*, I, sect. prior, 9 (597); Voetius, *Select. disp., pars prima*, 1.10 (141).

127. Aquinas comments that *dispositio* can signify either "a way leading to perfection" or "an effect proceeding from perfection" (*ST* IIIa.9.3 ad 2 [142]). The latter is applicable in the case of a *habitus*. Cf. also *ST* IIIa.11.5 corp. (163); Zanchi, *De incarn.*, 2.3 (377); Polanus, *Syntagma*, 2.29 (186), where a *habitus* is considered a "medium" between pure potency and a complete act or (in Polanus) "a power proximately determined toward acting."

128. See Aquinas, *ST* IaIIae.51.1 (325–26); Alsted, *Metaphysica*, 2.4 (257); Voetius, *Select. disp., pars prima*, 1.10 (140–41). A straightforward example is the human person's understanding of basic first principles, like the truth that a whole is greater than a part. The human person has an inchoate disposition to assent to such a principle but does not begin his or her existence with (would-be Platonic) concepts of wholes and parts already in the mind. He or she must therefore encounter wholes and parts in the external world in order to obtain actual and habitual knowledge of this principle.

129. See, e.g., Aquinas, *ST* IaIIae.51.4 (329); Maccovius, *Metaphysica*, 2.3 (218); Turretin, *Inst.*, 15.4.23 (2:573–74).

are considered to be "acquired" habits, developed through experience and inferential reasoning or repetition of certain acts.[130] When the capacity of a person is well formed or rightly disposed, the *habitus* present is considered to be a virtue as opposed to a vice, especially when that *habitus* is in the will, since it is by a habit of the will in particular that a person not only knows what is good but inclines to do what is good and to direct other powers or capacities of the person toward what is good.[131]

Given the material above about the Messiah's reception of Spirit-wrought wisdom, understanding, and delight in the fear of YHWH and about the Messiah's righteousness and faithfulness—and given God's concern in Scripture for the uprightness and holiness of the mind and heart—the concept of *habitus* can be appropriated in Christology to good effect. The wisdom and understanding that Christ receives from the Spirit are *habitus* of his human intellect. That is, they are determinations, dispositions, or aptitudes that he receives in order to think and, ultimately, to act truthfully before God the Father throughout his ministry. The delight of Christ in the fear of YHWH can be described as a *habitus* of his will, a continual inclination to love and enjoy the reverence for God that brings glory to God and justice and peace among God's image bearers. The righteousness of Christ can be described as a habitual rectitude and correspondence of his will with the law of God, a rectitude according to which he always does what is pleasing to the Father. The faithfulness of Christ likewise can be described as a *habitus* by which his mind and will are disposed to trust in the plan of God and to act loyally in the execution of that plan.

Whereas Barth worried about the notion of habitual graces weakening our understanding of Christ's humanity, I would suggest that appropriating the language of *habitus* actually helps us to confirm the fullness of Christ's humanity. Identifying Christ's wisdom or righteousness, for example, as a *habitus* helps to express the fact that Christ has and exercises a decidedly human wisdom and righteousness, not merely an undetermined human psyche through which the Spirit occasionally brings about certain divine works. By contrast, avoiding the notion that the man Jesus has permanent, holy inclinations in his mind and heart appears to omit something that belongs to the integrity of Christ's humanity and human agency. I do not presume that Barth would deny altogether the importance of the inward formation and

---

130. See, e.g., Aquinas, *ST* IaIIae.51.2 (327–28); Zanchi, *De incarn.*, 2.3.11 (362–63); Alsted, *Metaphysica*, 2.4 (257); Turretin, *Inst.*, 13.13.1 (2:379).

131. So, e.g., Aquinas, *ST* IaIIae.55.1–3 (349–52); 56.3 (356–57); Alsted, *Metaphysica*, 2.4 (257).

sanctity of Christ or Christian believers.[132] The point is just that when Barth's representation of Christ's correspondence with the will of God leads him to deny the presence of habitual graces in Christ, Barth's approach becomes counterproductive to understanding the fullness of Christ's holiness and fitness for office and the human agency of Christ within that office.[133]

(6) Finally, the affirmation of habitual graces in Christ does not overturn his human limitations or obviate his dependence on the Spirit. This point will be adumbrated here and then explored in more detail in the next chapter, on Christ's obedience. The graces communicated to Christ according to his humanity are received according to the human, finite "mode" and "capacity" of the one receiving. The graces are *created* gifts, so that Christ according to his humanity is still truly human.[134] Christ remains finite and subjected to the limitations and weaknesses of human nature—indeed, subjected to effects of the fall like bodily suffering and mental sorrow and anguish. The fact that Christ is wise and righteous and lives in the fear of YHWH does not cancel out the fact that he has natural appetites and various needs that render him susceptible to temptation.[135] Furthermore, that Christ exercises a habitual knowledge of divine things and a rectitude of will in resisting temptation underscores that he truly exerts himself as man in the midst of temptation, instead of having the human use of his faculties overridden by the Spirit. And it is the person of Christ who resists temptation in obedience to the Father, not a *habitus* abstracted from the person. The person is always the acting subject (the *principium quod* of action), obeying by use of the capacities of the human nature and its qualities (the *principia quo* of action). In other words, having infused habitual graces does not mean that Christ does not have to exercise them. He has to exercise them and in exercising them often has to deny certain natural human desires and bear the grief of doing so.

The finite *habitus* that Christ has according to his human nature do not render him self-sufficient according to his human nature or place him outside the sphere of dependence on the Spirit. The Spirit's presence and operation in the life of Jesus are not finished after his miraculous conception. The Spirit

132. For further reflection on Barth's vision for theological ethics, see Webster, *Barth's Moral Theology*; Nimmo, *Being in Action*; McKenny, *The Analogy of Grace*; Nolan, *Reformed Virtue after Barth*.

133. To the extent that Barth's (in many ways, understandable) focus on keeping the sovereign grace of God from human manipulation led him to neglect certain biblical themes, it may be a good reminder to us all that any quest for systematic coherence has to be constantly subjected to the concrete teaching of Scripture, which so often breaks up and corrects our intellectual trajectories.

134. So Zanchi, *De incarn.*, 2.3.11 (351–53, 366–67).

135. Whether this renders him capable of sinning will be discussed in the next chapter.

does not subsist in the human nature of Jesus, but he does rest and remain on the person of Jesus (Isa. 11:2; John 1:32–33; 3:34).[136] It seems fitting to infer from this that the Spirit continually upholds the intellectual, moral, spiritual endowments given to Jesus. And since Jesus grows in wisdom (Luke 2:52) and learns obedience by suffering (Heb. 2:10; 5:8), the Spirit's presence in Jesus's life implies that the Spirit superintends and advances Jesus's exercise of spiritual habits.[137] If Jesus is filled and led by the Spirit to go out into the wilderness in order to be tempted by the devil (Matt. 4:1; Luke 4:1), the Spirit moves and guides the intellect of Jesus to consider what he must do. And the Spirit evokes Jesus's exercise of his virtues to overcome the devil.[138] In addition, if Jesus offered himself on the cross by the "eternal Spirit" (Heb. 9:14), then the Spirit strengthens Jesus in his spiritual ascesis, in his application of his spiritual graces in the midst of the darkness of the cross, so that Jesus will not "grow faint or be crushed" (Isa. 42:4). In sum, while Jesus is endowed with habitual graces, he nevertheless has to look to the Spirit for the sustenance, movement, and evocation of these graces and for strength and comfort in his application of them.

VI. Conclusion

In this chapter, we have focused on the Son's relationship to the Holy Spirit. We began by exploring the Bible's teaching on the Spirit's eternal procession from the Father and Son, together with related matters like the unity of the Godhead and operations of the divine persons, the diverse modes of acting of the divine persons, and the Spirit's activity in empowering the Son throughout his earthly ministry. In order to examine the coherence of the Son's dependence on the Spirit and the unity of God's outward operations, we took into consideration the concerns of authors like LaCugna, Jenson, Gunton, and Spence. In response, the next section made a case that the unity of God's operations that is anchored in God's simplicity does cohere with the Spirit's empowerment of the Son by discussing the ways in which certain factors in God's operations are common or proper to certain persons, not

---

136. See further Zanchi, *De incarn.*, 2.3.11 (355); Owen, *Pneumatologia*, 2.3 (3:165, 168–88).

137. To clarify that Christ had the fullness of the Spirit from the onset of the Spirit's indwelling even as he still grew over time, one can say that the habitual grace or quality in itself does not increase but that the "efficacy of operation" does increase according to his age over time (see, e.g., Keckermann, *Systema s.s. theologiae*, 3.2 [177]).

138. As Aquinas points out, Christ's soul is intrinsically determined to the good, but not to *this or that good* (*ST* IIIa.18.4 ad 3 [234]), so it remains the case that Christ can be directed by the Spirit and choose a course of action.

least the principle and termination of the operations. The last main section of the chapter then addressed a particular question about whether the teaching of the Son's reception of habitual graces from the Spirit weakens our understanding of the Son's human life, limitations, and activity. That section did not provide an exhaustive treatment of the Son's human activity and exertion, but it did begin to sketch the positive relationship between his infused habits and his human exertion.

Before turning to the Son's human obedience in the next chapter, I will briefly note how the material in this chapter connects with the three main concerns discussed earlier in this volume about the Son's interaction with the Father and Spirit, the unity of the person of the Son, and the authentic human experience of the Son. This chapter has shown that the Son not only does all that he does in communion with the Father and the Spirit but also, according to his humanity, looks to the Spirit by whom he is equipped and strengthened for his work. That the Spirit eternally receives from the Father and Son the divine life and efficacy underscores the fact that the Spirit permanently rests upon and guides the Son *qua homo* in his incarnate work. Thus, a theology proper according to which God is simple and the divine persons are distinct from one another by their relations of origin illumines the scriptural involvement of all three persons in all of God's works and is capacious enough to offer description of the Spirit's peculiar way of operating in Christ's life.

This chapter has also at least gestured toward the fact that God's simplicity and aseity do not nullify the authenticity of the Son's human life and experience. On the one hand, the divine persons do always act together by the simple divine essence, which is all-powerful and complete without reference to the economy. As one divine person of the simple essence, the Son therefore shares in the divine operations that take place throughout his earthly ministry. On the other hand, given that the mode of union in the incarnation is hypostatic rather than essential, it is not the case that the Son's divine power and activity are communicated to the Son's human nature. The Son *qua homo* is still left in a position of finitude and dependence upon the Spirit of God.

SIX

"I Have Come to Do Your Will, O God": The Son's Obedience

I. Introduction

The previous chapter sought to show the coherence of the indivisibility of God's outward works and the Son's genuine dependence on the Spirit's empowerment and guidance throughout his earthly ministry. The end of the chapter also considered how Christ's reception of habitual graces from the Spirit (wisdom, understanding, righteousness, faithfulness, and so forth) coheres with and confirms the Son's genuine human agency. This material has prepared the way for a more concrete, detailed discussion of the Son's human obedience and exertion throughout his earthly trials. The present chapter, then, will examine Scripture's account of the Son's obedience during his earthly sojourn and elaborate on the material by engaging some historical debates that will shed light on how the resources of catholic Christology and theology proper can help us to expound the Bible's teaching. After looking directly at individual scriptural passages, the next section will turn to a broader discussion about whether Christ had to exercise faith on earth, the sense in which he shared in our human weaknesses, and the sense in which he grew through suffering in his role as a merciful high priest. The following section will look at some additional questions that have bearing on Christ's spiritual and moral exertion, particularly whether Christ assumed a fallen human nature and whether he was impeccable. The final section will then offer a response to these key questions.

II. Biblical Description

A. *The Son's Obedience and Trials*

According to Isaiah's prophecy, the servant of YHWH will fulfill the will of God for Israel. He is "the embodiment of the chosen nation."[1] He is the one in whom YHWH will be glorified and the one whom YHWH will establish to be a light for the nations (49:1–7). The servant rises each morning to be taught by YHWH and is prepared to suffer for the sake of accomplishing YHWH's plan (50:4–6). He sets his face like flint and entrusts himself to the care and vindication of YHWH (50:7–11). The servant will act wisely, but he will have a marred appearance and will suffer rejection by his fellow human beings (52:13–53:3). He bears the iniquities and sorrows of the people, going submissively like a sheep to the slaughter (53:4–9). But in doing this the servant accomplishes the will of God. He is the righteous one who secures the justification of many and receives his portion of the spoils of victory (53:11–12).

Matthew's Gospel takes up the theme of Jesus as the true and obedient Israel. After the Savior's birth, his family's flight to Egypt and subsequent return from Egypt fulfill what was spoken by the prophet Hosea: "Out of Egypt I called my son" (Matt. 2:15; cf. Hosea 11:1). Like Israel, Jesus then passes through the waters of baptism.[2] Jesus tells John the Baptist that it is fitting for him to be baptized in order "to fulfill all righteousness" (Matt. 3:15). By making this assertion, Jesus declares that it is necessary for him to undertake "the conduct which God expects of his people" (compare "righteousness" in Matt. 5:6, 10, 20; 6:1, 33; 21:32) and aligns himself with the righteous servant of Isaiah 53:11.[3] He submits to the entire will of God in the plan of salvation.[4] In the context of Matthew's Gospel, where various Old Testament precedents and promises reach their completion, the fact that this is described as a matter of "fulfilling" righteousness also suggests that it is a new development in the unfolding of God's plan.[5] In this fulfillment of God's plan, the divine Son condescends to associate himself with the sinful people of God in need of repentance and restoration and takes it upon himself to represent them and accomplish their salvation.[6] With an eye to Philippians 2,

---

1. Childs, *Isaiah*, 394.
2. On the Old Testament connections, see Beale, *A New Testament Biblical Theology*, 412–17. For more on Jesus's obedience in the Synoptic Gospels, see Crowe, *The Last Adam*.
3. For this rendering of "righteousness," see France, *Matthew*, 119. On the connection to the Isaianic servant, cf. France, *Matthew*, 120–21; Osborne, *Matthew*, 123–24.
4. Many commentators emphasize this aspect of the text—e.g., Calvin, *In harm.*, 125; Hagner, *Matthew 1–13*, 56–57; Luz, *Matthew 1–7*, 142–43.
5. Cf. Davies and Allison, *Matthew*, 326–27; Osborne, *Matthew*, 123–24.
6. Cf. Hagner, *Matthew 1–13*, 57; Keener, *Matthew*, 132; France, *Matthew*, 120.

Jerome paraphrases Jesus's statement: "I who have assumed the form of a servant should also fill out its humility."[7]

After the baptism in the Jordan and the descent of the Spirit in the form of a dove, Jesus goes into the wilderness to be tested. He is led by the Spirit himself to be tempted by the devil (Matt. 4:1). The fact that he is led in this way makes clear that it is the sovereign will of God that the Son should be tried in solidarity with his brothers and sisters. The verb used by Matthew (πειρασθῆναι) might be translated "to be tested" or "to be tempted." On the part of God, it is only a matter of acting to show the inner character of someone, for God never entices someone to sin (cf. James 1:13).[8] On the part of Satan, however, it is indeed an attempt to lead someone (here, Jesus himself) into sin. While Jesus had no indwelling sin to which Satan might appeal, Jesus certainly had natural human desires to which an external proposition of some apparent good might be directed.[9] On the one hand, Calvin points out, this period of trial sets the Son apart so that he will undertake a certain training regimen and emerge from the wilderness as "the highest teacher of the church and the ambassador of God." On the other hand, this is indeed an act of solidarity: "He descends into the arena in the common name of his own church." He is "tempted in the public person of all the faithful."[10] After fasting for forty days and nights, Jesus is hungry, at which point "the tempter" tries to cast doubt on his identity as the Son of God and encourages him to turn stones into bread and feed himself (Matt. 4:2–3). Calvin calls this is an attack on the faith of Christ,[11] and whether or in what sense it might be appropriate to say that Christ exercised faith on earth will come under discussion in the next major section of the chapter.

While it is true that Jesus ultimately hungered less for food than for the salvation of human beings,[12] it is also important not to spiritualize his experience to the point of overlooking his genuine hunger for ordinary food in Matthew 4:2. Being clothed with our flesh, the Son has assumed our infirmities and our "affections." "As many bodily affections as there are in man, so many occasions of tempting him Satan seizes."[13] Yet Matthew and Luke report no internal debate on the part of Jesus and portray Jesus responding with resolute

---

7. Jerome, *Sur Matt. I*, 1.3,15 (94).

8. Cf. Owen, *Of Temptation* 1 (91–96).

9. See further Owen, *Hebrews*, 3:477–79; 4:426–28.

10. Calvin, *In harm.*, 128, 130.

11. Calvin paraphrases the content of Satan's attack: "When you see yourself to be forsaken by God, necessity compels that you should provide for yourself. Therefore, make provision for yourself, which God does not supply for you" (*In harm.*, 132).

12. So Hilary of Poitiers, *Sur Matt. I*, 3,2 (112).

13. Calvin, *In harm.*, 130.

fidelity to God: "And answering, he said, 'It has been written, "Man lives not by bread alone but by every word coming forth from the mouth of God"'" (Matt. 4:4; Luke 4:4; cf. Deut. 8:3). Wielding the word of God, Jesus resolves "to conquer the devil by humility, not by force."[14] In fact, Jesus meets the next two temptations in the same way, quoting Old Testament Scripture to dismiss the devil's invitations to presume upon the Father's protection and to receive power through engaging in idolatry (Matt. 4:5–11).

Later in the Gospels, Jesus's loyalty and obedience are tested in the garden of Gethsemane. Matthew writes that Jesus took Peter, James, and John with him and "began to be sorrowful and distressed" (ἤρξατο λυπεῖσθαι καὶ ἀδημονεῖν) (Matt. 26:37). The language indicates that "Jesus experienced fear and dread before his death."[15] Indeed, Jesus tells the three disciples, "My soul is sorrowful to the point of death" (26:38)—as if by his own grief and sadness he is already "half-dead."[16] Going a little farther from the disciples, Jesus falls on his face and prays to the Father, "My Father, if it is possible, let this cup pass from me; nevertheless, not as I will but as you will" (26:39). After praying the first time, Jesus is "in agony," a phrase describing less the outward circumstances he is facing than the "interior distress" he is suffering.[17] His sweat becomes "like drops of blood coming down on the earth" (Luke 22:44). Thus, he prays a second and even a third time, "My Father, if it is not possible for this to pass from me unless I drink it, let your will be done" (Matt. 26:42, 44).

Both the real anguish and the unwavering obedience of Jesus ought to be highlighted here.[18] There is no need to explain away the sorrow and dread of Jesus, but, at the same time, recognition of the sorrow and dread should be paired with an equally robust recognition of Jesus's determination to fulfill the will of God. Various preachers and commentators in the exegetical tradition have endeavored to strike the right balance here. John Chrysostom, for example, emphasizes that Jesus does not "feign the agony." He exhibits "numerous signs of fear, so that no one may say that the words are contrived."

14. Jerome, *Sur Matt. I*, 1.4,4 (96).

15. *NIDNTTE* 3:178.

16. Calvin, *In harm.*, 721.

17. So Bovon, *Luke 3*, 203.

18. The former seems to be downplayed by the sort of comments that Hilary makes to the effect that Christ did not truly fear death or have anxiety for himself (see *Sur Matt. II*, 31,1–7 [224–34]). Cf. also Jerome, *Sur Matt. II*, 4.26, 37–38 (252, 254). Aquinas, however, contends that Hilary and Jerome intend to deny only that Christ felt anxiety with respect to the end of his suffering (i.e., our salvation) (*Super Matt.* 26.5.2225 [343]). For further charitable interpretation of such patristic comments, see Lombard, *Sent.* 3.15.3–4 (100–103); Aquinas, *ST* IIIa.15.5 ad 1 (190); 15.7 ad 2 (193).

Yet Jesus submits to the will of God and exhibits "virtue and discipline." When he prays "your will be done," he "very much harmonizes with the will of God."[19]

Calvin similarly comments, "Certainly those who imagine the Son of God to be immune from human passions truly and seriously do not acknowledge him to be a man." Appealing to Cyril of Alexandria, Calvin remarks that the passion of Christ was voluntary in some respects but not in others. It was voluntary with respect to the divine will for salvation and with respect to the fact that Christ as the God who is life does not fear death. But the passion had an "involuntary" element insofar as Christ as man would detest the prospect of pain and sorrow. Having been made flesh, "he allows to the flesh that it should suffer its proper things, and therefore as true man he fears the death now present at the door." However, whereas the affections in us are tainted by vice, Christ is disturbed by sadness at the thought of death and divine judgment and yet "remains composed toward the true rule of temperance."[20] For Calvin, the grief and anxiety temporarily draw Christ's attention away from the full scope of God's plan so that Christ prays for the cup to pass from him. But the prayer is not sinful. Christ is simply expressing his human desire to avoid the darkness before him. While it is "true rectitude to form all our affections toward the will of God, there is nevertheless a certain kind of indirect dissension [*obliquae dissensionis*] that lacks guilt and is not imputed as sin." Christ prays for something legitimate in itself but not ordered by God to take place, and Christ ultimately subjects his affections to obedience.[21]

In John's Gospel, at the Feast of Tabernacles in Jerusalem, Jesus makes a sweeping statement about his obedience to the Father: "He who sent me is with me; he has not left me alone, for I always do the things that are pleasing to him" (8:29). Later Jesus speaks of having received a "commandment" from the Father regarding his death: "On account of this the Father loves me, because I lay down my life, in order that I might take it up again. No one takes it from me, but I myself lay it down from myself. I have authority to lay it down, and I have authority to take it up again. This commandment [τὴν ἐντολὴν] I received from my Father" (10:17–18). Two chapters later he speaks again about the Father's "commandment." Warning his hearers not to reject him, Jesus says,

19. John Chrysostom, *In Matt.* 83.1 (746–47).
20. Calvin, *In harm.*, 719–20.
21. Calvin, *In harm.*, 722–23. Cf. Polanus, *Syntagma*, 6.15 (370–71), according to whom this is an *oratio infirmitatis* ("prayer of weakness"), the correction and revocation of which is due not to antecedent sin but to the consideration of a greater good (i.e., the salvation of humanity).

The one who rejects me and does not receive my words has one who judges him; that word which I have spoken will judge him on the last day. For I myself do not speak from myself, but the one who sent me, the Father himself, has given me the commandment [ἐντολήν]—what I should say and what I shall speak. And I know that his commandment [ἡ ἐντολὴ αὐτοῦ] is eternal life. Therefore, the things which I myself speak, just as the Father has spoken to me, so I speak. (12:48–50)

Similarly, in John 14:31 and 15:10, Jesus states that he does what the Father commands so the world will know that he loves the Father and that he has kept the Father's commands (ἐντολάς). Below we will return to the significance of the term ἐντολή in relation to the matter of Jesus undertaking a strictly *human* obedience, but for now the point is that in the Gospel of John Jesus always does what the Father wills.

The apostle Paul adds some other dimensions to the New Testament doctrine of the Son's obedience. In Romans 5:12–21, Jesus is the man who counteracts Adam's sin by his own fulfillment of God's righteous requirement. Sin and death came into the world through one man's transgression, but the gracious gift of God abounds to the many through "the righteous deed" of one man, Jesus Christ (5:12–18). Just as by one man's disobedience the many were made sinners, so by one man's obedience the many are made righteous (5:19). In 1 Corinthians, Paul touches upon Christ's submission to God the Father. When he is urging the Corinthians to embrace the wisdom of God, he writes that "all things are yours, and you are Christ's, and Christ is God's" (3:22–23). In his discussion of head coverings, Paul writes that "the head of every man is Christ, and the head of woman is man, and the head of Christ is God" (11:3). Near the end of the epistle, Paul describes Christ delivering the kingdom to the Father and concludes that the Son himself will be subjected to the Father "in order that God may be all in all" (15:24–28). Explaining the future implications for believers, the apostle also declares that the work of Christ, the "last Adam" and the "second man from heaven," guarantees that we will bear his image and receive imperishable bodies (15:45–49).

In Galatians, Paul informs us that "when the fullness of time came, God sent forth his son, born of a woman, born under the law, in order that he might redeem the ones under the law, in order that we might receive adoption" (4:4–5). As Matthew Poole comments, "He was born in a nation and of a parent under the law; he was circumcised, and submitted to the ceremonial law. He in all things conformed his life to the rule of the law, and subjected himself to the curse of the law, being made a curse for us."[22] The connection between the

---

22. Poole, *Annotations upon the Holy Bible*, on Gal. 4:4.

incarnation and the beginning of the Son's obedience appears in Philippians 2 as well. There Christ is the one "who, subsisting in the form of God, considered it not ἁρπαγμός [perhaps a thing to be seized or to be exploited] to be equal with God, but he emptied himself, taking the form of a servant and being made in the likeness of human beings." Indeed, "Being found in appearance as a man, he humbled himself, becoming obedient until death, even death on a cross" (2:6–8). In this hymn, the assumption of the *forma servi* yields a humble posture ("Being found in appearance as a man . . ."). Insofar as the participle "becoming" (γενόμενος) in 2:8 is used instrumentally, the self-humiliation is wrought *by* the Son becoming obedient even to the point of death on a Roman cross.

Finally, the book of Hebrews is particularly rich in its account of the Son's humility and obedience. In chapter 2, the author applies Psalm 8:4–6 to Jesus. With Psalm 8, the author highlights that God has taken the lowly human race or "son of man" and placed all things under his feet, but presently we do not see all things subjected to him. Identifying Jesus as the lowly and yet also exalted man of Psalm 8, the writer of Hebrews says that "for a little while we see Jesus having been made lower than the angels on account of the suffering of death, having been crowned with glory and honor, in order that by the grace of God he might taste death for everyone" (Heb. 2:8–9). As John Owen points out, the language of "tasting" implies that there is a "bitterness in the death he underwent."[23] The author explains why Jesus has been made lower than the angels and endures suffering: "For it was fitting for him, on account of whom all things are and through whom all things are, leading many sons [and daughters] to glory, to perfect the founder [or "pioneer," ἀρχηγὸν[24]] of their salvation through sufferings. For both the one sanctifying and the ones who are sanctified are all of one [ἐξ ἑνὸς]. For which reason he is not ashamed to call them brothers [and sisters]" (2:10–11). Jesus as "founder" or "pioneer" of our salvation leads us into the promised rest of God (chaps. 3–4). Indeed, he is the "forerunner" who goes before us into God's heavenly presence (6:20).

The perfection through suffering is rooted in the reality that Jesus and the beneficiaries of his priestly work are ἐξ ἑνὸς. He does not need God the Father to "perfect" him through suffering as though (*per impossibile*) he were once morally inclined to evil. Instead, in this context the verb arguably means that God the Father set him apart or consecrated him for his priestly office through suffering (see the use of τελειόω in the LXX of Exod. 29:9, 29, 33, 35; Lev. 4:5; 8:33; 16:32; 21:10; Num. 3:3).[25] In other words, this is a "vocational

23. Owen, *Hebrews*, 3:359.
24. On the semantic nuances of the word, see, e.g., Koester, *Hebrews*, 228–29.
25. So Owen, *Hebrews*, 3:384; 4:533–34; Lane, *Hebrews 1–8*, 57; Ellingworth, *Hebrews*, 162–63; Johnson, *Hebrews*, 97. At the same time, Moisés Silva ("Perfection and Eschatology

perfection."[26] In appointing the Son to his priestly office, the Father uses the Son's suffering as a means of consecrating him. On the one hand, Jesus was in an important sense appointed to his priestly office even prior to enduring suffering in his earthly life (cf. Heb. 10:7). On the other hand, the fulfillment and efficacy of Jesus's priestly office are attained through his suffering, and his capacity to comfort others who are suffering is informed by his own experience of it (cf. 2:18).[27] He and his brothers and sisters who face suffering and temptation are ἐξ ἑνὸς—from "the same mass of human nature."[28] Yet they are also united in that the Son is perfected through suffering with respect to his vocation and human compassion while his followers are trained in righteousness and holiness through God's fatherly discipline (cf. 12:10).

Since the children whom God has given to Jesus "have partaken of flesh and blood, he himself also likewise shares in the same" (Heb. 2:14). Jesus has come to help not the angels but the seed of Abraham, so "he had to be made like his brothers [and sisters] according to all things, in order that he might become a merciful and faithful high priest with the things toward God, in order to make propitiation for the sins of the people. For in that which he himself has suffered while being tempted, he is able to help the ones who are being tempted" (2:16–18). In Hebrews 4, the author reiterates that Christ has faced temptation and can sympathize with us: "We do not have a high priest who is unable to sympathize with our weaknesses, but one who has been tempted according to all things like us, without sin" (4:15). What does it mean that Christ is able to "sympathize" (συμπαθῆσαι)? The verb συμπαθέω appears in Hebrews 10:34 as well. There the addressees are said to have been "sharers" of the afflictions of others and to have "sympathized" with those in prison (10:33–34). It seems that if Christ is able to "sympathize," then he has had direct experience of the human condition and that this has some implications for the manner in which he cares for those who are in that same

---

in Hebrews") helpfully emphasizes the eschatological dimension of the perfection here. Jesus completes his work through suffering and sits down at the Father's right hand with a name and status superior to the angels (see Heb. 1:3–5).

26. Cockerill, *Hebrews*, 139.

27. Cf. Owen's comments (a) that Christ was "really" consecrated a priest before his sufferings but "openly declared" a high priest only in and by his sufferings; and (b) that even though he was already a priest, he could not fulfill all his priestly duties right away (*Hebrews*, 4:534). I am sympathetic to Owen's way of speaking about Christ's priesthood, but there are also contemporary exegetes who make a strong argument that, according to Hebrews, Christ takes up the role of high priest only after the resurrection (see Moffitt, *Atonement and the Logic of Resurrection*, 194–214; Jamieson, *Jesus' Death and Heavenly Offering in Hebrews*).

28. Owen, *Hebrews*, 3:418. Owen notes that the ἐξ ἑνὸς may indicate that Christ and his followers are "of one God," in "one covenant," "one mystical body." The interpretive options are not mutually exclusive.

condition. Discerning whether or in what sense Christ's obedience involved a real development in his compassion or his capacity to help sinners will be one of the tasks of the next section below. Presently it has to be noted that Christ's temptation occurred "without sin." Without diminishing the reality of the temptation, this important phrase sets Christ's temptation apart from that sort of temptation that the book of James describes, where evil desires already resident in the human person are integral to the logic of the temptation and give rise to acts of sin (James 1:15–16).

Hebrews 5 returns to Christ's obedience and suffering, pointedly teaching that Christ "in the days of his flesh" offered up "petitions and requests to the one able to save him from death, with great crying and tears." And he was heard due to his reverence (5:7). That Christ does the praying "in the days of his flesh" signals that he does it in "our nature as it is weak and infirm in this mortal life."[29] Though Christ is YHWH, the unchanging God, who created and outlasts all things (1:10–12), here he is depicted in the very human and humble act of prayer, crying out to the Father for help. His praying to the Father as the one "able to save him from death" suggests that he prayed for deliverance from death. Hence Owen writes that "it was his duty, to pray that he might be delivered from the absolute prevalency of [death]" or "that he might not be confounded or condemned. This he hoped, trusted, and believed."[30] The prayer is "heard" in the sense that his request is indeed accepted and will eventually be granted by the Father in his approval of the Son's obedient sacrifice and in his resurrection of the Son from the dead. The reason the prayer is heard is the Son's "reverence" or "piety" before God the Father. Furthermore, "although he was Son, he learned obedience from the things which he suffered, and, being perfected, he became the cause of eternal salvation for the ones obeying him" (5:8–9). The concessive clause "although he was Son" establishes a contrast between his identity as the divine Son and his obedience, impressing upon us the Son's gracious condescension. So genuine is the Son's participation in our condition that he "learns" obedience from the experience of suffering. Insofar as Christ never had to transition from being disposed toward disobedience to being disposed toward obedience, the "learning" here seems to consist in directly experiencing the difficulty of obedience via suffering.[31]

In Hebrews 10, the author explains the inadequacy of Old Testament animal sacrifices and states that when Jesus comes into the world, he says to

29. Owen, *Hebrews*, 4:498.
30. Owen, *Hebrews*, 4:509. Cf., e.g., Koester, *Hebrews*, 288.
31. So Owen, *Hebrews*, 4:524.

God, "Sacrifice and offering you did not desire, but a body you prepared for me. With burnt offerings and sin offerings you were not pleased. Then I said, 'Behold, I have come, in the scroll of the book it has been written about me, to do your will, O God'" (10:5–7). These verses refer back to Psalm 40:6–8, drawing upon and slightly modifying what is Psalm 39:7–9 in the LXX. Hebrews 10:7 omits that in both the MT and LXX the messianic king declares not only that he has come to do God's will but also that he "delights" to do God's will and God's law, which is in his "inward being." Even given this omission, in the context of the Hebrews passage there is an emphasis on the inward holiness and obedience of the people of God (see the invocation of Jer. 31:31–34 in Heb. 8:8–12 and 10:15–17), so it seems plausible that the text presents Jesus as the messianic figure who both exemplifies true inward devotion to God and procures such devotion for others.[32] Indeed, his principal devotion to the will of God over cultic sacrifice (regarded as though it were an end in itself) leads him to offer up the truly decisive sacrifice of his own body for our sanctification (Heb. 10:9).[33] His obedience, then, while beginning with his assumption of human flesh and thus encompassing his whole earthly life, especially culminates in his death.

Finally, in Hebrews 12, the writer instructs us to "run through perseverance the race set before us, fixing our eyes on Jesus, the ἀρχηγὸν ["founder" or "pioneer"] and perfecter of the faith, who for the joy set before him endured the cross, despising the shame, and sat down at the right hand of the throne of God. For consider him who has endured such opposition to himself by sinners, in order that you might not grow discouraged in your souls, giving up" (12:1–3). In the previous chapter, the author defined "faith" as "the substance of things hoped for" and "the assurance of things not being seen" (11:1) and described a "cloud of witnesses" who exemplified faith in God's promises (11:4–40). Given this preceding material in chapter 11, and given that Jesus is presented as the epitome of one who has completed his earthly course, it appears that in 12:2 Jesus is not only the object of our faith or the one who enables us to have faith but also the "pioneer" in the sense of being the preeminent example of trust in the promises of God laid out before him.[34]

32. See Guthrie, "Hebrews," 976–78.

33. So Peter C. Craigie: "In Christ, says the writer of the Epistle, there is a reversal; first, he affirms his intention to do the divine will . . . and that intention in turn leads back inevitably to sacrifice, but now to the sacrifice that ends all sacrifices" (Psalms 1–50, 317).

34. Other New Testament applications of the term ἀρχηγός to Jesus may work similarly. In Heb. 2:10 he is the ἀρχηγός of our salvation, the one who establishes our salvation and, according to 5:7, the first one saved from death (i.e., resurrected) by the Father. Cf. also Acts 3:15 and 5:31, where Jesus is, respectively, the ἀρχηγός of life, who has been raised by the Father, and the ἀρχηγός (without an accompanying genitive) exalted to the Father's right hand.

"As if all the former witnesses were not enough, [the author] adds a more excellent one than them all, even our Lord Jesus Christ, who is not only a pattern to them in their race and running of it, but a help."[35] The one who declared his trust in the Father in 2:13 (Ἐγὼ ἔσομαι πεποιθὼς ἐπ' αὐτῷ) and the one previously described as our "forerunner" into the presence of God in 6:20 is here the "pioneer" of that faith by which one has a foretaste of heavenly joy. He modeled "endurance" in the face of opposition so that we too would not give up (12:3).[36] As Peter puts it, when Christ was mistreated and suffered, he "entrusted himself to him who judges righteously," calling us to follow his example (1 Pet. 2:21–23).

B. The Human Character of the Son's Obedience

One of the aims of this chapter is to highlight the Son's full and humble participation in the human condition, particularly by considering his obedience to the Father. To underscore the Son's participation in our condition, it will be important to make the point that the Son's obedience is a decidedly *human* undertaking. In chapter 3, I examined Karl Barth's contention that the Son is obedient in his eternal relation to the Father. There I argued that Barth's view of a divine obedience on the part of the Son is problematic, not least because of the one will and authority shared by the divine persons. At this point I hope to show that some of the additional material covered here confirms that the Son's obedience is strictly human.[37]

First, the texts included in this section depict a novelty in the Son's obedience. When the incarnation takes place, the obedience begins. The Son is sent, and it is in being sent and being born of the virgin Mary that he enters a state in which he is "under the law" (Gal. 4:4).[38] It is upon assuming the *forma servi* and being made in the likeness of human beings that the Son "humbled himself

35. Poole, *Annotations upon the Holy Bible*, on Heb. 12:2. Cf. Lane, *Hebrews 9–13*, 410–12; Ellingworth, *Hebrews*, 640; Johnson, *Hebrews*, 317; deSilva, *Perseverance in Gratitude*, 431–32; Koester, *Hebrews*, 536; Cockerill, *Hebrews*, 606–8; Richardson, *Pioneer and Perfecter of Faith*.

36. The description of Jesus as πιστός in Heb. 3:2 may also prepare the way for the notion of Christ as the pioneer of faith in 12:2. While πιστός in 3:2 may mean something like "loyal" rather than "believing," the intervening definition of πίστις in 11:1 suggests that in 12:2 Jesus not only establishes the faith of others or displays loyalty to the Father but also trusts the Father to give what is not yet seen.

37. For a summary of recent debates in evangelical theology about the idea of an eternal submission or obedience of the Son to the Father, see Butner, *The Son Who Learned Obedience*, chap. 1. Note also the collection of essays in Bird and Harrower, *Trinity without Hierarchy*. On there being a correspondence between God's eternal being and the economy of salvation without a *divine* obedience of the Son, cf., e.g., Swain and Allen, "The Obedience of the Eternal Son."

38. On this text, Poole comments that the Son was "made under the law, to which as God he was not subject, being himself the law-maker" (*Annotations upon the Holy Bible*, on Gal. 4:4).

by becoming obedient" (Phil. 2:7–8). It is when the Son is "coming into the world" that he says, "Behold, I have come . . . to do your will, O God" (Heb. 10:5, 7).[39] And it is when the Son comes and suffers that he "learns" obedience in the sense of experiencing it firsthand (5:8). Furthermore, the human obedience is not an accompaniment or outworking of a prior divine obedience. For Philippians 2 in particular explicitly contrasts the obedience in the *forma servi* with the Son's prevenient divine subsistence. Christ is the one who, "subsisting in the form of God, considered it not ἁρπαγμός to be equal with God, but he emptied himself, taking the form of a servant and being made in the likeness of human beings." To subsist in the *forma Dei* and in this subsisting to be equal with God the Father stands in contrast to the assumption of the servant-form in which Christ becomes obedient.[40] Indeed, it is quite clear that the servant-form *is* the human nature assumed: the pairing of "taking the form of a servant" and "being made in the likeness of human beings" indicates that the phrases are two ways of expressing the same reality.[41] In other words, the servant-form in which the Son's service and obedience take place is the human nature that is dissimilar to the Son's divine subsistence.

Second, the obedience of Christ is representative. In Isaiah and in the beginning of Matthew's Gospel, Christ is the true Israel who obeys where the people of Israel failed to do so. He fulfills "all righteousness" in solidarity with a disobedient people in need of repentance and restoration. In Romans 5:12–21, Christ acts righteously to counteract the unrighteousness and the guilt incurred by the first Adam. And Christ's representative obedience can occur only by his acting according to his human nature. Third, Christ's obedience involves temptation and suffering so that he can share our human experience. It involves Christ relying on the power of the Spirit and learning firsthand the experience of suffering and self-denial in order to be a sympathetic high priest. Furthermore, according to Paul, Christ's obedience is an obedience "until death." If Christ as immortal God cannot die, then he undertakes this obedience according to his human nature.

39. However one understands the participle "coming" in "coming into the world" in Heb. 10:5 (for a reading according to which it is *by* coming that Christ exhibits his obedience to God, see Jobes, "Putting Words in His Mouth," 42–47), the text does not indicate that Christ began his obedience prior to assuming flesh. While coming, Christ says that God prepared a body for him. "*Then* he said, 'Behold, I *have come* to do your will, O God'" (10:7).

40. Various interpreters note the firm adversative ἀλλά here ("*but* he emptied himself, taking the form of a servant") (e.g., Wanamaker, "Philippians 2.6–11," 183; Bockmuehl, *Philippians*, 130; Hawthorne and Martin, *Philippians*, 115–16).

41. The "subsisting in the form of God" and the "to be equal with God" are parallel and mutually explanatory in Phil. 2, and so are "taking the form of a servant" and "being made in the likeness of human beings" (see, e.g., Fee, *Philippians*, 207, 213).

Fourth, there simply are no scriptural texts that affirm or imply a prein-carnate obedience in the Son's eternal, personally constitutive relation to the Father. Though the Father sending the Son and the Son being sent by the Father is logically (not temporally) prior to the Son's subsistence in his humanity, it is not a given that the sending and being-sent should entail a dominion proper to the Father alone and a corresponding divine obedience of the Son. Indeed, given the common will of the divine persons, the mission of the Son is not a matter of one person with a proper will and power of com-manding legislating that another person with a different will and no power of commanding must undertake some course of action. In this connection, it is significant that the Second Council of Constantinople (553) anathema-tizes those who do not confess the one authority (μίαν ἐξουσίαν) shared by the divine persons.[42] Positively, the Father and Son who share the one divine volition, having together established the plan of salvation, both effect the Son's coming into the world in the flesh. The Father, the one from whom the Son proceeds and always acts, is the one from whom the Son acts in coming into the world in the flesh. In this respect, the Father sends the Son. The Son, the one who proceeds and always acts from the Father, acts from the Father in coming into the world in the flesh. In this respect, the Son is sent by the Father.[43] According to Holy Scripture, the Son's coming into the world and acting in humble obedience to the Father is an act of grace on his part as well as the Father's (Rom. 5:15–17; 2 Cor. 8:9), which implies that the Son shares the Father's sovereign freedom and goodness in willing the incarnation to take place. As Cyril of Alexandria emphasizes, the Son is no less kind than the Father, and he too wills to give us life.[44]

Of course, in John's Gospel, Jesus says, "I do not seek my own will but the will of him who sent me" (5:30b; cf. 6:39–40). However, assuming this concerns Jesus's divine volition, it does not entail that Jesus in his divine volition subjects himself to something legislated by the Father. For earlier in

42. Second Council of Constantinople, "Anathema 1," in N. Tanner, *Decrees of the Ecu-menical Councils*, 114.

43. Thus, Ambrose states that in the Son's mission there is no "compulsion by an alien com-mand" (*alieno . . . coactus imperio*). Instead, he comes "with a voluntary choice" (*voluntario arbitratu*) (*De fide* 2.11.97 [2:322]). Ambrose also comments that the Son's generation by the Father is not a matter of the Father having a power or authority (*potentia*) that the Son lacks (*De fide* 4.8.81–82 and 85 [2:519–22]). Cf. Aquinas on the mission of the Son as just the act of the procession with the addition of a new habitude or *terminus* (i.e., the flesh) and on the distinction between the *principium personae* and the *principium effectus* in the mission (*ST* Ia.43.1–2 [445–46]; 43.8 corp. [454]).

44. Cyril of Alexandria, *Le Christ est un* 771e–772d (492, 494). Cf. Coccejus, *Summa doc-trinae*, 5.88 (86); 5.91 (90–91); 5.93 (91, 93), who remarks that the *exinanitio* of the Son occurs "spontaneously and with a free will."

this passage Jesus says that he does what the Father does and, indeed, does it "likewise" (ὁμοίως) (5:19). Commenting on John's use of the word "likewise," Gregory Nazianzen incisively notes that this does not concern not a "likeness" of the things that are done (as though the Son might do things separate from and "like" what the Father does) but rather an equal honor in the authority with which the Son acts.[45] The Son acts not in a servile or unlearned manner (οὐ δουλικῶς, οὐδὲ ἀμαθῶς), but in a knowledgeable and lordly manner (ἐπιστημονικῶς τε καὶ δεσποτικῶς), like the Father.[46] Gregory ultimately grounds this in the fact that the Son receives from the Father a "common" and "equal" being (τὸ εἶναι κοινὸν καὶ ὁμότιμον).[47] Cyril of Alexandria similarly comments that "in the being able to do exactly the same works of God the Father, and to work likewise [ὁμοίως] to the one begetting, [the Son] attests the identity of their substance."[48] Jesus also says that "just as the Father raises the dead and gives life, so also the Son gives life to whom he wills" (5:21). Evidently, there is an important sense in which the Son shares the Father's freedom to act and to give eschatological life to whomever he chooses.[49]

Are these two emphases coherent—the Son seeking not his own but the Father's will and the Son freely enacting the Son's will just as the Father freely enacts the Father's will? I think integrating these two emphases (and showing that the text does not invite us to posit a divine obedience on the Son's part) is a matter of seeing that the Son acts from the Father (John 5:19; 5:30a) and that the Father "gives" the Son the divine life, authority, and judgment (5:22, 25–27). The Son's enacting not his own but the Father's will reflects that he receives from the Father all that he has, while the Son's freely enacting the divine will just as the Father does reflects that what he receives from the Father is the same underived life, will, and authority that the Father has.[50] The point here is not obedience but natural reception and the reflection of that reception in the Son's economic action from the Father.[51] And since the Son receives

45. The Greek reads, οὐ κατὰ τὴν τῶν γινομένων ὁμοίωσιν, ἀλλὰ κατὰ τὴν τῆς ἐξουσίας ὁμο-τιμίαν.

46. Gregory Nazianzen, *Discours 27–31*, 30.11 (248).

47. Gregory Nazianzen, *Discours 27–31*, 30.11 (246).

48. Cyril of Alexandria, *In Joann.* 2.6 (1:318).

49. The Spirit, too, works "where he wills" and shares the divine freedom (3:8). Cf. B. Marshall, "What Does the Spirit Have to Do?," 64.

50. Cf. the material in chap. 2, sect. V, regarding the Son being personally from the Father and essentially *a se.*

51. Athanasius helpfully points out that the Son's receiving and the Father's giving do not imply that the Son once lacked what the Father previously had, for the text conveys a parity in the two having the divine life ("just as . . . so also" in 5:26), though the mode of having is different (either from the Father or from no other divine person) (*Oratio III*, 36,13–31 [348]).

from the Father, he does not rival the Father, which is arguably the primary point of the passage in the context of John's Gospel. Thus Cyril paraphrases Jesus's teaching: "'It is impossible for me,' he says, 'the Son from [the Father] according to nature, not to work and to will entirely, in all things, the things of the Father.'" For the Son, who shares the "uncreated nature," has "the same will and action as God the Father."[52] He cannot do anything that does not wholly agree with the Father's judgment.[53]

As noted above, Jesus also refers to a "command" (ἐντολή) that he receives from the Father (John 10:18; 12:49; 14:31; 15:10). In John 10:17–18 in particular, Jesus says that no one takes his life from him. He lays it down of his own accord, adding, "I have authority to lay it down, and I have authority to take it up. This commandment [τὴν ἐντολὴν] I received from my Father." The inexorability of Jesus's willing and acting here seems to entail that Jesus is talking about his divine operation, insofar as finite human operation is subject to compulsion or obstruction from without.[54] Does this mean that Jesus *as God* obeys God the Father? A number of earlier commentators encourage us to think carefully about the meaning of the Son receiving from the Father a commandment. Basil of Caesarea, for example, cautions that the Son is not "without purpose" or "without free choice" but is simply clarifying that he has the same will as the Father. To interpret the text in a manner befitting to God (θεοπρεπῶς) is to perceive that the Father has timelessly (ἀχρόνως) given the divine will to the Son.[55] Augustine takes a similar approach and argues that the Word does not receive a command by a word. Instead the Word eternally receives from the Father the divine substance and in so doing receives the divine authority. It is not as though an imperfect Son were generated by the Father and needed to receive something more. Thus, the Father giving a "command" to the Son is not the Father issuing a directive after the Son's generation or mission but the Father eternally giving the Son divine authority.[56]

Chrysostom comments that Jesus did not have to wait to hear a command from the Father or to learn something from the Father. Jesus's teaching in John

52. Cyril of Alexandria, *In Joann.* 2.6 (1:318).
53. Cyril of Alexandria, *In Joann.* 2.9 (1:354).
54. There is a line of interpretation according to which the reception of the command applies to Jesus only as human (so, e.g., Gregory Nazianzen, *Discours 27–31*, 30.16 [260]; Ambrose, *De fide* 5.10.131–32 [3:688]), but I am not convinced that this adequately expresses the meaning of the passage. As Augustine puts it, the laying down of Jesus's life is *ex potestate Verbi* ("from the power [or authority] of the Word") (*In Iohann.* 47.13 [412]). The reception of a command in the other texts (John 12:49; 14:31; 15:10) might be more easily attributed to the Son's humanity, so these texts are not treated in detail here.
55. Basil of Caesarea, *Sur le Saint-Esprit* 8,4–16 (316).
56. Augustine, *In Iohann.* 47.14 (412).

10:17–18 means only that what he does is what the Father regards as good. Given that Jesus says he lays down his life *from himself*, he does not mean that he needed a command to urge him to perform his duty. He is speaking in a human manner (ἀνθρωπίνως) so that his hearers will understand his unanimity with the Father.[57] Cyril of Alexandria offers an interpretation of John 10:18 that exhibits at least four interconnected strategies for clarifying that the Son is not inferior (ἐλάττων) to the Father. First, Jesus's point is not that he and the Father have competing wills. It is, in fact, the exact opposite: he and the Father will the same thing, and their works come forth from "one mind" or "one purpose." Second, the reception of a command accords with "the economy of the flesh" (τῇ μετὰ σαρκὸς οἰκονομίᾳ). Jesus simply seeks to express "the thing that is fitting to the incarnation [τῇ ἐνανθρωπήσει]" and thus speaks "economically" (οἰκονομικῶς). Third, receiving a command is not something that renders one inferior in substance or nature to the one commanding. While this might seem at first to give traction to the view that the Son might eternally obey as God without being a lesser deity, Cyril returns to stating that the Son receives a command from the Father *under the economy of the flesh*. The logic seems to be that in the case of human beings, for example, one commanded and one commanding remain equal in nature, so it should not surprise us that when the Son receives a command under the economy of the flesh, it does not diminish his divine substance. Indeed, to be commanded by the Father is not the "being" (τὸ εἶναι) of the Son, who is himself the very wisdom of the Father through whom any command would be issued. Fourth, Cyril encourages us not to be surprised when the Son speaks to us in "human words" about divine mysteries. The Son is explaining the unity of the purpose of the Father and Son with weak words inadequate to the things articulated.[58]

In Aquinas's commentary on John, he writes little on the commandment from the Father in John 10:18 but offers more on John 12:49 (the Father has given the Son a "commandment" regarding what he should speak). Aquinas takes up the concern that someone who commands appears to be greater than the one commanded. Indeed, this implies ignorance on the part of the one commanded, which would undermine the deity of the Son. Aquinas then clarifies that commandments are *rationes agendorum* ("reasons" or perhaps

57. John Chrysostom, *In Johann.* 60.3 (331). It is interesting that in John 5:16–30 Jesus does not act from himself but from the Father, while in John 10:17–18 he says he acts "from myself." In view of the discussion of the aseity of the Son earlier in chap. 2, this could be summarized by saying that the Son acts from the Father with regard to his personal mode of subsisting and from himself with regard to the essential power with which he acts.

58. Cyril of Alexandria, *In Joann.* 7 (2:244–46).

"bases" of things to be done). Just as the Son is called the wisdom of the Father and receives the divine understanding and *rationes* of all things from the Father by eternal generation, so he receives the *rationes agendorum* from the Father by eternal generation.[59] Polanus sheds a little more light on this in his discussion of the possible senses of the term "commandment" in places like John 10:18. For Polanus, there is an "ambiguity" in the word "commandment" (Latin *mandatum*), since it can signify "either the sort of command [*jussum*] a superior gives to an inferior, or the divine decree concerning our redemption." Reception of the former would be applicable to Christ according to his human nature. Reception of the latter is applicable to Christ according to his divine nature.[60]

How might these comments help to explain the meaning of John 10:17–18 and confirm the strictly human character of the Son's obedience? With Augustine, Chrysostom, and Aquinas, we will do well to bear in mind that the Son as God has never been ignorant of something, which entails that he, as God, has never needed a directive to complete a task. He has always received from the Father all that it is to be God, including the divine will, which entails that he, as God, has never needed a prompting to execute God's plan. Indeed, as Chrysostom observed, in this very passage Jesus says he operates from himself. Thus, if the Son receives a "command" that has some reference to his divine operation, he is not "commanded" in any ordinary sense. Accordingly, if the Son's operation of sovereignly giving up his flesh for the life of the world pertains to him as God and if he has in some sense received from the Father a "command" regarding that operation, this will have to be expressed carefully. The Son receives a "command" not in the sense of being supplied with instruction from one that has a different knowledge and will, but in the sense of receiving from the Father the divine knowledge, will, and authority with respect to their decretive application to the economy. On the one hand, the Son is not told what he must do as though an interval existed between his and the Father's divine knowledge and will. On the other hand, the Son is given by the Father's eternal generation the divine authority and efficacy by which he will inexorably offer his flesh on the cross.

In this connection, what the likes of Basil of Caesarea, Chrysostom, and Cyril of Alexandria have said about the accommodated, human manner of speaking is worth remembering here. Christ is speaking in a lowly human manner (ἀνθρωπίνως) to help us understand that his activity is undertaken in accord with the Father. The words are human, but the things conveyed by the

59. Aquinas, *Super Ioann*. 12.8.11.1723 (321).
60. Polanus, *Syntagma*, 3.10 (232).

words have to be understood in a manner that befits God (θεοπρεπῶς). One might wonder whether this implies something like a gnostic view of biblical interpretation, where verbal signs are disparaged and the things signified are to be grasped only by a knowledge possessed by the specially "enlightened." However, recognizing the lowly form and limited descriptive power of the words does not have to involve setting aside the words or the literal sense in favor of learning about God from somewhere else. Instead, understanding the substance of the text in a God-befitting way (θεοπρεπῶς) is a matter of bearing in mind what the whole canon of Scripture teaches us about God in order to avoid drawing conclusions from one statement or text that will end up conflicting with our conclusions from another text. In this case, Jesus's reception of a commandment conveys something that resonates with the literal sense of the words (he receives by his eternal generation the power and authority to do something), but the words of the passage should not be pressed in a direction that will bring about conflict with other Johannine teaching on the mystery of the Trinity.[61]

In addition, it seems to me that a number of early Reformed theologians may provide insight into relevant New Testament texts by developing the claim that the Father is "greater" than the Son (cf. John 14:28) with respect to his mediatorial office as well as his human nature per se. Polanus, for example, maps out diverse senses in which the Father is called "greater" than the Son. First, Polanus notes that a number of the fathers (e.g., Athanasius, Hilary, Basil of Caesarea, Gregory Nazianzen) call the Father "greater" than the Son with respect to his eternal origination of the Son (without negating the essential equality of the Father and Son). Second, the Father is greater than the Son "by reason of the mediatorial office in which the Son both has died in the state of humiliation and now functions in the state of exaltation." Finally, the Father is of course greater than the Son "by reason of the humanity assumed by the Son."[62] Polanus applies such reasoning in several places. The Son is "anointed" according to his divine nature in a qualified way (*secundum quid*) since he is "ordained according to [his divine nature]" to the mediatorial office of prophet, priest, and king, while he is "anointed" according to his human nature in an unrestricted way (*simpliciter*) since he receives the gifts of the Holy Spirit according to his human nature (see Ps. 45:7;

---

61. That teaching includes that the Son has eternally received by generation from the Father the divine life and knowledge (John 6:45–46; 7:28–29), that the Son acts in grace and freedom in the incarnation (1:16), and that the Son acts both from the Father and from himself like the Father (5:21; 10:18).

62. Polanus, *Syntagma*, 3.10 (230). Cf., e.g., Johann Alsted's threefold ramification of "attributes" of Christ: divine, human, economic (*Methodus s.s. theologiae*, 3.2 [209]).

Isa. 61:1; Heb. 1:9). Polanus addresses the Son being "of God" (cf. 1 Cor. 3:23) in a similar fashion. On the one hand, Christ is not of God "with respect to a dominion which the Father has toward Christ as he is God." On the other hand, Christ is of God "according to that economy and voluntary dispensation: first, according to his *suppositum*, as he is the God-man and mediator between God and human beings . . . voluntarily joining us to himself for the completion of our salvation; then, according to the human nature assumed, insofar as the condition of human nature is subject to God; lastly, according to the mystical body of the church, which he has united to himself as head."[63]

Herman Witsius also discusses the Son's "economic minority." He notes that the human nature of the mediator is never without the divine and asks the question whether the mediator can pledge subjection to the law of God without the divine nature also being led into the "company" (*consortium*) of this subjection. Witsius responds that the "divine nature as it is characterized in the Son" is not able "truly and really to be subject." In fact, although the Son has eternally chosen to stand in a mediatorial relation to the elect, that relation by itself introduces no subjection to the Father. The mediatorial relation stipulates only that, when the Son does assume a human nature, he will render a human obedience to the Father. Within the context of the Son's incarnation and earthly humiliation, the divine nature in the Son "will not have stretched forth nor shown all its magnificence in the servant-nature assumed, nor will it have hindered that [human] nature, united with itself in hypostatic union, from serving a true servitude under the law." This is not a "real denial of divine superiority" but a "certain economic hiding [*oeconomica occultatio*] for a time." Thus, "the relation of an inferior to a superior" may be predicated of the theandric person, just as obedience and passion are predicated of the person. Witsius then asks another question: whether Christ, as mediator, is

63. Polanus, *Syntagma*, 3.10 (232–33). Turretin has a comparable line of thought in arguing that Christ the mediator acts according to both natures in his mediatorial works. For Turretin, "the divine nature is not excluded from mediation." While Christ is not mediator according to the divine nature "absolutely, as it is common to the three persons," he is nevertheless mediator according to the divine nature "observed economically, by reason of his voluntary emptying [*ratione voluntariae suae exinanitionis*]" (*Inst.*, 14.2.13 [2:414–15]). "Although Christ is established as mediator according to the divine nature, the Logos is not therefore established as less than the Father. . . . For it is one thing to make the persons unequal according to essence, with the Arians. It is another thing to distinguish the Son from the Father according to a voluntary economy, in which he has emptied [*exinanivit*] himself" (*Inst.*, 14.2.23 [2:417]). (For an author like Turretin, the *exinanitio* is not a matter of giving up something divine but a matter of the Son assuming the lowly human nature and allowing his divinity in the state of humiliation to be veiled temporarily under the lowliness of the human nature; see Turretin, *Inst.*, 13.6.13 [2:340–41]. Cf. Owen's statements that the *exinanitio* involves, first, the Son's condescension or assumption of a lowly nature and, second, the temporary "hiding" of his divine glory [*Hebrews*, 4:526–27].)

"less than" and "subordinate" to the Father. He answers that if the mediator is considered "in the state of humiliation and in the *forma servi*," then he is less than and subordinate to the Father. The "mediatorial function in itself is to be considered to import a certain economic minority" that will be removed in the eschaton. Yet this mediation, leading human beings to glory, is not "below the eminence of deity." Its glory is not communicable to any creature.

> It is the glory of Jehovah to be the righteousness of Israel. He does not give this glory to what is not God. He does not call the mediator a mere servant of God but also the great God and Savior, who as first and principal cause of salvific grace, equal to the Father, works in himself our reconciliation with God, by the subjection and obedience of the human nature, without which the coequal Son had not been able to serve a servitude nor to obey the Father.[64]

My aim in drawing attention to these Reformed treatments of the Son's mediatorial "minority" is to suggest that they might add to the patristic and medieval material discussed above and help us to exegete other pertinent texts like 1 Corinthians 3:23 or 11:3. On the one hand, the Son's deity and divine operation as such can never be under a dominion that the Father alone might supposedly have. Thus, the Son with respect to his divine operation receives a "command" just in the sense that he receives from the Father by eternal generation the divine will and authority in their decretive direction toward the economy of salvation. On the other hand, the Son, in union with his lowly human nature, is the one divine person who assumes a human nature and is properly called the mediator (so 1 Tim. 2:5).[65] Thus, the God-man can be considered "less than" and "of" the Father with respect to his voluntary dispensation and office. Ultimately, the main point here is that the Scriptures teach a distinctly human obedience of the Son, not a divine obedience. The Scriptures do this by teaching that the Son's obedience is a novelty consequent upon his assumption of the *forma servi*, that his obedience has a representative character for our sake, and that his obedience tends toward a death that he could not undergo as immortal God. This is corroborated by the fact that even the Johannine texts about the Son willing from the Father or receiving from the Father a "command" do not require us to posit a divine obedience of the Son.

In this section, we have examined various threads of scriptural teaching regarding the Son's obedience according to his human nature. He is the Isaianic

64. Witsius, *De oeconomia foederum Dei*, 2.3.7, 16–20 (113, 115–17).

65. On the divine action in mediation principally belonging to the essence that is common to the divine persons while belonging in a special sense to the Son, cf. Turretin, *Inst.*, 14.2.15 (2:415).

figure who serves and fulfills YHWH's will, entrusting himself to the vindication of YHWH. In Matthew, he is the true Israel who acts righteously for the sake of God's people, not least in facing temptation from the devil and enduring the dread and anxiety of Gethsemane without compromising his determination to do the Father's will. For Paul, Christ the righteous second Adam representatively counteracts the disobedience and guilt of the first Adam. He is born "under the law" and humbles himself by becoming obedient even to the point of death. For the writer of Hebrews, the Son takes on flesh and blood like us, his brothers and sisters. He offers prayers, entrusting himself to the Father and undergoing a perfection by suffering and temptation. He is the pioneer and forerunner who leads the way into God's presence.

The next section of this chapter will explore in a little more detail three aspects of Christ's obedience for us. In particular, it will explore the question of whether Christ exercised faith on earth, the sense in which he shared in our human weaknesses without compromising his determination to obey the Father, and the sense in which he grew through suffering in his role as a merciful high priest. These elements of scriptural teaching—the faith, the weakness, and the growth of Christ—will be considered in dialogue with material from patristic, medieval, and early Reformed Christology under the following main points.

III. Faith, Weakness, and Growth in the Obedience of Christ

(1) The first two points here will be primarily historical and intended to provide a sense of theological context for the present discussion. The sense in which Christ exercised faith (or whether he did in fact exercise faith) while also possessing a unique human knowledge of God is a matter of debate in the Christian tradition.[66] Did Christ in his human intellect know all things, at least those pertaining to the plan of God? Did he enjoy the beatific vision even during his earthly life rather than exercising a pilgrim faith?[67] It seems

66. Discussion of Christ's faith (or "faithfulness") has also appeared recently in debates about the phrase πίστις Ἰησοῦ Χριστοῦ in Paul's writings (see Hays, *The Faith of Jesus Christ*; Bird and Sprinkle, *The Faith of Jesus Christ*; Allen, "'From the Time He Took On the Form of a Servant'"; Gaine, *Did the Saviour See the Father?*, 107–11; Downs and Lappenga, *The Faithfulness of the Risen Christ*; McCall, *Analytic Christology*, chap. 2). Although the interpretation of the Pauline phrase commands interest among biblical scholars and dogmatic theologians, the question of the objective or subjective genitive reading of that one phrase is not central to the argument here.

67. For recent discussion, see O'Collins and Kendall, "The Faith of Jesus"; Weinandy, "Jesus' Filial Vision of the Father"; Ashley, "The Extent of Jesus' Human Knowledge"; White, *Incarnate Lord*, 236–74; Weinandy, "The Beatific Vision and the Incarnate Son"; Mansini, *The Word*

wise to take into account some of the discussion on these matters insofar as it will help us to discern, on the one hand, the gravity of Christ's human endurance and obedience and, on the other hand, the preeminence and otherness of Christ without which he would not be fit to save sinners.

In light of the problem of Arianism, a number of church fathers reason that the apparent ignorance of Christ in a place like the eschatological discourse—not even the Son knows the hour of his return (Mark 13:32)—is something that pertains not to Christ's own (divine or human) understanding but to the needs of his listeners. Like God inquiring where Adam is in the garden, Jesus will not reveal what he knows all at once. He says he does not know the hour of his return in order to elicit a response from his hearers (in this case, a life of faithfulness rather than eschatological speculation).[68] At the same time, other patristic authors take Jesus's comment about not knowing the hour of his return to mean that Jesus in his human intellect does not know everything. Regarding this comment, Athanasius, for example, writes that Christ says this "on account of the flesh." For it is "proper" (ἴδιον) to the human nature "not to know" (ἀγνοεῖν).[69] Indeed, according to Athanasius, it is not merely that the human nature separate from the person of the Logos would not have knowledge of certain things. Rather, just as truly as the person of the Logos himself thirsts, hungers, and suffers, so he also does not know. Thus, "on the one hand, with men and as man he does not know, but, on the other hand, divinely being in the Father as Word and wisdom he knows, and there is nothing which he does not know [μετὰ μὲν ἀνθρώπων ὡς ἄνθρωπος οὐκ οἶδε, θεϊκῶς δὲ ἐν τῷ πατρὶ ὢν ὡς λόγος καὶ σοφία οἶδε, καὶ οὐδέν ἐστιν, ὃ ἀγνοεῖ]."[70] Furthermore, Ambrose affirms a true growth in the human knowledge of Christ. In light of Luke 2:52, where Christ grows "in wisdom and age and favor with God and human beings," Ambrose reasons that the growth in age, which pertains to Christ only as man, indicates that this is a growth in human wisdom. In addition, when Luke uses similar language in 2:40 ("The child grew and became strong, being filled with wisdom, and

---

Has Dwelt among Us, 45–71; Allen, *The Christ's Faith*; Wilkins, "Love and the Knowledge of God"; Healy, "*Simul viator et comprehensor*"; Gaine, *Did the Saviour See the Father?*; Legge, *The Trinitarian Christology of St Thomas Aquinas*, 173–82; Gaine, "The Beatific Vision and the Heavenly Mediation of Christ"; Gaine, "How Could the Earthly Jesus Have Taught Divine Truth?"

68. See, e.g., Hilary of Poitiers, *La Trinité* 9.58–68 (3:134–56); John Chrysostom, *In Matt.* 77.4 (705–6); Jerome, *Sur Matt. II*, 4.24, 36 (204, 206). Cf. also Ambrose, *De fide* 5.18 (3:758–66); John of Damascus, *Expos. fidei* 3.21 (163); 4.18 (216).

69. Athanasius, *Oratio III*, 43 (354–55). For the whole context of Athanasius's argument, see 42–50 (353–62).

70. Athanasius, *Oratio III*, 46,8–10 (357). Cf. Gregory Nazianzen, *Discours 27–31*, 30.15 (256, 258); Cyril of Alexandria, *Contra Theodoretum* 169,38–39 (124).

the grace of God was upon him"), he calls Christ a "child," a word used to express human age, which corroborates that the evangelist is speaking about Christ's human development in 2:52. Ambrose also takes Isaiah 8:4 ("before the child knows how to call 'My father' or 'My mother,' . . ." [NRSV]) to be a prophecy about Christ. For Ambrose, then, "future and hidden things do not slip past the wisdom of God, but, lacking knowledge, childhood certainly by human imprudence does not know what it has not yet learned." The growth in wisdom is rooted in a growth in "sense," for "wisdom grows by sense."[71]

In the medieval period, however, Peter Lombard writes that the human mind of Christ "knows all that God knows," though without the perspicuity with which God knows all things. Christ is, after all, the one who receives the Spirit and the Spirit's gifts "without measure" (cf. John 3:34). Indeed, he is the one in whom are hidden "all the storehouses of wisdom and knowledge" (Col. 2:3). Accordingly, Lombard is critical of Ambrose's interpretation of Luke's Gospel: "Ambrose is plainly seen to intimate that Christ will have grown according to human sense, and that in his childhood he will have been lacking cognition and will not have known his father and mother, which the church does not receive." For Lombard, the sense of Christ grew only with respect to the display of it before others (*secundum ostensionem et aliorum hominum opinionem*). In relation to Isaiah 8:4, Christ is said "not to have known his father and mother in infancy [or "childhood," *infantia*] because he comported and conducted himself as if [*ac si*] he were lacking knowledge."[72]

Subsequent discussion among medieval and early Reformed figures often ramifies the knowledge of Christ's human soul under a threefold consideration: beatific knowledge (i.e., direct vision of God's essence), infused knowledge (i.e., knowledge implanted in the mind of Christ by the Holy Spirit), and acquired knowledge (i.e., knowledge by sense perception or experience). In his commentary on the *Sentences*, Bonaventure, for example, follows Lombard's main conclusions but also considerably expands the material, dealing with the human knowledge of Christ's soul or mind (*anima*) with respect to the knowledge of the Word to which the soul is united,[73] the knowledge infused by the Spirit, and the knowledge acquired from sense or experience. Bonaventure reasons that Christ's human knowledge of the Word is a creaturely, habitual

71. Ambrose, *De incarnationis dominicae sacramento* 7,71–74 (260–62). Note also Cyril of Alexandria, *Scholia* 14 (532); 36 (568).

72. Lombard, *Sent.* 3.13.1 (88–89); 3.14.1 (90–91).

73. To avoid the impression that Bonaventure is speaking in a Nestorian manner here, it may be helpful to stress that he is speaking about the *anima Christi* not as a distinct person but as the human intellect of the one person. The discussion concerns Christ's human knowledge of his own divine person or divinity.

knowledge effected by the hypostatic union, assimilating Christ's human intellect to the Word and rendering it "clear," "bright," and "deiform" beyond any other human intellect possessing the beatific vision.[74] The human knowledge of Christ's soul remains finite; it does not strictly "comprehend" the Word. It apprehends the whole (*totum*), but not wholly (*totaliter*).[75] Yet this knowledge apprehends other things "in" the Word since the Word knows all things and is the "exemplar" of all things."[76] Thus, according to Bonaventure, Christ's human intellect knows all things in the Word by habit and knows some of these in act as well (i.e., by active consideration)—namely, those that pertain to Christ's uninterrupted beatific glory.[77] Beyond Christ's human knowledge, which he has "in" the Word, there is a human knowledge of things "from" the Word. This knowledge "from" the Word includes both the knowledge of "simple intelligence" (*cognitio simplicis intelligentiae* or *simplicis notitiae*) and the knowledge of "experience" (*cognitio experientiae*). Regarding the knowledge of simple intelligence, the species of all things are infused from the beginning in the human intellect of Christ. In this regard, the knowledge of Christ does not grow. Regarding the latter, the objects of sense experience are perceived by Christ at diverse times. In this regard alone, the knowledge of Christ is turned toward something new and grows over time. The knowledge of experience especially focuses on "penal experience" in the fallen world, according to which Christ learned while he suffered (so Heb. 5:8).[78]

74. Bonaventure, *In Sent.* 3.14.1.1 (296–97). For Bonaventure, Christ in his human soul, together with the blessed in heaven, sees not merely a certain "condescension" or "appearance" of the "font of light" that is God's own nature but rather the font of light itself (*In Sent.* 3.14.1.3 [303–5]).

75. Bonaventure, *In Sent.* 3.14.1.2 (300–301). Cf. Bonaventure, *De scientia Christi* 6 (34–35).

76. Bonaventure, *In Sent.* 3.14.2.1 (308).

77. Bonaventure, *In Sent.* 3.14.2.2 (311). The knowledge of Christ's human intellect is again restricted in the next question. While knowing *habitually* all things that the Word knows, the human intellect does not know *actually* (with active consideration) all that the Word knows, for a created intellect cannot judge an infinite number of things all at once. At the same time, the human intellect of Christ can freely "read" or attend to whatever is in the Word since the Word, who is the "mirror" (*speculum*) of all things, willingly manifests all that is in him. In this respect, Bonaventure posits a habitual omniscience of the human intellect of Christ (*In Sent.* 3.14.2.3 [314–16]; cf. the slightly different treatment in *De scientia Christi* 7 [39–40]). Interestingly, Bonaventure chooses this way of restricting the human knowledge of Christ over approaches in which Christ knows what God has planned and will actualize but not all that God could do. For Bonaventure, Christ not only sees what is included in the divine *scientia visionis* but also, at least habitually, knows what is included in the divine *scientia simplicis intelligentiae*. For, in Bonaventure's assessment, possession of the wisdom of God cannot exclude *possibilia*. Nor, in Bonaventure's judgment, can Christ be said to learn something *de novo* in a scenario where God actualizes more things than he has thus far made.

78. Bonaventure, *In Sent.* 3.14.3.1–2 (319–20, 322).

In the *Summa theologiae*, Aquinas introduces Christ's human knowledge in IIIa.9.1, where one of the driving principles of Aquinas's reasoning is that Christ assumed a complete human nature and that the powers or faculties of the human nature have attained to their ends and are perfect.[79] Aquinas then treats Christ's beatific, infused, and acquired or "experiential" (*experimentalis*) knowledge in successive questions. According to Aquinas, since Christ even in his humanity knows God fully (see John 8:55) and since Christ even in his humanity is the one leading many sons and daughters to glory (see Heb. 2:10), he must preeminently have the vision of God that God's people have in glory, for "it is proper for the cause to be greater than the thing caused."[80] Like Bonaventure, Aquinas still clarifies that this beatific knowledge is not a strict "comprehension" of the Word or the divine essence, for though Christ's human knowledge surpasses that of any other creature, it remains finite.[81] Christ as man knows all things "in" the Word, but, whereas Bonaventure restricts this human knowledge by appealing to the habit-act distinction, Aquinas restricts this human knowledge by appealing to the distinction between knowledge of all that God has actualized or will actualize (*scientia visionis*) and knowledge of all that God could possibly do (*scientia simplicis intelligentiae*).[82] Christ as man has the former but not the latter. As man, he has the former in its entirety, though without the infinite clarity of the divine knowing. He knows what is included in the divine *scientia visionis* because every blessed intellect knows all that pertains to it, and all things pertain to Christ's intellect insofar as all are subject to him and will be judged by him. Given that Christ knows all things that pertain to him, the comment in his eschatological discourse about not knowing the hour of his return indicates no lack of knowledge in him but rather a decision not to make the hour known (compare Acts 1:7).[83]

79. Aquinas, *ST* IIIa.9.1 (138–39). Cf. also IIIa.15.3 corp. (188).

80. Aquinas, *ST* IIIa.9.2 corp. (141); cf. Aquinas, *Compendium theologiae* 1.213 (166); 1.216 (170). See also Aquinas, *ST* IIIa.10.4 (154–55) and 11.5 ad 1 (163), where this knowledge is always active (never merely habitual). Recent treatments of the beatific vision from a Thomistic perspective (see the accounts of White, Mansini, Gaine, and Legge noted above) point out that Aquinas does not argue from a general "principle of perfection" but primarily from economic, soteriological considerations for the beatific vision of Christ on earth.

81. Aquinas, *ST* IIIa.10.1 (148–49); cf. Aquinas, *Compendium theologiae* 1.216 (170).

82. Strictly speaking, the *scientia visionis* is a knowledge of things present to the knowing subject, while the *scientia simplicis intelligentiae* is an abstractive knowledge of things that need not be in act or present to the knowing subject. The former pertains to what God has actualized or will actualize since these things have their own existence and were, are, or will be present to the human sense and intellect of Christ. The latter pertains to what God could possibly do since it is a knowledge God has by knowing his own essence and power without reference to the actualization of any *possibilia*.

83. Aquinas, *ST* IIIa.10.2 (149–50).

In Aquinas's exposition, Christ also knows all things by the infused knowledge that he has from the Spirit (see the various cognitive terms used in Isa. 11:2), though the infused knowledge itself does not include the beatific vision.[84] Moreover, because of Aquinas's commitment to the perfection of Christ's intellect, he reasons that Christ possesses acquired or experiential knowledge too. For, Aquinas says, it pertains to the perfection of the "active intellect" of the human person to access or act upon phantasms or images acquired by sense perception and render them intelligible to the intellect.[85] It was this acquired knowledge in which Christ grew in Luke 2:52. Aquinas appropriates Ambrose's comment that Christ "advanced according to human wisdom." According to Aquinas, "human wisdom is what is acquired in a human way, namely, by the light of the agent intellect. Therefore, Christ has advanced according to this knowledge." Aquinas then clarifies that growth in knowledge is twofold. The growth may take place either with respect to the essence of the knowledge itself, "insofar as the habit of knowledge itself is increased," or with respect to the effect of the knowledge, as when someone by the same knowledge shows "lesser things" to some and afterward "greater and more subtle things" to others. In his infused knowledge, which was complete in itself from its inception, Christ advanced in "knowledge and grace" in only the second way, for, "according to the increase of age, he did greater works, which showed greater wisdom and grace." In his acquired knowledge, however, Christ advanced in gaining new mental habits. Consciously abandoning his previous view of the matter in his *Sentences* commentary, Aquinas writes that Christ's knowledge increased not merely "by experience" (by connecting previously infused knowledge of universals to newly acquired sense perception), but even by

84. Aquinas, *ST* IIIa.11.1 (157–58). For Aquinas the infused knowledge is grounded in both the hypostatic union and the work of the Spirit, who proceeds and operates from the Son, to whom the human intellect is united (on which, see Legge, *The Trinitarian Christology of St Thomas Aquinas*, 175, 178, 181–82, 186). Aquinas also insists that Christ's infused knowledge did not require a turning of the intellect to phantasms (a utilization of impressions or images made by outward objects of sense perception) (IIIa.11.2 [159–60]). For Aquinas, the infused knowledge involved a capacity for *collatio*, or discursive reasoning. However, this was not for acquisition of new knowledge but for certain uses of knowledge already possessed (III.a.11.3 [161]). Furthermore, it includes both habitual and actual knowledge in accordance with its human nature. The "species" of things are "divinely imprinted" on Christ's human intellect, and he can actively consider them or reduce habit to act according to his will (IIIa.11.5 [163]). The use of the term "species," however, should not be taken to flatten out the infused knowledge as though it concerned only essences or abstract universals. For, as Aquinas makes clear, it includes diverse kinds of mental habits, including practical knowledge of singular things (IIIa.11.1 ad 3 [158] and 11.6 [164–65]).

85. Aquinas, *ST* IIIa.12.1 (166).

gaining new habits from the intellect's engagement of the objects of sense perception.[86]

In light of the simultaneity of Christ's beatific knowledge, on the one hand, and his corporeal and mental suffering, on the other, Aquinas concludes that Christ was at the same time a "comprehender" (comprehensor) who has obtained beatitude and a "pilgrim" (viator) who is en route to beatitude. On the one hand, Christ directly knew and enjoyed God even before his exaltation. On the other hand, both his body and soul were passible and underwent suffering. Thus, Christ already possessed a beatitude proper to the soul in the vision and enjoyment of God, but he also was still tending toward beatitude with regard to the passibility of body and soul.[87] Though Christ's beatific knowledge and passibility cohere during his earthly sojourn, his beatific knowledge, in Aquinas's judgment, does not fit with the notion of Christ having faith. For the object of faith is a "divine thing not seen." But, since Christ from the time of his conception fully sees God by the divine essence, there can be no faith in Christ. Though Aquinas affirms that true faith has a "certainty or firmness" with which one clings to God, he holds that there is a certain "defect" in it since it is not yet sight.[88] Likewise, the essence of hope is the expectation of the good that one does not yet see (cf. Rom. 8:24). But Christ had the full enjoyment of God from conception, so he did not have hope in that respect. Yet one can say that Christ did have hope at least with respect to anticipating the resurrection and glorification of his body.[89]

(2) In early Reformed theology, the human knowledge of Christ often appears in discussions of the various kinds of "ectypal" theological knowledge that God communicates to human beings.[90] For example, Polanus's treatment of ectypal theology uses a fundamental distinction between the knowledge of Christ's own human nature and the knowledge of the members of Christ's mystical body. Polanus applies the concept of "pilgrim theology" (theologia viatorum) not to Christ himself but only to Christ's members.[91] When the Reformed then treat Christ's own human knowledge, they often take up the

---

86. Aquinas, ST IIIa.12.2 (167–68). On whether Christ could grow in wisdom and grace, cf. also IIIa.7.12 (122–23), where Aquinas argues that Christ could not grow with respect to the form of the habits he received from the Spirit or with respect to himself as the subject who partakes of such habits, for he was someone who comprehended things (a comprehensor) from the moment of his conception. Thus, Christ increases only in the outward display of his wisdom and grace.

87. Aquinas, ST IIIa.15.10 (196).

88. Aquinas, ST IIIa.7.3 (109).

89. Aquinas, ST IIIa.7.4 (110).

90. See, e.g., Junius, De vera theologia 6 (45–52); Polanus, Syntagma, 1.7 (11); Turretin, Inst., 1.2.6 (1:5).

91. Polanus, Syntagma, 1.7–9 (11–12).

threefold division of beatific, infused, and acquired knowledge, but there is some diversity in their accounts, with frequent appeals to patristic figures like Athanasius and Ambrose. Within this Reformed diversity, there are some authors who maintain the doctrine of Christ's beatific knowledge on earth, while others reject that doctrine and explore the implications of Christ exercising faith on earth.

Girolamo Zanchi, for example, affirms that Christ always has beatific knowledge, for Christ's human intellect always immediately sees the Word and, in the Word as in a mirror, all other things.[92] Christ's direct vision of God is ingredient in his salvific efficacy. For it is from his own fullness that he communicates the beatific vision to the elect. Like his medieval predecessors, Zanchi also affirms the presence of a habitual knowledge infused by the Spirit, which Christ could consider actively when he willed, and a knowledge acquired by sense experience (in which Jesus grows according to Luke 2:52).[93] Yet Zanchi makes certain moves that might be considered somewhat eclectic in discussing the beatific and infused knowledge. On the one hand, Christ sees in the Word all that God has actualized or will actualize, though not all things that God could do. Christ knows all that human beings and angels can know. He knows all things that pertain to his own felicity and to his future judgment of all things.[94] On the other hand, in Zanchi's view, Christ's human knowledge does not include apprehension of the time of his return, for "that last day has been revealed to no one, either human beings or angels."[95] Furthermore, the Pauline statement that in Christ are "all the storehouses of wisdom and knowledge" (Col. 2:3) does not necessarily concern the knowledge of Christ's human intellect. Here Zanchi is wary of a Lutheran conception of a communication of divine omniscience to the human nature of Christ, so he takes Colossians 2:3 to mean that anyone who knows Christ has the fullness of spiritual wisdom. With regard to the infused knowledge, Zanchi comments that as Christ advanced in age, he also advanced in this knowledge in a certain way: not with respect to the habits themselves (which are "replete from the beginning") but with respect to the acts of knowing or the exercise of the Spirit's gifts. For just as Christ grew bodily and in sense experience, so he also grew in the powers of his soul for

92. Zanchi acknowledges the finitude of Christ's beatific knowledge and appeals to the *totum-totaliter* (ὅλον-ὅλως) distinction to clarify that Christ sees God by the divine essence but does not comprehend him. In addition, Zanchi also writes that Christ sees things in the Word not by "one intuition" but by one successive intuitive act after another.

93. Zanchi, *De incarn.*, 2.3 (362–64, 366–67, 369–71, 377–78).

94. Zanchi, *De incarn.*, 2.3 (367–69, 371, 373–77).

95. For Zanchi, Christ does know the hour of his return now that he is exalted to heaven.

discerning and ratiocinating.[96] Still, in accordance with his affirmation of Christ's beatific vision on earth, Zanchi holds that Christ does not have faith "properly speaking," for faith's object is something unseen (so Heb. 11:1). But insofar as faith is a gift of the Spirit, Christ must be said to have it in some sense. Zanchi thus reasons that Christ has faith "improperly" insofar as faith denotes a human knowledge of God.[97]

In a number of cases, the Reformed theologians address the Jesuit theologian Robert Bellarmine (1524–1621), who, more like Lombard and less like Bonaventure and Aquinas, was resistant to the affirmation of any growth in the knowledge of Christ.[98] In his treatment of Christ taking up human infirmities and being like us in everything (but without sin), Polanus engages Bellarmine, but Polanus states that there is no controversy over Christ's beatific or infused knowledge. By virtue of the hypostatic union and the Spirit's endowment, Christ has the fullness of beatific and infused knowledge "from the beginning of his own conception." For Polanus, there is no incremental growth in the infused or "donative" knowledge, except, as the "orthodox fathers" put it, according to the revelation of it to others (καθ' φανέρωσιν).[99] Yet, for Polanus, there is still a "negative" ignorance (though not a "privative" and culpable ignorance) in Christ. Indeed, when Christ says that he does not know the day or hour of his return, the interpretation that Christ simply wishes not to reveal the day and hour is false. Citing Cyril of Alexandria, Polanus judges that Christ himself in his human intellect did not know the day or the hour. Polanus also underscores that while Christ did not grow in the infused graces of the Spirit, he did grow in natural things, including his acquired knowledge.[100] In accordance with his affirmation of Christ's beatific knowledge on earth, Polanus denies that Christ has faith in the sense of a "gift by which these things are believed which are not seen."[101]

William Ames also addresses Bellarmine's position, appealing to Aquinas to make the point that Christ did grow in the habits of acquired knowledge. Like Zanchi, Ames also suggests that Christ's exercise of the habits of infused

96. Zanchi, *De incarn.*, 2.3 (357–58, 373–77). Zanchi attributes to John of Damascus (see *Expos. fidei* 3.22 [164–65]) the view that Christ advances not with respect to habit but only with respect to act. However, Zanchi himself expresses an openness to a view in which even the habits themselves undergo a certain "incremental" growth.

97. Zanchi, *De incarn.*, 2.3 (360–61).

98. See Bellarmine, *Disp.*, 1.2.4.1–5 (513–24).

99. However, while Polanus rejects advancement in Christ's infused knowledge, he does clarify that the unction of Christ is twofold: first, with regard to the Spirit's initial gifting and, second, with respect to his calling at his baptism to begin his public ministry, which completes the promise of Isa. 61:1 ("The Spirit of the Lord is upon me . . .").

100. Polanus, *Syntagma*, 6.15 (370–72).

101. Polanus, *Syntagma*, 9.6 (587).

knowledge, rather than being immediately perfect, grew over time in accordance with the growth of his human stature and "faculty of perceiving." For Ames, the wisdom of Christ can be regarded as perfect from the beginning "intensively and in the first act," but it still increased "in the second act" and "by extension to new objects." In fact, Ames goes on to utilize a distinction between the "right" (*jus*) and the "possession" of the Spirit's gifts. As Son of God and heir of all things, Christ has the right to all the Spirit's gifts, but under a "voluntary dispensation" Christ lives in a humble state and will come into full possession of certain gifts (or "degrees" of gifts) of both the soul and body only when he is raised and exalted. Within this framework, Ames then suggests that Christ in his human intellect truly did not know the hour of his return to judge the world. In fact, Ames reasons, it does not make sense to interpret the ignorance as only a denial of revelation. For if it were only a denial of revelation, and if, like Jesus, the Father, too, chose not to reveal the hour, then Jesus could not have said that the Father does know the hour of his return. But Jesus does say that the Father knows the hour in Mark 13:32, which entails that the ignorance cannot be just a matter of choosing not to reveal.[102]

Several Reformed theologians of the seventeenth century, like Gisbertus Voetius and Francis Turretin, affirm Christ's reception of infused knowledge from the Spirit but also argue that Christ exercised faith during his earthly life. Voetius[103] distances himself from those who attribute the beatific vision to Christ on earth and provides a number of reasons for attributing faith to Christ, several of which are included here.[104] First, the Scriptures expressly attribute faith or an "essential adjunct" of faith to Christ in various places (Ps. 22:9–11; Heb. 2:13). Second, the "formal object" of faith is proposed to Christ—namely, divine promises revealed by God, some of which concern blessings proposed to Christ himself as a man under the law of God and some of which concern the benefits that Christ will procure for others (see, e.g., Isa. 53:10–12; John 17:2, 20–21). Third, Christ's life exhibits the effects or consequences of faith, not least prayer, consolation, and hope (see Ps. 22:9–11; Matt. 26:39, 42, 44; John 17; Heb. 5:7).[105]

Fourth, the "proper external causes of faith" (at least those "conserving" faith) are offered to Christ, and Christ himself "uses these as appointed means and supports of faith." Some of the means that Voetius has in view

102. Ames, *Bellarminus enervatus*, 2.1 (82–86).

103. Or those who were authorized to give an account of the relevant disputations that occurred under Voetius's guidance at Utrecht.

104. For the comments on the beatific vision, see Voetius, *Select. disp., pars sec.*, 2.8 (156); 2.9 (186); 2.73 (1216).

105. Voetius, *Select. disp., pars sec.*, 2.8 (156, 159).

are "ordinary"—namely, the word of God, prayer, and sacraments like circumcision, Passover, baptism, and the Lord's Supper. Voetius recognizes that many commentators (*Postillistae*) and scholastic theologians have argued that Christ uses these sacraments only for the sake of others. Voetius maintains, though, that while Christ did not have to use the sacraments in the manner of sinners, that does not mean that he could not use them for himself at all. He used them both "legally" to fulfill the requirements of true religion and "evangelically" as signs sealing the divine promises and confirming and sustaining faith in the promises, including the promise of salvation from death (Heb. 5:7). Other means that Voetius has in view are "extraordinary," like the Father's speech at Christ's baptism and transfiguration (Matt. 3:17; 17:5), the ministry of angels after Christ's temptation (4:11), and the Father's speech after the triumphal entry in response to Jesus's prayer that the Father glorify his name (John 12:27–29).[106] Fifth, as a man subject to God's law, Christ ought to have faith as a "part" of divine worship and a "necessary act of religion." Sixth, Christ faces things that oppose (and therefore presuppose) faith—particularly, external temptations in the wilderness and "spiritual desertions" in Gethsemane.[107] Voetius is aware of potential objections. He clarifies, for example, that Christ did not have faith in the way that sinful pilgrims needing reconciliation have faith. Christ exercised faith in a mode that did not require the presence of sin, the work of regeneration, or the hearing of the word of God for the beginning of faith. Christ was not weakened by doubt, but for the conservation of faith and for eliciting acts of faith, he did use ordinary and extraordinary means and supports.[108]

Turretin adamantly contends that Christ receives the beatific vision only when he is glorified. Like Ames, Turretin employs a distinction between "right" and "possession" to make his case. There is, Turretin maintains, a distinction between the "right to all paternal goods" that Christ as Son of God had from the very beginning of the incarnation and the "possession" of these, some of which Christ could "lack for a time by a voluntary dispensation." The anointing of the Spirit abides from the conception of Christ and supplies all that Christ needs for his mediatorial office, but the "acts of anointing" progress through "their own order and degree according to the economy of the divine will." The "Spirit of wisdom . . . holds back his own acts and does not immediately pour out his own rays most fully into the intellect of Christ."

---

106. Voetius, *Select. disp., pars sec.*, 2.8 (157–62, 164).

107. Voetius, *Select. disp., pars sec.*, 2.8 (157).

108. Voetius, *Select. disp., pars sec.*, 2.8 (156–58). Voetius notes the apparently contrary view of Polanus in *Syntagma*, 6.55 (496), but there Polanus denies that Christ was baptized *pro se* only because Christ was not "polluted by sins" and thus did not need to be cleansed.

The union of the human soul with the person of the Logos "implies indeed possession of beatitude, but not immediately approaching or constantly being enjoyed, because, from the dispensation of God, passion ought to precede glory and felicity."[109] Indeed, for Turretin, the state of glory and beatitude and the suffering Christ experienced on earth are incompatible, so Christ is not simultaneously *comprehensor* and *viator* but rather *viator* and then *comprehensor* from his exaltation onward.[110] Thus, Christ could truly grow in human knowledge, and, in his human intellect, he did not know the exact time of his return. This follows from his being like us in everything except sin. And it does not create a logical problem, for contradictory propositions (i.e., that Christ knows something and Christ does not know something) can both be true in different respects (κατ᾽ ἄλλο καὶ ἄλλο), where the different respects in which they are affirmed have ontological bases (i.e., a divine and human nature) that are really distinct (not just formally distinct, like genus and species).[111]

Like Voetius, Turretin argues that several scriptural texts explicitly ascribe faith (or faithfulness) and hope to Christ (Acts 2:26; Heb. 2:17; 3:2) and imply faith in Christ where Christ calls the Father his God (e.g., Matt. 27:46). Yet faith is not applied to Christ as though he were a sinner in need of mercy. Nor is faith predicated of Christ "by reason of the mode of knowledge," as though there were an obscurity in Christ's human knowledge of God. For there is no imperfection in Christ's faith. Instead, a perfect faith with certitude is predicated of Christ "with respect to the substance of knowledge and with respect to assent to the thing known, that is, doctrine revealed by God, and with respect to the trust which rests in the goodness of God providing all things necessary for us." With this faith, Christ trusts and anticipates from the Father the full beatitude that awaits him after his resurrection (so Heb. 12:2).[112]

(3) With these historical considerations in view, what should be said about Christ's knowledge and faith during his earthly obedience? Given that some of the early Reformed affirm a beatific vision of Christ on earth while some

109. Turretin, *Inst.*, 13.13.2, 9, 14–16 (2:379, 381–83). Here Turretin says that Christ's seeing the Father in John 6:46 pertains not to his human nature "absolutely" (*praecise*) but rather to the person of the Logos, which has always been united to the Father and cannot fail to enjoy the beatific sight of him.

110. Turretin, *Inst.*, 13.13.12–13 (2:382). Turretin opines that the *Pontificii* wish to have Christ as simultaneously *comprehensor* and *viator* in order to claim that Christ's soul was not truly subject to spiritual suffering, but, in light of the material covered in this section, that charge should not be leveled against authors like Lombard, Bonaventure, and Aquinas.

111. Turretin, *Inst.*, 13.4–8 (2:380–81). Turretin's account also supplies interpretations of texts like Matt. 11:27, John 21:17, and Col. 2:3.

112. Turretin, *Inst.*, 13.12.5–8 (2:378).

recent Roman Catholics have questioned it (e.g., O'Collins and Weinandy), this is not an issue that can be settled simply by vague appeal to distinctive principles of Protestantism or Roman Catholicism. One must ultimately ask which view best expresses the concrete teaching of Holy Scripture. It seems to me that there are good reasons to affirm that Christ exercised faith before his exaltation and that the book of Hebrews in particular impresses upon us that this faith is ingredient in the Son's association with us human beings. However, the contrary statements and the cautions of eminent patristic, medieval, and early Reformed authors have to be taken seriously, especially in a contemporary context where theologians are often tempted to emphasize Jesus's solidarity with fallen human beings at the expense of his distinction from us—a distinction by virtue of which he can save us from our sin and misery.

On the one hand, then, before explicating the claim that Christ exercised faith on earth, it will be wise to take into account the importance of his unique human knowledge of God. In particular, the gifts of the Spirit attested in a text like Isaiah 11:1–5 should occupy a significant place in our Christology. Though the New Testament gives little information about Jesus's childhood, Luke's Gospel does bear witness to Jesus's wisdom from an early age. The boy miraculously conceived by the Spirit of God "grew and became strong, being filled with wisdom, and the grace of God was upon him" (Luke 2:40). At the age of twelve Jesus stayed in Jerusalem after his parents had left the Passover feast. He amazed the teachers there with his understanding (2:47). When asked why he remained behind, Jesus simply responded, "Why were you seeking me? Did you not know that it is necessary for me to be in the things of my Father [or "in my Father's house"]?" (2:49). Evidently, Jesus was aware of his filial identity and his divine appointment to a particular task ("It is necessary . . .") even prior to his baptism in the Jordan. Jesus's "sense of mission expresses itself early on."[113] From a negative angle, the Gospels do not present us with a Jesus who is unsure about his identity and mission or merely conjecturing about what he must do.[114] In light of what Scripture teaches about the intellectual gifts of the Spirit and about Jesus's wisdom at an early age, I take it that the infused knowledge of Christ secures his

113. Bock, *Jesus according to Scripture*, 75. While sonship in Luke can pertain to matters other than *eternal* or *divine* sonship, the cumulative teaching of Luke and the other Synoptic Gospels shows that sonship language in Jesus's case ultimately signifies a relationship to the Father that transcends something like messiahship alone (so, e.g., Gathercole, *The Pre-existent Son*, 272–83).

114. This is contrary to N. T. Wright's unfounded assertion that while Jesus "believed himself called to do and to be things which . . . only Israel's God, YHWH, was to do and be," he operated "with the knowledge that he could be making a terrible, lunatic mistake" ("Jesus' Self-Understanding," 59).

understanding of his filial identity and mission. Communicated immediately by the Spirit, this infused knowledge equips Christ with a certitude required to fulfill his office and reveal the Father, even if Christ in his human intellect does not directly see the divine essence throughout his earthly life.

Of course, Luke adds that Jesus still "advanced" in wisdom (2:52). It is true, as Lombard, Aquinas, and Polanus all point out, that Jesus advanced in the outward display of his gifts. As he progressed in age, he manifested his divine identity and spiritual gifts more fully. Yet it also seems, in accordance with Ambrose, that Christ's advancement in wisdom in Luke 2:52 corresponds to his own subjective advancement in age. In light of this, Bonaventure and Aquinas rightly affirm that Christ advanced in "acquired" or "experiential" knowledge, not least with respect to human suffering. Yet authors like Zanchi, Ames, and Turretin gesture toward some ways in which one might say that Christ advanced with regard to the infused knowledge as well: not with respect to its habits but with respect to its acts (Zanchi); not "intensively" or with respect to the "first act" (habit) but "extensively" and with respect to the "second act" (exercise) and "degree" (Ames); not with respect to the anointing of the Spirit per se but with respect to the subsequent outworking of the anointing and added degrees of knowledge (Turretin). I take these distinctions to be potentially fruitful, though it has to be admitted at some point that there are serious limits to our reasoning about the human intellect of the incarnate Son. Perhaps it is sufficient to say that the Son received at conception the intellectual habits from the Spirit and then, under the Spirit's constant presence and movement in his soul, exercised the habits over time in a greater degree or depth in correspondence with the growth of his human faculties and ratiocination.

On the other hand, it seems difficult to avoid the conclusion that Jesus in his human intellect truly did not know the hour of his return. In particular, given that the Father knows but does not reveal the hour, it is difficult to take Jesus not knowing in Mark 13:32 to be a matter of not revealing.[115] Furthermore, if

---

115. Gaine (*Did the Saviour See the Father?*, 140–58) has offered an alternative approach to Mark 13:32, arguing that while Jesus in the beatific vision possessed human knowledge of the time of his return, he did not possess at that moment a conceptual, communicable knowledge of the time of his return and did not endeavor then to render the content of the beatific knowledge intelligible to his hearers. It seems to me that one's broader exegetical conclusions about the person of Jesus will inform one's reading of Mark 13:32 and determine the manner in which one will need to qualify Jesus's ignorance and perhaps offer a reading like Gaine's. If one is committed to regarding Jesus as the omniscient God in the flesh, then one will of course clarify that Jesus according to his divinity is never ignorant of anything. But if one does not conclude from reading the canon of Scripture that Jesus according to his human intellect must have had the beatific vision before his resurrection, then one will not sense a need to reason that Jesus in his beatific knowledge is never ignorant but simply waits until the right time to communicate

the infused knowledge of Christ secures his fitness for his mediatorial work, it seems unnecessary to posit a beatific vision during his earthly life.[116] With Bonaventure, Aquinas, and many others, it is important to affirm that the human nature's union with the person of the Word does lead to the human nature receiving the gifts of the Spirit, including intellectual gifts. But Ames and Turretin, in my judgment, helpfully make the point that the "right" to the gifts does not mean there can be no development with regard to the "possession" of the gifts.[117] To be sure, as authors like Aquinas and Zanchi observe, Christ can give only what he has, and he is appointed to give us the glory

his human knowledge to others. Because I do not share the conclusion that Jesus in his human intellect must have had the beatific vision before his resurrection, I do not sense the need to follow Gaine's reading—though, if Jesus did have the beatific vision before his resurrection, it would be a viable reading of the text. Furthermore, though Gaine operates with a distinction between Agnoetism and orthodox affirmations of Jesus's human knowledge of the time of his return, a Reformed author like Turretin emphasizes that the claims of the Agnoetes ("who attributed ignorance to the Word, or to Christ as God") are different from the claims of Reformed authors who attribute a negative ignorance to Christ as man (*Inst.*, 13.13.11 [2:382]). Treatments of the Agnoetes in the context of monophysite Christologies of the sixth century can be found in Wickham, "The Ignorance of Christ"; Van Roey and Allen, *Monophysite Texts of the Sixth Century*. Whether Turretin had a full grasp of the teaching of the Agnoetes or not, I take it that the statements of authors like Athanasius, Gregory Nazianzen, and Cyril of Alexandria (see the notes above), together with the monophysite context that shaped the debates about Agnoetism, entail that it is well within the bounds of a two-natures, catholic Christology to conclude that Jesus in his human intellect did not know the hour of his return in Mark 13:32.

116. In addition, I do not think that a text like John 6:46, according to which only the Son has seen the Father, teaches that Jesus *as man* intuits the divine essence during his earthly ministry. It is reasonable to conclude that the seeing concerns Jesus *as God* and in his eternal procession from the Father. This divine seeing, together with the Spirit's operation on Jesus as man, would guide the human nature and intellect as the instrument of the divine Son and a medium of divine revelation, but that does not necessarily entail that Jesus in his human intellect has the beatific vision before his exaltation.

117. This point can be reinforced by the observations of Bonaventure (*In Sent.* 3.14.1.1 [297–98]) and Aquinas (*Quaestiones disputatae de veritate* 26.8 ad 10 [778]; 10 ad 8 [786]; Aquinas, *ST* IIIa.9.1 [138–39]; 9.2 ad 1–3 [141]; 10.4 ad 1 [155]) that the union of the human nature with the Logos by itself does not automatically entail the beatific vision. That is, the union of the human nature with the divine does not obviate the need for the human intellect to have its own proper light by which it possesses knowledge, beatific or otherwise. For while the human nature is directly united with the person of the Logos, the integrity of the human nature remains, so that the faculty of the intellect is not replaced by the divine knowledge or light of the Logos. This means that for Christ as man to have the immediate vision of the divine essence will require the light of glory, which is, for Aquinas and others, a supernaturally given elevation of the natural intellect. Though the beatific vision is immediate in the sense that the human intellect does not apprehend God by knowing something else as a medium in which to see God, the beatific vision still requires the light of glory as a facultative medium by which to see God (see Aquinas, *Super Sent.* 3.14.1 sol. 3 and ad 1–3; Aquinas, *ST* Ia.12.5 [123]; Turretin, *Inst.*, 20.8.8, 12–14 [3:682–84]; cf. Legge, *The Trinitarian Christology of St Thomas Aquinas*, 175, 177). All of this can be connected back to the point made by Owen that the only "necessary consequent" of the assumption of the flesh is the union itself of the flesh with the

of the beatific vision. But that does not require that Christ have the beatific vision from conception onward. It requires only that he obtain the beatific vision, along with knowledge of the time of his return, when he is raised and exalted.[118] After all, he is appointed to procure the resurrection of the body too (e.g., 1 Cor. 15:20; Phil. 3:20–21; Col. 1:18), but he himself obtains the resurrection body only after his passion.

Furthermore, while I am not quite convinced that Christ is fittingly called a *comprehensor* and *viator* at the same time,[119] the more decisive point seems to be that sight and faith are mutually exclusive (so, e.g., 2 Cor. 5:7; Heb. 11:1), and Christ had the latter prior to his exaltation. More specifically, as Voetius noted, Christ's vicarious obedience includes his exercise of faith. After Adam and Eve failed to trust in the goodness and provision of God (Gen. 3:1–7), and after Israel failed to trust the promises of God in the wilderness (Num. 14:11; Deut. 1:32; 9:23; Pss. 78:22, 32; 106:24), the second Adam and true Israel came to deliver us by fulfilling all righteousness, passing through the testing of the wilderness (so Matt. 3:13–4:11) and living by faith until he was vindicated and exalted to the Father's right hand. In addition to this broader biblical theme, there are a few texts that apply the language of faith to Christ more directly. For example, the evangelists apply Psalm 22:8 to Christ on the cross. In the Psalm, those who despise David mock him: "He trusts [LXX 21:8: "hopes"] in YHWH. Let him deliver him." Matthew then records the Jewish leaders mocking Jesus: "He trusts [πέποιθεν] in God. Let him save him now, if he wills" (27:43). Jesus himself and the evangelists confirm the applicability of Psalm 22, particularly where he utters the cry of dereliction and his clothes are divided by the soldiers (Matt. 27:46; Mark 15:34; John 19:24). The same verb (πείθω) is applied to Jesus in Hebrews 2:13. Jesus's speech in Hebrews

---

Son (*Pneumatologia*, 2.3 [3:160–61]). The additional consequents of the assumption are then wrought by the Spirit to render the Son as man fit for his mediatorial office.

118. To the extent that the beatific vision entails seeing in God all that he has planned, I think Zanchi and Polanus arguably have a logical problem in their argument that Christ had the beatific vision on earth without knowing the hour of his return.

119. It is not illogical to say that Christ is a *comprehensor* in certain respects and a *viator* in other respects, especially when the distinction is anchored in the soul of Christ having distinct "parts" or "powers." On this, see Aquinas's argument for the coherence of the beatific vision of Christ and the passibility of Christ's soul, where he invokes the distinction between the "higher" and "lower" parts of Christ's soul to locate enjoyment of God, on the one hand, and passion and sorrow, on the other (*ST* IIIa.46.7–8 [444–47]; see also Gaine, *Did the Saviour See the Father?*, 179–201). Aquinas asserts that the "overflow" (*redundantia*) of the beatitude of the higher part into the lower part does not automatically occur in Christ's earthly life. By divine omnipotence the beatitude is kept from "overflowing" (*ST* IIIa.15.5 ad 3 [191]; 15.6 corp. [191–92]). This avoids the logical problem, but, in my judgment, if a beatific vision *in via* is not soteriologically necessary, there may be grounds for questioning the fittingness of a beatific vision whose influence is contained in just one part of the human person.

2:13 echoes Isaiah 8:17–18, where the prophet awaits YHWH while YHWH hides his face from Jacob: "I will trust [ἔσομαι πεποιθὼς] in him."

To be fair, it is not as though a text like Hebrews 2:13 is overlooked by advocates of Christ's beatific vision on earth. As a prolific biblical commentator, Aquinas treats this passage in connection with the beatific vision. In his rendering of the text (*ego ero fidens in eum*; literally, "I will be trusting in him"), Aquinas exegetes the text by discussing Christ's "hope" (*spes*). Christ does not have just any "hope" but a "firm" hope that is "without fear," which is called *fiducia*. Christ has this *fiducia* in the help of the Father for "the glory of the body which he will raise again, both the members and the soul." However, Aquinas notes, some will question the applicability of *spes* and *fiducia* in the case of Christ. In response, Aquinas remarks that *spes* and *fiducia* must be distinguished. The former is "the expectation of future beatitude," which was not in Christ because he has been "blessed from the instant of his own conception." The latter is "the expectation of some help," which was in Christ since he "expected from the Father help in the passion." Hence, when the text says that Christ has hope, "it is not to be understood by reason of the principal object, which is beatitude, but by reason of the glory of the resurrection, and the glories collated to the body."[120]

Aquinas is certainly right to emphasize the firmness of Christ's confidence in the Father. However, if the infused knowledge of Christ sufficiently equipped him with a certitude about his identity and office, and if Christ's reception of the beatific vision upon his exaltation has enabled him to give the beatific vision to us, then there is no need to bring a prior commitment to a beatific vision of Christ *in via* to our exegesis of a text like Hebrews 2:13. In that case, it will be more fitting to take Christ's faith to be a confidence and rest in the Father's provision of future gifts that only anticipates the forthcoming sight of glory. For this aligns with the definition of faith in Hebrews 11:1 and with the fact that Jesus is the "pioneer" of this faith in Hebrews 12:2.[121]

To be clear, the presence of this faith does not entail that Christ merely held an opinion about his divine identity and mission or that he merely hoped someday to be sure about those matters. The infused knowledge communicated by the Spirit provided Christ a sure grasp of his identity and mission.[122]

120. Aquinas, *Super Heb.* 2.3.133–35 (366). In keeping with his reluctance to attribute faith to Christ, Aquinas takes Christ to be the *auctor fidei* and *consummatio fidei* ("author and consummation of faith") in the sense that Christ teaches the word and impresses it upon the heart and also confirms and rewards faith (*Super Heb.* 12.1.664 [482]).

121. See the discussion in the previous section on the meaning of ἀρχηγός ("founder" or "pioneer"), esp. n. 34.

122. White's account (*Incarnate Lord*, 236–74) aptly presses us to affirm the certainty of Christ's knowledge of his own identity in order to uphold the genuineness of his revelation of

On the one hand, attempts to establish the firmness of Christ's knowledge by positing a middle way between the beatific vision and the exercise of faith are open to objections.[123] Yet, on the other hand, the affirmation that Christ exercised faith need not jeopardize his certainty about his identity, mission, and teaching. In some ways his knowledge of these matters is profoundly dissimilar to the saints' common knowledge of them, a point that, I think, can be clarified by commenting on the subject, the mode, and the object of Christ's knowledge and faith.[124]

First, the subject is the Son of God according to his human nature, intellect, and will, who was sanctified from the moment of conception and filled with the Spirit beyond measure so that his understanding was never clouded by the sinful habits of mind and will against which even regenerate sinners must fight in the life of faith. Second, while Christ's mode of knowing bore a certain similarity to the supernatural theology and faith of the saints, it was also quite different. Insofar as Christ's infused knowledge did not include a direct seeing of the divine essence, it involved the use of created effects to understand divine things.[125] In this particular way it was indirect like the supernatural theology and faith common to the saints. Yet that infused knowledge did not depend on the witness of another human person (e.g., an apostle or a prophet) but came immediately from the Spirit. Thus, the infused knowledge was a direct knowledge relative to the supernatural theology and faith common to the saints and exceeded the certainty of that common theology and faith.[126] Furthermore, since Jesus received the Spirit without measure, his human cognition was always established and kept from error by the Spirit's inward movement so that his infused knowledge exceeded even the light of the prophets, who

---

the Father throughout his earthly ministry. My intention here is to argue that one can confirm that certainty and thus the genuineness of Jesus's revelation of the Father without positing a beatific vision of Christ *in via*. Gaine (*Did the Saviour See the Father?*, 159–78) also stresses the importance of Christ's unwavering determination to do the Father's will. I agree that worries about an abstract criterion of human free choice should not drive the discussion here, and I will make a case below that Jesus was unable to turn aside from the Father's will.

123. See the helpful discussion in Gaine, *Did the Saviour See the Father?*, 117–27.

124. I am presupposing that knowledge—*cognitio*, if not *intellectus* or *scientia* in the strictest Aristotelian sense—can be had by faith and that faith, in turn, is a kind of knowledge (cf., e.g., Aquinas, *SCG* 1.4 [11]; Aquinas, *ST* IIaIIae.4.8 ad 3 [53]; Polanus, *Syntagma*, 2.9 [144]; Turretin, *Inst.*, 1.6.2–3 [1:20–21]).

125. This does not mean that Christ observed created effects and haphazardly guessed what God might be like. The point is just that if Christ in his human intellect does not see the divine essence directly *in via*, then the human intellect with the infused knowledge must somehow draw upon an awareness of common wisdom or power, for example, in order to grasp the meaning of God's unique wisdom or power.

126. See Aquinas on the certainty of Christ's infused knowledge exceeding even that of angelic knowledge (*ST* IIIa.11.4 corp. [162]).

were only intermittently under the Spirit's supernatural guidance.[127] In light of the unique subject and mode of knowing involved and in light of Christ's filial reverence and love (Isa. 11:2; John 4:34; Heb. 5:7), Christ's faith did not entail a wavering on his part regarding the Father's provision. He set his face like flint to do the Father's will, confident that the Father would vindicate and glorify him (Isa. 50:7–11; Luke 9:51; John 12:27; Heb. 12:2).

Third, the object of Christ's faith has to be set forth carefully. Christ's divine identity, origin, and mediatorial office were included in the objects of Christ's infused knowledge. And as objects of the infused knowledge, they were presumably known by reference to created effects that would facilitate understanding of divine things. And yet these matters were present realities during Jesus's earthly life, which discourages identifying them as an object of faith. Matters that did lie in the future were Christ's beatific sight of the divine essence and the fulfillment of various other promises from the Father (e.g., his bodily resurrection, his royal outpouring of the Spirit as the Davidic ruler at Pentecost). These things most properly constitute the object of Christ's faith. And by the Spirit's infusion of habitual knowledge and faith and the Spirit's constant help throughout his life, Christ's faith in such promises always remained firm.[128]

After clarifying what Christ's faith did and did not involve, it is important to recall that he did have fear and anxiety in the face of trials and suffering. Perhaps this is a point where Voetius's discussion of Christ's use of signs and means of divine grace might play some role in our Christology. For example, when Christ completes his time of temptation in the wilderness and angels come and minister to him (Matt. 4:11), there are no crowds around him to benefit from this confirmation of Christ's identity. Presumably, he is the one

127. See Aquinas, *Super Ioann.* 3.6.4.541 (102); 14.4.3.1915 (359). On Christ knowing all that has ever been revealed to or prophesied by human beings, see Aquinas, *ST* IIIa.7.8 ad 1 (115–16); 11.1 corp. (157). Of course, Aquinas clarifies that he thinks Christ always has the beatific vision that is greater than any prophetic knowledge (e.g., *Super Ioann.* 4.6.2.667 [126]; 6.6.1.868 [164]).

128. In this connection, I would argue that direct perception or intuitive knowledge, though greater in clarity than faith, is not the only knowledge attended by certainty. This point might be developed by considering arguments from Aquinas and Reformed orthodox authors who contend that faith's knowledge of God, which draws upon created similitudes, exceeds the certainty of ordinary human sciences at least with respect to its cause (i.e., divine revelation) (see Aquinas, *ST* IIaIIae.4.8 [52–53]; Polanus, *Syntagma*, 2.18 [156]; Turretin, *Inst.*, 15.8.6 [2:613]). Cf. also Turretin's discussions of the distinction between a "habit of opining" and the "habit of believing" and the distinction between metaphysical and theological certainty (*Inst.*, 1.6.2–3 [1:20–21]; 2.4.22 [1:76–77]). In fact, Aquinas reasons, faith is subject to uncertainty and doubt not on the part of its cause but only *quoad nos* since we fail to adhere fully to the things believed (*ST* IIaIIae.4.8 ad 2 [53]). If that is so, then the faith of the Son of God disposed by the Spirit always to rest in the Father's love and provision would be attended by the certainty he needed to fulfill his mission.

who is helped and encouraged by the angels' ministry. Likewise, Christ is strengthened through prayer in Gethsemane. Though Christ is undeterred in his faith in the Father's promises, his soul is in some sense strengthened by such divinely ordained means. Considering the sense in which Christ might be both unshaken in his determination to do the Father's will and also subject to real mental infirmity leads us to the next point.

(4) In what way did Christ stand firm in faith while also experiencing sorrow and dread and even asking the Father to remove the cup of suffering? A number of insights in catholic Christology can help us to understand the Bible's portrayal of Christ's steadfastness and his genuine experience of the sorrow and dread on account of which he needed the comfort of the Father and Spirit. First, various authors call attention to the fact that in the incarnation the Son of God assumed the defects or infirmities of our human nature (cf. Ps. 88:3; Isa. 53:4, 11; Matt. 26:37–38; John 12:27). Ambrose writes, "[Christ] assumes my will, he assumes my sadness. Confidently I call it 'sadness,' for I preach the cross. . . . For me he suffers, for me he is sad, for me he is grieved. Therefore, for me and in me he has grieved, who for himself has had nothing that he should grieve."[129] As the sovereign God, the Son did not have to take up a human nature, much less these defects, so his bearing our infirmities was emphatically free.[130] But, under the decision to take up a human nature in which he would suffer for our sin and lead us to glory, the Son had to take up a nature with these defects. While the Son did not have in himself any cause of incurring such defects, since he came "in the likeness of sinful flesh" (Rom. 8:3) he still took up weaknesses consequent to the human race's fall into sin. In short, while he did not assume *defectus culpae* (defects rooted in one's own guilt), he still assumed *defectus poenae* (defects resulting from punishment common to the human race).[131] Thus, the Son did not assume a mere image

---

129. Ambrose, *De fide* 2.7.53 (2:284).

130. Lombard writes that Christ has "assumed these defects not by necessity of his own condition, but by a will of pity" (*Sent.* 3.15.1 [95]). As Aquinas puts it, Christ did not "contract" these defects, as though he should have in himself the cause of infirmity and death (i.e., sin) (*Super Matt.* 26.5.2226 [343]; Aquinas, *ST* IIIa.14.3 [182]; cf. 15.5 ad 2 [190–91]). See also Owen, *Hebrews*, 4:511–12. Hilary of Poitiers famously appears to minimize Christ's defects and suffering (e.g., *La Trinité* 10.23–41, 63 [3:206–36, 274]), though he does state that Christ had a "cause of sorrow" and "participation [*consortium*] of human anxiety in himself" concerning the welfare of his disciples, who would face trials (10.37 [3:228, 230]). Medieval authors often argue that Hilary's cautious statements are meant to deny only that Christ *necessarily* took up infirmities and underwent suffering, or that Christ had in himself a cause that merited the imposition of suffering (see, e.g., Lombard, *Sent.* 3.15.1, 2–4 [98, 100–103]; Aquinas, *Super Matt.* 26.5.2225 [343]; Aquinas, *ST* IIIa.15.5 ad 1 [190]; 15.7 ad 2 [193]).

131. Lombard, *Sent.* 3.15.1 (93, 95). Cf. Aquinas, *Compendium theologiae* 1.226 (176–78); Aquinas, *ST* IIIa.15.6 ad 3 (192). Aquinas also phrases the distinction as *malum culpae* versus *malum poenae*. Often the *defectus poenae* are called "natural" or "innocent" (see John of

or likeness of human passion and grief. He bore these infirmities in order to prove the truth of his humanity, to satisfy the justice of God by suffering in our place, and to set an example of patient endurance for us.[132]

These were defects or infirmities of both body and soul. Christ experienced not only bodily fatigue, hunger, and cold, for example, but also sorrow, fear, anxiety, anguish, and grief (tristia, timor, anxietas, angor, dolor).[133] He sensed and was affected in his soul by the pains of the body.[134] He also was affected in his soul by pains or griefs proper to the soul itself. He apprehended by his rational judgment the evils and afflictions set before him (and before others too) and abhorred those evils and afflictions by his human will, so that he was affected by sorrow, fear, and anxiety over present and future things that he had to face, including bodily harm and the eventual separation of the soul from the body at death.[135] He apprehended and abhorred things that were harmful or detestable not just with respect to the body but also with respect to the soul itself, like the sin and spiritual misery of the human race, the abandonment of his friends, or the loss of a good reputation through slander and mockery.[136]

There is some debate in the Christian tradition about whether Christ's mental and spiritual affliction affected not only the "lower reason" (ratio

Damascus, Expos. fidei 3.20 [162–63]; Aquinas, ST IIIa.14.4 corp. [183]). Polanus, for example, specifies that the defectus inculpabiles of Christ are "natural" or common to the human race rather than "non-natural" or "personal" (i.e., proper to the individual on account of some peculiar deformity or peculiar judgment of God) (Syntagma, 6.15 [370]).

132. See, e.g., John of Damascus, Expos. fidei 3.20 (162–63); Lombard, Sent. 3.15.1 (95–96); Aquinas, ST IIIa.14.1 (179–80); 15.1 (185–86); Polanus, Syntagma, 6.15 (370, 372); Voetius, Select. disp., pars sec., 2.9 (165–66, 187).

133. For different delineations of the mental, spiritual infirmities, see, e.g., John of Damascus, Expos. fidei 3.20, 23 (162, 165–66); Lombard, Sent. 3.15.1 (93); Aquinas, ST IIIa.15.5–7, 9 (190–93, 195); Turretin, Inst., 13.14.4 (2:384). Ambrose also says Christ as man "doubts" (Ut homo ergo dubitat, ut homo turbatur) (De fide 2.5.42–43 [276, 278]; 7.56 [286]). Uneasy with this language, Lombard suggests that Christ did not doubt so much as he "has borne the way of doubting" (Sent. 3.17.3 [110]). In my view, it is best to clarify that Christ had fear and anxiety but never uncertainty.

134. On the soul (not merely the body) performing the act of sensing by means of the organs of the body, see, e.g., Aquinas, ST Ia.78.3–4 (253–57); IIIa.15.4 corp. (189); 15.5 corp. (190).

135. Cf. Aquinas, Super Matt. 26.5.2225 (343); Aquinas, ST IIIa.15.4, 6–7 (189, 191–93). To clarify our thinking, it may be useful to observe that suffering or grief involves at least (a) the presence (or at least the possible, forthcoming, or imagined presence) of something evil and harmful to be endured, (b) apprehension of that thing as evil, and (c) the will's abhorrence of that thing as evil. Cf. John of Damascus, Expos. fidei 2.22 (88), and Aquinas's comments that dolor requires both the presence of evil or harm and a sense that this harm is joined to oneself (ST IaIIae.35.1 [240]; IIIa.15.5 corp. [190]).

136. See Aquinas, ST IIIa.46.5 corp. (441); 46.6 corp. and ad 4 (443–44). Aquinas thus speaks of the magnitude of not only Christ's dolor sensibilis but also Christ's dolor interior. I take this to be an important counterbalance to Aquinas's statements to the effect that the soul is affected with pain through the body (e.g., ST IIIa.46.8 ad 1 [447]).

inferior) of his soul but also the "higher reason" (*ratio superior*) of his soul.[137]
Did Christ endure things repugnant or disruptive not only to the well-being
or fulfillment of the *ratio inferior* but also to the well-being or fulfillment of
the *ratio superior*? If one is convinced that Christ possessed the beatific vision during his earthly sojourn, then one would logically deny that this was
the case.[138] If, however, one holds that Christ did not have the beatific vision
until his exaltation, then one may affirm that he did endure things repugnant
to the fulfillment of the *ratio superior*.

Some of the early Reformed authors (rightly, I think) affirm that when Christ
endured the wrath of God on the cross, it did affect the higher operation of
his soul.[139] He bore our sin and guilt as our covenant sponsor, becoming a
curse for us and facing the just judgment of God (Isa. 53:5–6; 2 Cor. 5:21;
Gal. 3:13; 1 Pet. 2:24). In order to atone fully for our sin, Christ was affected
in his "higher" mental and spiritual operation by *poenae infernales* ("hellish
punishments"): a *poena damni* (a privative "penalty of loss") and a *poena
sensus* (a positive "penalty of sense"). With respect to the *poena damni*, Christ
emphatically did *not* endure a deprivation of the Father's love or favor itself
(an *amissio* or *privatio realis*) (see John 10:17), but he did endure at least at
certain moments a deprivation of his active sense of the Father's love and favor

137. The distinction between *ratio inferior* and *ratio superior* is not a distinction between
two intellects or two sets of faculties but rather a distinction between two "offices" of human
reason. *Ratio inferior* signifies human reason in its consideration of temporal, lower matters,
and *ratio superior* signifies human reason in its contemplation of eternal, higher things (see
Augustine, *De trin.* 12.4.4 [1:358]; Aquinas, *ST* Ia.79.9 [275–76]).

138. See Aquinas, *ST* IIIa.46.7–8 (444–47). Aquinas argues that the subject of Christ's higher
reason (the soul) was affected by the things he endured, but he does not hold that the higher
reason as a distinct power was affected by those things.

139. See, e.g., Voetius, *Select. disp., pars sec.*, 2.9 (166–67); Turretin, *Inst.*, 13.14.3–4 (2:384),
where both authors take issue with the views of certain *Pontificii* who restrict the suffering of
Christ to his body or to the sensitive part of his soul. See, e.g., Bellarmine's polemic against
Calvin's view that Christ descended to the dead in the sense that he perceived the wrath of
God directed toward him on the cross (*Disp.*, 1.2.4.8 [526–36]). Against Bellarmine, see Ames,
Bellarminus enervatus, 2.2 (86–95). However, it is important to bear in mind that an earlier
author like Aquinas does not restrict the suffering of Christ's soul in this way. As noted above,
he acknowledges a suffering of the soul that concerns not just the *dolor sensibilis* of the "sensitive part" of the soul but also the *dolor interior* of the intellectual or rational part of the soul
regarding matters like human sin, the abandonment of friends, and so forth. For some of the
anthropological background, see Aquinas on the senses in which passion can pertain to the soul
(*ST* IaIIae.22.1 [168]; 22.3 [171]; 41.1 [272]). Indeed, Aquinas affirms that inward grief is more
potent than outward, sensible grief and that Christ had a greater capacity for grief than all
others (*ST* IaIIae.35.7 [246–47]; IIIa.46.6 [442–44]; cf. Owen, *Hebrews*, 3:485). For an excellent
treatment of Christ's beatific vision in connection with his suffering on the cross, see White,
Incarnate Lord, chap. 7. Where Reformed authors like Voetius and Turretin would disagree with
Aquinas is the point at which Aquinas, in light of his view of Christ's beatific vision, denies a
suffering of the soul in *the higher function* of the rational part (i.e., in the contemplation of God).

and of the joy and consolation following on that sense. With respect to the *poena sensus*, Christ apprehended the wrath of God directed toward him in his representation of sinners whose guilt was imputed to him. That apprehension of God in his severe wrath disturbed or suspended the joy of Christ's soul and induced in him the sort of grief to which we ourselves had become liable.[140]

Nevertheless, Christ remained steadfast in his faith and hope in the Father's provision while being affected by such sorrow and distress.[141] He knew in his human intellect that he remained the beloved Son of the Father. He knew that he was making satisfaction for our sin and not being eternally damned (Ps. 16:10–11), but he did lack at certain points the active sense and enjoyment of the Father's delight in him as the obedient Son. According to Voetius's disputation on the "agony and desertion of Christ," the Savior always had a habitual apprehension of the Father as his deliverer, which sustained his trust in the Father, but by another mental act he also apprehended the Father as the judge of the sin and guilt he bore for us, which yielded sorrow and anguish.[142] Thus, the cry of dereliction occurs "according to the flesh" and expresses Christ bearing the sins of others. Ambrose paraphrases Christ's words: "Because I have taken up alien sins, I have also taken up the words of alien sins."[143] As Christ himself faces the *poenae infernales* and endures a

---

140. Ames, *Bellarminus enervatus*, 2.2 (87–88, 91); Voetius, *Select. disp., pars sec.*, 2.9 (166–67); Turretin, *Inst.*, 13.14.5–7, 12, 14–15 (2:384–87); 16.9–10 (2:396); Owen, *Hebrews*, 4:504, 506–8, 510–11, 518, 528–29. Owen also notes that at a basic level only the divine *hypostasis* had to be communicated to the human nature in the incarnation, so the incarnation still allowed for a temporary suspension of the "comforting influences" of God (*Hebrews*, 4:507). In addition, the suffering of this kind of punishment is what makes sense of the magnitude of Christ's sorrow and fear (e.g., Owen, *Hebrews*, 4:503–4, 518). According to the Heidelberg Catechism, this promotes assurance of salvation in believers (see Heidelberg Catechism, Q. 44 [779]).

141. On Christ never despairing, see Ames, *Bellarminus enervatus*, 2.2 (89–90), where he argues that "despair is not of the essence of infernal punishment. The author of the punishment is God; the devil and the sinner is the author of despair." Again, "despair does not properly respect the punishment itself, but the continuation of it to eternity."

142. Voetius, *Select. disp., pars sec.*, 2.9 (168–70, 185–86); cf. Turretin, *Inst.*, 13.14.14 (2:386–87). Voetius's disputation argues that even if the soul of Christ could not be simultaneously confident and anxious in act, Christ would habitually trust in the Father's love and deliverance in the midst of active anxiety. A moment of active anxiety would not cause a "privative" infidelity, doubt, or despair. The habit of trust remains. There is only a temporary cessation of the act of trust (a *non-cogitatio* or *cessatio actus*) (*Select. disp., pars sec.*, 2.9 [170]).

143. Ambrose, *De incarnationis dominicae sacramento* 5,38 (242). For a somewhat different interpretation, see John of Damascus, *Expos. fidei* 3.24 (168); 4.18 (215–16), where he writes that while Christ was never disobedient to the Father, "assuming our person and arraying himself with us" (τὸ ἡμέτερον . . . οἰκειούμενος πρόσωπον καὶ μεθ' ἡμῶν τάσσων ἑαυτὸν) he speaks these things. Aquinas goes further in his Matthew commentary and states that the dereliction concerns Jesus himself being exposed to passion (*Super Matt.* 27.2.2383 [366]). Yet, drawing from John of Damascus and Augustine, Aquinas also notes that something like dereliction is predicated of Jesus by his having a certain "personal and habitudinal property" whereby what

suspension of his active enjoyment of the Father's delight and an apprehension of God's heavy wrath, he speaks "in his own person and about himself as our sponsor."[144]

Third, in order to grasp the sense in which Christ stood firm in his determination to do the Father's will while also having mental infirmities like sorrow, fear, and anxiety, it is important to consider the different ways in which he willed (or did not will) various things. Human volition includes at least (a) willing certain things as ends in themselves, (b) choosing certain things relative to certain ends under the deliberation and judgment of reason, and (c) having desires for things that concern the well-being of the body. The human will with respect to its act of desiring certain things as ends in themselves is sometimes called θέλησις, "natural will," "will as nature," or "simple will." The human will with respect to its act of choosing certain things relative to certain ends under rational deliberation and judgment is sometimes called βούλησις, "rational will," "will as reason," "conciliative will," or "deliberate will."[145] In addition, the will as the power of choosing or rational will is called the *liberum arbitrium* in Latin. It is a power or faculty involving both the rational intellect and the will since it involves both the judgment of reason about what is good and the will's consequent rational desire and determination to seek union with what is deemed good. The act of rational desire and determination about

applies to the members of his body is applied to him, so that he is speaking "in our person" in Ps. 22 and on the cross (*ST* IIIa.15.1 ad 1 [185–86]).

144. Voetius, *Select. disp., pars sec.*, 2.9 (185–86); cf. Ames, *Bellarminus enervatus*, 2.2 (93); Turretin, *Inst.*, 13.14.6, 14 (2:385–87). Voetius's joining of "in himself" and "as our sponsor" is helpful here. It expresses that Christ himself was affected by the *poenae infernales* and yet not as though he himself were guilty of sin but only as the innocent covenant head voluntarily bearing our guilt.

145. Aquinas, *ST* IIIa.18.3 (233). Aquinas also notes that what the natural will desires is what someone *would* will (*vellet*, imperfect subjunctive) if reason discerned no obstacles to it, so it can also be called *velleitas* (IIIa.21.4 corp. [254]). Put differently, while the natural will's desires can move the higher reason, they do not do so in an unqualified sense, for there is an important condition: *if* these desires do not conflict with the things that higher reason has to assess (Aquinas, *Super Matt.* 26.5.2231 [344]). Cf. Polanus, *Syntagma*, 6.15 (371). Of course, given that the human person is a rational creature, it is possible to speak broadly of the human will as "rational," but, beyond θέλησις or "will as nature," βούλησις or "will as reason" is "rational" in the stricter sense because it involves the counsel and judgment of the rational intellect. The "will as nature" can be called "absolute" or "simple" in that it is directed toward things as ends in themselves, without respect to considering things as good relative to certain ends (see Aquinas, *ST* IIIa.18.3 corp. [233]). Yet in another sense the "will as nature" or simple will is only a qualified (*secundum quid*) willing because, within the full context of human willing, it is subject to restriction by rational deliberation about potential obstacles and problems in pursuit of an end. In other words, what the simple will desires is not willed simply. In this connection, the "will as reason" is fittingly called the "absolute" will of the person because it reflects the settled judgment of reason (see *ST* IIIa.21.4 corp. [254]).

the way to obtain an end is called "choice" (*electio*).[146] Finally, the power of desiring things that concern the well-being of the body is sometimes called the "sensual" or "sensitive appetite" (*sensualitas*). It is, strictly speaking, located in the "sensitive power" of the soul and called "will" in only a participatory or extended sense, insofar as it is governed by the rational will's determination about seeking things that fulfill the desires of the body.[147]

As to the christological issues, Christ never faltered in his rational will (his rational judgment and determination) about either the end of his task (i.e., human salvation) or the means by which it would be accomplished (i.e., suffering and crucifixion). He did exercise "free choice" (*liberum arbitrium*) insofar as he desired and determined to do what his rational judgment had always deemed good, but his choosing was distinct from other human choosing insofar as he had no prior ignorance, uncertainty, or doubt about the good of his redemptive task and thus did not require counsel or deliberation.[148] Accordingly, Christ's rational will with respect to the end of his incarnation and even with respect to the painful means of suffering and crucifixion was always conformed to the divine will. At the same time, Christ did not will pain and death in his natural will (his will with respect to the power of desiring certain things as ends or goods in themselves) or in his sensitive appetite (his power of desiring things that concern the well-being of the body). Indeed, he naturally opposed and repudiated pain and death in his natural will and sensitive appetite.[149] While the end of his redemptive task (i.e., human salvation and the glory of God) was not at all repugnant to Christ's natural will or sensitive appetite, suffering and death were indeed repugnant to his natural will and sensitive appetite.[150] Thus, Christ as man

---

146. See Aquinas, *Sent. Ethic.* 3.5 (133–34); Aquinas, *ST* Ia.83.3–4 (310–12); IaIIae.13.1, 3 (98–101); IIIa.18.4 (234); cf. Mastricht, *TPT*, 2.15.5 (158). Significantly, "free will" is a translation of *liberum arbitrium* that appears to exclude the judgment of the rational intellect from the work of human choosing.

147. On the distinction between the apprehensive power of the intellect and the "appetitive" power of the will and the consequent distinction and connection between the "sensitive" and "intellective" appetites, see Aquinas, *ST* Ia.80.1–2 (282–84); 81.1 (288); IIIa.18.2 (232).

148. The absence of uncertainty and doubt on Christ's part is the reason that some have not predicated of Christ γνώμη (or a "gnomic will," roughly equivalent to *liberum arbitrium*) or προαίρεσις (roughly equivalent to *electio*) (see John of Damascus, *Expos. fidei* 3.14 [143–44]; for historical discussion, see Davidson, "'Not My Will but Yours Be Done'"; McFarland, "'Willing Is Not Choosing'"; Blowers, "Maximus the Confessor and John of Damascus"). However, Aquinas (*ST* IIIa.18.4 ad 1–2 [234]; cf. 34.2 [346–47]) points out that doubt and deliberation (unlike judgment) are not essential to free choice, so it is legitimate to say that Christ exercised a *liberum arbitrium* but without the doubt and deliberation typically ingredient in human choosing.

149. Lombard, *Sent.*, 3.17.2 (106–7); Aquinas, *ST* IIIa.14.2 (180–81); Ames, *Bellarminus enervatus*, 2.2 (92); Owen, *Hebrews*, 4:509.

150. Aquinas (*ST* IIIa.14.2 [180–81]) points out that while there was no coaction or compulsion in Christ's divine or human rational will, there was a certain coaction or compulsion in

in his natural will and sensitive appetite willed something other than the passion and death decreed by God.[151]

On the one hand, the desires of Christ's natural will and sensitive appetite did not, strictly speaking, contradict the divine will or his own human rational will. For Christ opposed and chose his passion and death for different reasons and in different capacities. Christ's natural and sensitive volition opposed pain and death as ends in themselves, and Christ's divine and human rational volition chose the pain and death not as ends in themselves but as means to a greater end. Likewise, since Christ was infallibly disposed to the fear of YHWH and to faithfulness by the grace of the Holy Spirit (Isa. 11:2, 5), his natural and sensitive repudiation of pain and death did not overwhelm or impede the determination of his divine and rational will. Moreover, the divine will and Christ's human rational will, while always governing the natural and sensitive will, permitted Christ's natural and sensitive displeasure in pain and death in accordance with the authenticity of his human nature.[152] On the other hand, then, it was granted to Christ as man genuinely to despise the suffering that had been decreed by God. The reality of the spiritual anguish of Christ discussed above is explained and corroborated by this natural and sensitive despising. For Christ was troubled that he had to face things that he naturally regarded as evil and despicable in themselves and that he naturally abhorred.[153]

Fourth, the fact that Christ was troubled and yet persevered in obedience to the Father is aptly set forth by employing a distinction between "passion" (*passio*) and "prepassion" (*propassio*). The language appears in Jerome's commentary on Matthew, for example, where Jesus "began to be sorrowful and distressed" (Matt. 26:37). Jerome observes that the Lord proves the truth of the humanity that he assumed by beginning to be sorrowful (*coepit contristari*). However, lest it be suggested that "*passio* should rule in his soul,"

Christ's natural and sensitive will with respect to his suffering and death. Thus, his suffering and death were "voluntary" as ordered to a greater end (our redemption) but "involuntary" considered as ends in themselves (*ST* IIIa.15.6 ad 4 [192]).

151. So Aquinas, *ST* IIIa.18.5 (235–36).

152. So Athanasius, *Oratio III*, 55,10–16 (366–67); John of Damascus, *Expos. fidei* 3.18 (157–60); Aquinas, *ST* IIIa.18.6 (236–37).

153. So John of Damascus, *Expos. fidei* 3.18, 23 (157–60, 165–66). In this connection, Lombard writes of Christ having a *duplex* or *geminus affectus*, one of reason and one of sensuality, the former willing death and the latter not willing it. Indeed, there is a *geminus affectus* of Christ according to his humanity and a *geminus affectus* in his members: "one of reason, informed by love, with which, on account of God, someone wills to die; the other of sensuality, near and therefore conjoined to the infirmity of the flesh, with which death is fled" (*Sent.* 3.17.2 [106–7]). See also Aquinas, *ST* IIIa.18.6 ad 3 (237). On *passio* being especially located in the "appetitive power" or the will, insofar as the will especially is affected by and ordered toward things as good or evil, see Aquinas, *ST* IaIIae.22.2 (169–70).

the Lord only "begins" to be sorrowful by *propassio*.[154] Jerome may overread the significance of Matthew including the verb "began," but the distinction between *passio* and *propassio* is a valuable one that is explained further by later writers.[155] In his commentary on Matthew's description of the scene in Gethsemane, Aquinas remarks that

> sadness sometimes occurs according to passion, sometimes according to pro-passion. According to passion, when something suffers and is changed; but when it suffers and is not changed, then it has propassion. But when things of this sort are in us, so that reason is changed, then there are complete passions. But in Christ reason has never been changed. Then there has been propassion, and not passion.[156]

While we often talk broadly about "passion" as a matter of one thing being affected by another and undergoing some sort of change, this *passio-propassio* distinction helps us to express that "passion" in the strictest and complete sense occurs when pain, grief, or anxiety deflects or hinders the will from following the sound judgment of reason about the best course of action. By contrast, "propassion" occurs when pain, grief, or anxiety are very much present in the soul and yet still subjected to sound rational judgment about the best course of action, which was true in Christ's life.[157] For, as Christ says, his soul was troubled, and yet he knew that he had come precisely for the hour of suffering that lay before him (John 12:27–28).

Significantly, the fact that Christ's sorrow, fear, and anxiety remained subject to his rational determination to do the Father's will takes nothing away from the genuineness of these mental infirmities. Indeed, one might say that he tasted them in an unmitigated form since he never attempted to insulate himself from them by taking the easier path of selfishness. What he did do to address these infirmities was to pray. Some authors in the Christian tradition assert that Christ did not have to pray for himself,[158] but even if a number of qualifications need to be made and even as he prayed to set an example for

154. Jerome, *Sur Matt. II*, 4.26, 37 (252).
155. It is picked up in Lombard's *Sentences* in 3.15.2 (98–99).
156. Aquinas, *Super Matt.*, 26.5.2226 (343).
157. Cf. Aquinas, *ST* IIIa.15.4 corp. (189), on *propassio* being "inchoate" and not extend-ing itself beyond sensitive desire. For further specification of the distinction between Christ's passion (or propassion) and ours, see, e.g., Aquinas, *ST* IIIa.15.4 corp. (189); 15.6 ad 1–2 (192); 15.7 ad 1 (193); Polanus, *Syntagma*, 6.15 (372–73).
158. E.g., Hilary of Poitiers, *La Trinité* 10.37–38 (228, 230, 232); Ambrose, *Traité sur l'Evangile de S. Luc* 5,41–42 (198–99); John of Damascus, *Expos. fidei* 3.24 (167–68); 4.18 (215). Lombard also stresses that Christ's praying is an example to help us submit our wills to God's (*Sent.* 3.17.2 [109]). Aquinas interprets these lines of thinking in a way that is compatible with

us, there is an important sense in which Christ truly prayed for himself. Just as the Son as God did not have to take up our infirmities, so he did not have to take up a posture of prayer. Nor did he have to pray as though he were unsure about the outcome of his passion. Nevertheless, having freely assumed a human nature with its infirmities, Christ genuinely expresses his natural and sensitive will to the Father when he asks that the cup should pass from him. He also expresses his rational determination when he adds, "Nevertheless, not as I will but as you will" (Matt. 26:39).[159] For the fulfillment of that rational determination Christ as man continually depends upon the empowerment of the Spirit. He therefore applies himself to the divinely appointed means of receiving help.[160] In this way, Christ follows in the tradition of the psalmists and provides both an example of unfolding our natural will and griefs before God and also an example of submitting our wills to the will of God.

(5) Finally, though we have already touched on the growth of Christ with respect to his knowledge, we should also comment on whether he grew with respect to his mercy and sympathy as high priest. Of course, the divine Son had previously understood the nature of human infirmity and emotion and operated with the Father and Spirit in God's work of comforting his people. In addition, the Son according to his humanity received a wisdom and understanding from the Spirit by which he always knew what sort of help sinners need. Yet the author of Hebrews anchors Jesus's ability to sympathize in his having been tempted like us: "For we do not have a high priest unable to sympathize with our weaknesses, but one having been tempted according to all things like us, without sin" (4:15). Is it fitting, then, to say that the Son in some sense *grew* in mercy?

In his commentary on Hebrews 4:15 Calvin denies that Christ grew in mercy. He says that "the Son of God will not have had necessarily to be formed by experience toward the affection of mercy." Yet the Son had to be "exercised in our miseries" in order to persuade us that he is merciful and inclined to help us. That Jesus experienced our misery is a gift to us.[161] For Calvin, the Son has clothed himself with our flesh and its affections and thereby proved himself to be true man and ready to help us, but the Son himself did not need such "les-

---

his view that Christ truly prays for himself (see *ST* IIIa.21.1 ad 1 [251]; 21.3 ad 1 [253–54]; 21.4 ad 1 [254–55]). On Christ praying for himself, see further Owen, *Hebrews*, 4:501–2.

159. Cf. Athanasius, *Oratio III*, 57 (368–70); Aquinas, *Super Matt.* 26.5.2231–32 (343–44); Aquinas, *ST* IIIa.21.2 (252–53); 21.3 corp. (253).

160. Aquinas, *ST* IIIa.21.1 corp. (251); cf. Owen, *Hebrews*, 4:509. Aquinas helpfully notes that Christ's certainty about receiving such help does not have to be in conflict with his prayer: "Among the things which Christ has known to be future, he has known some to be done on account of his own praying. And of this sort he not unfittingly asks from God" (*ST* IIIa.21.1 ad 2 [251]).

161. Calvin, *In Heb.*, 34.

sons." His experience of our condition is for our benefit, so that we can see how much he cares about our salvation. Whether the Son is still liable at present to experiencing our miseries is a "frivolous" question. The point is that, in view of the Son's human affections, we know not to be frightened by the majesty of Christ, because he is our brother.[162] When Christ is said to "learn" obedience in Hebrews 5:8, Calvin comments that the "proximate end" of Christ's suffering is to make him "accustomed" or "habituated" to obedience. But Christ did not need such habituation, for he was already willing to obey the Father from the beginning of his incarnate life. Christ does this for us, to give us a model of obedience. Calvin does acknowledge that Christ "by his own death has learned fully what it is to obey God," particularly since he is "led to the denial of himself." Yet in Calvin's exegesis the emphasis still falls not on Christ being equipped for his high priesthood but on the pedagogical aspect of Christ's experience of suffering. His suffering teaches us the extent to which we must obey God.[163]

Perhaps a charitable interpretation of Calvin's comments would suggest that he aims only (and rightly) to deny that Christ had to grow in mercy with respect to his divine love and with respect to his infused habits, while still leaving room for some genuine subjective growth on Christ's part. In any event, it seems to me that Bonaventure's aforementioned statement on Christ's "acquired knowledge" including a knowledge of penal suffering is important here. More than Calvin, exegetes like Aquinas and Owen allow such acquisition of knowledge by experience to influence their exposition of texts like Hebrews 4:15 and 5:8. Aquinas recognizes that God has eternally known our misery by a "simple knowledge" (*per simplicem notitiam*). Yet, according to Aquinas, the author of Hebrews intends to communicate that mercy and pity "agree" or "fit" with our high priest in a special way. The special ability to sympathize that is rooted in Christ's temptation does not concern a bare potential for showing pity (*nuda potentia*) but rather a certain "readiness" or "eagerness" (*promptitudo*) and "aptitude" (*aptitudo*) for coming to the aid of others—"and this because he knows, by experience, our misery."[164]

Owen also recognizes that the divine Son even prior to the assumption of a human nature was merciful. But mercy in that case was a "naked simple apprehension of misery, made effective by an act of his holy will to relieve." The human mercy of Christ, however, includes more.

> Mercy in Christ is a compassion, a condolency, and hath a moving of pity and sorrow joined with it. And this was in the human nature of Christ a grace of

162. Calvin, *In Heb.*, 54.
163. Calvin, *In Heb.*, 63.
164. Aquinas, *Super Heb.* 4.3.235 (387).

the Spirit in all perfection. Now, it being such a virtue as in the operation of it deeply affects the whole soul and body also, and being incomparably more excellent in Christ than in all the sons of men, it must needs produce the same effects in him wherewith in others in lesser degrees it is attended.[165]

For Owen, a text like Hebrews 2:17 is not describing mercy "in general" but "as excited, provoked, and drawn forth by [Christ's] own temptations and sufferings. He suffered and was tempted, that he might be merciful, not absolutely, but a merciful high priest." This particular mercy is

the gracious condolency and compassion of his whole soul with his people, in all their temptations, sufferings, dangers, fears, and sorrows, with a continual propensity of will and affection unto their relief, implanted in him by the Holy Ghost, as one of those graces which were to dwell in his nature in all fullness, excited and provoked, as to the continual exercise in his office of high priest, by the sense and experience which he himself had of those miseries which they undergo.[166]

Along with the habit of mercy originally implanted by the Spirit, Christ had a "ready enlargedness of heart" through "particular experience . . . of the weakness, sorrows, and miseries of human nature under the assaults of temptation; he tried it, felt it, and will never forget it." "In his throne of eternal peace and glory, he sees poor brethren labouring in that storm which with so much travail of soul himself passed through, and is intimately affected with their condition."[167]

Aquinas and Owen duly bring out the fact that while Christ as God already understood human misery and already was merciful, his experiential knowledge of temptation uniquely equipped him to care for sinners. Christ's divine omniscience and habitual graces from the Spirit were in no way defective, and yet the experience of suffering and acquired knowledge of human misery established in him a peculiar readiness and eagerness to help us in our weakness. What is new here is not the knowledge of misery in itself or the virtue of mercy in itself but the fact that Christ's human virtue of mercy is now informed by his own direct experience of suffering and incited to act in part by that experience. That is, upon seeing the saints' misery, Christ as man is moved to relieve us not just by what he sees outwardly but by his own inward experience and memory of what he himself went through on earth.[168]

---

165. Owen, *Hebrews*, 3:469–70.
166. Owen, *Hebrews*, 3:470.
167. Owen, *Hebrews*, 3:480.
168. Cf. Owen's comment that Christ is moved by both "external objects" and "sensible experience" (*Hebrews*, 3:485). To be clear, the memory of sorrow need not entail actual suffering

In this respect, then, Christ did grow in mercy and had to "become" a merciful and faithful high priest (Heb. 2:17).

IV. Questions about Christ's Sinlessness and Spiritual Exertion

Another set of questions to be addressed in exploring the connections between Scripture and catholic Christology pertains to Christ's sinlessness and exertion in his earthly life. Is the Bible's pointed representation of Christ's spiritual and moral striving blunted by talk of the union of two natures in Christ or the impeccability of Christ? Does the doctrine of the *communicatio operationum* (the sharing of the divine and human operations of Christ in all his mediatorial works) override the necessity and authenticity of his human activity? This section will take up these sorts of questions by describing how various authors have raised concerns about them in modern Christology. In order to take into account the concerns of different authors in a more manageable way, I will break up the material under two main considerations: (1) the question of whether the Son assumed a fallen human nature; and (2) the question of whether Christ is impeccable and, if so, how to understand the basis of his impeccability.

(1) A number of authors have rejected the claim that Christ assumed a fallen human nature, often stressing that this would undermine his holiness and saving power.[169] Others, however, have argued that Christ had to assume a fallen nature in order for him genuinely to share in the human condition and redeem sinful human beings.[170] Barth is an example of the latter group, framing his understanding of Christ's sinlessness in a way that leaves room for an assumption of a "fallen" nature. Barth's approach to Christ's unique "determination" or fitness for his mediatorial office is rooted in what Barth calls a "grace of

---

in Christ after his resurrection. Positively, given Christ's postresurrection enjoyment of the beatific vision and given the consolation and peace of the state of glory, he is no longer subject to suffering (see Heb. 12:2; Rev. 21:4; cf. Turretin, *Inst.*, 13.13.12–14 [2:382]; 16.9, 11 [2:396]). Owen at one point leaves open the question of "whatever may be the real effects on the mind of Christ from his temptations and sufferings now he is in heaven" (*Hebrews*, 3:485; cf. 4:422–26), but elsewhere Owen clarifies that Christ was susceptible to sorrow only on earth and now stands above all sorrow and trouble (*Hebrews*, 4:511, 514–15).

169. From different angles, see, e.g., Schleiermacher, *The Christian Faith*, §93 (571–72); Dods, *On the Incarnation of the Eternal Word*; A. B. Bruce, *The Humiliation of Christ*, 271–75; Crisp, "Did Christ Have a *Fallen* Human Nature?"

170. Along with the authors quoted below, see Irving, *The Doctrine of the Incarnation Opened*. A number of authors have also offered historical surveys and constructive clarifications of the issues at stake. See Weinandy, *In the Likeness of Sinful Flesh*; Kapic, "The Son's Assumption of a Human Nature"; McFarland, "Fallen or Unfallen?"; Hatzidakis, *Jesus: Fallen?*; Sumner, "Fallenness and *anhypostasis*"; King, "Assumption, Union and Sanctification"; Van Kuiken, *Christ's Humanity*; Crisp, "On the Vicarious Humanity of Christ."

origin." For the "existence of the man Jesus Christ is an event by and in the existence of the Son of God."[171] By this "grace of origin" Christ lives according to the divine will. At the same time, while Barth affirms that the "grace of origin" is also a "grace of sinlessness," he asserts that in the incarnation Christ assumed a "fallen" (even "sinful") human essence. On the one hand, Christ's humanity is determined by the electing grace of God, existing only in the Son of God who lives in obedience to the divine decision to atone for our sin and reconcile us to God. In this regard, Christ's humanity or the man Jesus is sinless. On the other hand, Christ's humanity is not sinless "as such." If it were, he would not be like us or be our brother. Christ is distinguished as the unique Son of Man in that he has the "unconditional affirmation" of the Father and the Spirit, but he is not a "superman in a middle essence."[172]

T. F. Torrance takes up a similar line of reasoning.[173] He states that when the Word is "made flesh" in John 1, this means that the Word became "true man and real man." "But are we to think of this flesh which he became as *our* flesh? Are we to think of it as describing some neutral human nature and existence, or as describing our actual human nature and existence in the bondage and estrangement of humanity fallen from God and under the divine judgment?" Torrance responds that there can be "no doubt that the New Testament speaks of the flesh of Jesus as the concrete form of our human nature marked by Adam's fall, the human nature which seen from the cross is at enmity with God and needs to be reconciled to God."[174] For Torrance, it is a weakness of the Chalcedonian formula that it does not specify that the Son assumed a "corrupt human nature, taken from our fallen creation, where human nature is determined and perverted by sin." The Chalcedonian formulation suggests that Christ assumed a "neutral and perfect humanity," leading to a "static" expression of the hypostatic union. The assumption of a "fallen humanity" is necessary for a "dynamic" understanding of the hypostatic union, in which Christ actively "heals" and "sanctifies" our humanity through his sinless, vicarious obedience.[175]

Thus, "the Word penetrated into hostile territory, into our human alienation and estrangement from God." He was made "in the likeness of sinful flesh" (Rom. 8:3), made sin and a curse for us (2 Cor. 5:21; Gal. 3:13). He

171. Barth construes this as an expression of the *anhypostasia* and *enhypostasia* of Christ's humanity.

172. Barth, *CD*, IV.2, 91–95. See also I.2, 151–59; II.1, 397–98.

173. On T. F. Torrance's approach, see Chiarot, *The Unassumed Is the Unhealed*; Habets, "The Fallen Humanity of Christ." For a recent critique of figures like Barth and T. F. Torrance on this topic, see Bello, *Sinless Flesh*.

174. T. F. Torrance, *Incarnation*, 61.

175. T. F. Torrance, *Incarnation*, 201, 205, 206.

entered our situation in such a way that with the psalmist he could cry, "My God, my God, why have you forsaken me?" Indeed, from the beginning of his public ministry, Christ was "identified with sinners" by undergoing John's baptism of repentance (see Matt. 3:11, 13–15) and by then going out into the desert to be tempted by Satan. In assuming our fallen flesh in this way, Christ takes our place. The "atoning exchange begins right away with the incarnation, with its assumption of our flesh of sin, its condemnation of sin in the flesh, its sanctification of our humanity through the gift of divine righteousness and sanctification of man in Christ."[176]

On the one hand, Torrance is clear that the person of Christ never sinned:

> While he, the holy Son of God, became what we are, he became what we are in a different way from us. We become what we are and continue to become what we are as sinners. He, however, who knew no sin became what we are, yet not by sinning himself. Christ the Word did not sin. He did not become flesh of our flesh in a sinful way, by sinning in the flesh.[177]

In fact, Torrance goes on to ask, "If God the Word became flesh, God the Word is the subject of the incarnation, and how could God sin? How could God deny God, be against himself, divest himself of his holiness and purity?"[178]

On the other hand, Torrance contends that while Christ was without sin, he "assumed our fallen human existence, our fallen flesh under the dominion of sin."[179] To set forth the origins and theological significance of this line of thought, Torrance invokes a number of patristic (especially Greek) sources, stating boldly that it is "a doctrine found everywhere in the early Church in the first five centuries."[180] For example, Torrance asserts that, according to Athanasius, "he who knew no sin became sin for us, exchanging his riches for our poverty, his perfection for our imperfection, his incorruption for our corruption, his eternal life for our mortality."[181] The axiom of Gregory Nazianzen (and other patristic sources) figures prominently: "The unassumed is the unhealed."[182] "If the Word of God did not really come into our fallen existence, if the Son of God did not actually come where we are, and join himself to us and range himself with us where we are in sin and under judgment, how could it be said that Christ really took our place, took our cause upon

---

176. T. F. Torrance, *Incarnation*, 61–63; cf. T. F. Torrance, *The Trinitarian Faith*, 179–90.
177. T. F. Torrance, *Incarnation*, 63.
178. T. F. Torrance, *Incarnation*, 63.
179. T. F. Torrance, *Incarnation*, 63.
180. T. F. Torrance, *The Mediation of Christ*, 39.
181. T. F. Torrance, *Incarnation*, 62, 201.
182. T. F. Torrance, *Incarnation*, 62; cf. T. F. Torrance, *The Trinitarian Faith*, 161–68.

himself in order to redeem us?" Under the assumption of our fallen flesh, he lived in perfect obedience and correspondence to the truth of God. And this obedience was "not light or sham obedience. It was agonisingly real in our flesh of sin." In the face of temptation, Christ had to "beat his way forward by blows." Throughout his life he "resisted the downward drag of our fallen nature." He "submitted our fallen humanity with our fallen will to the just and holy verdict of the Father, freely and gladly yielding it to the Father's judgement, and was therefore obedient unto the death of the cross."[183] Indeed, "far from sinning himself or being contaminated by what he appropriated from us, Christ triumphed over the forces of evil entrenched in our human existence, bringing his own holiness, his own perfect obedience to bear upon it in such a way as to condemn sin in the flesh and to deliver us from its power."[184]

(2) Another matter that has bearing on our understanding of Jesus's spiritual and moral exertion is the question of his impeccability. Some authors in the modern period have advocated the teaching of Jesus's impeccability, with their diverse christological frameworks bringing a different shape to the bases and character of the doctrine.[185] Others are concerned that impeccability will undermine the genuineness of Jesus's human experience and temptation. Trevor Hart articulates the pressing question: "If Jesus was at no time in his life faced with the real possibility of sinning (if, as we might say, he was never really 'free' to sin) then in what precise sense are we able to affirm the integrity of his human experience, and in particular the claim that he 'was tempted in all things as we are'? . . . Is the genuine potential for sin not analytic in some way in the very notion of temptation?"[186]

The nineteenth-century Scottish theologian A. B. Bruce's reflections shed light on some key issues to be addressed by those who would affirm the impeccability of Christ today. Bruce maintains Christ's sinlessness and judges that "sinless infirmity" (rather than a fallen nature or moral vice) is all that is required for the experience of genuine temptation. When Bruce inquires about the sense in which Christ's resistance to temptation is "guaranteed," he sympathizes with two different positions. In order to uphold the notion that Jesus faced true temptation, some would argue that Jesus had the capacity

---

183. T. F. Torrance, *Incarnation*, 62–64, 205. Cf. 105–7, 123–24, 137–38.

184. T. F. Torrance, *The Trinitarian Faith*, 161. Cf. T. F. Torrance, *Theology in Reconstruction*, 126, 132, 241.

185. See, e.g., Schleiermacher, *The Christian Faith*, §93 (571–72), §94 (575), §98 (608–10), §100 (622); Bavinck, *Sin and Salvation in Christ*, 314–16; McKinley, *Tempted for Us*; Crisp, "Was Christ Sinless or Impeccable?"; Pawl, "Conciliar Christology, Impeccability, and Temptation."

186. Hart, "Sinlessness and Moral Responsibility," 38. See also the recent essay of Adam C. Pelser, "Temptation, Virtue, and the Character of Christ," who argues that Christ was not fully virtuous from the beginning of his life and had to grow in virtue through his temptations.

to choose both what was right and what was wrong: *potuit non peccare* ("he has been able not to sin"). In order to uphold the notion that "any other than a sinless result in His case cannot be seriously contemplated as a real possibility," some would make the stronger statement: *non potuit peccare* ("he has not been able to sin"). For Bruce, the two positions must somehow be combined. "The *potuit non* signifies that Christ's experience of temptation was real. . . . The *non potuit*, on the other hand, signifies that there was in Christ a counter force stronger than the force of temptation, which certainly, though not without effort, ensured in every case a sinless result."[187]

According to Bruce, the temptation is real, which means "the force of temptation was strong enough to create the consciousness of a struggle." If it were not so, "then the whole curriculum of moral trial through which Jesus passed on earth degenerates at once into a mere stage performance." Bruce thus cautions against a docetic view of Christ's struggle in which "the essential divinity of Christ" functions as "an overwhelming force on the side of good, so as to make the force at work on the side of evil relatively zero."[188] In Bruce's words, Christ's resistance to temptation is not

the matter-of-course result of the physical ground of his being, but the effect brought about by the operations of the Holy Spirit dwelling in Him in plenary measure, helping Him to exercise strong faith and to cherish lively hope, and inspiring Him with a love to His Father and to men, which should be more than a match for all the temptations that might be directed against him.[189]

The "physical divine ground" in Christ is not an impediment to real struggle and "moral achievement" but is "simply the guarantee that gracious influences shall be supplied to the adequate extent." In light of the book of Hebrews (see esp. 2:10; 5:9; 7:28), Bruce aims to take seriously Christ's "moral development" and "curriculum of ethical discipline." Christ began life not in a sinful state but in a "morally incomplete" state, with a liability to temptation and a "bare possibility" of sinning. After the perfecting of Christ that occurs through his life and obedience, he is exalted and placed beyond the possibility of temptation and sin.[190]

H. R. Mackintosh provides another example of someone who highlights the sinlessness of Christ and traces it back to Christ's relationship to God, while at the same time insisting that this sinlessness does not automatically follow from Christ's divinity. After emphasizing that only a sinless person

187. A. B. Bruce, *The Humiliation of Christ*, 264, 273, 287–90.
188. A. B. Bruce, *The Humiliation of Christ*, 290–92.
189. A. B. Bruce, *The Humiliation of Christ*, 292.
190. A. B. Bruce, *The Humiliation of Christ*, 293, 295–304, 310–16.

could secure the remission of sins, Mackintosh asks whether the temptations of a sinless person would be "real." "How can evil find resonance where there is neither inherited bias to evil nor weakness due to previous transgression?" Mackintosh answers by noting that real temptation did occur in Jesus's case when the "solicitation" of a "lower end" came "knocking at His heart." "He was vulnerable in all His normal instincts, emotions, desires." A variety of "natural, innocent tendencies and the like [e.g., obtaining power, avoiding death] supplied very real opportunities of rebellion." Such tendencies brought a "pressure on the will against which force must be exerted in steadfast resistance and with a real pain of conflict. Thus the Holy One learned obedience." Further, the temptations of a sinless person "may be the most severe" inasmuch as they involve denying satisfaction to a purely "natural appetite" and, if resisted to the end, will last for a longer period of time. On the one hand, Mackintosh grounds the sinlessness of Jesus in his "vital and organic connection with the Father" or "that element in His being by virtue of which He is one with God." Indeed, the presence of God in Christ "formed the conditioning *prius* of His ethical self-determination" from childhood through adulthood. On the other hand, Mackintosh adds that "the holiness of Jesus was no automatic necessity of being. It was possessed only by being perpetually won anew, in a dependence of self-committal which . . . rested . . . on the felt need of an uninterrupted derivation of life and power from the Father."[191]

Mackintosh's representation of Jesus's sinlessness is located within his broader concern to jettison the category of amoral (or "unethical") "substance" in favor of the centrality of the will in theology and philosophy. Accordingly, Mackintosh is critical of those who would anchor the unity of Christ with God (or the reality of God in Christ) in a "Divine substance or nature, of which will and thought are but attributes, and which is somehow real apart from them." For, according to Mackintosh, "substance" is not a "category higher and more adequate than Subject, or intelligent conscious Will." Against the prioritization of "substance" the "history of philosophy since Kant has been one long and convincing protest." "Personality" or "self-consciousness" is the highest category. "For us, then, the proper inference is that the essential and noumenal divinity of Christ the Son ought to be formulated in conceptions other than substance or nature and the like, which really oppose the metaphysical aspect of Sonship to the ethical." For Mackintosh, the "ethical" just *is* the "metaphysical," which means that the "ultimate and central reality of things is Will." To say that Christ is one with God means, then, that he and God share one "central Will by which personality is constituted." In other words, "the

---

191. Mackintosh, *The Doctrine of the Person of Jesus Christ*, 400–404, 412–18, 421.

self-conscious active principle of the Son's life subsisted in perfect and identical union with the Father." Since the Son enjoys an "inherent and personal unity with the Father," it is the case that "no desire, motion, conception, or resolve existed in the soul of Jesus which was not the affirmation and execution of the will of God, dwelling in Him and informing His entire life."[192]

Within the context of what we might call an "actualist" Christology, Barth offers an alternative account of Christ's sinlessness and impeccability. Barth's exposition of the "determination" of Christ for his office affirms an "exaltation" of Christ to a correspondence with the divine will in true human freedom and obedience.[193] Thus, while Christ had a fallen human nature, he did not sin. He bore only an "alien guilt" that was properly ours. Nevertheless, Christ's sinlessness "was not a condition of His being as man." He became a "sinful creature." He had no "quality" by which he could not sin, but, nevertheless, given his "grace of origin," he exercised true human freedom and chose not to sin. Barth is still willing to say that by virtue of Christ's origin he was "unable" to choose sin, but he then turns to emphasizing that Christ was sustained by the Father's blessing and the Spirit's comfort and guidance. For Barth, Christ's sinlessness emerges not from an infused habit but from the "history" in which Christ by divine grace walks the road of obedience.[194]

Wolfhart Pannenberg surveys a number of patristic sources on Jesus's sinlessness, including statements of the Second Council of Constantinople (553), where, Pannenberg writes, Jesus's "inability to sin was not attributed to his human nature as such, nor derived directly from the hypostatic union and the hegemony of the divinity over the human nature." In Pannenberg's representation of the Council's teaching, Jesus's impeccability is a "gracious sinlessness" from the "community of the natures within the hypostatic union." Along the way, Pannenberg's remarks disclose his reservations about the notion of impeccability. For example: "Jesus' ability to be tempted and his assailment by doubts is no longer understandable if there was *a priori* no possibility that he could have sinned." Again, "it is still not understandable how a temptation could really have penetrated through his defense" if Jesus received grace from God so that he could not sin. In his constructive statements, Pannenberg is clear that Jesus's sinlessness is an important doctrine, but he agrees with Barth that "the Son of God assumed sinful flesh." Though Jesus was sinless from the beginning of his life, the point of the virgin birth narrative in the New Testament is not that it enabled Jesus to begin life sinless or impeccable. Ultimately, Jesus's sinlessness "is not an incapability for evil that belongs

192. Mackintosh, *The Doctrine of the Person of Jesus Christ*, 414, 416–18, 421.
193. Barth, *CD*, IV.2, 92.
194. Barth, *CD*, IV.2, 92–94.

naturally to his humanity but results only from his entire process of life." Jesus's victory over sin comes "only in the entire accomplishment of the course
of his existence." "For through the cross of Christ sin was condemned and
demolished," and through his resurrection his victory over sin was "decided"
or "became visible and became reality."[195]

In the field of philosophical theology, Thomas Morris reasons that "ad-
verting to the two-natures model and the reduplicative form of proposition"
(certain things are true of Christ *qua Deus*, others are true of Christ *qua
homo*) is unhelpful with respect to Christ's holiness and his temptation. Morris asks, "Could it have been that God the Son was necessarily good *qua*
God while only contingently good *qua* man? I think it is fairly easy to see
the impossibility of this." For Morris, a better way forward is to distinguish
between an "epistemic" and a "metaphysical" possibility of committing sin. In
particular, in his human knowledge, Jesus did not know that his divine nature
"prevented" him from sinning. "Thus, in his earthly stream of consciousness,
it was possible for Jesus to be tempted to sin." The human ignorance of the
metaphysical impossibility of sin yields an "epistemic" possibility of sin and
renders Jesus open to the mental struggle of temptation. At the same time,
the divine nature of Jesus establishes that there is in fact no "metaphysical"
possibility of sin.[196]

Drawing upon the Christology of Edward Irving, Colin Gunton states
that Christ was "not one automatically predetermined to innocence" but
rather "truly liable to the assaults of the enemy." Christ's sinlessness is not
grounded in a "prior endowment" but "in the fact that the incarnate one was
maintained in truth by the Spirit." For Gunton, the claim that Jesus "could
not have sinned" implies that his temptations were "unreal," so Gunton suggests that Jesus was "enabled by the Spirit not to sin."[197] Another theologian
who has recently stressed Jesus's dependence on the Spirit throughout his
obedient life is Bruce McCormack. Though McCormack (to my knowledge)
has not offered a proposal regarding the question of Christ's impeccability
in particular, it is relevant here that in a number of essays on the person and
work of Christ he contends that it is insufficient to envision the Logos acting
upon his human nature as an "instrument." Rather, the Logos himself must
undergo human suffering to ensure the efficacy of the atonement. Instead
of the Logos actively "divinizing" his humanity, McCormack argues, the
Logos is receptive to the characteristics and the suffering of his humanity.
The Logos, then, acting and suffering as true man, does what he does "in the

195. Pannenberg, *Jesus—God and Man*, 358–64.
196. Morris, *The Logic of God Incarnate*, 146–53.
197. Gunton, *Father, Son and Holy Spirit*, 154, 158, 162.

power of the Spirit."[198] It is significant for the present discussion that Mc-Cormack highlights well the problem of speaking about the incarnation as if the divinity of the Son obviated his human striving: "If the divine Logos has made this human nature to be the medium through which He exercised His omnipotent power what need is there for an outpouring of the Spirit upon him? Would this not make the Spirit's ministry in the life of Jesus superfluous to requirements?"[199] McCormack connects this concern to the doctrine of the *communicatio operationum*:

> I have a very hard time understanding how omnipotent power could function co-operatively—within the bounds of a single Subject, mind you—with the finite power proper to human nature without the latter being completely suppressed and finally eliminated by the former. Co-operation with the finite power of a human subject which remains ontologically distinct, yes. That is not a problem. . . . But co-operation within a single Subject? It would seem hard to avoid the conclusion that omnipotence would have to overwhelm and displace finite causality and the work of the God-human would, therefore, be a divine work only (a thought that always tempted the church Fathers).[200]

V. The Logic of Christ's Spiritual Exertion

What should be said in response to the concerns raised in the previous section? How might the resources of catholic Christology confirm and even illumine the Son's human striving? How would a Christology that affirms the impeccability of Christ and the doctrine of the *communicatio operationum* set forth Christ's real human exertion and temptation? I think the following points are important here.

(1) In order to address the question of whether Christ assumed a fallen human nature, there must be some clarification about what is meant by "fallen" in this case. In my view, the statements of Barth and Torrance canvassed above lack specificity. Does the assumption of a fallen nature mean only that Christ in his human nature is beset with various weaknesses that were not originally present before the fall but now are present after the fall (i.e., the *defectus poenae* discussed above)? Or does it mean that the Son in his human nature is not disposed to the good but is in fact inclined toward evil actions? Is the Son in his human nature beset with concupiscence? The assumption of a human nature that is subject to amoral weaknesses or living

198. McCormack, "The Only Mediator," 256–66.
199. McCormack, "The Only Mediator," 262, 266.
200. McCormack, "Karl Barth's Christology," 249–50.

in the midst of a hostile, broken world is quite different from operating with a human will inclined to hate God and other human beings, especially if evil inclinations of the heart are themselves violations of God's holy law and would render Christ unfit for his office.[201] It seems to me that those invested in the debate about whether Christ assumed a "fallen" human nature would do well to focus on the question of whether Christ was not only beset by the common infirmities of fallen humanity but also inclined toward evil actions. Whatever provocative language one might find in the patristic literature to describe the depth of Jesus's association with sinful humanity, one will be hard-pressed (to put it mildly) to conclude that the catholic fathers posited a Jesus disposed to rebel against the will of God.[202]

(2) Furthermore, the scriptural texts that might be adduced in favor of the fallenness of Christ's humanity do not stipulate a sinfulness of Christ or an inclination of Christ toward evil. In Romans 8:3, Paul writes that "what the law could not do in the thing in which it was weak through the flesh, God [did] by sending his own Son in the likeness of the flesh of sin, and concerning sin he condemned sin in the flesh."[203] Regarding this text, Chrysostom, for example, says that the word "likeness" (in the phrase "likeness of the flesh of sin") does not imply that Christ took up "another flesh" (ἄλλην ἐκείνην σάρκα), alien to ours. Yet, rather than proceeding to the opposite extreme and saying that Christ's flesh was itself sinful, Chrysostom contends that Paul includes the word "likeness," with its indication of some distinction, precisely because the flesh in the likeness of which Christ came was a flesh "of sin." For Chrysostom, Christ did not have "sinful flesh" but flesh "like to our sinful flesh and sinless."[204] Similarly, Aquinas reasons that the phrase "in the likeness of the flesh of sin" is "not to be understood as if [Christ] will not have had true flesh but only the likeness of flesh." Conceived by the power of the Holy Spirit, who takes away sin, Christ did not have "flesh of sin," but he nevertheless has "true flesh," which is passible, like ours.[205]

In his Romans commentary, John Calvin reasons, on the one hand, that "the flesh of Christ has been polluted with no stains" and, on the other hand,

201. On which, see, e.g., Polanus, *Syntagma*, 6.14 (366), and chap. 5, sect. V, of this volume.

202. Cf. the historical comments in Davidson, "Pondering the Sinlessness of Jesus Christ," 397–98; Bathrellos, "The Patristic Tradition on the Sinlessness of Jesus." Perhaps a word from one of the Latin fathers might be indulged here: "He who rescued others from the danger of the flesh, was he able to fear lest he himself should be conquered by any domination of this flesh?" (Ambrose, *De incarnationis dominicae sacramento* 7,64 [258]).

203. The Greek reads, τὸ γὰρ ἀδύνατον τοῦ νόμου ἐν ᾧ ἠσθένει διὰ τῆς σαρκός, ὁ θεὸς τὸν ἑαυτοῦ υἱὸν πέμψας ἐν ὁμοιώματι σαρκὸς ἁμαρτίας καὶ περὶ ἁμαρτίας κατέκρινεν τὴν ἁμαρτίαν ἐν τῇ σαρκί.

204. John Chrysostom, *In Rom.* 13.5 (514–15).

205. Aquinas, *Super Rom.* 8.1.

that "some image of the sinner's nature has appeared in part" in that Christ is subject to our infirmities and to death and punishment for our sin.[206] Drawing upon resources from Augustine, Peter Vermigli writes that the similarity here, with its presupposition of there being some distinction, concerns not so much the flesh itself but the sin. "For the human nature, which Christ has assumed, has had the appearance [*speciem*] of sin. Nevertheless, this has not been able truly to be contaminated by sin." Still, the word "likeness" does not call into question Christ's true humanity, which is a point confirmed by Philippians 2. There Paul writes that Christ has come "in the likeness of human beings," which means "not that in the thing itself he has not become man, but that he has so lowered himself that he has withdrawn nothing from the common custom of human beings." Furthermore, the suitability of the phrase "flesh of sin" can be seen in that Christ has assumed a human nature "with its affections, not those that are borne of malice but those that arise from the nature instituted by God. In sum, to have taken up the flesh of sin is nothing other than for Christ so to have become man that he is liable to hot, cold, hunger, thirst, indignities, and death. For these are effects of sin."[207]

Many recent commentators are sympathetic to such lines of thought. For example: "The flesh of Christ is 'like' ours inasmuch as it is flesh; 'like,' and only 'like,' because it is not sinful."[208] Again: Christ "came in the flesh, so that the incarnation was perfectly real, but only *in the likeness* of 'flesh of sin,' so that he remained sinless."[209] Even if "likeness" (ὁμοίωμα) might denote "form" in this text, one can still discern that the word does "introduce a note of distinction" or "some kind of reservation about identifying Christ with '*sinful* flesh.'" Christ is "in the flesh" so that he is "exposed" to the power of sin in the world, but he is not "imprisoned" in the flesh or "so subject to sin that he could be personally guilty of it."[210]

By contrast, in keeping with Barth, C. E. B. Cranfield holds that what he calls "the traditional solution" (i.e., that Paul uses the word "likeness" in Romans 8:3 to avoid suggesting that Christ's human nature was itself fallen)

---

206. Calvin, *In Rom.*, 139.

207. Vermigli, *In Rom.*, 261–62. For treatments in topical expositions of biblical doctrine, see Lombard, *Sent.* 3.3.4 (35–37); Polanus, *Syntagma*, 6.15 (368–69).

208. Sanday and Headlam, *A Critical and Exegetical Commentary on the Epistle to the Romans*, 193.

209. Barrett, *Romans*, 156.

210. Moo, *Romans*, 479–80. For other treatments similar to Barrett or Moo, see, e.g., Talbert, *Romans*, 203; Hultgren, *Romans*, 299; Kruse, *Romans*, 326; Schreiner, *Romans*, 398–99; cf. also Matera, *Romans*, 192. Without affirming that Jesus sinned, other interpreters make additional comments about Jesus being exposed to the presence of sin or being in some sense capable of sinning. For different views, see Barinck, "The Sinful Flesh of the Son of God"; Gillman, "Another Look at Romans 8:3"; Käsemann, *Romans*, 217; Wright, "Romans," 578.

is unlikely given that "it was not unfallen, but fallen, human nature which needed redeeming." According to Cranfield, it is more likely that Paul simply wished to convey that "the Son of God assumed the selfsame fallen human nature that is ours, but that in His case that fallen human nature was never the whole of Him—He never ceased to be the eternal Son of God."[211] However, Cranfield's exegesis seems to assume that an upright human being (whether Adam before the fall or the incarnate Son) must be essentially different from a sinful human being. But a human being inclined toward righteousness is not different *in essence* from a human being inclined toward sin, so it seems there is no reason that the former could not represent and redeem the latter. Furthermore, Cranfield's claim that the distinction introduced by ὁμοίωμα concerns Christ being the eternal Son does not quite reflect Paul's focus here. By speaking about "the likeness of sinful flesh," Paul seems to be focusing not on the distinctness of Christ in terms of his divinity but rather on something that specifically concerns distinction and similarity within the human flesh.

Texts like 2 Corinthians 5:21 and Galatians 3:13 also might be adduced in support of the fallen humanity view, but, like Romans 8:3, these do not stipulate that Christ was sinful or inclined toward sin. Indeed, 2 Corinthians 5:21 expressly states that Christ did not "know" sin, or did not "have personal acquaintance or experience" with it.[212] Of course, Paul says that God "made him who did not know sin [to be] sin for us." In certain LXX texts, "sin" (some form of ἁμαρτία) signifies a sin offering (see Exod. 29:14; Lev. 4:24; Num. 18:9), which may indicate that the particular event in which God made Christ to be sin is his atoning death.[213] Given that Christ did not "know" sin, it seems right to conclude from 2 Corinthians 5:21 that Christ should not be described as "sinful" but as the one who bears the consequences of sin and personally faces the wrath of God for our salvation.[214]

(3) While it is meant to reinforce Scripture's teaching that Christ is truly human and, indeed, our brother, the claim that Christ assumed a "sinful" and "corrupt" human nature—one that is, according to T. F. Torrance, "determined and perverted by sin" and needs reconciliation with God—is actually open to the charge that it minimizes the Son's participation in the human

211. Cranfield, *Romans*, 379–82. Cf. the statement of Dunn (*Romans 1–8*, 421) regarding Jesus's "complete identification with sinful flesh." Fitzmyer (*Romans*, 485) may go further in his comments that Paul's meaning is not "docetic" and that "in his own self Christ coped with the power of sin."

212. Harris, *Second Epistle to the Corinthians*, 450.

213. Cf. Thrall, *Second Epistle to the Corinthians*, 440; Harris, *Second Epistle to the Corinthians*, 452–53.

214. Cf., e.g., Barrett, *Second Epistle to the Corinthians*, 180; Thrall, *Second Epistle to the Corinthians*, 440; Harris, *Second Epistle to the Corinthians*, 453; Guthrie, *2 Corinthians*, 314. It is reasonable to interpret Gal. 3:13, where Christ becomes a "curse for us," in a similar manner.

condition. For if the Son genuinely operates according to his human nature in the incarnation, and if that nature were "determined and perverted by sin," then presumably the Son's operation in this nature would produce sinful works. As Paul says in Romans 8, "The mind of the flesh is hostile toward God, for it does not submit to the law of God, for it is not able. And the ones in the flesh are not able to please God" (8:7–8). If the Son does not produce sinful works, then is he keeping his distance from his purportedly sinful human nature? It seems to me that there are several potential responses to this problem, but, in my judgment, such responses will end up either implying that Christ's humanity is not sinful after all or else compromising Christ's human agency.

First, one might respond that Christ's purportedly "sinful" humanity did not have any evil inclinations (perhaps in accordance with Barth's "actualist" approach to Christology and anthropology), but that strategy would raise the question of why it would still be significant to say that Christ had not only common infirmities that afflict humanity but also a "sinful" human essence. If the descriptor "sinful" has a distinct, additional import in this discussion, what does it mean if not "inclined to sinful actions"? Second, one could say that Christ had evil inclinations but endeavored to combat and overcome them, but this strategy seems to face at least two problems, the first of which is more decisive: (a) evil inclinations are themselves violations of God's command to love him with one's whole heart; and (b) if these were genuine inclinations that could be overcome only gradually, then presumably the fight to overcome them would involve some deeds being tainted by sin along the way to victory. If one were to add that Christ overcame evil inclinations by the power of the Spirit, this would seem to entail that the Spirit would be nullifying the inclinations in view. But this arguably undermines the authenticity of Christ's human agency. On the one hand, the Spirit can and does cooperate with Christ as man in a way that upholds the authenticity of his human agency. Yet, on the other hand, this takes place not by the Spirit negating or overriding human capacities or inclinations but by the Spirit implanting holy inclinations and moving the man Jesus to act according to these holy inclinations.[215] Third, one could suggest that although Christ's humanity had evil inclinations, he had a holiness of his own (perhaps a divine holiness that transcends any human holiness) that he brought to bear on his human nature in his incarnate life. However, framing the matter in this way would imply that Christ acted only *upon* rather than also *within* and *according to* his humanity throughout his ministry, and this implication would undermine the integrity of Christ's human activity. This problem is exacerbated if one is led to speak about Christ

215. *Concursus*—if it is *concursus* and not mere obstruction—involves not so much a divine negation of human capacities and inclinations but an operation through or a use of them.

as if he were not the true subject of his own (purportedly sinful) humanity, as if there were features of Christ's humanity that could not really be attributed to the person of Christ himself. Torrance expresses himself in this manner in at least one place, where he writes that although Christ assumed a fallen, sinful human nature, Christ himself was "far from . . . being contaminated by what he appropriated from us."[216] Why would that which belongs to Christ's humanity (putatively, perversion or contamination by sin) not belong to the person of Christ himself and not then characterize his human acts? I think this illustrates that the statement that Christ assumed a fallen, sinful human nature leads to a conception of the incarnation in which, implicitly, Christ has to keep his distance from his humanity in order to make sure that he and his actions remain holy and pleasing to God the Father. In other words, the claim that Christ assumed a fallen, sinful human essence circles back to enervate the attempt to confirm that Christ truly acts as our brother.

In addition, denying that Christ assumed a sinful human nature does not entail that he is essentially different from us. A sinless human person and a sinful human person do not have two different essences. Within Christ's assumption of a sinless human nature, there is nothing that is not assumed that needs healing. Christ came to save and heal human beings who are sinners, not sin as such. Christ has assumed a genuine human body and soul—even a body and soul subject to the infirmities and griefs borne by sinful human beings. On that basis, he is the brother and redeemer of sinners. Furthermore, one can affirm the Son's assumption of a holy human nature without implying an entirely "static" conception of the Son's incarnate life. That Christ begins his incarnate work disposed to do what is good and right in the Father's eyes does not negate the fact that there is much that he still needs to accomplish under severe pressure along the path of obedience.

(4) To clarify that the doctrine of Christ's impeccability coheres with his subjection to severe trials, it will be important first to explicate the bases of his impeccability, which might be broken up under three headings. First, the ends of the incarnation should be considered. Given that God has decreed the incarnation in order that the Son would faithfully obey the Father, offer himself as a pure sacrifice for sin, and set an example of patient endurance under temptation, the Son must always act in a holy manner.[217] Yet, while the divine decree is infallible, its infallible execution in history may be opened up by looking at the ontological factors in the incarnation that have rendered the Son unfailingly obedient.

216. T. F. Torrance, *The Trinitarian Faith*, 161.
217. Cf., e.g., Aquinas, *Super Sent.* 3.12.2.1 sol. and ad 1; Aquinas, *ST* IIIa.15.1 (185–86); 41.1 (403–4).

Second, then, there is the Son's relationship to the Holy Spirit, including both the Spirit's activity in Mary's conception and the Spirit's communication of habitual graces. Because of the Spirit's activity in Mary's conception, the child begotten is "holy" (Luke 1:35). The Spirit's activity evidently distinguishes Jesus from other human persons. Whether the sense of the adjective "holy" in Luke 1:35 is focused on moral purity, and whether one finds a connection between the absence of a biological human father and the absence of the transmission of original guilt and sin,[218] the virgin conception is certainly the beginning of a narrative in which Jesus's relationship to the Spirit is such that he is free from sin and empowered to do the Father's will. By the Spirit's indwelling presence and activity, Jesus is full of wisdom, righteousness, and faithfulness (so Isa. 11:1–5). These gifts establish the Son in holiness and render him immutably inclined to obedience. Many authors in the Christian tradition identify the grace of the Spirit as a basis of the Son's impeccability, not least in the commentary tradition revolving around Lombard's *Sentences*. Arguing that free choice (*liberum arbitrium*) does not necessarily entail the potential to sin, Lombard points out that many angels, after all, are "confirmed in grace" so that they cannot sin. Lombard then states that this is all the more applicable to "that man, to whom the Spirit is given without measure."[219] Commenting on the *Sentences*, Bonaventure similarly writes that the "fullness of grace" in Christ is a "grace of confirmation" strengthening the *liberum arbitrium* in Christ so that he cannot sin or incur guilt of his own.[220] On the one hand, Christ has assumed a certain "power of sinning" (*potentia peccandi*) where that phrase signifies a created free choice or a faculty whereby the creature can act well or sinfully. On the other hand, Christ has not assumed a *potentia peccandi* where that phrase signifies a power ordered toward acts of sin. Furthermore, the "perfection of grace" in Christ is such that it will not endure or support the *potentia peccandi* taken in that first sense to proceed into sin.[221] Yet, it may be added, the fact that the

218. See, e.g., John of Damascus, *Expos. fidei* 3.1–2 (108–10); Lombard, *Sent.* 3.3.4 (36); Aquinas, *ST* IIIa.31.7 (330–31); Zanchi, *De incarn.*, 2.3 (154–73); Polanus, *Syntagma*, 6.14–15 (365–67, 374).

219. Lombard, *Sent.* 3.12.3 (82–83).

220. Bonaventure, *In Sent.* 3.12.2.1 (266). Here Bonaventure gives a threefold reason for Christ's impeccability: *plenitudo gratiae, consummatio gloriae, unio divinae naturae et humanae.* Cf. Aquinas, *Super Sent.* 3.12.2.1 sol. The second reason concerns the teaching of a beatific vision of Christ during his earthly life.

221. Bonaventure, *In Sent.* 3.12.2.2 ad 2 (269). The Latin reads, "*Animam Christi exire in actum peccati est impossibile, quamvis illam eandem potentiam habeat, quam habet peccator, et hoc propter perfectionem gratiae non sustinentis talem egressum sive defectum.*" See also Aquinas, *Super Sent.* 3.12.2.1 resp.; 3.12.2.2 ad 8. Cf. also Aquinas, *ST* IIIa.15.1–2 (185–87), where he argues that Christ does not have the *fomes peccati* (the "fuel" or "spark" of sin).

Son according to his humanity receives the Spirit "without measure" is itself rooted in the fact that the Son's humanity subsists in the one to whom the Father has communicated the divine life and handed over all things, including the act of spirating and sending the Spirit (cf. John 3:34–35; 15:26; 16:15). In other words, the Son's plenary reception of the Spirit's graces is ultimately grounded in the hypostatic union.[222]

Third, then, the hypostatic union is the principal ground of impeccability. The humanity of Christ has no subsistence or agency of its own apart from the person of the divine Son. It subsists in and only in the divine Son. On the one hand, if the human nature of the Son is mentally prescinded from the person himself, it can be called peccable. Hence Lombard writes that if the question about the ability to sin concerned the human nature on its own (*non unita Verbo*), then it would be capable of sin. But since the human nature is indissolubly united to the Word, it is incapable of sin.[223] Bonaventure comments that the *liberum arbitrium* is indeed a *potentia peccandi* that can be directed toward sin in human beings other than Christ. This *potentia peccandi* is a principle of sin and guilt *inasmuch as it is left to itself*. "But in Christ it is not able to be left to itself on account of the inseparable union with divinity."[224] On the other hand, then, given that the human nature subsists in and only in the divine Son, the human nature—or, better, the Son according to his human nature—cannot sin. For this divine person "cannot deny himself" (2 Tim. 2:13). In him there is no shadow of turning, no darkness at all (James 1:13, 17; 1 John 1:5). In light of the perfect goodness and holiness of God, Lombard frames the question about whether Christ could sin as a question of whether he could "not be God." For, according to Lombard, if Christ were able to sin, then he would be able to be damned and would then be able not to be God. Ultimately, to be God and to be able to will iniquity are simply not compatible.[225]

One might ask, however, whether the matter is so straightforward if God the Son according to his human nature can, for example, suffer or lack knowledge of something. If impassibility and omniscience are just as essential in

---

222. Cf., e.g., Athanasius, *Oratio I*, 46–47 (155–58); John of Damascus, *Expos. fidei* 3.21 (163); Aquinas, *ST* IIIa.7.13 (124–25); Zanchi, *De incarn.*, 2.2 (376); Polanus, *Syntagma*, 6.15 (371–72); Ames, *Bellarminus enervatus*, 2.1 (83); Turretin, *Inst.*, 13.12.1 (2:377).

223. Lombard, *Sent.* 3.12.3 (82).

224. Bonaventure, *In Sent.* 3.12.2.2 ad 2–3 (269). Likewise, Aquinas says, "It is able to be conceded under this sense, that Christ may be said to have the power of sinning because he has a power which in others is a power of sinning" (*Super Sent.* 3.12.2.2 resp. and ad 7). Significantly, there was no time at which Christ's humanity existed independently of the person of the Son. The creation and assumption of the human nature—and therefore the peculiar sanctification of the human nature—were simultaneous (see, e.g., Aquinas, *ST* IIIa.33.3 [343]; 34.1 [345–46]; Polanus, *Syntagma*, 6.16 [376]; Owen, *Pneumatologia*, 1.4 [3:168]).

225. Lombard, *Sent.* 3.12.3 (82). Cf. Bonaventure, *In Sent.* 3.12.2.1 concl. (266).

God as holiness, why is it that God the Son is able to suffer or lack knowledge according to his humanity but not able to sin according to his humanity? One might appeal to a text like Hebrews 4:14–15 (Christ is like us in everything but without sin) and take the question to be resolved on the authority of that text. But perhaps one can reflect a little more on the underlying rationale of the statement in Hebrews 4:14–15.

It seems to me that we may identify a few reasons why human passibility and human peccability have pertinent dissimilarities here. (a) Passibility and finitude with respect to something like knowledge will automatically follow from the reality of human nature, whereas sin is not a necessary feature or consequent of human nature. Thus, the Son could not assume a human nature without being passible according to that nature, whereas he could and did assume a human nature without being peccable according to that nature. This is confirmed by the fact that the Son was not born into the state of glory but was born into a fallen world and appointed to lead believers into the incorruptibility and immortality of the state of glory.[226] (b) Suffering does not obstruct human persons' fellowship with God; indeed, God draws near to the needy and the brokenhearted (e.g., Ps. 34:6, 15, 17–18). Sin, however, does obstruct human persons' fellowship with God (e.g., Pss. 5:5–6; 11:5; 34:16; Isa. 59:2; Hab. 1:13; Eph. 4:18; Rev. 21:27). Thus, given the inseparability of the two natures, the Son *qua homo* cannot sin, for that would compromise the union and (*per impossibile*) position the Son himself to need a mediator. (c) To suffer and to sin are distinct in that the Son's suffering according to his human nature affects the Son just according to his human nature. The suffering does not have to affect his deity. The suffering does involve on the Son's part a divine decision to experience suffering as man, but this does not mean that the divine volition or divine being is itself then undergoing suffering. However, if the Son were to sin, the scenario would be different. The sinning would involve on the Son's part a divine decision or consent to sin as man, but in this case the divine volition and divine being itself would participate in choosing sin.[227] Put differently, to will as God to suffer as man

226. Cf. Turretin, *Inst.*, 13.8.20 (2:355); 16.9 (2:396).
227. This line of argument presupposes (i) that the Son's human will can never be in conflict with the Son's divine willing, and (ii) that the Son in his divine will chooses whatever it is that the Son in his human will chooses. To imagine that the human will might conflict with the Son's divine willing, or that the Son in his divine will might repudiate what the Son in his human will chooses, is to forget that the human nature of the Son has no independence from the Son. It is individuated and characterized by (and only by) the divine Son. Thus, the enhypostatic human will operates only in accordance with the more fundamental choosing and approbation of the Son's divine willing. Accordingly, the Son's divine willing chooses whatever it is that the Son in his human will chooses to do. From this it follows that if the Son in his human

does not entail suffering as God, but to will as God to sin as man would entail sinning as God. For to desire and choose evil (even if it were ultimately wrought by the capacity of another nature that is assumed) is itself evil, but God cannot desire or choose evil. In sum, due to the ends of the incarnation infallibly decreed by God, the grace of the Holy Spirit, and the hypostatic union, Jesus is impeccable.

(5) It remains now to shed further light on the coherence of impeccability and human temptation and striving. Here I would emphasize that facing the pressures of temptation does not presuppose an inclination to evil or (as in Thomas Morris's proposal) an ignorance of the impeccability. Rather, the temptations of Christ are an occasion of painful, costly submission to the Father's will because they involve Christ denying his natural desires and forgoing things that often would be, in ordinary circumstances, legitimate human pursuits. For Christ's temptations to be true temptations, he does not need to have evil desires or to think that he can commit sin at any moment.[228] Rather, he must have a natural human desire for something like food or the preservation of his own life and a painful sense of the relief it would bring to accept whatever it is that has been proposed to him but contradicts the plan of God (e.g., bread in the wilderness or circumventing the crucifixion). Even amid his natural human aversion to deprivation and death, he drinks the cup of self-denial in full, which is why he knows firsthand the difficulty of temptation and why he is called our sympathetic high priest.

Furthermore, it is not as though the divinity of Christ or the infallible plan of God should cancel out the drama of Christ's human obedience. The fact that Christ cannot will to sin does not negate the fact that in concrete situations through his ministry Christ will have to be moved and directed by the Spirit to exercise his spiritual gifts and will have to taste the bitterness of forgoing good things (food, home, certain human relationships, a longer life, and so forth).[229] Thus, his endurance under temptation is decidedly experi-

---

will ever operated sinfully, then the Son's divine willing would have chosen and approved and effected sin, which, as God, the Son cannot do. On the characterization of the human will by the divine person of the Son and the importance of this for the harmony of the Son's two wills, see Third Council of Constantinople (680–81), "Exposition of Faith," in N. Tanner, *Decrees of the Ecumenical Councils*, 128. See also John of Damascus on the determination of the mode of willing (πῶς θέλειν) by the person, the subjection of Christ's human will to the divine, and the "deification" of the human will in the doctrine of Christ's "theandric energy" (*Expos. fidei* 3.14, 17–19 [138–39, 155–62]). See Aquinas, too, on the way in which the humanity of the Son as *organum Deitatis* informs the doctrine of Christ's impeccability (*Super Sent.* 3.12.2.1 sol.).

228. This distinguishes the temptations of Christ from the temptations of those who are led astray by their evil desires (cf. James 1:13–15), on which see Calvin, *In harm.*, 130–31; Owen, *Hebrews*, 3:477–78.

229. On this cf. Owen, *Hebrews*, 4:506.

ential and historical. He *learned* obedience from the things that he suffered (Heb. 5:8). Owen makes the point well in his Hebrews commentary:

> [Christ] can be said to learn obedience only on account of having an experience of it in the exercise. So a man knoweth the taste and savour of meat by eating it; as our Saviour is said to "taste of death," or to experience what was in it, by undergoing of it. And it was one especial kind of obedience that is here intended . . . namely, a submission to undergo great, hard, and terrible things, accompanied with patience and quiet endurance under them, and faith for deliverance from them. . . . Thus he learned obedience, or experienced in himself what difficulty it is attended withal, especially in cases like his own. And this way of learning obedience it is that is so useful unto us, and so full of consolation. For if he had only known obedience, though never so perfectly in the notion of it, what relief could have accrued unto us thereby?[230]

I take it that the Son's direct experience of temptation and its attendant sorrow and bitterness is fundamental to Scripture's teaching on the exemplary character of the Son's patient endurance. It is because the Son himself has taken up our infirmities and truly suffered while tempted that his work is instructive for us. In other words, it would be a mistake to overlook the genuine infirmity of Christ and the subjective costliness of his obedience while setting forth its significance relative to others. It is important to retain both aspects of Christ's obedience in our Christology: his own human striving for the fulfillment of his mission and his example for us.

Taking this approach, according to which Christ is impeccable and yet acutely aware of the pain of denying his natural desires, allows us to respond briefly to some of the main concerns brought up by recent authors in the previous section. With A. B. Bruce, we can affirm that Christ's divinity does not eliminate his human desires or render his temptations docetic. Impeccability is not mechanical. It leaves room for Christ's perception of and desire for the good things and comforts that a human person might ordinarily procure.[231] In this connection, the *non potuit peccare* coheres with the spiritual ascesis of Christ in the New Testament: he has to exercise his spiritual graces and trust in the goodness of God while tasting the bitterness of self-denial. With H. R. Mackintosh, we can affirm that the temptation of Christ was especially severe because he had to deny morally upright desires and, by never giving in, had to face the full duration of temptation. However, if the Son was permanently

---

230. Owen, *Hebrews*, 4:524.
231. Owen makes the important point that the grace of union does not "overbalance" Christ's temptation and suffering, as though the temptation were not a "great trouble unto him" (*Hebrews*, 3:484).

equipped by the Spirit, he did not have repeatedly to obtain anew the power of resisting temptation. He had to exercise his spiritual habits in moments of temptation even as he was permanently endowed by the Spirit with such habits. Furthermore, though a full discussion of Mackintosh's ethical revision of metaphysics goes beyond the limits of this section, the role of Christ's divinity in the doctrine of impeccability is not a matter of the metaphysical supplanting the ethical. For the key point is that the unfailing goodness and holiness of God are incompatible with willing evil.

With Pannenberg, we can affirm that Christ's divinity must not be taken to nullify his human experience. But the forcefulness of Christ's temptation does not turn on Christ being able to choose sin but rather on Christ having to deny his natural desires. And the determination of Christ's life in the way of holiness is not established only at the resurrection but is present from the beginning by virtue of the hypostatic union and the Spirit's indwelling. With Gunton, we can affirm that Christ was truly liable to the assaults of Satan. But in Christ's case this liability consisted not in Christ having competing motives of action in his heart but rather in Christ having a true vulnerability to the sorrow and bitterness of self-denial. Furthermore, Christ's reliance on the Spirit to endure times of temptation need not be set in opposition to the role of Christ's divinity. The Spirit moves and comforts the Savior *qua homo* in the midst of deprivation and grief, and the Spirit does so since he is the Spirit of the divine Son, who would never choose sin.

(6) Finally, a word should be said about the doctrine of the *communicatio operationum*. While traditional Protestant formulations of the doctrine stress that Christ always acts according to both of his natures in all his mediatorial works,[232] this does not necessarily obviate Christ's human activity in the power of the Spirit. It seems to me that this can be broken up into three considerations: first, that Christ's divine power does not obviate his human power and efficacy; second, that each of Christ's mediatorial works has a distinctly human aspect; third, that Christ's human activity is empowered by the Spirit.

First, it is true that in almost all cases the *concursus* of divine and human operation takes place with two distinct acting subjects (i.e., God and a given creature), but this does not entail that, in the unique case of the incarnation, divine and human power must then be placed in a zero-sum game. Within the single subject of Christ, it remains that divinity and humanity are not located in the same order of being. The divinity of Christ (or Christ according

---

232. See Duby, "Atonement, Impassibility, and the *Communicatio Operationum*."

to his divinity) transcends the order of created being. In principle, then, if Christ should act by his divine power and by his human power to effect something, the one operation does not automatically obviate or exclude the other. Second, this is corroborated by the consideration that each of Christ's mediatorial works has a distinctly human aspect to it. Indeed, each of these mediatorial works has an element that is *necessarily* human and could not be supplied by divine operation alone. For example, Christ's crucifixion involves him sovereignly operating as God to lay down his human life, but it also involves him submissively willing and operating as man to undergo death on a cross. That second aspect of the work cannot be accomplished by divine operation and therefore cannot be obviated by divine operation. Christ's sending of the Spirit (with the Father) involves him operating as a divine person from whom the Spirit proceeds and receives the divine power and efficacy, but it also involves him operating as the newly exalted Davidic king who "receives" the promised Spirit from the Father and pours out the Spirit's gifts at Pentecost (Acts 2:33). Likewise, Christ's heavenly intercession involves him, as the omniscient Word, knowing the prayers of the saints and, as man and covenant head, seeing in his own divine essence and knowledge those same prayers and interceding before the Father on behalf of the members of his body.[233] Finally, as discussed in chapter 5, within the unity of God's outward works, the Spirit empowers Christ's human action. The Spirit's empowerment does not exclude the divine activity of the other two persons, but the empowerment does pertain in a special way to the Spirit as the third person of the Trinity who is fittingly said to confer grace and perfect God's works as the person who proceeds from the other two divine persons and receives the divine power, efficacy, and gracious operation from them.[234]

VI. Conclusion

This chapter has focused on expounding the scriptural account of Christ's obedience to the Father. We began by exploring Old and New Testament material on his faithful obedience and submission to the Father in the midst of

233. Cf. Maccovius, *Loci communes* 57 (495); Polanus, *Syntagma*, 6.16 (378–79). On the priestly aspect of Christ's mediatorial office especially requiring the assumption of a human nature, see Owen, *Hebrews*, 4:472.

234. Cf. Mastricht, *TPT*, 2.24.12 (239); 2.27.11 (264), who calls the Holy Spirit the "emissary of the Trinity," whose economic office is a matter of "perfecting the things which have been decreed."

trials and suffering. Certain features of this material elicited further consideration in the next section of the chapter—namely, the knowledge and faith of Christ, the human weaknesses to which Christ was subject in his earthly life, and the sense in which Christ grew through suffering in his role as a merciful high priest. After considering these issues, the next section took into account questions about how the spiritual and moral exertion of Christ relates to his sinlessness. The last main section then argued that Christ assumed a sinless human nature and was impeccable in his human activity without that compromising the authenticity of his trials and temptations, which consisted chiefly in his tasting the bitterness of self-denial while declining to satisfy natural human desires in deference to the plan of God.

This material has bearing on the ways in which a catholic Christology and theology proper can secure some of the desiderata found in modern Christologies. First, this material underscores the centrality of Christ's relationship to the other two divine persons throughout his earthly life and ministry. Having eternally proceeded from the Father in his deity, the Son temporally rendered obedience to the Father in his humanity in every moment of his incarnate life. The fact that he obeyed only as man underscores that he had to trust in the Father's provision and consolation throughout his work and had to depend on the Spirit's graces to empower him to complete this work. Second, Christ's sinless fulfillment of the will of God reflects that he is none other than the divine and impeccable Son, who, with the Father and Spirit, eternally willed our salvation and eternally willed to accomplish that salvation through the instrument of a human nature that he would assume in the fullness of time. That point corroborates the unity of his person. Third, the material in this chapter underscores the authenticity of Christ's human nature and experience. Among other things, he truly despised in his natural and sensitive will the pain and grief that he had to undergo, trusting the Father's love while tasting the bitterness of self-denial and divine judgment upon sin. How this suffering fits together with the doctrine of divine impassibility will be the subject of the final chapter of this study.

SEVEN

"A Man of Sorrows":
The Son's Suffering

I. Introduction

The previous chapter has already emphasized the genuineness of Christ's mental and spiritual suffering in the midst of his earthly trials. This chapter will now seek to integrate the suffering of Christ with the doctrine of divine impassibility. The first main section of the chapter will look further at the biblical account of Christ's suffering. It will highlight the fact that its unique redemptive efficacy turns on it belonging to a divine person, which will ultimately require us to ask whether Christ's suffering can have this redemptive efficacy without Christ suffering as God. But in order to clarify why divine impassibility ought to be upheld in the first place, the next section will examine what passions are and why they do not apply to God in his deity. To anticipate the direction of the argument, the heart of the issue is not whether God cares about his creatures (he certainly does) but whether God himself can gain something from us or be harmed by us. The following section will connect this line of argument to biblical passages in which God repents or grieves, for example. It will maintain that such passages offer metaphorical descriptions of God and that these passages fit with the doctrine of divine impassibility. Finally, returning to the person of Christ, the last main section of the chapter will argue that Christ's suffering and divine impassibility are legitimately brought together by the practice of reduplicative speech about Christ.

II. Biblical Description

It is appropriate to begin with Isaiah's portrayal of the true Israel and true
servant of YHWH that is Jesus of Nazareth. The Davidic king enthroned
for eternity in Isaiah 9 and anointed by the Spirit for judgment in Isaiah 11
is also the one revealed to be a suffering servant later in Isaiah's prophecy.
Much of this suffering is due to mistreatment from other human beings.
The servant is despised by others (49:7). He subjects himself to bodily harm
and humiliation, though he will ultimately triumph in his work (50:6). The
servant's appearance is disfigured and causes people to shudder (52:14). He is
despised and rejected by human beings. He is a "man of sorrows [מַכְאֹבוֹת]"
and "acquainted with infirmity [חֹלִי]" (53:3). The Hebrew word מַכְאוֹב can
signify both corporeal and mental pain. It is the common lot of the human
race laboring in vain under the sun (Eccles. 2:23). It is what evokes God's
deliverance of his people from the oppression of Egypt (Exod. 3:7–8). It is
what David feels because of God's opposition to David's sin and because of
the hatred of his enemies (Ps. 38:18 MT; cf. 69:27 MT). It is the state of Israel
and Judah after their destruction: "Incurable is your sorrow [מַכְאֹבֵךְ]" (Jer.
30:15a). Jerusalem herself laments that there is no מַכְאוֹב like hers, which
YHWH inflicted on the day of his anger (Lam. 1:12, 18). Given that the servant
in Isaiah 53 experiences things like bodily disfigurement and abandonment, his
sorrow is evidently both corporeal and mental. The Hebrew word חֹלִי often
signifies corporeal weakness or sickness (e.g., Deut. 7:15; 28:59, 61; 2 Chron.
21:15, 19; Isa. 38:9), but it may also signify a weakness or ailment affecting
the inner person (e.g., Isa. 1:5; Jer. 6:7; 10:19; Eccles. 6:2; Hosea 5:13). In the
case of the servant in Isaiah 53, he has done no wrong of his own, but his
life is marked by the ailments of fallen humanity. Indeed, he not only experiences sorrow and infirmity but even bears our sorrow and infirmity (53:4a).
The servant suffers not only according to the will of human beings but also
according to the will of God. He not only was thought to be struck down
and afflicted by God (53:4b) but in fact *was* wounded and punished by God.
He was "wounded for our transgressions," "crushed for our iniquities." He
bore the punishment that secured our peace (53:5). God laid upon him the
iniquity of us all (53:6).

The rest of Isaiah 53 persists in the affirmation that the servant suffers according to both human action and divine choice. Though he does no wrong,
the servant endures oppression and burial with the wicked (53:7–9). At the
same time, God is executing his own purpose: he is pleased to crush his
servant, to make him infirm and an offering for sin. Yet the servant is not
ultimately forsaken, for he procures "seed" or descendants for himself. The

good pleasure of YHWH prospers in his hand (53:10). Out of the trouble of his soul the servant is satisfied. By his knowledge he justifies many and bears their iniquities (53:11). God gives him a great portion because of his saving work (53:12a). And it is not as though the servant is merely a passive victim. He has actively poured out his soul to death and intercedes for transgressors (53:12b).

According to Isaiah 53, then, the suffering servant would experience both bodily and spiritual grief. And he would do this not as though it were an unintended consequent of his coming but precisely because it was the will of God for him to face punitive suffering that would lead to the acquittal and deliverance of the people of God. Unlike those who offered the ordinary sacrifices of the Levitical system, YHWH's servant would actively give himself to atone for sins. In addition, he justifies people and obtains a "seed" or progeny for himself. In this connection, it is worth observing that in Isaiah 45:24–25 YHWH has made clear that in or by him alone there is righteousness. In or by YHWH all the "seed" or progeny of Israel are declared righteous or justified. In Isaiah 54:17, YHWH says that the righteousness of the servants of YHWH is from him. Apparently, the suffering servant who is revealed in the New Testament to be Jesus will do something that YHWH alone could do (i.e., justify Israel). Isaiah does not expressly teach the divinity of the servant of YHWH, but he does attribute to the servant a power to justify and to deliver that, according to YHWH, belongs to YHWH alone. Among other things, this means that our discussion of Christ's redemptive suffering in this chapter will have to take into account that its unique salvific efficacy in some way turns on it belonging to a divine person.

In the New Testament, the suffering of Christ takes place all throughout the "days of his flesh" when he learns obedience (so Heb. 5:7–8), but it is particularly acute in his last days. It is not only a corporeal but also a mental suffering. During his final week, Christ says, "Now my soul has been troubled, and what shall I say? 'Father, save me from this hour?' But on account of this I came for this hour" (John 12:27–28). In Gethsemane, Jesus becomes sorrowful and anxious and expresses that his soul is sorrowful even to the point of death (Matt. 26:37–38). Then, in addition to the bodily suffering of crucifixion, Jesus faces on the cross the *poenae infernales* discussed in the previous chapter. Without losing the Father's approbation or his own trust in the Father's goodness, Jesus undergoes a temporary suspension of his active sense of the Father's consolation, crying out, "My God, my God, why have you forsaken me?" (27:46).

As in Isaiah, so too in Acts Jesus's suffering and death are ordained by God. Peter announces at Pentecost that Jesus was "delivered up by the set counsel and foreknowledge of God" (Acts 2:23; cf. 3:18). Again, God's anointed servant Jesus suffered at the hands of human beings who did "as many things as [God's] hand and counsel foreordained to happen" (4:27–28). Although the New Testament does not provide technical analysis of the doctrine of *concursus*, it is plain that what happens on the cross is the outworking of God's purpose. The evil intentions involved in the crucifixion belong to sinful creatures alone, but the event itself is ultimately orchestrated by God for our salvation. God the Father set forth the Son to atone for sin (Rom. 3:25; 1 John 4:10). He made the Son, who knew no sin, to be sin for us "so that in him we might become the righteousness of God" (2 Cor. 5:21).

At the same time, the eternal Son himself, together with the Father and Spirit, ordained this particular plan. The Son did not have it imposed upon him by the Father as though the Father might have possessed a higher volition or dominion than the Son. For the Son had no servant-form until the incarnation (Phil. 2:6–7).[1] The eternal Son actively chose this plan, and then within that plan the Father in his economic office delivers up the Son and the Son in his economic office lays down his own life. The divine volition and authority of the Son in laying down his life can be seen in John 10:17–18: "On account of this the Father loves me, that I myself lay down my life, in order that I might take it up again. No one takes it from me, but I myself lay it down from myself." Likewise, the apostle Paul attests the active love of Christ in his sacrificial death: "The life I now live in the flesh I live by faith in the Son of God, who loved me and gave himself up for me" (Gal. 2:20). "Christ redeemed us from the curse of the law by becoming a curse for us" (3:13). He has "reconciled [you] in the body of his flesh through death to present you holy and unblemished and blameless before him" (Col. 1:22).

In order to appreciate the fullness of the New Testament's teaching on Christ's suffering, it is important to take into account both that suffering's decidedly human character and the fact that its efficacy comes from it belonging to a divine person. On the one hand, it is clear that the suffering Jesus undergoes in the *forma servi* is unlike the richness of his subsistence in the *forma Dei* (2 Cor. 8:9; Phil. 2:6–8). Indeed, the suffering that he undergoes is consequent upon his being "made like" his brothers and sisters, Abraham's children (Heb. 2:14–18). And what is made like something has been "other according to nature."[2] According to the logic of Christ's incarnation and

---

1. See chap. 3, sect. IV, and chap. 6, sect. II.B.
2. Cyril of Alexandria, *Le Christ est un* 725e–726a (338). One might respond that the novelty of Christ's suffering in Heb. 2:17–18 (cf. 4:15) is a matter of him suffering "while being tempted" (πειρασθείς), which might mean only that Christ had not suffered before *in this particular manner*, leaving open the question of whether there was a novelty of Christ's suffering

humiliation, then, his divine life is other than and unlike his human suffering. Furthermore, the suffering that Jesus undergoes is designed to equip him to be a sympathetic high priest acquainted with our weakness (Heb. 2:17–18; 4:14–15). He was not merciful in this particular sense before and had to *become* merciful in this sense. The point is not that Jesus would undergo a would-be divine version of suffering but rather that he undergoes a truly human suffering that enables him in a special way to help us. In addition, the suffering that Jesus undergoes is designed to provide an example of patient endurance for us (so Heb. 12:1–3). "Therefore, since Jesus has suffered *in the flesh*, arm yourselves also with the same intention" (1 Pet. 4:1; cf. 4:13). This is a human example for human persons. Given the New Testament teaching about the dissimilarity between Christ's divinity and humanity and about the purposes of Christ's suffering, it seems to me that biblical Christology does not invite us to posit divine passibility. The teaching of Scripture in fact leads in the opposite direction.

On the other hand, though, it is crucial that the Son's voluntary suffering belongs to a divine person. Its efficacy could not be what it is if it were a suffering willed and undertaken by a mere creature. When Paul urges the elders from Ephesus to keep watch over the flock, he says that the Holy Spirit has appointed them "overseers to shepherd the church of God, which he acquired through his own blood [διὰ τοῦ αἵματος τοῦ ἰδίου]" (Acts 20:28). Some manuscripts have Paul speaking of the church "of the Lord" (τοῦ κυρίου instead of τοῦ θεοῦ), which, by making the subject "the Lord" rather than "God," might have made the following clause seem less awkward ("which he [the Lord] acquired through his own blood"). But critical editions of the New Testament retain τοῦ θεοῦ, not least because it is arguably the more difficult reading and would thus explain the emergence of divergent textual traditions.[3] Given the apparent awkwardness of the statement that God "acquired" or "bought" the church through his own blood, it is perhaps not surprising that various commentators suggest that the phrase ought to be understood as "the blood

---

in general. However, it seems to me that two factors in the text indicate the novelty (and hence the decidedly human character) of Christ's suffering in general. First, throughout Hebrews Christ's suffering is a matter of him being perfected in the days of his flesh in his priestly capacity (2:10; 5:8). Second, the verb πειρασθείς in 2:18 (see also πεπειρασμένον in 4:15) signifies in a broader way being tried or tested, not merely being tempted by one enticing another to do evil (cf. Ellingworth, *Hebrews*, 191; Koester, *Hebrews*, 283; Cockerill, *Hebrews*, 151–52). In this respect, one might point out that there really is no way to suffer except by being in a trying circumstance, which means that a novelty in Christ suffering while being tried indicates a novelty of Christ's suffering in general.

3. See DeVine, "The 'Blood of God' in Acts 20.28," 395–97; Metzger, *A Textual Commentary on the Greek New Testament*, 425–27.

of his own [i.e., his own Son]," sometimes appealing to Luke 22:20, where
Jesus institutes the new covenant by his blood, or to a parallel in Roman 8:32,
where God did not spare "his own Son" (τοῦ ἰδίου υἱοῦ).[4] There are places in
the New Testament where a plural form of ἴδιος functions as a substantive (see
John 1:11; 13:1; Acts 4:23; 24:23). Some interpreters also refer to extrabiblical
sources in which ἴδιος functions substantively as a "term of endearment."[5]

Inasmuch as both interpretations ("his own blood" or "the blood of his
own") recognize that it is not the person of God the Father but the person of
God the Son, Jesus, who partook of flesh and blood and died on the cross,
neither conflicts with orthodox trinitarianism. In the former interpretation
("his own blood"), Jesus would be designated by the term "God," whereas
in the latter Jesus would be called God's "own" or "own Son." Though this
one passage is not the sole foundation of the argument of this section, if the
former reading is correct, it has pertinent implications for our understanding
of Christ's suffering in the present chapter. Taking the singular genitive τοῦ
ἰδίου to have an adjectival function here (as in, "his own blood") accords with
the more common use of ἴδιος.[6] This is why Joseph Fitzmyer, for example,
calls the substantive interpretation ("the blood *of his own*") a "last-ditch
solution."[7] In biblical thought, there is nothing untoward about God acquiring
or purchasing his people. Positively, Paul's description of God acquiring or
purchasing his people echoes certain Old Testament texts. "Remember your
congregation, which you have purchased of old, which you have redeemed to
be the tribe of your heritage!" (Ps. 74:2 ESV). Isaiah 43:21 in the LXX uses the
same verb that Luke has Paul using in Acts 20:28 (a form of περιποιέω): "my
people, whom I have bought [περιεποιησάμην] to recount my excellencies"
(cf. 1 Pet. 2:9). And in his epistles Paul exhibits a readiness to identify Jesus as
the God of Israel (e.g., 1 Cor. 8:6; Phil. 2:9–11) and even explicitly to call him
θεός (Rom. 9:5; Titus 2:13).[8] In fact, Colossians mentions Christ's deity even
in connection with the shedding of his blood: in Christ all fullness, presumably

4. E.g., F. F. Bruce, *Acts*, 391; Johnson, *Acts*, 363; Witherington, *Acts*, 623–24; cf. Harris,
Jesus as God, 131–41. Another line of interpretation posits that Paul is simply speaking hyper-
bolically in order to arrest the attention of his listeners (see Keener, *Acts*, 3039).

5. On which, see Moulton et al., *A Grammar of New Testament Greek*, 90–91; Robertson,
A Grammar of the Greek New Testament, 691–92. Cf. also Bock, *Acts*, 630, who asserts that
τοῦ ἰδίου "implies sonship" and then comments that "the death of Jesus, God's own Son, is
described here."

6. So, e.g., Metzger, *Textual Commentary*, 426.

7. Fitzmyer, *Acts*, 680.

8. Cf. Keener, *Acts*, 3038–39; Harris, *Jesus as God*, 143–85; Capes, *The Divine Christ*. Some
exegetes who prefer the rendering "through the blood of his own" still remark that Paul very
closely connects (perhaps identifies?) God's action and Jesus's action (see Fitzmyer, *Acts*, 680;
Gaventa, "Theology and Ecclesiology in the Miletus Speech," 48–49).

the "fullness of deity" (cf. Col. 2:9), dwells and through him reconciles all things, making peace through the blood of his cross (1:19–20). In light of all this, I think it is best to conclude that Paul in Acts 20:28 teaches that God, in the person of the Son, who has assumed flesh and blood and is also called Jesus, bought the church with his own blood.[9] In John Calvin's exegesis of this passage, he observes that while nothing is "more absurd" than to think that God is corporeal or mortal, Acts 20:28 sets forth the unity of the person of Christ. Since there are two natures in Christ, Scripture does not separate Christ's deity from his humanity. Sometimes Scripture individually mentions that which is proper to one nature, and other times, Calvin writes, it will take what belongs to one of the natures and transfer it to the other. In this way, Paul attributes blood to God: "because the man Jesus Christ, who has poured out his own blood for us, was also God." "This figure of speaking by the ancients is called the *communicatio idiomatum*, because the property of one nature is adapted to another."[10]

If it is correct that "God (the Son) bought the church through his own blood," this interpretation has some pertinent implications for our understanding of Christ's suffering. It sheds light on the unique worth and efficacy of the sacrificial death that took place at Calvary.[11] While it is not the only text that roots the efficacy of Christ's suffering in it belonging to a divine person, it is one text that contributes to this broader pattern of scriptural teaching. The phrase τοῦ αἵματος τοῦ ἰδίου in Acts 20:28, with the adjectival modifier in what is sometimes called the "second attributive position,"[12] arguably underscores that what is signified by the noun is indeed characterized by the descriptive content of the adjective. Moreover, the adjective ἴδιος is itself a "strong possessive."[13] In this case, then, the blood of God the Son is emphatically *his*.

The preeminent book of the New Testament that addresses the unique efficacy of Christ's suffering and death is Hebrews. There the unique efficacy of Christ's saving work and in particular his suffering and death is rooted in it belonging to a person who is both human and divine. On the one hand, Christ could not accomplish what he accomplishes without being truly human. He must be the one who partakes of flesh and blood and tastes death for us all in order to deliver us from death's power (Heb. 2:5–18). Having been tempted

9. Cf. DeVine, "The 'Blood of God' in Acts 20:28," 397–408.
10. Calvin, *In Acta*, 469. However, if the argument of chap. 4, sect. V, in this volume is on target, there is a real communication of properties to the person (though not to the other nature itself) that is ontologically prior to a verbal or predicative communication of properties.
11. On the cost of the redemption that God the Son procures, cf. Bock, *Acts*, 630; Keener, *Acts*, 3037.
12. See, e.g., Wallace, *Greek Grammar beyond the Basics*, 306–7.
13. Robertson, *A Grammar of the Greek New Testament*, 691.

himself, he sympathizes with our weaknesses (4:14–15). Having been perfected through obedience, he is the cause of eternal salvation (5:7–10). His human sinlessness sets him apart so that he has no need to offer sacrifices for any sins of his own (7:26–28).

On the other hand, Christ could not accomplish what he accomplishes without being the Son who is the radiance of the Father's glory and who is himself YHWH, the eternal God (Heb. 1:3, 10–12). His salvation is "so great a salvation" (2:3) because he is superior to all creatures. Christ's priesthood in particular could not accomplish what it accomplishes without it belonging to a divine person. There are debates about when Christ is appointed a priest and when he offers himself to God according to the teaching of Hebrews,[14] but, whatever the precise timing of the actual inception of his priesthood, his priesthood is informed by him being the divine Son. For he is appointed a priest by the one who says to him, "You are my son, today I have begotten you" (5:5). The Father has already said the same thing to the Son in 1:5: "You are my son, today I have begotten you." The pronouncement is an outward declaration of Christ's sonship and an advancement of Christ's economic office that arguably takes place at his resurrection or ascension.[15] But the content of that declaration is not just that Christ is raised from the dead or called "Son" in the sense of being the exalted Messiah. For Christ's sonship in Hebrews 1 involves him being the radiance of the Father's glory, the representation of the Father's substance, and the one through whom the Father made all things (1:2–3). If the *occasion* of the declaration of Christ's sonship is his resurrection or ascension, its *material content* includes that Christ is the divine Son.[16] Thus, when the Father installs Christ as high priest in 5:5 with a statement of his begetting, it follows that Christ's high priesthood is informed and given its superiority not only by his resurrection but also by his divine sonship, which fitted him for his economic work in the first place.[17]

This claim is reinforced by the link between Christ's priesthood and Melchizedek's. Right after teaching that Christ has entered the presence of God, having become a high priest "according to the order of Melchizedek" (Heb. 6:20), the author of Hebrews elaborates on the unusual nature of Melchizedek's priesthood. Melchizedek is "without father, without mother, without

14. On this issue, see Peterson, *Hebrews and Perfection*, 191–95; Moffitt, *Atonement and the Logic of Resurrection*, 194–214; Jamieson, "When and Where Did Jesus Offer Himself?"; Jamieson, *Jesus' Death and Heavenly Offering in Hebrews*.

15. So, e.g., Ellingworth, *Hebrews*, 113–14; Cockerill, *Hebrews*, 103–4.

16. Cf. Owen, *Hebrews*, 3:135–37.

17. Regarding the connection between Christ's priesthood and sonship, cf. also Heb. 10:21 with 3:1–6. On Hebrews using the designation "Son" to refer to Christ's *divine* sonship (though not only to his divine sonship), see Jamieson, *The Paradox of Sonship*, chap. 2.

genealogy, having neither beginning of days nor end of life, and, resembling the Son of God, he remains a priest forever" (7:3). The point is not that in reality Melchizedek had no biological father or mother but rather that in the text of Scripture no account is given of the beginning or end of his life, which enables him in this qualified way to prefigure the Son of God, who truly has no beginning or end of days (cf. 1:10–12). Melchizedek is without beginning in writing; the eternal Son is without beginning in reality.[18] "The direction of thought is important: the Son of God is not like Melchizedek; rather Melchizedek is like the Son of God, who is the principal reality."[19] While the forward perpetuity of Christ's priesthood might be explained by his (human) resurrection (see, e.g., 7:16, 28), the absence of temporal beginning that is included in what renders his priesthood superior can be ascribed to his divinity alone.[20]

As an aspect of Christ's priesthood, Christ's atoning death is efficacious at least in part because of his divine sonship. Even if Christ formally began his priesthood after his resurrection and offered himself up to God after his ascension in the particular descriptions of Hebrews (see 2:17; 5:5–6; 6:20; 7:15–16), it remains the case that what Christ the high priest offers up to God is "the life he gave in death" (cf. 9:11–14, 28).[21] And the superior worth of Christ's death could not have been grounded in his human resurrection life that he obtained only after his death. Instead, it must have been grounded in the death being the death of God's eternal Son and in the sinlessness of the eternal Son, a conclusion borne out in a number of interconnected passages in Hebrews that contrast the inadequacy of Levitical sacrifices with the supremacy of Christ's sacrifice.

The Levitical priesthood could not achieve "perfection" (Heb. 7:11). Its gifts and sacrifices, dealing in the end only with matters of food and drink and bodily regulations until the "time of reformation," could not perfect the worshiper "according to conscience" (9:9–10). Again, the repetition of the same sacrifices under the Mosaic law could not perfect the ones offering them—otherwise, they would have ceased (10:1–2). Ultimately, it is "impossible for the blood of bulls and goats to take away sins" (10:4). However, Christ entered the heavenly tabernacle not through the blood of goats and

18. John Chrysostom, *In Heb.* 7.12 (97). Cf., e.g., Lane, *Hebrews 1–8*, 164–66.

19. Koester, *Hebrews*, 343.

20. Peterson, e.g., calls into question the place of the two natures of Christ in the conception of Christ's priesthood in Hebrews, arguing for "the centrality of making expiation for the sins of the people" (*Hebrews and Perfection*, 194). It seems to me that Heb. 6:20, taken with the material on Jesus's divinity in Heb. 1, implies that the divinity of Christ is included in the conception of Christ's priesthood. And Jesus's divinity and the act of making expiation are hardly mutually exclusive.

21. See Jamieson, *Jesus' Death and Heavenly Offering*, 165–77.

calves but "through his own blood" (τοῦ ἰδίου αἵματος) and "once for all," thereby securing an "eternal redemption" (9:11–12). If the blood of animals provided a purification of the flesh, "how much more will the blood of Christ, who through the eternal Spirit offered himself without blemish to God, purify our conscience from dead works" (9:13–14). Christ purified the things of the heavenly tabernacle "with better sacrifices" (9:23). And he does not enter the heavenly tabernacle to offer himself repeatedly. Rather, "he has been revealed once for all at the end of the ages for the removal of sins through his sacrifice" (9:25–26). Hebrews repeats that Christ's sacrifice did not need repeating. The offering of Christ's body has sanctified us "once for all" (10:10). He offered only one sacrifice, which has perfected us forever (10:12, 14). The supreme worth of Christ's sacrifice is then a warning not to apostatize: if breaking the Mosaic covenant led to punishment, "how much worse do you think the one trampling the Son of God underfoot and regarding the blood of the covenant as profane will be considered worthy of punishment?" (10:28–29). Thus, instead of being ashamed of Christ, the readers are told to bear the reproach of Jesus, who "suffered outside the gate in order that he might sanctify the people through his own blood [τοῦ ἰδίου αἵματος]" (13:12–13).

The goal of covering this material in Isaiah, Acts, Hebrews, and other places is to show that the salvific efficacy of Christ's suffering and death hinges on that suffering and death being undertaken by the divine Son himself. It is to show that we cannot separate Christ's suffering from his deity even as we make a case that in the midst of his suffering he remains impassible according to his deity. If we take the exegetical material seriously, we will have to be alert to the care that is required to integrate the human suffering and the divine impassibility of Christ.

Earlier Christian authors have picked up on the need to draw together the efficacy of Christ's atoning death and his divinity. This can be found in medieval commentaries on the *Sentences*, for example. Bonaventure writes that "no pure creature has been able to make satisfaction for the whole human race." For Bonaventure, this applies with respect to both the grave injustice done to God and the penalty owed because of the injustice.[22] Aquinas contends that Christ could make satisfaction for the sin of the human race by his passion on account of his divinity and divine action. Christ's human nature was an "instrument" of a divine person, which means that Christ's human operation "had in itself the force of divinity." Thus, "the meritorious action of Christ, although it was a human operation, nevertheless acted with divine power." Therefore, the meritorious action of Christ surpasses that of someone who

---

22. Bonaventure, *In Sent.* 3.20.1.3 (423).

is a mere man. His humanity and his meritorious action have a greater worth than the entire human race.[23] Though Christ did not suffer as God, his human operation and passion "have power from divine conjunction [ex divino consortio]." Christ's action in meriting salvation for us is efficacious because it is the action of one who is at once God and man, and his passion has an infinite efficacy in satisfying for sin because of the union of the two natures in him.[24]

In early Reformed thought, Christ's operation according to both his divinity and his humanity is often distilled in the notion of the communicatio operationum. William Ames, for example, takes it to be an axiom that "by the God-man the reparation of the human race has been done, since he is capable as God [and] ought to satisfy as man." "We say that he has suffered according to the human nature, but he has endured and overcome the things which he has suffered by the force and power of the divine nature." Again, "In the human nature he has satisfied, but by the divine nature the worth [pretium], dignity, efficacy, and application of that satisfaction come forth."[25] Such reflections on the efficacy of Christ's death of course presuppose that his passion has a penal and substitutionary aspect according to which the question of its worth and dignity is intelligible. But perhaps this should not surprise us since the Spirit himself has told us in Scripture that Christ bore our punishment and gave his life as a ransom. His blood, the apostle Peter tells us, outvalues silver and gold since it is "the precious blood as of the Lamb without blemish and without defect" (1 Pet. 1:18–19).

In this section we have considered the teaching of Scripture on Christ's suffering, particularly the fact that the efficacy of Christ's suffering and death is rooted in his identity as the divine Son. Christ's suffering and death accomplish what they accomplish by virtue of being the suffering and death of a divine person. Before we directly take up the work of integrating Christ's suffering and his impassibility in greater detail, the next two sections of the chapter aim to show why impassibility is worth holding on to in the first place. After this, the final main section of the chapter will return to the issue of integrating Christ's passion and impassibility.

III. Impassibility and the Nature of Passions

Various theologians in recent times have contended that God is passible. The arguments given for divine passibility involve a range of considerations,

23. Aquinas, *Super Sent.* 3.18.1.6 sol. 1. Cf. 3.18.1.1 ad 1.
24. Aquinas, *Super Sent.* 3.19.1.1, quaestiuncula 1 ad 1; sol. 2.
25. Ames, *Bellarminus enervatus*, 2.3.3 (116).

including the suffering of Christ, the biblical passages in which God is said to have passions like grief or wrath, and the prima facie moral or existential appeal of a God who can experience pain.[26] The previous section and the final main section of this chapter address the coherence of divine impassibility and the suffering of Christ. The next section of this chapter addresses the coherence of divine impassibility and the biblical passages that speak of God's grief, wrath, and so forth. Along the way, the next section will also touch upon the question of whether divine impassibility is a morally or existentially viable teaching. The goal of the present section is to argue that God is impassible by examining more carefully what passions are and why they do not apply to God. Positively, I will aim to clarify what it does mean to attribute affections of the will (e.g., love, delight, hatred) to God. I will break up the material under the following four points.

(1) It will be helpful first to clarify the different senses in which the term "passion" has been used in classical philosophy and earlier Christian theology.[27] In general, the term "passion" signifies being acted upon by an agent or receiving something from an agent in such a way that the recipient or patient is somehow conformed to or shaped by the act of the agent. In a loose sense, "passion" can signify receiving something without losing anything (e.g., gaining new understanding), but in that case the subject is in fact being perfected more than it is being acted upon or disturbed. In another sense, "passion" can signify the introduction of a new quality in a subject, perhaps together with consequent actions performed according to that new quality.[28]

---

26. See, e.g., Barth, CD, IV.1, 186–88; IV.2, 357; IV.3.2, 414–15; von Balthasar, *Mysterium Paschale*, esp. 23–36; T. F. Torrance, *The Christian Doctrine of God*, 246–50; Moltmann, *The Crucified God*; Jüngel, *God as the Mystery of the World*; Jenson, *Systematic Theology*, 125, 144, 234 and passim; Wolterstorff, *Inquiring about God*, chaps. 8–9; Fretheim, *What Kind of God?*

27. There is a large body of recent literature dealing with the passions or emotions from historical and constructive perspectives, including James, *Passion and Action*; Griffiths, *What Emotions Really Are*; Nussbaum, *Upheavals of Thought*; Lagerlund and Yrjönsuuri, *Emotions and Choice from Boethius to Descartes*; Roberts, *Emotions*; Hatzimoysis, *Philosophy and the Emotions*; Knuuttila, *Emotions in Ancient and Medieval Philosophy*; Solomon, *Thinking about Feeling*; Gondreau, "The Passions and the Moral Life"; Goldie, "Emotion"; Cates, *Aquinas on the Emotions*; Goldie, *The Oxford Handbook of Philosophy of Emotion*; Lombardo, *The Logic of Desire*; Scrutton, *Thinking through Feeling*; Peckham, *The Love of God*, chap. 6; Kahm, *Aquinas on Emotion's Participation in Reason*; LaPine, *The Logic of the Body*; Mullins, *God and Emotion*; F. Spencer, *Passions of the Christ*. In recent works, there are some debates about the different connotations of "passion" and "emotion." While I use the terms "passion" and "affection" here, I suspect that, if carefully defined, the word "emotion" also can be serviceable in theological discussion.

28. Passion taken as a quality is still distinct from a settled habit or virtue. Indeed, passion in itself may be amoral and then rendered moral or immoral insofar as the habits of the intellect and will govern (or fail to govern) the passion well or evilly.

In addition, "passion" can signify receiving something good from an agent while losing something bad (e.g., undergoing the good effects of a medicine that eliminates sickness). Most properly, though, "passion" signifies receiving something bad while losing something good. In other words, it signifies the reception of an effect that involves a change in which the subject is harmed and loses something ingredient in its well-being, a change in which the subject loses a disposition agreeable to its nature and telos and, in place of that disposition, now has a contrary disposition.[29] In this strict sense, passion is "corruptive" or "destructive" of what is good.[30] Thus, the term "passion" designates something like sorrow more properly than something like joy.[31]

Given the unity of body and soul in traditional Aristotelian psychology and, more importantly, in biblical anthropology, and given the accompanying principle that sense experience is needed to incite understanding and volition in the soul, treatments of the passions sometimes state that the passions involve bodily change and pertain to the soul just in connection with the body.[32] Thus, Aquinas writes that, strictly speaking, passions apply to the soul *per accidens*, inasmuch as the whole person composed of both body and soul suffers.[33] In particular, the passions of the composite subject pertain to the subject's "appetitive power" (i.e., the will). For in the case of passion, being acted upon affects the patient in such a way that the patient is now either drawn to or repulsed by the agent, and attraction and repulsion pertain to the will as the power of the soul that inclines to what is good and agreeable and abhors what is evil or disagreeable. And, in this line of thought, if passions involve bodily change and affect the soul just in connection with the body, then they pertain especially to the subject's "sensitive appetite" (i.e., the soul's power of willing taken with respect to things that concern the well-being of the body).[34] At the same time, older authors still suggest that passions in a certain sense do apply to the soul's "rational appetite" as well (i.e., the soul's power of willing under the deliberation and judgment of reason, a power that concerns not merely corporeal but incorporeal and spiritual things).

29. See further John of Damascus, *Dial.*, fus. νγ' (123–24); Aquinas, *In Metaphys.* 5.14.958 (256); 16.993, 998–1000 (263–64); 20.1065–68 (277–78); Aquinas, *ST* IaIIae.22.1 (168); 24.1 (179); Keckermann, *Systema logicae, tribus libris adornatum*, I, sect. prior, 11 (601–2); Keckermann, *Scientiae metaphysicae*, 2.2 (2038); Alsted, *Metaphysica*, 2.7 (265–66); Maccovius, *Metaphysica*, 2.5 (244–45).

30. So Alsted, *Metaphysica*, 2.7 (265).

31. See, e.g., Aquinas, *ST* IaIIae.22.1 corp. (168).

32. See Aristotle, *De anima* 1.403a3–403b24 (3–5). Cf. John of Damascus, *Expos. fidei* 2.22 (87–88); Aquinas, *Sent. De anima* 1.2 (9–12); Mastricht, *TPT*, 2.15.19 (161).

33. Aquinas, *ST* IaIIae.22.1 (168).

34. See John of Damascus, *Expos. fidei* 2.22 (88); Aquinas, *ST* Ia.80.1–2 (282–84); 81.1 (288); IaIIae.22.2–3 (169–71).

For example, Aquinas comments that *passio divinorum* is "affection toward divine things, and conjunction to them by love, which nevertheless happens without corporeal transmutation."[35] There are inward delights and griefs that are determined not by corporeal objects but by incorporeal and spiritual objects and that are thus ultimately applicable to the rational will.[36]

The term "passion" often connotes something problematic like violence, irrationality, or immoral desire (cf. Rom. 1:26; Col. 3:5; 1 Thess. 4:5).[37] However, earlier Christian writers often recognize that the term can be used in a variety of ways, not necessarily signifying things that are morally evil.[38] Whether one translates the Greek πάθος with the Latin *passio*, *affectio*, or *affectus*, it is a "movement" or a "motion of the soul."[39] In the classical metaphysical tradition, the term "motion" (κίνησις, *motio*, *motus*) can be used in several ways. Broadly speaking, it is the actualization (ἐντελέχεια) of potential, or the attainment of the proper end of potential.[40] It is often taken to be the incomplete act of a corporeal thing (e.g., being warmed up but not yet fully hot), the incomplete act of something being acted upon (e.g., by something that produces heat).[41] However, it is often applied even to incorporeal things to signify a transition from inactive potential to actuality or activity, not least in cases where such a transition is induced by some object that the subject comes to apprehend or desire.[42]

35. Aquinas, *ST* IaIIae.22.3 ad 1 (171).

36. John of Damascus, *Expos. fidei* 2.13 (80–81); Aquinas, *ST* IaIIae.31.4–5 (217–20); 35.7 (246–47); IIIa.46.5 corp. (441); 46.6 corp. and ad 4 (443–44). In the case of incorporeal, strictly spiritual creatures (i.e., angels), it is sometimes said that would-be "passions" like delight or anger are applied to them just with respect to the "simple" acts of the rational will (cf. Augustine, *De civ.* 9.5; Aquinas, *ST* Ia.59.4 ad 2 [96]; IaIIae.22.3 ad 3 [171]). At the same time, the intellectual and volitional acts of angels still involve the transition from passive potential to actuality that also characterizes the passions of the human will, with pure actuality belonging to God alone (so Aquinas, *ST* Ia.10.5 corp. [100]; 54.1–3 [39–40, 45, 47]; 59.1 ad 3 [92]; 59.2 corp. [93]; 60.1 ad 2 [98]).

37. Cf. remarks from John of Damascus, *Expos. fidei* 2.22 (88); Mastricht, *TPT*, 2.15.32 (166).

38. On this point, and on the superficial difference between Stoic and Aristotelian or "Peripatetic" use of the language, see Augustine, *De civ.* 9.4–5; Aquinas, *Sent. Ethic.* 2.4 (84–85); Aquinas, *ST* IaIIae.24.1–4 (179–82); 31.1 ad 3 (216).

39. See Augustine, *De civ.* 9.4; Aquinas, *Sent. Ethic.* 2.4 (84); Aquinas, *ST* IaIIae.23.1 sed contra (173); Polanus, *Syntagma*, 2.35 (193); Owen, *Vindiciae evangelicae* 4 (110); Mastricht, *TPT*, 2.15.32 (166).

40. E.g., John of Damascus, *Dial.*, fus. ξβ' (129–30).

41. E.g., Aquinas, *Commentaria in octo libros Physicorum Aristotelis* 3.1.2.3, 6–7 (105–6); 3.1.3.2 (107–8); 3.2.4.1 (109); cf. Aquinas, *Sent. De anima* 3.6 (229–30).

42. Cf. Aquinas, *In De div. nom.* 4.7.368–79 (121–22); Aquinas, *SCG* 1.13 (30–34); 1.68 (198–99); Aquinas, *ST* Ia.10.5 ad 1 (100–101); 18.3 corp. (228); 54.1–3 (39–40, 45, 47); 59.1 ad 3 (92); 59.2 corp. (93); 60.1 ad 2 (98); IaIIae.9.1–4 (74–79). See also the slightly different discussion in Alsted's *Metaphysica*, 1.13 (127–28, 131), and *Theologia naturalis*, 1.16 (141).

Accordingly, the *passio* or *affectio* that concerns us here is a motion of the soul that occurs when a subject is acted upon and drawn to or repulsed by an agent and undergoes a transition from passive potential to actuality that yields a new disposition in the will.[43] The affections of the will in view in this section may be marked by motion in two senses in that they involve (a) an actualization of passive potential in a subject and (b) at least in some cases, an imperfect act of desiring something good without yet acquiring it or being able to acquire it.[44]

In common ramifications of the specific affections, they are differentiated by their objects.[45] The affection of love (*amor*) is a basic inclination or attraction toward some object, a basic complacency in some object that is caused by the goodness of the object, whether the lover has already obtained the object or not.[46] Hatred (*odium*) is opposed to love and is a basic disinclination or repulsion from some object that is caused by the evil or harmfulness of the object, whether the one doing the hating is already joined to the object or not. Desire (*desiderium*) is a longing or seeking after a good thing that is not present to the subject. If the absent good is perceived to be difficult to obtain, then in this respect the desire is also called "hope" (*spes*). If the absent good is perceived to be unattainable, then the affection is called

43. This kind of motion is sometimes called ἀλλοίωσις or *alteratio* (the introduction of a new quality or disposition in the subject) (see Aristotle, *Metaphysica* 12.1069b [243–44]; John of Damascus, *Dial.*, fus. ξβʹ [129–30]; Aquinas, *In Metaphys.* 12.2.2424–40 [569–72]). Ἀλλοίωσις or *alteratio* is commonly identified as a qualitative kind of motion alongside a quantitative kind of motion of "increase" or "diminution" (αὔξησις or φθίσις) and a local kind of motion of spatial change (κατὰ τόπον or ποῦ). To these three kinds of motion is added the more fundamental change of "simple generation" or "corruption" (γένεσις or φθορά), concerning substance itself (κατὰ τόδε), making a taxonomy of four kinds of change.

44. On this second point, see Owen, *Vindiciae evangelicae* 4 (109–10).

45. See, e.g., Aquinas, *ST* IaIIae.23.1 (173–74); 23.4 (176–77); Mastricht, *TPT*, 2.15.20 (161–62). One of the key distinctions drawn is between "concupiscible" passions (those that pertain simply to what is good and agreeable or to what is bad and disagreeable) and "irascible" passions (those that pertain to what is good and agreeable or to what is bad and disagreeable with respect to the good being difficult to obtain or the bad being difficult to avoid).

46. A variety of terms are used to designate love in its various aspects, so the explanation here is only a précis that is open to more clarification and precision. Among other things, the term *dilectio* can be used to designate a basic propensity or attraction toward some good as an end. *Complacentia* can be used as a rough synonym of *dilectio*, but it can also be referred to a chosen means (rather than an end). *Delectatio intenta* ("intended delight") can also signify or accompany this initial *dilectio*. Typically, though, *delectatio* signifies a perfection of desire, a *complacentia* or *quietatio* (repose) in a present good that is really joined to oneself. *Gaudium* can signify a *quietatio* in a present good whether it is really joined to oneself or in some sense still extrinsic to oneself. In addition, *delectatio* can signify a delight and repose whether the subject is a rational creature or not, whereas *gaudium* can signify the same in the case of rational creatures only. Cf. Aquinas, *SCG* 1.90 (243–44); Aquinas, *ST* IaIIae.25.2 (184–85); 31.3 (217); Turretin, *Inst.*, 3.20.5 (1:267); Mastricht, *TPT*, 2.15.5 (158).

"despair" (*desperatio*). Flight (*fuga*) is an aversion toward an evil or harmful thing that is not present to the subject. If the absent evil is perceived to be difficult to avoid and insuperable, then the affection is called "fear" (*timor*). If the absent evil is perceived to be difficult to avoid but elicits in the subject a readiness to fight against it, then the affection is called "daring" (*audacia*). Joy (*gaudium*) is a repose and satisfaction in a good thing already obtained by the subject. Sorrow (*tristia*) is an aversion to an evil thing that is already joined to the subject and causes harm. Finally, anger (*ira*) is sorrow with a desire or hope to punish wrongdoing.

In creaturely or ordinary circumstances, both the affections that pertain to good things and the affections that pertain to evil or unsuitable things presuppose some lack in the subject. In the case of those that pertain to good things, there is initially a lack of inclination toward the good, an unfulfilled potential even to have the inclination. Then, with the inclination in place, there is often still a lack of the good itself, an unfulfilled desire to be connected with an absent good. In addition, when the good is obtained, it remains the case that the subject initially lacked the good and thus that the subject's satisfaction and well-being had to be established from without.[47] In the case of the affections that pertain to evil or disagreeable things, there is often a lack involved as well. There is a passive potential to be perturbed or a vulnerability to the loss of what is good, by which the subject can be harmed and disposed contrary to its nature and proper telos.

(2) A careful discussion of divine impassibility will have to take into account the technical use of the aforementioned terms. One can take up the received, technical use of these terms and then either affirm or deny that "passion" in the technical signification applies to God. Or one can reject the received, technical use of the terms, produce a new arrangement of terms and definitions, and then either affirm or deny that some new signification of "passion" applies to God. But if one makes an unarticulated shift away from the older definitions and then attempts to critique older accounts of divine impassibility, one will simply generate confusion. In my judgment, the treatments of passion offered by authors like Aristotle, John of Damascus, and Aquinas do provide sufficiently accurate descriptions of what happens when created beings are affected by objects that they encounter, even if such treatments might be clarified or supplemented at some points for constructive theology today. In other words, I think these descriptions express in formal ways a natural knowledge that ordinary human beings already have about the

47. As Aquinas notes, the passions are formed according to the "active power" of their objects (*ST* IaIIae.23.4 corp. [176]).

way things happen in the world. Readers who disagree on this point might venture a new understanding of what passion involves, work out an alternative semantic system by which to express that understanding, and then put that system forward for philosophical and theological debate about its heuristic value. The present discussion, however, will utilize these established technical treatments of what passion involves with the aim of facilitating knowledge of God.

(3) If passions that pertain to good things are movements of the will with which the subject begins to seek some good or begins to enjoy some good not originally possessed, then these passions in an ordinary sense do not apply to God insofar as God himself is the highest good and the source of all creaturely good. Here it is important to pause and note that both Scripture and the Aristotelian or Peripatetic philosophical tradition speak about what is good and about the goodness of God in particular in several interconnected ways.[48] Something can be called "good" in the sense that it has what befits its nature or its given purpose, or in the sense that it befits the nature and purpose of something by which it may be possessed (e.g., Gen. 2:18; Exod. 18:17; Num. 14:7; Deut. 1:14; Ps. 111:10; Eccles. 5:18; Matt. 7:11, 17; Luke 5:39; 8:8; 16:25; Rom. 8:28). This is goodness that concerns the perfection of a thing's essential constitution, its qualities, its operations, or its attainment of an end.[49] A person or a deed can be called "good" in the sense that the person or the deed has a moral alignment with a rule of conduct (e.g., Gen. 2:17–18; Deut. 6:18; 12:28; 1 Sam. 26:16; 2 Kings 20:3; 2 Chron. 14:2; Ps. 14:1, 3; Eccles. 9:2; Mic. 6:8; Isa. 1:17; Matt. 19:16; Luke 23:50; Acts 11:24; Rom. 7:12–13; 16:19; 2 Cor. 5:10). Something can also be called "good" in the sense that it is useful (so Eccles. 7:11, 18; Luke 14:34; James 2:14, 16). Finally, something can be called "good" in the sense that it is pleasing or evokes delight: "God

48. Concerning the scriptural language, see BDB, 373–75; Louw and Nida, *Greek-English Lexicon*, 57.109–10 (570); 65.20–25 (623–24); 88.1–11 (743–44); *NIDNTTE* 1:92–100. For the use of pertinent philosophical concepts and distinctions, see Augustine, *De trin.* 8.3.4 (1:271–73); Boethius, *Philosophiae consolationis* 3.10 (276–85); Aquinas, *Sent. Ethic.* 1.1 (5); 2.3 (83–85); Aquinas, *SCG* 1.37 (111); Aquinas, *ST* Ia.5.1, 6 (56, 64–65); 6.2–4 (67–68, 70); 20.2 corp. (254); Keckermann, *Scientiae metaphysicae*, 1.3–4 (2018–19); Alsted, *Metaphysica*, 1.8 (92–102); Maccovius, *Metaphysica*, 1.8 (51–63); Leigh, *A Treatise of Divinity*, 2.10 (78–81); Mastricht, *TPT*, 2.16.1–2, 4, 6–8 (170–72).

49. In the Peripatetic tradition, at the most fundamental level, something is good insofar as it exists. For if something exists, then its essence (which will include something desirable) is actualized, and in this minimal way the thing is "perfect" and desirable. This is often called a "transcendental" goodness (i.e., goodness as a mode of being applicable in all the categories of being). A being may then be good or perfect insofar as it has not just its essence but also those qualities, operations, or attainments that befit its nature or use, which may be called a "natural" goodness.

saw everything that he had made, and indeed, it was very good" (Gen. 1:31 NRSV; cf. Gen. 6:2; 49:15; 2 Sam. 18:27; 19:38; 1 Kings 21:2; Neh. 9:36; Job 21:25; Pss. 34:12; 103:5; 107:9; 133:1; Prov. 15:23, 30; 24:13, 25; Eccles. 6:3, 6; Isa. 55:2).[50] Such modes of goodness are unified in that the good (considered as the perfect, the morally virtuous, the pleasing) is always what is desirable (*appetibile*) or what ought to be desired.[51] In other words, the good is what elicits and terminates the motion of the will. In this regard, the good is communicative or self-diffusive: as an end to be willed by others, it orients and draws others to union with itself.[52]

God himself is good in similar senses. God has in himself all that befits his own nature and lacks nothing of what it is to be the true God (Isa. 41:21–24; 43:9–10; 44:6–8; Jer. 10:1–16; John 17:5). In this regard, he alone is absolutely and originally "good" or "perfect" (Matt. 5:48; Mark 10:18; Luke 18:19). "God cannot be a better God."[53] In addition, God is good with respect to his will. He is good in that his will inclines or propends to communicating or giving what is good: "You are good and do good" (Ps. 119:68; cf. Neh. 9:25; Pss. 25:7; 31:19; 68:10; 73:1; 86:5; 143:10; 145:9; Isa. 63:7; Lam. 3:25, 31–33; Zech. 8:15; Matt. 20:15; Acts 14:17; Titus 3:4). This inclination or propensity of will is commonly called "love" or "benevolence" or, in its outward manifestation, "beneficence."[54] God is also good in that he is always morally inclined to do

50. The good in these last three senses is often expressed in terms of an "honest" or "virtuous good" (*bonum honestum*), a "useful good" (*bonum utile*), and a "pleasing good" (*bonum jucundum*). In some cases, the *bonum honestum* is described without overt moral connotation as that which is desirable per se, while in other cases it is described as that which is desirable per se over against any moral deficiency that might be found in the *bonum jucundum* taken as that which is pleasing or delectable or as the act of delight itself (see Aquinas, ST Ia.5.6 corp. and ad 2 [65]; Alsted, *Metaphysica*, 1.8 [99]; Leigh, *A Treatise of Divinity*, 2.10 [80]; Mastricht, *TPT*, 2.16.4 [171]).

51. Desirability in this case is not necessarily a matter of haphazard human preference. It is fundamentally a matter of correspondence with the being and will of God (cf. Alsted, *Metaphysica*, 1.8 [92]).

52. On the good as communicative in this sense, see Aquinas, *In Metaphys.* 12.7.2519–35 (590–92); Aquinas, *ST* Ia.5.4 (61); 19.2 (233). Cf. Maccovius, *Metaphysica*, 1.8 (53): "An end communicates itself because it perfects a thing."

53. Leigh, *A Treatise of Divinity*, 2.10 (80).

54. See, e.g., Turretin, *Inst.*, 3.20.2–5 (1:266–67); Mastricht, *TPT*, 2.16.1 (170). It may be worth noting that God's goodness can be described as "communicative" or "self-diffusive" in at least two ways. The first way concerns the goodness of God that is all the perfection God has in himself. By virtue of this perfection, he is eminently desirable. If God decides to create the world, then God will orient and direct all things to himself as their end (so Rom. 11:36; 1 Cor. 8:6; 10:31). The second way concerns the goodness of God as a particular attribute or virtue of his will, which is his propensity to communicate or give good to others. In the first sense, God's goodness is necessarily communicative (apt to be the chief end and desire of anything that might exist). In the second sense, God's goodness might be considered naturally and necessarily communicative or contingently communicative: naturally and necessarily communicative with

what is right (Ps. 25:8; James 1:13; cf. James 1:17; 1 John 1:5), which is often called "righteousness" (e.g., Deut. 32:4; Pss. 9:7–8; 11:7; 96:13; 97:2; Dan. 9:14). Finally, God is good in that he is the one in whom the highest delight, joy, and satisfaction may be found and the one from whom all creaturely, secondary pleasures come forth (Pss. 16:2, 5–6, 11; 34:8, 10; 36:8–9; 37:4; 42:1–2; 65:4; 84:1–2, 4, 10–11; 103:5; 107:9; 145:16, 19; Isa. 51:3; Jer. 31:12; Zech. 9:17; John 16:24; 17:13; 1 Pet 2:3). Indeed, in God's triune existence, God the Father beholds and delights in the goodness of the Son, who is the radiance of divine glory (Matt. 3:17; 17:5; John 17:5, 24; Eph. 1:6; Heb. 1:3).

Inasmuch as God would not fail to appreciate his own infinite, sufficient, original goodness, and inasmuch as Scripture gives us a glimpse of the divine persons' mutual enjoyment of one another, it follows that the triune God eternally delights and reposes in himself as the primary object of his own will. Moreover, in relation to creatures, God is the source and archetype of all created goodness, so creatures are good only insofar as they imitate him (Gen. 1:26–27; Pss. 16:2; 24:1; 19:1; 94:9; Matt. 5:48; Luke 6:36; Rom. 11:36; 1 Cor. 8:6; Eph. 3:15; 4:24; Col. 3:10; 1 Tim. 4:4; James 1:17; 2 Pet. 1:4). In this respect, God himself is "the good of every good."[55] Accordingly, God does not acquire new goodness or supplement his goodness by his decision to create us or by our existence and actions (Ps. 50:7–15; Acts 17:24–25; Rom. 11:35–36). The will and operation of God *ad extra* do not presuppose but rather produce the goodness of created beings.[56]

In view of all this, it is important not to take passions or affections directed toward good things and apply them in their ordinary sense to God. God in his perfection and omnipotence does not have to struggle to obtain something that might be requisite to his well-being, but affections like *amor* and *delectatio* or *gaudium* do still have a positive application to God.[57] On the one hand, divine love and joy do not involve a motion or change in God whereby he might become newly inclined toward or newly satisfied by some good that he previously did not have—some good of which he was not the archetype and source. One therefore has to remove from the signification of these terms (a) change from passive potential to attainment, (b) incomplete longing for an absent good, and (c) novel acquisition of something good and

---

respect to the eternal processions in God, contingently communicative with respect to the order of created being. On divine goodness in connection with communication *ad intra* and *ad extra*, cf. Maccovius on God's *duplex communicatio* in *Metaphysica*, 1.8 (54–57).

55. Augustine, *De trin.* 8.3.4 (272).

56. Aquinas, *ST* Ia.20.2 corp. (254); Mastricht, *TPT*, 2.15.9 (159).

57. Cf. Aquinas's remarks about love and joy considered under the genus of passion versus love and joy considered in themselves or in their own "species," the latter containing nothing repugnant to God's perfection (*SCG* 1.90 [243–44]; *ST* Ia.20.1 ad 2 [253]).

satisfying. On the other hand, there is a positive sense in which love and joy do belong preeminently to God. As noted above, the term "love" can have various significations, including a basic propensity to or complacency in what is good and a propensity to give what is good to another. With respect to the former, God's love is the eternal act of his will in which he enjoys his own goodness.[58] With respect to the latter, God's benevolence may be taken as a virtue or perfection of his will—though, if God is simple, such a virtue is not really distinct from a faculty or act of willing in God but rather is God's eternal act of willing in its readiness to work good for creatures.[59] Benefi-cence, then, is God's eternal act of willing with respect to his outward work-ing of good for creatures. Furthermore, with the existence and activities of creatures in place, God's love of complacency applies to them as well. This divine complacency is the simple act of God's will with a relation to creatures in whom he rejoices as representations of his goodness, wisdom, power, and glory.[60] It is worth underscoring that the object of God's joy includes cre-ated being and action. God does not receive something good from creatures that he once lacked, so his joy does not have to be completed by creatures. Yet God has created a world that is truly valuable and pleasing to him. God beholds and rejoices in the good to be found in created being and action that ultimately comes from his own generous hand (e.g., Pss. 104:31; 149:4; Isa. 62:4–5; Zeph. 3:17; Luke 15:10; 2 Cor. 9:7; Heb. 13:15–16). In this sense, while God is not happy *because of* creatures being or doing good, he is genuinely happy *about* creatures being and doing good.[61]

58. On which, see Aquinas, *Sent. Ethic.* 7.14 (438–39); Aquinas, *SCG* 1.90 (243–44); Aquinas, *ST* Ia.19.1–2 (231, 233); Leigh, *A Treatise of Divinity*, 2.8 (71); Owen, *Christologia* 12 (144–45); Owen, *Posthumous Sermons, Part IV* 22 (613–14); Mastricht, *TPT*, 2.15.8 (159).

59. Cf. Aquinas, *SCG* 1.92 (251); Ames, *Medulla theologica*, 1.4.63–64 (15); Leigh, *A Treatise of Divinity*, 2.10 (78).

60. I take it that affirming something like this *amor complacentiae* may be one of the aims of a proposal like Peckham's in *The Love of God*, chap. 8, where he stresses that God's rela-tionship to creation is not "unilateral" but "reciprocal." I would not use the adjective "recipro-cal," because it suggests that God's fulfillment or well-being is dependent upon creatures, but I would certainly affirm that God enjoys creatures' acts of love toward God and toward one another. The central point in the doctrine of divine impassibility is that God is neither fulfilled nor harmed by creatures. It leaves room for a number of ways in which one might still discuss the positive application of affections to God and the positive value of created being and agency.

61. Cf. Aquinas, *SCG* 1.90–91 (243–44, 246–47); Aquinas, *ST* IaIIae.22.3 ad 3 (171); Turretin, *Inst.*, 3.14.8 (1:242); 3.20.5 (1:267). God delights both in the outward exercise of his perfections and in the beneficiaries of that exercise, especially his own people (see esp. Owen, *Christologia* 4 [54–60]; 12 [146, 148]; 15 [175]; Owen, *Meditations and Discourses on the Glory of Christ* 3 [314]; Charnock, *The Existence and Attributes of God*, 2:219, 227–28). In a recent essay, R. T. Mullins suggests that God either must be moved from without to create or must not value crea-tures and thus create with no reason ("The Problem of Arbitrary Creation for Impassibility"). But one need not choose between God being moved from without and God not valuing creatures. As

(4) Finally, if passions that pertain to evil things are movements of the will in which the subject either seeks to avoid something harmful or undergoes some harm, then these passions in an ordinary sense do not apply to God insofar as God himself cannot be harmed or made to undergo the loss of something good. For the true God is not ὁμοιοπαθής with us—"of like passions" or "subject to being affected in similar ways" (Acts 14:15).[62] Even when creatures divert their worship from God, no creature has the power to deprive God of something that is constitutive of his well-being: he remains the "incorruptible God" (ἄφθαρτος θεός) (Rom. 1:23; cf. 1 Tim. 1:17).

When Paul calls God the "incorruptible God" in Romans 1:23, he is echoing Old Testament teaching on idolatry (cf. Ps. 106:20; Jer. 2:11) and contrasting God with "corruptible" creatures, who are unworthy of worship.[63] Sometimes in the pertinent ancient literature the adjective φθαρτός and related words deal with a subject being mortal or inclined to morally evil actions.[64] But in Romans 8:21 Paul speaks about creation's bondage to "corruption" (φθορά) not just in the sense of mere mortality but also in the sense of deterioration and the loss of fulfillment or well-being.[65] In Romans 8:21 the corruption of the nonhuman creation is contrasted with its eventual participation in the "freedom of the glory of the children of God," which is then explained in terms of the saints' reception of the resurrection body (8:23). As Paul teaches in 1 Corinthians 15, the body that will be buried presently exists in a state of "corruption" (φθορά) but will be raised in "incorruptibility" or "imperishability" (ἐν ἀφθαρσίᾳ) (15:42). This contrast concerns not only whether the

---

Scripture emphasizes, God does not gain something from us, something external to himself that might move him to create. Apart from God himself, there just is no other source of goodness from which God could be fulfilled. And yet creatures are good and valuable and an object of God's joy. Creatures are good and valuable without God being moved from outside himself to create because creatures are good and valuable by participating in God's own goodness. And the fact that they are good by participating in God's own goodness does not diminish their goodness or value at all. Participating in God's own goodness is the only way to have goodness. Creation's likeness to God actually explains God's enjoyment of creation: "Anything naturally rejoices in its own like. . . . But every good is a similitude of divine goodness. . . . It remains, then, that God rejoices in every good" (Aquinas, *SCG* 1.90 [243–44]).

62. See the lexical analysis in Erich Beyreuther and Günter Finkenrath, "ὅμοιος κτλ.," in *NIDNTT* 2:501; Louw and Nida, *Greek-English Lexicon*, 25.32 (292). Cf. Johnson, *Acts*, 249; Wilson, *The Embodied God*, 43, 51.

63. Cf. Philo, *Legum allegoriae* 3.36 (324); Philo, *De aeternitate mundi* 44 (214).

64. For the usage of the word group φθείρω, φθορά, and so forth in the LXX and New Testament, see Günther Harder, "φθείρω κτλ.," in *TDNT* 9:93–106; Louw and Nida, *Greek-English Lexicon*, 23.127–28 (268); 88.43 (747); Traugott Holtz, "φθείρω κτλ.," in *EDNT* 3:422–23; *NIDNTTE* 4:597–602.

65. Cf. Fitzmyer, *Romans*, 505, 509; Moo, *Romans*, 517; Jewett, *Romans*, 515; Kruse, *Romans*, 347–48.

body might continue functioning indefinitely but also whether the body is equipped by the Spirit for the abundance of eschatological life (15:43–44).[66] The first Adam even before the fall was but a man "of dust" and in this regard capable of subjection to decay, but the second Adam and those who follow him are "of heaven" (15:45–49). Ultimately, "flesh and blood," human beings in their weakness, vulnerability, and sinfulness, cannot inherit the kingdom of God (15:50).[67] This is the problem to which "incorruptibility" is the solution. And here to be incorruptible is to have a certain "wholeness"[68] that is broader than just the power to go on existing indefinitely, a point perhaps corroborated by the fact that Paul uses the word "incorruptibility" (ἀφθαρσία) in addition to the word "immortality" (ἀθανασία) (15:53–54).

The point of considering Romans 1:23 in connection with the teaching of Romans 8 and 1 Corinthians 15 is to note that if God is "incorruptible" in a Pauline sense, then God is dissimilar to created being not just in its mortality or sinfulness but also in its weakness, vulnerability, and loss of well-being. God is not only removed from corporeal decay, mortality, and the possibility of sin. He is also removed from the potential to be harmed or to lose something that is constitutive of one's well-being.[69] In a word, he is impassible.[70]

Therefore, it is important not to take passions or affections directed toward evil things and apply them in their ordinary sense to God. Predicates like hatred, grief, sorrow, anger, and jealousy are applied to God in Scripture, but, given the whole sweep of canonical teaching, such predicates do not mean that God himself might be harmed by something evil.[71] Applied to God, these predicates signify acts or the one simple act of God's will under a relation to various objects

66. Cf. Thiselton, *First Epistle to the Corinthians*, 1271–81.

67. On "flesh and blood" see again Thiselton, *First Epistle to the Corinthians*, 1291.

68. Thiselton, *First Epistle to the Corinthians*, 1297.

69. It might be objected that just as creation and the saints presently "groan" while awaiting the fullness of redemption, so too the Spirit intercedes for us with "inexpressible groans" (Rom. 8:21, 23, 26). However, Paul's point is not that the Spirit himself is caught up in a state of corruptibility but rather that he helps us in the midst of ours. In fact, it is precisely because the Spirit is not stuck in our situation that he can help us. Cf. Kruse, *Romans*, 351–52.

70. On the connection between incorruptibility and impassibility, note Basil of Caesarea, *Contre Eunome* 2.23 (2:92); Cyril of Alexandria, *Ad Theodosium* 7,10–11 (48–49); Cyril, *Explanatio XII cap*. 148,31 (25). The fact that created beings in the eschaton can be incorruptible or impassible in a certain sense does not necessarily trivialize God's impassibility. For the finite creature and the infinite God will each be incorruptible or impassible in a manner proper to their being, God alone being absolutely impassible.

71. In the works of older authors examined here, anger is commonly considered to be an effect of sorrow, with a desire for revenge, and jealousy or envy a species of sorrow that is occupied with the good of another (e.g., Aquinas, *ST* IaIIae.46.1–3 [292–94]; 47.1–2 [300–301]; IIaIIae.36.1 [290]; IIIa.15.9 [195]).

and effects, or else the effects themselves.[72] For example, divine hatred may signify God's act of willing and delighting in the good viewed with respect to its negative side: God's negative opposition and disdain toward evil. Alternatively, it may signify the effects of that opposition and disdain (e.g., withdrawal of favor, elimination or punishment of evil) (Pss. 5:4–6; 11:5–6; Isa. 1:14; Zech. 8:17; Mal. 1:2–3; cf. Isa. 59:2).[73] Whichever sense divine hatred bears in any given text, it provides an opportunity to clarify that divine impassibility does not mean indifference to evil. The impassible God is not harmed by evil, but he nevertheless sees it as it is and, in his perfect holiness, disdains and condemns it.[74]

Given the scriptural teaching on God's goodness and incorruptibility, it is fitting to offer readings of divine sorrow, anger, and jealousy according to which these predicates also signify God's act of willing with a relation to certain objects and effects, or the effects themselves. Offering that sort of reading of these divine attributes involves defending the claim that the biblical passages in which they appear are employing metaphorical descriptions of God. Because this sort of reading is sometimes misunderstood or rejected outright in contemporary exegesis and theology, the next section will take up the question of whether a metaphorical reading of the relevant passages remains viable today.

IV. Impassibility and Metaphorical Attribution of Passions to God

Though exegetes of the past regularly took descriptions of God repenting or grieving, for example, to be metaphorical, that reading cannot be assumed

72. The affections predicated of God have been variously considered virtues, acts, or metaphorical attributes applied to God on the basis of his outward effects (e.g., Aquinas, SCG 1.89 [240–41]; 1.91 [247]; Aquinas, ST Ia.19.11 corp. [249]; 20.1 ad 2 [253]; Polanus, Syntagma, 2.35 [192–94]; Ames, Medulla theologica, 1.4.62–64 [15]; Leigh, A Treatise of Divinity, 2.7 [70]; 2.9 [74]; 2.10 [78]; Mastricht, TPT, 2.15.19 [161]). Each of those designations can be helpful but can also obscure important points. For example, virtues in God like love, mercy, or patience are not additions to his essence or will but are simply the readiness of God's one act of being and willing to do good, which we learn about diversely from his diverse effects (cf. Mastricht, TPT, 2.15.21 [162]). And metaphorical attributes like hatred or wrath that are applied to God only "effectively" (on the basis of a resemblance between his outward effects and the outward effects of human beings with the relevant affections) still point back to some eternal perfection in God (e.g., hatred and wrath are a manifestation of God's eternal justice and holiness).

73. Aquinas, SCG 1.96 (259–60); Polanus, Syntagma, 2.35 (194); Mastricht, TPT, 2.15.17, 20 (161); 2.17.11 (180). As these authors point out, since God's will is not positively inclined to evil, his hatred is not malevolence but rather the negation of benevolence toward what is evil.

74. In light of this, it seems to me that divine impassibility may in fact be compatible with some (though not necessarily all) of the concerns of those who believe they need to qualify or reject impassibility in order to maintain that God's affections involve an evaluation of good and evil (see Peckham, The Love of God, chaps. 5–6; Mullins, God and Emotion, 28–29 and passim).

today. More fundamentally, it cannot be assumed that older exegetes' views of what a metaphor is will be shared by their critics. A recent advocate of divine passibility like Terence Fretheim, for example, asserts that virtually all of our descriptions of God are metaphorical. He emphasizes that while there is no "one-to-one correspondence" between a metaphor and its referent, metaphors nevertheless can "say some things about God that correspond to the reality which is God." For Fretheim, "metaphor does not stand over against the literal. Though the use of the metaphor is not literal there is literalness intended in the relationship to which the metaphor has reference." In particular, metaphorical descriptions of God in the Bible "reveal that God is literally related to the world." Thus, according to Fretheim, though a metaphorical description of God involves something "discontinuous with the reality which is God," God still suffers and repents (presumably, on Fretheim's logic, in a kind of "literal" manner). Within Fretheim's hermeneutic, this is based on the doctrine of the *imago Dei*, a doctrine from which Fretheim reasons that God is "relational" in the sense of having an "openness to change" that is "integral to genuine relationship." While acknowledging the discontinuity or the "no" involved in any metaphorical description, Fretheim chastises older exegetes of the Jewish and Christian traditions for being "anti-anthropomorphic" in their refusal to predicate suffering and repentance of God in what exegetes throughout history would typically have called a literal manner.[75] Though it is not quite clear why it would be antimetaphorical to read metaphorical descriptions of God as metaphorical, I take it that Fretheim is concerned that older readings denigrate the truthfulness or descriptive import of passages like those in which God repents or grieves.

In this section, I will make an argument that claims like Fretheim's rest on a misunderstanding of metaphor and its place in the Christian exegetical tradition. I will also argue that descriptions of God that attribute to him repentance, grief, jealousy, and wrath are metaphorical in that these descriptions do not posit change or deprivation in God but rather tell us something striking about God's action relative to his creatures. The argument will also involve pointing out that this approach upholds the cognitive import of these descriptions. I will first seek to provide some clarity on the nature of metaphorical locutions by looking briefly at the works of authors like Aristotle,

75. Fretheim, *What Kind of God?*, 25, 44, 79, 91–94, 96, 116, 310. Cf. Walter Brueggemann's comments that "classical Christian theology" envisions a God "completely apart from and unaffected by the reality of the world" and is therefore beset with an "embarrassment" on account of which it attempts to "explain away" biblical anthropomorphisms (*An Unsettling God*, 1–2). For a look at several influential biblical scholars on divine "pathos," see Schlimm, "Different Perspectives on Divine Pathos."

Augustine, Aquinas, Bartholomäus Keckermann, and others and then move toward a reading of pertinent biblical texts under the following main points.

(1) Aristotle's comments on metaphor in his *Poetics* and *Rhetoric* have long functioned as a point of reference in discussions of metaphor. Though there are critics of Aristotle's so-called substitution theory of metaphor and a swath of newer proposals on the nature and use of metaphor,[76] it is fitting to take note of his definition of metaphor in order to understand how classical philosophy of language and rhetoric has influenced the history of scriptural exegesis. Furthermore, if some or even much of the concern about Aristotle rests on the worry that his approach makes the communicative import of metaphor entirely reducible to literal speech, it is worth keeping in mind that that is not a necessary commitment for those who would consider the potential fecundity of more traditional treatments of metaphor in contemporary exegesis.

In the *Poetics*, Aristotle deems a "prevalent name" (ὄνομα κύριον) to be one that is used by all who speak a given language. Though it is not drawn from a foreign language, a metaphor (μεταφορά), by contrast, is "an application of an alien name [ὀνόματος ἀλλοτρίου ἐπιφορά] either from genus to species, from species to genus, from species to species, or according to analogy [κατὰ τὸ ἀνάλογον]." The examples that Aristotle gives show that the "alien names" that are so applied can include verbs. For example, "There my ship stands" illustrates a metaphorical application of an alien name from genus to species, "standing" being the genus here and "being anchored" a certain species of "standing." In the examples of a metaphor "according to analogy," Aristotle has in mind a four-term analogy that is sometimes called an analogy of "proper proportion." For example: "Old age is to life as evening is to day," so that evening can be called the "old age of the day," or old age the "evening of life."[77]

According to Aristotle's *Rhetoric*, the "prevalent" words (τὰ κύρια) make speech clear, while others, including metaphor, make it "ornamented." Yet both may be used in the persuasive speeches Aristotle describes. In fact, a metaphor especially combines clarity and pleasantness. Though a metaphor "according to analogy" (κατ' ἀναλογίαν) is one of the four kinds of metaphor and, indeed, the most highly esteemed kind, Aristotle remarks more broadly

76. For various recent treatments, see, e.g., Black, *Models and Metaphors*; Lakoff and Johnson, *Metaphors We Live By*; Ricoeur, *The Rule of Metaphor*; Soskice, *Metaphor and Religious Language*. Overviews that touch on the issues in contemporary discussion can be found in Moran, "Metaphor"; Vanhoozer, *Is There a Meaning in This Text?*, 126–40; Gibbs, *The Cambridge Handbook of Metaphor and Thought*; Gibbs, *Metaphor Wars*; Lancaster, "Metaphor Research and the Hebrew Bible."

77. Aristotle, *Poetics* 21.1457b (200–202).

that metaphors should always emerge from some analogy. It is necessary to "carry over" or "transfer" (μεταφέρειν) names not "from afar" but "from the same genera and species" to whatever needs to be signified and understood.[78] Located between prevalent names, which are already familiar, and entirely foreign names, which are unknown, metaphor is especially apt to produce learning. For a metaphor involves a "transfer" of a name between things that are akin but not in an entirely obvious way (ἀπὸ οἰκείων καὶ μὴ φανερῶν), facilitating a moment of discovery on the part of the hearer.[79]

Of course, Aristotle was not the only significant ancient writer on the nature of metaphor. Cicero's work on rhetoric, for example, provides a noteworthy treatment as well. Cicero states that some words are "proper" and "certain" names of things and "almost born together with things themselves." Others are "transferred, and, as it were, positioned in an alien place." The practice of "transferring" words originally came from necessity due to a lack of words but then became frequent due to the delight that this transfer can bring about. Metaphors (*translationes*) are "exchanges" (*mutationes*) in which "what you do not have, you take up from elsewhere." Cicero then defines a metaphor as a "brevity of similitude contracted to one word" (*similitudinis ad verbum unum contracta brevitas*). The word is "put in an alien place as if it were its own." A metaphor requires a resemblance between the thing that the word properly designates and the "alien" thing it newly designates and illumines.[80]

Within the context of the Christian tradition, Augustine's work *De doctrina christiana* discusses the "figures of speech" (*figurae locutionis*) that are handed down in the art of speaking and appear in Holy Scripture as well. According to Augustine, these figures of speech or *tropoi* that may be learned in a liberal art apart from the study of Holy Scripture are found in the common speech of the ordinary person and in Scripture itself. Augustine states that with "proper words" the thing said is the thing understood. In the case of figurative or "tropical" speech (*tropica locutio*), however, where a transfer or "translation" of a word takes place, someone says one thing in order to make another understood. Students of Scripture should both learn the "kinds of locutions" in Scripture and pray to gain understanding of them. It is, after all, part of the "eloquence of the prophets" to use metaphors or

78. Aristotle, *Ars Rhetorica* 3.2.1404b–1405a (148–51); 3.10.1410b36–1411a1 (170). See also 3.4.1406b–1407a (155–56), according to which one kind of metaphor is a simile or "likeness" (εἰκών), the difference being that instead of just transferring a name to a thing other than what it ordinarily signifies, the simile explicitly includes the particle "as" or "like."

79. Aristotle, *Ars Rhetorica* 3.10.1410b12–15 (169); 3.11.1412a9–11 (174).

80. Cicero, *De oratore Book III* 37.149–38.157 (83–84); 41.166 (86).

"transferred words," which are sometimes opaque but cause delight all the more when they become clear.[81]

Augustine emphasizes that interpretation of particular biblical texts with "transferred words" demands great care, lest one interpret a "figured locution" as a literal one. We should not mistake signs for the things themselves, and we have to be ready to rise above corporeal things. Yet Augustine recognizes that we come to Scripture with cultural mores and individual opinions that may hinder our discernment of what is proper and what is metaphorical in Scripture. In order to interpret Scripture correctly, then, Augustine commends a number of guidelines, including the promotion of love and holiness, adherence to the catholic faith, and what is often called the *analogia Scripturae*. If things that are seen to be "shameful to the ignorant" are said or done "from the person of God or men whose holiness is commended to us," they are entirely figurative. According to Augustine, such things include the wrath of God and Jesus indulgently allowing a woman to anoint his feet with oil.[82] Though the variety of usage in the Bible can present interpretive difficulties, it is ultimately a gift from the Holy Spirit. And ascertaining the will of the author may be facilitated by drawing conclusions that do not oppose "right faith" and are attested elsewhere in the Bible.[83]

In his discussion of metaphor in the *Summa theologiae*, Aquinas affirms the fittingness of Scripture's use of metaphors by appealing to Hosea 12:10, where God says that he has multiplied visions and given parables. Aquinas affirms that "it is agreeable to holy Scripture to pass down divine and spiritual things under a similitude of corporeal things. For God provides to all according to what belongs to their natures. And it is natural to man that he should come to intelligible things by sensible things. Because all our cognition has a beginning from sense." Thus, it is a matter of necessity that Scripture employs metaphors. In the use of metaphors, the "ray of divine revelation" is not "destroyed," for the use of metaphors does not "permit the minds to which revelation comes to remain in the similitudes but elevates them to the cognition of intelligible things." In fact, the "hiding of figures" (*occultatio figurarum*) is useful in part because it promotes diligent study of the Scriptures. Furthermore, the things conveyed by metaphors in some places are "expounded more expressly in other places."[84]

The early Reformer Philipp Melanchthon also treats the nature and use of metaphor in his works on rhetoric and dialectic. Melanchthon writes that

---

81. Augustine, *De doct.* 3.29.40–41 (100–102); 3.37.56 (115–16); 4.7.14–15 (126–28).
82. Augustine, *De doct.* 3.4.9 (82–83); 3.10.15–18 (86–89); 3.24.34 (97).
83. Augustine, *De doct.* 3.25.35–28.39 (97–99).
84. Aquinas, *ST* Ia.1.9 (23–24).

the greatest part of oration consists in "primary speech," but because of "necessity" or "ornament" sometimes figures ought to be added. For where proper words are lacking, "need compels other words from nearby to be exchanged." Moreover, sometimes when a proper word is available, it may still be fitting to use a figurative word insofar as it is "more meaningful" or "more expressive" (*significantius*). Melanchthon then observes that the Greeks call it a *tropos* when a word is changed from "proper signification to a similar or near thing." First in the list of *tropoi* is metaphor, which occurs when "on account of a similitude a word is transferred from proper signification." By a similitude "this thing is declared which is signified by metaphor." The use of metaphor increases clarity for the hearer, especially when the similitude involved appeals to sense perception.[85]

In Melanchthon's work on dialectic he takes up the distinction between "proper" and "figured" or "improper" speech in the treatment of predication. According to Melanchthon, "true predication" occurs when the attribution of a predicate to a subject "agrees with the thing about which something is affirmed or negated." True predication is either "regular," "figured," or "strange."[86] "Regular" predication is the sort that agrees with one of the modes of the five "predicables" (genus, species, difference, property, accident). That is, "regular" predication occurs when genus is predicated of a species or an individual in the genus, when species is predicated of an individual in the species, or when the differentiating mark of the species or a property or accident is predicated of the species or an individual in the species. "Figured" predication involves "improper speech, where nevertheless the sentence is true, and with a similitude signified, as in metaphor." The "figured" sort of true predication accords with ordinary rules of interpretation. It agrees with "regular" predication in that it is a matter of attributing an accident to a subject. Melanchthon offers biblical examples: "'Christ is the lamb,' that is, 'similar to a lamb,' which is a victim. For he is called a 'lamb' because he is a victim."[87]

The early Reformed Hebrew professor, theologian, and philosopher Bartholomäus Keckermann offers a detailed treatment of metaphor and also locates it within the distinction between proper and improper predication. In Keckermann's *Systema rhetoricae*, he defines a trope or figure of speech as a "translation of a word from its own proper signification to the signification

---

85. Melanchthon, *Elementorum rhetorices libri duo* 2 (463–64).

86. In Melanchthon's taxonomy, the "strange" (*inusitata*) sort of predication pertains to christological statements like "God is man" that do not have ordinary precedents or analogies.

87. Melanchthon, *Erotemata dialectica* 1 (518–26). Although Melanchthon distinguishes rhetoric and dialectic by saying that the latter avoids use of improper, ornamental words, Melanchthon still acknowledges that dialectical argument has some place for improper words (515).

of another thing not completely dissimilar," or a "translation of signification to signification." The word is "transferred" or "translated" from the thing it originally signified and applied to another thing. "Tropical" or "improper" words are thus called "translated" words. Sometimes the term "metaphor" more generally designates all tropical speech; other times "metaphor" more strictly designates a certain species of trope. Use of tropes can arise from both lack of available words and also the pursuit of "delight" and "sweetness" in speech. According to Keckermann, proper words (τὰ κύρια) still precede tropes in both nature and dignity, but, it should be noted, this is because an understanding of the original signification of a word is required for understanding any figurative use of it.[88]

In its stricter definition, a metaphor occurs when "the name of a thing is put for the name of another similar thing," or when "from one similar thing another similar thing is signified." A metaphor more closely aligns with things themselves than other tropes do. Being more closely bound to reality, a metaphor is less dependent on the free choice of the one speaking. While all tropes involve the transfer of a word from its "native signification" to another signification, a metaphor especially involves transferring a word "with a certain reason" to another thing that is similar "by nature." Thus, understanding a metaphor requires considering the basis of the commonality from which the comparison arises.[89]

Keckermann produced multiple treatments of the discipline of logic, and there he locates the use of tropes within the context of the distinction between proper and improper predication. His treatment of the material demands some patience with technical linguistic analysis, but it can help to shed light on the role of metaphor in exegeting biblical passages like those in which God repents or grieves. Proper predication, Keckermann writes, is the sort where both (a) the "disposition" of the predicate toward the subject and also (b) the "words" themselves used to designate the predicate and subject are "proper." "Disposition" here refers to the relationship between the predicate and the subject, and it is "proper" when the predicate is applied to the subject by virtue of something pertaining to the subject in itself or in its own right (rather than by virtue of an extrinsic relation between predicate and subject). The "words," of course, are the terms used to signify the subject and predicate, and they are proper when they are used to signify what they originally and normally signify.[90]

88. Keckermann, *Systema rhetoricae*, 2.2 (1456–57).
89. Keckermann, *Systema rhetoricae*, 2.4 (1464–66).
90. Keckermann, *Systema logicae, tribus libris adornatum*, II, sect. post., 2 (728–32).

By contrast, improper predication occurs when the predicate is "improperly" disposed to the subject. This occurs when either the "disposition" itself is "improper" (i.e., the predicate is applied to the subject by virtue of an outward relation to it) or the words are improper (i.e., they have been "transferred" from their native signification to a new thing that needs to be signified). For example, one kind of predication that is improper by virtue of the disposition itself (i.e., by virtue of the fact that the predicate is applied to the subject according to an outward relation) is the sacramental kind that is built on the sacramental union of the sacred sign and the spiritual reality signified: for example, circumcision is God's covenant (Gen. 17:10); baptism washes away sins (Acts 22:16).[91] For our purposes, it is important that metaphor does not fall under predication that is "improper" by reason of the disposition itself. Rather, it falls under predication that is improper by reason of the words alone. In the case of predication that is improper by reason of the words alone, a word is transferred from its native signification to an initially "alien" signification, but the "impropriety is only in the words, because contrary to the words the disposition of the predicate with the subject is most proper." In other words, a trope concerns the words and leaves untouched the propriety of the onto-logical relationship between the thing signified by the predicate and the thing signified by the subject. One of Keckermann's examples is, "The meadows laugh" (*Prata rident*). He explains,

> When I say, "The meadows laugh," by laughter I understand "pleasantness," which truly and properly is in the meadows. Therefore all impropriety is in the simple term "to laugh," which is transferred from the native signification of a human action, which is called "laughter," toward signifying the pleasantness of the meadows, which is said properly about them.[92]

Significantly, then, such an approach to metaphorical description would entail interpreting a statement like "God repented" to involve an improper use of the verb "repent" without at all questioning that what the verb "repent" has come to signify in this case truly pertains to God himself.

Finally, Reformed authors often seek to provide some rules for distinguishing between literal and figurative locutions in the Bible in their analyses of Christ's words about the bread and wine at the Last Supper ("This is my

91. From a Reformed perspective, while God uses the sacraments as means of sealing and conferring grace (with faith receiving the promises of God), the signs included in the matter of the sacraments do not physically contain the grace they signify—hence the attribution of the spiritual reality to the sign would be based on the sign having a divinely ordained outward relation to the spiritual reality.

92. Keckermann, *Systema logicae, tribus libris adornatum*, II, sect. post., 2 (732–34).

body" and "This is my blood").[93] Before identifying such criteria, Turretin, for example, clarifies that while proper speech belongs "immediately" to the *sensus literalis* of a text, figurative speech can still belong "mediately" to the *sensus literalis*, insofar as it may be referred back to "proper words" and "resolved" into these proper words by considering "the intention of the one speaking" and the "nature of the subject." That is, even if a trope is not included in the *sensus literalis* with respect to what is said (κατὰ τὸ ῥητὸν), it may still be included in the *sensus literalis* with respect to the author's intent or judgment (κατὰ τήν διάνοιαν).[94]

Prioritizing the *sensus literalis* in scriptural exegesis and including any figurative speech in Scripture at least "mediately" within the *sensus literalis* will require the exegete to interpret tropes under the conditions set by the author's own communicative purpose (to the extent that that can be gathered from a careful reading of the text). But when debate arises about whether a trope is present or not, how should the exegete proceed? Turretin lays out several interpretive rules. In addition to pointing out the importance of consulting other relevant biblical passages and relevant articles of faith that ought to shape our theological judgment, Turretin appeals to a number of "rules of speech" (*regula sermonis*), some of which are pertinent here. First, "When a propriety of the letter involves something of the absurd and contradictory, there is necessarily recourse to the figured sense." Turretin writes, "Since the human intellect is not able to accept that a thing is and is not at the same time, it is compelled to have recourse to a figure." Furthermore, "When the letter attributes unworthy things to God and Christ, there should be recourse to a figure, because it cannot happen that the word of God would prescribe something that is injurious to that highest majesty or indeed that does not tend to his glory." In other words, when "piety and reverence of the divine majesty conflict with the letter," "a figured locution is detected." In addition, "When the subject not only easily admits a figure but also necessarily demands it," the locution is figured, "for the words ought to follow the nature of things."[95] Considering whether such rules are sufficient to identify metaphorical locutions will be part of our task below.

(2) What might we draw from these historical observations when we come to the task of interpreting biblical statements about God "repenting" or "grieving" or being "jealous"? First, it seems to me that while more nuance regarding the nature and use of metaphor could be added to the discussion

---

93. See, e.g., Keckermann, *Systema s.s. theologiae*, 3.8 (213–15); Polanus, *Syntagma*, 6.56 (497); Mastricht, *TPT*, 7.5.23 (938–39).

94. Turretin, *Inst.*, 19.26.3 (3:520–21).

95. Turretin, *Inst.*, 19.26.15–17 (3:530–33).

by taking into account recent work in the philosophy of language and biblical interpretation, the basic insight that a metaphor involves transferring a word from its original signification to another signification is something that holds up. On the one hand, it may be that not all of a metaphor's communicative import can be reduced to or conveyed by literal description. As Melanchthon put it, even when a proper locution is available, a figurative one may be "more meaningful" or "more expressive." After all, communication is more than the bare use of signs. On the other hand, it remains the case at a basic level that if one does not first grasp the original or native signification of the words involved, one cannot grasp the sense of a metaphorical locution. Recourse to "proper" words is not a matter of rationalism but a normal element of verbal communication. For example, if one does not first know what the word "rock" or "fortress" ordinarily signifies, then one will not understand the sense of the psalmist's prayer "You are indeed my rock and my fortress" (Ps. 31:3 NRSV). Moreover, whatever distinctives one might find in Old Testament Hebrew—the peculiar metaphors and "dead" metaphors, the poetic meter, and so on—its use of metaphor is commensurable with the use of metaphor in other languages. As Augustine noted in *De doctrina christiana*, figurative patterns of speaking do not belong only to the rhetorical analysis undertaken in the study of the liberal arts. They are common in the speech of the average person, including the biblical authors.

Second, the idea that all or nearly all human language used in the biblical canon and in Christian theology is metaphorical needs to be challenged. To be sure, as Aquinas noted, all our cognition begins with sense perception, and our use of verbal signs draws upon our experience of sensible objects. It is therefore not surprising that the Bible would often take up language originally used to signify sensible objects in order to signify spiritual realities. Furthermore, the human language used in the Bible to describe God is truthful but still finite and, strictly speaking, always inadequate to God's being. At the same time, if a metaphor involves the transfer of a word from its native signification to another signification, then the use of metaphor assumes an antecedent nonmetaphorical signification from which the word is transferred. Without an initial proper signification from which to draw, a word could not be "carried over" to a new thing that needs to be signified, and thus the use of metaphor could not occur at all. Moreover, the biblical authors do not take up only words that remain bound to the sphere of sensible objects. For example, a word like "good" or "powerful" that can be predicated of God is not directly bound to the sensible realm in the way that the word "rock" or "fortress" is. In short, while the human language employed in the biblical canon and in Christian doctrine is always applied to God analogically, it is sometimes literal and sometimes metaphorical, which makes discerning the presence of metaphor an important aspect of exegesis.[96]

Third, authors like Cicero, Melanchthon, and Keckermann indicate that the most fundamental reason for using metaphors is the paucity of human language. Metaphors arise from need and are not merely ornamental. They are designed to shed light on reality and therefore have to be based upon a real similitude between the thing ordinarily signified and the thing newly signified. Indeed, if Keckermann is correct that in metaphorical locutions the thing improperly signified by the predicate is nevertheless properly "disposed" or truly applicable to the subject in reality, then a metaphorical interpretation of divine repentance, grief, wrath, and so on will involve accounting for the ontological resemblance between what takes place in the case of a repentant, grieving, or wrathful human person and what takes place in God's case.

Fourth, authors like Augustine and Turretin call attention to the need for criteria or rules of interpretation that help us to distinguish between literal and metaphorical predication. Both of those authors insist on comparing one biblical text with other pertinent biblical texts in situations where the exegete must determine whether a locution is metaphorical. That rule has the advantage of recognizing the authority and the perspicuity of Holy Scripture. But does an additional appeal to certain "rules of speech" undermine the authority of Scripture by placing the norms of interpretation in the hands of the interpreter? At this point, I think it is worth keeping in mind that even the most ardent supporter of Scripture's authority and the greatest skeptic

---

96. Perhaps a comment on what constitutes analogical description and what distinguishes it from metaphor will be useful here. An analogical view of theological language is situated between a univocal view and a purely equivocal view. A univocal view would hold that something like "being" or "wisdom" or "goodness," for example, would apply equally to God and the creature (which is not the case), or that human consideration of such predicates can prescind from the fact that what they signify will always be present in either a finite way (in creatures) or an infinite way (in God). A purely equivocal view would hold that such predicates apply in entirely distinct senses to God and the creature, which would undermine human knowledge of God. By contrast, an analogical view holds that such perfections are not equally applicable to God and the creature since they are infinite in God and identical with God's essence. Moreover, human consideration of such perfections inevitably includes a recognition that they will always be present in either a finite way (in creatures) or an infinite way (in God). Yet an analogical view also holds that while such perfections are in God in an absolute and unique way, what something like "wisdom" ordinarily signifies in the case of creatures (e.g., understanding of higher things in light of which one can make good judgments) is present in an eminent manner in God (see further Duby, *God in Himself*, chap. 5). All human speech about God is analogical given God's infinity and simplicity and given the creature's finite participation in God's perfections, but it is often still literal. For although attributes like wisdom or goodness are in God and creatures in distinct ways, what such attributes ordinarily and properly signify is present in God (albeit in an eminent manner), so that no "transfer" from a native signification to an alien one has to occur.

of the use of philosophy will have to do exegesis with the help of natural, extrabiblical knowledge. For example, Scripture does not explain the law of noncontradiction, and yet every exegete assumes that an accurate interpretation of a text will accord with the rule that a thing is not able to be and not to be in the same way and at the same time. For a mundane example, every exegete will assume that Babylon was not able to conquer Jerusalem and also not conquer Jerusalem in the same way and at the same time. But this use of natural, extrabiblical knowledge is no threat to the authority of Scripture. Likewise, drawing upon a rudimentary understanding of how metaphorical language functions is something that, in and of itself, represents an innocuous use of reason in exegesis and theology.

Of course, if Augustine in *De doctrina christiana* was incorrect to argue that Jesus would never allow a woman literally to anoint his feet with oil, then this illustrates that particular deployments of "rules of speech" can err. Augustine was right to contend that Jesus would not act out of selfishness, but I take it that he was wrong to infer that Jesus allowing a woman literally to anoint his feet would have necessarily been an act of selfishness. To combat misguided use of rules of speech, I would suggest that it is important to prioritize two of the rules identified by Turretin—namely, those addressing whether a proper sense would involve contradiction and whether a proper sense would conflict with the nature of the subject signified. These rules are in fact two sides of the same coin, for there would be a contradiction when the words taken in a proper sense would conflict with the nature of the subject signified. To borrow Keckermann's example again, taking "The meadows laugh" to be a literal locution would mean claiming that "meadows" (nonrational created things) have a property (the ability to laugh) that only rational creatures have. It seems to me that in scriptural exegesis this rule concerning contradiction or conflict with the nature of the subject also enfolds the other rule of Turretin mentioned above, which addresses whether a proper sense would conflict with the majesty of God.

Commendation of these "rules" (or this one composite rule) presupposes that the exegete can have a knowledge of God's nature that suffices for discerning whether a predicate's proper signification accords or conflicts with God's nature. In my view, it is possible and legitimate for Christians to argue from natural or philosophical knowledge of God to make the point that the proper signification of "repentance" or "grief" does not accord with God's nature. However, for readers who do not share that presupposition it will be important to argue that scriptural revelation itself gives us a sufficient knowledge of God's nature to discern that the proper signification of "repentance" or "grief" does not accord with God's nature. While neither natural nor supernatural revelation gives us a knowledge of God's essence as such and in its entirety, both teach us at least what pertains and does not pertain to God's essence. For example, according to Scripture, God in his own being is spiritual and invisible rather than corporeal (Deut. 4:12, 15; John 4:24; Rom. 1:20; Col. 1:15; 1 Tim. 1:17). He is complete and sufficient in himself rather than dependent on his creatures for his completeness or sufficiency (Ps. 50:7–15; John 17:5; Acts 17:24–25; Rom. 11:34–35). He is incorruptible in his life rather than capable of diminishment (Ps. 102:25–27; John 5:26; Rom. 1:23, 25; 1 Tim. 6:15–16; Rev. 1:8). He is infinite rather than limited in knowledge or power (Pss. 115:3; 139:1–18; Isa. 40:12–31; 41:21–24; 44:6–8; 45:18–21; 46:8–10). He is unfailingly good rather than susceptible to evil or cruel motives (Pss. 119:68; 145:9; Lam. 3:33; Ezek. 18:23, 32; 1 John 1:5; James 1:13, 17). Much more could be said about what pertains and does not pertain to God's essence, but these brief observations will help us begin to discern why certain biblical locutions should be read metaphorically.

(3) Beginning with a less contentious metaphorical description of God may help to illustrate the logic of the approach advocated here. For example, when God is said to have "wings" under which human beings take refuge (e.g., Ruth 2:12; Ps. 36:7), the exegete immediately recognizes that a proper sense would not accord with God's nature since he is incorporeal.[97] The exegete at least implicitly acknowledges that the word "wings" is transferred from its native or proper signification on account of a certain similitude or resemblance: as the wings of a corporeal creature provide protection, so God provides protection for those who call upon him. Such a metaphorical locution offers a true description of divine action. While the fullness of its spiritual impact on the reader cannot be captured by a literal locution, its meaning can be clarified in literal terms.

More contentious in the present time are texts that predicate of God things like "repentance," "grief," "jealousy," or "wrath." Genesis 6:6 tells us that when human wickedness increased in the world, "YHWH repented [וַיִּנָּחֶם] that he made humankind on the earth. And he was grieved [וַיִּתְעַצֵּב] in his heart." Other similar texts that speak of God repenting or grieving also could be collated here (e.g., Exod. 32:14; 1 Sam. 15:11, 35; Isa. 63:10; Jon. 3:10; 4:2; Eph. 4:30; cf. Hosea 11:8).[98] In the approach advocated in this section, the

---

97. Some contemporary interpreters argue that God literally has a body in the Bible (e.g., Sommer, *The Bodies of God*; Wilson, *The Embodied God*), but my sense is that this position is not making significant inroads in orthodox Christian communions today.

98. For recent discussion of the repentance texts, see Kuyper, "The Repentance of God"; Kuyper, "The Suffering and Repentance of God"; van Dyke Parunak, "A Semantic Survey of NḤM"; Janzen, "Metaphor and Reality in Hosea 11"; Balzer, "Gottes Reue"; Amit, "'The

exegete would not have to propose a novel definition for the verbs "repent" and "grieve." Rather, the exegete would recognize that a proper sense of the verb "repent" would not accord with the nature of the subject since God's wisdom includes all that will ever come to pass and entails that he would never have to alter his intention on the basis of acquiring new knowledge or a new alignment with what is good. The exegete would then recognize that the verb "repent" has been transferred from its native or proper signification (e.g., to change one's intention in view of new knowledge or sorrow about wrong actions) on account of a certain similitude: as a repentant human person acts to produce new and different works, so God in Genesis 6 and similar texts produces something new and different in the world. In Genesis 6, he no longer permits the advancement of evil and violence but begins the work of eliminating the wicked from the earth (so Gen. 6:7). Thus, repentance in God's case is not a "change of counsel" but a "change of works." Indeed, it is not an abrogation but an unfolding of God's eternal counsel, which preveniently encompasses all the turning points of salvation history.[99] The metaphor strikingly exhibits the heinousness of sin and the greatness of the change that God is effecting.

Likewise, in the approach advocated here the exegete would recognize that a proper sense of "grief" would not accord with the nature of the subject since God is sufficient in himself, in perfect possession of his own infinite goodness rather than being susceptible to harm or deprivation caused by creatures. While God cares for his creatures and attends to them with a delight in their well-being, creatures' sin harms creatures, not God himself. Creatures' sin does not diminish God's sufficiency or well-being. The exegete would then recognize that the verb "grieve" has been transferred from its native or proper signification (to undergo pain from the loss of some good that is ingredient in one's wholeness or well-being) on account of a certain similitude: as an aggrieved or injured human person shows displeasure by withdrawing from fellowship with the offending party, so God withdraws his favor or the consolation of his presence from the wicked.[100] The metaphor strikingly exhibits

Glory of Israel Does Not Deceive or Change His Mind'"; J. Willis, "The 'Repentance' of God"; Jeremias, Die Reue Gottes; Brueggemann, "The Recovering God of Hosea"; Döhling, Der bewegliche Gott; Sonnet, "God's Repentance and 'False Starts'"; Moberly, Old Testament Theology, chap. 4; Cornell, "Holy Mutability." While these studies provide a number of useful insights into textual and literary details, in my view they sometimes need a greater attentiveness to the theological implications of our statements about God.

99. Polanus, Syntagma, 2.13 (152); 2.35 (194). Cf. Jerome, Commentaire sur Jonas 3,10 (284); Mastricht, TPT, 2.7.

100. See Aquinas, Super Eph. 4.10; Poole, Annotations upon the Holy Bible, on Eph. 4:30. Johannes Coccejus offers the important clarification that this does not mean that the Holy

the severity of sin's consequences and the profundity of God's opposition and disdain toward sin.

A number of texts also predicate "jealousy" of God. Because God is "jealous" (קַנָּא), Israel must not worship other gods (Exod. 20:5; cf. 34:14; Deut. 4:24; 5:9; 6:15; 29:20; Josh. 24:19; cf. 1 Cor. 10:22). God is provoked to jealousy by Israel's disobedience and idolatry, or by human sin in general (Num. 25:11; Deut. 32:16, 21; 1 Kings 14:22; Pss. 78:58; 79:5; Nah. 1:2; Zeph. 1:18; 3:8). Sometimes God's jealousy in relation to idol worship is framed by spousal imagery. In Ezekiel 16, YHWH reminds Jerusalem of his tender care and rebukes her for being an adulterous wife. "I will judge you as women who commit adultery and shed blood are judged, and bring blood upon you in wrath and jealousy" (Ezek. 16:38 NRSV; cf. 23:1–49; Hosea 2:1–13).

Throughout the Bible the word "jealousy" and its cognates and synonyms can have different significations, some righteous and some unrighteous. First, on a human level there is righteous love and commitment to God and God's ways, which is sometimes translated as "zeal" (Num. 25:11, 13; 1 Kings 19:10, 14; 2 Kings 10:16; Ezra 7:23; Pss. 69:9; 119:139; John 2:17; Acts 22:3; Rom. 10:2; 12:11; Titus 2:14). Second, there is also jealousy in the sense of a sorrow about what someone else has or has taken (Gen. 37:11; Num 5:14; Prov. 23:17; Eccles. 4:4; Rom. 10:19; 11:11, 14), which sometimes includes a readiness to exact revenge (Prov. 6:32–35). Third, in some cases a desire for what another has is predicated of persons who may not have been wronged by another but still greedily want some good thing that the other has (Ps. 106:16; Matt. 27:18; Acts 5:17; 13:45; Rom. 13:13; 1 Cor. 3:3; 2 Cor. 12:20; Gal. 5:20–21, 26; Phil. 1:15; James 3:16).

Jealousy in the first signification, of righteous love and commitment, is predicated of God with respect to his own name, his people, and his purposes (2 Kings 19:31; Isa. 9:7; 26:11; 37:32; Ezek. 39:25; Zech. 1:14; 8:2). In light of all that Scripture teaches us about God's being, jealousy as love is predicated of God in a proper sense.[101] Love and loyalty very much accord with the nature of God. In this connection, commenting on Nahum 1:2, Johannes Coccejus states that "zeal is [God's] immutable will of demonstrating his own glory and asserting the truth of all his own perfections and of his grace and union with the church in Christ, against those who assault and despise it."[102] The

---

Spirit in Eph. 4:30 withdraws altogether from believers but that, while still indwelling us, he "hides" himself and withdraws his light in order to bring about our repentance (S. apostoli Pauli epistola ad Ephesios, 262–63).

101. On zeal as love or an effect of love, cf., e.g., Aquinas, Expositio super Isaiam ad litteram 11.151–54 (69); Aquinas, ST IaIIae.28.4 (200–201); Polanus, Syntagma, 2.35 (193).

102. Coccejus, Prophetae duodecim minores, 338.

English Reformed divine Thomas Watson calls this God's jealousy *for* (rather than *of*) his people in whom he delights.[103] It may be that in all or most cases in Scripture, this first signification is in view when jealousy is predicated of God. If, however, jealousy in the second signification outlined above (a sorrow about the gains of another, sometimes with a desire to avenge wrongdoing) is predicated of God, particularly in the context of spousal imagery, its proper signification would not accord with the nature of the subject since God is not subject to harm or lack. The predicate will have been transferred from its native or proper signification on account of a certain similitude: as a jealous human husband may withdraw favor from an adulterous wife, bring about legal consequences for adultery, or seek the restoration of his wife's fidelity, so God withdraws favor from his idolatrous people, brings judgment upon them, and restores their fidelity and righteousness. Watson calls this God's jealousy *of* (rather than *for*) his people.[104]

Divine jealousy is related to divine "wrath." In Ezekiel 5:13, for example, God says regarding the judgment of Jerusalem, "My anger shall spend itself, and I will vent my fury on them and satisfy myself; and they shall know that I, the LORD, have spoken in my jealousy, when I spend my fury on them" (NRSV). Here Coccejus remarks that "zeal" or "jealousy" is the "cause of wrath." For jealousy incites wrath against the one who "injures and violates the thing loved."[105] Various scriptural passages attest the close relationship between divine jealousy and divine wrath (Num. 25:11; Deut. 6:15; 29:20; 32:16; Ps. 78:58–59; Ezek. 16:38, 42–43; 23:25; 36:6; 38:19; Nah. 1:2; Zech. 8:2), but in many places wrath by itself is attributed to God (e.g., Exod. 32:10; Num. 16:46; Deut. 9:7–8, 20–22; 2 Kings 22:17; Ezra 8:22; 10:14; Pss. 2:5; 21:9; 88:7; Isa. 9:19; 51:17, 22; 63:36; Jer. 7:20; 10:10; Hosea 8:5; Mic. 5:15; John 3:36; Rom. 1:18; 9:22; 12:19; Eph. 5:6; Rev. 11:18; 19:15).

When righteous anger or wrath is predicated of God, insofar as it ordinarily signifies grief or sorrow with a desire for retribution, its proper signification

---

103. Watson, *A Body of Practical Divinity*, 282.

104. Watson, *Body of Practical Divinity*, 282. One might ask if this approach posits an unfitting serenity in God in face of the real dangers to which God's creatures and especially his covenant people are exposed. Is God not concerned about their well-being? Would he not be devastated if his creation or his covenant people came to ruin? In response, I would first point out that if (*per impossibile*) God were the sort of being whose counsel could come to ruin, then, yes, he would be devastated if that counsel came to ruin. But God is not of that sort. His counsel stands, and he will accomplish all his purpose (Isa. 46:9–10; cf. Job 42:2; Ps. 115:3; Rom. 9:19–24). In an important sense God's glory (not his essential glory but the economic display of it) is contingent upon the accomplishment of his purpose, but there is no risk of him failing to accomplish his purpose. This distinguishes the real God from idols (so Deut. 32:39; Isa. 43:10–15).

105. Coccejus, *Prophetia Ezechielis*, 33.

does not accord with the nature of the subject since God in his incorruptible goodness is not subject to harm or deprivation. Anger or wrath is transferred from its native signification on account of a certain similitude: as a wrathful human being opposes wrongdoing and endeavors to punish the wrongdoer, so God opposes wrongdoing and punishes those who rebel against him and harm his creation. So Coccejus, for example, on Nahum 1:2: in God's case wrath is his "will of punishing that befits his most holy nature." Coccejus observes that God cannot approve of the malice of those who attempt to harm what he loves, so Nahum's prophecy attributes a burning ardor to God in that God wills the destruction of his enemies.[106] Similarly, Aquinas comments on Romans 1:18 that God's wrath is God's vengeance, which is called "wrath" "according to a similitude of men who are angry, who seek vengeance." Nevertheless, Aquinas adds, "God inflicts vengeance from a tranquility of mind."[107] To catch up the variety in this metaphorical sense of wrath, Polanus aptly notes that the wrath of God can signify either the "certain and just will of God against sins" or the "punishment itself inflicted or to be inflicted by God."[108]

Given the injustice and suffering that we see in the world—and given that we are rightly angered by injustice—it may be important to underscore that taking wrath to be a metaphorical attribute of God does not at all entail that he is indifferent or flippant about evil and injustice. The metaphorical element in the attribution of wrath to God lies only in that God himself is not harmed or impoverished by the unjust actions of creatures. It remains the case that God is robustly opposed to injustice and cares for the downtrodden. He is committed to punishing the unrepentant. In fact, one might make the point that it is good news that the God who alone can ultimately eradicate evil is never endangered or weakened by it. Moreover, it may be good news that God's justice and opposition to evil is already perfect in God himself rather than having to be brought into being or formed as a corollary to evil creatures' actions.[109]

Within the Christian exegetical tradition, this reading of predicates like "repentance," "grief," "jealousy," and "wrath" is generally anchored and summed up in the notion of a "similitude of effect." That is, such predicates are applied to God on the basis of a similarity between the effects or works

---

106. Coccejus, *Prophetae duodecim minores*, 338.
107. Aquinas, *Super Rom.* 1.6; cf. Aquinas, *ST* Ia.19.11 corp. (249).
108. Polanus, *Syntagma*, 2.35 (194); cf. Owen, *Vindiciae evangelicae* 4 (111–12).
109. Among other things, if God's justice were formed as a corollary to evil creatures' actions, that would imply that the perfection of God's justice would require evil, which would itself suggest that God could be fully God only by setting up evil as a counterpart—a suggestion that would compromise God's freedom in the act of creation and raise the question of whether he needed our suffering to actualize himself.

that a repentant, aggrieved, jealous, or wrathful human person brings about and the effects that God brings about.[110] There is a distinction observed here between the "affective" and the "effective," between someone undergoing something that changes and informs their disposition and someone performing certain actions. Turretin, for example, comments that repentance is attributed to God ἀνθρωποπαθῶς but has to be understood θεοπρεπῶς (in a manner that befits God). More specifically, repentance applies to God not by reason of "affect and internal sorrow, but of effect and external work." Thus, God repents not παθητικῶς or "affectively" but rather ἐνεργητικῶς or "effectively."[111] Mastricht writes similarly that God is said to repent ἀνθρωποπαθῶς, "according to effect, not affect."[112] Within the British Reformed tradition Owen's opposition to Socinianism in the seventeenth century led to the same kind of statements.[113] Owen denies that passions like anger are "ascribed properly unto God, denoting such passions and affections in him as those in us which are so termed." Owen contends instead that such passions are "spoken of [God] metaphorically only, in reference to his outward works and dispensations, correspondent and answering to the actings of men in whom such affections are."[114]

(4) At this point it is worth considering a potential objection: Why not say that, although God by virtue of his own perfection and sufficiency is not *unwillingly* subject to deprivation from without, he has chosen to limit himself or make himself vulnerable to his creatures with the result that "repentance," "grief," "jealousy," "wrath," and the like might literally be predicated of God? A number of theologians have offered proposals of this sort, sometimes taking up the concept of *kenōsis* to make their case.[115] Though one could take the idea of divine vulnerability in a number of different directions, it seems that by definition it would have to involve a potential in God to be harmed or wounded by creatures, a potential to be bereft of something good that he would need for his own wholeness and sufficiency. Perhaps this manner of expression does not flatter the idea of divine vulnerability, but to be vulnerable

---

110. See, e.g., Aquinas, *Super Eph.* 4.10; Aquinas, *ST* Ia.19.11 corp. (249).

111. Turretin, *Inst.*, 3.11.11 (1:227).

112. Mastricht, *TPT*, 2.23.7 (233).

113. Owen's arguments against Socinianism may be particularly relevant today to the extent that something like a Socinian literalistic reading of certain biblical passages in isolation from the rest of the canon has been taken up and reinvigorated in some modes of biblical interpretation.

114. Owen, *Vindiciae evangelicae* 4 (108).

115. See, from various angles, Moltmann, *God in Creation*, 86–89; Childs, *Biblical Theology of the Old and New Testaments*, 356–58; Polkinghorne, "Kenotic Creation and Divine Action"; Pool, *God's Wounds*; Fretheim, *What Kind of God?*, 159–71; Lohmann, "God's Freedom." See also the critique of such lines of reasoning in Oord, *The Uncontrolling Love of God*, chaps. 6–7, esp. 163–64.

is to be susceptible to harm and to depend on another for one's own good. And to be harmed is to undergo the loss of some good thing that is requisite to one's wholeness and sufficiency. In response to the idea of divine self-limitation or divine vulnerability, it has to be said that Holy Scripture offers us no indication that in God's decision to create the world or in God's actual creation of the world a transition occurred in which God altered himself to become subject to either losing or acquiring something good that would be necessary for his own wholeness and sufficiency. The Genesis creation narrative and other biblical passages on the origin of creation give us no ground for speaking about such an event in God. To be frank, then, the idea of a divine self-limitation or a transition in God from plenitude and self-sufficiency to insufficiency and vulnerability is a mythological posit or a theogony that attempts to account for a would-be new version of God whose wholeness turns on receiving from creatures something that we may give or withhold.[116] Furthermore, if such a shift had taken place, it would make little sense for Scripture still to include a passage like Acts 17:24–25: "The God who made the world and all things in it, he, being the Lord of heaven and earth, does not dwell in temples built by human hands, nor is he served by human hands as though needing something, he himself giving to all life and breath and all things." As the sum and origin and giver of all that is good, God, even in his relation to the world, is not subject to losing or gaining something at the hands of creatures. He remains incorruptible (Rom. 1:23). No one gives to God as though God should have gained something from them and been indebted to them, "for from him and through him and to him are all things" (11:35–36).

That God has remained fully and unabatedly himself in his relation to us is significant in Paul's teaching on the incarnation. It is because all the fullness of deity dwells bodily in Christ that Christ's revealing and reconciling work is decisive, never to be supplemented by other religious or spiritual resources (Col. 1:20; 2:3, 9). While God's infinite being is not reducible to what takes place in the incarnation, God the Son genuinely subsists in his divine fullness while subsisting in human flesh, so that his revelation of God and atonement for sin are efficacious. It is the sameness of God *in se* and *pro nobis* that rules

---

116. Although he would have presumably disagreed with almost all the arguments of this volume, it may be of interest to note that in the nineteenth century Wilhelm Herrmann called the idea of divine self-limitation a "mythological view" (*Die Metaphysik in der Theologie*, 38). In the context of Herrmann's reasoning about metaphysics and theology, he was critiquing Otto Pfleiderer's "metaphysical" understanding of divine causality and arguing that its undermining of divine and human freedom could not be salvaged by introducing "the mythological view of a self-limitation of God" (*die mythologische Anschauung einer Selbstbeschränkung Gottes*).

out the possibility of an aloof or elusive *Deus absconditus* and that secures
our redemption.[117]

Happily, it is true that God is "related" to the world. He brought us creatures into being and sustains and governs our life. He enters covenant relationships with human beings and grants human beings genuine agency in the
world. As Aquinas has put it, God gives creatures the "dignity of causality."[118]
But to exist with a relation to another does not automatically entail passibility
or vulnerability. Whether it entails passibility or vulnerability is a question
that can be answered only by considering who is the one existing in relation.
If the one existing in relation is a finite being dependent on others for its
fulfillment and wholeness, then existing in relation typically does entail vulnerability. However, if the one in view is the triune God in perfect possession
of his own incorruptible goodness, then existing in relation does not entail
vulnerability. If our words are answerable to the realities that they signify,
and if God is not the sort of being who has given up or even could give up
some good that is ingredient in his wholeness and well-being, then we should
not take the ordinary entailments of creaturely relations and project them
onto God as if he existed with us in the same order of being. What God's
covenantal relationship to human beings does entail is his ongoing care and
fidelity and his delight in doing good for us (e.g., Deut. 31:6; Isa. 62:4–5; Jer.
32:41). Indeed, given that God has life and perfect goodness in and of himself,
his covenant fidelity is unwavering. Instead of God's impassibility entailing
that he is only tentatively involved in human affairs, it entails the opposite: he
cannot be deflected from being "all in" regarding the accomplishment of his
purposes even in the face of creatures' sin and infidelity. Thus, he tells Israel
in Hosea 11:9 that despite their rejection of him, he will not utterly destroy
them: "For I am God and not a man, the holy one in your midst."

There are additional reasons that might be adduced in favor of concluding that predicates like "repentance," "grief," "jealousy," and "wrath" are
applied metaphorically to God since God is not susceptible to being harmed
or deprived by creatures. For example, the idea of a divine self-limitation or
movement to vulnerability would presuppose that it is possible for God to
pass from having an infinite goodness in which he is content to a finite goodness or satisfaction whose degree of fulfillment is determined by creatures'
actions. But is it possible for God's infinite goodness to be reduced to a finite
goodness? Can an incorruptible goodness be diminished? Can the infinite be

---

117. The importance of the sameness of God *in se* and *pro nobis* is highlighted well by Barth,
for example, in *CD*, IV.1, 183–85. I think one can appreciate this emphasis in Barth even if one
disagrees with some inferences that he draws from it.

118. Aquinas, *ST* Ia.22.3 corp. (267).

reduced to (not merely united with) the finite, to which it has no proportion?[119] Furthermore, if God is not composed of parts held together by something more ultimate than himself, then it is not possible to insulate a would-be part of God from diminution or vulnerability while rendering another would-be part vulnerable. And if that is so, then a purported vulnerability of God would render God capable of impoverishment in his wisdom, love, and justice and in all aspects of his perfection.

Here one might respond that it is incorrect to assume that a self-limitation or vulnerability on God's part would constitute a lessening or imperfection. Perhaps one could argue that, *pace* sub-Christian versions of "perfect being theology," it is actually included in God's perfection that he is able to assume a relation to creatures in which he does not have a self-sufficient goodness, knowledge, or beatitude in himself. Perhaps one could attempt to base such a claim on the notion that the incarnation and crucifixion of the Son controvert human wisdom about divine things (so 1 Cor. 1:18–2:16). Yet, despite the initial rhetorical power of such a claim, it would not actually correspond to what Scripture teaches about God's incorruptibility or about the incarnation and suffering of the Son. On the one hand, Scripture does of course present the jarring fact of God incarnate and crucified, challenging the assumption that the true God would not take on a lowly servant's form and suffer in it. On the other hand, Scripture does not teach us that the incarnate and crucified God who willed to be vulnerable in the form of a servant was vulnerable in the form of God also. In fact, Scripture positively teaches us that the poverty and suffering in the form of a servant are dissimilar to the richness in the form of God (2 Cor. 8:9; Phil. 2:6–7). The wonder of the incarnation is rooted not in the idea that the human suffering of the Son accords with his divine life but rather in the fact that it is radically unlike his divine life.[120]

Accordingly, a Christian doctrine of God that is alert to the significance of the incarnation does not stipulate an utterly paradoxical view of God in which his perfection would consist in being imperfect (i.e., lacking what pertains to his own well-being and having to acquire it from elsewhere). Christian theology does not overturn reason's rudimentary, innocuous knowledge of the fact that to be perfect is not to lack something, and that to lack something is to be imperfect. Of course, one could add that God's perfection includes

119. Cf. Gregory of Nyssa, *Contra Eunomium, pars prior* 1.167–71 (1:77–78), regarding the immutability of God's infinite goodness and the impossibility of any degeneration in it, a notion that, in context, Gregory uses to uphold the equality of Father, Son, and Spirit.

120. Cyril of Alexandria, for example, aptly notes that God does not leave behind his own nature when he takes on flesh. Indeed, the "God of the universe" cannot be "damaged" or "injured" (ἀδικεῖται) when coming to do us good (*Contra Theodoretum* 169,74 [138–39]).

both the divine persons' inward relations and God's ability (freely) to assume an external relation to agents other than himself, but that does not mean that his perfection should include a potential to lose or gain some good at the hands of those other agents.[121] In light of this, the Christian doctrine of God ought to maintain that God does not limit or make himself vulnerable to creatures and that passions are metaphorically attributed to God in the biblical canon.

(5) Finally, one might conclude that God in himself is not vulnerable and does not undergo any loss of goodness and yet also wonder whether God's love for suffering creatures should entail some sort of passibility. To conclude this section, then, it is worth briefly making a case that God's mercy does not entail passibility and, moreover, that it is precisely God's impassibility that clarifies the richness of his mercy.

The biblical authors use a variety of Hebrew and Greek words to describe God's love and kindness toward the suffering, which are expressed with English words like "mercy," "pity," and "compassion."[122] My goal here is not to offer a fine-tuned analysis of any one biblical word and how it might overlap or differ from other similar words. Rather, my goal is to discuss at a broader level what it means when Scripture and Christian theology attribute mercy to God. According to Scripture, God's mercy is great and rich, free and wide-ranging in its application (Exod. 33:19; 34:6; 2 Sam. 24:14; Neh. 9:31; Ps. 145:9; Eph. 2:4; James 5:11; 1 Pet. 1:3). It is the origin of all creaturely comfort and mercy (Luke 6:36; 2 Cor. 1:3–4). Mercy is something God prefers to wrath and judgment (Jer. 32:41; Lam. 3:33; Mic. 7:18). Indeed, according

---

121. This may be pastorally helpful on at least two levels. First, it means that God did not have a choice of either (a) remaining incomplete in himself without us or (b) making creatures whose suffering would move and enable him to become more loving or just. God simply is what he is and does not need our gifts or our suffering in order to fulfill himself. Having no need of evil as a counterpart, he is emphatically not the author of evil. Second, this line of thought reminds us that the Christian faith does not glamorize suffering. Though it is ordained that Christian believers suffer for a time, it really is good to get rid of suffering. Thus, instead of insisting that the highest state of created being should be one of openness to suffering, God will finally end our mourning (Rev. 21:1–5). This is not to say that creatures will become *absolutely* impassible as God alone is. Rather, it is to celebrate that the creature's glorification does not involve endless suffering caused by others but rather an impassibility and beatitude that befits the finite mode of created being.

122. In the Old Testament, for example, the verb רחם and its cognates are prominent (e.g., Exod. 33:19; 34:6; Deut. 30:3; 2 Kings 13:23; Pss. 25:6; 51:3 MT; 69:17 MT; 102:14 MT; 103:8–14; 145:9; Isa. 49:13, 15; 54:7–8, 10; Jer. 31:20; Lam. 3:22, 32; Hosea 2:21 MT; Jon. 4:2). The relevant adjective רחון is also applied somewhat frequently to God (see Exod. 22:27; Neh. 9:17; Pss. 86:15; 116:5; 145:8). In the New Testament, the verbs ἐλεέω, οἰκτίρω, and σπλαγχνίζω and their cognates are predicated of God (e.g., Luke 1:58, 78; Rom. 9:15–16, 18, 23; Titus 3:5; 1 Pet. 1:3; 2:10; James 5:11).

to Thomas Watson, "It is the great design of the Scripture to represent God as merciful."[123]

The biblical authors sometimes express God's mercy with language involving corporeal change. In Jeremiah 31:20, for example, God says regarding his "dear son" Ephraim, "My inward parts are stirred for him. I will surely have mercy on him." Comparing this verse to Hosea 11:8, Aquinas comments here that the disturbance of the "bowels" or "heart" (*viscera*) anthropopathically indicates an "inward compassion."[124] John Calvin similarly writes that "God transfers to himself human affections." For a disturbance of the inward parts occurs when one experiences an "immoderate grief" and "great sorrow." Thus, "God takes to himself the affection of a tender father." This does not belong "properly" to God, but God speaks this way in order to "express the greatness of his love for us." That is, he "speaks coarsely in order to accommodate himself to our crudeness."[125] Of course, if such an expression (the stirring or disturbance of "inward parts") retained its original signification and was not a "dead" metaphor at the time of its use in the Bible, then it would constitute a metaphorical description since God is incorporeal.

However, mercy does not necessarily have reference to any corporeal change. Mercy might ordinarily signify an incorporeal grief or sorrow from a sense of the misery of another—a sense of "alien" misery—that leads one to help another.[126] "Mercy" in this signification would be predicated metaphorically of God. For God himself does not undergo a loss through the loss of another. For God's own wholeness and well-being are not imperiled by what happens in the world. This view of divine mercy is implied by Hebrews 2:17–18 and 4:14–15, where the Son being merciful and sympathetic in the sense of having experienced suffering himself is a new thing consequent upon his assumption of flesh and blood. Taken in this way, mercy would be applied to God on account of his operations and effects: as a merciful human being helps those who suffer, so God wills and acts to help those who suffer.[127] Yet mercy might not have reference to grief or sorrow and might simply signify an

123. Watson, *A Body of Practical Divinity*, 53. From the Bible's witness to God's mercy, Owen infers that the chief distortion of the image of God is human cruelty (*Hebrews*, 4:423).

124. Aquinas, *In Jeremiam prophetam expositio* 31.6 (649).

125. Calvin, *Praelectiones in Ieremiam prophetam*, 677.

126. See, e.g., Aquinas, *ST* Ia.21.3 corp. (260); IaIIae.35.8 corp. (247); Polanus, *Syntagma*, 2.23 (174–75); Turretin, *Inst.*, 3.20.10 (1:269); Owen, *Hebrews*, 4:419–22; Mastricht, *TPT*, 2.17.21 (182).

127. See, e.g., Aquinas, *ST* Ia.21.3 (260–61). Cf. Coccejus, *Prophetae duodecim minores*, 28, who calls God's mercy his "will of consoling in afflictions." As noted in the previous section, the affections of the divine will are acts or the one simple act of the will with a relation to certain objects and effects (e.g., miserable human persons). A similar explanation could be given for the use of English words like "sympathy" and "compassion."

inclination and readiness of the will to help those who are suffering. In that case, mercy belongs properly and preeminently to God.[128] For there is a preeminent readiness in God to help those who are stuck in their sin and misery.[129]

Perhaps at first an understanding of God's mercy that negates grief on his part and focuses on affirming his eagerness to help the miserable will sound somewhat cold and inadequate. However, I would suggest that there are at least four reasons why this understanding is not necessarily cold or existentially inadequate. First, it is important to bear in mind that in this discussion of divine impassibility the predicate "grief" is being used in a strict sense to denote a harm or loss of good in a subject, together with an awareness on the part of the subject that he or she is the subject of such harm or loss.[130] If God as God is never the subject of harm or of the loss of what is good, then it follows that his mercy never involves grief in this strict sense. But the relatively modest claim that God as God is never the subject of harm or loss leaves room for us to underscore in a multitude of ways that God cares for miserable sinners. In fact, it may impress upon us the purity of God's benevolence, liberality, and delight in our well-being to consider that this God who does not have to gain or recover something for himself has pledged to alleviate our misery.[131]

Second, while it is true that in human situations participation in the grief of another is frequently a result of love, this does not entail that, in all cases or in God's case in particular, being harmed is the criterion of love. Even in human situations, one's participation in the grief of another in and of itself is not what is virtuous. It is one's attentiveness to the well-being of someone who suffers, one's readiness to remain present with them and help them in their suffering, that is virtuous. And sometimes when that propensity to help and comfort has no reference to alleviating any suffering of one's own, the benevolence involved is all the more brilliant.

128. Cf. Zanchi, *De natura Dei*, 2.2 (68–69); Polanus, *Syntagma*, 2.23 (174–75); Leigh, *A Treatise of Divinity*, 2.2 (86); Watson, *A Body of Practical Divinity*, 53. If God is simple and without a real distinction between faculty and virtue or virtue and act, then, more precisely, mercy would signify God's eternal act of willing in his readiness to help the suffering.

129. On this approach, when Isa. 63:9, for example, tells us that God was afflicted in his people's affliction, this means not that God himself was harmed or made to lose something belonging to his own wholeness but rather that God, being united in covenant love and fidelity to his people, took his people's misery as his own concern and took their deliverance as his responsibility.

130. Cf., e.g., John of Damascus, *Expos. fidei* 2.22 (88); Aquinas, *ST* IaIIae.35.1 (240–41); IIIa.15.5 corp. (190).

131. On the connection between God being impassible and his being supremely generous, cf. Gregory Nazianzen, *Discours 27–31*, 28.11 (122); Charnock, *The Existence and Attributes of God*, 2:218–19, 227.

It seems, then, that in God's case, if his propensity to help his people in their sin and suffering does not entail his being harmed or impoverished by their suffering, that does not mean that God's love is deficient. He just is not the sort of being who could be harmed, which ends up being good news for those who face sorrow and need a Father who deems their salvation a worthwhile endeavor even when there is nothing he has to gain or recover for himself.[132]

Third, it is good for one to be moved by the suffering of another only if one is the sort of being who needs to be moved in order to love. It is good and right for creatures to be moved by their fellow creatures' suffering since their love is incomplete and often inactive, but God's love is never inactive or inadequate to new circumstances. His love is already complete in the fellowship of Father, Son, and Spirit. It does not need to acquire mercy as an accident by which it might begin to have a power of helping creatures. Thus, God's mercy toward creatures is just an inflection or egression of God's essential goodness and love. Or, as Mastricht puts it, attributes like benevolence, beneficence, grace, mercy, and patience are just God's one inclination to the good "variously modified."[133] Accordingly, the creature's suffering is not an external cause that has to excite or initiate love in God but rather a condition or circumstance according to which God applies his perfect love to the creature.[134] God does not become greater in his love; at the same time, he is still not mechanical in his love. Without having to become greater, he still affirms created agency and the diverse situations issuing from it, suiting the manifestation of his love to what is really happening in the world. And it may be an encouragement in suffering to know that instead of God only beginning to love adequately from the onset of

---

132. Of course, the end and fulfillment of the creature is God himself—to manifest and enjoy the glory of God. The creature is ordered to the triune God and must worship him alone. And, on his side, God enjoys creatures' manifestation and enjoyment of himself as the supreme good. But creatures have God as their end not because they are means by which God actualizes himself but because God is the only one in whom the creature ever could find fulfillment. For God alone is the source of all goodness and joy. God then orders creatures to himself because it is the only good and right thing to do for them. And he enjoys their manifestation and enjoyment of himself because he is the one from whom all perfection and goodness proceed. God enjoys in creatures only what manifests God because apart from what comes forth from him and manifests him there is nothing else to enjoy. Thus, God taking pleasure in creatures glorifying him is nothing other than God taking pleasure in acting generously for their sake and giving them what is best for them. In recognizing this, we are in a position to confirm that while creatures have God as their end—while they exist *for* God—they do so in such a way that they retain an integrity of their own. They are genuinely other than God and an object of God's unselfish benevolence and delight.

133. Mastricht, *TPT*, 2.17.5 (179).

134. Turretin, *Inst.*, 3.20.11 (1:269). Cf. Owen, *Hebrews*, 4:423.

our suffering, God's mercy is his eternal goodness and love directed toward us in all their infinite strength.[135]

Finally, God's mercy has still manifested itself in God suffering. It has appeared to us not as God suffering as God but rather as God suffering as man and as our brother. It is not the case that God willed to avoid association with human beings in their misery. Rather, in God's eternal decision to permit the fall and save sinners, God the Son chose to assume a nature in which he could partake of human misery in order to deliver us from it. We can negate passibility in a certain respect (i.e., with regard to God or God the Son according to his deity) and still affirm passibility in another respect (i.e., with regard to God the Son according to his humanity and human experience). And if the Son is "no less true man than he is true God,"[136] then it cannot be said that this suffering is not truly his or that it does not matter. It is as truly predicated of the Son as divine aseity or divine immutability is predicated of the Son. Indeed, since it is truly *his* suffering, it is a revelation or human representation of divine love. For the Son's human nature with all its passibility subsists only in the divine Son and is an instrument of the divine Son. All the operation and the suffering of the Son according to his humanity exhibits the perfection of God, including his grace and mercy. The human mercy of the Son, which involves weeping at the death of Lazarus, manifests on a human level impassible divine love. That human mercy does not translate suffering back into the Son's divine essence, but it is the freely chosen experience of a divine person and a revelation of divine goodness, love, and trustworthiness.[137]

135. Recent proposals concerning "divine omnisubjectivity" (see, e.g., Zagzebski, *Omnisubjectivity*; Zagzebski, "Omnisubjectivity"; Mullins, *God and Emotion*, 60–69) contend that God in his omniscience acquires a version of creatures' emotions and that while God may not agree with a creature's emotion, it is still beneficial at both the theological and existential levels to fill out the concept of divine omniscience in this way. However, if having an emotion or empathizing in an ordinary sense presupposes receiving something good or harmful in another's good or harm and assessing such a thing as good or harmful, it is not clear that God could have in his own divine will the likeness of a creature's emotion without himself sharing the creature's assessment of the good or evil producing the emotion. He would simply be aware of what the creature's emotion is and what the creature needs. More decisively, if scriptural texts like Heb. 2:17–18 and 4:15 teach that God the Son did not have experience of our suffering prior to the incarnation, then the idea of God as God having in himself his own version of our suffering is not viable.

136. Zanchi, *De incarn.*, 2.2 (82, 84).

137. Owen offers the intriguing suggestion that the anthropopathic descriptions of God's love in the Old Testament (esp. Isa. 63:9) not only show God's condescension to our manner of understanding but also anticipate the incarnation. For Owen, God intimated in those descriptions his eternal plan to represent himself to us in the Son's human compassion (*Christologia* 7 [89]; *Hebrews*, 4:421, 424).

This section has aimed to clarify that God's impassibility fits with the biblical authors' (metaphorical) attribution of passions to God. This has led to an exposition of God's repentance, jealousy, wrath, and so on that accords with God's incorruptible perfection and goodness. It has also led to an exposition of God's mercy that has just ended with a note on the passibility of the Son according to his humanity. But drawing such a distinction between what pertains to the Son as God and what pertains to the Son as human has come under scrutiny in recent Christology. Is it legitimate to employ "reduplicative" speech and predicate certain things of Christ as God and other contrary things of Christ as human? This will be the topic of the next section.

V. Impassibility and Reduplicative Predication in Christology

This section seeks to develop the claim that divine impassibility and the human suffering of God the Son cohere with one another and that this coherence can be articulated through the use of reduplicative speech (predicating certain things of Christ as God and others of Christ as human). From the start, though, I should clarify that at this point I am no longer constructing an argument for divine impassibility or the genuineness and immediacy of the Son's human suffering. If the exegesis from earlier in this chapter is accurate, then divine impassibility has been set in place as a biblical doctrine with which one just does have to work in the field of Christology. And given the emphasis in the exegetical material on the divine Son's suffering being truly his own, I take that too to be an established reality with which one has to work in Christology. Thus, the discernment of coherence and the consideration of reduplicative speech here is not a matter of trying to prove divine impassibility or the Son's human passibility. It is a matter of recognizing that if the divinity and thus the divine impassibility of the Son explains why he can accomplish our salvation by his human suffering, then Christology will benefit from having a stronger understanding of how these things fit together. In pursuit of a stronger understanding, then, I will offer the following four points, enfolding some recent objections along the way for ultimately constructive ends.[138]

138. The secondary literature on reduplication and related issues is rapidly expanding. Here I will not attempt to engage with any one author in an exhaustive manner but will try to touch on what I take to be some salient points from different analyses and critiques. For recent discussion, see Cross, *The Metaphysics of the Incarnation*, 192–205; Cross, "The Incarnation"; Stump, "Aquinas' Metaphysics of the Incarnation"; Leftow, "A Timeless God Incarnate"; Leftow, "Composition and Christology"; Senor, "Incarnation, Timelessness, and Leibniz's Law Problems"; Senor, "The Compositional Account of the Incarnation"; Adams, *Christ and Horrors*, 128–38; Le Poidevin, "Identity and the Composite Christ"; Le Poidevin, "Incarnation"; Le Poidevin,

(1) It is significant that while Scripture teaches that God the Son bought the church with his own blood (Acts 20:28), Scripture also specifies that it was in the form of a servant that the Son undertook his obedience until death (Phil. 2:7–8). He had to take on flesh in order to suffer (Heb. 2:17–18), and, having taken on flesh, he suffered *in the flesh* (1 Pet. 4:1).[139] In this way, Scripture itself implies the patristic logic wherein certain things (e.g., impassibility) are attributed to Christ with respect to his deity and others (e.g., passibility) are attributed to Christ with respect to his humanity.[140] This logic is formally expressed in the Christology of Chalcedon: the Son's deity remains impassible since the Son is "consubstantial with the Father according to the deity" (ὁμοούσιος τῷ πατρὶ κατὰ τὴν θεότητα), and yet the Son is also "consubstantial with us . . . according to the humanity" (ὁμοούσιος ἡμῖν . . . κατὰ τὴν ἀνθρωπότητα).[141] Medieval theologians take up this manner of speaking and analyze the ways in which it can help to assess the veracity of statements like "Christ as man is God," "Christ as man is a person," or "Christ as man is a creature."[142] For example, Aquinas in his *Sentences* commentary remarks that whatever is "redoubled" (*reduplicatur*) in a proposition by the phrase "according to" or "insofar as" (*secundum quod*) is "that by which the predicate agrees with the subject."[143]

(2) Underlying recent concerns about reduplicative speech in Christology are deeper ontological questions, which is fitting since our speech is not an end in itself but has to signify and describe the reality of the God-man. One

"Euthyphro and the Goodness of God Incarnate"; Marmodoro and Hill, "Composition Models of the Incarnation"; K. Rogers, "The Incarnation as Action Composite"; M. Gorman, "Christological Consistency and the Reduplicative Qua"; M. Gorman, "Two Problems concerning Divine Immutability and the Incarnation"; Pawl, "Conciliar Christology and the Problem of Incompatible Predications"; Pawl, "Conciliar Christology and the Consistency of Divine Immutability"; Crisp, *The Word Enfleshed*, chap. 6; Hasker, "A Compositional Incarnation"; Beall and Henderson, "A Neglected Qua Solution to the Fundamental Problem of Christology"; Beall, "Christ—a Contradiction"; Moser, "Tools for Interpreting Christ's Saving Mysteries in Scripture"; Beall, *The Contradictory Christ*.

139. Cf. the observations in Moser, "Tools for Interpreting Christ's Saving Mysteries in Scripture," esp. 292–93.

140. See, e.g., Gregory Nazianzen, *Discours 27–31*, 29.20 (220, 222); Ambrose, *De incarnationis dominicae sacramento* 5,34–39, 44–45 (240–43, 246–47); 6,56–57 (252–54); Augustine, *De trin.* 2.1–4 (81–87); Cyril of Alexandria, *Altera ad Nestorium* 4,4–5 (27–28); Cyril, *Tertia ad Nestorium* 6,6–7 (37–38); Cyril, *Scholia* 36 (564–68); Cyril, *Contra Orientales* 24,109–12 (62–63). John of Damascus (*Expos. fidei* 4.18 [212–18]) elaborates further on the number of modes in which one can speak of Christ.

141. Council of Chalcedon, "Definition of the Faith," in N. Tanner, *Decrees of the Ecumenical Councils*, 86.

142. See, e.g., Aquinas, *Super Sent.* 3.10.1.1–2; 3.11.1–4; Aquinas, *ST* IIIa.16.10 (215); Duns Scotus, *Ordinatio* 3.11.2. Medieval treatments of reduplication are discussed in Bäck, *On Reduplication*; Bäck, "Scotus on the Consistency of the Incarnation and the Trinity."

143. Aquinas, *Super Sent.* 3.10.1.1 sol. 1.

of the issues is whether Christ is a "composite" person. If there were distinct parts in the "composite" Christ, then, so the logic goes, that would make it easier to attribute, say, impassibility to Christ with regard to one "part" and passibility to Christ with regard to another "part." Senor, for example, writes that according to a "compositional" Christology, "God the Son became a human being by adding on a human body and a human mind, and by doing it in such a way that God the Son, the human body, and the human mind of Christ together composed the Incarnate God." Thus, "God the Son is one part of the composite that is God Incarnate." Senor reasons that this "compositional" view will undermine the claim that God the Son is identical to Jesus Christ: "If [God the Son] is but a proper part of the individual who is Jesus Christ, then [the "compositional account"] is committed to saying that [God the Son] and [Jesus Christ] are not identical." For Senor, this entails either that there would be two persons in the incarnation or, if there were still only one person (i.e., God the Son), that "the composite Christ is not a person." In other words, one would have either Nestorianism or the idea that the incarnate Christ is "an impersonal conglomerate."[144] Moreover, Senor doubts that the "composite whole" (i.e., the person of Christ) could sufficiently have or "borrow" the properties from each of his "parts" (i.e., the divinity and humanity) in order to be the one subject of whom they are truly predicated. At the same time, Senor suggests, if such "borrowing" did take place, the divine properties and human properties could not be "insulated" from one another, producing a logical inconsistency wherein, for example, Christ would be both omnipotent and not omnipotent.[145]

Taking a similar approach to reduplication and composition, Le Poidevin reasons that composition in the incarnation implies that there are two persons involved: "the divine person, and the human person. For, prior to the Incarnation, what became the divine part of Christ was the Second Person of the Trinity. And Christ's human part contains everything that is possessed by human persons." Le Poidevin suggests a way of qualifying the personhood of the second person of the Trinity and the purported personhood of Christ's humanity in order to avoid the implication of two persons in the incarnation. The second person of the Trinity could be considered a person in his own right prior to the incarnation, but then he "becomes the divine part of Christ" in the incarnation. That "divine part" does persist in the incarnation, but since it is "part" of Christ, it is not a person per se and "not identical to Christ."

---

144. Senor, "Compositional Account," 53, 55–56. It should be borne in mind that Senor is responding to "mereological" accounts of the incarnation that he finds in authors like Stump and Leftow.

145. Senor, "Compositional Account," 64–65, 69.

And, on the other side, Christ's humanity could be thought to "constitute a person in its own right" only in the absence of the second person of the Trinity, so that it is not an additional person in union with the person of the Son. As Le Poidevin traces out the logic, the Son is not identical to Christ, so when the incarnation takes place, "a new person comes into existence, namely the composite of divine and human elements." But Le Poidevin recognizes a problem here: "If we say that the Second Person of the Trinity is not Christ, but Christ, as it were, *replaced* the Second Person, then the Second Person *as a person* ceased to exist. Thus, during the Incarnation, the Second *Person* of the Trinity was not in existence."[146]

In response, it is worth clarifying that the sense in which earlier Christian theologians spoke of Christ as a "composite" person is different from what authors like Senor and Le Poidevin have in mind in their criticisms of reduplication. As discussed in chapter 4, section III, writers like Aquinas, Polanus, and Turretin state clearly that the point of calling the incarnate Son a "composite person" (*persona synthetos*) is to express that, after subsisting only in the divine nature prior to the incarnation, the Son now subsists in two natures. Aquinas remarks quite simply that Christ can be called "composite" since "everything in which two convene can be called 'composed' from these."[147] But neither the Son's deity nor his personal subsistence is a "part" in the ordinary sense of an incomplete thing ordered to the constitution of a greater whole. His deity transcends the order of common, created being altogether, so, strictly speaking, it cannot enter into composition with any part of that order. By transcending the order of common being God can be immediately present throughout that order and even assume and individuate a created nature within it, but he never becomes one more part of a greater whole. And the Son's personal subsistence or proper mode of subsisting is already complete in the divine essence and by his eternal, personally constitutive relation to the Father. Thus, the Son's proper subsistence never becomes part of a greater whole or a whole itself founded upon and completed by parts. In his assumption of a human nature, then, the Son actualizes, sustains, and perfects the human nature without being composed or completed by it. In the unique situation of God the Son, his subsistence is shared by the human nature, so he is the immediate subject of his human nature and suffering, but, because of the prevenient completeness of his subsistence, his subsistence is still not established or composed or put together by his human nature.

146. Le Poidevin, "Identity and the Composite Christ," 173–74, 177–78, 180, 182–83. Cf. Le Poidevin, "Incarnation," 707–9.
147. Aquinas, *ST* IIIa.2.4 (31).

These considerations about the person of the Son never being a part composing a whole or a whole composed of parts have bearing in at least two ways on the question about God the Son being identical to the person of Jesus Christ. First, if the person of God the Son does not enter into composition even in his assumption of a human nature, then there are no logical conundrums that Christology needs to address regarding how a "part" of something (purportedly, God the Son) might be identical with the whole (purportedly, Jesus Christ). Second, the eternal completeness of the Son by virtue of which he does not enter into composition also entails that what constitutes him as the person that he is does not change in the incarnation. His proper mode of subsisting is complete in the divine essence and in relation to the Father. This is what constitutes him as the person of the Son. Accordingly, the Son is not constituted a person *absolutely* by his assumption of a human nature. He is only contingently constituted a person *of a human nature* by his assumption of a human nature.[148] In light of this reality, the Son's personal identity (who he fundamentally is) is not affected or altered by the human nature even as he himself is now the subject of the human nature and of his own human activity and suffering in it. The person of God the Son, then, is the person of Jesus Christ even as the person of God the Son has taken up something new (i.e., the human nature) in the economic office according to which he is called "Jesus Christ."[149]

The clarification about Christ not having parts in a proper sense also helps to address the concern about whether Christ might sufficiently "borrow" a property from one of his natures while also "insulating" that property from

148. So Aquinas: "The human nature does not constitute the divine person absolutely [*simpliciter*], but it constitutes [the divine person] insofar as it is denominated by such a nature. For not from the human nature does the Son exist absolutely [*habet . . . quod sit simpliciter*], because he has been from eternity, but only as he is man" (*ST* IIIa.3.1 ad 3 [53–54]). Cf., e.g., Polanus, *Syntagma*, 6.16 (376); Owen, *Christologia* 18 (229). For related material qualifying the sense in which the person of Christ might be called a "creature," or a "man," see John of Damascus, *Expos. fidei* 4.5 (177); Aquinas, *Super Sent.* 3.10.1.2; 3.11.1–3; Aquinas, *ST* IIIa.16.8 (211).

149. Cf. Turretin, *Inst.*, 14.2.14 (2:415) regarding the person of the Son being distinguishable from Christ the mediator only by a (nonconstitutive) relation to his economic office. On a related note, because of the uniqueness of the incarnation, it seems wise to avoid getting caught up in recent debates about the idea of "relative identity" (i.e., things that are identical to each other may be identical with respect to one sort of thing and distinct with respect to another sort of thing) and its potential applicability to the doctrine of the incarnation. In favor of using the idea, see van Inwagen, "Not by Confusion of Substance." For critiques of "relative identity," see, e.g., Rea, "Relative Identity and the Trinity"; Cross, "Incarnation," 457–58; Le Poidevin, "Identity and the Composite Christ," 174, 180–82; Le Poidevin, "Incarnation," 708–9. Whether a general theory of "relative identity" is workable or not in a range of ordinary scenarios, dogmatic Christology can still carry out its work of expressing the content of scriptural teaching on the incarnation and making sure to avoid logical contradiction along the way.

a contrary property. Christ does not have his humanity as a "part," so there is no need to ponder how to ensure that he, the whole person, would sufficiently possess the properties of a would-be "part." Instead, the person of Christ is constituted as man by his human nature, so, having this constitutive natural principle, Christ is of course the subject of all his human properties and experiences. And there is no need to worry about how to "insulate" one property from its contrary. The impassible, omnipotent deity and the passible, finite humanity do not occupy the same order of being. Therefore, they are not confused or in conflict with one another.

(3) If God the Son remains the same person in the incarnation, should one still be concerned that Christ's humanity itself (composed of body and soul with rational intellect and will) might yield a second person in the incarnation? As noted above, Le Poidevin, for example, suggests that Christ's humanity might "constitute a person in its own right." However, if one holds to something like Boethius's definition of "person" (an individual substance of a rational nature), it is important to recall that rational intellect and will per se are included in the common nature of human beings. And if rational intellect and will per se are included in the common nature of human beings, then rational intellect and will per se do not suffice for establishing an individual human person. In view of this, the human nature of Christ with its rational intellect and will on its own does not have the potential to introduce a second person in the incarnation. If the human nature is to constitute a human person, it requires completion or actualization and termination in a proper mode of subsisting.[150] The human nature of Christ receives this actualization and termination only in the person of the Son, so it exists only in the Son. Thus, it cannot and does not constitute a new person as human; it constitutes the prevenient person of the Son as human. In this connection, the teaching of the *enhypostasia* of the human nature (i.e., its subsisting only in the person of the Son) is not an ad hoc dismissal of an independent human person in the incarnation. Instead, it is an expression of the fact that the human nature inevitably would have to be actualized and terminated in a proper mode of subsisting and in fact is actualized and terminated only in the Son.[151]

150. Given that it is not the common nature but the individual that is designated by the term "person," a person is not a constituent feature of the common nature but the *terminus* or "endpoint" of an actual instance of the common nature. Personality pertains to the *terminus* and proper mode of subsisting of the nature. This is not to separate person from nature, for the person is still always a person of the nature with all that it includes. However, person or personality as such adds the distinct mode of subsisting to the nature.

151. Cf. Davidson, "Theologizing the Human Jesus." For a helpful account of the diverse uses of ἀνυπόστατος and ἐνυπόστατος, see John of Damascus, *Dial.*, fus. κη'-κθ' (109–10). A

Recent discussion about whether Christ's humanity is "concrete" or "abstract" has caused some confusion regarding this point that Christ's humanity includes a human intellect and will without being a distinct person in its own right.[152] Alvin Plantinga's use of these terms posits that in a "concrete" view of Christ's humanity, the human nature is "a 'human nature' in the sense of a human being," which entails that there would be two intellects and two wills in Christ. By contrast, in an "abstract" view of Christ's humanity (exemplified by Cyril of Alexandria according to Plantinga's reading), the human nature is a "property" (or "group of properties") and thus an "abstract object," "which is such that necessarily, every human being has P, and necessarily, whatever has P is a human being."[153]

There are several problems in this sort of description. First, on a historical level, while intended to describe some real differences among competing christological views in the patristic period, this way of framing the distinction between the "concrete" and the "abstract" is misguided. Among other things, it implies that the major authors in the patristic and medieval tradition were left with a choice of either (a) a "concrete" view that *over*stated the content of Christ's human nature so that it logically entailed a second (human) person in the incarnation or (b) an "abstract" view that *under*stated the content of Christ's human nature so that it was considered a "property" (or set of properties) without a human intellect and will. This suggests that someone like Cyril of Alexandria (taken to be a proponent of an "abstract" view) would not have affirmed that there are two intellects and wills in Christ, which is false.[154]

Furthermore, this framing of the distinction obscures earlier usage of the distinction between the "concrete" and the "abstract." The "concrete" is commonly regarded as the person of the nature or the person constituted as human by the nature, while the "abstract" is commonly regarded as the nature

broader discussion of historical developments in the use of ἐνυπόστατος can be found in Gleede, *The Development of the Term* ἐνυπόστατος.

152. See esp. Alvin Plantinga's essay "On Heresy, Mind, and Truth." For pertinent material on the relationship between nature and person and attempts at clarifying what the descriptors "concrete" and "abstract" entail, see, e.g., Swinburne, *The Christian God*, 212–15; Wolterstorff, *Inquiring about God*, 91–95, 100–109; DeWeese, "One Person, Two Natures," 121–35; Loke, "Solving a Paradox against Concrete-Composite Christology"; Loke, "On the An-Enhypostasia Distinction and Three-Part Concrete-Nature Christology"; Loke, "On the Divine Preconscious Model of the Incarnation and Concrete-Nature Christology"; Crisp, "Desiderata for Models of the Hypostatic Union"; Arcadi, "Kryptic or Cryptic?"; Farris, "Loke on the Abstractist/Concretist Christological Distinction." See also Pawl and Spencer, "Christologically Inspired, Empirically Motivated Hylomorphism."

153. Plantinga, "On Heresy, Mind, and Truth," 183–84.

154. See Cyril of Alexandria, *Ad Theodosium* 7,6 (45), 17–18 (52–53), 21 (55); Cyril, *Contra Orientales* 24,31 (40).

as such or the principle constituting the subject as human.[155] In this respect, what is "concrete" is indeed a person, and natures exist only in concrete persons. But the nature as such is not what is concrete or a person.[156] And what is "abstract" is indeed not a person but the nature as such. But the nature as such is not a "property" or "abstract object" but a constitutive principle by which something is of a certain kind, ordered to a certain end and with a capacity to have properties and virtues and to undertake actions that befit its end.[157]

Second, on a more constructive level, aside from the question of whether it makes sense to call a nature a "property" that is instantiated and yet also an "abstract object," the key point is that human intellect and will per se are included in the common nature of humanity and not in that which individuates a person. On the one hand, this means, against what Plantinga calls a "concrete" view, that human intellect and will per se do not automatically establish a distinct person (or, in particular, a second person in the incarnation). On the other hand, against what Plantinga calls an "abstract" view, an instance of human nature cannot be without human intellect and will, as though the subject of the human nature might possess an intellect and will from elsewhere and join them to whatever the human nature itself might still include.[158] Thus, because the human nature (not what individuates a person) is what includes the human intellect and will per se, the human intellect and will of Christ do not introduce an additional person in the incarnation but are, rather, terminated in the one person of the Son. And, at the same time, because all that the human nature includes is terminated in the one person of the Son, the Son has a distinctly human intellect and will.[159]

155. See, e.g., Aquinas, *Super Sent.* 3.11.4; Aquinas, *De hebdomadibus* 2 (272); Aquinas, *ST* IIIa.16.1–2, 4–5 (197–98, 201, 203–5); Keckermann, *Systema s.s. theologiae*, 3.2 (175–76); Turretin, *Inst.*, 13.8.5–6 (2:350).

156. Regarding the distinction between nature and an individual ὑπόστασις or person, see, e.g., John of Damascus, *Dial.*, fus. λα' (94–95); Aquinas, *De hebdomadibus* 2 (272); Aquinas, *Quaestiones de quolibet* 2.2.2 [4] (215–18); Aquinas, *ST* Ia.3.3 (40).

157. Cf., e.g., John of Damascus, *Dial.*, fus. λα' (93–94); Aquinas, *De unione* q. un., art. 1 corp. (422).

158. To elaborate, if one posited that what individuates or what is proper to a human person supplied intellect and will in the human species, then there would be no guarantee that all human beings would have intellect and will. If one clarified that what individuates or what is proper to a human person always includes a human intellect and will, then the human intellect and will would not truly be included in what individuates or what is proper to a human person. For the intellect and will would have been tacitly relocated back to the common nature shared by all.

159. When the distinction between nature and person is not worked out carefully in Christology, there is often a tendency to assume that the Word's divine intellect and will must somehow become the seat of human thoughts and volition, which inevitably leads to perplexing (and unnecessary) questions about how a divine intellect or "mind" can accommodate two apparently conflicting streams of consciousness (on which, see, e.g., Morris, *The Logic of God Incarnate*,

(4) Finally, given the biblical impetus and the logical viability of the teaching that the one person of the Son is the immediate subject of the diverse properties of his two natures, this section can conclude with a summation of the coherence of the Son's divine impassibility and human suffering. Beyond making the basic point that the Son remains impassible according to his deity even as he suffers according to his humanity, it is important to consider how the Son's deity and divine impassibility positively ground the efficacy of his human suffering.

First, the Son's deity secures the infinite dignity of his person and thus the infinite worth and efficacy of his redemptive suffering. As Paul put it in Acts 20:28, God bought the church with his own blood, which underscores the inestimable price paid in the Son's vicarious death. Since all the fullness of deity dwells in Christ, he is able by the shedding of his blood to reconcile us to God and cleanse us of sin (Col. 1:19–22). While the Son does not suffer according to his deity in the crucifixion, the Son does act according to his deity in sovereignly laying down his life and offering his flesh for the life of the world. For he says, "No one takes [my life] from me, but I myself lay it down from myself" (John 10:18).

In describing the efficacy of Christ's satisfaction for our sin, Aquinas addresses a pertinent objection here: "Satisfaction imports some equality to the guilt. . . . But the passion of Christ is not seen to be equal to all the sins of the human race, because Christ has not suffered according to the divinity but according to the flesh." Aquinas responds that "the dignity of the flesh of Christ is not to be estimated only according to the nature of the flesh but according to the person assuming, inasmuch as it actually was the flesh of God, from which it has an infinite dignity."[160] Whatever questions might need to be addressed regarding the ascription of an infinite dignity to the finite human nature of Christ, it remains that the divine person, with an infinite dignity, is the efficient cause of the satisfaction. The person (not a nature as such) performs the act.[161] And Christ does operate according to his deity in his atoning work even though he does not suffer according to his deity in this work.

153–62; Swinburne, The Christian God, 199–209; Cross "Incarnation," 466–71; Marmodoro and Hill, "Composition Models of the Incarnation"; Loke, "The Incarnation and Jesus' Apparent Limitation in Knowledge").

160. Aquinas, ST IIIa.48.2 ad 3 (464). See also Aquinas, Super Sent. 3.20.1.2 sol.; 3.20.1.3 ad 2. Without necessarily asserting that the flesh of Christ itself has an infinite dignity, Reformed authors often speak of a "grace of eminence" given to the humanity of Christ whereby Christ according to his humanity has a dignity that surpasses that of all created beings (e.g., Keckermann, Systema s.s. theologiae, 3.2 [176–77]; Turretin, Inst., 13.8.1 [2:349]).

161. Cf. Ames, Bellarminus enervatus, 2.3.9 (118); Voetius, Select. disp., pars sec., 2.9 (168); Turretin, Inst., 14.2.5 (2:412–13); 14.12.7 (2:478); Owen, Pneumatologia, 2.4 (3:177).

William Ames makes this point well in his discussion of Christ's mediatorial office. He notes that the infinite dignity and efficacy of the person of Christ will not "overflow" into his work of satisfaction and reconciliation unless Christ is acting according to his deity as well as his humanity. The dignity and efficacy will not characterize the work unless Christ operates according to the nature to which his divine majesty belongs. But Christ does indeed operate according to that nature. Commenting on John 10:17–18, where Christ teaches that he will lay down his life and will take it up again, Ames observes that "although to put aside the life passively is to die and to take up the life passively is to rise," Christ is speaking about his authority to lay down and take up his life, which means that he is speaking about *actively* laying down and taking up his life. In this sense, "to put aside the life is freely to dismiss the life in death and to take up the life is to raise up the dead." Christ cannot do this by mere human operation; he does this by divine operation. Accordingly, the "worth, dignity, efficacy, and application of that satisfaction come forth from the divine nature."[162]

Second, because of the union of the deity and humanity in Christ, he is able to bear the weight of his human suffering.[163] While the *communicatio idiomatum* does not mean that the omnipotence of Christ's deity was communicated to Christ's human nature itself, the hypostatic union of the deity with the humanity entails that Christ can endure the weight of punishment for our sin. There may be various aspects of this point to bring forward in working through a theology of Christ's atonement. For example, the deity and divine subsistence of Christ entails that the person in whom the human nature is actualized and sustained cannot be destroyed or divided. It entails that the person in whom the human nature is actualized and sustained is the same person who sovereignly chose the duration of the suffering and the time and manner of death (so John 10:17–18). The filial identity of Christ and the filial characterization of Christ's human life and activity entail that Christ as man will always have the love and approbation of the Father. Even on the cross as he bears our guilt, he is the object of the Father's delight (see again John 10:17–18). The divine subsistence and filial identity of Christ also entail that he will always have the help of the Spirit in his human exertion. For Christ, together with the Father, is the one from whom the Spirit proceeds. Thus, Christ as man is the one who has the Spirit without measure and offers himself up as a sacrifice for sin through the eternal Spirit (John 3:34; Heb. 9:14). If one considers Christ's deity more particularly under the aspect of his impassibility, it can be added that because his deity is above harm, deprivation,

162. Ames, *Bellarminus enervatus*, 2.3.3, 10–11, 14 (116, 118–21).
163. On which, see, e.g., Turretin, *Inst.*, 14.2.7 (2:413); Owen, *Pneumatologia*, 2.4 (3:176).

and diminishment, the infinite dignity of the person of Christ never wanes in the midst of his act of laying down his life. Since Christ as God is impassible, when he suffers and dies there is no attenuation of the divine fullness and majesty by virtue of which his atoning work has its unlimited worth and efficacy and can redeem us from our sin.

Finally, because Christ as God is impassible, he overcomes death and brings us life. Because Christ as God is unharmed and undiminished in his divine life and immortality, he can do as he promised in John 10:18 and take his life up once again. Because Christ has all the fullness of deity in himself, he is the firstborn from the dead, who has preeminence in the resurrection and gives us resurrection life (Col. 1:18–19; cf. John 11:25–26). By the divine power according to which Christ subjects all things to himself he will come and transform our lowly bodies to be like his glorious body (Phil. 3:21).[164]

It may seem plausible at first to suggest that Christ as God could undergo suffering and, in that way, absorb and eradicate suffering and death by his immortal life. However, beyond the scriptural texts (e.g., Rom. 1:23; Heb. 2:17–18; 4:15; 1 Pet. 4:1) that press us to conclude that Christ suffered only according to the flesh, the prima facie plausibility of the idea of divine suffering overcoming death does not hold up on closer examination. Suffering involves being harmed and no longer being in possession of one's fullness and well-being. If Christ was really harmed according to his deity or divested himself of his fullness and well-being according to his deity, then that would raise the question of whether his divine life and divine power to overcome death would remain intact. Some aspect or "part" of his divine being would somehow have to remain insulated from the suffering and damage in order to ensure that Christ could regenerate or heal, as it were, those aspects or "parts" of his divine being that were supposed to have been harmed. But the deity of Christ is not composed of parts, and the fullness of that deity is undiminished before, during, and after the suffering of the cross.[165] The teaching of Scripture, then, entails that by his impassible divine life and power Christ has overcome death's power and become the firstborn from the dead. "By the grace of God he tasted death for everyone, giving to [death] his own body though by nature he is life and is himself the resurrection." And "trampling death by unspeakable power," he "became in his own flesh the firstborn from the dead and the firstfruits of the ones who have fallen asleep and made the way for a return for human nature to incorruptibility."[166]

164. Cf., e.g., Bockmuehl, *Philippians*, 236.
165. Cf. Mastricht's critique of the idea that God might absorb and convert divine suffering into something good (*TPT*, 2.15.32 [166–67]).
166. Cyril of Alexandria, *Tertia ad Nestorium* 6,6 (37).

VI. Conclusion

This chapter began by considering the Bible's teaching on the suffering of Christ, particularly its emphasis upon the fact that the efficacy of that suffering turns on it belonging to the divine person of the Son—a point that elicits care in setting out the coherence of the teaching on the Son's suffering and his divine impassibility. Before proceeding to comment further on the coherence of the Son's suffering and impassibility, I sought to clarify in the next section of the chapter what passions actually involve and why they do not apply in any ordinary sense to the biblical God, who cannot be harmed or deprived of his goodness and is the one who gives rather than gains in his relation to creatures. The following section elaborated on the metaphorical way in which passions like jealousy or wrath are predicated of God in Scripture, arguing that such predication is both meaningful and compatible with the doctrine of divine impassibility. Finally, the last main section of the chapter returned to the question of integrating the Son's suffering and impassibility by clarifying the logic involved in reduplicative speech that attributes impassibility to Christ as God and possibility to Christ as human.

There are a number of evident connections here with some of the key concerns of modern Christology that have been revisited throughout this volume. Among other things, the claims of this chapter underscore the unity of the person of Christ and the genuineness of his suffering. On the one hand, by virtue of his divine impassibility he does not become a different person in his incarnate activity and suffering. On the other hand, his human suffering is never allocated to another person. The divine Son is not "part" of a greater whole in which some other "part" might truly bear the suffering. Though the prevenient Son is not constituted a *new* person by his human nature, he is still constituted a *truly human* person by his human nature, which means that he is the immediate subject of his own human suffering. And, in keeping with the emphases of Hebrews 2:14–18 and 4:14–16, the Son's suffering is not divine or a divine-human hybrid. It is the genuine, unalloyed human suffering of a brother who tasted death for us and is leading us to eternal glory.

Conclusion

This study has explored the relationship between the Bible's Christology and the central claims of the catholic Christology and theology proper developed by major figures in patristic, medieval, and Reformed orthodox thought. I have made a case that those claims in catholic Christology and theology proper not only fit together with the Bible's Christology but in fact emerge from it and shed light on its meaning and implications. Making that case has involved showing how orthodox trinitarianism and Christology help us understand Christ's relationship to the Father and Spirit, his personal unity, and his genuinely human life and suffering.

Chapter 1 examined various criticisms of earlier Christian accounts of God and the person of Christ—criticisms focused on both the content of those accounts and the formal concepts and categories utilized in them. In response, I sketched a brief rationale for continuing to affirm divine attributes like aseity, immutability, impassibility, eternity, and simplicity. I also provided a rationale for continuing the use of broadly Aristotelian metaphysical concepts and categories in our exposition of the doctrine of the person of Christ today. Chapter 2 then considered the Son's eternal relation to the Father or eternal procession from the Father. There I sought to integrate the distinctions among the divine persons with God's simplicity. Chapter 3 turned to the election and mission of the Son and argued that the eternal appointment of the Son to be the mediator who takes on flesh fits together with a robust doctrine of God's aseity and immutability, according to which the divine Son both is who he is without reference to the economy and also is unchanged by his determination to take on flesh in the economy. Chapter 3 also made a case for the doctrine of the *pactum salutis* in connection with God's aseity

375

and simplicity and described the Son's temporal mission in connection with his divine transcendence of temporal succession.

Chapter 4 described the Son's relationship to the human nature that he has assumed. In that chapter I discussed the communication of the Son's subsistence to his human nature, the actualization and individuation of all that the human nature includes in the one person of the Son, the sense in which the human nature is an instrument of the Son, and the sameness of the person of the Son after his assumption of a human nature. I also discussed the doctrine of the *communicatio idiomatum* and related concerns about the notion of the *extra Calvinisticum*, making a case that the communication of properties in the person of the Son fits together with his divine immutability. Chapter 5 addressed the Son's relationship to the Holy Spirit and contended that the undividedness of the Trinity's outward works is capacious enough to make sense of the Spirit's empowerment of Christ's earthly ministry. In treating the Spirit's empowerment of Christ's ministry, I argued that the Spirit communicates habitual graces to Christ and that, instead of undermining Christ's human activity and experience, this communication helps us to confirm his human activity and experience.

Chapter 6 dealt with the obedience of the Son and underscored that it is strictly and truly a human obedience. In that chapter I sought to illumine the sense in which Christ exercised faith on earth, the sense in which Christ bore our infirmities and yet persevered in fulfilling the Father's will, and the sense in which Christ grew in his role as a merciful high priest. I also sought to respond to claims about Christ having a "fallen" or "sinful" human nature and to set out Christ's impeccability in connection with the real pain involved in his temptation. Finally, chapter 7 considered the suffering of Christ. There I aimed to integrate Christ's suffering with his divine impassibility by discussing what passions are and why they do not apply to God in a literal sense and by addressing concerns about reduplicative speech in Christology, wherein one attributes impassibility to Christ according to his deity and passibility to Christ according to his humanity.

Having proceeded through the argument of this study, I am inclined to conclude with three observations relative to future work in Christology and theology proper. First, in spite of the sometimes overwhelming intricacy of ancient and modern accounts of the person of Christ, the goal of Christology is still to set forth what Scripture teaches about Christ for the benefit of the church and its mission in the world. Accordingly, the deployment of refined concepts and patterns of reasoning taken up from the Christian theological tradition has to show how those concepts and patterns of reasoning first emerged from the material content of Scripture's teaching and can then serve to open up the sense of that teaching for those who hear and receive the gospel today. In this respect, theological "retrieval" cannot be a distinct theological program. Examining the contributions of earlier Christian thinkers is one part of a larger exegetical and constructive task.

Second, it seems to me that our exegetical work in Christology and theology proper will profit from a greater patience in reading earlier Christian theologians. For the ultimate aim of theologians like Athanasius and Ambrose, Bonaventure and Aquinas was to exegete the sense of Scripture and draw out its implications for the purity and enrichment of Christian doctrine and preaching. Even if certain things that such theologians have to say about this or that biblical text may elicit some modification today, their level of attentiveness to the broader entailments of exegetical claims can be instructive in an age of specialization that sometimes leads us to neglect the theological implications of what we say.

Third, the magnitude of the work to be done in Christology and theology proper underscores how important it is for biblical scholars, historical theologians, and dogmatic theologians to cooperate. Reading Scripture today without an alertness to the history of Christian exegesis and dogmatic theology severely limits one's interpretive resources and may lead to advocating a reading of a text that has already been tried and duly found wanting. At the same time, undertaking topical exposition of scriptural doctrine in dogmatic theology in isolation from the yield of biblical scholarship may cause us to miss insights that can refine our thinking and add a richer texture to our confession of what God has revealed.

In the end, it is Christian theology's greatest privilege to confess and bear witness to the triune God, who both transcends the economy of salvation and, in the person of the Son, has partaken of flesh and blood to deliver us from our sin. If the claims of this study are accurate, then grasping that the triune God does indeed transcend the economy is precisely what is needed to understand the meaning and efficacy of the incarnate Son's work. Because he always remains the Son who has life in himself, he can give his flesh for the life of the world. Because he always remains rich even in the midst of his human lowliness, he can make us rich with the gift of salvation.

Bibliography

Abba, Raymond. "The Divine Name of Yahweh." *JBL* 80 (1961): 320–28.

Abecina, Alexander L. "The Unity of Christ and the Anointing of the Spirit in Gregory of Nyssa's *Antirrheticus adversus Apolinarium*." *MT* 35 (2019): 728–45.

à Brakel, Wilhelmus. *The Christian's Reasonable Service*. Vol. 1, *God, Man, and Christ*. Edited by Joel R. Beeke. Translated by Bartel Elshout. Grand Rapids: Reformation Heritage, 1992.

Adams, Marilyn McCord. *Christ and Horrors: The Coherence of Christology*. CIT. Cambridge: Cambridge University Press, 2006.

Allen, R. Michael. *The Christ's Faith: A Dogmatic Account*. T&T Clark Studies in Systematic Theology. London: T&T Clark, 2009.

———. "Exodus 3 after the Hellenization Thesis." *JTI* 3 (2009): 179–96.

———. "'From the Time He Took On the Form of a Servant': The Christ's Pilgrimage of Faith." *IJST* 16 (2014): 4–24.

Alsted, Johann. *Metaphysica*. Herborn, 1613.

———. *Methodus s.s. theologiae*. Hanover, 1634.

———. *Theologia naturalis*. Frankfurt, 1615.

Ambrose. *De fide (ad Gratianum)*. 3 vols. Edited by Christoph Markschies. Fontes Christiani 47/1–3. Turnhout: Brepols, 2005.

———. *De incarnationis dominicae sacramento*. In *Sancti Ambrosii opera, pars VIIII*. Edited by Otto Faller. CSEL 79. Vienna: Hölder-Pichler-Tempsky, 1964.

———. *De Spiritu Sancto libri tres*. In *Sancti Ambrosii opera, pars VIIII*. Edited by Otto Faller. CSEL 79. Vienna: Hölder-Pichler-Tempsky, 1964.

———. *Traité sur l'Évangile de S. Luc*. Vol. 1. Translated by Gabriel Tissot. SC 45. Paris: Cerf, 1956.

Ames, William. *Bellarminus enervatus*. Vol. 1. Amsterdam: Iohannes Ianssonius, 1628.

———. *Medulla theologica.* 2nd ed. Amsterdam, 1659.

———. *Utriusque epistolae divi Petri Apostoli explicatio analytica.* Amsterdam: Cornelius Blavius, 1635.

Amit, Yairah. "'The Glory of Israel Does Not Deceive or Change His Mind': On the Reliability of the Narrator and Speakers in the Biblical Narrative." *Prooftexts* 12 (1992): 201–12.

Anatolios, Khaled. "Personhood, Communion, and the Trinity in Some Patristic Texts." In *The Holy Trinity in the Life of the Church*, edited by Khaled Anatolios, 147–64. Grand Rapids: Baker Academic, 2014.

———. *Retrieving Nicaea: The Development and Meaning of Trinitarian Doctrine.* Grand Rapids: Baker Academic, 2011.

Anselm. *Monologion.* In vol. 1 of *S. Anselmi Cantuariensis Archiepiscopi opera omnia.* Edited by F. S. Schmitt. Edinburgh: Thomas Nelson and Sons, 1946.

Aquinas, Thomas. *See* Thomas Aquinas

Arcadi, James M. "Kryptic or Cryptic? The Divine Preconscious Model of the Incarnation as a Concrete-Nature Christology." *NZSTh* 58 (2016): 229–43.

Archer, Joel. "Kenosis, Omniscience, and the Anselmian Concept of Divinity." *RS* 54 (2017): 201–13.

Aristotle. *Aristotelis Ars Rhetorica.* Edited by Rudolf Kassel. Berlin: de Gruyter, 1976.

———. *Aristotelis De anima.* Edited by W. D. Ross. Oxford Classic Texts. Oxford: Oxford University Press, 1956.

———. *Aristotelis Metaphysica.* Edited by W. Jaeger. Oxford: Clarendon, 1957.

———. *Poetics: Editio Maior of the Greek Text with Historical Introductions and Philological Commentaries.* Edited by Leonardo Tarán and Dimitri Gutas. Leiden: Brill, 2012.

Arminius, Jacob. *Declaratio sententiae I. Arminii de praedestinatione, providentia Dei, libero arbitrio, gratia Dei, divinitate Filii Dei, et de iustificatione hominis coram Deo.* In *Opera theologica.* Leiden, 1629.

Arnold, Clinton E. *Ephesians.* ZECNT. Grand Rapids: Zondervan, 2010.

Ashley, Benedict M. "The Extent of Jesus' Human Knowledge according to the Fourth Gospel." In *Reading John with St. Thomas Aquinas: Theological Exegesis and Speculative Theology*, edited by Michael Dauphinais and Matthew Levering, 241–53. Washington, DC: Catholic University of America Press, 2005.

Athanasius. *De decretis.* In vol. 2.1 of *Athanasius Werke.* Edited by Hans-George Opitz. Berlin: de Gruyter, 1935.

———. *De incarnatione.* In *"Contra gentes" and "De incarnatione."* Edited and translated by Robert W. Thomson. Oxford: Clarendon, 1971.

———. *De synodis.* In vol. 2.1 of *Athanasius Werke.* Edited by Hans-Georg Opitz. Berlin: de Gruyter, 1941.

———. *Epistulae I–IV ad Serapionem*. In vol. 1.1.4 of *Athanasius Werke*. Edited by Kyriakos Savvidis and Dietmar Wyrwa. Berlin: de Gruyter, 2010.

———. *Orationes I et II contra Arianos*. In vol. 1.1.2 of *Athanasius Werke*. Edited by Karin Metzler and Kyriakos Savvidis. Berlin: de Gruyter, 1998.

———. *Oratio III contra Arianos*. In vol. 1.1.3 of *Athanasius Werke*. Edited by Karin Metzler and Kyriakos Savvidis. Berlin: de Gruyter, 2000.

———. *Oratio IV contra Arianos*. PG 26. Paris, 1857.

Augustine. *Confessionum libri XIII*. Edited by L. Verheijen. 2nd ed. CCSL 27. Turnhout: Brepols, 1981.

———. *De civitate Dei*. 2 vols. CCSL 47–48. Turnhout: Brepols, 1955.

———. *De doctrina christiana libri IV*. In *De doctrina christiana; De vera religione*. Edited by K. D. Daur and J. Martin. CCSL 32. Turnhout: Brepols, 1962.

———. *De trinitate libri XV*. 2 vols. Edited by W. J. Mountain. CCSL 50–50A. Turnhout: Brepols, 1968.

———. *In Iohannis Evangelium tractatus CXXIV*. CCSL 36. Turnhout: Brepols, 1954.

Aus der Au, Christina. "Das Extra Calvinisticum—mehr al sein reformiertes Extra." *TZ* 64 (2008): 358–69.

Averbeck, Richard E. "Breath, Wind, Spirit and the Holy Spirit in the Old Testament." In *Presence, Power and Promise: The Role of the Spirit of God in the Old Testament*, edited by David G. Firth and Paul D. Wegner, 25–37. Downers Grove, IL: InterVarsity, 2011.

Ayres, Lewis. *Augustine and the Trinity*. Cambridge: Cambridge University Press, 2010.

———. *Nicaea and Its Legacy: An Approach to Fourth-Century Trinitarian Theology*. Oxford: Oxford University Press, 2004.

———. "'Remember That You Are Catholic' (*serm.* 52, 2): Augustine on the Unity of the Triune God." *JECS* 8 (2000): 39–82.

Baars, Arie. "'*Opera Trinitatis ad Extra Sunt Indivisa*' in the Theology of John Calvin." In *Calvinus Sacrarum Literarum Interpres: Papers of the International Congress of Calvin Research*, edited by Herman J. Selderhuis, 131–41. Gottingen: Vandenhoeck & Ruprecht, 2008.

Bac, J. Martin. *Perfect Will Theology: Divine Agency in Reformed Scholasticism as against Suárez, Episcopius, Descartes, and Spinoza*. Leiden: Brill, 2010.

Bäck, Allan. *On Reduplication: Logical Theories of Qualification*. Studien und Texte zur Geistesgeschichte des Mittelalters 49. Leiden: Brill, 1996.

———. "Scotus on the Consistency of the Incarnation and the Trinity." *Vivarium* 36 (1998): 83–107.

Baird, William. *History of New Testament Research*. Vol. 1, *From Deism to Tübingen*. Minneapolis: Augsburg Fortress, 1992.

Balzer, H. R. "Gottes Reue: Zum theologischen Verständnis Gottes als Subjekt der hebräischen Wurzel *nhm*." *Verbum et Ecclesia* 12 (1991): 1–16.

Barinck, Vincent P. "The Sinful Flesh of the Son of God (Rom. 8:3): A Key Image of Pauline Theology." *CBQ* 47 (1985): 246–62.

Barnes, Michel René. "Augustine in Contemporary Trinitarian Theology." *TS* 56 (1995): 237–50.

———. "De Régnon Reconsidered." *Augustinian Studies* 26 (1995): 51–79.

Barr, James. *The Semantics of Biblical Language*. Oxford: Oxford University Press, 1961.

Barrett, C. K. *A Commentary on the Epistle to the Romans*. New York: Harper & Row, 1957.

———. *Commentary on the Second Epistle to the Corinthians*. HNTC. Peabody, MA: Hendrickson, 1973.

———. *The Gospel according to St. John: An Introduction with Commentary and Notes on the Greek Text*. London: SPCK, 1962.

Barth, Karl. *Church Dogmatics*. Edited by G. W. Bromiley and T. F. Torrance. Translated by G. W. Bromiley et al. London: T&T Clark, 2009.

———. *Die kirchliche Dogmatik*. Zürich: Theologischer Verlag Zürich, 1986–93.

Basil of Caesarea. *Contre Eunome*. 2 vols. Edited by Bernard Seboüé et al. SC 299, 305. Paris: Cerf, 1982–83.

———. *Sur le Saint-Esprit*. Edited by Benoît Pruche. Paris: Cerf, 2013.

Bates, Matthew W. *The Birth of the Trinity: Jesus, God, and Spirit in New Testament and Early Christian Interpretations of the Old Testament*. Oxford: Oxford University Press, 2015.

Bathrellos, Demetrios. *The Byzantine Christ: Person, Nature, and Will in the Christology of Saint Maximus the Confessor*. Oxford: Oxford University Press, 2004.

———. "The Patristic Tradition on the Sinlessness of Jesus." In *Studia Patristica Vol. LXIII: Papers Presented at the Sixteenth International Conference on Patristic Studies Held in Oxford 2011*. Vol. 11, *Biblica, Philosophica, Theologica, Ethica*, edited by Markus Vinzent, 236–41. Leuven: Peeters, 2013.

Bauckham, Richard. *Gospel of Glory: Major Themes in Johannine Theology*. Grand Rapids: Baker Academic, 2015.

———. "Is 'High Human Christology' Sufficient? A Critical Response to J. R. Daniel Kirk's *A Man Attested by God*." *BBR* 27 (2017): 503–25.

———. *Jesus and the God of Israel: "God Crucified" and Other Studies on the New Testament's Christology of Divine Identity*. Grand Rapids: Eerdmans, 2008.

———. *The Testimony of the Beloved Disciple: Narrative, History, and Theology in the Gospel of John*. Grand Rapids: Baker Academic, 2007.

———. *Theology of the Book of Revelation*. New Testament Theology. Cambridge: Cambridge University Press, 1993.

———. *Who Is God? Key Moments of Biblical Revelation*. Grand Rapids: Baker Academic, 2020.

Bavinck, Herman. *Sin and Salvation in Christ*. Vol. 3 of *Reformed Dogmatics*. Edited by John Bolt. Translated by John Vriend. Grand Rapids: Baker Academic, 2006.

Beach, J. Mark. *Christ and the Covenant: Francis Turretin's Federal Theology as a Defense of the Doctrine of Grace*. RHT 1. Göttingen: Vandenhoeck & Ruprecht, 2007.

Beale, G. K. *Colossians and Philemon*. BECNT. Grand Rapids: Baker Academic, 2019.

———. *A New Testament Biblical Theology: The Unfolding of the Old Testament in the New*. Grand Rapids: Baker Academic, 2011.

———. *The Temple and the Church's Mission: A Biblical Theology of the Dwelling Place of God*. Downers Grove, IL: IVP Academic, 2004.

Beale, G. K., and D. A. Carson, eds. *Commentary on the New Testament Use of the Old*. Grand Rapids: Baker Academic, 2007.

Beall, Jc. "Christ—a Contradiction: A Defense of Contradictory Christology." *JAT* 7 (2019): 400–433.

———. *The Contradictory Christ*. OSAT. Oxford: Oxford University Press, 2021.

Beall, Jc, and Jared Henderson. "A Neglected Qua Solution to the Fundamental Problem of Christology." *Faith and Philosophy* 36 (2019): 157–72.

Beasley-Murray, George. *John*. WBC 36. Nashville: Nelson, 1999.

Beeke, Joel R., and Mark Jones. *Puritan Theology: Doctrine for Life*. Grand Rapids: Reformation Heritage, 2012.

Behr, John. *The Formation of Christian Theology*. Vol. 2, *The Nicene Faith, Part Two: One of the Holy Trinity*. Crestwood, NY: St. Vladimir's Seminary Press, 2004.

———. *John the Theologian and His Paschal Gospel: A Prologue to Theology*. Oxford: Oxford University Press, 2019.

Beiser, Frederick. *The German Historicist Tradition*. Oxford: Oxford University Press, 2011.

———. *German Idealism: The Struggle against Subjectivism, 1781–1801*. Cambridge, MA: Harvard University Press, 2002.

Bellarmine, Robert. *Disputationum Roberti Bellarmini de controversiis Christianae fidei, adversus huius temporis haereticos*. Vol. 1. Ingolstadt: Sartorii, 1601.

Belleville, Linda. *Reflections of Glory: Paul's Polemical Use of the Moses-Doxa Tradition in 2 Corinthians 3.1–18*. JSNTSS 52. Sheffield: JSOT Press, 1991.

Bello, Rafael. *Sinless Flesh: A Critique of Karl Barth's Fallen Christ*. Bellingham, WA: Lexham, 2020.

Best, Ernest. *Second Corinthians*. Interpretation. Louisville: John Knox, 1987.

Bird, Michael F. *Jesus the Eternal Son: Answering Adoptionist Christology*. Grand Rapids: Eerdmans, 2017.

Bird, Michael F., and Scott Harrower, eds. *Trinity without Hierarchy: Reclaiming Nicene Orthodoxy in Evangelical Theology.* Grand Rapids: Kregel, 2019.

Bird, Michael F., and Preston M. Sprinkle, eds. *The Faith of Jesus Christ: Exegetical, Biblical, and Theological Studies.* Milton Keynes, UK: Paternoster, 2009.

Black, Max. *Models and Metaphors: Studies in Language and Philosophy.* Ithaca, NY: Cornell University Press, 1962.

Block, Daniel I. "The View from the Top: The Holy Spirit in the Prophets." In *Presence, Power and Promise: The Role of the Spirit of God in the Old Testament,* edited by David G. Firth and Paul D. Wegner, 175–207. Downers Grove, IL: InterVarsity, 2011.

Blowers, Paul M. "Maximus the Confessor and John of Damascus on Gnomic Will (γνώμη) in Christ: Clarity and Ambiguity." *USQR* 63 (2012): 44–50.

Bock, Darrell L. *Acts.* BECNT. Grand Rapids: Baker Academic, 2007.

———. *Jesus according to Scripture: Restoring the Portrait from the Gospels.* Grand Rapids: Baker Academic, 2002.

Bockmuehl, Markus. *The Epistle to the Philippians.* 4th ed. Black's New Testament Commentaries. London: A&C Black, 1997.

Boethius. *Contra Eutychen.* In *Theological Tractates; The Consolation of Philosophy,* 72–129.

———. *De trinitate.* In *Theological Tractates; The Consolation of Philosophy,* 2–31.

———. *Philosophiae consolationis.* In *Theological Tractates; The Consolation of Philosophy,* 130–435.

———. *The Theological Tractates; The Consolation of Philosophy.* LCL 74. Translated by S. J. Tester. Cambridge, MA: Harvard University Press, 1973.

Bonaventure. *Commentaria in quatuor libros Sententiarum.* Vol. 1. In vol. 1 of *Doctoris seraphici S. Bonaventurae opera omnia.* Florence: ex Typographia Collegii Bonaventurae, 1882.

———. *Commentaria in quatuor libros Sententiarum.* Vol. 3. In vol. 3 of *Doctoris seraphici S. Bonaventurae opera omnia.* Florence: ex Typographia Collegii Bonaventurae, 1887.

———. *Quaestiones disputatae de scientia Christi.* In vol. 5 of *Doctoris seraphici S. Bonaventurae opera omnia.* Florence: ex Typographia Collegii Bonaventurae, 1891.

Bovon, François. *Luke 3: A Commentary on the Gospel of Luke 19:28–24:53.* Edited by Helmut Koester. Translated by James Crouch. Hermeneia. Minneapolis: Fortress, 2012.

Brown, David. *Divine Humanity: Kenosis and the Construction of a Christian Theology.* Waco: Baylor University Press, 2011.

Brown, Raymond E. *The Epistles of John: Translated with Introduction, Notes, and Commentary.* AB 30. Garden City, NY: Doubleday, 1982.

———. *The Gospel according to John I–XII.* AB 29. Garden City, NY: Doubleday, 1966.

———. *The Gospel according to John XIII–XXI: A New Translation with Introduction and Commentary.* AB 29A. Garden City, NY: Doubleday, 1970.

Bruce, A. B. *The Humiliation of Christ: In Its Physical, Ethical, and Official Aspects.* Edinburgh: T&T Clark, 1876.

Bruce, F. F. *The Book of Acts.* Rev. ed. NICNT. Grand Rapids: Eerdmans, 1998.

Brueggemann, Walter. *Old Testament Theology: Essays on Structure, Theme, and Text.* Edited by Patrick D. Miller. Minneapolis: Fortress, 1992.

———. "The Recovering God of Hosea." *HBT* 30 (2008): 5–20.

———. *An Unsettling God: The Heart of the Hebrew Bible.* Minneapolis: Fortress, 2009.

Bultmann, Rudolf. *The Gospel of John: A Commentary.* Edited by R. W. N. Hoare and J. K. Riches. Translated by G. R. Beasley-Murray. Oxford: Basil Blackwell, 1971.

Butner, D. Glenn, Jr. "For and against de Régnon: Trinitarianism East and West." *IJST* 17 (2015): 399–412.

———. *The Son Who Learned Obedience: A Theological Case against the Eternal Submission of the Son.* Eugene, OR: Wipf & Stock, 2018.

Byrne, Brendan. "Christ's Pre-existence in Pauline Soteriology." *TS* 58 (1997): 308–30.

Calvin, John. *Commentarius in Acta Apostolorum.* In vol. 48 of *CO.*

———. *Commentarius in epistolam ad Hebraeos.* In vol. 55 of *CO.*

———. *Commentarius in epistolam ad Philippenses.* In vol. 52 of *CO.*

———. *Commentarius in epistolam Pauli ad Romanos.* In vol. 49 of *CO.*

———. *Commentarius in harmoniam evangelicam.* In vol. 45 of *CO.*

———. *Institutio Christianae religionis* (1559). In vol. 2 of *CO.*

———. *Praelectiones in Ieremiam prophetam, pars altera cap. VIII–XXXI.* In vol. 38 of *CO.*

Campbell, Constantine R. *Advances in the Study of Greek: New Insights for Reading the Old Testament.* Grand Rapids: Zondervan, 2015.

Capes, David B. *The Divine Christ: Paul, the Lord Jesus, and the Scriptures of Israel.* Grand Rapids: Baker Academic, 2018.

Carroll R., M. Daniel. "Hosea." In *The Expositor's Bible Commentary*, edited by Tremper Longman III and David E. Garland, 8:213–305. Rev. ed. Grand Rapids: Zondervan, 2008.

Carson, D. A. *The Gospel according to John.* PNTC. Grand Rapids: Eerdmans, 1991.

Carter, Craig A. *Interpreting Scripture with the Great Tradition: Recovering the Genius of Premodern Exegesis.* Grand Rapids: Baker Academic, 2018.

Cassuto, Umberto. *A Commentary on the Book of Exodus.* Translated by Israel Abrahams. Jerusalem: Magnes, 1983.

Cates, Diana Fritz. *Aquinas on the Emotions: A Religious-Ethical Inquiry*. Moral Traditions. Washington, DC: Georgetown University Press, 2009.

Chalamet, Christophe. "Immutability or Faithfulness?" *MT* 34 (2018): 457–68.

Charnock, Stephen. *The Existence and Attributes of God*. 2 vols. in 1. Reprint, Grand Rapids: Baker, 1996.

Chemnitz, Martin. *De duabis naturis in Christo*. Leipzig, 1580.

Chiarot, Kevin. *The Unassumed Is the Unhealed: The Humanity of Christ in the Christology of T. F. Torrance*. Eugene, OR: Wipf & Stock, 2013.

Childs, Brevard S. *Biblical Theology of the Old and New Testaments: Theological Reflection on the Christian Bible*. Minneapolis: Fortress, 1993.

———. *The Book of Exodus: A Critical Theological Commentary*. Philadelphia: Westminster, 1974.

———. *Isaiah: A Commentary*. OTL. Louisville: Westminster John Knox, 2001.

Ciampa, Roy E., and Brian S. Rosner. *The First Epistle to the Corinthians*. PNTC. Grand Rapids: Eerdmans, 2010.

Cicero. *De oratore Book III*. Edited by David Mankin. Cambridge: Cambridge University Press, 2011.

Clayton, Paul B. *Theodoret of Cyrus: Antiochene Christology from the Council of Ephesus (431) to the Council of Chalcedon (451)*. Oxford: Oxford University Press, 2007.

Coccejus, Johannes. *Prophetae duodecim minores*. Leiden, 1652.

———. *Prophetia Ezechielis, cum commentario*. Amsterdam: á Someren, 1669.

———. *S. apostoli Pauli epistola ad Ephesios, cum commentario*. Leiden: à Gaasbeeck, 1667.

———. *S. Pauli apostoli epistola ad Philippenses, cum commentario*. Amsterdam: á Someren, 1669.

———. *Summa doctrinae de foedere et testamento Dei*. Amsterdam, 1683.

Cockerill, Gareth Lee. *The Epistle to the Hebrews*. NICNT. Grand Rapids: Eerdmans, 2012.

Coffey, David. "The Theandric Nature of Christ." *TS* 60 (1999): 405–31.

Cornell, Collin. "Holy Mutability: *Religionsgeschichte* and Theological Ontology." *HBT* 38 (2016): 200–220.

Craig, William Lane. "Is God the Son Begotten in His Divine Nature?" *Theologica* 3 (2019): 22–32.

———. *Time and Eternity: Exploring God's Relationship to Time*. Wheaton: Crossway, 2001.

———. "Toward a Tenable Social Trinitarianism." In *Philosophical and Theological Essays on the Trinity*, edited by Thomas H. McCall and Michael C. Rea, 89–99. Oxford: Oxford University Press, 2009.

Craigie, Peter C. *Psalms 1–50*. WBC 19. Waco: Word, 1983.

Cranfield, C. E. B. *The Epistle to the Romans*. Vol. 1. ICC. London: T&T Clark, 1975.

Cremer, Hermann. *Die christliche Lehre von den Eigenschaften Gottes*. Gütersloh: Bertelsmann, 1897.

Crisp, Oliver. "Desiderata for Models of the Hypostatic Union." In *Christology Ancient and Modern: Explorations in Constructive Dogmatics*, edited by Oliver D. Crisp and Fred Sanders, 19–41. Grand Rapids: Zondervan, 2013.

———. "Did Christ Have a *Fallen* Human Nature?" *IJST* 6 (2004): 270–88.

———. *Divinity and Humanity: The Incarnation Reconsidered*. CIT. Cambridge: Cambridge University Press, 2007.

———. *Jonathan Edwards on God and Creation*. Oxford: Oxford University Press, 2012.

———. "On the Vicarious Humanity of Christ." *IJST* 21 (2019): 235–50.

———. *Revisioning Christology: Theology in the Reformation Tradition*. London: Routledge, 2016.

———. "Was Christ Sinless or Impeccable?" *ITQ* 72 (2007): 168–86.

———. *The Word Enfleshed: Exploring the Person and Work of Christ*. Grand Rapids: Baker Academic, 2016.

Cross, Richard. *Communicatio Idiomatum: Reformation Christological Debates*. CPHST. Oxford: Oxford University Press, 2019.

———. "The Incarnation." In *The Oxford Handbook of Philosophical Christology*, edited by Thomas P. Flint and Michael C. Rea, 452–75. Oxford: Oxford University Press, 2009.

———. *The Metaphysics of the Incarnation: Thomas Aquinas to Duns Scotus*. Oxford: Oxford University Press, 2002.

Crowe, Brandon D. *The Last Adam: A Theology of the Obedient Life of Jesus in the Gospel*. Grand Rapids: Baker Academic, 2017.

Cullmann, Oscar. *The Christology of the New Testament*. Translated by Shirley C. Guthrie and Charles A. M. Hall. Rev. ed. Philadelphia: Westminster, 1963.

Cyril of Alexandria. *Apologia XII capitulorum contra Orientales*. In vol. 1.1.7 of *ACO*.

———. *Apologia XII capitulorum contra Theodoretum*. In vol. 1.1.6 of *ACO*.

———. *Commentaire sur Jean*. Vol. 1. Translated by Bernard Meunier. SC 600. Paris: Cerf, 2018.

———. *Dialogues sur la Trinité*. 3 vols. Edited by G. M. Durand. SC 231, 237, 246. Paris: Cerf, 1976–78.

———. *Epistula ad monachos*. In vol. 1.1.1 of *ACO*.

———. *Epistula altera ad Nestorium*. In vol. 1.1.1 of *ACO*.

———. *Epistula tertia ad Nestorium*. In vol. 1.1.1 of *ACO*.

———. *Explanatio XII capitulorum*. In vol. 1.1.5 of *ACO*.

———. *In d. Joannis Evangelium*. 3 vols. Edited by P. E. Pusey. Oxford: Clarendon, 1872.

———. *Le Christ est un*. In *Deux Dialogues Christologiques*, edited by G. M. de Durand, 302–515. SC 97. Paris: Cerf, 2008.

———. *Oratio ad Theodosium*. In vol. 1.1.1 of *ACO*.

———. *Scholia de incarnatione Unigeniti*. In *Sancti patris nostri Cyrilli archiepiscopi Alexandrini, Epistolae tres oecumenicae et al.*, edited by P. E. Pusey, 498–579. Oxford: Parker, 1875.

Daley, Brian E. *God Visible: Patristic Christology Reconsidered*. CPHST. Oxford: Oxford University Press, 2018.

Davidson, Ivor J. "'Not My Will but Yours Be Done': The Ontological Dynamics of Incarnational Intention." *IJST* 7 (2005): 178–204.

———. "Pondering the Sinlessness of Jesus Christ: Moral Christologies and the Witness of Scripture." *IJST* 10 (2008): 372–98.

———. "Theologizing the Human Jesus: An Ancient (and Modern) Approach to Christology Reassessed." *IJST* 3 (2001): 129–53.

Davies, W. D., and Dale C. Allison. *A Critical and Exegetical Commentary on the Gospel according to Saint Matthew*. Vol. 1. ICC. London: T&T Clark, 1988.

Davis, Stephen T. *Logic and the Nature of God*. Grand Rapids: Eerdmans, 1983.

———. "The Metaphysics of Kenosis." In *The Metaphysics of the Incarnation*, edited by Anna Marmodoro and Jonathan Hill, 114–33. Oxford: Oxford University Press, 2011.

del Colle, Ralph. *Christ and the Spirit: Spirit-Christology in Trinitarian Perspective*. Oxford: Oxford University Press, 1994.

Dempsey, Michael T., ed. *Trinity and Election in Contemporary Theology*. Grand Rapids: Eerdmans, 2011.

Dempster, Stephen G. *Dominion and Dynasty: A Theology of the Hebrew Bible*. NSBT. Downers Grove, IL: InterVarsity, 2003.

Deng, Natalja. *God and Time*. EPR. Cambridge: Cambridge University Press, 2018.

De Nys, Martin J. *Hegel and Theology*. London: T&T Clark, 2009.

deSilva, David A. *Perseverance in Gratitude: A Socio-Rhetorical Commentary on the Epistle "to the Hebrews."* Grand Rapids: Eerdmans, 2000.

de Vaux, Roland. "The Revelation of the Divine Name YHWH." In *Proclamation and Presence: Old Testament Essays in Honour of Gwynne Henton Davies*, edited by John I. Durham and J. R. Porter, 48–75. Richmond: John Knox, 1970.

DeVine, Charles F. "The 'Blood of God' in Acts 20.28." *CBQ* 9 (1947): 381–408.

DeWeese, Garrett J. "One Person, Two Natures: Two Metaphysical Models of the Incarnation." In *Jesus in Trinitarian Perspective: An Intermediate Christology*, edited by Fred Sanders and Klaus Issler, 114–53. Nashville: B&H, 2007.

Dods, Marcus. *On the Incarnation of the Eternal Word*. London: Seeley and Burnside, 1831.

Döhling, Jan-Dirk. *Der bewegliche Gott: Eine Untersuchung des Motivs der Reue Gottes in der Hebräischen Bibel*. Freiburg: Herder, 2009.

Dolezal, James E. *God without Parts: Divine Simplicity and the Metaphysics of God's Absoluteness*. Eugene, OR: Pickwick, 2011.

Dorner, Isaak A. *Divine Immutability: A Critical Reconsideration*. Translated by Claude Welch. Minneapolis: Fortress, 1994.

———. *History of the Development of the Doctrine of the Person of Christ*. Vol. 2. Translated by D. W. Simon. Edinburgh: T&T Clark, 1866.

Dorrien, Gary. *Kantian Reason and Hegelian Spirit: The Idealistic Logic of Modern Theology*. Oxford: Wiley Blackwell, 2012.

Downs, David J., and Benjamin J. Lappenga. *The Faithfulness of the Risen Christ: Pistis and the Exalted Lord in the Pauline Letters*. Waco: Baylor University Press, 2019.

Drake, K. J. *The Flesh of the Word: The* extra Calvinisticum *from Zwingli to Early Orthodoxy*. OSHT. Oxford: Oxford University Press, 2021.

Drecoll, Volker Henning. "Ferdinand Christian Baur's View of Christian Gnosis, and the Philosophy of Religion of His Own Day." In *Ferdinand Christian Baur and the History of Early Christianity*, edited by Martin Bauspiess et al., 116–46. Translated by Robert F. Brown and Peter C. Hodgson. Oxford: Oxford University Press, 2017.

Duby, Steven J. "Atonement, Impassibility and the *Communicatio Operationum*." *IJST* 17 (2015): 284–95.

———. "Divine Action and the Meaning of Eternity." *JRT* 11 (2017): 353–76.

———. "Divine Immutability, Divine Action and the God-World Relation." *IJST* 19 (2017): 144–62.

———. *Divine Simplicity: A Dogmatic Account*. T&T Clark Studies in Systematic Theology. London: T&T Clark, 2016.

———. "Divine Simplicity, Divine Freedom, and the Contingency of Creation." *JRT* 6 (2012): 125–41.

———. "Election, Actuality and Divine Freedom: Thomas Aquinas, Bruce McCormack and Reformed Orthodoxy in Dialogue." *MT* 32 (2016): 325–40.

———. *God in Himself: Scripture, Metaphysics and the Task of Christian Theology*. SCDS. Downers Grove, IL: IVP Academic, 2019.

———. "Goodness, Gratitude, and Divine Freedom." *SJT* (forthcoming).

Dunn, James D. G. "Christ, Adam, and Preexistence." In *Where Christology Began: Essays on Philippians 2*, edited by Ralph P. Martin and Brian J. Dodd, 74–83. Louisville: Westminster John Knox, 1998.

———. *The Christ and the Spirit*. Vol. 1, *Christology*. Grand Rapids: Eerdmans, 1998.

———. *The Epistles to the Colossians and to Philemon: A Commentary on the Greek Text*. NIGTC. Grand Rapids: Eerdmans, 1996.

———. *Romans 1–8*. WBC 38A. Dallas: Word, 1988.

———. *The Theology of Paul the Apostle*. Grand Rapids: Eerdmans, 1998.

Duns Scotus, John. *Ordinatio*. In vol. 3 of *Opera omnia*. Edited by P. Carolo Balić. Vatican: Typis Polyglottis Vaticanis, 1954.

Edwards, James R. *The Gospel according to Luke*. PNTC. Grand Rapids: Eerdmans, 2015.

Edwards, Jonathan. *Concerning the End for Which God Created the World*. In *Ethical Writings*, edited by Paul Ramsey, 405–63. Vol. 8 of *The Works of Jonathan Edwards*. New Haven: Yale University Press, 1989.

Ellingworth, Paul. *The Epistle to the Hebrews: A Commentary on the Greek Text*. NIGTC. Grand Rapids: Eerdmans, 1993.

Ellis, Brannon. *Calvin, Classical Trinitarianism, and the Aseity of the Son*. Oxford: Oxford University Press, 2012.

Emery, Gilles. *The Trinitarian Theology of St Thomas Aquinas*. Translated by Francesca Aran Murphy. Oxford: Oxford University Press, 2007.

Evans, C. Stephen, ed. *Exploring Kenotic Christology: The Self-Emptying of God*. Oxford: Oxford University Press, 2006.

Evans, Craig A. *Word and Glory: On the Exegetical and Theological Background of John's Prologue*. JSNTSS 89. Sheffield, UK: Sheffield Academic, 1993.

Expositio rectae fidei. In vol. 3.1 of *Iustini Philosophi et Martyris opera quae feruntur omnia*. In vol. 4 of *Corpus Apologetarum Christianorum saeculi secondi*. Edited by J. C. T. Otto. 3rd ed. Jena, 1880.

Farris, Joshua R. "Loke on the Abstractist/Concretist Christological Distinction: A Semantic Problem or a Metaphysical Problem?" *NZSTh* 62 (2020): 222–32.

Fee, Gordon D. "Christology and Pneumatology in Romans 8:9–11—and Elsewhere: Some Reflections on Paul as a Trinitarian." In *Jesus of Nazareth: Lord and Christ*, edited by Joel B. Green and Max Turner, 312–31. Grand Rapids: Eerdmans, 1999.

———. *The First Epistle to the Corinthians*. Rev. ed. NICNT. Grand Rapids: Eerdmans, 2014.

———. *Paul's Letter to the Philippians*. NICNT. Grand Rapids: Eerdmans, 1995.

Feldmeier, Reinhard, and Hermann Spieckermann. *God of the Living: A Biblical Theology*. Translated by Mark E. Biddle. Waco: Baylor University Press, 2011.

Feser, Edward. *Aristotle's Revenge: The Metaphysical Foundations of Physical and Biological Science*. Neunkirchen-Seelscheid: Editiones Scholasticae, 2019.

———. "The Medieval Principle of Motion and the Modern Principle of Inertia." In *Skepticism, Causality and Skepticism about Causality*. Vol. 10 of *Proceedings of the Society of Medieval Logics and Metaphysics*, edited by Gyula Klima and Alexander W. Hall, 5–21. Newcastle upon Tyne: Cambridge Scholars Publishing, 2013.

———. "Motion in Aristotle, Newton, and Einstein." In *Aristotle on Method and Metaphysics*, edited by Edward Feser, 236–58. New York: Palgrave Macmillan, 2013.

Fesko, J. V. *The Covenant of Redemption: Origins, Development, and Reception.* RHT 35. Göttingen: Vandenhoeck & Ruprecht, 2015.

Fichte, J. G. *A Crystal Clear Report to the General Public concerning the Actual Essence of the Newest Philosophy: An Attempt to Force the Reader to Understand, 1801.* In *Philosophy of German Idealism*, edited by Ernst Behler, 39–115. Translated by John Botterman and William Rasch. New York: Continuum, 1987.

Fitzmyer, Joseph. *The Acts of the Apostles: A New Translation with Introduction and Commentary.* AB 31. New York: Doubleday, 1997.

———. *Romans: A New Translation with Introduction and Commentary.* AB 33. New York: Doubleday, 1992.

Fletcher-Louis, Crispin. *Jesus Monotheism.* Vol. 1, *Christological Origins: The Emerging Consensus and Beyond.* Eugene, OR: Cascade Books, 2015.

Forsyth, P. T. *The Person and Place of Jesus Christ.* London: Hodder & Stoughton, 1909.

Fowl, Stephen E. *Engaging Scripture: A Model for Theological Interpretation.* Oxford: Blackwell, 1998.

———. *Philippians.* THNTC. Grand Rapids: Eerdmans, 2005.

———. *The Story of Christ in the Ethics of Paul: An Analysis of the Function of Hymnic Material in the Pauline Corpus.* Sheffield: Sheffield Academic, 1990.

Fox, Michael V. *Proverbs 1–9: A New Translation with Introduction and Commentary.* AB 18A. New York: Doubleday, 2000.

France, R. T. *The Gospel of Matthew.* NICNT. Grand Rapids: Eerdmans, 2007.

Fretheim, Terence E. *What Kind of God? The Collected Essays of Terence E. Fretheim.* Edited by Michael J. Chan and Brent A. Strawn. Winona Lake, IN: Eisenbrauns, 2015.

Friedman, Russell L. *Intellectual Traditions at the Medieval University: The Use of Philosophical Psychology in Trinitarian Theology among the Franciscans and Dominicans, 1250–1350.* 2 vols. Leiden: Brill, 2012.

Froula, John. "*Esse Secundarium*: An Analogical Term Meaning That by Which Christ Is Human." *The Thomist* 78 (2014): 557–80.

Gabler, J. P. *De iusto discrimine theologiae biblicae et dogmaticae regundisque recte utriusque finibus oratio.* In vol. 2 of *D. Johann Philipp Gablers kleinere theologische Schriften.* Edited by Theodor August Gabler and Johann Gottfried Gabler. Ulm: Verlag der Stettinischen Buchhandlung, 1831.

Gaine, Simon Francis. "The Beatific Vision and the Heavenly Mediation of Christ." *Theologica* 2 (2018): 116–28.

———. *Did the Saviour See the Father? Christ, Salvation and the Vision of God.* London: T&T Clark, 2015.

———. "How Could the Earthly Jesus Have Taught Divine Truth?" In *Christ Unabridged: Knowing and Loving the Son of Man*, edited by George Westhaver and Rebekah Vince, 82–93. London: SCM, 2020.

Gathercole, Simon. *The Pre-existent Son: Recovering the Christologies of Matthew, Mark, and Luke*. Grand Rapids: Eerdmans, 2006.

Gaventa, Beverly Roberts. "Theology and Ecclesiology in the Miletus Speech: Reflections on Content and Context." *NTS* 50 (2004): 36–52.

Gavrilyuk, Paul L. *The Suffering of the Impassible God: Dialectics of Patristic Thought*. Oxford Early Christian Studies. Oxford: Oxford University Press, 2004.

Gerhard, Johann. *Loci theologici*. Vol. 1. Edited by Eduard Preuss. Berlin: Gustav Schlawitz, 1863.

Gibbs, Raymond W., Jr., ed. *The Cambridge Handbook of Metaphor and Thought*. Cambridge: Cambridge University Press, 2008.

———. *Metaphor Wars: Conceptual Metaphors in Human Life*. Cambridge: Cambridge University Press, 2017.

Gibson, David. "A Mirror for God and for Us: Christology and Exegesis in Calvin's Doctrine of Election." *IJST* 11 (2009): 448–65.

Gillman, Florence Morgan. "Another Look at Romans 8:3: 'In the Likeness of Sinful Flesh.'" *CBQ* 49 (1987): 597–604.

Gleede, Benjamin. *The Development of the Term ἐνυπόστατος from Origen to John of Damascus*. VCSup 113. Leiden: Brill, 2012.

Goldie, Peter. "Emotion." *Philosophy Compass* 2 (2007): 928–38.

———, ed. *The Oxford Handbook of Philosophy of Emotion*. Oxford: Oxford University Press, 2010.

Goldingay, John. *Biblical Theology: The God of the Christian Scriptures*. Downers Grove, IL: IVP Academic, 2016.

Goldingay, John, and David Payne. *Isaiah 40–55*. 2 vols. ICC. London: T&T Clark, 2006.

Gondreau, Paul. "The Passions and the Moral Life: Appreciating the Originality of Aquinas." *Thomist* 71 (2007): 419–50.

Gordon, James R. *The Holy One in Our Midst: An Essay on the Flesh of Christ*. Minneapolis: Fortress, 2016.

Gorman, Michael. *Aquinas on the Metaphysics of the Hypostatic Union*. Cambridge: Cambridge University Press, 2017.

———. "Christ as Composite according to Aquinas." *Traditio* 55 (2000): 143–57.

———. "Christological Consistency and the Reduplicative Qua." *JAT* (2014): 86–100.

———. "Two Problems concerning Divine Immutability and the Incarnation." *Nova et Vetera* 16 (2018): 899–912.

Gorman, Michael J. "'Although/Because He Was in the Form of God': The Theological Significance of Paul's Master Story (Phil. 2:6–11)." *JTI* 1 (2007): 147–69.

————. "The Spirit, the Prophets, and the End of the 'Johannine Jesus.'" *JTI* 12 (2018): 3–23.

Gregory Nazianzen. *Discours 27–31 [Discours Théologiques]*. Translated by Paul Gallay. SC 250. Paris: Cerf, 1978.

Gregory of Nyssa. *Ad Ablabium, Quod non sint tres dei*. In vol. 3.1 of GNO.

————. *Contra Eunomium libri*. In vols. 1–2 of GNO.

————. *Refutatio confessionis Eunomii*. In vol. 2 of GNO.

Griffiths, Paul E. *What Emotions Really Are: The Problem of Psychological Categories*. Chicago: University of Chicago Press, 1997.

Grudem, Wayne. "Doctrinal Deviations in Evangelical-Feminist Arguments about the Trinity." In *One God in Three Persons: Unity of Essence, Distinction of Persons, Implications for Life*, edited by Bruce A. Ware and John Starke, 17–46. Wheaton: Crossway, 2015.

Gunton, Colin E. *Father, Son and Holy Spirit: Toward a Fully Trinitarian Theology*. London: T&T Clark, 2003.

————. *The Promise of Trinitarian Theology*. 2nd ed. London: T&T Clark, 1997.

Guthrie, George H. "Hebrews." In *Commentary on the New Testament Use of the Old*, edited by G. K. Beale and D. A. Carson, 919–95. Grand Rapids: Baker Academic, 2007.

————. *2 Corinthians*. BECNT. Grand Rapids: Baker Academic, 2015.

Habets, Myk. *The Anointed Son: A Trinitarian Spirit Christology*. Eugene, OR: Wipf & Stock, 2010.

————. "The Fallen Humanity of Christ: A Pneumatological Clarification of the Theology of Thomas F. Torrance." *Participatio* 5 (2015): 18–44.

————. "Putting the 'Extra' Back into Calvinism." *SJT* 62 (2009): 441–56.

Hafeman, Scott. "'Divine Nature' in 2 Peter 1, 4 within Its Eschatological Context." *Biblica* 94 (2013): 80–99.

Haga, Joar. *Was There a Lutheran Metaphysics? The Interpretation of* communicatio idiomatum *in Early Modern Lutheranism*. Refo500 Academic Studies 2. Göttingen: Vandenhoeck & Ruprecht, 2012.

Hagner, Donald A. *Matthew 1–13*. WBC 33A. Dallas: Word, 1993.

Haight, Roger. "The Case for Spirit Christology." *TS* 53 (1992): 257–87.

Hansen, G. Walter. *The Letter to the Philippians*. PNTC. Grand Rapids: Eerdmans, 2009.

Harnack, Adolf. *History of Dogma*. Vol. 1. Translated by Neil Buchanan. New York: Dover, 1961.

————. *Outlines of the History of Dogma*. Translated by Edwin Knox Mitchell. London: Hodder & Stoughton, 1893.

Harris, Murray J. *Jesus as God: The New Testament Use of* Theos *in Reference to Jesus*. Grand Rapids: Baker, 1992.

———. *Prepositions and Theology in the Greek New Testament: An Essential Reference Resource for Exegesis*. Grand Rapids: Zondervan, 2012.

———. *The Second Epistle to the Corinthians: A Commentary on the Greek Text*. NIGTC. Grand Rapids: Eerdmans, 2005.

Harrisville, Roy A., and Walter Sundberg. *The Bible in Modern Culture: Spinoza to Brevard Childs*. 2nd ed. Grand Rapids: Eerdmans, 2002.

Hart, Trevor A. "Sinlessness and Moral Responsibility: A Problem in Christology." *SJT* 48 (1995): 37–54.

Hasker, William. "A Compositional Incarnation." *RS* 53 (2017): 433–47.

———. *Metaphysics and the Tri-personal God*. OSAT. Oxford: Oxford University Press, 2013.

———. "The One Divine Nature." *Theologica* 3 (2019): 57–76.

Hatzidakis, Emmanuel. *Jesus: Fallen? The Human Nature of Christ Examined from an Eastern Orthodox Perspective*. Clearwater, FL: Orthodox Witness, 2013.

Hatzimoysis, Anthony, ed. *Philosophy and the Emotions*. Royal Institute of Philosophy Supplement 52. Cambridge: Cambridge University Press, 2003.

Hawthorne, Gerald F. "In the Form of and Equal with God (Philippians 2:6)." In *Where Christology Began: Essays on Philippians 2*, edited by Ralph P. Martin and Brian J. Dodd, 96–110. Louisville: Westminster John Knox, 1998.

Hawthorne, Gerald F., and Ralph P. Martin. *Philippians*. Edited by Ralph P. Martin. Rev. ed. WBC 43. Grand Rapids: Zondervan, 2004.

Hayes, John H., and Frederick Prussner. *Old Testament Theology: Its History and Development*. Atlanta: John Knox, 1985.

Hays, Richard B. *Echoes of Scripture in the Gospels*. Waco: Baylor University Press, 2016.

———. *Echoes of Scripture in the Letters of Paul*. New Haven: Yale University Press, 1989.

———. *The Faith of Jesus Christ: The Narrative Substructure of Galatians 3:1–4:11*. Grand Rapids: Eerdmans, 2002.

———. "The Story of God's Son: The Identity of Jesus in the Letters of Paul." In *Seeking the Identity of Jesus: A Pilgrimage*, edited by Beverly Roberts Gaventa and Richard B. Hays, 180–99. Grand Rapids: Eerdmans, 2008.

Healy, Nicholas M. "*Simul viator et comprehensor*: The Filial Mode of Christ's Knowledge." *Nova et Vetera* 11 (2013): 341–55.

Hegel, G. W. F. *Lectures on the Philosophy of Religion*. Edited by Peter C. Hodgson. Translated by Robert F. Brown et al. 3 vols. Oxford: Oxford University Press, 2007.

———. *The Phenomenology of Spirit*. Edited and translated by Terry Pinkard. Cambridge: Cambridge University Press, 2018.

Heidelberg Catechism. In *Reformed Confessions of the 16th and 17th Centuries in English Translation*, edited by James T. Dennison, 769–99. Grand Rapids: Reformation Heritage, 2010.

Hengel, Martin. "The Prologue of the Gospel of John as the Gateway to Christological Truth." In *The Gospel of John and Christian Theology*, edited by Richard Bauckham and Carl Mosser, 265–94. Grand Rapids: Eerdmans, 2008.

Hermann, Wilhelm. *Die Metaphysik in der Theologie*. Halle: Max Niemeyer, 1876.

Hilary of Poitiers. *La Trinité*. 3 vols. Edited by G. M. de Durand et al. SC 443, 448, 462. Paris: Cerf, 1999–2001.

———. *Sur Matthieu I–II*. Translated by Jean Doignon. SC 254, 258. Paris: Cerf, 2007.

Hill, Jonathan. "Introduction." In Marmadoro and Hill, *The Metaphysics of the Incarnation*, 1–19.

Hill, Wesley. *Paul and the Trinity: Persons, Relations, and the Pauline Letters*. Grand Rapids: Eerdmans, 2015.

Hodgson, Peter C. *Hegel and Christian Theology: A Reading of the Lectures on the Philosophy of Religion*. Oxford: Oxford University Press, 2005.

Holland, Richard A., Jr. *God, Time, and the Incarnation*. Eugene, OR: Wipf & Stock, 2012.

Holmes, Christopher R. J. *The Holy Spirit*. NSD. Grand Rapids: Zondervan, 2015.

Holmes, Stephen R. "Asymmetrical Assumption: Why Lutheran Christology Does Not Lead to Kenoticism or Divine Passibility." *SJT* 72 (2019): 357–74.

———. *The Quest for the Trinity: The Doctrine of God in Scripture, History and Modernity*. Downers Grove, IL: InterVarsity, 2012.

———. "Trinitarian Action and Inseparable Operations: Some Historical and Dogmatic Reflections." In *Advancing Trinitarian Theology: Explorations in Constructive Dogmatics*, edited by Oliver D. Crisp and Fred Sanders, 60–74. Grand Rapids: Zondervan, 2014.

Hoover, Roy W. "The HARPAGMOS Enigma: A Philological Solution." *HTR* 64 (1971): 95–119.

Howard, Thomas Albert. *Religion and the Rise of Historicism: W. M. L. de Wette, Jacob Burckhardt, and the Theological Origins of Nineteenth-Century Historical Consciousness*. Cambridge: Cambridge University Press, 2000.

Hultgren, Arland J. *Paul's Letter to the Romans: A Commentary*. Grand Rapids: Eerdmans, 2011.

Hunsinger, George. *Reading Barth with Charity: A Hermeneutical Proposal*. Grand Rapids: Baker Academic, 2015.

Hurst, Lincoln D. "Christ, Adam, and Preexistence Revisited." In *Where Christology Began: Essays on Philippians 2*, edited by Ralph P. Martin and Brian J. Dodd, 84–95. Louisville: Westminster John Knox, 1998.

Hurtado, Larry W. *God in New Testament Theology*. Nashville: Abingdon, 2010.

———. *Lord Jesus Christ: Devotion to Jesus in Earliest Christianity*. Grand Rapids: Eerdmans, 2003.

Ingraffia, Brian D. *Postmodern Theory and Biblical Theology: Vanquishing God's Shadow*. Cambridge: Cambridge University Press, 1995.

Irving, Edward. *The Doctrine of the Incarnation Opened*. In vol. 5 of *The Collected Writings of Edward Irving*, edited by G. Carlyle, 114–46. London: Alexander Strahan, 1865.

James, Susan. *Passion and Action: The Emotions in Seventeenth-Century Philosophy*. Oxford: Clarendon, 1997.

Jamieson, R. B. "1 Corinthians 15.28 and the Grammar of Paul's Christology." *NTS* 66 (2020): 187–207.

———. *Jesus' Death and Heavenly Offering in Hebrews*. SNTSMS 172. Cambridge: Cambridge University Press, 2019.

———. *The Paradox of Sonship: Christology in the Epistle to the Hebrews*. SCDS. Downers Grove, IL: IVP Academic, 2021.

———. "When and Where Did Jesus Offer Himself? A Taxonomy of Recent Scholarship." *CBR* 15 (2017): 338–68.

Janzen, J. Gerald. "Metaphor and Reality in Hosea 11." *Semeia* 24 (1982): 7–44.

Jauhiainen, Marko. "Turban and Crown Lost and Regained: Ezekiel 21:29–32 and Zechariah's Zemah." *JBL* 127 (2008): 501–11.

Jenson, Robert W. *Systematic Theology*. Vol. 1, *The Triune God*. Oxford: Oxford University Press, 1997.

Jeremias, Jörg. *Die Reue Gottes: Aspekte alttestamentlicher Gottesvorstellung*. 2nd ed. Neukirchen-Vluyn: Neukirchener, 1997.

Jerome. *Commentaire sur Jonas*. Translated by Yves-Marie Duval. SC 323. Paris: Cerf, 1985.

———. *Commentaire sur Saint Matthieu I–II*. Translated by Émile Bonnard. SC 242, 259. Paris: Cerf, 2008–13.

Jewett, Robert. *Romans*. Hermeneia. Minneapolis: Fortress, 2007.

Jobes, Karen H. *1 Peter*. BECNT. Grand Rapids: Baker Academic, 2005.

———. "Putting Words in His Mouth: The Son Speaks in Hebrews." In *So Great a Salvation: A Dialogue on the Atonement in Hebrews*, edited by Jon C. Laansma et al., 40–50. Library of New Testament Studies 516. London: T&T Clark, 2019.

———. "Sophia Christology: The Way of Wisdom?" In *The Way of Wisdom: Essays in Honor of Bruce K. Waltke*, edited by J. I. Packer and Sven K. Soderlund, 226–50. Grand Rapids: Zondervan, 2000.

John Chrysostom. *Homiliae XV in epistolam ad Philippenses*. PG 62. Paris, 1862.

———. *Homiliae XXXII in epistolam ad Romanos*. PG 60. Paris, 1862.

———. *Homiliae XXXIV in epistolam ad Hebraeos*. PG 63. Paris, 1862.

———. *Homiliae CXXXVIII in Johannem*. PG 59. Paris, 1862.

———. *Homiliae in Matthaeum*. PG 58. Paris, 1862.

John of Damascus. *Dialectica*. In vol. 1 of *Die Schriften des Johannes von Damaskos*, edited by P. Bonifatius Kotter, 51–146. Berlin: de Gruyter, 1969.

———. *Expositio fidei*. Vol. 2 of *Die Schriften des Johannes von Damaskos*. Edited by Bonifatius Kotter. Berlin: de Gruyter, 1973.

Johnson, Luke Timothy. *Acts of the Apostles*. SP. Collegeville, MN: Liturgical Press, 1992.

———. *Hebrews: A Commentary*. NTL. Louisville: Westminster John Knox, 2006.

———. *The Letter of James: A New Translation and Commentary*. AB 37A. New York: Doubleday, 1995.

Jones, Paul Dafydd. *The Humanity of Christ: Christology in Karl Barth's "Church Dogmatics."* London: T&T Clark, 2008.

Jüngel, Eberhard. *God as the Mystery of the World: On the Foundation of the Theology of the Crucified One in the Dispute between Theism and Atheism*. Translated by Darrell L. Guder. Grand Rapids: Eerdmans, 1983.

Junius, Franciscus. *De vera theologia*. Leiden, 1594.

Kahm, Nicholas. *Aquinas on Emotion's Participation in Reason*. Washington, DC: Catholic University of America Press, 2019.

Kant, Immanuel. *Critique of Practical Reason*. Translated by Mary Gregor. Rev. ed. Cambridge: Cambridge University Press, 2015.

———. *Critique of Pure Reason*. Edited and translated by Paul Guyer and Allen W. Wood. Cambridge: Cambridge University Press, 1998.

———. *Groundwork of the Metaphysics of Morals*. Edited by Mary Gregor and Jens Timmermann. Rev. ed. Cambridge: Cambridge University Press, 2012.

———. *Prolegomena to Any Future Metaphysics*. Edited and translated by Gary Hatfield. Rev. ed. Cambridge: Cambridge University Press, 2004.

———. *Religion within the Bounds of Mere Reason*. Edited by Allen Wood and George di Giovanni. Rev. ed. Cambridge: Cambridge University Press, 1998.

Kapic, Kelly M. "The Son's Assumption of a Human Nature: A Call for Clarity." *IJST* 3 (2001): 154–66.

Käsemann, Ernst. *Commentary on Romans*. Edited and translated by Geoffrey W. Bromiley. Grand Rapids: Eerdmans, 1980.

———. "A Critical Analysis of Philippians 2:5–11." *JTC* 5 (1968): 45–88.

Kashow, Robert C. "Two Philological Notes on Zechariah 6,12–13 Relevant for the Identification of Ṣemaḥ." *ZAW* 128 (2016): 476–77.

Kasper, Walter. *Jesus the Christ*. New ed. London: T&T Clark, 2011.

Keckermann, Bartholomäus. *Scientiae metaphysicae brevissima synopsis et compendium*. In vol. 1 of *Operum omnium quae extant*. Geneva, 1614.

———. *Systema logicae, tribus libris adornatum*. In vol. 1 of *Operum omnium quae extant*. Geneva, 1614.

———. *Systema logica minus*. In vol. 1 of *Operum omnium quae extant*. Geneva, 1614.

———. *Systema rhetoricae*. In vol. 2 of *Operum omnium quae extant*. Geneva, 1614.

———. *Systema s.s. theologiae*. In vol. 2 of *Operum omnium quae extant*. Geneva, 1614.

Keener, Craig S. *Acts: An Exegetical Commentary*. Vol. 3, *15:1–23:35*. Grand Rapids: Baker Academic, 2014.

———. *A Commentary on the Gospel of Matthew*. Grand Rapids: Eerdmans, 1999.

———. *The Gospel of John: A Commentary*. 2 vols. Peabody, MA: Hendrickson, 2003. Reprint, Grand Rapids: Baker Academic, 2012.

Kieser, Ty. "Is the *Filioque* an Obstacle to a Pneumatologically Robust Christology? A Response from Reformed Resources." *JRT* 12 (2018): 394–412.

King, Rolfe. "Assumption, Union and Sanctification: Some Clarifying Distinctions." *IJST* 19 (2017): 53–72.

Kirk, J. R. Daniel. *A Man Attested by God: The Human Jesus of the Synoptic Gospels*. Grand Rapids: Eerdmans, 2016.

Klinge, Heinrich. *Verheißene Gegenwart: Die Christologie des Martin Chemnitz*. Forschungen zur systematischen und ökumenischen Theologie 152. Göttingen: Vandenhoeck & Ruprecht, 2015.

Knuuttila, Simo. *Emotions in Ancient and Medieval Philosophy*. Oxford: Oxford University Press, 2004.

Koester, Craig R. *Hebrews: A New Translation with Introduction and Commentary*. AB 36. New York: Doubleday, 2001.

Krötke, Wolf. *Gottes Klarheiten: Eine Neuinterpretation der Lehre von Gottes "Eigenschaften."* Tübingen: Mohr Siebeck, 2001.

Kruse, Colin G. *Paul's Letter to the Romans*. PNTC. Grand Rapids: Eerdmans, 2012.

Kuyper, Lester J. "The Repentance of God." *Reformed Review* 18 (1965): 3–16.

———. "The Suffering and Repentance of God." *SJT* 22 (1969): 257–77.

LaCugna, Catherine Mowry. *God for Us: The Trinity and the Christian Life*. Reprint, San Francisco: HarperCollins, 1991.

Lagerlund, Henrik, and Mikko Yrjönsuuri, eds. *Emotions and Choice from Boethius to Descartes*. Studies in the History of the Philosophy of Mind 1. Dordrecht: Kluwer, 2002.

Lakoff, George, and Mark Johnson. *Metaphors We Live By*. Chicago: University of Chicago Press, 1980.

Lancaster, Mason D. "Metaphor Research and the Hebrew Bible." *CBR* 19 (2021): 235–85.

Lane, William L. *Hebrews 1–8*. WBC 47A. Waco: Word, 1991.

———. *Hebrews 9–13*. WBC 47B. Dallas: Word, 1991.

LaPine, Matthew A. *The Logic of the Body: Retrieving Theological Psychology*. Bellingham, WA: Lexham, 2020.

Lee, Dorothy. *Flesh and Glory: Symbolism, Gender and Theology in the Gospel of John*. New York: Crossroad, 2002.

Leftow, Brian. "Composition and Christology." *Faith and Philosophy* 28 (2011): 310–22.

———. "A Timeless God Incarnate." In *The Incarnation: An Interdisciplinary Symposium on the Incarnation of the Son of God*, edited by Stephen T. Davis et al., 273–99. Oxford: Oxford University Press, 2002.

Legaspi, Michael C. *The Death of Scripture and the Rise of Biblical Studies*. Oxford: Oxford University Press, 2010.

Legge, Dominic. *The Trinitarian Christology of St Thomas Aquinas*. Oxford: Oxford University Press, 2017.

Leigh, Edward. *A Treatise of Divinity*. London: Griffin, 1646.

Lenow, Joseph E. "Shoring Up Divine Simplicity against Modal Collapse: A Powers Account." *RS* (2021): 10–29.

Le Poidevin, Robin. "Euthyphro and the Goodness of God Incarnate." *Ratio* 24 (2011): 206–21.

———. "Identity and the Composite Christ: An Incarnational Dilemma." *RS* 45 (2009): 167–86.

———. "Incarnation: Metaphysical Issues." *Philosophy Compass* (2009): 703–14.

———. "Kenosis, Necessity and Incarnation." *Heythrop Journal* 54 (2012): 214–27.

Levering, Matthew. "Christ, the Trinity, and Predestination: McCormack and Aquinas." In *Trinity and Election in Contemporary Theology*, edited by Michael T. Dempsey, 244–73. Grand Rapids: Eerdmans, 2011.

———. *Christ's Fulfillment of Torah and Temple: Salvation according to Thomas Aquinas*. Notre Dame, IN: University of Notre Dame Press, 2002.

———. *Engaging the Doctrine of the Holy Spirit: Love and Gift in the Trinity and the Church*. Grand Rapids: Baker Academic, 2016.

———. *Scripture and Metaphysics: Aquinas and the Renewal of Trinitarian Theology*. Challenges in Contemporary Theology. Oxford: Blackwell, 2004.

Lightfoot, J. B. *St. Paul's Epistle to the Philippians*. Rev. ed. Grand Rapids: Zondervan, 1953.

Lincoln, Andrew T. *Ephesians*. WBC 42. Dallas: Word, 1990.

Liston, Greg. "A 'Chalcedonian' Spirit Christology." *ITQ* 81 (2016): 74–93.

Lohmann, Friedrich. "God's Freedom: Free to Be Bound." *MT* 34 (2018): 368–85.

Loke, Andrew Ter Ern. "The Incarnation and Jesus' Apparent Limitation in Knowledge." *New Blackfriars* 94 (2013): 583–602.

———. *A Kryptic Model of the Incarnation*. London: Routledge, 2016.

————. "On the An-Enhypostasia Distinction and Three-Part Concrete-Nature Christology: The Divine Preconscious Model." *JAT* 2 (2014): 101–16.

————. "On the Divine Preconscious Model of the Incarnation and Concrete-Nature Christology: A Reply to James Arcadi." *NZSTh* 59 (2017): 26–33.

————. "Solving a Paradox against Concrete-Composite Christology: A Modified Hylomorphic Proposal." *RS* 47 (2011): 493–502.

Lombard, Peter. *Sententiae in IV libris distinctae.* 3rd ed. Spicilegium Bonaventurianum 4B–5. Rome: Grottaferrata, 1971–81.

Lombardo, Nicholas E. *The Logic of Desire: Aquinas on Emotion.* Washington, DC: Catholic University of America Press, 2011.

Long, D. Stephen. *The Perfectly Simple Triune God: Aquinas and His Legacy.* Minneapolis: Fortress, 2016.

Longman, Tremper, III. *The Fear of the Lord Is Wisdom: A Theological Introduction to Wisdom in Israel.* Grand Rapids: Baker Academic, 2017.

Louw, Johannes P., and Eugene A. Nida. *Greek-English Lexicon of the New Testament Based on Semantic Domains.* Vol. 1. New York: United Bible Societies, 1988.

Luy, David J. *Dominus Mortis: Martin Luther on the Incorruptibility of God in Christ.* Minneapolis: Fortress, 2014.

Luz, Ulrich. *Matthew 1–7: A Commentary.* Edited by Helmut Koester. Translated by James E. Crouch. Hermeneia. Minneapolis: Fortress, 2007.

Macaskill, Grant. "Identifications, Articulations, and Proportions in Practical Theological Interpretation." *JTI* 14 (2020): 3–15.

————. *Living in Union with Christ: Paul's Gospel and Christian Moral Identity.* Grand Rapids: Baker Academic, 2019.

————. "Name Christology, Divine Aseity, and the I Am Sayings in the Fourth Gospel." *JTI* 12 (2018): 217–41.

Maccovius, Johannes. *Loci communes.* Edited by Nicolaus Arnoldus. 2nd ed. Amsterdam, 1658.

————. *Metaphysica.* Edited by Adrianus Heereboord. 3rd ed. Leiden, 1658.

Mackintosh, H. R. *The Doctrine of the Person of Jesus Christ.* New York: Scribner's Sons, 1912.

MacLeod, David J. "Imitating the Incarnation of Christ: An Exposition of Philippians 2:5–8." *BS* 158 (2001): 308–30.

Mansini, Guy. "Can Humility and Obedience Be Trinitarian Realities?" In *Thomas Aquinas and Karl Barth: An Unofficial Catholic-Protestant Dialogue*, edited by Bruce L. McCormack and Thomas Joseph White, 71–98. Grand Rapids: Eerdmans, 2013.

————. *The Word Has Dwelt among Us: Explorations in Theology.* Ave Maria, FL: Sapientia Press, 2008.

Marmodoro, Anna, and Jonathan Hill. "Composition Models of the Incarnation: Unity and Unifying Relations." *RS* 46 (2010): 469–88.

———, eds. *The Metaphysics of the Incarnation*. Oxford: Oxford University Press, 2011.

Marshall, Bruce D. "The Dereliction of Christ and the Impassibility of God." In *Divine Impassibility and the Mystery of Human Suffering*, edited by James F. Keating and Thomas Joseph White, 246–98. Grand Rapids: Eerdmans, 2009.

———. "What Does the Spirit Have to Do?" In *Reading John with St. Thomas Aquinas: Theological Exegesis and Speculative Theology*, edited by Michael Dauphinais and Matthew Levering, 62–77. Washington, DC: Catholic University of America Press, 2005.

Marshall, I. Howard. *New Testament Theology: One Gospel, Many Witnesses*. Downers Grove, IL: InterVarsity, 2004.

Martin, Michael Wade. "ἁρπαγμός Revisited: A Philological Reexamination of the New Testament's 'Most Difficult Word.'" *JBL* 135 (2016): 175–94.

Martin, Ralph P. *A Hymn of Christ: Philippians 2:5–11 in Recent Interpretation and in the Setting of Early Christian Worship*. Downers Grove, IL: IVP Academic, 1997.

———. *2 Corinthians*. WBC 40. Waco: Word, 1986.

Mastricht, Petrus van. *Theoretico-practica theologia*. 2nd ed. Utrecht, 1724.

Matera, Frank J. *Romans*. Paideia. Grand Rapids: Baker Academic, 2010.

———. *II Corinthians: A Commentary*. NTL. Louisville: Westminster John Knox, 2003.

Maximus the Confessor. *Opusculum 7*. PG 91. Paris, 1863.

McCall, Thomas H. *Analytic Christology and the Theological Interpretation of the New Testament*. OSAT. Oxford: Oxford University Press, 2021.

McCormack, Bruce L. "The Actuality of God: Karl Barth in Conversation with Open Theism." In *Engaging the Doctrine of God: Contemporary Protestant Perspectives*, edited by Bruce L. McCormack, 185–242. Grand Rapids: Baker Academic, 2008.

———. "Atonement and Human Suffering." In *Locating Atonement: Explorations in Constructive Dogmatics*, edited by Oliver D. Crisp and Fred Sanders, 189–208. Grand Rapids: Zondervan, 2015.

———. "Christ and the Decree: An Unsettled Question for the Reformed Churches Today." In *Reformed Theology in Contemporary Perspective: Yesterday, Today—and Tomorrow?*, edited by Lynn Quigley, 124–43. Edinburgh: Rutherford House, 2006.

———. "Divine Impassibility or Simply Divine Constancy? Implications of Karl Barth's Later Christology for Debates over Impassibility." In *Divine Impassibility and the Mystery of Human Suffering*, edited by James F. Keating and Thomas Joseph White, 150–86. Grand Rapids: Eerdmans, 2009.

———. "The Doctrine of the Trinity after Barth: An Attempt to Reconstruct Barth's Doctrine of the Trinity in the Light of His Later Christology." In *Trinitarian*

Theology after Barth, edited by Myk Habets and Phillip Tolliday, 87–117. Cambridge: James Clark & Co., 2012.

———. "Election and the Trinity: Theses in Response to George Hunsinger." *SJT* 63 (2010): 203–24.

———. "Grace and Being." In *The Cambridge Companion to Karl Barth*, edited by John Webster, 92–110. Cambridge: Cambridge University Press, 2000.

———. *The Humility of the Eternal Son: Reformed Kenoticism and the Repair of Chalcedon.* Cambridge: Cambridge University Press, 2021.

———. "Karl Barth's Christology as a Resource for a Reformed Version of Kenoticism." *IJST* 8 (2006): 243–51.

———. "Let's Speak Plainly: A Response to Paul Molnar." *Theology Today* 67 (2010): 57–65.

———. "The Lord and Giver of Life: A 'Barthian' Defense of the Filioque." In *Rethinking Trinitarian Theology: Disputed Questions and Contemporary Issues in Trinitarian Theology*, edited by Robert J. Wozniak and Giulio Maspero, 230–53. London: T&T Clark, 2012.

———. "The Only Mediator: The Person and Work of Christ in Evangelical Perspective." In *Renewing the Evangelical Mission*, edited by Richard Lints, 250–69. Grand Rapids: Eerdmans, 2013.

———. *Orthodox and Modern: Studies in the Theology of Karl Barth.* Grand Rapids: Baker Academic, 2008.

———. "Processions and Missions: A Point of Convergence between Thomas Aquinas and Karl Barth." In *Thomas Aquinas and Karl Barth: An Unofficial Catholic-Protestant Dialogue*, edited by Bruce L. McCormack and Thomas Joseph White, 99–126. Grand Rapids: Eerdmans, 2013.

———. "Seek God Where He May Be Found: A Response to Edwin Chr. Van Driel." *SJT* 60 (2007): 62–79.

———. "Trinity and Election: A Progress Report." In *Ontmoetingen—Tijdgenoten en getuigen: Studies aangeboden aan Gerrit Neven*, edited by Akke van der Kooi et al., 14–35. Kampen: Kok, 2009.

———. "'With Loud Cries and Tears': The Humanity of the Son in the Epistle to the Hebrews." In *The Epistle to the Hebrews and Christian Theology*, edited by Richard Bauckham et al., 37–68. Grand Rapids: Eerdmans, 2009.

McFarland, Ian. "Fallen or Unfallen? Christ's Human Nature and the Ontology of Human Sinfulness." *IJST* 10 (2008): 399–415.

———. "Spirit and Incarnation: Toward a Pneumatic Chalcedonianism." *IJST* 16 (2014): 143–58.

———. "'Willing Is Not Choosing': Some Anthropological Dynamics of Dyothelite Christology." *IJST* 9 (2007): 3–23.

———. *The Word Made Flesh: A Theology of the Incarnation*. Louisville: Westminster John Knox, 2019.

McGinnis, Andrew M. *The Son of God beyond the Flesh: A Historical and Theological Study of the* extra Calvinisticum. T&T Clark Studies in Systematic Theology. London: Bloomsbury, 2014.

McGuckin, John A. *Saint Cyril of Alexandria and the Christological Controversy*. Crestwood, NY: St. Vladimir's Seminary Press, 2004.

McKenny, Gerald. *The Analogy of Grace: Karl Barth's Moral Theology*. Oxford: Oxford University Press, 2010.

McKinley, John E. *Tempted for Us: Theological Models and the Practical Relevance of Christ's Impeccability and Temptation*. Eugene, OR: Wipf & Stock, 2009.

Melanchthon, Philipp. *Elementorum rhetorices libri duo*. In vol. 13 of *Philippi Melanthonis opera quae supersunt omnia*. Edited by Carolus Gottlieb Bretschneider. Brunswick: Schwetschke, 1846.

———. *Erotemata dialectica*. In vol. 13 of *Philippi Melanthonis opera quae supersunt omnia*. Edited by Carolus Gottlieb Bretschneider. Brunswick: Schwetschke, 1846.

Metzger, Bruce M. *A Textual Commentary on the Greek New Testament*. 2nd ed. Stuttgart: Deutsche Bibelgesellschaft, 1994.

Michaels, J. Ramsey. *The Gospel of John*. NICNT. Grand Rapids: Eerdmans, 2010.

Moberly, R. W. L. *Old Testament Theology: Reading the Hebrew Bible as Christian Scripture*. Grand Rapids: Baker Academic, 2013.

Moffitt, David M. *Atonement and the Logic of Resurrection in the Epistle to the Hebrews*. Supplements to Novum Testamentum 141. Leiden: Brill, 2013.

Molnar, Paul D. *Faith, Freedom and the Spirit: The Economic Trinity in Barth, Torrance and Contemporary Theology*. Downers Grove, IL: IVP, 2015.

Moloney, Raymond. "Approaches to Christ's Knowledge in the Patristic Era." In *Studies in Patristic Christology*, edited by Thomas Finan and Vincent Twomey, 37–66. Dublin: Four Courts, 1998.

Moltmann, Jürgen. *The Crucified God: The Cross of Christ as the Foundation and Criticism of Christian Theology*. Translated by Margaret Kohl. Minneapolis: Fortress, 1993.

———. *God in Creation: A New Theology of Creation and the Spirit of God*. Translated by Margaret Kohl. Minneapolis: Fortress, 1993.

———. *The Trinity and the Kingdom: The Doctrine of God*. Translated by Margaret Kohl. Minneapolis: Fortress, 1993.

———. *The Way of Jesus Christ: Christology in Messianic Dimensions*. Translated by Margaret Kohl. Minneapolis: Fortress, 1993.

Moo, Douglas J. *The Epistle to the Romans*. NICNT. Grand Rapids: Eerdmans, 1996.

———. *Galatians*. BECNT. Grand Rapids: Baker Academic, 2013.

———. *The Letters to the Colossians and Philemon*. PNTC. Grand Rapids: Eerdmans, 2008.

Moran, Richard. "Metaphor." In *A Companion to the Philosophy of Language*, edited by Bob Hale and Crispin Wright, 248–68. Blackwell Companions to Philosophy. Oxford: Blackwell, 1997.

Moreland, J. P., and William Lane Craig. *Philosophical Foundations for a Christian Worldview*. Downers Grove, IL: InterVarsity, 2003.

Morris, Thomas V. *The Logic of God Incarnate*. Ithaca, NY: Cornell University Press, 1986.

Moser, J. David. "Tools for Interpreting Christ's Saving Mysteries in Scripture: Aquinas on Reduplicative Propositions in Christology." *SJT* 73 (2020): 285–94.

Motyer, J. Alec. *The Prophecy of Isaiah: An Introduction and Commentary*. Downers Grove, IL: InterVarsity, 1993.

Moule, C. F. D. "Further Reflexions on Philippians 2:5–11." In *Apostolic History and the Gospel: Biblical and Historical Essays Presented to F. F. Bruce on His 60th Birthday*, edited by W. Ward Gasque and Ralph P. Martin, 264–76. Grand Rapids: Eerdmans, 1970.

Moulton, James Hope, et al. *A Grammar of New Testament Greek*. Vol. 1, *Prolegomena*. 3rd ed. Edinburgh: T&T Clark, 1908.

Mounce, William. *The Analytical Lexicon to the Greek New Testament*. Grand Rapids: Zondervan, 1993.

Mowinckel, Sigmund. "The Name of the God of Moses." *HUCA* 32 (1961): 121–33.

Muller, Richard A. *Post-Reformation Reformed Dogmatics: The Rise and Development of Reformed Orthodoxy, ca. 1520 to ca. 1725*. 4 vols. Grand Rapids: Baker Academic, 2003.

———. "Toward the *Pactum Salutis*: Locating the Origins of a Concept." *MAJT* 18 (2007): 11–65.

Mullins, R. T. *The End of the Timeless God*. OSAT. Oxford: Oxford University Press, 2016.

———. *God and Emotion*. EPR. Cambridge: Cambridge University Press, 2020.

———. "The Problem of Arbitrary Creation for Impassibility." *Open Theology* 6 (2020): 392–406.

———. "Simply Impossible: A Case against Divine Simplicity." *JRT* 7 (2013): 181–203.

Murphy-O'Connor, J. "Christological Anthropology in Phil., II, 6–11." *RB* 83 (1976): 25–50.

Naugle, David K. *Worldview: The History of a Concept*. Grand Rapids: Eerdmans, 2002.

Nemes, Steven. "Divine Simplicity Does Not Entail Modal Collapse." In *Roses & Reasons: Philosophical Essays*, edited by Carlos Frederico Calvet da Silveira and Alin Tat, 101–19. Bucharest: Eikon, 2020.

Newman, Paul W. *A Spirit Christology: Recovering the Biblical Paradigm of Christian Faith*. Lanham, MD: University Press of America, 1987.

Ngien, Dennis. "Chalcedonian Christology and Beyond: Luther's Understanding of the *Communicatio Idiomatum*." *Heythrop Journal* 45 (2004): 54–68.

Nimmo, Paul T. *Being in Action: The Theological Shape of Barth's Ethical Vision*. London: T&T Clark, 2007.

Nolan, Kirk J. *Reformed Virtue after Barth: Developing Moral Virtue Ethics in the Reformed Tradition*. Louisville: Westminster John Knox, 2014.

Nolland, John. *The Gospel of Matthew*. NIGTC. Grand Rapids: Eerdmans, 2005.

Noonan, John T. "Hegel and Strauss: The Dialectic and the Gospels." *CBQ* 12 (1950): 136–52.

Nussbaum, Martha C. *Upheavals of Thought: The Intelligence of Emotions*. Cambridge: Cambridge University Press, 2001.

O'Collins, Gerald, and Daniel Kendall. "The Faith of Jesus." *TS* 53 (1992): 403–23.

Ollenburger, Ben C. "Old Testament Theology before 1933." In *Old Testament Theology: Flowering and Future*, edited by Ben C. Ollenburger, 3–11. Winona Lake, IN: Eisenbrauns, 2004.

O'Neill, John Cochrane. "Hoover on *Harpagmos* Reviewed, with a Modest Proposal Concerning Philippians 2:6." *HTR* 81 (1988): 445–49.

Oord, Thomas Jay. *The Uncontrolling Love of God: An Open and Relational Account of Providence*. Downers Grove, IL: IVP, 2015.

Osborne, Grant R. *Matthew*. ZECNT. Grand Rapids: Zondervan, 2010.

Oswalt, John N. *The Bible among the Myths: Unique Revelation or Just Ancient Literature?* Grand Rapids: Zondervan, 2009.

Owen, John. *A Brief Declaration and Vindication of the Doctrine of the Trinity*. In *The Works of John Owen*, edited by William H. Goold, 2:377–439. Edinburgh: Banner of Truth, 1965.

———. *Christologia*. In *The Works of John Owen*, edited by William H. Goold, 1:29–272. Edinburgh: Banner of Truth, 1965.

———. *A Dissertation on Divine Justice*. In *The Works of John Owen*, edited by William H. Goold, 10:495–624. Edinburgh: Banner of Truth, 1967.

———. *An Exposition of the Epistle to the Hebrews, with Preliminary Exercitations*. In vols. 17–23 of *The Works of John Owen*. Edited by William H. Goold. Edinburgh: Banner of Truth, 1991.

———. *Meditations and Discourses on the Glory of Christ*. In *The Works of John Owen*, edited by William H. Goold, 1:285–415. Edinburgh: Banner of Truth, 1965.

———. *Of Temptation*. In *The Works of John Owen*, edited by William H. Goold, 6:91–151. Edinburgh: Banner of Truth, 1967.

———. *Pneumatologia*. Vols. 3–4 of *The Works of John Owen*. Edited by William H. Goold. Edinburgh: Banner of Truth, 1965–67.

———. *Posthumous Sermons, Part IV*. In *The Works of John Owen*, edited by William H. Goold, 9:521–622. Edinburgh: Banner of Truth, 1965.

———. *Vindiciae evangelicae*. In *The Works of John Owen*, edited by William H. Goold, 12:85–590. Edinburgh: Banner of Truth, 1966.

Padgett, Alan G. *God, Eternity and the Nature of Time*. New York: St. Martin's Press, 1992.

Pannenberg, Wolfhart. *Jesus—God and Man*. Translated by Lewis L. Wilkins and Duane A. Priebe. 2nd ed. Philadelphia: Westminster, 1977.

Pasnau, Robert. "On Existing All at Once." In *God, Eternity, and Time*, edited by Christian Tapp and Edmund Runggaldier, 13–28. Farnham, UK: Ashgate, 2011.

Paul, Shalom M. *Isaiah 40–66: Translation and Commentary*. Grand Rapids: Eerdmans, 2012.

Pawl, Timothy. "Conciliar Christology and the Consistency of Divine Immutability with a Mutable, Incarnate God." *Nova et Vetera* 16 (2018): 913–37.

———. "Conciliar Christology and the Problem of Incompatible Predications." *Scientia et Fides* 3 (2015): 85–106.

———. "Conciliar Christology, Impeccability, and Temptation." In *Impeccability and Temptation: Understanding Christ's Divine and Human Will*, edited by Johannes Grössl and Klaus von Stosch, 94–115. Routledge Studies in Analytic and Systematic Theology. London: Routledge, 2021.

———. *In Defense of Conciliar Christology*. OSAT. Oxford: Oxford University Press, 2016.

———. *In Defense of Extended Conciliar Christology: A Philosophical Essay*. OSAT. Oxford: Oxford University Press, 2019.

Pawl, Timothy, and Mark K. Spencer. "Christologically Inspired, Empirically Motivated Hylomorphism." *Res Philosophica* 93 (2016): 137–60.

Peckham, John C. *The Love of God: A Canonical Model*. Downers Grove, IL: IVP Academic, 2015.

Pedersen, Daniel J. "Schleiermacher and Reformed Scholastics on the Divine Attributes." *IJST* 17 (2015): 413–31.

Pelser, Adam C. "Temptation, Virtue, and the Character of Christ." *Faith and Philosophy* 36 (2019): 81–101.

Peppiatt, Lucy. "Life in the Spirit: Christ's and Ours." In *The Christian Doctrine of Humanity: Explorations in Constructive Dogmatics*, edited by Oliver D. Crisp and Fred Sanders, 165–81. Grand Rapids: Zondervan, 2018.

Perrin, Nicholas. *Jesus the Temple*. Grand Rapids: Baker Academic, 2010.

Peterson, David. *Hebrews and Perfection: An Examination of the Concept of Perfection in the 'Epistle to the Hebrews.'* SNTSMS 47. Cambridge: Cambridge University Press, 1982.

Philo. *De aeternitate mundi*. In *Philo IX*, translated by F. H. Colson, 184–291. LCL 363. Cambridge, MA: Harvard University Press, 1941.

———. *Legum allegoriae*. In *Philo I*, translated by F. H. Colson and G. H. Whitaker, 146–473. LCL 226. Cambridge, MA: Harvard University Press, 1929.

Pierce, Madison N. *Divine Discourse in the Epistle to the Hebrews: The Contextualization of Spoken Quotations of Scripture*. SNTSMS 178. Cambridge: Cambridge University Press, 2020.

———. "Hebrews 1 and the Son Begotten 'Today.'" In *Retrieving Eternal Generation*, edited by Fred Sanders and Scott R. Swain, 117–31. Grand Rapids: Zondervan, 2017.

Pike, Nelson. *God and Timelessness*. London: Routledge & Kegan Paul, 1970.

Pinkard, Terry. *German Philosophy, 1760–1860: The Legacy of Idealism*. Cambridge: Cambridge University Press, 2002.

———. *Hegel: A Biography*. Cambridge: Cambridge University Press, 2000.

Plantinga, Alvin. "On Heresy, Mind, and Truth." *Faith and Philosophy* 16 (1999): 182–93.

Poe, Shelli M. *Essential Trinitarianism: Schleiermacher as Trinitarian Theologian*. London: Bloomsbury, 2019.

Pokorný, Petr. *Colossians: A Commentary*. Translated by Siegfried S. Schatzmann. Peabody, MA: Hendrickson, 1991.

Polanus, Amandus. *Logicae libri duo*. Herbornae Nassaviorum, 1590.

———. *Syntagma theologiae christianae*. Hanover, 1615.

Polkinghorne, John C. "Kenotic Creation and Divine Action." In *The Work of Love: Creation as Kenosis*, edited by John C. Polkinghorne, 90–106. Grand Rapids: Eerdmans, 2001.

Pool, Jeff B. *God's Wounds: Hermeneutic of the Christian Symbol of Divine Suffering*. Vol. 1, *Divine Vulnerability and Creation*. Princeton Theological Monograph Series 100. Eugene, OR: Pickwick, 2009.

Poole, Matthew. *Annotations upon the Holy Bible*. Vol. 2. London: Parkhurst, 1700.

Quenstedt, Johann. *Theologia didactico-polemica*. Leipzig: Fritsch, 1702.

Rahner, Karl. *The Trinity*. Translated by Joseph Donceel. Reprint, London and New York: Burns and Oates, 2001.

Rainbow, Paul A. *Johannine Theology: The Gospel, the Epistles and the Apocalypse*. Downers Grove, IL: IVP Academic, 2014.

Rea, Michael C. "Relative Identity and the Trinity." In *Philosophical and Theological Essays on the Trinity*, edited by Thomas McCall and Michael C. Rea, 248–62. Oxford: Oxford University Press, 2009.

Reumann, John. *Philippians: A New Translation with Introduction and Commentary*. AB 33B. New Haven: Yale University Press, 2008.

Richard of St. Victor. *De trinitate*. Translated by Gaston Salet. SC 63. Paris: Cerf, 1999.

Richardson, Christopher A. *Pioneer and Perfecter of Faith: Jesus' Faith as the Climax of Israel's History in the Epistle to the Hebrews*. WUNT 2.338. Tübingen: Mohr Siebeck, 2012.

Riches, Aaron. *Ecce Homo: On the Divine Unity of Christ*. Interventions. Grand Rapids: Eerdmans, 2016.

Ricoeur, Paul. *The Rule of Metaphor: The Creation of Meaning in Language*. Translated by Robert Czerny et al. 3rd ed. London: Routledge, 2004.

Ridderbos, Herman. *The Gospel of John: A Theological Commentary*. Translated by John Vriend. Grand Rapids: Eerdmans, 1997.

Ridgley, Thomas. *A Body of Divinity*. Vol. 1. Philadelphia, 1814.

Ritschl, Albrecht. *The Christian Doctrine of Justification and Reconciliation*. Translated by H. R. Mackintosh and A. B. Macaulay. 2nd ed. Edinburgh: T&T Clark, 1902.

———. *Theology and Metaphysics: Towards Rapprochement and Defense*. In *Three Essays*, translated by Philip Hefner, 151–217. Minneapolis: Fortress, 1972.

Roberts, Robert C. *Emotions: An Essay in Aid of Moral Psychology*. Cambridge: Cambridge University Press, 2003.

Robertson, A. T. *A Grammar of the Greek New Testament in Light of Historical Research*. 4th ed. New York: Hodder & Stoughton, 1923.

Rogers, Katherin A. "The Incarnation as Action Composite." *Faith and Philosophy* 30 (2013): 251–70.

Rogers, Trent A. *God and the Idols: Representations of God in 1 Corinthians 8–10*. WUNT 2.427. Tübingen: Mohr Siebeck, 2016.

Rogerson, John W. *Old Testament Criticism in the Nineteenth Century: England and Germany*. London: SPCK, 1984.

———. *W. M. L. de Wette, Founder of Modern Biblical Criticism: An Intellectual Biography*. Sheffield, UK: Sheffield Academic, 1992.

Rowe, C. Kavin. "Biblical Pressure and Trinitarian Hermeneutics." *Pro Ecclesia* 11 (2002): 295–312.

———. *Early Narrative Christology: The Lord in the Gospel of Luke*. Grand Rapids: Baker Academic, 2009.

Salas, Victor. "There Can Only Be One: Thomas Aquinas on Christ's *Esse*." *Divus Thomas* 120 (2017): 243–72.

———. "Thomas Aquinas on Christ's *Esse*: A Metaphysics of the Incarnation." *The Thomist* 70 (2006): 577–603.

Sanday, William, and Arthur C. Headlam. *A Critical and Exegetical Commentary on the Epistle to the Romans*. 5th ed. ICC. Edinburgh: T&T Clark, 1902.

Sanders, Fred. "The Spirit Who Is from God: The Pneumatology of Procession and Mission." In *The Third Person of the Trinity: Explorations in Constructive*

Dogmatics, edited by Oliver D. Crisp and Fred Sanders, 1–20. Grand Rapids: Zondervan, 2020.

———. *The Triune God*. NSD. Grand Rapids: Zondervan, 2016.

Saner, Andrea D. *"Too Much to Grasp": Exodus 3:13–15 and the Reality of God*. Journal of Theological Interpretation Supplements 11. Winona Lake, IN: Eisenbrauns, 2015.

Sarisky, Darren. *Reading the Bible Theologically*. CIT. Cambridge: Cambridge University Press, 2019.

Schelling, F. W. J. *System of Transcendental Idealism (1800)*. Translated by Peter Heath. Charlottesville: University Press of Virginia, 1978.

Schlatter, Adolf. *Der Evangelist Johannes: Wie er spricht, denkt und glaubt; Ein Kommentar zum vierten Evangelium*. Stuttgart: Calwer Verlag, 1975.

Schleiermacher, Friedrich. *The Christian Faith: A New Translation and Critical Edition*. Vol. 2. Edited by Catherine L. Kelsey and Terrence N. Tice. Translated by Terrence N. Tice et al. Louisville: Westminster John Knox, 2016.

———. *On Religion: Speeches to Its Cultured Despisers*. Edited and translated by Richard Crouter. Cambridge: Cambridge University Press, 1988.

Schlimm, Matthew R. "Different Perspectives on Divine Pathos: An Examination of Hermeneutics in Biblical Theology." *CBQ* 69 (2007): 673–94.

Schnelle, Udo. *Antidocetic Christology in the Gospel of John*. Translated by Linda M. Maloney. Minneapolis: Fortress, 1992.

Schrage, Wolfgang. *Unterwegs zur Einzigheit und Einheit Gottes: Zum "Monotheismus" des Paulus und seiner alttestamentlich-frühjüdischen Tradition*. Neukirchen-Vluyn: Neukirchener Verlag, 2002.

Schreiner, Thomas R. *Galatians*. ZECNT. Grand Rapids: Zondervan, 2010.

———. *New Testament Theology: Magnifying God in Christ*. Grand Rapids: Baker Academic, 2008.

———. *Romans*. 2nd ed. BECNT. Grand Rapids: Baker Academic, 2018.

Schwöbel, Christoph. "The Eternity of the Triune God: Preliminary Considerations on the Relationship between the Trinity and the Time of Creation." *MT* 34 (2018): 345–55.

Scrutton, Anastasia Philippa. *Thinking through Feeling: God, Emotion and Passibility*. London: Bloomsbury, 2011.

Seitz, Christopher R. *Colossians*. Brazos Theological Commentary on the Bible. Grand Rapids: Brazos, 2014.

———. *Figured Out: Typology and Providence in Christian Scripture*. Louisville: Westminster John Knox, 2001.

Senor, Thomas D. "The Compositional Account of the Incarnation." *Faith and Philosophy* 24 (2007): 52–71.

———. "Drawing on Many Traditions: An Ecumenical Kenotic Christology." In Marmodoro and Hill, *The Metaphysics of the Incarnation*, 88–113.

———. "Incarnation, Timelessness, and Leibniz's Law Problems." In *God and Time: Essays on the Divine Nature*, edited by Gregory E. Ganssle and David M. Woodruff, 220–35. Oxford: Oxford University Press, 2002.

Silva, Moisés. "Perfection and Eschatology in Hebrews." *WTJ* 39 (1976): 60–71.

———. *Philippians*. 2nd ed. BECNT. Grand Rapids: Baker Academic, 2005.

Simut, Corneliu. F. C. *Baur's Synthesis of Böhme and Hegel: Redefining Christian Theology as a Gnostic Philosophy of Religion*. Leiden: Brill, 2015.

Smith, Gary V. *Isaiah 1–39*. New American Commentary 15A. Nashville: B&H, 2007.

Solomon, Robert C. *Thinking about Feeling: Contemporary Philosophers of Emotion*. Series in Affective Science. Oxford: Oxford University Press, 2004.

Sommer, Benjamin D. *The Bodies of God and the World of Ancient Israel*. Cambridge: Cambridge University Press, 2009.

Sonderegger, Katherine. *Systematic Theology*. Vol. 1, *The Doctrine of God*. Minneapolis: Fortress, 2015.

———. *Systematic Theology*. Vol. 2, *The Doctrine of the Holy Trinity: Processions and Persons*. Minneapolis: Fortress, 2020.

Sonnet, Jean-Pierre. "God's Repentance and 'False Starts' in Biblical History (Gen. 6–9; Exodus 32–34; 1 Samuel 15 and 2 Samuel 7)." In *Congress Volume Ljubljana 2007*, edited by André Lemaire, 469–94. Vetus Testamentum Supplements 133. Leiden: Brill, 2007.

Soskice, Janet Martin. *Metaphor and Religious Language*. Oxford: Clarendon, 1985.

Spence, Alan. *Incarnation and Inspiration: John Owen and the Coherence of Christology*. London: Bloomsbury, 2007.

Spencer, F. Scott. *Passions of the Christ: The Emotional Life of Jesus in the Gospels*. Grand Rapids: Baker Academic, 2021.

Spencer, Mark K. "The Flexibility of Divine Simplicity." *IPQ* 57 (2017): 123–39.

Spinoza, Baruch (Benedictus). *Tractatus theologico-politicus*. In vol. 3 of *Spinoza opera*. Edited by Carl Gebhardt. Heidelberg: Carl Winters, 1925.

Stanglin, Keith D. *The Letter and Spirit of Biblical Interpretation: From the Early Church to Modern Practice*. Grand Rapids: Baker Academic, 2018.

Sterling, Gregory E. "Prepositional Metaphysics in Jewish Wisdom Speculation and Early Christological Hymns." In *The Studia Philonica Annual: Studies in Hellenistic Judaism, Volume IX*, edited by David T. Runia et al., 219–38. Atlanta: Scholars Press, 1997.

Stuart, Douglas. *Hosea–Jonah*. WBC 31. Waco: Word, 1987.

Stump, Eleonore. "Aquinas' Metaphysics of the Incarnation." In *The Incarnation: An Interdisciplinary Symposium on the Incarnation of the Son of God*, edited by Stephen T. Davis et al., 197–218. Oxford: Oxford University Press, 2002.

Sumner, Darren O. "Fallenness and *anhypostasis*: A Way Forward in the Debate over Christ's Humanity." *SJT* 67 (2014): 195–212.

———. *Karl Barth and the Incarnation: Christology and the Humility of God*. T&T Clark Studies in Systematic Theology. London: Bloomsbury, 2014.

———. "Obedience and Subordination in Karl Barth's Trinitarian Theology." In *Advancing Trinitarian Theology: Explorations in Constructive Dogmatics*, edited by Oliver D. Crisp and Fred Sanders, 130–46. Grand Rapids: Zondervan, 2014.

———. "The Twofold Life of the Word: Karl Barth's Critical Reception of the *Extra Calvinisticum*." *IJST* 15 (2012): 42–57.

Swain, Scott R. "Covenant of Redemption." In *Christian Dogmatics: Reformed Theology for the Church Catholic*, edited by Michael Allen and Scott R. Swain, 107–25. Grand Rapids: Baker Academic, 2016.

———. "The Radiance of the Father's Glory: Eternal Generation, the Divine Names, and Biblical Interpretation." In *Retrieving Eternal Generation*, edited by Fred Sanders and Scott R. Swain, 29–43. Grand Rapids: Zondervan, 2017.

Swain, Scott R., and Michael Allen. "The Obedience of the Eternal Son: Catholic Trinitarianism and Reformed Christology." In *Christology Ancient and Modern: Explorations in Constructive Dogmatics*, edited by Oliver D. Crisp and Fred Sanders, 74–95. Grand Rapids: Zondervan, 2013.

Swinburne, Richard. *The Christian God*. Oxford: Oxford University Press, 1994.

Talbert, Charles H. "The Problem of Pre-existence in Philippians 2:6–11." *JBL* 86 (1967): 141–53.

———. *Romans*. SHBC. Macon, GA: Smyth & Helwys, 2002.

Tanner, Kathryn. *Christ the Key*. CIT. Cambridge: Cambridge University Press, 2010.

Tanner, Norman P., ed. *Decrees of the Ecumenical Councils*. Vol. 1, *Nicaea I to Lateran V*. Washington, DC: Georgetown University Press, 1990.

te Velde, Dolf. *Paths beyond Tracing Out: The Connection of Method and Content in the Doctrine of God, Examined in Reformed Orthodoxy, Karl Barth, and the Utrecht School*. Delft: Eburon, 2010.

Thigpen, J. Michael. "The Storm of YHWH: Jeremiah's Theology of God's Heart and Motives." *BS* 176 (2019): 418–28.

Thiselton, Anthony C. *The First Epistle to the Corinthians: A Commentary on the Greek Text*. NIGTC. Grand Rapids: Eerdmans, 2000.

Thomas Aquinas. *Commentaria in octo libros Physicorum Aristotelis*. In vol. 2 of *Opera omnia*. Leonine ed. Rome: ex Typographia Polyglotta, 1884.

———. *Compendium theologiae*. In vol. 42 of *Opera omnia*. Leonine ed. Rome: Editori di San Tommaso, 1979.

———. *Contra errores Graecorum*. In vol. 40A of *Opera omnia*. Leonine ed. Rome: ad Sanctae Sabinae, 1967.

————. *De potentia.* In vol. 2 of *Quaestiones disputatae.* Edited by P. Bazzi et al. 10th ed. Rome and Turin: Marietti, 1965.

————. *Expositio libri Boethii De hebdomadibus.* In vol. 50 of *Opera omnia.* Leonine ed. Rome: Commissio Leonina; Paris: Cerf, 1992.

————. *Expositio super Isaiam ad litteram.* In vol. 28 of *Opera omnia.* Leonine ed. Rome: Editori di San Tommaso, 1974.

————. *In duodecim libros Metaphysicorum Aristotelis expositio.* Edited by M. R. Cathala and R. M. Spiazzi. Rome: Marietti, 1950.

————. *In Jeremiam prophetam expositio.* In vol. 14 of *Sancti Thomae Aquinatis opera omnia.* Parma: Petrus Fiaccadorus, 1863.

————. *In librum Beati Dionysii De divinis nominibus expositio.* Edited by Ceslai Pera. Rome-Turin: Marietti, 1950.

————. *Quaestio disputata De unione Verbi incarnati.* In vol. 2 of *Quaestiones disputatae.* Edited by P. Bazzi et al. 10th ed. Rome and Turin: Marietti, 1965.

————. *Quaestiones de quolibet.* In vol. 25/2 of *Opera omnia.* Leonine ed. Rome: Commissio Leonina; Paris: Cerf, 1996.

————. *Quaestiones disputatae de veritate.* In vols. 22/1.2 and 22/3.1 of *Opera omnia.* Leonine ed. Rome: ad Sanctae Sabinae, 1970.

————. *Scriptum super libros Sententiarum.* Edited by R. P. Mandonnet. 2 vols. Paris: Lethielleux, 1929.

————. *Sentencia libri De anima.* In vol. 45/1 of *Opera Omnia.* Leonine ed. Rome: Commissio Leonina; Paris: J. Vrin, 1984.

————. *Sententia libri Ethicorum.* In vol. 47 of *Opera omnia.* Leonine ed. Rome: ad Sanctae Sabinae, 1969.

————. *Summa contra Gentiles.* In vols. 13–15 of *Opera omnia.* Leonine ed. Rome: Typis Ricardi Garroni, 1918–30.

————. *Summa theologiae.* In vols. 4–12 of *Opera omnia.* Leonine ed. Rome: ex Typographia Polyglotta, 1888–1906.

————. *Super Boetium De trinitate.* In vol. 50 of *Opera omnia.* Leonine ed. Rome: Commissio Leonina; Paris: Cerf, 1992.

————. *Super epistolam ad Ephesios lectura.* In vol. 2 of *Super epistolas S. Pauli lectura.* Edited by R. Cai. 8th ed. Rome: Marietti, 1953.

————. *Super epistolam ad Hebraeos lectura.* In vol. 2 of *Super epistolas S. Pauli lectura.* Edited by P. Raphaelis Cai. 8th ed. Rome: Marietti, 1953.

————. *Super epistolam ad Philippenses lectura.* In vol. 2 of *Super epistolas S. Pauli lectura.* Edited by P. Raphaelis Cai. 8th ed. Rome: Marietti, 1953.

————. *Super epistolam ad Romanos lectura.* In vol. 1 of *Super epistolas S. Pauli lectura.* Edited by P. Raphaelis Cai. 8th ed. Rome: Marietti, 1953.

————. *Super Evangelium S. Iohannis lectura.* Edited by P. Raphaelis Cai. 5th ed. Rome: Marietti, 1952.

———. *Super Evangelium S. Matthaei lectura.* Edited by R. Cai. 5th ed. Rome: Marietti, 1951.

Thomasius, Gottfried. *Christi Person und Werk—Zweiter Teil: Die Person des Mittlers.* 2nd ed. Erlangen: Theodor Bläsing, 1857.

———. *Christ's Person and Work.* In *God and Incarnation: In Mid-Nineteenth Century German Theology,* edited and translated by Claude Welch, 30–101. Oxford: Oxford University Press, 1965.

Thompson, James W., and Bruce W. Longenecker. *Philippians and Philemon.* Paideia. Grand Rapids: Baker Academic, 2016.

Thompson, Marianne Meye. *Colossians and Philemon.* THNTC. Grand Rapids: Eerdmans, 2005.

———. *The God of the Gospel of John.* Grand Rapids: Eerdmans, 2001.

Thrall, Margaret E. *A Critical and Exegetical Commentary on the Second Epistle to the Corinthians.* Vol. 1. ICC. Edinburgh: T&T Clark, 1994.

Tilling, Chris. *Paul's Divine Christology.* Grand Rapids: Eerdmans, 2015.

Tomaszewski, Christopher. "Collapsing the Modal Collapse Argument: On an Invalid Argument against Divine Simplicity." *Analysis* 79 (2019): 275–84.

Torrance, Alan. *Persons in Communion: An Essay on Trinitarian Description and Human Participation, with Special Reference to Volume One of Karl Barth's Church Dogmatics.* Edinburgh: T&T Clark, 1996.

———. "Reclaiming the Continuing Priesthood of Christ." In *Christology Ancient and Modern: Explorations in Constructive Dogmatics,* edited by Oliver D. Crisp and Fred Sanders, 184–204. Grand Rapids: Zondervan, 2013.

Torrance, James B. "Covenant or Contract? A Study of the Theological Background of Worship in Seventeenth-Century Scotland." *SJT* 23 (1970): 51–76.

Torrance, Thomas F. *The Christian Doctrine of God: One Being, Three Persons.* London: T&T Clark, 1996.

———. *Incarnation: The Person and Life of Christ.* Downers Grove, IL: IVP Academic, 2008.

———. *The Mediation of Christ.* Edinburgh: T&T Clark, 1992.

———. *Theology in Reconstruction.* Eugene, OR: Wipf & Stock, 1996.

———. *The Trinitarian Faith: The Evangelical Theology of the Ancient Catholic Church.* Edinburgh: T&T Clark, 1988.

———. *Trinitarian Perspectives: Toward Doctrinal Agreement.* Edinburgh: T&T Clark 1994.

Trueman, Carl. "From Calvin to Gillespie: Mythological Excess or an Exercise in Doctrinal Development?" *IJST* 11 (2009): 378–97.

Turcescu, Lucian. *Gregory of Nyssa and the Concept of Divine Persons.* Oxford: Oxford University Press, 2005.

Turner, Max. "The Spirit of Christ and 'Divine Christology.'" In *Jesus of Nazareth: Lord and Christ*, edited by Joel B. Green and Max Turner, 413–36. Grand Rapids: Eerdmans, 1999.

Turretin, Francis. *Institutio theologiae elencticae*. 3 vols. 2nd ed. Geneva, 1688.

Ursinus, Zacharias. *Doctrinae Christianae compendium*. Leiden, 1584.

van Asselt, Willem. *The Federal Theology of Johannes Cocceius (1603–1669)*. Studies in the History of Christian Thought 100. Leiden: Brill, 2001.

van der Kooi, Cornelis. "The Identity of Israel's God: The Potential of the So-Called Extra Calvinisticum." In *Tradition and Innovation in Biblical Interpretation*, edited by W. Th. Van Peursen and J. W. Dyk, 209–22. Leiden: Brill, 2011.

———. *This Incredibly Benevolent Force: The Holy Spirit in Reformed Theology and Spirituality*. Grand Rapids: Eerdmans, 2018.

van Dyke Parunak, H. "A Semantic Survey of NḤM." *Biblica* 56 (1975): 512–32.

Vanhoozer, Kevin J. *Is There a Meaning in This Text? The Bible, the Reader, and the Morality of Literary Knowledge*. Grand Rapids: Zondervan, 1998.

van Inwagen, Peter. "And Yet They Are Not Three Gods but One God." In *Philosophical and Theological Essays on the Trinity*, edited by Thomas McCall and Michael C. Rea, 217–48. Oxford: Oxford University Press, 2009.

———. "Not by Confusion of Substance, but by Unity of Person." In *Reason and the Christian Religion: Essays in Honor of Richard Swinburne*, edited by Alan G. Padgett, 201–26. Oxford: Clarendon, 1994.

Van Kuiken, Jerome. *Christ's Humanity in Current and Ancient Controversy: Fallen or Not?* London: Bloomsbury, 2017.

van Loon, Hans. *The Dyophysite Christology of Cyril of Alexandria*. VCSup 96. Leiden: Brill, 2009.

Van Roey, Alvert, and Pauline Allen, eds. *Monophysite Texts of the Sixth Century*. Orientalia Lovaniensia Analecta 56. Leuven: Peters, 1994.

Venema, Cornelis P. "Recent Criticisms of the 'Covenant of Works' in the Westminster Confession of Faith." *MAJT* 9 (1993): 165–98.

Vermigli, Peter. *In epistolam S. Pauli Apostoli ad Romanos*. Heidelberg: Cambierus, 1613.

Vidu, Adonis. "The Incarnation and Trinitarian Inseparable Operations." *JAT* 4 (2016): 106–27.

———. *The Same God Who Works All Things: Inseparable Operations in Trinitarian Theology*. Grand Rapids: Eerdmans, 2021.

Voetius, Gisbertus. *Selectarum disputationum theologicarum, pars prima*. Utrecht, 1648.

———. *Selectarum disputationum theologicarum, pars secunda*. Utrecht, 1655.

von Balthasar, Hans Urs. *Mysterium Paschale: The Mystery of Easter*. Translated by Aidan Nichols. San Francisco: Ignatius, 2000.

————. *Theo-Drama*. Vol. 3, *The Dramatis Personae: The Person in Christ*. Translated by Graham Harrison. San Francisco: Ignatius, 1992.

von Rad, Gerhard. *Old Testament Theology*. Vol. 1, *The Theology of Israel's Historical Traditions*. Translated by D. M. G. Stalker. New York: Harper & Row, 1962.

Wallace, Daniel B. *Greek Grammar beyond the Basics: An Exegetical Syntax of the New Testament*. Grand Rapids: Zondervan, 1996.

Waltke, Bruce K. *The Book of Proverbs: Chapters 1–15*. NICOT. Grand Rapids: Eerdmans, 2004.

Walton, John H. *Ancient Near Eastern Thought and the Old Testament: Introducing the Conceptual World of the Hebrew Bible*. Grand Rapids: Baker Academic, 2006.

Wanamaker, C. A. "Philippians 2.6–11: Son of God or Adamic Christology?" *NTS* 33 (1987): 179–93.

Watson, Thomas. *A Body of Practical Divinity*. London: Parkhurst, 1692.

Watts, John D. W. *Isaiah 1–33*. Rev. ed. WBC 24. Nashville: Nelson, 2005.

Webster, John. *Barth's Moral Theology: Human Action in Barth's Thought*. Grand Rapids: Eerdmans, 1998.

————. *God without Measure: Working Papers in Christian Theology*. Vol. 1, *God and the Works of God*. London: Bloomsbury, 2015.

————. "The Place of Christology in Systematic Theology." In *The Oxford Handbook of Christology*, edited by Francesca Aran Murphy and Troy A. Stefano, 611–27. Oxford: Oxford University Press, 2015.

————. "Trinity and Creation." *IJST* 12 (2010): 4–19.

Weinandy, Thomas G. "The Beatific Vision and the Incarnate Son: Furthering the Discussion." *The Thomist* 70 (2006): 605–15.

————. *Does God Suffer?* Notre Dame, IN: University of Notre Dame Press, 2000.

————. *In the Likeness of Sinful Flesh: An Essay on the Humanity of Christ*. Edinburgh: T&T Clark, 1993.

————. *Jesus: Essays in Christology*. Ave Maria, FL: Sapientia Press, 2014.

————. "Jesus' Filial Vision of the Father." *Pro Ecclesia* 13 (2004): 189–201.

Welker, Michael. *God the Revealed: Christology*. Translated by Douglas W. Stott. Grand Rapids: Eerdmans, 2013.

Westcott, B. F. *The Gospel according to St. John*. Reprint, Grand Rapids: Eerdmans, 1971.

White, Thomas Joseph. *The Incarnate Lord: A Thomistic Study in Christology*. Washington, DC: Catholic University of America Press, 2015.

Whybray, R. N. *Wisdom in Proverbs: The Concept of Wisdom in Proverbs 1–9.45*. SBT. London: SCM, 1965.

Wickham, Lionel. "The Ignorance of Christ: A Problem for the Ancient Theology." In *Christian Faith and Greek Philosophy in Late Antiquity: Essays in Tribute* to *Christopher George Stead in Celebration of His Eightieth Birthday 9th April 1993*, edited by Lionel R. Wickham and Caroline P. Bammel, 213–26. VCSup 19. Leiden: Brill, 1993.

Wiedenroth, Ulrich. *Krypsis und Kenosis: Studien zu Thema und Genese der Tübinger Christologie im 17. Jahrhundert.* Beiträge zur historischen Theologie 162. Tübingen: Mohr Siebeck, 2011.

Wilkins, Jeremy. "Love and the Knowledge of God in the Human Life of Christ." *Pro Ecclesia* 21 (2012): 77–99.

Williams, Rowan. *Christ the Heart of Creation.* London: Bloomsbury, 2018.

Willis, E. David. *Calvin's Catholic Christology: The Function of the So-Called* Extra Calvinisticum *in Calvin's Theology.* Leiden: Brill, 1966.

Willis, John T. "The 'Repentance' of God in the Books of Samuel, Jeremiah, and Jonah." *HBT* 16 (1994): 156–75.

Wilson, Brittany E. *The Embodied God: Seeing the Divine in Luke-Acts and the Early Church.* Oxford: Oxford University Press, 2021.

Witherington, Ben, III. *The Acts of the Apostles: A Socio–Rhetorical Commentary.* Grand Rapids: Eerdmans, 1998.

Witsius, Herman. *De oeconomia foederum Dei cum hominibus, libri quatuor.* Leeuwarden, 1685.

———. *Exercitationes sacrae in symbolum quod Apostolorum dicitur.* 4th ed. Herborn, 1712.

Wittman, Tyler R. "The End of the Incarnation: John Owen, Trinitarian Agency and Christology." *IJST* 15 (2013): 284–300.

———. *God and Creation in the Theology of Thomas Aquinas and Karl Barth.* Cambridge: Cambridge University Press, 2019.

———. "On the Unity of the Trinity's External Works: Archaeology and Grammar." *IJST* 20 (2018): 359–80.

Wolterstorff, Nicholas. *Inquiring about God: Selected Essays.* Vol. 1. Edited by Terence Cuneo. Cambridge: Cambridge University Press, 2010.

Woo, B. Hoon. *The Promise of the Trinity: The Covenant of Redemption in the Theologies of Witsius, Owen, Dickson, Goodwin, and Cocceius.* Göttingen: Vandenhoeck & Ruprecht, 2018.

Work, Telford C. "Jesus' New Relationship with the Holy Spirit, and Ours: How Biblical Spirit-Christology Helps Resolve a Chalcedonian Dilemma." In *Christology Ancient and Modern: Explorations in Constructive Dogmatics*, edited by Oliver D. Crisp and Fred Sanders, 171–83. Grand Rapids: Zondervan, 2013.

Wright, N. T. *The Climax of the Covenant: Christ and the Law in Pauline Theology.* Minneapolis: Fortress, 1993.

———. "Historical Paul and 'Systematic Theology': To Start a Discussion." In *Biblical Theology: Past, Present, and Future*, edited by Carey Walsh and Mark W. Elliott, 147–64. Eugene, OR: Cascade Books, 2016.

———. *How God Became King: The Forgotten Story of the Gospels.* New York: HarperCollins, 2012.

———. "Jesus' Self-Understanding." In *The Incarnation: An Interdisciplinary Symposium on the Incarnation of the Son of God*, edited by Stephen T. Davis et al., 47–61. Oxford: Oxford University Press, 2002.

———. *Paul and the Faithfulness of God.* 2 vols. Minneapolis: Fortress, 2013.

———. "Romans." In *The New Interpreter's Bible*, edited by Leander E. Keck, 10:393–770. Nashville: Abingdon, 2002.

Yandell, Keith. "How Many Times Does Three Go into One?" In *Philosophical and Theological Essays on the Trinity*, edited by Thomas H. McCall and Michael C. Rea, 151–68. Oxford: Oxford University Press, 2009.

Yang, Eric. "Kenoticism and Essential Divine Properties." *RS* 56 (2020): 409–18.

Young, Edward J. *The Book of Isaiah: The English Text, with Introduction, Exposition, and Notes.* Vol. 3, *Chapters 40 through 66.* Grand Rapids: Eerdmans, 1972.

Youngs, Samuel J. *The Way of the Kenotic Christ: The Christology of Jürgen Moltmann.* Eugene, OR: Cascade Books, 2019.

Zachhuber, Johannes. *Theology as Science in Nineteenth-Century Germany: From F. C. Baur to Ernst Troeltsch.* Oxford: Oxford University Press, 2013.

———. *Zwischen Idealismus und Historismus: Theologie als Wissenschaft in der Tübinger Schule und in der Ritschlschule.* Leipzig: Evangelische Verlagsanstalt, 2015.

Zagzebski, Linda. *Omnisubjectivity: A Defense of a Divine Attribute.* The Aquinas Lecture, 2013. Milwaukee: Marquette University Press, 2013.

———. "Omnisubjectivity: Why It Is a Divine Attribute." *Nova et Vetera* 14 (2016): 435–50.

Zanchi, Girolamo. *De incarnatione Filii Dei.* Heidelberg, 1593.

———. *De natura Dei.* Neustadt, 1598.

———. *De tribus Elohim.* Neustadt, 1597.

———. *In d. Pauli apostoli epistolam ad Philippenses.* Neustadt: Wilhelmus Harnisius, 1601.

Zizioulas, John. *Being as Communion: Studies in Personhood and the Church.* Crestwood, NY: St. Vladimir's Seminary Press, 1985.

Index of Authors

Index of Subjects

Index of Selected Greek Terms

Index of Scripture and Other
Primary Sources